NEW PERSPECTIVES

Microsoft® Office 365™ & Access® 2016

COMPREHENSIVE

Mark Shellman

Gaston College

Sasha Vodnik

CENGAGE
Learning·

Australia • Brazil • Mexico • Singapore • United Kingdom • United States

CENGAGE
Learning®

**New Perspectives Microsoft® Office 365™ &
Access® 2016, Comprehensive**
Mark Shellman, Sasha Vodnik

SVP, GM Science, Technology & Math: Balraj S. Kalsi

Senior Product Director: Kathleen McMahon

Senior Product Team Manager: Lauren Murphy

Product Team Manager: Andrea Topping

Associate Product Manager: Melissa Stehler

Senior Director, Development: Julia Caballero

Product Development Manager: Leigh Hefferon

Senior Content Developer: Marjorie Hunt

Developmental Editors: Kim T. M. Crowley,
	Sasha Vodnik

Manuscript Quality Assurance: Danielle Shaw,
	Serge Palladino

Product Assistant: Erica Chapman

Marketing Director: Michele McTighe

Marketing Manager: Stephanie Albracht

Marketing Coordinator: Cassie Cloutier

Senior Production Director: Wendy Troeger

Production Director: Patty Stephan

Senior Content Project Managers: Jennifer Goguen
	McGrail, Stacey Lamodi

Art Director: Diana Graham

Text Designer: Althea Chen

Composition: GEX Publishing Services

Cover Template Designer: Wing-Ip Ngan, Ink
	Design, Inc.

Cover image(s): asharkyu/Shutterstock.com

For product information and technology assistance, contact us at
Cengage Learning Customer & Sales Support, 1-800-354-9706

For permission to use material from this text or product, submit all requests online at **www.cengage.com/permissions**.
Further permissions questions can be e-mailed to
permissionrequest@cengage.com

Some of the product names and company names used in this book have been used for identification purposes only and may be trademarks or registered trademarks of their respective manufacturers and sellers.

Windows® is a registered trademark of Microsoft Corporation. © 2012 Microsoft. Microsoft and the Office logo are either registered trademarks or trademarks of Microsoft Corporation in the United States and/or other countries. Cengage Learning is an independent entity from Microsoft Corporation and not affiliated with Microsoft in any manner.

Disclaimer: Any fictional data related to persons or companies or URLs used throughout this text is intended for instructional purposes only. At the time this text was published, any such data was fictional and not belonging to any real persons or companies.

Disclaimer: The material in this text was written using Microsoft Office 365 ProPlus and Microsoft Access 2016 running on Microsoft Windows 10 Professional and was Quality Assurance tested before the publication date. As Microsoft continually updates the Microsoft Office suite and the Windows 10 operating system, your software experience may vary slightly from what is presented in the printed text.

Microsoft product screenshots used with permission from Microsoft Corporation. Unless otherwise noted, all clip art is courtesy of openclipart.org.

Library of Congress Control Number: 2016934377
ISBN: 978-1-305-88013-9

Cengage Learning
20 Channel Center Street
Boston, MA 02210
USA

Cengage Learning is a leading provider of customized learning solutions with employees residing in nearly 40 different countries and sales in more than 125 countries around the world. Find your local representative at **www.cengage.com.**

Cengage Learning products are represented in Canada by Nelson Education, Ltd.

To learn more about Cengage Learning, visit **www.cengage.com**

Purchase any of our products at your local college store or at our preferred online store **www.cengagebrain.com**

Printed in the United States of America
Print Number: 01   Print Year: 2016

TABLE OF CONTENTS

Module 9 Using Action Queries and Advanced Table Relationships

Enhancing User Interaction with the Veterinary Database . . . . **AC 497**

Module 10 Automating Tasks with Macros

Creating a User Interface for the Veterinary Database . . . . **AC 547**

Module 11 Using and Writing Visual Basic for Applications Code

Creating VBA Code for the Veterinary Database . . . . **AC 601**

Productivity Apps for School and Work

OneNote
Sway
Office Mix
Edge

Corinne Hoisington

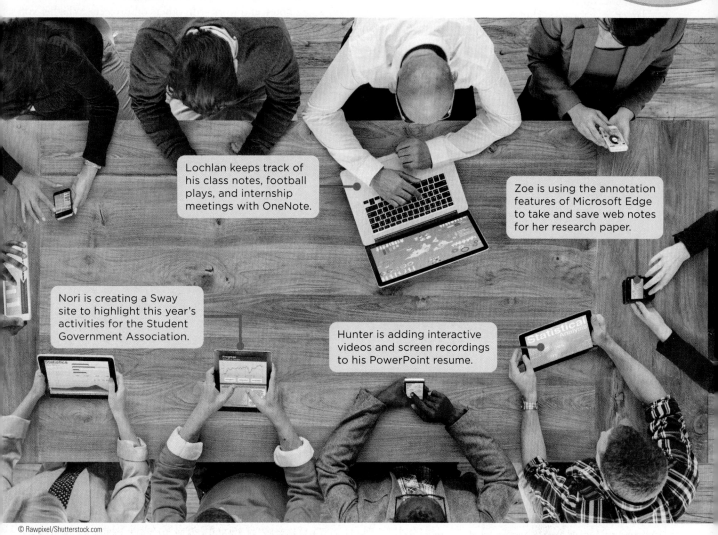

Lochlan keeps track of his class notes, football plays, and internship meetings with OneNote.

Zoe is using the annotation features of Microsoft Edge to take and save web notes for her research paper.

Nori is creating a Sway site to highlight this year's activities for the Student Government Association.

Hunter is adding interactive videos and screen recordings to his PowerPoint resume.

© Rawpixel/Shutterstock.com

Being computer literate no longer means mastery of only Word, Excel, PowerPoint, Outlook, and Access. To become technology power users, Hunter, Nori, Zoe, and Lochlan are exploring Microsoft OneNote, Sway, Mix, and Edge in Office 2016 and Windows 10.

In this Module

Learn to use productivity apps!
Links to companion **Sways**, featuring **videos** with hands-on instructions, are located on www.cengagebrain.com.

Introduction to OneNote 2016

notebook | section tab | To Do tag | screen clipping | note | template | Microsoft OneNote Mobile app | sync | drawing canvas | inked handwriting | Ink to Text

As you glance around any classroom, you invariably see paper notebooks and notepads on each desk. Because deciphering and sharing handwritten notes can be a challenge, Microsoft OneNote 2016 replaces physical notebooks, binders, and paper notes with a searchable, digital notebook. OneNote captures your ideas and schoolwork on any device so you can stay organized, share notes, and work with others on projects. Whether you are a student taking class notes as shown in **Figure 1** or an employee taking notes in company meetings, OneNote is the one place to keep notes for all of your projects.

Figure 1: OneNote 2016 notebook

Each **notebook** is divided into sections, also called **section tabs**, by subject or topic.

Use **To Do tags**, icons that help you keep track of your assignments and other tasks.

Type on a page to add a **note**, a small window that contains text or other types of information.

Personalize a page with a **template**, or stationery.

Write or draw directly on the page using drawing tools.

Pages can include pictures such as **screen clippings**, images from any part of a computer screen.

Attach files and enter equations so you have everything you need in one place.

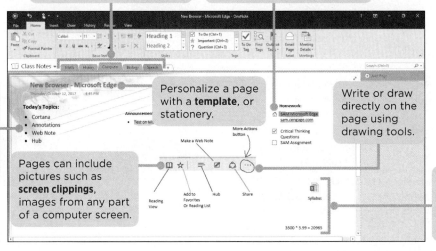

Creating a OneNote Notebook

OneNote is divided into sections similar to those in a spiral-bound notebook. Each OneNote notebook contains sections, pages, and other notebooks. You can use One-Note for school, business, and personal projects. Store information for each type of project in different notebooks to keep your tasks separate, or use any other organization that suits you. OneNote is flexible enough to adapt to the way you want to work.

When you create a notebook, it contains a blank page with a plain white background by default, though you can use templates, or stationery, to apply designs in categories such as Academic, Business, Decorative, and Planners. Start typing or use the buttons on the Insert tab to insert notes, which are small resizable windows that can contain text, equations, tables, on-screen writing, images, audio and video recordings, to-do lists, file attachments, and file printouts. Add as many notes as you need to each page.

Syncing a Notebook to the Cloud

OneNote saves your notes every time you make a change in a notebook. To make sure you can access your notebooks with a laptop, tablet, or smartphone wherever you are, OneNote uses cloud-based storage, such as OneDrive or SharePoint. **Microsoft OneNote Mobile app**, a lightweight version of OneNote 2016 shown in **Figure 2**, is available for free in the Windows Store, Google Play for Android devices, and the AppStore for iOS devices.

If you have a Microsoft account, OneNote saves your notes on OneDrive automatically for all your mobile devices and computers, which is called **syncing**. For example, you can use OneNote to take notes on your laptop during class, and then open OneNote on your phone to study later. To use a notebook stored on your computer with your OneNote Mobile app, move the notebook to OneDrive. You can quickly share notebook content with other people using OneDrive.

Figure 2: Microsoft OneNote Mobile app

Notes synced to OneDrive and displayed on a smartphone

Taking Notes

Use OneNote pages to organize your notes by class and topic or lecture. Beyond simple typed notes, OneNote stores drawings, converts handwriting to searchable text and mathematical sketches to equations, and records audio and video.

OneNote includes drawing tools that let you sketch freehand drawings such as biological cell diagrams and financial supply-and-demand charts. As shown in **Figure 3**, the Draw tab on the ribbon provides these drawing tools along with shapes so you can insert diagrams and other illustrations to represent your ideas. When you draw on a page, One-Note creates a **drawing canvas**, which is a container for shapes and lines.

On the Job Now

OneNote is ideal for taking notes during meetings, whether you are recording minutes, documenting a discussion, sketching product diagrams, or listing follow-up items. Use a meeting template to add pages with content appropriate for meetings.

Figure 3: Tools on the Draw tab

Draw tab

Pens and highlighters are in the Tools group.

Insert rectangles and lines from the Shapes group.

Lines and shapes are in the Shapes group.

Make drawings using pens in the Tools group.

Insert text using the Type button in the Tools group.

Files syncing over the Internet

Microsoft OneDrive

Converting Handwriting to Text

When you use a pen tool to write on a notebook page, the text you enter is called **inked handwriting**. OneNote can convert inked handwriting to typed text when you use the **Ink to Text** button in the Convert group on the Draw tab, as shown in **Figure 4**. After OneNote converts the handwriting to text, you can use the Search box to find terms in the converted text or any other note in your notebooks.

Figure 4: Converting handwriting to text

On the Job Now

Use OneNote as a place to brainstorm ongoing work projects. If a notebook contains sensitive material, you can password-protect some or all of the notebook so that only certain people can open it.

Recording a Lecture

If your computer or mobile device has a microphone or camera, OneNote can record the audio or video from a lecture or business meeting as shown in **Figure 5**. When you record a lecture (with your instructor's permission), you can follow along, take regular notes at your own pace, and review the video recording later. You can control the start, pause, and stop motions of the recording when you play back the recording of your notes.

Figure 5: Video inserted in a notebook

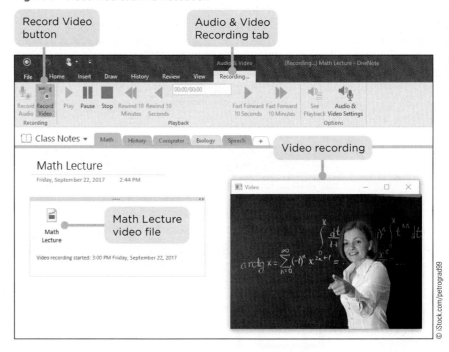

Try This Now

1: Taking Notes for a Week

As a student, you can get organized by using OneNote to take detailed notes in your classes. Perform the following tasks:

a. Create a new OneNote notebook on your Microsoft OneDrive account (the default location for new notebooks). Name the notebook with your first name followed by "Notes," as in **Caleb Notes**.

b. Create four section tabs, each with a different class name.

c. Take detailed notes in those classes for one week. Be sure to include notes, drawings, and other types of content.

d. Sync your notes with your OneDrive. Submit your assignment in the format specified by your instructor.

2: Using OneNote to Organize a Research Paper

You have a research paper due on the topic of three habits of successful students. Use OneNote to organize your research. Perform the following tasks:

a. Create a new OneNote notebook on your Microsoft OneDrive account. Name the notebook **Success Research**.

b. Create three section tabs with the following names:

- **Take Detailed Notes**
- **Be Respectful in Class**
- **Come to Class Prepared**

c. On the web, research the topics and find three sources for each section. Copy a sentence from each source and paste the sentence into the appropriate section. When you paste the sentence, OneNote inserts it in a note with a link to the source.

d. Sync your notes with your OneDrive. Submit your assignment in the format specified by your instructor.

3: Planning Your Career

Note: This activity requires a webcam or built-in video camera on any type of device.

Consider an occupation that interests you. Using OneNote, examine the responsibilities, education requirements, potential salary, and employment outlook of a specific career. Perform the following tasks:

a. Create a new OneNote notebook on your Microsoft OneDrive account. Name the notebook with your first name followed by a career title, such as **Kara - App Developer**.

b. Create four section tabs with the names **Responsibilities, Education Requirements, Median Salary**, and **Employment Outlook**.

c. Research the responsibilities of your career path. Using OneNote, record a short video (approximately 30 seconds) of yourself explaining the responsibilities of your career path. Place the video in the Responsibilities section.

d. On the web, research the educational requirements for your career path and find two appropriate sources. Copy a paragraph from each source and paste them into the appropriate section. When you paste a paragraph, OneNote inserts it in a note with a link to the source.

e. Research the median salary for a single year for this career. Create a mathematical equation in the Median Salary section that multiplies the amount of the median salary times 20 years to calculate how much you will possibly earn.

f. For the Employment Outlook section, research the outlook for your career path. Take at least four notes about what you find when researching the topic.

g. Sync your notes with your OneDrive. Submit your assignment in the format specified by your instructor.

Introduction to Sway

Sway site | responsive design | Storyline | card | Creative Commons license | animation emphasis effects | Docs.com

Bottom Line
- Drag photos, videos, and files from your computer and content from Facebook and Twitter directly to your Sway presentation.
- Run Sway in a web browser or as an app on your smartphone, and save presentations as webpages.

Expressing your ideas in a presentation typically means creating PowerPoint slides or a Word document. Microsoft Sway gives you another way to engage an audience. Sway is a free Microsoft tool available at Sway.com or as an app in Office 365. Using Sway, you can combine text, images, videos, and social media in a website called a **Sway site** that you can share and display on any device. To get started, you create a digital story on a web-based canvas without borders, slides, cells, or page breaks. A Sway site organizes the text, images, and video into a **responsive design**, which means your content adapts perfectly to any screen size as shown in **Figure 6**. You store a Sway site in the cloud on OneDrive using a free Microsoft account.

Figure 6: Sway site with responsive design

You can display a Sway presentation in a web browser.

Sway uses responsive design to make sure pages fit perfectly on any device.

Learn to use Sway!
Links to companion **Sways**, featuring **videos** with hands-on instructions, are located on www.cengagebrain.com.

Creating a Sway Presentation

You can use Sway to build a digital flyer, a club newsletter, a vacation blog, an informational site, a digital art portfolio, or a new product rollout. After you select your topic and sign into Sway with your Microsoft account, a **Storyline** opens, providing tools and a work area for composing your digital story. See **Figure 7**. Each story can include text, images, and videos. You create a Sway by adding text and media content into a Storyline section, or **card**. To add pictures, videos, or documents, select a card in the left pane and then select the Insert Content button. The first card in a Sway presentation contains a title and background image.

Figure 7: Creating a Sway site

Design and create Sway presentations.

Share and play published Sway sites.

Arrange content in a Storyline, which contains all the text, pictures, videos, and other media in a Sway presentation.

To add content, select a card, which is designed to hold a particular type of information.

After selecting a card, click the Insert Content button to add the content to the Sway presentation.

Adding Content to Build a Story

As you work, Sway searches the Internet to help you find relevant images, videos, tweets, and other content from online sources such as Bing, YouTube, Twitter, and Facebook. You can drag content from the search results right into the Storyline. In addition, you can upload your own images and videos directly in the presentation. For example, if you are creating a Sway presentation about the market for commercial drones, Sway suggests content to incorporate into the presentation by displaying it in the left pane as search results. The search results include drone images tagged with a **Creative Commons license** at online sources as shown in **Figure 8**. A Creative Commons license is a public copyright license that allows the free distribution of an otherwise copyrighted work. In addition, you can specify the source of the media. For example, you can add your own Facebook or OneNote pictures and videos in Sway without leaving the app.

On the Job Now

If you have a Microsoft Word document containing an outline of your business content, drag the outline into Sway to create a card for each topic.

Figure 8: Images in Sway search results

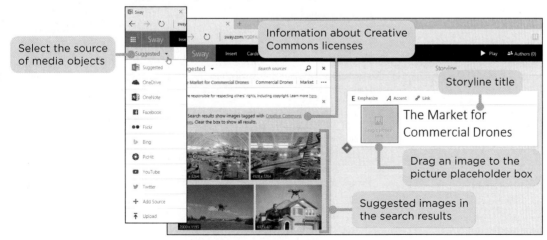

Select the source of media objects

Information about Creative Commons licenses

Storyline title

The Market for Commercial Drones

Drag an image to the picture placeholder box

Suggested images in the search results

On the Job Now

If your project team wants to collaborate on a Sway presentation, click the Authors button on the navigation bar to invite others to edit the presentation.

Designing a Sway

Sway professionally designs your Storyline content by resizing background images and fonts to fit your display, and by floating text, animating media, embedding video, and removing images as a page scrolls out of view. Sway also evaluates the images in your Storyline and suggests a color palette based on colors that appear in your photos. Use the Design button to display tools including color palettes, font choices, **animation emphasis effects**, and style templates to provide a personality for a Sway presentation. Instead of creating your own design, you can click the Remix button, which randomly selects unique designs for your Sway site.

Publishing a Sway

Use the Play button to display your finished Sway presentation as a website. The Address bar includes a unique web address where others can view your Sway site. As the author, you can edit a published Sway site by clicking the Edit button (pencil icon) on the Sway toolbar.

Sharing a Sway

When you are ready to share your Sway website, you have several options as shown in **Figure 9**. Use the Share slider button to share the Sway site publically or keep it private. If you add the Sway site to the Microsoft **Docs.com** public gallery, anyone worldwide can use Bing, Google, or other search engines to find, view, and share your Sway site. You can also share your Sway site using Facebook, Twitter, Google+, Yammer, and other social media sites. Link your presentation to any webpage or email the link to your audience. Sway can also generate a code for embedding the link within another webpage.

Figure 9: Sharing a Sway site

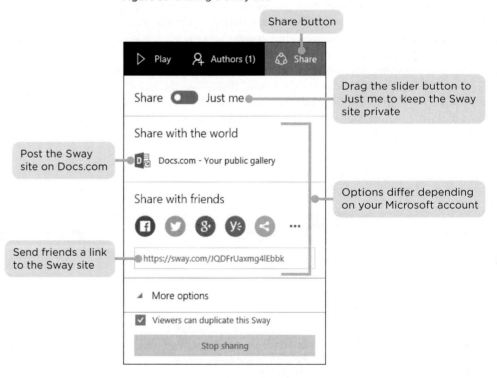

Try This Now

Learn to use Sway!
Links to companion **Sways**, featuring **videos** with hands-on instructions, are located on www.cengagebrain.com.

1: Creating a Sway Resume

Sway is a digital storytelling app. Create a Sway resume to share the skills, job experiences, and achievements you have that match the requirements of a future job interest. Perform the following tasks:

    a. Create a new presentation in Sway to use as a digital resume. Title the Sway Storyline with your full name and then select a background image.

    b. Create three separate sections titled **Academic Background, Work Experience**, and **Skills**, and insert text, a picture, and a paragraph or bulleted points in each section. Be sure to include your own picture.

    c. Add a fourth section that includes a video about your school that you find online.

    d. Customize the design of your presentation.

    e. Submit your assignment link in the format specified by your instructor.

2: Creating an Online Sway Newsletter

Newsletters are designed to capture the attention of their target audience. Using Sway, create a newsletter for a club, organization, or your favorite music group. Perform the following tasks:

    a. Create a new presentation in Sway to use as a digital newsletter for a club, organization, or your favorite music group. Provide a title for the Sway Storyline and select an appropriate background image.

    b. Select three separate sections with appropriate titles, such as Upcoming Events. In each section, insert text, a picture, and a paragraph or bulleted points.

    c. Add a fourth section that includes a video about your selected topic.

    d. Customize the design of your presentation.

    e. Submit your assignment link in the format specified by your instructor.

3: Creating and Sharing a Technology Presentation

To place a Sway presentation in the hands of your entire audience, you can share a link to the Sway presentation. Create a Sway presentation on a new technology and share it with your class. Perform the following tasks:

    a. Create a new presentation in Sway about a cutting-edge technology topic. Provide a title for the Sway Storyline and select a background image.

    b. Create four separate sections about your topic, and include text, a picture, and a paragraph in each section.

    c. Add a fifth section that includes a video about your topic.

    d. Customize the design of your presentation.

    e. Share the link to your Sway with your classmates and submit your assignment link in the format specified by your instructor.

Introduction to Office Mix

add-in | clip | slide recording | Slide Notes | screen recording | free-response quiz

Bottom Line
- Office Mix is a free PowerPoint add-in from Microsoft that adds features to PowerPoint.
- The Mix tab on the PowerPoint ribbon provides tools for creating screen recordings, videos, interactive quizzes, and live webpages.

To enliven business meetings and lectures, Microsoft adds a new dimension to presentations with a powerful toolset called Office Mix, a free add-in for PowerPoint. (An **add-in** is software that works with an installed app to extend its features.) Using Office Mix, you can record yourself on video, capture still and moving images on your desktop, and insert interactive elements such as quizzes and live webpages directly into PowerPoint slides. When you post the finished presentation to OneDrive, Office Mix provides a link you can share with friends and colleagues. Anyone with an Internet connection and a web browser can watch a published Office Mix presentation, such as the one in **Figure 10**, on a computer or mobile device.

Figure 10: Office Mix presentation

Adding Office Mix to PowerPoint

Learn to use Office Mix!
Links to companion **Sways**, featuring **videos** with hands-on instructions, are located on www.cengagebrain.com.

To get started, you create an Office Mix account at the website mix.office.com using an email address or a Facebook or Google account. Next, you download and install the Office Mix add-in (see **Figure 11**). Office Mix appears as a new tab named Mix on the PowerPoint ribbon in versions of Office 2013 and Office 2016 running on personal computers (PCs).

Figure 11: Getting started with Office Mix

Capturing Video Clips

A **clip** is a short segment of audio, such as music, or video. After finishing the content on a PowerPoint slide, you can use Office Mix to add a video clip to animate or illustrate the content. Office Mix creates video clips in two ways: by recording live action on a webcam and by capturing screen images and movements. If your computer has a webcam, you can record yourself and annotate the slide to create a **slide recording** as shown in **Figure 12**.

Figure 12: Making a slide recording

When you are making a slide recording, you can record your spoken narration at the same time. The **Slide Notes** feature works like a teleprompter to help you focus on your presentation content instead of memorizing your narration. Use the Inking tools to make annotations or add highlighting using different pen types and colors. After finishing a recording, edit the video in PowerPoint to trim the length or set playback options.

The second way to create a video is to capture on-screen images and actions with or without a voiceover. This method is ideal if you want to show how to use your favorite website or demonstrate an app such as OneNote. To share your screen with an audience, select the part of the screen you want to show in the video. Office Mix captures everything that happens in that area to create a **screen recording**, as shown in **Figure 13**. Office Mix inserts the screen recording as a video in the slide.

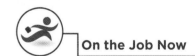
Figure 13: Making a screen recording

Inserting Quizzes, Live Webpages, and Apps

To enhance and assess audience understanding, make your slides interactive by adding quizzes, live webpages, and apps. Quizzes give immediate feedback to the user as shown in **Figure 14**. Office Mix supports several quiz formats, including a **free-response quiz** similar to a short answer quiz, and true/false, multiple-choice, and multiple-response formats.

Figure 14: Creating an interactive quiz

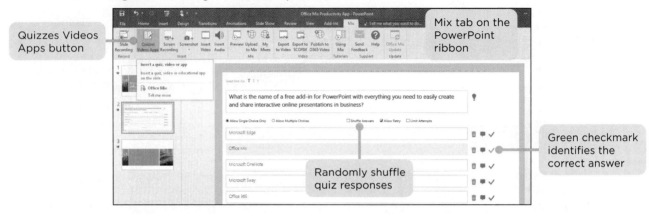

Sharing an Office Mix Presentation

When you complete your work with Office Mix, upload the presentation to your personal Office Mix dashboard as shown in **Figure 15**. Users of PCs, Macs, iOS devices, and Android devices can access and play Office Mix presentations. The Office Mix dashboard displays built-in analytics that include the quiz results and how much time viewers spent on each slide. You can play completed Office Mix presentations online or download them as movies.

Figure 15: Sharing an Office Mix presentation

Try This Now

1: Creating an Office Mix Tutorial for OneNote

Note: This activity requires a microphone on your computer.

Office Mix makes it easy to record screens and their contents. Create PowerPoint slides with an Office Mix screen recording to show OneNote 2016 features. Perform the following tasks:

a. Create a PowerPoint presentation with the Ion Boardroom template. Create an opening slide with the title **My Favorite OneNote Features** and enter your name in the subtitle.
b. Create three additional slides, each titled with a new feature of OneNote. Open OneNote and use the Mix tab in PowerPoint to capture three separate screen recordings that teach your favorite features.
c. Add a fifth slide that quizzes the user with a multiple-choice question about OneNote and includes four responses. Be sure to insert a checkmark indicating the correct response.
d. Upload the completed presentation to your Office Mix dashboard and share the link with your instructor.
e. Submit your assignment link in the format specified by your instructor.

Learn to use Office Mix!
Links to companion **Sways**, featuring **videos** with hands-on instructions, are located on www.cengagebrain.com.

2: Teaching Augmented Reality with Office Mix

Note: This activity requires a webcam or built-in video camera on your computer.

A local elementary school has asked you to teach augmented reality to its students using Office Mix. Perform the following tasks:

a. Research augmented reality using your favorite online search tools.
b. Create a PowerPoint presentation with the Frame template. Create an opening slide with the title **Augmented Reality** and enter your name in the subtitle.
c. Create a slide with four bullets summarizing your research of augmented reality. Create a 20-second slide recording of yourself providing a quick overview of augmented reality.
d. Create another slide with a 30-second screen recording of a video about augmented reality from a site such as YouTube or another video-sharing site.
e. Add a final slide that quizzes the user with a true/false question about augmented reality. Be sure to insert a checkmark indicating the correct response.
f. Upload the completed presentation to your Office Mix dashboard and share the link with your instructor.
g. Submit your assignment link in the format specified by your instructor.

3: Marketing a Travel Destination with Office Mix

Note: This activity requires a webcam or built-in video camera on your computer.

To convince your audience to travel to a particular city, create a slide presentation marketing any city in the world using a slide recording, screen recording, and a quiz. Perform the following tasks:

a. Create a PowerPoint presentation with any template. Create an opening slide with the title of the city you are marketing as a travel destination and your name in the subtitle.
b. Create a slide with four bullets about the featured city. Create a 30-second slide recording of yourself explaining why this city is the perfect vacation destination.
c. Create another slide with a 20-second screen recording of a travel video about the city from a site such as YouTube or another video-sharing site.
d. Add a final slide that quizzes the user with a multiple-choice question about the featured city with five responses. Be sure to include a checkmark indicating the correct response.
e. Upload the completed presentation to your Office Mix dashboard and share your link with your instructor.
f. Submit your assignment link in the format specified by your instructor.

Introduction to Microsoft Edge

Reading view | Hub | Cortana | Web Note | Inking | sandbox

Bottom Line

- Microsoft Edge is the name of the new web browser built into Windows 10.
- Microsoft Edge allows you to search the web faster, take web notes, read webpages without distractions, and get instant assistance from Cortana.

Microsoft Edge is the default web browser developed for the Windows 10 operating system as a replacement for Internet Explorer. Unlike its predecessor, Edge lets you write on webpages, read webpages without advertisements and other distractions, and search for information using a virtual personal assistant. The Edge interface is clean and basic, as shown in **Figure 16**, meaning you can pay more attention to the webpage content.

Figure 16: Microsoft Edge tools

Learn to use Edge!

Links to companion **Sways**, featuring **videos** with hands-on instructions, are located on www.cengagebrain.com.

Browsing the Web with Microsoft Edge

One of the fastest browsers available, Edge allows you to type search text directly in the Address bar. As you view the resulting webpage, you can switch to **Reading view**, which is available for most news and research sites, to eliminate distracting advertisements. For example, if you are catching up on technology news online, the webpage might be difficult to read due to a busy layout cluttered with ads. Switch to Reading view to refresh the page and remove the original page formatting, ads, and menu sidebars to read the article distraction-free.

Consider the **Hub** in Microsoft Edge as providing one-stop access to all the things you collect on the web, such as your favorite websites, reading list, surfing history, and downloaded files.

Locating Information with Cortana

Cortana, the Windows 10 virtual assistant, plays an important role in Microsoft Edge. After you turn on Cortana, it appears as an animated circle in the Address bar when you might need assistance, as shown in the restaurant website in **Figure 17**. When you click the Cortana icon, a pane slides in from the right of the browser window to display detailed information about the restaurant, including maps and reviews. Cortana can also assist you in defining words, finding the weather, suggesting coupons for shopping, updating stock market information, and calculating math.

On the Job Now

Businesses started adopting Internet Explorer more than 20 years ago simply to view webpages. Today, Microsoft Edge has a different purpose: to promote interaction with the web and share its contents with colleagues.

Figure 17: Cortana providing restaurant information

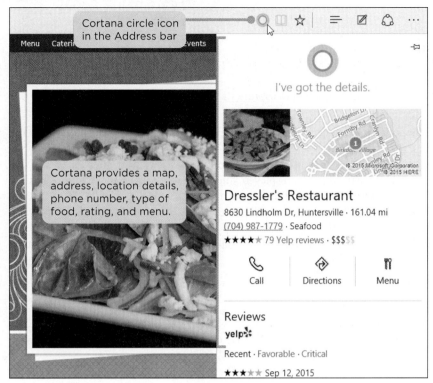

Annotating Webpages

One of the most impressive Microsoft Edge features are the **Web Note** tools, which you use to write on a webpage or to highlight text. When you click the Make a Web Note button, an **Inking** toolbar appears, as shown in **Figure 18**, that provides writing and drawing tools. These tools include an eraser, a pen, and a highlighter with different colors. You can also insert a typed note and copy a screen image (called a screen clipping). You can draw with a pointing device, fingertip, or stylus using different pen colors. Whether you add notes to a recipe, annotate sources for a research paper, or select a product while shopping online, the Web Note tools can enhance your productivity. After you complete your notes, click the Save button to save the annotations to OneNote, your Favorites list, or your Reading list. You can share the inked page with others using the Share Web Note button.

On the Job Now

To enhance security, Microsoft Edge runs in a partial sandbox, an arrangement that prevents attackers from gaining control of your computer. Browsing within the **sandbox** protects computer resources and information from hackers.

Figure 18: Web Note tools in Microsoft Edge

Inking toolbar with Web Note tools for making annotations

Writing and drawing created with the Pen tool

Highlighted text

Save a copy of the webpage with annotations

Typed note

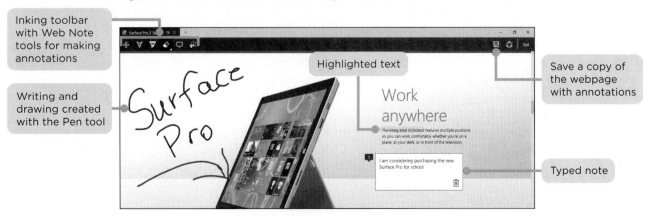

Try This Now

Learn to use Edge!
Links to companion **Sways**, featuring **videos** with hands-on instructions, are located on www.cengagebrain.com.

1: Using Cortana in Microsoft Edge

Note: This activity requires using Microsoft Edge on a Windows 10 computer.

Cortana can assist you in finding information on a webpage in Microsoft Edge. Perform the following tasks:

a. Create a Word document using the Word Screen Clipping tool to capture the following screenshots.

- Screenshot A—Using Microsoft Edge, open a webpage with a technology news article. Right-click a term in the article and ask Cortana to define it.
- Screenshot B—Using Microsoft Edge, open the website of a fancy restaurant in a city near you. Make sure the Cortana circle icon is displayed in the Address bar. (If it's not displayed, find a different restaurant website.) Click the Cortana circle icon to display a pane with information about the restaurant.
- Screenshot C—Using Microsoft Edge, type **10 USD to Euros** in the Address bar without pressing the Enter key. Cortana converts the U.S. dollars to Euros.
- Screenshot D—Using Microsoft Edge, type **Apple stock** in the Address bar without pressing the Enter key. Cortana displays the current stock quote.

b. Submit your assignment in the format specified by your instructor.

2: Viewing Online News with Reading View

Note: This activity requires using Microsoft Edge on a Windows 10 computer.

Reading view in Microsoft Edge can make a webpage less cluttered with ads and other distractions. Perform the following tasks:

a. Create a Word document using the Word Screen Clipping tool to capture the following screenshots.

- Screenshot A—Using Microsoft Edge, open the website **mashable.com**. Open a technology article. Click the Reading view button to display an ad-free page that uses only basic text formatting.
- Screenshot B—Using Microsoft Edge, open the website **bbc.com**. Open any news article. Click the Reading view button to display an ad-free page that uses only basic text formatting.
- Screenshot C—Make three types of annotations (Pen, Highlighter, and Add a typed note) on the BBC article page displayed in Reading view.

b. Submit your assignment in the format specified by your instructor.

3: Inking with Microsoft Edge

Note: This activity requires using Microsoft Edge on a Windows 10 computer.

Microsoft Edge provides many annotation options to record your ideas. Perform the following tasks:

a. Open the website **wolframalpha.com** in the Microsoft Edge browser. Wolfram Alpha is a well-respected academic search engine. Type **US$100 1965 dollars in 2015** in the Wolfram Alpha search text box and press the Enter key.

b. Click the Make a Web Note button to display the Web Note tools. Using the Pen tool, draw a circle around the result on the webpage. Save the page to OneNote.

c. In the Wolfram Alpha search text box, type the name of the city closest to where you live and press the Enter key. Using the Highlighter tool, highlight at least three interesting results. Add a note and then type a sentence about what you learned about this city. Save the page to OneNote. Share your OneNote notebook with your instructor.

d. Submit your assignment link in the format specified by your instructor.

Creating a Database

Tracking Animal, Visit, and Billing Data

ACCESS

OBJECTIVES

Session 1.1
- Learn basic database concepts and terms
- Start and exit Access
- Explore the Microsoft Access window and Backstage view
- Create a blank database
- Create and save a table in Datasheet view
- Enter field names and records in a table datasheet
- Open a table using the Navigation Pane

Session 1.2
- Open an Access database
- Copy and paste records from another Access database
- Navigate a table datasheet
- Create and navigate a simple query
- Create and navigate a simple form
- Create, preview, navigate, and print a simple report
- Use Help in Access
- Learn how to compact, back up, and restore a database

Case | *Riverview Veterinary Care Center*

Riverview Veterinary Care Center, a veterinary care center in Cody, Wyoming, provides care for pets and livestock in the greater Cody area. In addition to caring for household pets, such as dogs and cats, the center specializes in serving the needs of livestock on ranches in the surrounding area. Kimberly Johnson, the office manager for Riverview Veterinary Care Center, oversees a small staff and is responsible for maintaining the medical records for all of the animals the care center serves.

In order to best manage the center, Kimberly and her staff rely on electronic medical records for information on the animals and their owners, billing, inventory control, purchasing, and accounts payable. Several months ago, the center upgraded to **Microsoft Access 2016** (or simply **Access**), a computer program used to enter, maintain, and retrieve related data in a format known as a database. Kimberly and her staff want to use Access to store information about the animals, their owners, billing, vendors, and products. She asks for your help in creating the necessary Access database.

STARTING DATA FILES

Access1 → Module	Review	Case1
Kimberly.accdb	Company.accdb	BeautyToGo.accdb

Case2	Case3	Case4
ProgPros.accdb	Diane.accdb	HikeApp.accdb

Session 1.1 Visual Overview:

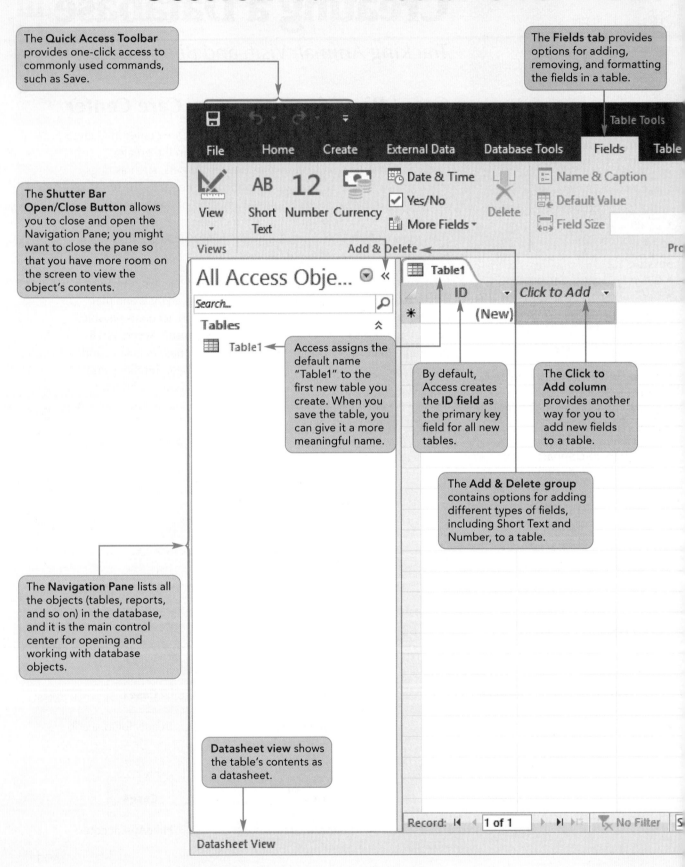

The **Quick Access Toolbar** provides one-click access to commonly used commands, such as Save.

The **Fields tab** provides options for adding, removing, and formatting the fields in a table.

The **Shutter Bar Open/Close Button** allows you to close and open the Navigation Pane; you might want to close the pane so that you have more room on the screen to view the object's contents.

Access assigns the default name "Table1" to the first new table you create. When you save the table, you can give it a more meaningful name.

By default, Access creates the **ID field** as the primary key field for all new tables.

The **Click to Add column** provides another way for you to add new fields to a table.

The **Add & Delete group** contains options for adding different types of fields, including Short Text and Number, to a table.

The **Navigation Pane** lists all the objects (tables, reports, and so on) in the database, and it is the main control center for opening and working with database objects.

Datasheet view shows the table's contents as a datasheet.

The Access Window

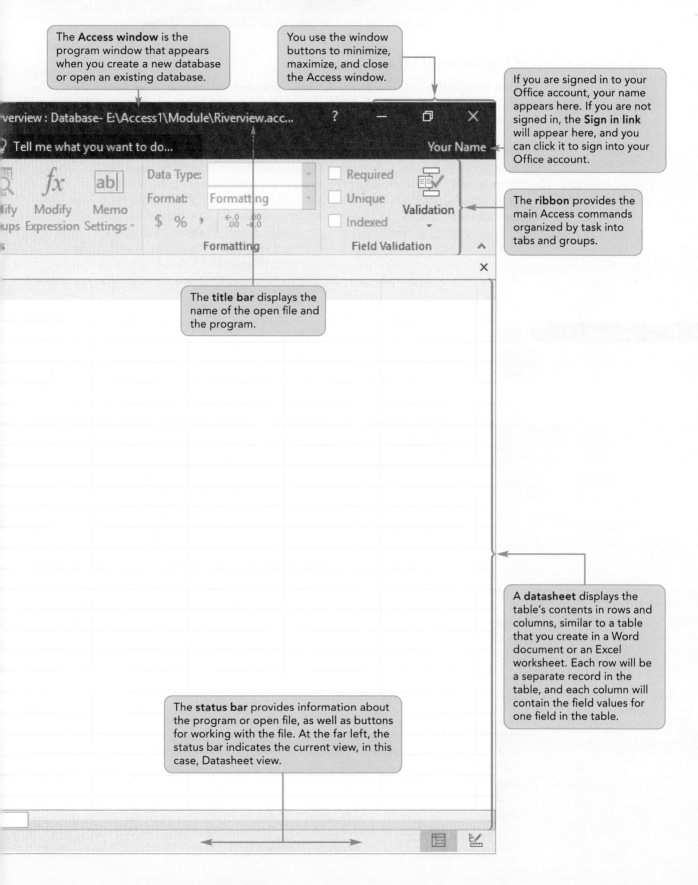

The **Access window** is the program window that appears when you create a new database or open an existing database.

You use the window buttons to minimize, maximize, and close the Access window.

If you are signed in to your Office account, your name appears here. If you are not signed in, the **Sign in link** will appear here, and you can click it to sign into your Office account.

The **ribbon** provides the main Access commands organized by task into tabs and groups.

The **title bar** displays the name of the open file and the program.

A **datasheet** displays the table's contents in rows and columns, similar to a table that you create in a Word document or an Excel worksheet. Each row will be a separate record in the table, and each column will contain the field values for one field in the table.

The **status bar** provides information about the program or open file, as well as buttons for working with the file. At the far left, the status bar indicates the current view, in this case, Datasheet view.

Introduction to Database Concepts

Before you begin using Access to create the database for Kimberly, you need to understand a few key terms and concepts associated with databases.

Organizing Data

Data is a valuable resource to any business. At Riverview Veterinary Care Center, for example, important data includes the names of the animals, owners' contact information, visit dates, and billing information. Organizing, storing, maintaining, retrieving, and sorting this type of data are critical activities that enable a business to find and use information effectively. Before storing data on a computer, however, you must organize the data.

Your first step in organizing data is to identify the individual fields. A **field** is a single characteristic or attribute of a person, place, object, event, or idea. For example, some of the many fields that Riverview Veterinary Care Center tracks are the animal ID, animal name, animal type, breed, visit date, reason for visit, and invoice amount.

Next, you group related fields together into tables. A **table** is a collection of fields that describes a person, place, object, event, or idea. Figure 1-1 shows an example of an Animal table that contains the following four fields: AnimalID, AnimalName, AnimalType, and AnimalBreed. Each field is a column in the table, with the field name displayed as the column heading.

Figure 1-1	Data organization for a table of animals

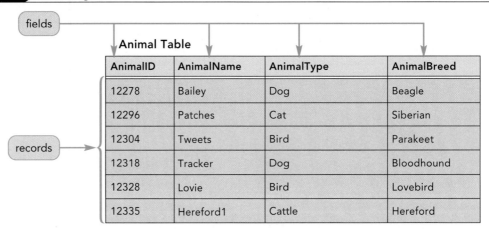

The specific content of a field is called the **field value**. In Figure 1-1, the first set of field values for AnimalID, AnimalName, AnimalType, and AnimalBreed are, respectively: 12278; Bailey; Dog; and Beagle. This set of field values is called a **record**. In the Animal table, the data for each animal is stored as a separate record. Figure 1-1 shows six records; each row of field values in the table is a record.

Databases and Relationships

A collection of related tables is called a **database**, or a **relational database**. In this module, you will create the database for Riverview Veterinary Care Center, and within that database, you'll create a table named Visit to store data about animal visits. Later on, you'll create three more tables, named Animal, Owner, and Billing, to store related information about animals, their owners, and invoices related to their care.

As Kimberly and her staff use the database that you will create, they will need to access information about animals and their visits. To obtain this information, you must have a way to connect records in the Animal table to records in the Visit table. You connect the records in the separate tables through a **common field** that appears in both tables.

In the sample database shown in Figure 1-2, each record in the Animal table has a field named AnimalID, which is also a field in the Visit table. For example, the beagle named Bailey is the first animal in the Animal table and has an AnimalID field value of 12278. This same AnimalID field value, 12278, appears in two records in the Visit table. Therefore, the beagle named Bailey is the animal that was seen at these two visits.

| Figure 1-2 | Database relationship between tables for animals and visits |

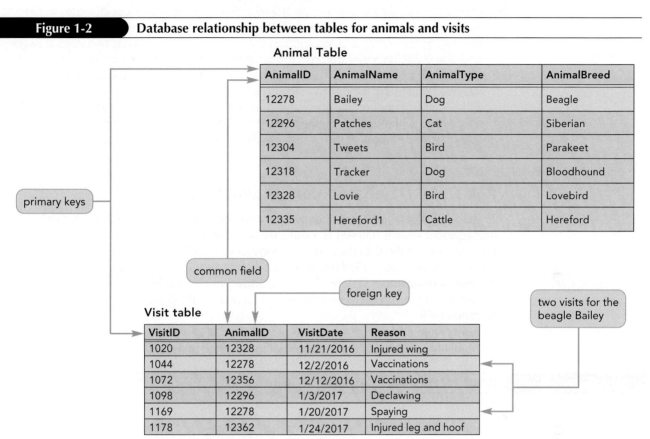

Each AnimalID value in the Animal table must be unique so that you can distinguish one animal from another. These unique AnimalID values also identify each animal's specific visits in the Visit table. The AnimalID field is referred to as the primary key of the Animal table. A **primary key** is a field, or a collection of fields, whose values uniquely identify each record in a table. No two records can contain the same value for the primary key field. In the Visit table, the VisitID field is the primary key because Riverview Veterinary Care Center assigns each visit a unique identification number.

When you include the primary key from one table as a field in a second table to form a relationship between the two tables, it is called a **foreign key** in the second table, as shown in Figure 1-2. For example, AnimalID is the primary key in the Animal table and a foreign key in the Visit table. The AnimalID field must have the same characteristics in both tables. Although the primary key AnimalID contains unique values in the Animal table, the same field as a foreign key in the Visit table does not necessarily contain unique values. The AnimalID value 12278, for example, appears two times in the Visit table because the beagle named Bailey made two visits to the center. Each foreign key value, however, must match one of the field values for the primary key in the other table. In the example shown in Figure 1-2, each AnimalID value in the Visit table must match an AnimalID value in the Animal table. The two tables are related, enabling users to connect the facts about animals with the facts about their visits to the center.

INSIGHT

Storing Data in Separate Tables

When you create a database, you must create separate tables that contain only fields that are directly related to each other. For example, in the Riverview database, the animal and visit data should not be stored in the same table because doing so would make the data difficult to update and prone to errors. Consider the beagle Bailey and her visits to the center, and assume that she has many more than just two visits. If all the animal and visit data was stored in the same table, so that each record (row) contained all the information about each visit and the animal, the animal data would appear multiple times in the table. This causes problems when the data changes. For example, if the phone number of Bailey's owner changed, you would have to update the multiple occurrences of the owner's phone number throughout the table. Not only would this be time-consuming, it would increase the likelihood of errors or inconsistent data.

Relational Database Management Systems

To manage its databases, a company uses a database management system. A **database management system (DBMS)** is a software program that lets you create databases and then manipulate the data they contain. Most of today's database management systems, including Access, are called relational database management systems. In a **relational database management system**, data is organized as a collection of tables. As stated earlier, a relationship between two tables in a relational DBMS is formed through a common field.

A relational DBMS controls the storage of databases and facilitates the creation, manipulation, and reporting of data, as illustrated in Figure 1-3.

Figure 1-3   **Relational database management system**

Specifically, a relational DBMS provides the following functions:

- It allows you to create database structures containing fields, tables, and table relationships.
- It lets you easily add new records, change field values in existing records, and delete records.
- It contains a built-in query language, which lets you obtain immediate answers to the questions (or queries) you ask about your data.
- It contains a built-in report generator, which lets you produce professional-looking, formatted reports from your data.
- It protects databases through security, control, and recovery facilities.

An organization such as Riverview Veterinary Care Center benefits from a relational DBMS because it allows users working in different groups to share the same data. More than one user can enter data into a database, and more than one user can retrieve and analyze data that other users have entered. For example, the database for Riverview Veterinary Care Center will contain only one copy of the Visit table, and all employees will use it to access visit information.

Finally, unlike other software programs, such as spreadsheet programs, a DBMS can handle massive amounts of data and can be used to create relationships among multiple tables. Each Access database, for example, can be up to two gigabytes in size, can contain up to 32,768 objects (tables, reports, and so on), and can have up to 255 people using the database at the same time. For instructional purposes, the databases you will create and work with throughout this text contain a relatively small number of records compared to databases you would encounter outside the classroom, which would likely contain tables with very large numbers of records.

Starting Access and Creating a Database

Now that you've learned some database terms and concepts, you're ready to start Access and create the Riverview database for Kimberly.

To start Access:

▶ **1.** On the Windows taskbar, click the **Start** button ⊞. The Start menu opens.

▶ **2.** Click **All apps** on the Start menu, and then click **Access 2016**. Access starts and displays the Recent screen in Backstage view. See Figure 1-4.

Figure 1-4	Recent screen in Backstage view

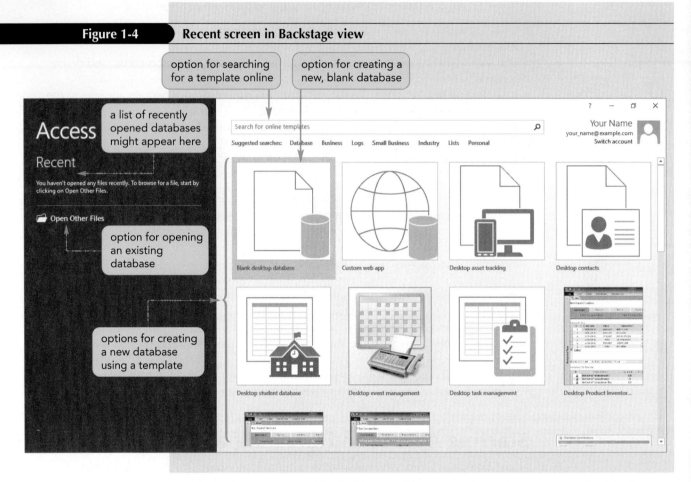

When you start Access, the first screen that appears is Backstage view, which is the starting place for your work in Access. **Backstage view** contains commands that allow you to manage Access files and options. The Recent screen in Backstage view provides options for you to create a new database or open an existing database. To create a new database that does not contain any data or objects, you use the Blank desktop database option. If the database you need to create contains objects that match those found in common databases, such as databases that store data about contacts or tasks, you can use one of the templates provided with Access. A **template** is a predesigned database that includes professionally designed tables, reports, and other database objects that can make it quick and easy for you to create a database. You can also search for a template online using the Search for online templates box.

In this case, the templates provided do not match Kimberly's needs for the center's database, so you need to create a new, blank database from scratch.

To create the new Riverview database:

▶ **1.** Make sure you have the Access starting Data Files on your computer.

Trouble? If you don't have the starting Data Files, you need to get them before you can proceed. Your instructor will either give you the Data Files or ask you to obtain them from a specified location (such as a network drive). If you have any questions about the Data Files, see your instructor or technical support person for assistance.

▶ **2.** On the Recent screen, click **Blank desktop database** (see Figure 1-4). The Blank desktop database screen opens.

Be sure to type **Riverview** or you'll create a database named Database1.

▶ **3.** In the File Name box, type **Riverview** to replace the selected database name provided by Access, Database1. Next you need to specify the location for the file.

▶ **4.** Click the **Browse** button 📁 to the right of the File Name box. The File New Database dialog box opens.

▶ **5.** Navigate to the drive and folder where you are storing your files, as specified by your instructor.

▶ **6.** Make sure the Save as type box displays "Microsoft Access 2007–2016 Databases."

   Trouble? If your computer is set up to show filename extensions, you will see the Access filename extension ".accdb" in the File name box.

TIP

If you don't type the filename extension, Access adds it automatically.

▶ **7.** Click the **OK** button. You return to the Blank desktop database screen, and the File Name box now shows the name Riverview.accdb. The filename extension ".accdb" identifies the file as an Access 2007–2016 database.

▶ **8.** Click the **Create** button. Access creates the new database, saves it to the specified location, and then opens an empty table named Table1.

   Trouble? If you see only ribbon tab names and no buttons, click the Home tab to expand the ribbon, and then in the bottom-right corner of the ribbon, click the Pin the ribbon button 📌.

Refer back to the Session 1.1 Visual Overview and spend some time becoming familiar with the components of the Access window.

INSIGHT

Understanding the Database File Type

Access 2016 uses the .accdb file extension, which is the same file extension used for databases created with Microsoft Access 2007, 2010, and 2013. To ensure compatibility between these earlier versions and the Access 2016 software, new databases created using Access 2016 have the same file extension and file format as Access 2007, Access 2010, and Access 2013 databases. This is why the File New Database dialog box provides the Microsoft Access 2007–2016 Databases option in the Save as type box. In addition, the notation "(Access 2007–2016 file format)" appears in the title bar next to the name of an open database in Access 2016, confirming that database files with the .accdb extension can be used in Access 2007, Access 2010, Access 2013, and Access 2016.

Working in Touch Mode

TIP

On a touch device, you tap instead of click.

If you are working on a touch device, such as a tablet, you can switch to Touch Mode in Access to make it easier for you to tap buttons on the ribbon and perform other touch actions. Your screens will not match those shown in the book exactly, but this will not cause any problems.

Note: The following steps assume that you are using a mouse. If you are instead using a touch device, please read these steps but don't complete them, so that you remain working in Touch Mode.

To switch to Touch Mode:

▶ **1.** On the Quick Access Toolbar, click the **Customize Quick Access Toolbar** button ▤. A menu opens listing buttons you can add to the Quick Access Toolbar as well as other options for customizing the toolbar.

Trouble? If the Touch/Mouse Mode command on the menu has a checkmark next to it, press the Esc key to close the menu, and then skip to Step 3.

▶ **2.** Click **Touch/Mouse Mode**. The Quick Access Toolbar now contains the Touch/Mouse Mode button ▤, which you can use to switch between Mouse Mode, the default display, and Touch Mode.

▶ **3.** On the Quick Access Toolbar, click the **Touch/Mouse Mode** button ▤. A menu opens with two commands: Mouse, which shows the ribbon in the standard display and is optimized for use with the mouse; and Touch, which provides more space between the buttons and commands on the ribbon and is optimized for use with touch devices. The icon next to Mouse is shaded red to indicate that it is selected.

Trouble? If the icon next to Touch is shaded red, press the Esc key to close the menu and skip to Step 5.

▶ **4.** Click **Touch**. The display switches to Touch Mode with more space between the commands and buttons on the ribbon. See Figure 1-5.

| Figure 1-5 | Ribbon displayed in Touch Mode |

The figures in this text show the standard Mouse Mode display, and the instructions assume you are using a mouse to click and select options, so you'll switch back to Mouse Mode.

Trouble? If you are using a touch device and want to remain in Touch Mode, skip Steps 5 and 6.

▶ **5.** On the Quick Access Toolbar, click the **Touch/Mouse Mode** button ▤, and then click **Mouse**. The ribbon returns to the standard display, as shown in the Session 1.1 Visual Overview.

▶ **6.** On the Quick Access Toolbar, click the **Customize Quick Access Toolbar** button ▤, and then click **Touch/Mouse Mode** to deselect it. The Touch/Mouse Mode button is removed from the Quick Access Toolbar.

Creating a Table in Datasheet View

Tables contain all the data in a database and are the fundamental objects for your work in Access. There are different ways to create a table in Access, including entering the fields and records for the table directly in Datasheet view.

REFERENCE

Creating a Table in Datasheet View

- On the ribbon, click the Create tab.
- In the Tables group, click the Table button.
- Rename the default ID primary key field and change its data type, if necessary; or accept the default ID field with the AutoNumber data type.
- In the Add & Delete group on the Fields tab, click the button for the type of field you want to add to the table (for example, click the Short Text button), and then type the field name; or, in the table datasheet, click the Click to Add column heading, click the type of field you want to add from the list that opens, and then press the Tab or Enter key to move to the next column in the datasheet. Repeat this step to add all the necessary fields to the table.
- In the first row below the field names, enter the value for each field in the first record, pressing the Tab or Enter key to move from one field to the next.
- After entering the value for the last field in the first record, press the Tab or Enter key to move to the next row, and then enter the values for the next record. Continue this process until you have entered all the records for the table.
- On the Quick Access Toolbar, click the Save button, enter a name for the table, and then click the OK button.

For Riverview Veterinary Care Center, Kimberly needs to track information about each animal visit at the center. She asks you to create the Visit table according to the plan shown in Figure 1-6.

Figure 1-6   **Plan for the Visit table**

Field	Purpose
VisitID	Unique number assigned to each visit; will serve as the table's primary key
AnimalID	Unique number assigned to each animal; common field that will be a foreign key to connect to the Animal table
VisitDate	Date on which the animal visited the center or was seen offsite
Reason	Reason/diagnosis for the animal visit
OffSite	Whether the animal visit was offsite at a home or ranch

As shown in Kimberly's plan, she wants to store data about visits in five fields, including fields to contain the date of each visit, the reason for the visit, and if the visit was offsite. These are the most important aspects of a visit and, therefore, must be tracked. Also, notice that the VisitID field will be the primary key for the table; each visit at Riverview Veterinary Care Center has a unique number assigned to it, so this field is the logical choice for the primary key. Finally, the AnimalID field is needed in the Visit table as a foreign key to connect the information about visits to animals. The data about animals, as well as the data about their owners, and the bills for the animals' care, will be stored in separate tables, which you will create later.

Notice the name of each field in Figure 1-6. You need to name each field, table, and object in an Access database.

PROSKILLS

Decision Making: Naming Fields in Access Tables

One of the most important tasks in creating a table is deciding what names to specify for the table's fields. Keep the following guidelines in mind when you assign field names:

- A field name can consist of up to 64 characters, including letters, numbers, spaces, and special characters, except for the period (.), exclamation mark (!), grave accent ('), and square brackets ([ ]).
- A field name cannot begin with a space.
- Capitalize the first letter of each word in a field name that combines multiple words, for example VisitDate.
- Use concise field names that are easy to remember and reference and that won't take up a lot of space in the table datasheet.
- Use standard abbreviations, such as Num for Number, Amt for Amount, and Qty for Quantity, and use them consistently throughout the database. For example, if you use Num for Number in one field name, do not use the number sign (#) for Number in another.
- Give fields descriptive names so that you can easily identify them when you view or edit records.
- Although Access supports the use of spaces in field names (and in other object names), experienced database developers avoid using spaces because they can cause errors when the objects are involved in programming tasks.

By spending time obtaining and analyzing information about the fields in a table, and understanding the rules for naming fields, you can create a well-designed table that will be easy for others to use.

Renaming the Default Primary Key Field

As noted earlier, Access provides the ID field as the default primary key for a new table you create in Datasheet view. Recall that a primary key is a field, or a collection of fields, whose values uniquely identify each record in a table. However, according to Kimberly's plan, the VisitID field should be the primary key for the Visit table. You'll begin by renaming the default ID field to create the VisitID field.

To rename the ID field to the VisitID field:

TIP

A **shortcut menu** opens when you right-click an object and provides options for working with that object.

1. Right-click the **ID** column heading to open the shortcut menu, and then click **Rename Field**. The column heading ID is selected, so that whatever text you type next will replace it.

2. Type **VisitID** and then click the row below the heading. The column heading changes to VisitID, and the insertion point moves to the row below the heading. The **insertion point** is a flashing cursor that shows where text you type will be inserted. In this case, it is hidden within the selected field value (New). See Figure 1-7.

    Trouble? If you make a mistake while typing the field name, use the Backspace key to delete characters to the left of the insertion point or the Delete key to delete characters to the right of the insertion point. Then type the correct text. To correct a field name by replacing it entirely, press the Esc key, and then type the correct text.

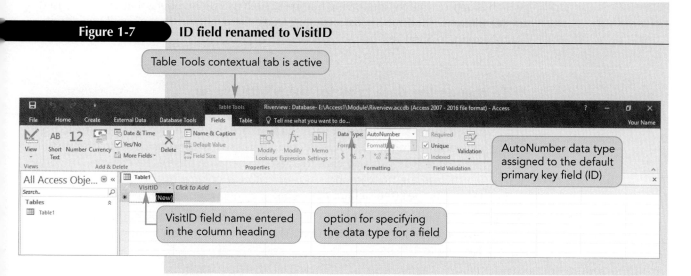

Figure 1-7   **ID field renamed to VisitID**

Table Tools contextual tab is active

AutoNumber data type assigned to the default primary key field (ID)

VisitID field name entered in the column heading

option for specifying the data type for a field

Notice that the Table Tools tab is active on the ribbon. This is an example of a **contextual tab**, which is a tab that appears and provides options for working with a specific object that is selected—in this case, the table you are creating. As you work with other objects in the database, other contextual tabs will appear with commands and options related to each selected object.

Buttons and Labels on the Ribbon

INSIGHT

Depending on the size of the monitor you are using and your screen resolution settings, you might see more or fewer buttons on the ribbon, and you might not see labels next to certain buttons. The screenshots in these modules were created using a screen resolution setting of 1366 x 768 with the program window maximized. If you are using a smaller monitor or a lower screen resolution, some buttons will appear only as icons, with no labels next to them, because there is not enough room on the ribbon to display the labels.

You have renamed the default primary key field, ID, to VisitID. However, the VisitID field still retains the characteristics of the ID field, including its data type. Your next task is to change the data type of this field.

Changing the Data Type of the Default Primary Key Field

Notice the Formatting group on the Table Tools Fields tab. One of the options available in this group is the Data Type option (see Figure 1-7). Each field in an Access table must be assigned a data type. The **data type** determines what field values you can enter for the field. In this case, the AutoNumber data type is displayed. Access assigns the AutoNumber data type to the default ID primary key field because the **AutoNumber** data type automatically inserts a unique number in this field for every record, beginning with the number 1 for the first record, the number 2 for the second record, and so on. Therefore, a field using the AutoNumber data type can serve as the primary key for any table you create.

Visit numbers at the Riverview Veterinary Care Center are specific, four-digit numbers, so the AutoNumber data type is not appropriate for the VisitID field, which is the primary key field in the table you are creating. A better choice is the **Short Text** data type, which allows field values containing letters, digits, and other characters, and which is appropriate for identifying numbers, such as visit numbers, that are never used in calculations. So, Kimberly asks you to change the data type for the VisitID field from AutoNumber to Short Text.

To change the data type for the VisitID field:

▶ 1. Make sure that the VisitID column is selected. A column is selected when you click a field value, in which case the background color of the column heading changes to orange (the default color) and the insertion point appears in the field value. You can also click the column heading to select a column, in which case the background color of both the column heading and the field value changes (the default colors are gray and blue, respectively).

▶ 2. On the Table Tools Fields tab, in the Formatting group, click the **Data Type arrow**, and then click **Short Text**. The VisitID field is now a Short Text field. See Figure 1-8.

Figure 1-8   Short Text data type assigned to the VisitID field

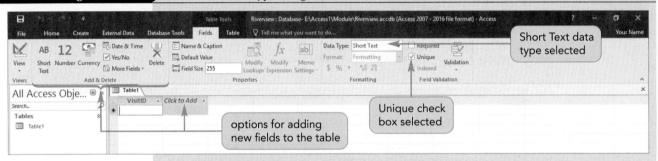

Note the Unique check box in the Field Validation group. This check box is selected because the VisitID field assumed the characteristics of the default primary key field, ID, including the fact that each value in the field must be unique. Because this check box is selected, no two records in the Visit table will be allowed to have the same value in the VisitID field.

With the VisitID field created and established as the primary key, you can now enter the rest of the fields in the Visit table.

Adding New Fields

When you create a table in Datasheet view, you can use the options in the Add & Delete group on the Table Tools Fields tab to add fields to your table. You can also use the Click to Add column in the table datasheet to add new fields. (See Figure 1-8.) You'll use both methods to add the four remaining fields to the Visit table. The next field you need to add is the AnimalID field. Similar to the VisitID field, the AnimalID field will contain numbers that will not be used in calculations, so it should be a Short Text field.

To add the rest of the fields to the Visit table:

▶ 1. On the Table Tools Fields tab, in the Add & Delete group, click the **Short Text** button. A new field named "Field1" is added to the right of the VisitID field. See Figure 1-9.

| Figure 1-9 | New Short Text field added to the table |

The text "Field1" is selected, so you can simply type the new field name to replace it.

2. Type **AnimalID**. The second field is added to the table. Next, you'll add the VisitDate field. Because this field will contain date values, you'll add a field with the **Date/Time** data type, which allows field values in a variety of date and time formats.

3. In the Add & Delete group, click the **Date & Time** button. Access adds a third field to the table, this time with the Date/Time data type.

4. Type **VisitDate** to replace the selected name "Field1." The fourth field in the Visit table is the Reason field, which will contain brief descriptions of the reason for the visit to the center. You'll add another Short Text field—this time using the Click to Add column.

5. Click the **Click to Add** column heading. Access displays a list of available data types from which you can choose the data type for the new field you're adding.

6. Click **Short Text** in the list. Access adds a fourth field to the table.

7. Type **Reason** to replace the highlighted name "Field1," and then press the **Enter** key. The Click to Add column becomes active and displays the list of field data types.

The fifth and final field in the Visit table is the OffSite field, which will indicate whether or not the visit was at an offsite venue, such as at a home or ranch (that is, not within the center). The **Yes/No** data type is suitable for this field because it is used to define fields that store values representing one of two options—true/false, yes/no, or on/off.

TIP

You can also type the first letter of a data type to select it and close the Click to Add list.

8. Click **Yes/No** in the list, and then type **OffSite** to replace the highlighted name "Field1."

Trouble? If you pressed the Tab or Enter key after typing the OffSite field name, press the Esc key to close the Click to Add list.

9. Click in the row below the VisitID column heading. All five fields are now entered for the Visit table. See Figure 1-10.

| Figure 1-10 | Table with all fields entered |

five fields entered

record (row) selector

field (column) selector

values for first record will go in this row

The table contains three Short Text fields (VisitID, AnimalID, and Reason), one Date/Time field (VisitDate), and one Yes/No field (OffSite). You'll learn more about field data types in the next module.

As noted earlier, Datasheet view shows a table's contents in rows (records) and columns (fields). Each column is headed by a field name inside a field selector, and each row has a record selector to its left (see Figure 1-10). Clicking a **field selector** or a **record selector** selects that entire column or row (respectively), which you then can manipulate. A field selector is also called a **column selector**, and a record selector is also called a **row selector**.

Entering Records

With the fields in place for the table, you can now enter the field values for each record. Kimberly requests that you enter eight records in the Visit table, as shown in Figure 1-11.

| Figure 1-11 | Visit table records |

VisitID	AmimalID	VisitDate	Reason	OffSite
1072	12356	12/12/2016	Vaccinations	Yes
1169	12278	1/20/2017	Spaying	No
1184	12443	1/25/2017	Neutering	No
1016	12345	11/18/2016	Vaccinations	Yes
1196	12455	2/1/2017	Vaccinations	No
1098	12296	1/3/2017	Declawing	No
1178	12362	1/24/2017	Injured leg and hoof	Yes
1044	12278	12/2/2016	Vaccinations	No

To enter records in a table datasheet, you type the field values below the column headings for the fields. The first record you enter will go in the first row (see Figure 1-10).

To enter the first record for the Visit table:

Be sure to type the numbers "0" and "1" and not the letters "O" and "l" in the field value.

1. In the first row for the VisitID field, type **1072** (the VisitID field value for the first record), and then press the **Tab** key. Access adds the field value and moves the insertion point to the right, into the AnimalID column. See Figure 1-12.

| Figure 1-12 | First field value entered |

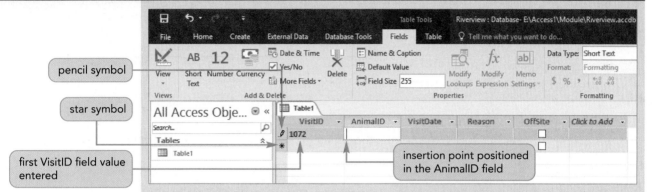

pencil symbol

star symbol

first VisitID field value entered

insertion point positioned in the AnimalID field

Trouble? If you make a mistake when typing a value, use the Backspace key to delete characters to the left of the insertion point or the Delete key to delete characters to the right of the insertion point. Then type the correct value. To correct a value by replacing it entirely, press the Esc key, and then type the correct value.

Notice the pencil symbol that appears in the row selector for the new record. The **pencil symbol** indicates that the record is being edited. Also notice the star symbol that appears in the row selector for the second row. The **star symbol** identifies the second row as the next row available for a new record.

2. Type **12356** (the AnimalID field value for the first record), and then press the **Tab** key. Access enters the field value and moves the insertion point to the VisitDate column.

3. Type **12/12/16** (the VisitDate field value for the first record), and then press the **Tab** key. Access displays the year as "2016" even though you entered only the final two digits of the year. This is because the VisitDate field has the Date/Time data type, which automatically formats dates with four-digit years.

4. Type **Vaccinations** (the Reason field value for the first record), and then press the **Tab** key to move to the OffSite column.

Recall that the OffSite field is a Yes/No field. Notice the check box displayed in the OffSite column. By default, the value for any Yes/No field is "No"; therefore, the check box is initially empty. For Yes/No fields with check boxes, you press the Tab key to leave the check box unchecked, or you press the spacebar to insert a checkmark in the check box. The record you are entering in the table is for an offsite visit, so you need to insert a checkmark in the check box to indicate "Yes."

TIP

You can also click a check box in a Yes/No field to insert or remove a checkmark.

5. Press the **spacebar** to insert a checkmark, and then press the **Tab** key. The first record is entered into the table, and the insertion point is positioned in the VisitID field for the second record. The pencil symbol is removed from the first row because the record in that row is no longer being edited. The table is now ready for you to enter the second record. See Figure 1-13.

Figure 1-13   **Datasheet with first record entered**

next row available for a new record

value displayed with a four-digit year

field values for the first record entered

Now you can enter the remaining seven records in the Visit table.

To enter the remaining records in the Visit table:

TIP

You can also press the Enter key instead of the Tab key to move from one field to another and to the next row.

1. Referring to Figure 1-11, enter the values for records 2 through 8, pressing the **Tab** key to move from field to field and to the next row for a new record. Keep in mind that you do not have to type all four digits of the year in the VisitDate field values; you can enter only the final two digits, and Access will display all four. Also, for any OffSite field values of "No," be sure to press the Tab key to leave the check box empty.

   Trouble? If you enter a value in the wrong field by mistake, such as entering a Reason field value in the VisitDate field, a menu might open with options for addressing the problem. If this happens, click the "Enter new value" option in the menu. You'll return to the field with the incorrect value selected, which you can then replace by typing the correct value.

   Notice that not all of the Reason field values are fully displayed. To see more of the table datasheet and the full field values, you'll close the Navigation Pane and resize the Reason column.

2. At the top of the Navigation Pane, click the **Shutter Bar Open/Close Button** «. The Navigation Pane closes, and only the complete table datasheet is displayed.

3. Place the pointer on the vertical line to the right of the Reason field name until the pointer changes to ↔, and then double-click the vertical line. All the Reason field values are now fully displayed. See Figure 1-14.

Figure 1-14   **Datasheet with eight records entered**

Navigation Pane is closed

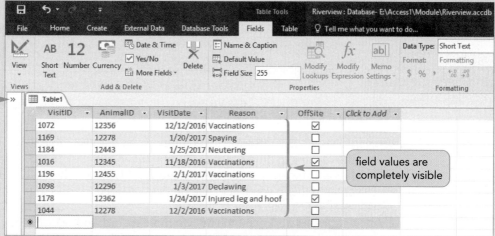

field values are completely visible

When you resize a datasheet column by double-clicking the column dividing line, you are sizing the column to its **best fit**—that is, so the column is just wide enough to display the longest visible value in the column, including the field name.

Carefully compare your VisitID and AnimalID values with those in the figure, and correct any errors before continuing.

4. Compare your table to the one in Figure 1-14. If any of the field values in your table do not match those shown in the figure, you can correct a field value by clicking to position the insertion point in the value, and then using the Backspace key or Delete key to delete incorrect text. Then type the correct text and press the Enter key. To correct a value in the OffSite field, simply click the check box to add or remove the checkmark as appropriate. Also, be sure the spelling and capitalization of field names in your table match those shown in the figure exactly and that there are no spaces between words. To correct a field name, double-click it to select it, and then type the correct name; or use the Rename Field option on the shortcut menu to rename a field with the correct name.

Saving a Table

The records you enter are immediately stored in the database as soon as you enter them; however, the table's design—the field names and characteristics of the fields themselves, plus any layout changes to the datasheet—are not saved until you save the table. When you save a new table for the first time, you should give it a name that best identifies the information it contains. Like a field name, a table name can contain up to 64 characters, including spaces.

REFERENCE

Saving a Table

- Make sure the table you want to save is open.
- On the Quick Access Toolbar, click the Save button. The Save As dialog box opens.
- In the Table Name box, type the name for the table.
- Click the OK button.

According to Kimberly's plan, you need to save the table with the name "Visit."

To save and name the Visit table:

TIP

You can also use the Save command in Backstage view to save and name a new table.

1. On the Quick Access Toolbar, click the **Save** button 🖫. The Save As dialog box opens.

2. With the default name Table1 selected in the Table Name box, type **Visit**, and then click the **OK** button. The tab for the table now displays the name "Visit," and the Visit table design is saved in the Riverview database.

Notice that after you saved and named the Visit table, Access sorted and displayed the records in order by the values in the VisitID field because it is the primary key. If you compare your screen to Figure 1-11, which shows the records in the order you entered them, you'll see that the current screen shows the records in order by the VisitID field values.

Kimberly asks you to add two more records to the Visit table. When you add a record to an existing table, you must enter the new record in the next row available for a new record; you cannot insert a row between existing records for the new record. In a table with just a few records, such as the Visit table, the next available row is visible on the screen. However, in a table with hundreds of records, you would need to scroll the datasheet to see the next row available. The easiest way to add a new record to a table is to use the New button, which scrolls the datasheet to the next row available so you can enter the new record.

To enter additional records in the Visit table:

1. If necessary, click the first record's VisitID field value (**1016**) to make it the current record.

2. On the ribbon, click the **Home** tab.

3. In the Records group, click the **New** button. The insertion point is positioned in the next row available for a new record, which in this case is row 9. See Figure 1-15.

Figure 1-15 **Entering a new record**

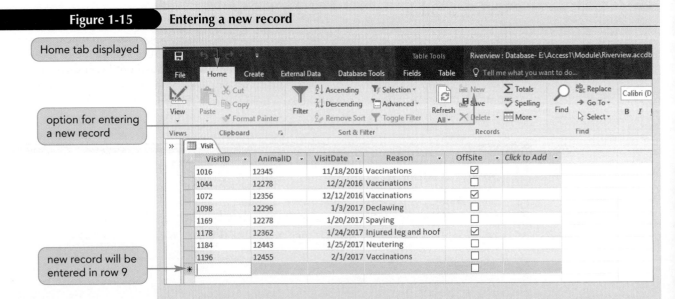

Home tab displayed

option for entering a new record

new record will be entered in row 9

VisitID	AnimalID	VisitDate	Reason	OffSite	Click to Add
1016	12345	11/18/2016	Vaccinations	☑	
1044	12278	12/2/2016	Vaccinations	☐	
1072	12356	12/12/2016	Vaccinations	☑	
1098	12296	1/3/2017	Declawing	☐	
1169	12278	1/20/2017	Spaying	☐	
1178	12362	1/24/2017	Injured leg and hoof	☑	
1184	12443	1/25/2017	Neutering	☐	
1196	12455	2/1/2017	Vaccinations	☐	
*				☐	

4. With the insertion point in the VisitID field for the new record, type **1036** and then press the **Tab** key.

5. Complete the entry of this record by entering each value shown below, pressing the **Tab** key to move from field to field:

AnimalID = **12294**

VisitDate = **11/29/2016**

Reason = **Declawing**

OffSite = **No (unchecked)**

6. Enter the values for the next new record, as follows, and then press the **Tab** key after entering the OffSite field value:

VisitID = **1152**

AnimalID = **12318**

VisitDate = **1/13/2017**

Reason = **Not eating**

OffSite = **No (unchecked)**

Your datasheet should now look like the one shown in Figure 1-16.

Figure 1-16 **Datasheet with additional records entered**

The new records you added appear at the end of the table, and are not sorted in order by the primary key field values. For example, VisitID 1036 should be the second record in the table, placed between VisitID 1016 and VisitID 1044. When you add records to a table datasheet, they appear at the end of the table. The records are not displayed in primary key order until you either close and reopen the table or switch between views.

7. Click the **Close 'Visit'** button ☒ on the object tab (see Figure 1-16 for the location of this button). The Visit table closes, and the main portion of the Access window is now blank because no database object is currently open. The Riverview database file is still open, as indicated by the filename in the Access window title bar.

Opening a Table

The tables in a database are listed in the Navigation Pane. You open a table, or any Access object, by double-clicking the object name in the Navigation Pane. Next, you'll open the Visit table so you can see all the records you've entered in the correct primary key order.

To open the Visit table:

1. On the Navigation Pane, click the **Shutter Bar Open/Close Button** >> to open the pane. Note that the Visit table is listed.

2. Double-click **Visit** to open the table in Datasheet view. See Figure 1-17.

| Figure 1-17 | Table with 10 records entered and displayed in primary key order |

Visit table object in the Riverview database

last two records added

records listed in order by the values in the primary key field

Current Record box

VisitID	AnimalID	VisitDate	Reason	OffSite	Click to Add
1016	12345	11/18/2016	Vaccinations	☑	
1036	12294	11/29/2016	Declawing	☐	
1044	12278	12/2/2016	Vaccinations	☐	
1072	12356	12/12/2016	Vaccinations	☑	
1098	12296	1/3/2017	Declawing	☐	
1152	12318	1/13/2017	Not eating	☐	
1169	12278	1/20/2017	Spaying	☐	
1178	12362	1/24/2017	Injured leg and hoof	☑	
1184	12443	1/25/2017	Neutering	☐	
1196	12455	2/1/2017	Vaccinations	☐	

Record: 1 of 10   No Filter   Search

Datasheet View

The two records you added, with VisitID field values of 1036 and 1152, now appear in the correct primary key order. The table now contains a total of 10 records, as indicated by the Current Record box at the bottom of the datasheet. The **Current Record box** displays the number of the current record as well as the total number of records in the table.

Each record contains a unique VisitID value because this field is the primary key. Other fields, however, can contain the same value in multiple records; for example, note the four values of "Vaccinations" in the Reason field.

Closing a Table and Exiting Access

When you are finished working in an Access table, it's a good idea to close the table so that you do not make unintended changes to the table data. You can close a table by clicking its Close button on the object tab, as you did earlier. Or, if you want to close the Access program as well, you can click the program's Close button. When you do, any open tables are closed, the active database is closed, and you exit the Access program.

To close the Visit table and exit Access:

1. Click the **Close** button ☒ on the program window title bar. The Visit table and the Riverview database close, and then the Access program closes.

TIP

To close a database without exiting Access, click the File tab to display Backstage view, and then click Close.

Saving a Database

INSIGHT

Unlike the Save buttons in other Office programs, the Save button on the Quick Access Toolbar in Access does not save the active document (database). Instead, you use the Save button to save the design of an Access object, such as a table (as you saw earlier), or to save datasheet format changes, such as resizing columns. Access does not have a button or option you can use to save the active database.

Access saves changes to the active database automatically when you change or add a record or close the database. If your database is stored on a removable storage device, such as a USB drive, you should never remove the device while the database file is open. If you do, Access will encounter problems when it tries to save the database, which might damage the database. Make sure you close the database first before removing the storage device.

Now that you've become familiar with database concepts and Access, and created the Riverview database and the Visit table, Kimberly wants you to add more records to the table and work with the data stored in it to create database objects including a query, form, and report. You'll complete these tasks in the next session.

Session 1.1 Quick Check

REVIEW

1. A(n) _____ is a single characteristic of a person, place, object, event, or idea.

2. You connect the records in two separate tables through a(n) _____ that appears in both tables.

3. The _____, whose values uniquely identify each record in a table, is called a(n) _____ when it is placed in a second table to form a relationship between the two tables.

4. The _____ is the area of the Access window that lists all the objects in a database, and it is the main control center for opening and working with database objects.

5. What is the name of the field that Access creates, by default, as the primary key field for a new table in Datasheet view?

6. Which group on the Fields tab contains the options you use to add new fields to a table?

7. What does a pencil symbol at the beginning of a record represent? What does a star symbol represent?

8. Explain how the saving process in Access is different from saving in other Office programs.

Session 1.2 Visual Overview:

The **Create tab** provides options for creating various database objects, including tables, forms, and reports. The options appear on the tab grouped by object type.

The **Query Wizard button** opens a dialog box with different types of wizards that guide you through the steps to create a query. One of these, the **Simple Query Wizard**, allows you to select records and fields quickly to display in the query results.

You use the options in the Tables group to create a table in Datasheet view or in Design view.

The Forms group contains options for creating a **form**, which is a database object you use to enter, edit, and view records in a database.

The **Form tool** quickly creates a form containing all the fields in the table (or query) on which you're basing the form.

The **Form Wizard** guides you through the process of creating a form.

The Queries group contains options for creating a **query**, which is a question you ask about the data stored in a database. In response to a query, Access displays the specific records and fields that answer your question.

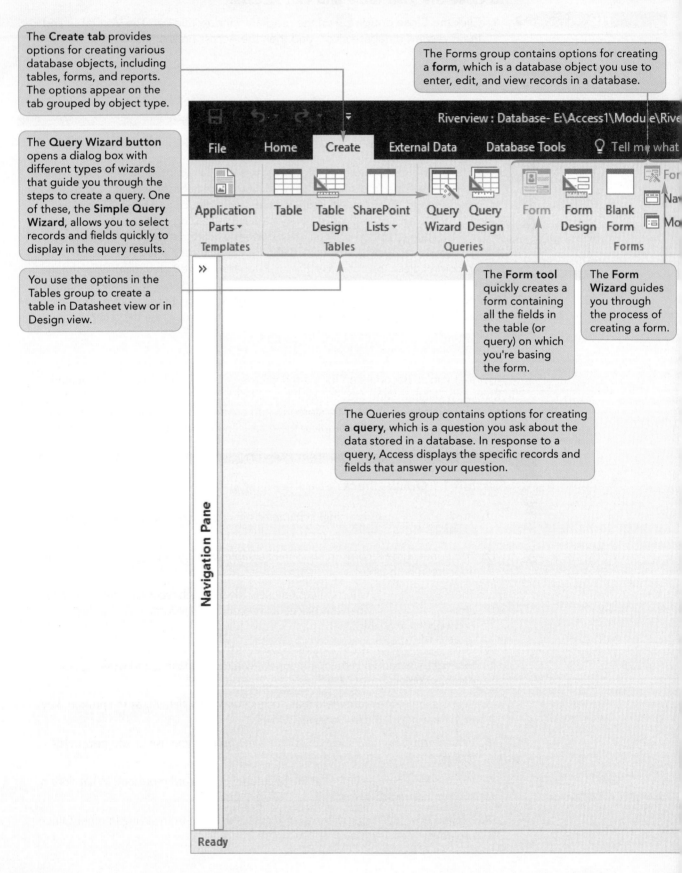

Riverview : Database- E:\Access1\Module\Rive

File   Home   Create   External Data   Database Tools   Tell me what

Application Parts ·   Table   Table Design   SharePoint Lists ·   Query Wizard   Query Design   Form   Form Design   Blank Form

Templates   Tables   Queries   Forms

Navigation Pane

Ready

The Create Tab Options

The Reports group contains options for creating a **report**, which is a formatted printout (or screen display) of the contents of one of more tables (or queries) in a database.

The Microsoft Access Help button opens the **Access 2016 Help** window, where you can find information about Access commands and features as well as instructions for using them.

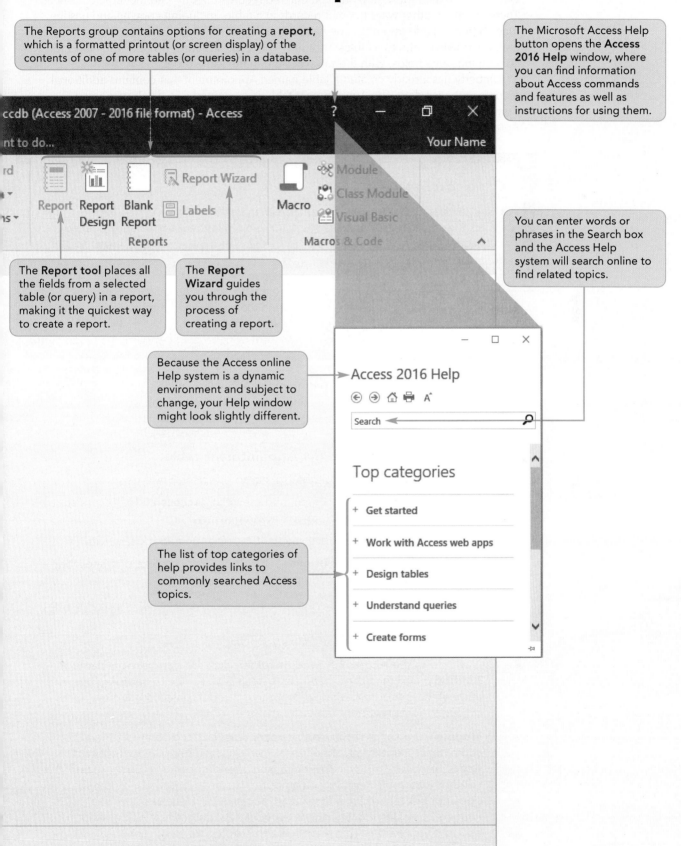

The **Report tool** places all the fields from a selected table (or query) in a report, making it the quickest way to create a report.

The **Report Wizard** guides you through the process of creating a report.

You can enter words or phrases in the Search box and the Access Help system will search online to find related topics.

Because the Access online Help system is a dynamic environment and subject to change, your Help window might look slightly different.

Access 2016 Help

Search

Top categories

+ Get started

+ Work with Access web apps

+ Design tables

+ Understand queries

+ Create forms

The list of top categories of help provides links to commonly searched Access topics.

Copying Records from Another Access Database

When you created the Visit table, you entered records directly into the table datasheet. There are many other ways to enter records in a table, including copying and pasting records from a table into the same database or into a different database. To use this method, however, the two tables must have the same structure—that is, the tables must contain the same fields, with the same design, in the same order.

Kimberly has already created a table named Appointment that contains additional records with visit data. The Appointment table is contained in a database named Kimberly located in the Access1 > Module folder included with your Data Files. The Appointment table has the same table structure as the Visit table you created.

Opening a Database

- Start Access and display the Recent screen in Backstage view.
- Click the name of the database you want to open in the list of recently opened databases.

or

- Start Access and display the Recent screen in Backstage view.
- In the navigation bar, click Open Other Files to display the Open screen.
- Click the Browse button to open the Open dialog box, and then navigate to the drive and folder containing the database file you want to open.
- Click the name of the database file you want to open, and then click the Open button.

Your next task is to copy the records from the Appointment table and paste them into your Visit table. To do so, you need to open the Kimberly database.

To copy the records from the Appointment table:

1. Click the **Start** button 🔳 on the taskbar to open the Start menu.

2. Click **All apps** on the Start menu, and then click **Access 2016**. Access starts and displays the Recent screen in Backstage view.

3. Click **Open Other Files** to display the Open screen in Backstage view.

4. On the Open screen, click **Browse**. The Open dialog box opens, showing folder information for your computer.

   Trouble? If you are storing your files on OneDrive, click OneDrive, and then log in if necessary.

5. Navigate to the drive that contains your Data Files.

6. Navigate to the **Access1 > Module** folder, click the database file named **Kimberly**, and then click the **Open** button. The Kimberly database opens in the Access program window. Note that the database contains only one object, the Appointment table.

   Trouble? If a security warning appears below the ribbon indicating that some active content has been disabled, click the Enable Content button. Access provides this warning because some databases might contain content that could harm your computer. Because the Kimberly database does not contain objects that could be harmful, you can open it safely. If you are accessing the file over a network, you might also see a dialog box asking if you want to make the file a trusted document; click Yes.

7. In the Navigation Pane, double-click **Appointment** to open the Appointment table in Datasheet view. The table contains 65 records and the same five fields, with the same characteristics, as the fields in the Visit table. See Figure 1-18.

| Figure 1-18 | Appointment table in the Kimberly database |

Kimberly wants you to copy all the records in the Appointment table. You can select all the records by clicking the **datasheet selector**, which is the box to the left of the first field name in the table datasheet, as shown in Figure 1-18.

8. Click the **datasheet selector** to the left of the VisitID field. All the records in the table are selected.

9. On the Home tab, in the Clipboard group, click the **Copy** button. All the records are copied to the Clipboard.

10. Click the **Close 'Appointment'** button [X] on the object tab. A dialog box opens asking if you want to save the data you copied to the Clipboard. This dialog box opens only when you copy a large amount of data to the Clipboard.

11. Click the **Yes** button. The dialog box closes, and then the Appointment table closes.

With the records copied to the Clipboard, you can now paste them into the Visit table. First you need to close the Kimberly database while still keeping the Access program open, and then open the Riverview database.

To close the Kimberly database and then paste the records into the Visit table:

▶ 1. Click the **File** tab to open Backstage view, and then click **Close** in the navigation bar to close the Kimberly database. You return to a blank Access program window, and the Home tab is the active tab on the ribbon.

▶ 2. Click the **File** tab to return to Backstage view, and then click **Open** in the navigation bar. Recent is selected on the Open screen, and the recently opened database files are listed. This list should include the Riverview database.

▶ 3. Click **Riverview** to open the Riverview database file.

Trouble? If the Riverview database file is not in the list of recent files, click Browse. In the Open dialog box, navigate to the drive and folder where you are storing your files, and then open the Riverview database file.

Trouble? If the security warning appears below the ribbon, click the Enable Content button, and then, if necessary, click Yes to identify the file as a trusted document.

▶ 4. In the Navigation Pane, double-click **Visit** to open the Visit table in Datasheet view.

▶ 5. On the Navigation Pane, click the **Shutter Bar Open/Close Button** ⟨⟨ to close the pane.

▶ 6. Position the pointer on the star symbol in the row selector for row 11 (the next row available for a new record) until the pointer changes to ➡, and then click to select the row.

▶ 7. On the Home tab, in the Clipboard group, click the **Paste** button. The pasted records are added to the table, and a dialog box opens asking you to confirm that you want to paste all the records (65 total).

Trouble? If the Paste button isn't active, click the ➡ pointer on the row selector for row 11, making sure the entire row is selected, and then repeat Step 7.

▶ 8. Click the **Yes** button. The dialog box closes, and the pasted records are selected. See Figure 1-19. Notice that the table now contains a total of 75 records—10 records that you entered previously and 65 records that you copied and pasted.

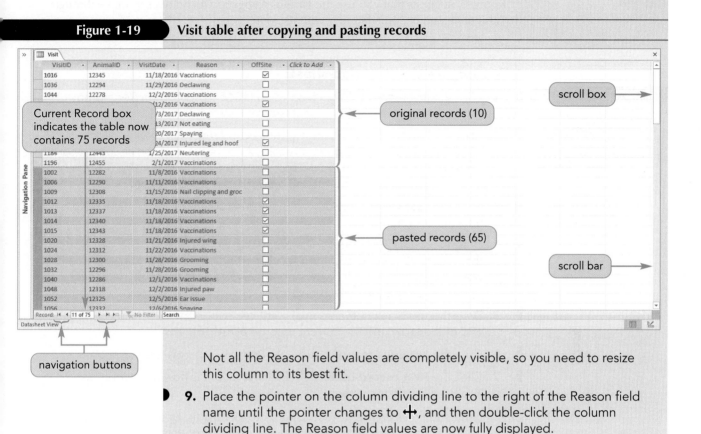

Figure 1-19   Visit table after copying and pasting records

Not all the Reason field values are completely visible, so you need to resize this column to its best fit.

▶ **9.** Place the pointer on the column dividing line to the right of the Reason field name until the pointer changes to ↔, and then double-click the column dividing line. The Reason field values are now fully displayed.

Navigating a Datasheet

The Visit table now contains 75 records, but only some of the records are visible on the screen. To view fields or records not currently visible on the screen, you can use the horizontal and vertical scroll bars to navigate the data. The **navigation buttons**, shown in Figure 1-19 and also described in Figure 1-20, provide another way to move vertically through the records. The Current Record box appears between the two sets of navigation buttons and displays the number of the current record as well as the total number of records in the table. Figure 1-20 shows which record becomes the current record when you click each navigation button. Note the New (blank) record button, which works in the same way as the New button on the Home tab you used earlier to enter a new record in the table.

Figure 1-20   Navigation buttons

Navigation Button	Record Selected	Navigation Button	Record Selected
⏮	First record	⏭	Last record
◀	Previous record	▶✳	New (blank) record
▶	Next record		

Kimberly suggests that you use the various navigation techniques to move through the Visit table and become familiar with its contents.

To navigate the Visit datasheet:

TIP

You can make a field the current field by clicking anywhere within the column for that field.

1. Click the first record's VisitID field value (**1016**). The Current Record box shows that record 1 is the current record.

2. Click the **Next record** button ▶ . The second record is now highlighted, which identifies it as the current record. Also, notice that the second record's value for the VisitID field is selected, and the Current Record box displays "2 of 75" to indicate that the second record is the current record.

3. Click the **Last record** button ▶▌ . The last record in the table, record 75, is now the current record.

4. Drag the scroll box in the vertical scroll bar up to the top of the bar. Notice that record 75 is still the current record, as indicated in the Current Record box. Dragging the scroll box changes the display of the table datasheet, but does not change the current record.

5. Drag the scroll box in the vertical scroll bar back down until you can see the end of the table and the current record (record 75).

6. Click the **Previous record** button ◀ . Record 74 is now the current record.

7. Click the **First record** button ▐◀ . The first record is now the current record and is visible on the screen.

   Earlier you resized the Reason column to its best fit, to ensure all the field values were visible. However, when you resize a column to its best fit, the column expands to fully display only the field values that are visible on the screen at that time. If you move through the complete datasheet and notice that not all of the field values are fully displayed after conducting the resizing process on the records initially visible, you need to repeat the resizing process.

8. Scroll down through the records and observe if the field values are fully displayed. In this case, all of the fields are fully visible, so there is no need to resize any of the field columns.

The Visit table now contains all the data about animal visits for Riverview Veterinary Care Center. To better understand how to work with this data, Kimberly asks you to create simple objects for the other main types of database objects— queries, forms, and reports.

Creating a Simple Query

As noted earlier, a query is a question you ask about the data stored in a database. When you create a query, you tell Access which fields you need and what criteria it should use to select the records that will answer your question. Then Access displays only the information you want, so you don't have to navigate through the entire database for the information. In the Visit table, for example, Kimberly might create a query to display only those records for visits that occurred in a specific month. Even though a query can display table information in a different way, the information still exists in the table as it was originally entered.

Kimberly wants to see a list of all the visit dates and reasons for visits in the Visit table. She doesn't want the list to include all the fields in the table, such as AnimalID and OffSite. To produce this list for Kimberly, you'll use the Simple Query Wizard to create a query based on the Visit table.

To start the Simple Query Wizard:

▶ **1.** On the ribbon, click the **Create** tab.

▶ **2.** In the Queries group, click the **Query Wizard** button. The New Query dialog box opens.

▶ **3.** Make sure **Simple Query Wizard** is selected, and then click the **OK** button. The first Simple Query Wizard dialog box opens. See Figure 1-21.

Figure 1-21   First Simple Query Wizard dialog box

Because the Visit table is the only object in the Riverview database, it is listed in the Tables/Queries box by default. If the database contained more objects, you could click the Tables/Queries arrow and choose another table or a query as the basis for the new query you are creating. The Available Fields box lists all the fields in the Visit table.

You need to select fields from the Available Fields box to include them in the query. To select fields one at a time, click a field and then click the > button. The selected field moves from the Available Fields box on the left to the Selected Fields box on the right. To select all the fields, click the >> button. If you change your mind or make a mistake, you can remove a field by clicking it in the Selected Fields box and then clicking the < button. To remove all fields from the Selected Fields box, click the << button.

Each Simple Query Wizard dialog box contains buttons on the bottom that allow you to move to the previous dialog box (Back button), move to the next dialog box (Next button), or cancel the creation process (Cancel button). You can also finish creating the object (Finish button) and accept the wizard's defaults for the remaining options.

Kimberly wants her query results to list to include data from only the following fields: VisitID, VisitDate, and Reason. You need to select these fields to include them in the query.

To create the query using the Simple Query Wizard:

1. Click **VisitID** in the Available Fields box to select the field (if necessary), and then click the ⟩ button. The VisitID field moves to the Selected Fields box.

2. Repeat Step 1 for the fields **VisitDate** and **Reason**, and then click the **Next** button. The second, and final, Simple Query Wizard dialog box opens and asks you to choose a name (title) for your query. The suggested name is "Visit Query" because the query you are creating is based on the Visit table. You'll change the suggested name to "VisitList."

3. Click at the end of the suggested name, use the **Backspace** key to delete the word "Query" and the space, and then type **List**. Now you can view the query results.

4. Click the **Finish** button to complete the query. The query results are displayed in Datasheet view, on a new tab named "VisitList." A query datasheet is similar to a table datasheet, showing fields in columns and records in rows—but only for those fields and records you want to see, as determined by the query specifications you select.

5. Place the pointer on the column divider line to the right of the Reason field name until the pointer changes to ↔, and then double-click the column divider line to resize the Reason field. See Figure 1-22.

Figure 1-22   Query results

only the three specified fields are displayed in the query datasheet

all 75 records are included in the results

VisitID	VisitDate	Reason
1002	11/8/2016	Vaccinations
1006	11/11/2016	Vaccinations
1009	11/15/2016	Nail clipping and grooming
1012	11/18/2016	Vaccinations
1013	11/18/2016	Vaccinations
1014	11/18/2016	Vaccinations
1015	11/18/2016	Vaccinations
1016	11/18/2016	Vaccinations
1020	11/21/2016	Injured wing
1024	11/22/2016	Vaccinations
1028	11/28/2016	Grooming
1032	11/28/2016	Grooming
1036	11/29/2016	Declawing
1040	12/1/2016	Vaccinations
1044	12/2/2016	Vaccinations
1048	12/2/2016	Injured paw
1052	12/5/2016	Ear issue
1056	12/6/2016	Spaying
1060	12/8/2016	Vaccinations
1064	12/9/2016	Injured paw
1070	12/12/2016	Vaccinations
1071	12/12/2016	Vaccinations
1072	12/12/2016	Vaccinations
1073	12/12/2016	Vaccinations
1074	12/12/2016	Vaccinations

Record: 1 of 75   No Filter   Search

Datasheet View

The VisitList query datasheet displays the three fields in the order you selected them in the Simple Query Wizard, from left to right. The records are listed in order by the primary key field, VisitID. Even though the query datasheet displays only the three fields you chose for the query, the Visit table still includes all the fields for all records.

Notice that the navigation buttons are located at the bottom of the window. You navigate a query datasheet in the same way that you navigate a table datasheet.

6. Click the **Last record** button ▶|. The last record in the query datasheet is now the current record.

7. Click the **Previous record** button ◀. Record 74 in the query datasheet is now the current record.

8. Click the **First record** button |◀. The first record is now the current record.

9. Click the **Close 'VisitList'** button ✕ on the object tab. A dialog box opens asking if you want to save the changes to the layout of the query. This dialog box opens because you resized the Reason column.

10. Click the **Yes** button to save the query layout changes and close the query.

The query results are not stored in the database; however, the query design is stored as part of the database with the name you specified. You can re-create the query results at any time by opening the query again. When you open the query at a later date, the results displayed will reflect up-to-date information to include any new records entered in the Visit table.

Next, Kimberly asks you to create a form for the Visit table so that Riverview Veterinary Care Center staff can use the form to enter and work with data in the table easily.

Creating a Simple Form

As noted earlier, you use a form to enter, edit, and view records in a database. Although you can perform these same functions with tables and queries, forms can present data in many customized and useful ways.

Kimberly wants a form for the Visit table that shows all the fields for one record at a time, with fields listed one below another in a column. This type of form will make it easier for her staff to focus on all the data for a particular visit. You'll use the Form tool to create this form quickly and easily.

To create the form using the Form tool:

1. Make sure the Visit table is still open in Datasheet view. The table or other database object you're using as the basis for the form must either be open or selected in the Navigation Pane when you use the Form tool.

   Trouble? If the Visit table is not open, click the Shutter Bar Open/Close Button ≫ to open the Navigation Pane. Then double-click Visit to open the Visit table in Datasheet view. Click the Shutter Bar Open/Close Button ≪ to close the pane.

2. On the ribbon, click the **Create** tab if necessary.

3. In the Forms group, click the **Form** button. The Form tool creates a simple form showing every field in the Visit table and places it on a tab named "Visit" because the form is based on the Visit table. See Figure 1-23.

Figure 1-23	Form created by the Form tool

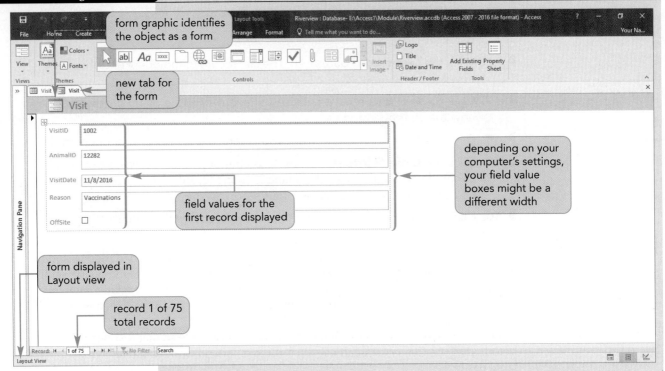

Trouble? Depending on the size of your monitor and your screen resolution settings, the fields in your form might appear in multiple columns instead of a single column. This difference will not present any problems.

The form displays one record at a time in the Visit table, providing another view of the data that is stored in the table and allowing you to focus on the values for one record. Access displays the field values for the first record in the table and selects the first field value (VisitID) as indicated by the border that appears around the value. Each field name appears on a separate line and on the same line as its field value, which appears in a box to the right. Depending on your computer's settings, the field value boxes in your form might be wider or narrower than those shown in the figure. As indicated in the status bar, the form is displayed in Layout view. In **Layout view**, you can make design changes to the form while it is displaying data, so that you can see the effects of the changes you make immediately.

To view, enter, and maintain data using a form, you must know how to move from field to field and from record to record. Notice that the form contains navigation buttons, similar to those available in Datasheet view, which you can use to display different records in the form. You'll use these now to navigate the form; then you'll save and close the form.

To navigate, save, and close the form:

▶ **1.** Click the **Next record** button ▶. The form now displays the values for the second record in the Visit table.

▶ **2.** Click the **Last record** button ▶| to move to the last record in the table. The form displays the information for VisitID 1196.

▶ **3.** Click the **Previous record** button ◀ to move to record 74.

▶ **4.** Click the **First record** button |◀ to return to the first record in the Visit table.

▶ **5.** Next, you'll save the form with the name "VisitData" in the Riverview database. Then the form will be available for later use.

▶ **6.** On the Quick Access Toolbar, click the **Save** button 🖫. The Save As dialog box opens.

▶ **7.** In the Form Name box, click at the end of the selected name "Visit," type **Data**, and then press the **Enter** key. The dialog box closes and the form is saved as VisitData in the Riverview database. The tab containing the form now displays the name VisitData.

▶ **8.** Click the **Close 'VisitData'** button ☒ on the object tab to close the form.

Saving Database Objects

INSIGHT

In general, it is best to save a database object—query, form, or report—only if you anticipate using the object frequently or if it is time-consuming to create, because all objects use storage space and increase the size of the database file. For example, you most likely would not save a form you created with the Form tool because you can re-create it easily with one mouse click. (However, for the purposes of this text, you usually need to save the objects you create.)

Kimberly would like to see the information in the Visit table presented in a more readable and professional format. You'll help Kimberly by creating a report.

Creating a Simple Report

As noted earlier, a report is a formatted printout (or screen display) of the contents of one or more tables or queries. You'll use the Report tool to quickly produce a report based on the Visit table for Kimberly. The Report tool creates a report based on the selected table or query.

To create the report using the Report tool:

▶ **1.** On the ribbon, click the **Create** tab.

▶ **2.** In the Reports group, click the **Report** button. The Report tool creates a simple report showing every field in the Visit table and places it on a tab named "Visit" because the object you created (the report) is based on the Visit table. See Figure 1-24.

Figure 1-24   **Report created by the Report tool**

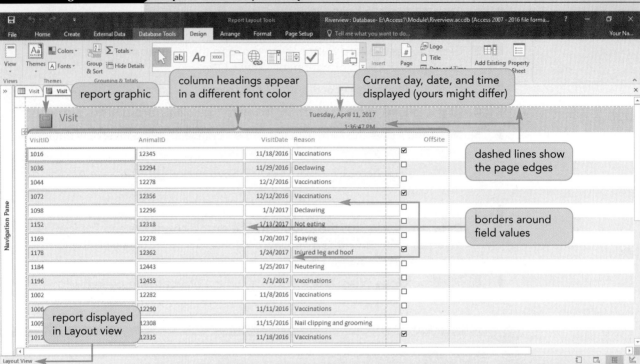

Trouble? The records in your report might appear in a different order from the records shown in Figure 1-24. This difference will not cause any problems.

The report shows each field in a column, with the field values for each record in a row, similar to a table or query datasheet. However, the report offers a more visually appealing format for the data, with the column headings in a different color, borders around each field value, a graphic of a report at the top left, and the current day, date, and time at the top right. Also notice the dashed horizontal and vertical lines on the top and right, respectively; these lines mark the edges of the page and show where text will print on the page.

The report needs some design changes to better display the data. The columns are much wider than necessary for the VisitID and AnimalID fields, and the Reason and OffSite field values and borders are not completely displayed within the page area defined by the dashed lines, which means they would not appear on the same page as the rest of the fields in the printed report. You can resize the columns easily in Layout view.

To resize the VisitID and AnimalID columns:

1. Position the pointer on the right border of any field value in the VisitID column until the pointer changes to ↔.

2. Click and drag the mouse to the left. Notice the dark outlines surrounding the field names and field values indicating the changing column width.

3. Drag to the left until the column is slightly wider than the VisitID field name, and then release the mouse button. The VisitID column is now narrower, and the other four columns have shifted to the left. The Reason and OffSite fields, values, and borders are now completely within the page area. See Figure 1-25.

Figure 1-25   **Report after resizing the VisitID column**

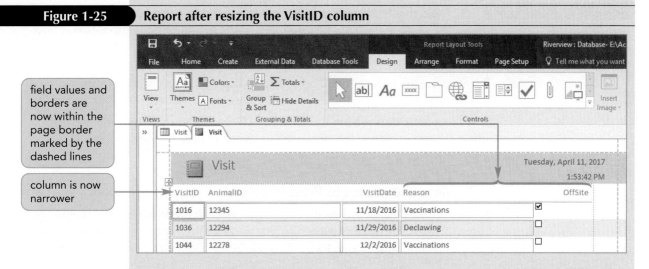

field values and borders are now within the page border marked by the dashed lines

column is now narrower

4. Click the first field value for AnimalID. AnimalID is now the current field.

5. Position the pointer on the right border of the first value in the AnimalID column until the pointer changes to ↔, click and drag to the left until the column is slightly wider than its field name, and then release the mouse button.

6. Drag the scroll box on the vertical scroll bar down to the bottom of the report to check its entire layout.

   The Report tool displays the number "75" at the bottom left of the report, showing the total number of records in the report and the table on which it is based—the Visit table. The Report tool also displays the page number at the bottom right, but the text "Page 1 of 1" appears cut off through the vertical dashed line. This will cause a problem when you print the report, so you need to move this text to the left.

7. Click anywhere on the words **Page 1 of 1**. An orange outline appears around the text, indicating it is selected. See Figure 1-26.

Figure 1-26   **Report page number selected**

text to the right of this dashed line will print on a separate page

selected text to be moved

total number of records in the report

With the text selected, you can use the keyboard arrow keys to move it.

TIP

You can also use the mouse to drag the selected page number, but the arrow key is more precise.

8. Press the ← key repeatedly until the selected page number is to the left of the vertical dashed line (roughly 35 times). The page number text is now completely within the page area and will print on the same page as the rest of the report.

9. Drag the vertical scroll box up to redisplay the top of the report.

The report is displayed in Layout view, which doesn't show how many pages there are in the report. To see this, you need to switch to Print Preview.

To view the report in Print Preview:

1. On the Design tab, in the Views group, click the **View button arrow**, and then click **Print Preview**. The first page of the report is displayed in Print Preview. See Figure 1-27.

Figure 1-27 **First page of the report in Print Preview**

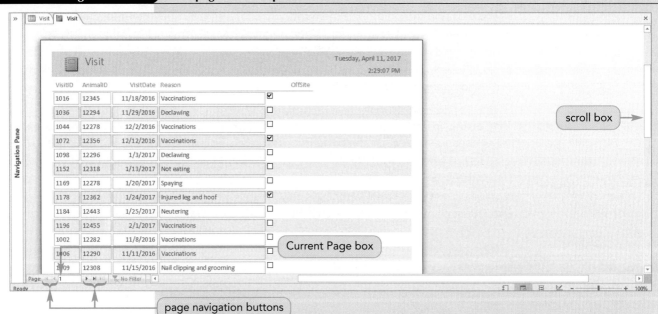

Print Preview shows exactly how the report will look when printed. Notice that Print Preview provides page navigation buttons at the bottom of the window, similar to the navigation buttons you've used to move through records in a table, query, and form.

2. Click the **Next Page** button ▶. The second page of the report is displayed in Print Preview.

3. Click the **Last Page** button ▶| to move to the last page of the report.

4. Drag the scroll box in the vertical scroll bar down until the bottom of the report page is displayed. The notation "Page 3 of 3" appears at the bottom of the page, indicating that you are on page 3 out of a total of 3 pages in the report.

Trouble? Depending on the printer you are using, your report might have more or fewer pages, and some of the pages might be blank. If so, don't worry. Different printers format reports in different ways, sometimes affecting the total number of pages and the number of records printed per page.

5. Click the **First Page** button ⏮ to return to the first page of the report, and then drag the scroll box in the vertical scroll bar up to display the top of the report.

Next you'll save the report as VisitDetails, and then print it.

6. On the Quick Access Toolbar, click the **Save** button 💾. The Save As dialog box opens.

7. In the Report Name box, click at the end of the selected word "Visit," type **Details**, and then press the **Enter** key. The dialog box closes and the report is saved as VisitDetails in the Riverview database. The tab containing the report now displays the name "VisitDetails."

Printing a Report

After creating a report, you might need to print it to distribute it to others who need to view the report's contents. You can print a report without changing any print settings, or display the Print dialog box and select options for printing.

REFERENCE

Printing a Report

- Open the report in any view, or select the report in the Navigation Pane.
- Click the File tab to display Backstage view, click Print, and then click Quick Print to print the report with the default print settings.

or

- Open the report in any view, or select the report in the Navigation Pane.
- Click the File tab, click Print, and then click Print (or, if the report is displayed in Print Preview, click the Print button in the Print group on the Print Preview tab). The Print dialog box opens, in which you can select the options you want for printing the report.

Kimberly asks you to print the entire report with the default settings, so you'll use the Quick Print option in Backstage view.
Note: To complete the following steps, your computer must be connected to a printer. Check with your instructor first to see if you should print the report.

To print the report and then close it:

1. On the ribbon, click the **File** tab to open Backstage view.

2. In the navigation bar, click **Print** to display the Print screen, and then click **Quick Print**. The report prints with the default print settings, and you return to the report in Print Preview.

Trouble? If your report did not print, make sure that your computer is connected to a printer, and that the printer is turned on and ready to print. Then repeat Steps 1 and 2.

3. Click the **Close 'VisitDetails'** button ✕ on the object tab to close the report.

4. Click the **Close 'Visit'** button ✕ on the object tab to close the Visit table.

Trouble? If you are asked to save changes to the layout of the table, click the Yes button.

You can also use the Print dialog box to print other database objects, such as table and query datasheets. Most often, these objects are used for viewing and entering data, and reports are used for printing the data in a database.

Viewing Objects in the Navigation Pane

The Riverview database now contains four objects—the Visit table, the VisitList query, the VisitData form, and the VisitDetails report. When you work with the database file—such as closing it, opening it, or distributing it to others—the file includes all the objects you created and saved in the database. You can view and work with these objects in the Navigation Pane.

To view the objects in the Riverview database:

▶ **1.** On the Navigation Pane, click the **Shutter Bar Open/Close Button** ≫ to open the pane. See Figure 1-28.

Figure 1-28	First page of the report in Print Preview

The Navigation Pane currently displays the default category, **All Access Objects**, which lists all the database objects in the pane. Each object type (Tables, Queries, Forms, and Reports) appears in its own group. Each database object (the Visit table, the VisitList query, the VisitData form, and the VisitDetails report) has a unique icon to its left to indicate the type of object. This makes it easy for you to identify the objects and choose which one you want to open and work with.

The arrow on the All Access Objects bar displays a menu with options for various ways to group and display objects in the Navigation Pane. The Search box enables you to enter text for Access to find; for example, you could search for all objects that contain the word "Visit" in their names. Note that Access searches for objects only in the categories and groups currently displayed in the Navigation Pane.

As you continue to build the Riverview database and add more objects to it in later modules, you'll use the options in the Navigation Pane to manage those objects.

Using Microsoft Access Help

Access includes a Help system you can use to search for information about specific program features. You start Help by clicking the Microsoft Access Help button in the top right of the Access window, or by pressing the F1 key.

You'll use Help now to learn more about the Navigation Pane.

To search for information about the Navigation Pane in Help:

TIP

You can also get help by typing keywords in the Tell Me box on the ribbon to access information about topics related to those words in the Access Help window.

1. Click the **Microsoft Access Help** button ? on the title bar. The Access 2016 Help window opens, as shown earlier in the Session 1.2 Visual Overview.

2. Click in the **Search** box, type **Navigation Pane**, and then press the **Enter** key. The Access 2016 Help window displays a list of topics related to the Navigation Pane.

3. Click the topic **Manage Access database objects in the Navigation Pane**. The Access Help window displays the article you selected. See Figure 1-29.

Figure 1-29   Article displayed in the Access Help window

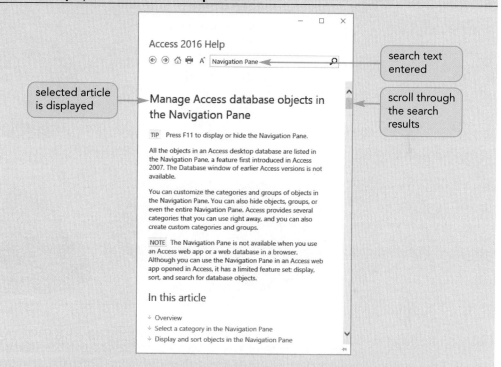

Trouble? If the article on managing database objects is not listed in your Help window, choose another article related to the Navigation Pane to read.

4. Scroll through the article to read detailed information about working with the Navigation Pane.

5. When finished, click the **Close** button X on the Access 2016 Help window to close it.

The Access Help system is an important reference tool for you to use if you need additional information about databases in general, details about specific Access features, or support with problems you might encounter.

Managing a Database

One of the main tasks involved in working with database software is managing your databases and the data they contain. Some of the activities involved in database management include compacting and repairing a database and backing up and restoring a database. By managing your databases, you can ensure that they operate in the most efficient way, that the data they contain is secure, and that you can work with the data effectively.

Compacting and Repairing a Database

Whenever you open an Access database and work in it, the size of the database increases. Further, when you delete records or when you delete or replace database objects—such as queries, forms, and reports—the storage space that had been occupied by the deleted or replaced records or objects does not automatically become available for other records or objects. To make the space available, and also to increase the speed of data retrieval, you must compact the database. **Compacting** a database rearranges the data and objects in a database to decrease its file size, thereby making more storage space available and enhancing the performance of the database. Figure 1-30 illustrates the compacting process.

Figure 1-30 **Compacting a database**

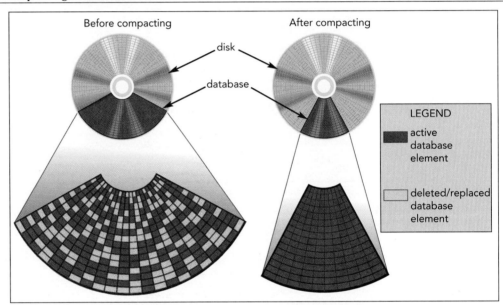

When you compact a database, Access repairs the database at the same time, if necessary. In some cases, Access detects that a database is damaged when you try to open it and gives you the option to compact and repair it at that time. For example, the data in your database might become damaged, or corrupted, if you exit the Access program suddenly by turning off your computer. If you think your database might be damaged because it is behaving unpredictably, you can use the Compact & Repair Database option to fix it.

REFERENCE

Compacting and Repairing a Database

- Make sure the database file you want to compact and repair is open.
- Click the File tab to display the Info screen in Backstage view.
- Click the Compact & Repair Database button.

Access also allows you to set an option to compact and repair a database file automatically every time you close it. The Compact on Close option is available in the Current Database section of the Access Options dialog box, which you open from

Backstage view by clicking the Options command in the navigation bar. By default, the Compact on Close option is turned off.

Next, you'll compact the Riverview database manually using the Compact & Repair Database option. This will make the database smaller and allow you to work with it more efficiently. After compacting the database, you'll close it.

To compact and repair the Riverview database:

▶ **1.** On the ribbon, click the **File** tab to open the Info screen in Backstage view.

▶ **2.** Click the **Compact & Repair Database** button. Although nothing visible happens on the screen, the Riverview database is compacted, making it smaller, and repairs it at the same time. The Home tab is again the active tab on the ribbon.

▶ **3.** Click the **File** tab to return to Backstage view, and then click **Close** in the navigation bar. The Riverview database closes.

Backing Up and Restoring a Database

Backing up a database is the process of making a copy of the database file to protect your database against loss or damage. The Back Up Database command enables you to back up your database file from within the Access program, while you are working on your database. To use this option, click the File tab to display the Info screen in Backstage view, click Save As in the navigation bar, click Back Up Database in the Advanced section of the Save Database As pane, and then click the Save As button. In the Save As dialog box that opens, a default filename is provided for the backup copy that consists of the same filename as the database you are backing up (for example, "Riverview"), and an underscore character, plus the current date. This filenaming system makes it easy for you to keep track of your database backups and when they were created. To restore a backup database file, you simply copy the backup from the location where it is stored to your hard drive, or whatever device you use to work in Access, and start working with the restored database file. (You will not actually back up the Riverview database in this module unless directed by your instructor to do so.)

INSIGHT

Planning and Performing Database Backups

Experienced database users make it a habit to back up a database before they work with it for the first time, keeping the original data intact. They also make frequent backups while continuing to work with a database; these backups are generally on flash drives, recordable CDs or DVDs, external or network hard drives, or cloud-based storage (such as OneDrive). Also, it is recommended to store the backup copy in a different location from the original. For example, if the original database is stored on a flash drive, you should not store the backup copy on the same flash drive. If you lose the drive or the drive is damaged, you would lose both the original database and its backup copy.

If the original database file and the backup copy have the same name, restoring the backup copy might replace the original. If you want to save the original file, rename it before you restore the backup copy. To ensure that the restored database has the most current data, you should update the restored database with any changes made to the original between the time you created the backup copy and the time the original database became damaged or lost.

By properly planning for and performing backups, you can avoid losing data and prevent the time-consuming effort required to rebuild a lost or damaged database.

PROSKILLS

Decision Making: When to Use Access vs. Excel

Using a spreadsheet application like Microsoft Excel to manage lists or tables of information works well when the data is simple, such as a list of contacts or tasks. As soon as the data becomes complex enough to separate into tables that need to be related, you start to see the limitations of using a spreadsheet application. The strength of a database application such as Access is in its ability to easily relate one table of information to another. Consider a table of contacts that includes home addresses, with a separate row for each person living at the same address. When an address changes, it's too easy to make a mistake and not update the home address for each person who lives there. To ensure you have the most accurate data at all times, it's important to have only one instance of each piece of data. By creating separate tables that are related and keeping only one instance of each piece of data, you'll ensure the integrity of the data. Trying to accomplish this in Excel is a complex process, whereas Access is specifically designed for this functionality.

Another limitation of using Excel instead of Access to manage data has to do with the volume of data. Although a spreadsheet can hold thousands of records, a database can hold millions. A spreadsheet containing thousands of pieces of information is cumbersome to use. Think of large-scale commercial applications such as enrollment at a college or tracking customers for a large company. It's hard to imagine managing such information in an Excel spreadsheet. Instead, you'd use a database. Finally, with an Access database, multiple users can access the information it contains at the same time. Although an Excel spreadsheet can be shared, there can be problems when users try to open and edit the same spreadsheet at the same time.

When you're trying to decide whether to use Excel or Access, ask yourself the following questions.

1. Do you need to store data in separate tables that are related to each other?
2. Do you have a very large amount of data to store?
3. Will more than one person need to access the data at the same time?

If you answer "yes" to any of these questions, an Access database is most likely the appropriate application to use.

In the following modules, you'll help Kimberly complete and maintain the Riverview database, and you'll use it to meet the specific information needs of the employees of the care center.

REVIEW

Session 1.2 Quick Check

1. To copy the records from a table in one database to another table in a different database, the two tables must have the same _____.

2. A(n) _____ is a question you ask about the data stored in a database.

3. The quickest way to create a form is to use the _____.

4. Which view enables you to see the total number of pages in a report and navigate through the report pages?

5. In the Navigation Pane, each database object has a unique _____ to its left that identifies the object's type.

6. _____ a database rearranges the data and objects in a database to decrease its file size and enhance the speed and performance of the database.

7. _____ a database is the process of making a copy of the database file to protect the database against loss or damage.

Review Assignments

Data File needed for the Review Assignments: Company.accdb

For Riverview Veterinary Care Center, Kimberly asks you to create a new database to contain information about the vendors that the care center works with to obtain supplies, equipment, and resale items, and the vendors who service and maintain the equipment. Complete the following steps:

1. Create a new, blank database named **Vendor** and save it in the folder where you are storing your files, as specified by your instructor.
2. In Datasheet view for the Table1 table, rename the default ID primary key field to **SupplierID**. Change the data type of the SupplierID field to Short Text.
3. Add the following 10 fields to the new table in the order shown; all of them are Short Text fields *except* InitialContact, which is a Date/Time field: **Company, Category, Address, City, State, Zip, Phone, ContactFirst, ContactLast,** and **InitialContact**. Resize the columns as necessary so that the complete field names are displayed. Save the table as **Supplier**.
4. Enter the records shown in Figure 1-31 in the Supplier table. For the first record, be sure to enter your first name in the ContactFirst field and your last name in the ContactLast field.
   Note: When entering field values that are shown on multiple lines in the figure, do not try to enter the values on multiple lines. The values are shown on multiple lines in the figure for page spacing purposes only.

Figure 1-31   Supplier table records

SupplierID	Company	Category	Address	City	State	Zip	Phone	ContactFirst	ContactLast	InitialContact
YUM345	Yummy Dog Food	Resale	345 Riverside Dr	Charlotte	NC	28201	704-205-8725	Student First	Student Last	2/1/2017
FTS123	Flea & Tick Supplies	Resale	123 Overlook Ln	Atlanta	GA	30301	404-341-2981	Robert	Jackson	3/6/2017
PMC019	Pet Medical	Equipment	19 Waverly Ct	Blacksburg	VA	24061	540-702-0098	Julie	Baxter	2/21/2017
APL619	A+ Labs	Equipment	619 West Dr	Omaha	NE	68022	531-219-7206	Jacques	Dupont	4/10/2017
CWI444	Cat World Inc.	Supplies	444 Boxcar Way	San Diego	CA	92110	619-477-9482	Amelia	Kline	5/1/2017

5. Kimberly created a database named Company that contains a Business table with supplier data. The Supplier table you created has the same design as the Business table. Copy all the records from the **Business** table in the **Company** database (located in the Access1 > Review folder provided with your Data Files) and then paste them at the end of the Supplier table in the Vendor database.
6. Resize all datasheet columns to their best fit, and then save the Supplier table.
7. Close the Supplier table, and then use the Navigation Pane to reopen it. Note that the records are displayed in primary key order by the values in the SupplierID field.
8. Use the Simple Query Wizard to create a query that includes the Company, Category, ContactFirst, ContactLast, and Phone fields (in that order) from the Supplier table. Name the query **SupplierList**, and then close the query.
9. Use the Form tool to create a form for the Supplier table. Save the form as **SupplierInfo**, and then close it.

10. Use the Report tool to create a report based on the Supplier table. In Layout view, resize all fields except the Company field, so that each field is slightly wider than the longest entry (either the field name itself or an entry in the field). Display the report in Print Preview and verify that all the fields fit across one page in the report. Save the report as **SupplierDetails**, and then close it.

11. Close the Supplier table, and then compact and repair the Vendor database.

12. Close the Vendor database.

Case Problem 1

APPLY

Data File needed for this Case Problem: BeautyToGo.accdb

Beauty To Go   Sue Miller, an owner of a nail and hair salon in Orlando, Florida, regularly checks in on her grandmother, who resides in a retirement community. On some of her visits, Sue does her grandmother's hair and nails. Her grandmother recently asked if Sue would also be willing to do the hair and nails of some of her friends in her retirement community and other surrounding communities. She said that these friends would happily pay for her services. Sue thinks this is an excellent way to expand her current business and serve the needs of the retirement community at the same time. In discussing the opportunity with some of the members of the retirement community, she found that the ladies would very much like to pay Sue in advance for her services and have them scheduled on a regular basis; however, the frequency and types of the services vary from person to person. Sue decides to come up with different options that would serve the needs of the ladies in the retirement community. Sue wants to use Access to maintain information about the customers and the types of options offered. She needs your help in creating this database. Complete the following:

1. Create a new, blank database named **Beauty** and save it in the folder where you are storing your files, as specified by your instructor.

2. In Datasheet view for the Table1 table, rename the default primary key ID field to **OptionID**. Change the data type of the OptionID field to Short Text.

3. Add the following three fields to the new table in the order shown: **OptionDescription** (a Short Text field), **OptionCost** (a Currency field), and **FeeWaived** (a Yes/No field). Save the table as **Option**.

4. Enter the records shown in Figure 1-32 in the Option table. *Hint*: When entering the OptionCost field values, you do not have to type the dollar signs, commas, or decimal places; they will be entered automatically.

Figure 1-32   Option table records

when entering currency values, you do not have to type the dollar signs, commas, or decimal places

OptionID	OptionDescription	OptionCost	FeeWaived
136	Wash/cut bi-weekly for 6 months	$500.00	Yes
101	Manicure weekly for 1 month	$125.00	No
124	Manicure/pedicure weekly for 3 months	$700.00	Yes
142	Wash/cut/color monthly for 6 months	$600.00	Yes
117	Pedicure bi-weekly for 3 months	$190.00	No

5. Sue created a database named BeautyToGo that contains a MoreOptions table with plan data. The Option table you created has the same design as the MoreOptions table. Copy all the records from the **MoreOptions** table in the **BeautyToGo** database (located in the Access1 > Case1 folder provided with your Data Files), and then paste them at the end of the Option table in the Beauty database.

6. Resize all datasheet columns to their best fit, and then save the Option table.

7. Close the Option table, and then use the Navigation Pane to reopen it. Note that the records are displayed in primary key order by the values in the OptionID field.

8. Use the Simple Query Wizard to create a query that includes the OptionID, OptionDescription, and OptionCost fields from the Option table. In the second Simple Query Wizard dialog box, select the Detail option if necessary. (This option appears because the query includes a Currency field.) Save the query as **OptionData**, and then close the query.

9. Use the Form tool to create a form for the Option table. Save the form as **OptionInfo**, and then close it.

10. Use the Report tool to create a report based on the Option table. In Layout view, resize the OptionID field so it is slightly wider than the longest entry, which is the field name in this case. Resize the OptionDescription field so there are no entries with multiple lines. Also, resize the box containing the total amount that appears below the OptionCost column by clicking the box and then dragging its bottom border down so that the amount is fully displayed. (The Report Tool calculated this total automatically.) Display the report in Print Preview; then verify that all the fields are within the page area and all field values are fully displayed. Save the report as **OptionList**, print the report (only if asked by your instructor to do so), and then close it.

11. Close the Option table, and then compact and repair the Beauty database.

12. Close the Beauty database.

Case Problem 2

APPLY

Data File needed for this Case Problem: ProgPros.accdb

Programming Pros   While in college obtaining his bachelor's degree in Raleigh, North Carolina, Brent Hovis majored in computer science and learned programming. Brent found that many of his fellow classmates found it difficult to write code, and he was constantly assisting them with helpful tips and techniques. Prior to graduating, Brent began tutoring freshman and sophomore students in programming to make some extra money. As his reputation grew, high school students began contacting him for help with their programming classes. When Brent entered graduate school, he started Programming Pros, a company offering expanded tutoring service for high school and college students through group, private, and semi-private tutoring sessions. As demand for the company's services grew, Brent hired many of his fellow classmates to assist him. Brent wants to use Access to maintain information about the tutors who work for him, the students who sign up for tutoring, and the contracts they sign. He needs your help in creating this database. Complete the following steps:

1. Create a new, blank database named **Programming** and save it in the folder where you are storing your files, as specified by your instructor.

2. In Datasheet view for the Table1 table, rename the default primary key ID field to **TutorID**. Change the data type of the TutorID field to Short Text.

3. Add the following five fields to the new table in the order shown; all of them are Short Text fields *except* HireDate, which is a Date/Time field: **FirstName**, **LastName**, **Major**, **YearInSchool**, **School**, and **HireDate**. Resize the columns, if necessary, so that the complete field names are displayed. Save the table as **Tutor**.

4. Enter the records shown in Figure 1-33 in the Tutor table. For the first record, be sure to enter your first name in the FirstName field and your last name in the LastName field.

Figure 1-33	Tutor table records

TutorID	FirstName	LastName	Major	YearInSchool	School	HireDate
1060	*Student First*	*Student Last*	Computer Science	Senior	Ellings College	2/14/2017
1010	Cathy	Cowler	Computer Engineering	Graduate	Eikenville College	2/1/2017
1051	Donald	Gallager	Computer Science	Graduate	Hogan University	1/18/2017
1031	Nichole	Schneider	Computer Science	Junior	Switzer University	2/28/2017
1018	Fredrik	Karlsson	Mechatronics	Junior	Smith Technical College	2/6/2017

5. Brent created a database named ProgPros that contains a MoreTutors table with tutor data. The Tutor table you created has the same design as the MoreTutors table. Copy all the records from the **MoreTutors** table in the **ProgPros** database (located in the Access1 > Case2 folder provided with your Data Files), and then paste them at the end of the Tutor table in the Programming database.

6. Resize all datasheet columns to their best fit, and then save the Tutor table.

7. Close the Tutor table, and then use the Navigation Pane to reopen it. Note that the records are displayed in primary key order by the values in the TutorID field.

8. Use the Simple Query Wizard to create a query that includes the FirstName, LastName, and HireDate fields from the Tutor table. Save the query as **StartDate**, and then close the query.

9. Use the Form tool to create a form for the Tutor table. Save the form as **TutorInfo**, and then close it.

10. Use the Report tool to create a report based on the Tutor table. In Layout view, resize the TutorID, FirstName, LastName, Major, YearInSchool, School, and HireDate fields so they are slightly wider than the longest entry (either the field name itself or an entry in the field). All seven fields should fit within the page area after you resize the fields. At the bottom of the report, move the text "Page 1 of 1" to the left so it is within the page area. Display the report in Print Preview; then verify that the fields and page number fit within the page area and that all field values are fully displayed. Save the report as **TutorList**, print the report (only if asked by your instructor to do so), and then close it.

11. Close the Tutor table, and then compact and repair the Programming database.

12. Close the Programming database.

CHALLENGE

Case Problem 3

Data File needed for this Case Problem: Diane.accdb

Diane's Community Center   Diane Coleman is a successful businesswoman in Dallas, Georgia, but things were not always that way. Diane experienced trying times and fortunately had people in the community come into her life to assist her and her children when times were difficult. Diane now wants to give back to her community and support those in need, just as she was supported many years ago, by creating a community center in Dallas where those in need can come in for goods and services. Diane plans to open a thrift store as well to sell donated items to support the center. Diane has been contacted by many people in the community wishing to donate materials to the center as well as items to be sold at the thrift store. Diane has asked you to create an Access database to manage information about the center's patrons and donations. Complete the following steps:

1. Create a new, blank database named **Center** and save it in the folder where you are storing your files, as specified by your instructor.

2. In Datasheet view for the Table1 table, rename the default primary key ID field to **PatronID**. Change the data type of the PatronID field to Short Text.

3. Add the following five Short Text fields to the new table in the order shown: **Title**, **FirstName**, **LastName**, **Phone**, and **Email**. Save the table as **Patron**.

4. Enter the records shown in Figure 1-34 in the Patron table. For the first record, be sure to enter your title in the Title field, your first name in the FirstName field, and your last name in the LastName field.

Figure 1-34   **Patron table records**

PatronID	Title	FirstName	LastName	Phone	Email
3001	*Student Title*	*Student First*	*Student Last*	404-987-1234	student@example.com
3030	Mr.	David	Hampton	404-824-3381	thehamptons@example.net
3006	Dr.	Elbert	Schneider	678-492-9101	countrydoc@example.com
3041	Mr.	Frank	Miller	404-824-3431	frankmiller12@example.net
3019	Mrs.	Jane	Michaels	706-489-3310	jjmichaels@example.com

5. Diane created a database named Diane that contains a MorePatrons table with data about additional patrons. The Patron table you created has the same design as the MorePatrons table. Copy all the records from the **MorePatrons** table in the **Diane** database (located in the Access1 > Case3 folder provided with your Data Files), and then paste them at the end of the Patron table in the Center database.

6. Resize all datasheet columns to their best fit, and then save the Patron table.

7. Close the Patron table, and then use the Navigation Pane to reopen it. Note that the records are displayed in primary key order by the values in the PatronID field.

⊕ **Explore** 8. Use the Simple Query Wizard to create a query that includes all the fields in the Patron table *except* the Title field. (*Hint*: Use the >> and < buttons to select the necessary fields.) Save the query using the name **PatronContactList**.

⊕ **Explore** 9. The query results are displayed in order by the PatronID field values. You can specify a different order by sorting the query. Display the Home tab. Then, click the insertion point anywhere in the LastName column to make it the current field. In the Sort & Filter group on the Home tab, click the Ascending button. The records are now listed in order by the values in the LastName field. Save and close the query.

⊕ **Explore** 10. Use the Form tool to create a form for the Patron table. In the new form, navigate to record 13 (the record with PatronID 3028), and then print the form *for the current record only*. (*Hint*: You must use the Print dialog box in order to print only the current record. Go to Backstage view, click Print in the navigation bar, and then click Print to open the Print dialog box. Click the Selected Record(s) option button, and then click the OK button to print the current record.) Save the form as **PatronInfo**, and then close it.

11. Use the Report tool to create a report based on the Patron table. In Layout view, resize each field so it is slightly wider than the longest entry (either the field name itself or an entry in the field). All six fields should fit within the page area after resizing. At the bottom of the report, move the text "Page 1 of 1" to the left so it is within the page area. Display the report in Print Preview, then verify that the fields and page number fit within the page area and that all field values are fully displayed. Save the report as **PatronList**. Print the report (only if asked by your instructor to do so), and then close it.

12. Close the Patron table, and then compact and repair the Center database.

13. Close the Center database.

Case Problem 4

CHALLENGE

Data File needed for this Case Problem: HikeApp.accdb

Hike Appalachia   Molly and Bailey Johnson grew up in the Blue Ridge Mountains of North Carolina. Their parents were avid outdoors people and loved to take the family on long hikes and teach the girls about the great outdoors. During middle school and high school, their friends would ask them to guide them in the surrounding area because it could be quite dangerous. One summer, the girls had an idea to expand their hiking clientele beyond their friends and help earn money for college; this was the start of their business, which they named Hike Appalachia. The girls advertised in local and regional outdoor magazines and were flooded with requests from people all around the region. They would like you to build an Access database to manage information about the hikers they guide, the tours they provide, and tour reservations. Complete the following:

1. Create a new, blank database named **Appalachia** and save it in the folder where you are storing your files, as specified by your instructor.

2. In Datasheet view for the Table1 table, rename the default primary key ID field to **HikerID**. Change the data type of the HikerID field to Short Text.

3. Add the following seven Short Text fields to the new table in the order shown: **HikerFirst**, **HikerLast**, **Address**, **City**, **State**, **Zip**, and **Phone**. Save the table as **Hiker**.

4. Enter the records shown in Figure 1-35 in the Hiker table. For the first record, be sure to enter your first name in the HikerFirst field and your last name in the HikerLast field.

Figure 1-35 **Hiker table records**

HikerID	HikerFirst	HikerLast	Address	City	State	Zip	Phone
501	*Student First*	*Student Last*	123 Jackson St	Boone	NC	28607	828-497-9128
547	Heather	Smith	412 Sentry Ln	Gastonia	NC	28052	704-998-0987
521	Zack	Hoskins	2 Hope Rd	Atlanta	GA	30301	404-998-2381
535	Elmer	Jackson	99 River Rd	Blacksburg	SC	29702	864-921-2384
509	Sarah	Peeler	32 Mountain Ln	Ridgeview	WV	25169	703-456-9381

5. Molly and Bailey created a database named HikeApp that contains a MoreHikers table with data about hikers. The Hiker table you created has the same design as the MoreHikers table. Copy all the records from the **MoreHikers** table in the **HikeApp** database (located in the Access1 > Case4 folder provided with your Data Files), and then paste them at the end of the Hiker table in the Appalachia database.

6. Resize all datasheet columns to their best fit, and then save the Hiker table.

7. Close the Hiker table, and then use the Navigation Pane to reopen it. Note that the records are displayed in primary key order.

8. Use the Simple Query Wizard to create a query that includes the following fields from the Hiker table, in the order shown: HikerID, HikerLast, HikerFirst, State, and Phone. Name the query **HikerData**.

⊕ **Explore** 9. The query results are displayed in order by the HikerID field values. You can specify a different order by sorting the query. Display the Home tab. Then, click the insertion point anywhere in the State column to make it the current field. In the Sort & Filter group on the Home tab, click the Ascending button. The records are now listed in order by the values in the State field. Save and close the query.

⊕ **Explore** 10. Use the Form tool to create a form for the Hiker table. In the new form, navigate to record 10 (the record with HikerID 527), and then print the form *for the current record only*. (*Hint*: You must use the Print dialog box in order to print only the current record. Go to Backstage view, click Print in the navigation bar, and then click Print to open the Print dialog box. Click the Selected Record(s) option button, and then click the OK button to print the current record.) Save the form as **HikerInfo**, and then close it.

11. Use the Report tool to create a report based on the Hiker table. In Layout view, resize each field so it is slightly wider than the longest entry (either the field name itself or an entry in the field). At the bottom of the report, move the text "Page 1 of 1" to the left so it is within the page area on the report's first page. All fields should fit on one page. Save the report as **HikerList**.

12. Print the report (only if asked by your instructor to do so), and then close it.

a. Close the Hiker table, and then compact and repair the Appalachia database.

b. Close the Appalachia database.

MODULE **2**

OBJECTIVES

Session 2.1
- Learn the guidelines for designing databases and setting field properties
- Create a table in Design view
- Define fields, set field properties, and specify a table's primary key
- Modify the structure of a table
- Change the order of fields in Design view
- Add new fields in Design view
- Change the Format property for a field in Datasheet view
- Modify field properties in Design view

Session 2.2
- Import data from Excel
- Import an existing table structure
- Add fields to a table with the Data Type gallery
- Delete and rename fields
- Change the data type for a field in Design view
- Set the Default Value property for a field
- Import a text file
- Define a relationship between two tables

Building a Database and Defining Table Relationships

Creating the Billing, Owner, and Animal Tables

Case | *Riverview Veterinary Care Center*

The Riverview database currently contains one table, the Visit table. Kimberly Johnson also wants to track information about the clinic's animals, their owners, and the invoices sent to them for services provided by Riverview Veterinary Care Center. This information includes such items as each owner's name and address, animal information, and the amount and billing date for each invoice.

In this module, you'll create three new tables in the Riverview database—named Billing, Owner, and Animal—to contain the additional data Kimberly wants to track. You will use two different methods for creating the tables, and learn how to modify the fields. After adding records to the tables, you will define the necessary relationships between the tables in the Riverview database to relate the tables, enabling Kimberly and her staff to work with the data more efficiently.

STARTING DATA FILES

Access1 ➤ **Module**

AllAnimals.accdb
Invoices.xlsx
Kelly.accdb
Owner.txt
Riverview.accdb (*cont.*)

Review

Supplies.xlsx
Vendor.accdb (*cont.*)

Case1

Beauty.accdb (*cont.*)
Customers.txt

Case2

Agreements.xlsx
Client.accdb
Programming.accdb (*cont.*)
Students.txt

Case3

Auctions.txt
Center.accdb (*cont.*)
Donations.xlsx

Case4

Appalachia.accdb (*cont.*)
Bookings.txt
Travel.accdb

Session 2.1 Visual Overview:

Design view allows you to define or modify a table structure or the properties of the fields in a table.

The default name for a new table you create in Design view is Table1. This name appears on the tab for the new table.

The top portion of the Table window in Design view is called the **Table Design grid**. Here, you enter values for the Field Name, Data type, and Description field properties.

In the Field Name column, you enter the name for each new field in the table. When you first open a new Table window in Design view, Field Name is the current property.

In the Data Type column, you select the appropriate data type for each new field in the table. The data type determines what field values you can enter for a new field and what other properties the field will have. The default data type for a new field is Short Text.

After you assign a data type to a field, the General tab displays additional field properties for that data type. Initially, most field properties are assigned default values.

When defining the fields in a table, you can move from the Table Design grid to the Field Properties pane by pressing the **F6 key**.

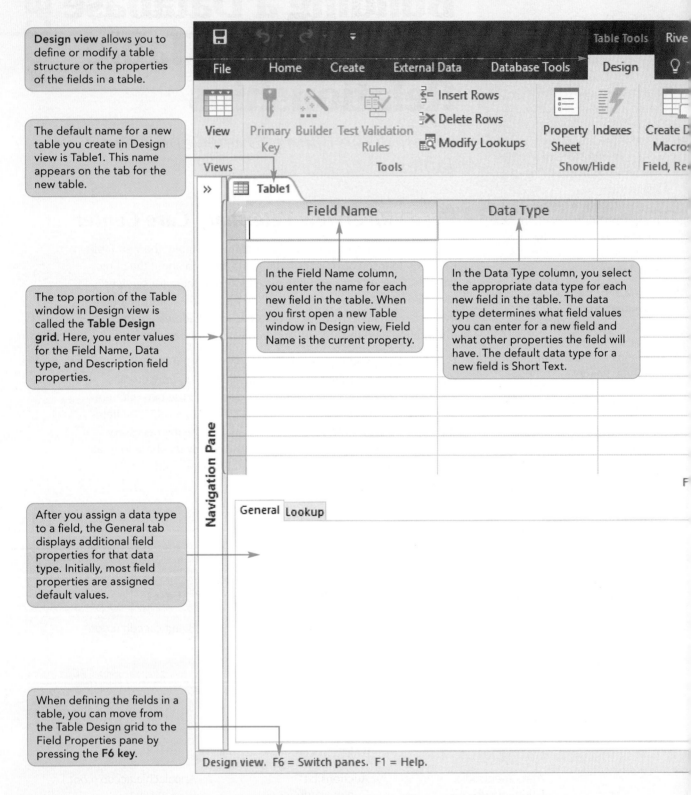

Table Window in Design View

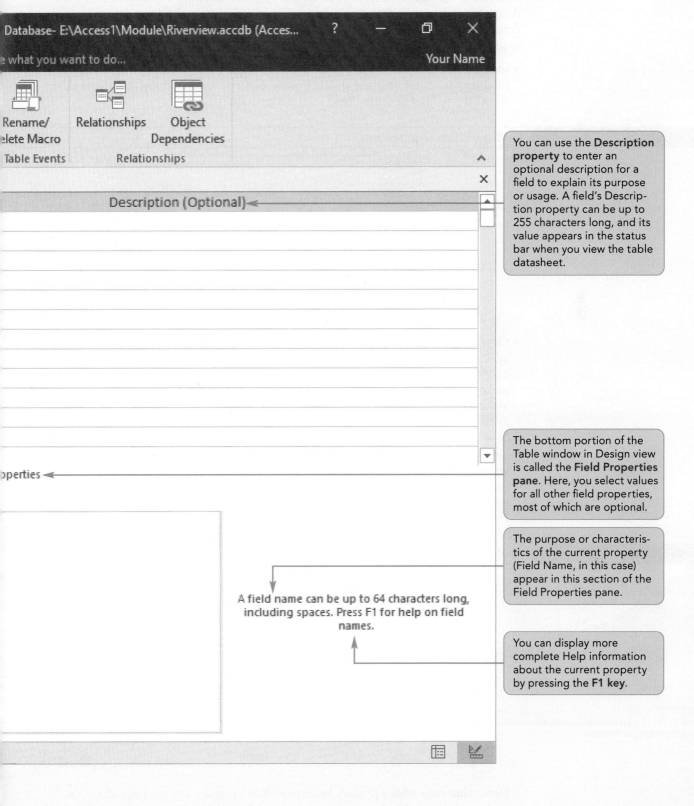

Database- E:\Access1\Module\Riverview.accdb (Acces...   ?   □   ✕

e what you want to do...   Your Name

Rename/
elete Macro   Relationships   Object
Dependencies

Table Events   Relationships

Description (Optional)

You can use the **Description property** to enter an optional description for a field to explain its purpose or usage. A field's Description property can be up to 255 characters long, and its value appears in the status bar when you view the table datasheet.

The bottom portion of the Table window in Design view is called the **Field Properties pane**. Here, you select values for all other field properties, most of which are optional.

operties

The purpose or characteristics of the current property (Field Name, in this case) appear in this section of the Field Properties pane.

A field name can be up to 64 characters long, including spaces. Press F1 for help on field names.

You can display more complete Help information about the current property by pressing the **F1 key**.

Guidelines for Designing Databases

A database management system can be a useful tool, but only if you first carefully design the database so that it meets the needs of its users. In database design, you determine the fields, tables, and relationships needed to satisfy the data and processing requirements. When you design a database, you should follow these guidelines:

- **Identify all the fields needed to produce the required information.** For example, Kimberly needs information about animals, owners, visits, and invoices. Figure 2-1 shows the fields that satisfy these information requirements.

Figure 2-1   **Kimberly's data requirements**

VisitID	AnimalBreed	Zip
VisitDate	OwnerID	Email
Reason	FirstName	InvoiceNum
OffSite	LastName	InvoiceDate
AnimalID	Phone	InvoiceAmt
AnimalName	Address	InvoiceItem
AnimalBirthDate	City	InvoicePaid
AnimalType	State	

- **Organize each piece of data into its smallest useful part.** For example, Kimberly could store each owner's complete name in one field called Name instead of using two fields called FirstName and LastName, as shown in Figure 2-1. However, doing so would make it more difficult to work with the data. If Kimberly wanted to view the records in alphabetical order by last name, she wouldn't be able to do so with field values such as "Reggie Baxter" and "Aaron Jackson" stored in a Name field. She could do so with field values such as "Baxter" and "Jackson" stored separately in a LastName field.
- **Group related fields into tables.** For example, Kimberly grouped the fields related to visits into the Visit table, which you created in the previous module. The fields related to invoices are grouped into the Billing table, the fields related to owners are grouped into the Owner table, and the fields related to animals are grouped into the Animal table. Figure 2-2 shows the fields grouped into all four tables for the Riverview database.

Figure 2-2   **Kimberly's fields grouped into tables**

Visit table	Billing table	Owner table	Animal table
VisitID	InvoiceNum	OwnerID	AnimalID
AnimalID	VisitID	FirstName	OwnerID
VisitDate	InvoiceDate	LastName	AnimalName
Reason	InvoiceAmt	Phone	AnimalBirthDate
OffSite	InvoiceItem	Address	AnimalType
	InvoicePaid	City	AnimalBreed
		State	
		Zip	
		Email	

- **Determine each table's primary key.** Recall that a primary key uniquely identifies each record in a table. For some tables, one of the fields, such as a credit card number, naturally serves the function of a primary key. For other tables, two or more fields might be needed to function as the primary key. In these cases, the primary key is called a **composite key**. For example, a school grade table would use a combination of student number, term, and course code to serve as the primary key. For a third category of tables, no single field or combination of fields can uniquely identify a record in a table. In these cases, you need to add a field whose sole purpose is to serve as the table's primary key. For Kimberly's tables, VisitID is the primary key for the Visit table, InvoiceNum is the primary key for the Billing table, OwnerID is the primary key for the Owner table, and AnimalID is the primary key for the Animal table.

- **Include a common field in related tables.** You use the common field to connect one table logically with another table. For example, Kimberly's Visit and Animal tables include the AnimalID field as a common field. Recall that when you include the primary key from one table as a field in a second table to form a relationship, the field in the second table is called a foreign key; therefore, the AnimalID field is a foreign key in the Visit table. With this common field, Kimberly can find all visits to the clinic made by a particular animal; she can use the AnimalID value for an animal and search the Visit table for all records with that AnimalID value. Likewise, she can determine which animal made a particular visit by searching the Animal table to find the one record with the same AnimalID value as the corresponding value in the Visit table. Similarly, the VisitID field is a common field, serving as the primary key in the Visit table and a foreign key in the Billing table. Since animals have owners responsible for their bills, there must be a relationship between the animals and owners for the clinic to contact; therefore, the OwnerID field is a foreign key in the Animal table.

- **Avoid data redundancy.** When you store the same data in more than one place, **data redundancy** occurs. With the exception of common fields to connect tables, you should avoid data redundancy because it wastes storage space and can cause inconsistencies. An inconsistency would exist, for example, if you type a field value one way in one table and a different way in the same table or in a second table. Figure 2-3, which contains portions of potential data stored in the Animal and Visit tables, shows an example of incorrect database design that has data redundancy in the Visit table. In Figure 2-3, the AnimalName field in the Visit table is redundant, and one value for this field was entered incorrectly, in three different ways.

Figure 2-3   Incorrect database design with data redundancy

AnimalID	AnimalName	AnimalBirthDate	AnimalType
12286	Lady	8/12/2015	Dog
12304	Tweets	11/12/2010	Bird
12332	Smittie	5/19/2014	Cat
12345	Herford5	4/28/2015	Cattle
12359	Merino4	8/2/2014	Sheep

data redundancy

VisitID	AnimalID	AnimalName	VisitDate	OffSite
1202	12500	Bonkers	12/11/2016	No
1250	12332	Smitty	12/19/2016	No
1276	12492	Bessie	1/10/2017	Yes
1308	12332	Smity	1/23/2017	No
1325	12612	Tweets	2/6/2017	No
1342	12595	Angus	2/27/2017	Yes
1367	12332	Smittee	3/7/2017	No

Inconsistent data

- **Determine the properties of each field.** You need to identify the **properties**, or characteristics, of each field so that the DBMS knows how to store, display, and process the field values. These properties include the field's name, data type, maximum number of characters or digits, description, valid values, and other field characteristics. You will learn more about field properties later in this module.

The Billing, Owner, and Animal tables you need to create will contain the fields shown in Figure 2-2. Before creating these new tables in the Riverview database, you first need to learn some guidelines for setting field properties.

Guidelines for Setting Field Properties

As just noted, the last step of database design is to determine which values to assign to the properties, such as the name and data type, of each field. When you select or enter a value for a property, you **set** the property. Access has rules for naming fields and objects, assigning data types, and setting other field properties.

Naming Fields and Objects

You must name each field, table, and other object in an Access database. Access stores these items in the database, using the names you supply. It's best to choose a field or object name that describes the purpose or contents of the field or object so that later you can easily remember what the name represents. For example, the four tables in the Riverview database are named Visit, Billing, Owner, and Animal because these names suggest their contents. Note that a table or query name must be unique within a database. A field name must be unique within a table, but it can be used again in another table.

Assigning Field Data Types

Each field must have a data type, which is either assigned automatically by Access or specifically by the table designer. The data type determines what field values you can enter for the field and what other properties the field will have. For example, the Billing table will include an InvoiceDate field, which will store date values, so you will assign the Date/Time data type to this field. Then Access will allow you to enter and manipulate only dates or times as values in the InvoiceDate field.

Figure 2-4 lists the most commonly used data types in Access, describes the field values allowed for each data type, explains when you should use each data type, and indicates the field size of each data type. You can find more complete information about all available data types in Access Help.

Figure 2-4	Common data types

Data Type	Description	Field Size
Short Text	Allows field values containing letters, digits, spaces, and special characters. Use for names, addresses, descriptions, and fields containing digits that are *not used in calculations*.	0 to 255 characters; default is 255
Long Text	Allows field values containing letters, digits, spaces, and special characters. Use for long comments and explanations.	1 to 65,535 characters; exact size is determined by entry
Number	Allows positive and negative numbers as field values. A number can contain digits, a decimal point, commas, a plus sign, and a minus sign. Use for fields that will be used in calculations, except those involving money.	1 to 15 digits
Date/Time	Allows field values containing valid dates and times from January 1, 100 to December 31, 9999. Dates can be entered in month/day/year format, several other date formats, or a variety of time formats, such as 10:35 PM. You can perform calculations on dates and times, and you can sort them. For example, you can determine the number of days between two dates.	8 bytes
Currency	Allows field values similar to those for the Number data type, but is used for storing monetary values. Unlike calculations with Number data type decimal values, calculations performed with the Currency data type are not subject to round-off error.	Accurate to 15 digits on the left side of the decimal point and to 4 digits on the right side
AutoNumber	Consists of integer values created automatically by Access each time you create a new record. You can specify sequential numbering or random numbering, which guarantees a unique field value, so that such a field can serve as a table's primary key.	9 digits
Yes/No	Limits field values to yes and no, on and off, or true and false. Use for fields that indicate the presence or absence of a condition, such as whether an order has been filled or whether an invoice has been paid.	1 character
Hyperlink	Consists of text used as a hyperlink address, which can have up to four parts: the text that appears in a field or control; the path to a file or page; a location within the file or page; and text displayed as a ScreenTip.	Up to 65,535 characters total for the four parts of the hyperlink

Setting Field Sizes

The **Field Size property** defines a field value's maximum storage size for Short Text, Number, and AutoNumber fields only. The other data types have no Field Size property because their storage size is either a fixed, predetermined amount or is determined automatically by the field value itself, as shown in Figure 2-4. A Short Text field has a default field size of 255 characters; you can also set its field size by entering a number from 0 to 255. For example, the FirstName and LastName fields in the Owner table will be Short Text fields with sizes of 20 characters and 25 characters, respectively. These field sizes will accommodate the values that will be entered in each of these fields.

PROSKILLS

Decision Making: Specifying the Field Size Property for Number Fields

When you use the Number data type to define a field, you need to decide what the Field Size setting should be for the field. You should set the Field Size property based on the largest value that you expect to store in that field. Access processes smaller data sizes faster, using less memory, so you can optimize your database's performance and its storage space by selecting the correct field size for each field. Field Size property settings for Number fields are as follows:

- **Byte**: Stores whole numbers (numbers with no fractions) from 0 to 255 in one byte
- **Integer**: Stores whole numbers from –32,768 to 32,767 in two bytes
- **Long Integer** (default): Stores whole numbers from –2,147,483,648 to 2,147,483,647 in four bytes
- **Single**: Stores positive and negative numbers to precisely seven decimal places in four bytes
- **Double**: Stores positive and negative numbers to precisely 15 decimal places in eight bytes
- **Replication ID**: Establishes a unique identifier for replication of tables, records, and other objects in databases created using Access 2003 and earlier versions in 16 bytes
- **Decimal**: Stores positive and negative numbers to precisely 28 decimal places in 12 bytes

Choosing an appropriate field size is important to optimize efficiency. For example, it would be wasteful to use the Long Integer field size for a Number field that will store only whole numbers ranging from 0 to 255 because the Long Integer field size uses four bytes of storage space. A better choice would be the Byte field size, which uses one byte of storage space to store the same values. By first gathering and analyzing information about the number values that will be stored in a Number field, you can make the best decision for the field's Field Size property and ensure the most efficient user experience for the database.

Setting the Caption Property for Fields

The **Caption property** for a field specifies how the field name is displayed in database objects, including table and query datasheets, forms, and reports. If you don't set the Caption property, Access displays the field name as the column heading or label for a field. For example, field names such as InvoiceAmt and InvoiceDate in the Billing table can be difficult to read. Setting the Caption property for these fields to "Invoice Amt" and "Invoice Date" would make it easier for users to read the field names and work with the database.

INSIGHT

Setting the Caption Property vs. Naming Fields

Although Access allows you to include spaces in field names, this practice is not recommended because the spaces cause problems when you try to perform more complex tasks with the data in your database. Setting the Caption property allows you to follow best practices for naming fields, such as not including spaces in field names, while still providing users with more readable field names in datasheets, forms, and reports.

In the previous module, you created the Riverview database file and, within that file, you created the Visit table working in Datasheet view. According to her plan for the Riverview database, Kimberly also wants to track information about the invoices the care center sends to the owners of the animals. Next, you'll create the Billing table for Kimberly—this time, working in Design view.

Creating a Table in Design View

Creating a table in Design view involves entering the field names and defining the properties for the fields, specifying a primary key for the table, and then saving the table structure. Kimberly documented the design for the new Billing table by listing each field's name and data type; each field's size and description (if applicable); and any other properties to be set for each field. See Figure 2-5.

Figure 2-5 Design for the Billing table

Field Name	Data Type	Field Size	Description	Other
InvoiceNum	Short Text	5	Primary key	Caption = Invoice Num
VisitID	Short Text	4	Foreign key	Caption = Visit ID
InvoiceAmt	Currency			Format = Currency
				Decimal Places = 2
				Caption = Invoice Amt
InvoiceDate	Date/Time			Format = mm/dd/yyyy
				Caption = Invoice Date
InvoicePaid	Yes/No			Caption = Invoice Paid

You'll use Kimberly's design as a guide for creating the Billing table in the Riverview database.

To begin creating the Billing table:

1. Start Access and open the **Riverview** database you created in the previous module.

   Trouble? If the security warning is displayed below the ribbon, click the **Enable Content** button.

2. If the Navigation Pane is open, click the **Shutter Bar Open/Close Button** « to close it.

3. On the ribbon, click the **Create** tab.

4. In the Tables group, click the **Table Design** button. A new table named Table1 opens in Design view. Refer to the Session 2.1 Visual Overview for a complete description of the Table window in Design view.

Defining Fields

When you first create a table in Design view, the insertion point is located in the first row's Field Name box, ready for you to begin defining the first field in the table. You enter values for the Field Name, Data Type, and Description field properties, and then select values for all other field properties in the Field Properties pane. These other properties will appear when you move to the first row's Data Type box.

REFERENCE

Defining a Field in Design View

- In the Field Name box, type the name for the field, and then press the Tab key.
- Accept the default Short Text data type, or click the arrow and select a different data type for the field. Press the Tab key.
- Enter an optional description for the field, if necessary.
- Use the Field Properties pane to type or select other field properties, as appropriate.

The first field you need to define is the InvoiceNum field. This field will be the primary key for the Billing table. Each invoice at Riverview Veterinary Care Center is assigned a specific five-digit number. Although the InvoiceNum field will contain these number values, the numbers will never be used in calculations; therefore, you'll assign the Short Text data type to this field. Any time a field contains number values that will not be used in calculations—such as phone numbers, zip codes, and so on—you should use the Short Text data type instead of the Number data type.

To define the InvoiceNum field:

TIP

You can also press the Enter key to move from one property to the next in the Table Design grid.

1. Type **InvoiceNum** in the first row's Field Name box, and then press the **Tab** key to advance to the Data Type box. The default data type, Short Text, is selected in the Data Type box, which now also contains an arrow, and the field properties for a Short Text field appear in the Field Properties pane. See Figure 2-6.

Figure 2-6 Table window after entering the first field name

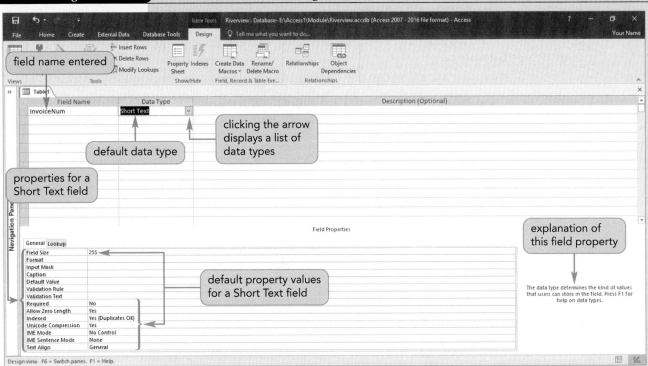

Notice that the right side of the Field Properties pane now provides an explanation for the current property, Data Type.

Trouble? If you make a typing error, you can correct it by clicking to position the insertion point, and then using either the Backspace key to delete characters to the left of the insertion point or the Delete key to delete characters to the right of the insertion point. Then type the correct text.

Because the InvoiceNum field values will not be used in calculations, you will accept the default Short Text data type for the field.

2. Press the **Tab** key to accept Short Text as the data type and to advance to the Description (Optional) box.

3. Next you'll enter the Description property value as "Primary key." The value you enter for the Description property will appear in the status bar when you view the table datasheet. Note that specifying "Primary key" for the Description property does *not* establish the current field as the primary key; you use a button on the ribbon to specify the primary key in Design view, which you will do later in this session.

4. Type **Primary key** in the Description (Optional) box.

Notice the Field Size property for the field. The default setting of 255 for Short Text fields is displayed. You need to change this number to 5 because all invoice numbers at Riverview Veterinary Care Center contain only five digits.

5. Double-click the number **255** in the Field Size property box to select it, and then type **5**.

Finally, you need to set the Caption property for the field so that its name appears with a space, as "Invoice Num."

6. Click the **Caption** property box, and then type **Invoice Num**. The definition of the first field is complete. See Figure 2-7.

Figure 2-7	InvoiceNum field defined

Kimberly's Billing table design (Figure 2-5) shows VisitID as the second field. Because Kimberly and other staff members need to relate information about invoices to the visit data in the Visit table, the Billing table must include the VisitID field, which is the Visit table's primary key. Recall that when you include the primary key from one table as a field in a second table to connect the two tables, the field is a foreign key in the second table. The field must be defined in the same way in both tables—that is, the field properties, including field size and data type, must match exactly.

Next, you will define VisitID as a Short Text field with a field size of 4. Later in this session, you'll change the Field Size property for the VisitID field in the Visit table to 4 so that the field definition is the same in both tables.

To define the VisitID field:

▶ **1.** In the Table Design grid, click the second row's **Field Name** box, type **VisitID**, and then press the **Tab** key to advance to the Data Type box.

▶ **2.** Press the **Tab** key to accept Short Text as the field's data type. Because the VisitID field is a foreign key to the Visit table, you'll enter "Foreign key" in the Description (Optional) box to help users of the database understand the purpose of this field.

▶ **3.** Type **Foreign key** in the Description (Optional) box. Next, you'll change the Field Size property.

▶ **4.** Press the **F6** key to move to the Field Properties pane. The current entry for the Field Size property, 255, is selected.

▶ **5.** Type **4** to set the Field Size property. Finally, you need to set the Caption property for this field.

▶ **6.** Press the **Tab** key three times to position the insertion point in the Caption box, and then type **Visit ID** (be sure to include a space between the two words). You have completed the definition of the second field.

The third field in the Billing table is the InvoiceAmt field, which will display the dollar amount of each invoice the clinic sends to the animals' owners. Kimberly wants the values to appear with two decimal places because invoice amounts include cents. She also wants the values to include dollar signs, so that the values will be formatted as currency when they are printed in bills sent to owners. The Currency data type is the appropriate choice for this field.

To define the InvoiceAmt field:

▶ **1.** Click the third row's **Field Name** box, type **InvoiceAmt** in the box, and then press the **Tab** key to advance to the Data Type box.

▶ **2.** Click the **Data Type** arrow, click **Currency** in the list, and then press the **Tab** key to advance to the Description (Optional) box. According to Kimberly's design (Figure 2-5), you do not need to enter a description for this field. If you've assigned a descriptive field name and the field does not fulfill a special function (such as primary key), you usually do not enter a value for the optional Description property. InvoiceAmt is a field that does not require a value for its Description property.

Kimberly wants the InvoiceAmt field values to be displayed with two decimal places. The **Decimal Places property** specifies the number of decimal places that are displayed to the right of the decimal point.

TIP

You can display the arrow and the list simultaneously by clicking the right side of a box.

3. In the Field Properties pane, click the **Decimal Places** box to position the insertion point there. An arrow appears on the right side of the Decimal Places box, which you can click to display a list of options.

4. Click the **Decimal Places** arrow, and then click **2** in the list to specify two decimal places for the InvoiceAmt field values.

5. Press the **Tab** key twice to position the insertion point in the Caption box, and then type **Invoice Amt**. The definition of the third field is now complete. Notice that the Format property is set to "Currency," which formats the values with dollar signs. See Figure 2-8.

Figure 2-8 | **Table window after defining the first three fields**

The fourth field in the Billing table is the InvoiceDate field. This field will contain the dates on which invoices are generated for the animals in the care center. You'll define the InvoiceDate field using the Date/Time data type. Also, according to Kimberly's design (Figure 2-5), the date values should be displayed in the format mm/dd/yyyy, which is a two-digit month, a two-digit day, and a four-digit year.

To define the InvoiceDate field:

▶ **1.** Click the fourth row's **Field Name** box, type **InvoiceDate**, and then press the **Tab** key to advance to the Data Type box.

You can select a value from the Data Type list as you did for the InvoiceAmt field. Alternately, you can type the property value in the box or type just the first character of the property value.

▶ **2.** Type **d**. Access completes the entry for the fourth row's Data Type box to "date/Time," with the letters "ate/Time" selected. See Figure 2-9.

Figure 2-9	Selecting a value for the Data Type property

completed entry for Data Type

▶ **3.** Press the **Tab** key to advance to the Description (Optional) box. Note that the value for the Data Type property changes to "Date/Time."

Kimberly wants the values in the InvoiceDate field to be displayed in a format showing the month, the day, and a four-digit year, as in the following example: 03/10/2017. You use the Format property to control the display of a field value.

▶ **4.** In the Field Properties pane, click the right side of the **Format** box to display the list of predefined formats for Date/Time fields. See Figure 2-10.

Figure 2-10	Displaying available formats for Date/Time fields

formats for Date/Time fields

Click to display a list of predefined formats

Trouble? If you see an arrow instead of a list of predefined formats, click the arrow to display the list.

As noted in the right side of the Field Properties pane, you can either choose a predefined format or enter a custom format. Even though the Short Date format seems to match the format Kimberly wants, it displays only one digit for months that contain only one digit. For example, it would display the month of March with only the digit "3"—as in 3/10/2017—instead of displaying the month with two digits, as in 03/10/2017.

Because none of the predefined formats matches the exact layout Kimberly wants for the InvoiceDate values, you need to create a custom date format. Figure 2-11 shows some of the symbols available for custom date and time formats.

Figure 2-11 ▶ **Symbols for some custom date formats**

Symbol	Description
/	date separator
d	day of the month in one or two numeric digits, as needed (1 to 31)
dd	day of the month in two numeric digits (01 to 31)
ddd	first three letters of the weekday (Sun to Sat)
dddd	full name of the weekday (Sunday to Saturday)
w	day of the week (1 to 7)
ww	week of the year (1 to 53)
m	month of the year in one or two numeric digits, as needed (1 to 12)
mm	month of the year in two numeric digits (01 to 12)
mmm	first three letters of the month (Jan to Dec)
mmmm	full name of the month (January to December)
yy	last two digits of the year (01 to 99)
yyyy	full year (0100 to 9999)

Kimberly wants the dates to be displayed with a two-digit month (mm), a two-digit day (dd), and a four-digit year (yyyy).

5. Click the **Format** arrow to close the list of predefined formats, and then type **mm/dd/yyyy** in the Format box.

6. Press the **Tab** key twice to position the insertion point in the Caption box, and then type **Invoice Date**. See Figure 2-12.

Figure 2-12	Specifying the custom date format

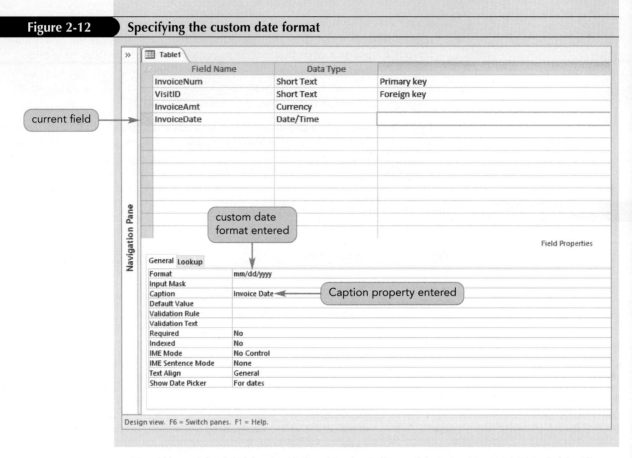

current field

The fifth and final field to be defined in the Billing table is InvoicePaid. This field will be a Yes/No field to indicate the payment status of each invoice record stored in the Billing table. Recall that the Yes/No data type is used to define fields that store true/false, yes/no, and on/off field values. When you create a Yes/No field in a table, the default Format property is set to Yes/No.

To define the InvoicePaid field:

1. Click the fifth row's **Field Name** box, type **InvoicePaid**, and then press the **Tab** key to advance to the Data Type box.

2. Type **y**. Access completes the data type as "yes/No".

3. Press the **Tab** key to select the Yes/No data type and move to the Description (Optional) box. In the Field Properties pane, note that the default format of "Yes/No" is selected, so you do not have to change this property.

4. In the Field Properties pane, click the **Caption** box, and then type **Invoice Paid**.

You've finished defining the fields for the Billing table. Next, you need to specify the primary key for the table.

Specifying the Primary Key

As you learned earlier, the primary key for a table uniquely identifies each record in the table.

Specifying a Primary Key in Design View

- Display the table in Design view.
- Click in the row for the field you've chosen to be the primary key to make it the active field. If the primary key will consist of two or more fields, click the row selector for the first field, press and hold the Ctrl key, and then click the row selector for each additional primary key field.
- In the Tools group on the Table Tools Design tab, click the Primary Key button.

According to Kimberly's design, you need to specify InvoiceNum as the primary key for the Billing table. You can do so while the table is in Design view.

To specify InvoiceNum as the primary key:

1. Click in the row for the InvoiceNum field to make it the current field.

TIP

This button is a toggle; you can click it to remove the key symbol.

2. On the Table Tools Design tab, in the Tools group, click the **Primary Key** button. The Primary Key button in the Tools group is now selected, and a key symbol appears in the row selector for the first row, indicating that the InvoiceNum field is the table's primary key. See Figure 2-13.

| Figure 2-13 | InvoiceNum field selected as the primary key |

Primary Key button

key symbol

Understanding the Importance of the Primary Key

Although Access does not require a table to have a primary key, including a primary key offers several advantages:

- A primary key uniquely identifies each record in a table.
- Access does not allow duplicate values in the primary key field. For example, if a record already exists in the Visit table with a VisitID value of 1550, Access prevents you from adding another record with this same value in the VisitID field. Preventing duplicate values ensures the uniqueness of the primary key field.
- When a primary key has been specified, Access forces you to enter a value for the primary key field in every record in the table. This is known as **entity integrity**. If you do not enter a value for a field, you have actually given the field a **null value**. You cannot give a null value to the primary key field because entity integrity prevents Access from accepting and processing that record.
- You can enter records in any order, but Access displays them by default in order of the primary key's field values. If you enter records in no specific order, you are ensured that you will later be able to work with them in a more meaningful, primary key sequence.
- Access responds faster to your requests for specific records based on the primary key.

Saving the Table Structure

The last step in creating a table is to name the table and save the table's structure. When you save a table structure, the table is stored in the database file (in this case, the Riverview database file). Once the table is saved, you can enter data into it. According to Kimberly's plan, you need to save the table you've defined as "Billing."

To name and save the Billing table:

▶ **1.** On the Quick Access Toolbar, click the **Save** button ⊞. The Save As dialog box opens.

▶ **2.** Type **Billing** in the Table Name box, and then press the **Enter** key. The Billing table is saved in the Riverview database. Notice that the tab for the table now displays the name "Billing" instead of "Table1."

Modifying the Structure of an Access Table

Even a well-designed table might need to be modified. Some changes that you can make to a table's structure in Design view include changing the order of fields and adding new fields.

After meeting with her assistant, Kelly Flannagan, and reviewing the structure of the Billing table, Kimberly has changes she wants you to make to the table. First, she wants the InvoiceAmt field to be moved so that it appears right before the InvoicePaid field. Then, she wants you to add a new Short Text field named InvoiceItem to the table to include information about what the invoice is for, such as office visits, lab work, and so on. Kimberly would like the InvoiceItem field to be inserted between the InvoiceAmt and InvoicePaid fields.

Moving a Field in Design View

To move a field, you use the mouse to drag it to a new location in the Table Design grid. Although you can move a field in Datasheet view by dragging its column heading to a new location, doing so rearranges only the *display* of the table's fields; the table structure is not changed. To move a field permanently, you must move the field in Design view.

Next, you'll move the InvoiceAmt field so that it is before the InvoicePaid field in the Billing table.

To move the InvoiceAmt field:

1. Position the pointer on the row selector for the InvoiceAmt field until the pointer changes to ➡.

2. Click the **row selector** to select the entire InvoiceAmt row.

3. Place the pointer on the row selector for the InvoiceAmt field until the pointer changes to ▷, press and hold the mouse button and then drag to the row selector for the InvoicePaid field. Notice that as you drag, the pointer changes to ▷. See Figure 2-14.

Figure 2-14   **Moving the InvoiceAmt field in the table structure**

4. Release the mouse button. The InvoiceAmt field now appears between the InvoiceDate and InvoicePaid fields in the table structure.

Trouble? If the InvoiceAmt field did not move, repeat Steps 1 through 4, making sure you hold down the mouse button during the drag operation.

Adding a Field in Design View

To add a new field between existing fields, you must insert a row. You begin by selecting the row below where you want the new field to be inserted.

REFERENCE

Adding a Field Between Two Existing Fields

- In the Table window in Design view, select the row below where you want the new field to be inserted.
- In the Tools group on the Table Tools Design tab, click the Insert Rows button.
- Define the new field by entering the field name, data type, optional description, and any property specifications.

Next, you need to add the InvoiceItem field to the Billing table structure between the InvoiceAmt and InvoicePaid fields.

To add the InvoiceItem field to the Billing table:

1. Click the **InvoicePaid Field Name** box. You need to establish this field as the current field so that the row for the new record will be inserted above this field.

2. On the Table Tools Design tab, in the Tools group, click the **Insert Rows** button. A new, blank row is added between the InvoiceAmt and InvoicePaid fields. The insertion point is positioned in the Field Name box for the new row, ready for you to type the name for the new field. See Figure 2-15.

Figure 2-15 Table structure after inserting a row

new, blank row inserted

Trouble? If you selected the InvoicePaid field's row selector and then inserted the new row, you need to click the new row's Field Name box to position the insertion point in it.

You'll define the InvoiceItem field in the new row of the Billing table. This field will be a Short Text field with a field size of 40, and you need to set the Caption property to include a space between the words in the field name.

3. Type **InvoiceItem**, press the **Tab** key to move to the Data Type property, and then press the **Tab** key again to accept the default Short Text data type.

4. Press the **F6** key to select the default field size in the Field Size box, and then type **40**.

5. Press the **Tab** key three times to position the insertion point in the Caption box, and then type **Invoice Item**. The definition of the new field is complete. See Figure 2-16.

| Figure 2-16 | InvoiceItem field added to the Billing table |

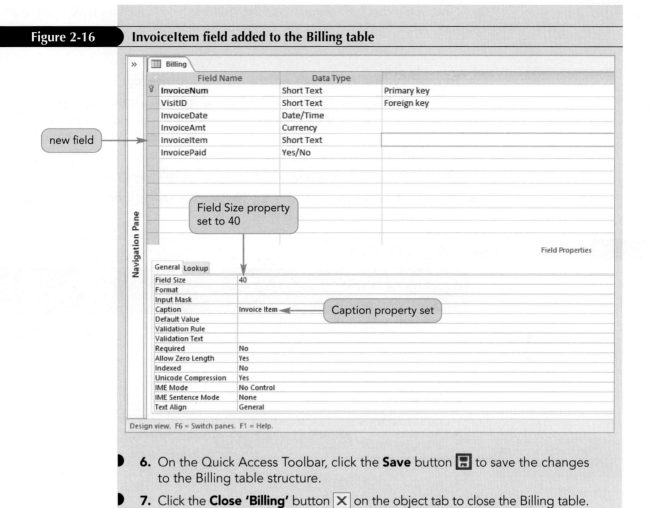

new field

Field Size property set to 40

Caption property set

6. On the Quick Access Toolbar, click the **Save** button 💾 to save the changes to the Billing table structure.

7. Click the **Close 'Billing'** button ✕ on the object tab to close the Billing table.

Modifying Field Properties

With the Billing table design complete, you can now go back and modify the properties of the fields in the Visit table you created in the previous module, as necessary. You can make some changes to properties in Datasheet view; for others, you'll work in Design view.

Changing the Format Property in Datasheet View

The Formatting group on the Table Tools Fields tab in Datasheet view allows you to modify some formatting for certain field types. When you format a field, you change the way data is displayed, but not the actual values stored in the table.

Next, you'll check the properties of the VisitDate field in the Visit table to see if any changes are needed to improve the display of the date values.

To modify the VisitDate field's Format property:

1. In the Navigation Pane, click the **Shutter Bar Open/Close Button** to open the pane. Notice that the Billing table is listed above the Visit table in the Tables section. By default, objects are listed in alphabetical order in the Navigation pane.

2. Double-click **Visit** to open the Visit table in Datasheet view.

3. In the Navigation Pane, click the **Shutter Bar Open/Close Button** to close the pane. See Figure 2-17.

| Figure 2-17 | Visit table datasheet |

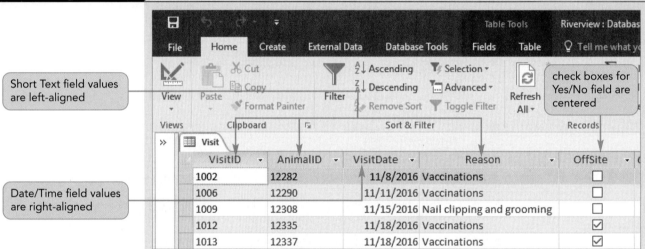

Notice that the values in the three Short Text fields—VisitID, AnimalID, and Reason—appear left-aligned within their boxes, and the values in the Date/Time field (VisitDate) appear right-aligned. In Access, values for Short Text fields are left-aligned, and values for Number, Date/Time, and Currency fields are right-aligned. The Offsite field is a Yes/No field, so its values appear in check boxes that are centered within the column.

4. On the ribbon, click the **Table Tools Fields** tab.

5. Click the **first field value** in the VisitDate column. The Data Type option shows that this field is a Date/Time field.

   By default, Access assigns the General Date format to Date/Time fields. Note the Format box in the Formatting group, which you use to set the Format property (similar to how you set the Format property in the Field Properties pane in Design view.) Even though the Format box is empty, the VisitDate field has the General Date format applied to it. The General Date format includes settings for date or time values, or a combination of date and time values. However, Kimberly wants *only date values* to be displayed in the VisitDate field, so she asks you to specify the Short Date format for the field.

6. In the Formatting group, click the **Format** arrow, and then click **Short Date**. See Figure 2-18.

| Figure 2-18 | VisitDate field after modifying the format |

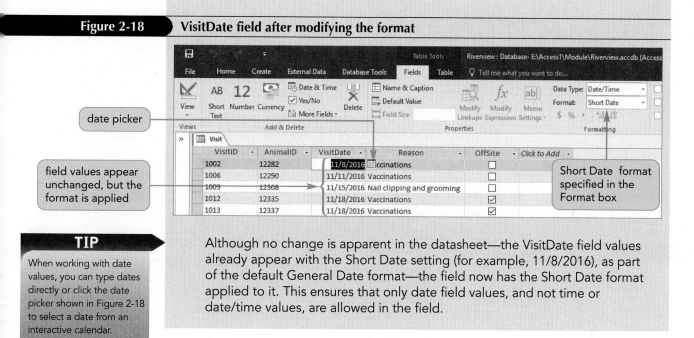

Although no change is apparent in the datasheet—the VisitDate field values already appear with the Short Date setting (for example, 11/8/2016), as part of the default General Date format—the field now has the Short Date format applied to it. This ensures that only date field values, and not time or date/time values, are allowed in the field.

Changing Properties in Design View

Recall that each of the Short Text fields in the Visit table—VisitID, AnimalID, and Reason—still has the default field size of 255, which is too large for the data contained in these fields. Also, the VisitID and AnimalID fields need descriptions to identify them as the primary and foreign keys, respectively, in the table. Finally, each of these fields needs a caption either to include a space between the words in the field name or to make the name more descriptive. You can make all of these property changes more easily in Design view.

To modify the Field Size, Description, and Caption field properties:

1. On the Table Tools Fields tab, in the Views group, click the **View** button. The table is displayed in Design view with the VisitID field selected. You need to enter a Description property value for this field, the primary key in the table, and change its Field Size property to 4 because each visit number at Riverview Veterinary Care Center consists of four digits.

2. Press the **Tab** key twice to position the insertion point in the Description (Optional) box, and then type **Primary key**.

3. Press the **F6** key to move to and select the default setting of 255 in the Field Size box in the Fields Properties pane, and then type **4**. Next you need to set the Caption property for this field.

4. Press the **Tab** key three times to position the insertion point in the Caption box, and then type **Visit ID**.

   Next you need to enter a Description property value for the AnimalID field, a foreign key in the table, and set its Field Size property to 5 because each AnimalID number at Riverview Veterinary Care Center consists of five digits. You also need to set this field's Caption property.

5. Click the **VisitDate** Field Name box, click the **Caption** box, and then type **Date of Visit**.

For the Reason field, you will set the Field Size property to 60. This size can accommodate the longer values in the Reason field. You'll also set this field's Caption property to provide a more descriptive name.

6. Click the **Reason** Field Name box, press the **F6** key, type **60**, press the **Tab** key three times to position the insertion point in the Caption box, and then type **Reason/Diagnosis**.

Finally, you'll set the Caption property for the OffSite field.

7. Click the **OffSite** Field Name box, click the **Caption** box, and then type **Off-Site Visit?**. See Figure 2-19.

Figure 2-19 | **Visit table after modifying field properties**

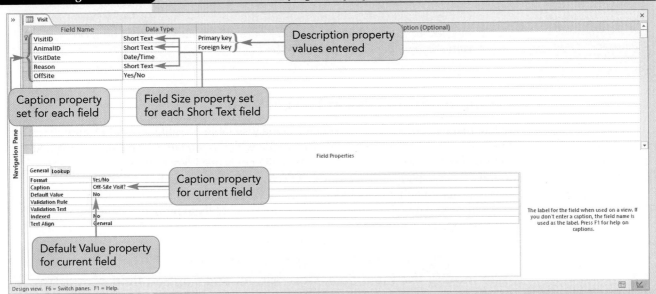

Notice that the OffSite field's Default Value property is automatically set to "No," which means the check box for this field will be empty for each new record. This is the default for this property for any Yes/No field. You can set the Default Value property for other types of fields to make data entry easier. You'll learn more about setting this property in the next session.

The changes to the Visit table's properties are now complete, so you can save the table and view the results of your changes in Datasheet view.

To save and view the modified Visit table:

1. On the Quick Access Toolbar, click the **Save** button 💾 to save the modified table. A dialog box opens informing you that some data may be lost because you decreased the field sizes. Because all of the values in the VisitID, AnimalID, and Reason fields contain the same number of or fewer characters than the new Field Size properties you set for each field, you can ignore this message.

2. Click the **Yes** button.

3. On the Table Tools Design tab, in the Views group, click the **View** button to display the Visit table in Datasheet view. Notice that each column (field) heading now displays the text you specified in the Caption property for that field. However, now the Off-Site Visit? field caption doesn't fully display.

4. Place the pointer on the column border to the right of the Off-Site Visit? field name until the pointer changes to **↔**, and then double-click the column border to fully display this field name. See Figure 2-20.

Figure 2-20	Modified Visit table in Datasheet view

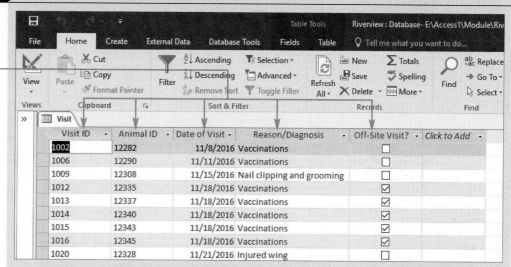

column headings display Caption property values

5. Click the **Close 'Visit'** button **X** on the object tab to close the Visit table, and click **Yes** to save the changes to the Visit table.

6. If you are not continuing to Session 2.2, click the **File** tab, and then click **Close** in the navigation bar of Backstage view to close the Riverview database.

You have created the Billing table and made modifications to its design. In the next session, you'll add records to the Billing table and create the Animal and Owner tables in the Riverview database.

REVIEW

Session 2.1 Quick Check

1. What guidelines should you follow when designing a database?

2. What is the purpose of the Data Type property for a field?

3. The _____ property specifies how a field's name is displayed in database objects, including table and query datasheets, forms, and reports.

4. For which three types of fields can you assign a field size?

5. The default Field Size property setting for a Short Text field is _____.

6. In Design view, which key do you press to move from the Table Design grid to the Field Properties pane?

7. List three reasons why you should specify a primary key for an Access table.

Session 2.2 Visual Overview:

Click the Close button to close the Relationships window.

You click the **Show Table button** to open the Show Table dialog box. From there, you can choose a table to add to the Relationships window.

The **Relationships window** illustrates the relationships among a database's tables. Using this window, you can view or change existing relationships, define new relationships between tables, and rearrange the layout of the tables in the window.

The key symbol next to a field name indicates that the field is the table's primary key. For example, OwnerID is the primary key for the Owner table.

A **one-to-many relationship** exists between two tables when one record in the first table matches zero, one, or many records in the second table, and when one record in the second table matches at most one record in the first table. Here, the Owner and Animal tables have a one-to-many relationship because an Owner can own many animals, and each animal is associated with only one owner. The two tables are still separate tables, but because they are joined, you can use the data in them as if they were one table.

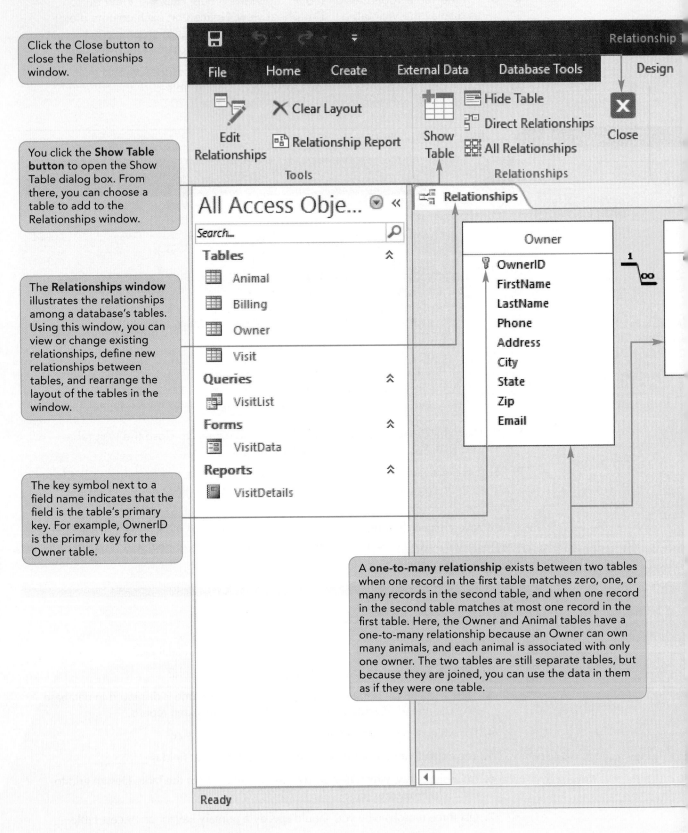

Modified Visit table in Datasheet view

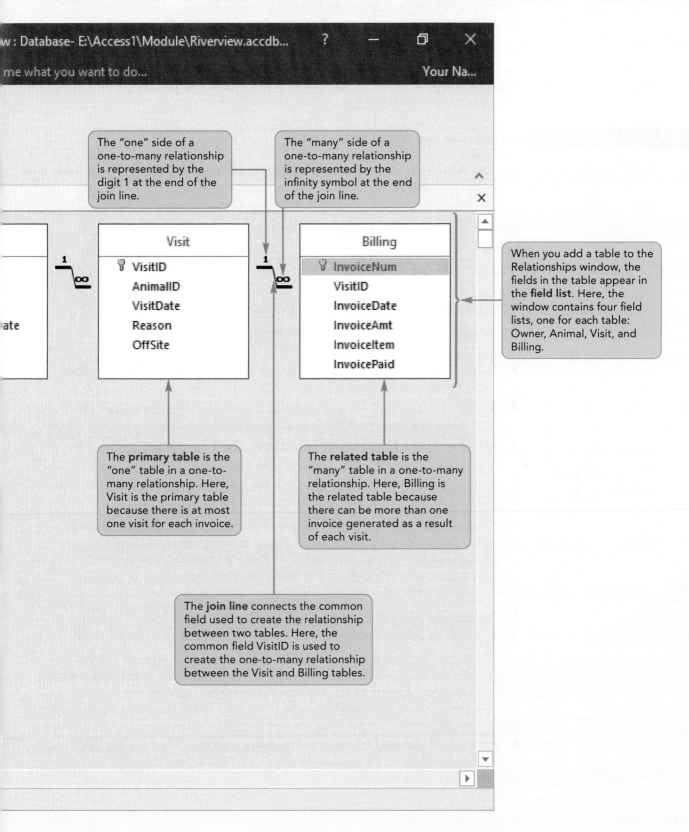

w : Database- E:\Access1\Module\Riverview.accdb...   ?   —   □   ✕

me what you want to do...   Your Na...

The "one" side of a one-to-many relationship is represented by the digit 1 at the end of the join line.

The "many" side of a one-to-many relationship is represented by the infinity symbol at the end of the join line.

Visit
- VisitID
- AnimalID
- VisitDate
- Reason
- OffSite

Billing
- InvoiceNum
- VisitID
- InvoiceDate
- InvoiceAmt
- InvoiceItem
- InvoicePaid

When you add a table to the Relationships window, the fields in the table appear in the **field list**. Here, the window contains four field lists, one for each table: Owner, Animal, Visit, and Billing.

The **primary table** is the "one" table in a one-to-many relationship. Here, Visit is the primary table because there is at most one visit for each invoice.

The **related table** is the "many" table in a one-to-many relationship. Here, Billing is the related table because there can be more than one invoice generated as a result of each visit.

The **join line** connects the common field used to create the relationship between two tables. Here, the common field VisitID is used to create the one-to-many relationship between the Visit and Billing tables.

Adding Records to a New Table

Before you can begin to define the table relationships illustrated in the Session 2.2 Visual Overview, you need to finish creating the tables in the Riverview database.

The Billing table design is complete. Now, Kimberly would like you to add records to the table so it will contain the invoice data for Riverview Veterinary Care Center. As you learned earlier, you add records to a table in Datasheet view by typing the field values in the rows below the column headings for the fields. You'll begin by entering the records shown in Figure 2-21.

Figure 2-21 Records to be added to the Billing table

Invoice Num	Visit ID	Invoice Date	Invoice Amt	Invoice Item	Invoice Paid
42098	1002	11/09/2016	$50.00	Lab work	Yes
42125	1012	11/21/2016	$50.00	Off-site visit	No
42271	1077	12/15/2016	$45.00	Flea & tick medications	Yes
42518	1181	01/26/2017	$35.00	Heartworm medication	No

To add the first record to the Billing table:

1. If you took a break after the previous session, make sure the Riverview database is open and the Navigation Pane is open.

2. In the Tables section of the Navigation Pane, double-click **Billing** to open the Billing table in Datasheet view.

3. Close the Navigation Pane, and then use the ✛ pointer to resize columns, as necessary, so that the field names are completely visible.

4. In the Invoice Num column, type **42098**, press the **Tab** key, type **1002** in the Visit ID column, and then press the **Tab** key.

5. Type **11/9/2016** and then press the **Tab** key. The date "11/09/2016" in the Invoice Date column reflects the custom date format you set.

   Next you need to enter the invoice amount for the first record. This is a Currency field with the Currency format and two decimal places specified. Because of the field's properties, you do not need to type the dollar sign, comma, or zeroes for the decimal places; these items will display automatically.

6. Type **50** and then press the **Tab** key. The value displays as "$50.00."

7. In the Invoice Item column, type **Lab work**, and then press the **Tab** key.

   The last field in the table, InvoicePaid, is a Yes/No field. Recall that the default value for any Yes/No field is "No"; therefore, the check box is initially empty. For the record you are entering in the Billing table, the invoice has been paid, so you need to insert a checkmark in the check box in the Invoice Paid column.

8. Press the **spacebar** to insert a checkmark, and then press the **Tab** key. The values for the first record are entered. See Figure 2-22.

Be sure to type the numbers "0" and "1" and *not* the letters "O" and "I" in the field values.

| Figure 2-22 | First record entered in the Billing table |

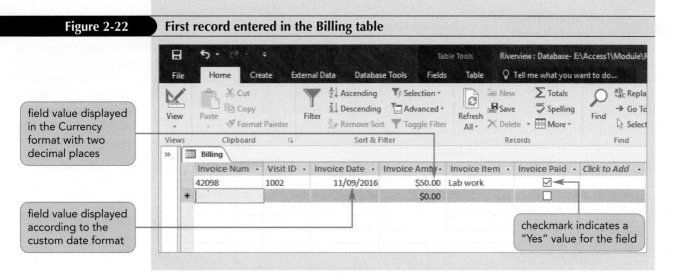

field value displayed in the Currency format with two decimal places

field value displayed according to the custom date format

checkmark indicates a "Yes" value for the field

Now you can add the remaining three records. As you do, you'll learn a keyboard shortcut for inserting the value from the same field in the previous record. A **keyboard shortcut** is a key or combination of keys you press to complete an action more efficiently.

To add the next three records to the Billing table:

▶ **1.** Refer to Figure 2-21 and enter the values in the second record's Invoice Num, Visit ID, and Invoice Date columns.

Notice that the value in the second record's Invoice Amt column is $50.00. This value is the exact same value as in the first record. You can quickly insert the value from the same column in the previous record using the Ctrl + ' (apostrophe) keyboard shortcut. To use this shortcut, you press and hold the Ctrl key, press the ' key once, and then release both keys. (The plus sign in the keyboard shortcut indicates you're pressing two keys at once; you do not press the + key.)

▶ **2.** With the insertion point in the Invoice Amt column, press the **Ctrl + ' keys**. The value "$50.00" is inserted in the Invoice Amt column for the second record.

▶ **3.** Press the **Tab** key to move to the Invoice Item column, and then type **Off-site visit**.

▶ **4.** Press the **Tab** key to move to the Invoice Paid column, and then press the **Tab** key to leave the Invoice Paid check box unchecked to indicate the invoice has not been paid. The second record is entered in the Billing table.

▶ **5.** Refer to Figure 2-21 to enter the values for the third and fourth records. Your table should look like the one in Figure 2-23.

Figure 2-23	Billing table with four records entered

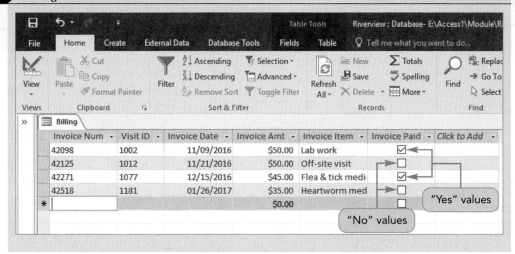

To finish entering records in the Billing table, you'll use a method that allows you to import the data.

Importing Data from an Excel Worksheet

Often, the data you want to add to an Access table exists in another file, such as a Word document or an Excel workbook. You can bring the data from other files into Access in different ways. For example, you can copy and paste the data from an open file, or you can **import** the data, which is a process that allows you to copy the data from a source without having to open the source file.

TIP

Caption property values set for fields are not considered in the import process. Therefore make sure that the field names match the Excel worksheet column headings. If there are differences, change the column headings in the Excel worksheet to match the Access table field names.

Kimberly had been using Excel to track invoice data for Riverview Veterinary Care Center and already created a worksheet, named "Invoices," containing this data. You'll import this Excel worksheet into your Billing table to complete the entry of data in the table. To use the import method, the columns in the Excel worksheet must match the names and data types of the fields in the Access table.

The Invoices worksheet contains the following columns: InvoiceNum, VisitID, InvoiceDate, InvoiceAmt, InvoiceItem, and InvoicePaid. These column headings match the field names in the Billing table exactly, so you can import the data. Before you import data into a table, you need to close the table.

To import the Invoices worksheet into the Billing table:

1. Click the **Close 'Billing'** button ☒ on the object tab to close the Billing table, and then click the **Yes** button in the dialog box asking if you want to save the changes to the table layout.

2. On the ribbon, click the **External Data** tab.

3. In the Import & Link group, click the **Excel** button. The Get External Data - Excel Spreadsheet dialog box opens. See Figure 2-24.

| Figure 2-24 | Get External Data – Excel Spreadsheet dialog box |

click to navigate to the Excel workbook containing the data you want to import

you might see a different path here

option for adding records to an existing table

The dialog box provides options for importing the entire worksheet as a new table in the current database, adding the data from the worksheet to an existing table, or linking the data in the worksheet to the table. You need to add, or append, the worksheet data to the Billing table.

4. Click the **Browse** button. The File Open dialog box opens. The Excel workbook file is named "Invoices" and is located in the Access1 > Module folder provided with your Data Files.

5. Navigate to the **Access1 > Module** folder, where your Data Files are stored, and then double-click the **Invoices** Excel file. You return to the dialog box.

6. Click the **Append a copy of the records to the table** option button. The box to the right of this option becomes active and displays the Billing table name, because it is the first table listed in the Navigation Pane.

7. Click the **OK** button. The first Import Spreadsheet Wizard dialog box opens. The dialog box confirms that the first row of the worksheet you are importing contains column headings. The bottom section of the dialog box displays some of the data contained in the worksheet. See Figure 2-25.

Figure 2-25 **First Import Spreadsheet Wizard dialog box**

selected check box
confirms that the
first row contains
column headings

data from the worksheet
to be imported

8. Click the **Next** button. The second, and final, Import Spreadsheet Wizard dialog box opens. Notice that the Import to Table box shows that the data from the spreadsheet will be imported into the Billing table.

9. Click the **Finish** button. A dialog box opens asking if you want to save the import steps. If you needed to repeat this same import procedure many times, it would be a good idea to save the steps for the procedure. However, you don't need to save these steps because you'll be importing the data only one time. Once the data is in the Billing table, Kimberly will no longer use Excel to track invoice data.

10. Click the **Close** button in the dialog box to close it without saving the steps.

The data from the Invoices worksheet has been added to the Billing table. Next, you'll open the table to view the new records.

To open the Billing table and view the imported data:

1. Open the Navigation Pane, and then double-click **Billing** in the Tables section to open the table in Datasheet view.

2. Resize the Invoice Item column to its best fit, scrolling the worksheet and resizing, as necessary.

3. Press the **Ctrl + Home** keys to scroll to the top of the datasheet. Notice that the table now contains a total of 204 records—the four records you entered plus 200 records imported from the Invoices worksheet. The records are displayed in primary key order by the values in the Invoice Num column. See Figure 2-26.

| Figure 2-26 | Billing table after importing data from Excel |

records displayed in order by the values in the Invoice Num column

table contains a total of 204 records

4. Save and close the Billing table, and then close the Navigation Pane.

Two of the tables—Visit and Billing—are now complete. According to Kimberly's plan for the Riverview database, you still need to create the Owner and Animal tables. You'll use a different method to create these tables.

Creating a Table by Importing an Existing Table or Table Structure

If another Access database contains a table—or even just the design, or structure, of a table—that you want to include in your database, you can import the table and any records it contains or import only the table structure into your database. To create the new Owner and Animal tables per Kimberly's plan shown in Figure 2-2, you will import a table structure from a different Access database to create the Owner table and an existing table structure and records from another database to create the Animal table.

Importing an Existing Table Structure

Kimberly documented the design for the new Owner table by listing each field's name and data type, as well as any applicable field size, description, and caption property values, as shown in Figure 2-27. Note that each field in the Owner table will be a Short Text field, and the OwnerID field will be the table's primary key.

Figure 2-27   **Design for the Owner table**

Field Name	Data Type	Field Size	Description	Caption
OwnerID	Short Text	4	Primary key	Owner ID
FirstName	Short Text	20		First Name
LastName	Short Text	25		Last Name
Phone	Short Text	14		
Address	Short Text	35		
City	Short Text	25		
State	Short Text	2		
Zip	Short Text	10		
Email	Short Text	50		

Kimberly's assistant Kelly already created an Access database containing an Owner table design, however, she hasn't entered any records into the table. After reviewing the table design, both Kelly and Kimberly agree that it contains some of the fields they want to track, but that some changes are needed. You will import the table structure in Kelly's database to create the Owner table in the Riverview database, and later in this session, you will modify the imported table to produce the final table structure according to Kimberly's design.

To create the Owner table by importing the structure of another table:

1. Make sure the External Data tab is the active tab on the ribbon.

2. In the Import & Link group, click the **Access** button. The Get External Data - Access Database dialog box opens. This dialog box is similar to the one you used earlier when importing the Excel spreadsheet.

3. Click the **Browse** button. The File Open dialog box opens. The Access database file from which you need to import the table structure is named "Kelly" and is located in the Access1 > Module folder provided with your Data Files.

4. Navigate to the **Access1 > Module** folder, where your Data Files are stored, and then double-click the **Kelly** database file. You return to the dialog box.

5. Make sure the **Import tables, queries, forms, reports, macros, and modules into the current database** option button is selected, and then click the **OK** button. The Import Objects dialog box opens. The dialog box contains tabs for importing all the different types of Access database objects—tables, queries, forms, and so on. The Tables tab is the current tab.

6. Click the **Options** button in the dialog box to see all the options for importing tables. See Figure 2-28.

| Figure 2-28 | Import Objects dialog box |

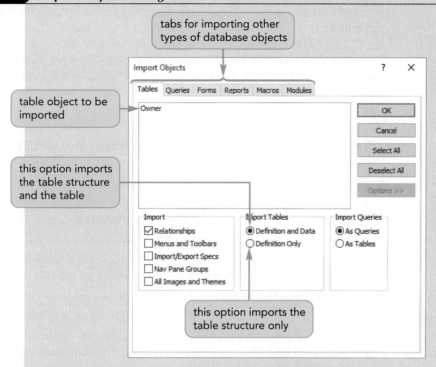

tabs for importing other types of database objects

table object to be imported

this option imports the table structure and the table

this option imports the table structure only

▶ **7.** On the Tables tab, click **Owner** to select this table.

▶ **8.** In the Import Tables section of the dialog box, click the **Definition Only** option button, and then click the **OK** button. Access creates the Owner table in the Riverview database using the structure of the Owner table in the Kelly database, and opens a dialog box asking if you want to save the import steps.

▶ **9.** Click the **Close** button to close the dialog box without saving the import steps.

▶ **10.** Open the Navigation Pane, double-click **Owner** in the Tables section to open the table, and then close the Navigation Pane. The Owner table opens in Datasheet view. The table contains no records. See Figure 2-29.

| Figure 2-29 | Imported Owner table in Datasheet view |

Before you add records to the Owner table and fine-tune its design, you need to first add the Animal table to the Riverview database. You will do this by importing a table and its data from another database.

Importing an Existing Table

Kelly has already created a database called "AllAnimals" that contains a table called "Animal." To import this Animal table into the Riverview database, you will follow the same process you used to import the table structure from the Kelly database to create the Owner table; however, this time you will choose the Definition and Data option, instead of the Definition only option in the Import Objects dialog box. This will import the structure and the data that Kelly has created and verified in the Animal table in the AllAnimals database.

To create the Animal table by importing the structure and data of another table:

▶ **1.** Close the Owner table, make sure the External Data tab is the active tab on the ribbon, and then in the Import & Link group, click the **Access** button. The Get External Data - Access Database dialog box opens.

▶ **2.** Click the **Browse** button. The File Open dialog box opens. The Access database file from which you need to import the table is named "AllAnimals" and is located in the Access1 > Module folder provided with your Data Files.

▶ **3.** Navigate to the **Access1 > Module** folder, where your Data Files are stored, and then double-click the **AllAnimals** database file. You return to the dialog box.

▶ **4.** Make sure the **Import tables, queries, forms, reports, macros, and modules into the current database** option button is selected, and then click the **OK** button to open the Import Objects dialog box opens. The Tables tab is the current tab.

▶ **5.** Click **Animal** to select this table, click the **Options** button to display the options for importing tables, and then, in the Import Tables section, make sure the **Definition and Data** option button is selected.

▶ **6.** Click the **OK** button, and then click the **Close** button to close the dialog box without saving the import steps. Access creates the Animal table in the Riverview database using the records and structure of the Animal table in the AllAnimals database.

▶ **7.** Open the Navigation Pane, double-click **Animal** in the Tables section to open the table, and then close the Navigation Pane. The Animal table opens in Datasheet view. Kimberly reviews the new Animal table and is satisfied with its structure and the records it contains, so you can close this table.

▶ **8.** Close the Animal table.

Now Kimberly asks you to complete the Owner table. She notes that the table structure you imported earlier for this table contains some of the fields she wants, but not all (see Figure 2-27); it also contains some fields she does not want in the Owner table. You can add the missing fields using the Data Type gallery.

Adding Fields to a Table Using the Data Type Gallery

The **Data Type gallery**, available from the More Fields button located on the Add & Delete group on the Table Tools Fields tab, allows you to add a group of related fields to a table at the same time, rather than adding each field to the table individually.

The group of fields you add is called a **Quick Start selection**. For example, the **Address Quick Start selection** adds a collection of fields related to an address, such as Address, City, State, and so on, to the table at one time. When you use a Quick Start selection, the fields added already have properties set. However, you need to review and possibly modify the properties to ensure the fields match your design needs for the database.

Next, you'll use the Data Type gallery to add the missing fields to the Owner table.

To add fields to the Owner table using the Data Type gallery:

1. Open the **Owner** table, and then on the ribbon, click the **Table Tools Fields** tab. Before inserting fields from the Data Type gallery, you need to place the insertion point in the field to the right of where you want to insert the new fields. According to Kimberly's design, the Address field should come after the Phone field, so you need to make the next field, Email, the active field.

Make sure the correct field is active before adding new fields.

2. Click the **first row** in the Email field to make it the active field.

3. In the Add & Delete group, click the **More Fields** button. The Data Type gallery opens and displays options for different types of fields you can add to your table.

4. Scroll down the gallery until the Quick Start section is visible. See Figure 2-30.

| Figure 2-30 | Owner table with the Data Type gallery displayed |

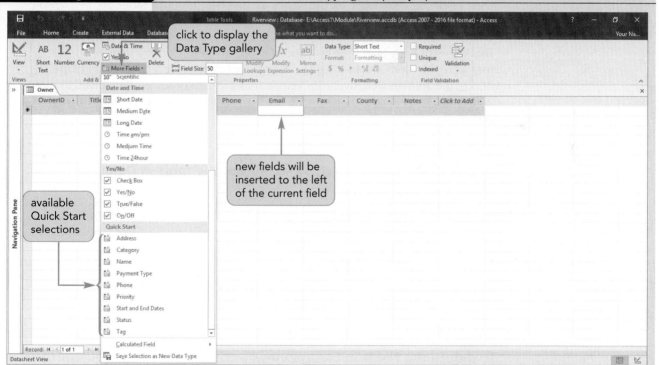

The Quick Start section provides options that will add multiple, related fields to the table at one time. The new fields will be inserted to the left of the current field.

5. In the Quick Start section, click **Address**. Five fields are added to the table: Address, City, State Province, ZIP Postal, and Country Region. See Figure 2-31.

Figure 2-31   Owner table after adding fields from the Data Type gallery

Modifying the Structure of an Imported Table

Refer back to Kimberly's design for the Owner table (Figure 2-27). To finalize the table design, you need to modify the imported table by deleting fields, renaming fields, and changing field data types. You'll begin by deleting fields.

Deleting Fields from a Table Structure

After you've created a table, you might need to delete one or more fields. When you delete a field, you also delete all the values for that field from the table. So, before you delete a field, you should make sure that you want to do so and that you choose the correct field to delete. You can delete fields in either Datasheet view or Design view.

The Address Quick Start selection added a field named "Country Region" to the Owner table. Kimberly doesn't need a field to store country data because all of the owners of the animals that Riverview Veterinary Care Center serves are located in the United States. You'll begin to modify the Owner table structure by deleting the Country Region field.

To delete the Country Region field from the table in Datasheet view:

1. Click the **first row** in the Country Region field (if necessary).

2. On the Table Tools Fields tab, in the Add & Delete group, click the **Delete** button. The Country Region field is removed and the first field, OwnerID, is now the active field.

You can also delete fields from a table structure in Design view. You'll switch to Design view to delete the other unnecessary fields.

To delete the fields in Design view:

1. On the Table Tools Fields tab, in the Views group, click the **View** button. The Owner table opens in Design view. See Figure 2-32.

Figure 2-32   **Owner table in Design view**

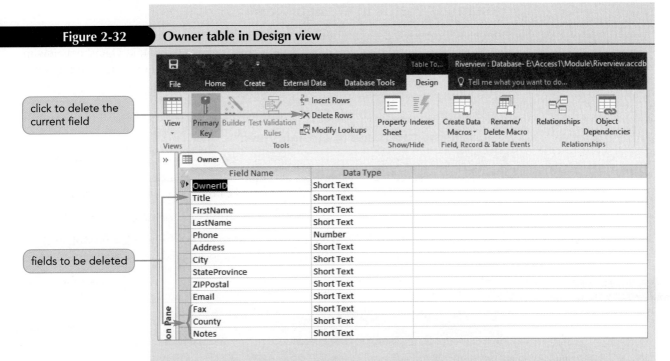

click to delete the current field

fields to be deleted

> **2.** Click the **Title** Field Name box to make it the current field.

> **3.** On the Table Tools Design tab, in the Tools group, click the **Delete Rows** button. The Title field is removed from the Owner table structure. You'll delete the Fax, County, and Notes fields next. Instead of deleting these fields individually, you'll select and delete them at the same time.

> **4.** On the row selector for the **Fax** field, press and hold the mouse button and then drag the mouse to select the **County** and **Notes** fields.

> **5.** Release the mouse button. The rows for the three fields are outlined in red, indicating all three fields are selected.

> **6.** In the Tools group, click the **Delete Rows** button. See Figure 2-33.

Figure 2-33   **Owner table after deleting fields**

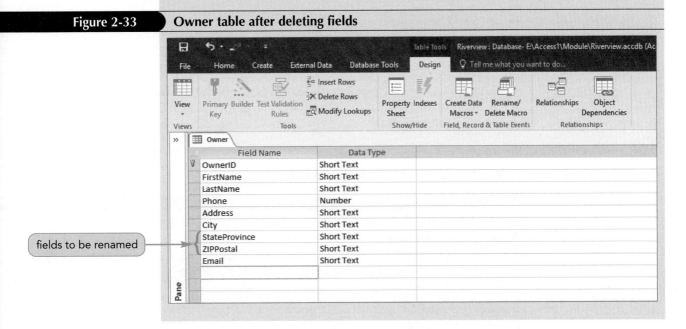

fields to be renamed

Renaming Fields in Design View

To match Kimberly's design for the Owner table, you need to rename some of the fields. You already have renamed the default primary key field (ID) in Datasheet view in the previous module. You can also rename fields in Design view by simply editing the names in the Table Design grid.

To rename the fields in Design view:

1. Click to position the insertion point to the right of the text StateProvince in the seventh row's Field Name box, and then press the **Backspace** key eight times to delete the word "Province." The name of the seventh field is now State.

   You can also select an entire field name and then type new text to replace it.

2. In the eighth row's Field Name box, drag to select the text **ZIPPostal**, and then type **Zip**. The text you type replaces the original text. See Figure 2-34.

Figure 2-34   **Owner table after renaming fields**

renamed fields

data type to be changed

Changing the Data Type for a Field in Design View

In the table structure you imported earlier, you used an option in Datasheet view to change a field's data type. You can also change the data type for a field in Design view. According to Kimberly's plan, all of the fields in the Owner table should be Short Text fields.

To change the data type of the Phone field in Design view:

1. Click the right side of the Data Type box for the Phone field to display the list of data types.

2. Click **Short Text** in the list. The Phone field is now a Short Text field. Note that, by default, the Field Size property is set to 255. According to Kimberly's plan, the Phone field should have a Field Size property of 14. You'll make this change next.

3. Press the **F6** key to move to and select the default Field Size property, and then type **14**.

Each of the remaining fields you added using the Address Quick Start selection—Address, City, State, and Zip—also has the default field size of 255. You need to change the Field Size property for these fields to match Kimberly's design. You'll also delete any Caption property values for these fields because the field names match how Kimberly wants them displayed, so captions are unnecessary.

To change the Field Size and Caption properties for the fields:

▶ **1.** Click the **Address Field Name** box to make it the current field.

▶ **2.** Press the **F6** key to move to and select the default Field Size property, and then type **35**. Note that the Caption property setting for this field is the same as the field name. This field doesn't need a caption, so you can delete this value.

▶ **3.** Press the **Tab** key three times to select Address in the Caption box, and then press the **Delete** key. The Caption property value is removed.

▶ **4.** Repeat Steps 1 through 3 for the City field to change the Field Size property to **25** and delete its Caption property value.

▶ **5.** Change the Field Size property for the State field to **2**, and then delete its Caption property value.

▶ **6.** Change the Field Size property for the Zip field to **10**, and then delete its Caption property value.

▶ **7.** On the Quick Access Toolbar, click the **Save** button 🖫 to save your changes to the Owner table.

Finally, Kimberly would like you to set the Description property for the OwnerID field and the Caption property for the OwnerID, FirstName, and LastName fields. You'll make these changes now.

To enter the Description and Caption property values:

▶ **1.** Click the **Description (Optional)** box for the OwnerID field, and then type **Primary key**.

▶ **2.** In the Field Properties pane, click the **Caption** box.

After you leave the Description (Optional) box, the Property Update Options button 📝 appears below this box for the OwnerID field. When you change a field's property in Design view, you can use this button to update the corresponding property on forms and reports that include the modified field. For example, if the Riverview database included a form that contained the OwnerID field, you could choose to propagate, or update, the modified Description property in the form by clicking the Property Update Options button, and then choosing the option to make the update everywhere the field is used. The ScreenTip on the Property Update Options button and the options it lists vary depending on the task; in this case, if you click the button, the option is "Update Status Bar Text everywhere OwnerID is used." Because the Riverview database does not include any forms or reports that are based on the Owner table, you do not need to update the properties, so you can ignore the button for now. In most cases, however, it is a good idea to perform the update.

▶ **3.** In the Caption box for the OwnerID field, type **Owner ID**.

▶ **4.** Click the **FirstName** Field Name box to make it the current field, click the **Caption** box, and then type **First Name**.

▶ **5.** Click the **LastName** Field Name box to make it the current field, click the
Caption box, and then type **Last Name**. See Figure 2-35.

Figure 2-35	Owner table after entering descriptions and captions

▶ **6.** On the Quick Access Toolbar, click the **Save** button 🖫 to save your changes
to the Owner table.

▶ **7.** On the Table Tools Design tab, in the Views group, click the **View** button to
display the table in Datasheet view.

▶ **8.** Resize each column to its best fit, and then click in the first row for the **Owner ID**
column. See Figure 2-36.

Figure 2-36	Modified Owner table in Datasheet view

Kimberly feels that data entry would be made easier if the State field value of "WY"
was automatically filled in for each new record added to the table, because all of the
owners live in Wyoming. You can accomplish this by setting the Default Value property
for the field.

Setting the Default Value Property for a Field

The **Default Value property** for a field specifies what value will appear, by default, for the field in each new record you add to a table.

Because all of the owners at Riverview Veterinary Care Center live in Wyoming, you'll specify a default value of "WY" for the State field in the Owner table. With this setting, each new record in the Owner table will have the correct State field value entered automatically.

To set the Default Value property for the State field:

▶ **1.** On the Home tab, in the Views group, click the **View** button to display the Owner table in Design view.

▶ **2.** Click the **State** Field Name box to make it the current field.

▶ **3.** In the Field Properties pane, click the **Default Value** box, type **WY**, and then press the **Tab** key. See Figure 2-37.

Figure 2-37	Specifying the Default Value property for the State field

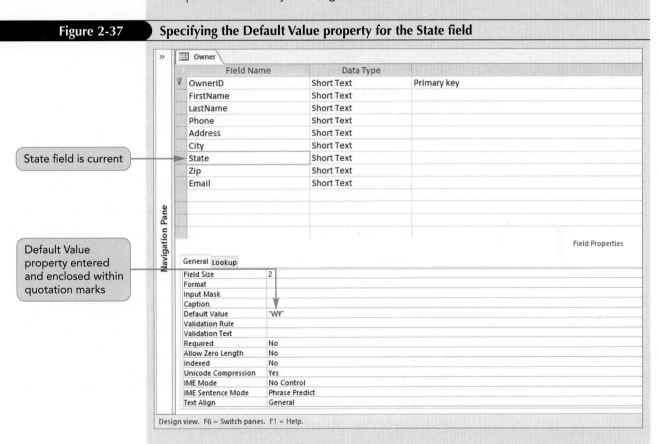

State field is current

Default Value property entered and enclosed within quotation marks

Note that a text entry in the Default Value property must be enclosed within quotation marks. If you do not type the quotation marks, Access adds them for you. However, for some entries, you would receive an error message indicating invalid syntax if you omitted the quotation marks. In such cases, you have to enter the quotation marks yourself.

▶ **4.** On the Quick Access Toolbar, click the **Save** button 🖫 to save your changes to the Owner table.

5. Display the table in Datasheet view. Note that the State field for the first row now displays the default value "WY" as specified by the Default Value property. Each new record entered in the table will automatically have this State field value entered.

With the Owner table design set, you can now enter records in it. You'll begin by entering two records, and then you'll use a different method to add the remaining records.

Note: Be sure to enter your last name and first name where indicated.

To add two records to the Owner table:

1. Enter the following values in the columns in the first record; note that you can press **Tab** to move past the default State field value:

Owner ID = **2310**

First Name = **[student's first name]**

Last Name = **[student's last name]**

Phone = **307-824-1245**

Address = **12 Elm Ln**

City = **Cody**

State = **WY**

Zip = **82414**

Email = **student@example.com**

2. Enter the following values in the columns in the second record:

Owner ID = **2314**

First Name = **Sally**

Last Name = **Cruz**

Phone = **307-406-4321**

Address = **199 18th Ave**

City = **Ralston**

State = **WY**

Zip = **82440**

Email = **scruz@example.com**

3. Resize columns to their best fit, as necessary, and then save and close the Owner table.

Before Kimberly decided to store data using Access, Kelly managed the owner data for the care center in a different system. She exported that data into a text file and now asks you to import it into the new Owner table. You can import the data contained in this text file to add the remaining records to the Owner table.

Adding Data to a Table by Importing a Text File

There are many ways to import data into an Access database. So far, you've learned how to add data to an Access table by importing an Excel spreadsheet, and you've created a new table by importing the structure of an existing table. You can also import data contained in text files.

To complete the entry of records in the Owner table, you'll import the data contained in Kelly's text file. The file is named "Owner" and is located in the Access1 > Module folder provided with your Data Files.

To import the data contained in the Owner text file:

▶ **1.** On the ribbon, click the **External Data** tab.

▶ **2.** In the Import & Link group, click the **Text File** button. The Get External Data - Text File dialog box opens. This dialog box is similar to the one you used earlier when importing the Excel spreadsheet and the Access table structure.

▶ **3.** Click the **Browse** button. The File Open dialog box opens.

▶ **4.** Navigate to the **Access1 > Module** folder, where your Data Files are stored, and then double-click the **Owner** file. You return to the dialog box.

▶ **5.** Click the **Append a copy of the records to the table** option button. The box to the right of this option becomes active. Next, you need to select the table to which you want to add the data.

▶ **6.** Click the arrow on the box, and then click **Owner**.

▶ **7.** Click the **OK** button. The first Import Text Wizard dialog box opens. The dialog box indicates that the data to be imported is in a delimited format. A **delimited text file** is one in which fields of data are separated by a character such as a comma or a tab. In this case, the dialog box shows that data is separated by the comma character in the text file.

▶ **8.** Make sure the **Delimited** option button is selected in the dialog box, and then click the **Next** button. The second Import Text Wizard dialog box opens. See Figure 2-38.

| Figure 2-38 | Second Import Wizard dialog box |

fields in the text file are separated by commas

preview of the data being imported

This dialog box asks you to confirm the delimiter character that separates the fields in the text file you're importing. Access detects that the comma character is used in the Owner text file and selects this option. The bottom area of the dialog box provides a preview of the data you're importing.

9. Make sure the **Comma** option button is selected, and then click the **Next** button. The third and final Import Text Wizard dialog box opens. Notice that the Import to Table box shows that the data will be imported into the Owner table.

10. Click the **Finish** button, and then click the **Close** button in the dialog box that opens to close it without saving the import steps.

Kimberly asks you to open the Owner table in Datasheet view so she can see the results of importing the text file.

To view the Owner table datasheet:

1. Open the Navigation Pane, and then double-click **Owner** to open the Owner table in Datasheet view. The Owner table contains a total of 25 records.

2. Close the Navigation Pane, and then resize columns to their best fit, scrolling the table datasheet as necessary, so that all field values are displayed. When finished, scroll back to display the first fields in the table, and then click the first row's **Owner ID** field, if necessary. See Figure 2-39.

| Figure 2-39 | Owner table after importing data from the text file |

Owner ID	First Name	Last Name	Phone	Address	City	State	Zip	Email	Click to Add
2310	Student First	Student Last	307-824-1245	12 Elm Ln	Cody	WY	82414	student@example.com	
2314	Sally	Cruz	307-406-4321	199 18th Ave	Ralston	WY	82440	scruz@example.com	
2318	Sandra	Pincher	307-982-8401	12 Rock Ln	Cody	WY	82414	sp231@example.com	
2322	Billy	Ruffton	307-843-9810	21 Simple Cir	Garland	WY	82435	br299@example.com	
2325	Barbara	Fishman	307-987-0092	2 Lakeview Rd	Cody	WY	82414	fishy@example.com	
2330	Jimmy	Gonzalez	307-987-0334	16 Rockway Rd	Wapiti	WY	82450	gonzo@example.com	
2335	Joey	Smith	307-888-4239	17 Fourth St	Cody	WY	82414	smittyj@example.com	
2340	Melanie	Jackson	307-882-1925	42 Blackwater Way	Elk Butte	WY	82433	mj@example.com	
2345	Dan	Poleman	307-887-8873	75 Stream Rd	Cody	WY	82414	poleman@example.net	
2350	Samantha	Smith	307-887-1239	14 Rock Ln	Ralston	WY	82440	ssmith@example.com	
2354	Randy	Blacksmith	307-882-9987	245 18th Ave	Cody	WY	82414	blacksmith@example.com	
2358	Angie	Hendricks	307-943-2234	27 Locklear Ln	Powell	WY	82440	angie@example.com	
2362	Thomas	Jones	307-985-9981	622 Bobcat Tr	Ralston	WY	82440	tj@example.com	
2366	Aaron	Jackson	307-984-1182	17 Ridge Rd	Cody	WY	82414	aj17@example.com	
2370	Curt	Billings	307-824-1802	14 Elm Ln	Cody	WY	82414	curtbillings@example.com	
2375	Joseph	Otterman	307-824-9863	42 Rock Ln	Cody	WY	82414	otterman42@example.com	
2380	Billy	Smith	307-887-4829	312 Oak Rd	Ralston	WY	82440	bsmith@example.com	
2384	Susan	Miller	307-824-2756	1283 Old Roundabout Rd	Cody	WY	82414	susanfarms@example.com	
2388	Jack	Sprawling	307-824-8305	1 Sprawling Farm Rd	Cody	WY	82414	sprawlingfarms@example.com	
2392	Elmer	Jackson	307-843-8472	22 Jackson Farm Rd	Garland	WY	82435	ElmerJ22@example.com	
2396	Richie	Upton	307-824-9876	155 Cherry Canyon Rd	Cody	WY	82414	uptonfarms@example.com	
2400	Leslie	Smith	307-883-9481	123 Sheepland Rd	Elk Butte	WY	82433	sheepland@example.com	
2404	Reggie	Baxter	307-943-2469	880 Powell-Cody Rd	Powell	WY	82440	baxterfarms@example.com	
2408	Tom	Rascal	307-824-3575	1 Rascal Farm Rd	Cody	WY	82414	rascalfarms@example.com	
2412	Taylor	Johnson	307-868-8862	412 River Rd	Cody	WY	82414	taylorj@example.com	

▶ **3.** Save and close the Owner table, and then open the Navigation Pane.

The Riverview database now contains four tables—Visit, Billing, Owner, and Animal—and the tables contain all the necessary records. Your final task is to complete the database design by defining the necessary relationship between its tables.

Defining Table Relationships

One of the most powerful features of a relational database management system is its ability to define relationships between tables. You use a common field to relate one table to another. The process of relating tables is often called performing a **join**. When you join tables that have a common field, you can extract data from them as if they were one larger table. For example, you can join the Animal and Visit tables by using the AnimalID field in both tables as the common field. Then you can use a query, form, or report to extract selected data from each table, even though the data is contained in two separate tables, as shown in Figure 2-40. The AnimalVisits query shown in Figure 2-40 includes the AnimalID, AnimalName, AnimalType, and AnimalBreed fields from the Animal table, and the VisitDate and Reason fields from the Visit table. The joining of records is based on the common field of AnimalID. The Animal and Visit tables have a type of relationship called a one-to-many relationship.

| Figure 2-40 | One-to-many relationship and sample query |

One-to-Many Relationships

As shown earlier in the Session 2.2 Visual Overview, a one-to-many relationship exists between two tables when one record in the first table matches zero, one, or many records in the second table, and when one record in the second table matches at most one record in the first table. For example, as shown in Figure 2-40, Animal 12278 has two visits in the Visit table. Other animals have one or more visits. Every visit has a single matching animal.

In Access, the two tables that form a relationship are referred to as the primary table and the related table. The primary table is the "one" table in a one-to-many relationship; in Figure 2-40, the Animal table is the primary table because there is only one animal for each visit. The related table is the "many" table; in Figure 2-40, the Visit table is the related table because an animal can have zero, one, or many visits.

Because related data is stored in two tables, inconsistencies between the tables can occur. Referring to Figure 2-40, consider the following three scenarios:

- Kimberly adds a record to the Visit table for a new animal, Fluffy (a Siberian cat), using Animal ID 12500. She did not first add the new animal's information to the animal table, so this visit does not have a matching record in the animal table. The data is inconsistent, and the visit record is considered to be an **orphaned record**.
- In another situation, Kimberly changes the AnimalID in the Animal table for Bailey the beagle from 12278 to 12510. Because there is no longer an animal with the AnimalID 12278 in the Animal table, this change creates two orphaned records in the Visit table, and the database is inconsistent.

- In a third scenario, Kimberly deletes the record for Bailey the beagle, Animal 12278, from the Animal table because this animal and its owner have moved and so the animal no longer receives care from Riverview. The database is again inconsistent; two records for Animal 12278 in the Visit table have no matching record in the Animal table.

You can avoid these types of problems and avoid having inconsistent data in your database by specifying referential integrity between tables when you define their relationships.

Referential Integrity

Referential integrity is a set of rules that Access enforces to maintain consistency between related tables when you update data in a database. Specifically, the referential integrity rules are as follows:

- When you add a record to a related table, a matching record must already exist in the primary table, thereby preventing the possibility of orphaned records.
- If you attempt to change the value of the primary key in the primary table, Access prevents this change if matching records exist in a related table. However, if you choose the **Cascade Update Related Fields option**, Access permits the change in value to the primary key and changes the appropriate foreign key values in the related table, thereby eliminating the possibility of inconsistent data.
- When you attempt to delete a record in the primary table, Access prevents the deletion if matching records exist in a related table. However, if you choose the **Cascade Delete Related Records option**, Access deletes the record in the primary table and also deletes all records in related tables that have matching foreign key values. However, you should rarely select the Cascade Delete Related Records option because doing so might cause you to inadvertently delete records you did not intend to delete. It is best to use other methods for deleting records that give you more control over the deletion process.

Defining a Relationship Between Two Tables

At the Riverview Veterinary Care Center, the owners own animals, the animals visit the clinic, and the owner receives the bill for the visits. It is important to understand these relationships in order to determine which owner to send the bill to for the visit each animal makes. Understanding these relationships also allows you to establish relationships between the tables of records in the Riverview database. When two tables have a common field, you can define a relationship between them in the Relationships window, as shown in the Session 2.2 Visual Overview.

Next, you need to define a series of relationships in the Riverview database. First, you will define a one-to-many relationship between the Owner and Animal tables, with Owner as the primary table and Animal as the related table and with OwnerID as the common field (primary key in the Owner table and a foreign key in the Animal table). Second, you will define a one-to-many relationship between the Animal and Visit tables, with Animal as the primary table and Visit as the related table and with AnimalID as the common field (the primary key in the Animal table and a foreign key in the Visit table). Finally, you will define a one-to-many relationship between the Visit and Billing tables, with Visit as the primary table and Billing as the related table and with VisitID as the common field (the primary key in the Visit table and a foreign key in the Billing table).

To define the one-to-many relationship between the Owner and Animal tables:

▶ **1.** On the ribbon, click the **Database Tools** tab.

▶ **2.** In the Relationships group, click the **Relationships** button to display the Relationship window and open the Show Table dialog box. See Figure 2-41.

Figure 2-41 **Show Table dialog box**

add these two tables to the Relationship window

You must add each table participating in a relationship to the Relationships window. Because the Owner table is the primary table in the relationship, you'll add it first.

TIP

You can also double-click a table in the Show Table dialog box to add it to the Relationships window.

▶ **3.** Click **Owner**, and then click the **Add** button. The Owner table's field list is added to the Relationships window.

▶ **4.** Click **Animal**, and then click the **Add** button. The Animal table's field list is added to the Relationships window.

▶ **5.** Click the **Close** button in the Show Table dialog box to close it.

So that you can view all the fields and complete field names, you'll resize the Owner table field list.

▶ **6.** Position the mouse pointer on the bottom border of the Owner table field list until it changes to ↕, and then drag the bottom of the Owner table field list to lengthen it until the vertical scroll bar disappears and all the fields are visible.

To form the relationship between the two tables, you drag the common field of OwnerID from the primary table to the related table. Then Access opens the Edit Relationships dialog box, in which you select the relationship options for the two tables.

7. Click **OwnerID** in the Owner field list, and then drag it to **OwnerID** in the Animal field list. When you release the mouse button, the Edit Relationships dialog box opens. See Figure 2-42.

Figure 2-42   **Edit Relationships dialog box**

The primary table, related table, common field, and relationship type (One-To-Many) appear in the dialog box. Note that Access correctly identifies the "One" side of the relationship and places the primary table Owner in the Table/Query section of the dialog box; similarly, Access correctly identifies the "Many" side of the relationship and places the related table Animal in the Related Table/Query section of the dialog box.

8. Click the **Enforce Referential Integrity** check box. After you click the Enforce Referential Integrity check box, the two cascade options become available. If you select the Cascade Update Related Fields option, Access will update the appropriate foreign key values in the related table when you change a primary key value in the primary table. You will *not* select the Cascade Delete Related Records option because doing so could cause you to delete records that you do not want to delete; this option is rarely selected.

9. Click the **Cascade Update Related Fields** check box.

10. Click the **Create** button to define the one-to-many relationship between the two tables and to close the dialog box. The completed relationship appears in the Relationships window, with the join line connecting the common field of OwnerID in each table. See Figure 2-43.

Figure 2-43   **Defined relationship in the Relationship window**

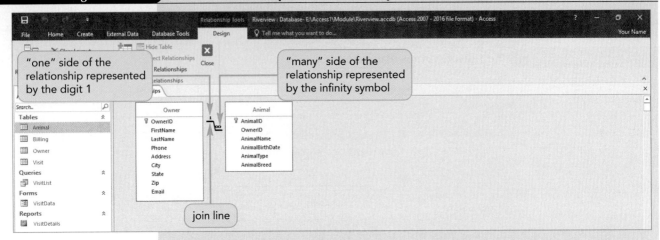

Trouble? If a dialog box opens indicating a problem that prevents you from creating the relationship, you most likely made a typing error when entering the two records in the Owner table. If so, click the OK button in the dialog box and then click the Cancel button in the Edit Relationships dialog box. Refer back to the earlier steps instructing you to enter the two records in the Owner table and carefully compare your entries with those shown in the text, especially the OwnerID field values. Make any necessary corrections to the data in the Owner table, and then repeat Steps 7 through 10. If you still receive an error message, ask your instructor for assistance.

The next step is to define the one-to-many relationship between the Animal and Visit tables. In this relationship, Animal is the primary ("one") table because there is at most one animal for each visit. Visit is the related ("many") table because there are zero, one, or many visits that are generated for each animal. Similarly, you need to define the one-to-many relationship between the Visit and Billing tables. In this relationship, Visit is the primary ("one") table because there is at most one visit for each invoice. Billing is the related ("many") table because there are zero, one, or many invoices that are generated for each animal visit. For example, some visits require lab work, which is invoiced separately.

To define the relationship between the Animal and Visit tables and to define the relationship between the Visit and billing tables:

1. On the Relationship Tools Design tab, in the Relationships group, click the **Show Table** button to open the Show Table dialog box.

2. Click **Visit** on the Tables tab, click the **Add** button, and then click the **Close** button to close the Show Table dialog box. The Visit table's field list appears in the Relationships window to the right of the Animal table's field list.

   Because the Animal table is the primary table in this relationship, you need to drag the AnimalID field from the Animal field list to the Visit field list.

3. Drag the **AnimalID** field in the Animal field list to the **AnimalID** field in the Visit field list. When you release the mouse button, the Edit Relationships dialog box opens.

TIP

You can also use the mouse to drag a table from the Navigation Pane to add it to the Relationships window.

4. Click the **Enforce Referential Integrity** check box, click the **Cascade Update Related Fields** check box, and then click the **Create** button. The Edit Relationships dialog box closes and the completed relationship appears in the Relationships window.

Finally, you will define the relationship between the Visit and Billing tables.

5. On the Relationship Tools Design tab, in the Relationships group, click the **Show Table** button to open the Show Table dialog box.

6. Click **Billing** on the Tables tab, click the **Add** button, and then click the **Close** button to close the Show Table dialog box. The Billing table's field list appears in the Relationships window to the right of the Visit table's field list.

7. Click and drag the **VisitID** field in the Visit field list to the **VisitID** field in the Billing field list. The Edit Relationships dialog box opens.

8. In the Edit Relationships dialog box, click the **Enforce Referential Integrity** check box, click the **Cascade Update Related Fields** check box, and then click the **Create** button to define the one-to-many relationship between the two tables and to close the dialog box. The completed relationships for the Riverview database appear in the Relationships window. See Figure 2-44.

Figure 2-44   **All three relationships now defined**

9. On the Quick Access Toolbar, click the **Save** button to save the layout in the Relationships window.

10. On the Relationship Tools Design tab, in the Relationships group, click the **Close** button to close the Relationships window.

11. Compact and repair the Riverview database, and then close the database.

PROSKILLS

Problem Solving: Creating a Larger Database

The Riverview database is a relatively small database containing only a few tables, and the data and the reports you will generate from it will be fairly simple. A larger database would most likely have many more tables and different types of relationships that can be quite complex. When creating a large database, follow this standard process:

- Consult people who will be using the data to gain an understanding of how it will be used. Gather sample reports and representative data if possible.
- Plan the tables, fields, data types, other properties, and the relationships between the tables.
- Create the tables and define the relationships between them.
- Populate the tables with sample data.
- Design some queries, forms, and reports that will be needed, and then test them.
- Modify the database structure, if necessary, based on the results of your tests.
- Enter the actual data into the database tables.

Testing is critical at every stage of creating a database. Once the database is finalized and implemented, it's not actually finished. The design of a database evolves as new functionality is required and as the data that is gathered changes.

REVIEW

Session 2.2 Quick Check

1. What is the keyboard shortcut for inserting the value from the same field in the previous record into the current record?

2. _____ data is a process that allows you to copy the data from a source without having to open the source file.

3. The _____ gallery allows you to add a group of related fields to a table at the same time, rather than adding each field to the table individually.

4. What is the effect of deleting a field from a table structure?

5. A(n) _____ text file is one in which fields of data are separated by a character such as a comma or a tab.

6. The _____ is the "one" table in a one-to-many relationship, and the _____ is the "many" table in the relationship.

7. _____ is a set of rules that Access enforces to maintain consistency between related tables when you update data in a database.

Review Assignments

PRACTICE

Data File needed for the Review Assignments: Vendor.accdb (*cont. from Module 1*) **and Supplies.xlsx**

In addition to tracking information about the vendors Riverview Veterinary Care Center works with, Kimberly also wants to track information about their products and services. First, Kimberly asks you to modify the necessary properties in the existing Supplier table in the Vendor database; then she wants you to create a new table in the Vendor database to contain product data. Complete the following:

1. Open the **Vendor** database you created in the previous module.
2. Open the **Supplier** table in Design view, and set the field properties as shown in Figure 2-45.

Figure 2-45 Field properties for the Supplier table

Field Name	Data Type	Description	Field Size	Other
SupplierID	Short Text	Primary key	6	Caption = Supplier ID
Company	Short Text		50	
Category	Short Text		15	
Address	Short Text		35	
City	Short Text		25	
State	Short Text		2	
Zip	Short Text		10	
Phone	Short Text		14	Caption = Contact Phone
ContactFirst	Short Text		20	Caption = Contact First Name
ContactLast	Short Text		25	Caption = Contact Last Name
InitialContact	Date/Time			Format = Short Date
				Caption = Initial Contact

3. Save the Supplier table. Click the **Yes** button when a message appears, indicating some data might be lost. Switch to Datasheet view and resize columns, as necessary, to their best fit. Then save and close the Supplier table.
4. Create a new table in Design view, using the table design shown in Figure 2-46.

Figure 2-46 Design for the Product table

Field Name	Data Type	Description	Field Size	Other
ProductID	Short Text	Primary key	5	Caption = Product ID
SupplierID	Short Text	Foreign key	6	Caption = Supplier ID
ProductName	Short Text		75	Caption = Product Name
Price	Currency			Format = Standard
				Decimal Places = 2
TempControl	Yes/No			Caption = Temp Controlled?
Sterile	Yes/No			Caption = Sterile?
Units	Number		Integer	Decimal Places = 0
				Caption = Units/Case
				Default Value = [no entry]

5. Specify ProductID as the primary key, and then save the table as **Product**.

6. Modify the table structure by adding a new field between the Price and TempControl fields. Name the new field **Weight** (data type: **Number**; field size: **Single**; Decimal Places: **2**; Caption: **Weight in Lbs**; Default Value: [no entry]). Then move the **Units** field so that it is positioned between the Price and Weight fields.

7. Enter the records shown in Figure 2-47 in the Product table. Resize all datasheet columns to their best fit. When finished, save and close the Product table.

Figure 2-47   **Records for the Product table**

Product ID	Supplier ID	Product Name	Price	Units/Case	Weight in Lbs	Temp Controlled?	Sterile?
PT100	KLS321	Paper tape roll	20.00	12	3	No	No
TC050	QLS002	Thermometer covers	27.00	50	1	No	Yes

8. Use the Import Spreadsheet Wizard to add data to the Product table. The data you need to import is contained in the Supplies workbook, which is an Excel file located in the Access1 > Review folder provided with your Data Files.

   a. Specify the Supplies workbook as the source of the data.

   b. Select the option for appending the data.

   c. Select Product as the table.

   d. In the Import Spreadsheet Wizard dialog boxes, make sure Access confirms that the first row contains column headings, and import to the Product table. Do not save the import steps.

9. Open the **Product** table in Datasheet view, and resize columns to their best fit, as necessary. Then save and close the Product table.

10. Define a one-to-many relationship between the primary Supplier table and the related Product table. Resize the table field lists so that all field names are visible. Select the referential integrity option and the cascade updates option for the relationship.

11. Save the changes to the Relationships window and close it, compact and repair the Vendor database, and then close the database.

Case Problem 1

APPLY

Data Files needed for this Case Problem: Beauty.accdb (cont. from Module 1) and Customers.txt

Beauty To Go   Sue Miller wants to use the Beauty database to track information about customers who subscribe to her business, which provides a variety of salon services on a subscription basis, and the plans in which customers are enrolled. She asks you to help maintain this database. Complete the following:

1. Open the **Beauty** database you created in the previous module, open the **Option** table in Design view, and then change the following field properties:

   a. OptionID: Enter **Primary key** for the description, change the field size to **3**, and enter **Option ID** for the caption.

   b. OptionDescription: Change the field size to **45** and enter **Option Description** for the caption.

   c. OptionCost: Change the format to **Standard**, specify **0** decimal places, enter **Option Cost** for the caption, no default value.

   d. FeeWaived: Enter **Fee Waived** for the caption.

2. Save and close the Option table. Click the Yes button when a message appears, indicating some data might be lost.

3. Create a new table in Design view, using the table design shown in Figure 2-48.

Figure 2-48   Design for the Member table

Field Name	Data Type	Description	Field Size	Other
MemberID	Short Text	Primary key	4	Caption = Member ID
OptionID	Short Text	Foreign key	3	Caption = Option ID
FirstName	Short Text		20	Caption = First Name
LastName	Short Text		25	Caption = Last Name
Phone	Short Text		14	
OptionEnd	Date/Time	Date Option Ends		Format = Short Date
				Caption = Option Ends

4. Specify **MemberID** as the primary key, and then save the table as **Member**.
5. Use the Address Quick Start selection in the Data Type gallery to add five fields between the LastName and Phone fields.
6. Switch to Design view, and then make the following changes to the Member table design:
   a. Address field: Change the name of this field to **Street**, change the field size to **40**, and delete the entry for the caption.
   b. City field: Change the field size to **25**, and delete the entry for the caption.
   c. StateProvince field: Change the name of this field to **State**, change the field size to **2**, delete the entry for the caption, and enter **FL** for the default value.
   d. ZIPPostal field: Change the name of this field to **Zip**, change the field size to **10**, and delete the entry for the caption.
   e. Delete the **CountryRegion** field from the Member table structure.
   f. Between the Phone and OptionEnd fields, add a new field named **OptionBegin** (data type: **Date/Time**; format: **Short Date**; Caption: **Option Begins**).
7. Enter the records shown in Figure 2-49 in the Member table. Resize all datasheet columns to their best fit. When finished, save and close the Member table. Be sure to enter your first and last name in the appropriate fields in the first record.

Figure 2-49   Records for the Member table

Member ID	Option ID	First Name	Last Name	Street	City	State	Zip	Phone	Option Begins	Option Ends
2103	123	Student First	Student Last	22 Oak St	Orlando	FL	32801	407-832-3944	2/1/17	3/1/17
2118	120	Susan	Reyes	3 Balboa St	Orlando	FL	32804	407-216-0091	11/2/16	2/2/17

8. Use the Import Text File Wizard to add data to the Member table. The data you need to import is contained in the Customers text file, which is located in the Access1 > Case1 folder provided with your Data Files.
   a. Specify the Customers text file as the source of the data.
   b. Select the option for appending the data.
   c. Select Member as the table.
   d. In the Import Text File Wizard dialog boxes, choose the options to import delimited data, to use a comma delimiter, and to import the data into the Member table. Do not save the import steps.
9. Open the **Member** table in Datasheet view and resize columns to their best fit, as necessary. Then save and close the Member table.

10. Define a one-to-many relationship between the primary Option table and the related Member table. Resize the Member table field list so that all field names are visible. Select the referential integrity option and the cascade updates option for this relationship.

11. Save the changes to the Relationships window and close it, compact and repair the Beauty database, and then close the database.

APPLY

Case Problem 2

Data Files needed for this Case Problem: Programming.accdb *(cont. from Module 1)***, Client.accdb, Students.txt, and Agreements.xlsx**

Programming Pros   Brent Hovis plans to use the Programming database to maintain information about the students, tutors, and contracts for his tutoring services company. Brent asks you to help him build the database by updating one table and creating two new tables in the database. Complete the following:

1. Open the **Programming** database you created in the previous module, open the **Tutor** table in Design view, and then set the field properties as shown in Figure 2-50.

Figure 2-50	Field properties for the Tutor table

Field Name	Data Type	Description	Field Size	Other
TutorID	Short Text	Primary key	4	Caption = Tutor ID
FirstName	Short Text		20	Caption = First Name
LastName	Short Text		25	Caption = Last Name
Major	Short Text		25	
YearInSchool	Short Text		12	Caption = Year In School
School	Short Text		30	
HireDate	Date/Time			Format = Short Date
				Caption = Hire Date

2. Add a new field as the last field in the Tutor table with the field name **Groups**, the **Yes/No** data type, and the caption **Groups Only**.

3. Save the Tutor table. Click the **Yes** button when a message appears, indicating some data might be lost.

4. In the table datasheet, specify that the following tutors conduct group tutoring sessions only: Carey Billings, Fredrik Karlsson, Ellen Desoto, and Donald Gallager. Close the Tutor table.

5. Brent created a table named Student in the Client database that is located in the Access1 > Case2 folder provided with your Data Files. Import the structure of the Student table in the Client database into a new table named Student in the Programming database. Do not save the import steps.

6. Open the **Student** table in Datasheet view, and then add the following two fields to the end of the table: **BirthDate** (Date/Time field) and **Gender** (Short Text field).

7. Use the Phone Quick Start selection in the Data Type gallery to add four fields related to phone numbers between the Zip and BirthDate fields. (*Hint:* Be sure to make the BirthDate field the active field before adding the new fields.)

8. Display the Student table in Design view, delete the BusinessPhone and FaxNumber fields, and then save and close the Student table.

9. Reopen the Student table and modify its design so that it matches the design in Figure 2-51, *including the revised field names and data types.*

Figure 2-51   Field properties for the Student table

Field Name	Data Type	Description	Field Size	Other
StudentID	Short Text	Primary key	7	Caption = Student ID
LastName	Short Text		25	Caption = Last Name
FirstName	Short Text		20	Caption = First Name
Address	Short Text		35	
City	Short Text		25	
State	Short Text		2	Default Value = NC
Zip	Short Text		10	
HomePhone	Short Text		14	Caption = Home Phone
CellPhone	Short Text		14	Caption = Cell Phone
BirthDate	Date/Time			Format = Short Date
				Caption = Birth Date
Gender	Short Text		1	

10. Move the LastName field so it follows the FirstName field.
11. Save your changes to the table design, and then add the records shown in Figure 2-52 to the Student table.

Figure 2-52   Records for the Student table

Student ID	First Name	Last Name	Address	City	State	Zip	Home Phone	Cell Phone	Date of Birth	Gender
LOP4015	Henry	Lopez	19 8th St	Raleigh	NC	27601	919-264-9981	919-665-8110	2/19/1998	M
PER4055	Rosalyn	Perez	421 Pine Ln	Cary	NC	27511	984-662-4761	919-678-0012	4/12/1996	F

12. Resize the fields to their best fit, and then save and close the Student table.
13. Use the Import Text File Wizard to add data to the Student table. The data you need to import is contained in the Students text file, which is located in the Access1 > Case2 folder provided with your Data Files.

    a. Specify the Students text file as the source of the data.

    b. Select the option for appending the data.

    c. Select Student as the table.

    d. In the Import Text File Wizard dialog boxes, choose the options to import delimited data, to use a comma delimiter, and to import the data into the Student table. Do not save the import steps.

14. Open the **Student** table in Datasheet view, resize columns in the datasheet to their best fit (as necessary), and then save and close the table.
15. Create a new table in Design view, using the table design shown in Figure 2-53.

Figure 2-53	Design for the Contract table

Field Name	Data Type	Description	Field Size	Other
ContractID	Short Text	Primary key	4	Caption = Contract ID
StudentID	Short Text	Foreign key	7	Caption = Student ID
TutorID	Short Text	Foreign key	4	Caption = Tutor ID
SessionType	Short Text		15	Caption = Session Type
Length	Number		Integer	Decimal Places = 0
				Caption = Length (Hrs)
				Default Value = [no entry]
NumSessions	Number		Integer	Decimal Places = 0
				Caption = Number of Sessions
				Default Value = [no entry]
Cost	Currency			Format = Currency
				Decimal Places = 0
				Default Value = [no entry]
Assessment	Yes/No	Pre-assessment exam complete		Caption = Assessment Complete

16. Specify ContractID as the primary key, and then save the table using the name **Contract**.
17. Add a new field to the Contract table, between the TutorID and SessionType fields, with the field name **ContractDate**, the **Date/Time** data type, the description **Date contract is signed**, the **Short Date** format, and the caption **Contract Date**. Save and close the Contract table.
18. Use the Import Spreadsheet Wizard to add data to the Contract table. The data you need to import is contained in the Agreements workbook, which is an Excel file located in the Access1 > Case2 folder provided with your Data Files.
    a. Specify the Agreements workbook as the source of the data.
    b. Select the option for appending the data to the table.
    c. Select Contract as the table.
    d. In the Import Spreadsheet Wizard dialog boxes, choose the Agreements worksheet, make sure Access confirms that the first row contains column headings, and import to the Contract table. Do not save the import steps.
19. Open the **Contract** table, and add the records shown in Figure 2-54. (*Hint:* Use the New (blank) record button in the navigation buttons to add a new record.)

Figure 2-54	Records for the Contract table

Contract ID	Student ID	Tutor ID	Contract Date	Session Type	Length (Hrs)	Number of Sessions	Cost	Assessment Complete
6215	PER4055	1018	7/6/2017	Group	2	5	$400	Yes
6350	LOP4015	1010	10/12/2017	Private	3	4	$720	Yes

20. Resize columns in the datasheet to their best fit (as necessary), and then save and close the Contract table.
21. Define the one-to-many relationships between the database tables as follows: between the primary Student table and the related Contract table, and between the primary Tutor table and the related Contract table. Resize the table field lists so that all field names are visible. Select the referential integrity option and the cascade updates option for each relationship.
22. Save the changes to the Relationships window and close it, compact and repair the Programming database, and then close the database.

Case Problem 3

CHALLENGE

Data Files needed for this Case Problem: Center.accdb *(cont. from Module 1)*, Donations.xlsx, and Auctions.txt

Diane's Community Center   Diane Coleman wants to use the Center database to maintain information about the patrons and donations for her not-for-profit community center. Diane asks you to help her maintain the database by updating one table and creating two new ones. Complete the following:

1. Open the **Center** database you created in the previous module, open the **Patron** table in Design view, and then change the following field properties:

   a. PatronID: Enter **Primary key** for the description, change the field size to **5**, and enter **Patron ID** for the caption.

   b. Title: Change the field size to **4**.

   c. FirstName: Change the field size to **20**, and enter **First Name** for the caption.

   d. LastName: Change the field size to **25**, and enter **Last Name** for the caption.

   e. Phone: Change the field size to **14**.

   f. Email: Change field size to **35**.

2. Save and close the Patron table. Click the Yes button when a message appears, indicating some data might be lost.

⊕ **Explore** 3. Use the Import Spreadsheet Wizard to create a table in the Center database. As the source of the data, specify the Donations workbook, which is located in the Access1 > Case3 folder provided with your Data Files. Select the option to import the source data into a new table in the database.

⊕ **Explore** 4. Complete the Import Spreadsheet Wizard dialog boxes as follows:

   a. Select Donation as the worksheet you want to import.

   b. Specify that the first row contains column headings.

   c. Accept the field options suggested by the wizard, and do not skip any fields.

   d. Choose DonationID as your own primary key.

   e. Import the data to a table named **Donation**, and do not save the import steps.

⊕ **Explore** 5. Open the Donation table in Datasheet view. Left-justify the DonationDescription field by clicking the column heading, and then on the Home tab, clicking the Align Left button in the Text Formatting group.

6. Open the Donation table in Design view, and then modify the table so it matches the design shown in Figure 2-55, including changes to data types, field name, and field position. For the Short Text fields, delete any formats specified in the Format property boxes.

Figure 2-55   **Design for the Donation table**

Field Name	Data Type	Description	Field Size	Other
DonationID	Short Text	Primary key	4	Caption = Donation ID
PatronID	Short Text	Foreign key	5	Caption = Patron ID
DonationDate	Date/Time			Format = mm/dd/yyyy
				Caption = Donation Date
Description	Short Text		30	
DonationValue	Currency	Dollar amount or estimated value		Format = Currency
				Decimal Places = 2
				Caption = Donation Value
				Default Value = [no entry]
CashDonation	Yes/No			Caption = Cash Donation?
AuctionItem	Yes/No			Caption = Possible Auction Item?

7. Save your changes to the table design, click Yes for the message about lost data, and then switch to Datasheet view.
8. Resize the columns in the Donation datasheet to their best fit.
⊕ **Explore** 9. Diane decides that the values in the Donation Value column would look better without the two decimal places. Make this field the current field in the datasheet. Then, on the Table Tools Fields tab, in the Formatting group, use the Decrease Decimals button to remove the two decimal places and the period from these values. Switch back to Design view, and note that the Decimal Places property for the DonationValue field is now set to 0.
10. Save and close the Donation table.
11. Use Design view to create a table using the table design shown in Figure 2-56.

Figure 2-56   **Design for the Auction table**

Field Name	Data Type	Description	Field Size	Other
AuctionID	Short Text	Primary key	3	Caption = Auction ID
AuctionDate	Date/Time			Format = mm/dd/yyyy
				Caption = Date of Auction
DonationID	Short Text		4	Caption = Donation ID
MinPrice	Currency			Format = Currency
				Decimal Places = 0
				Caption = Minimum Sale Price
ItemSold	Yes/No			Caption = Item Sold at Auction?

12. Specify **AuctionID** as the primary key, save the table as **Auction**, and then close the table.
13. Use the Import Text File Wizard to add data to the Auction table. The data you need to import is contained in the Auctions text file, which is located in the Access1 > Case3 folder provided with your Data Files.
    a. Specify the Auctions text file as the source of the data.
    b. Select the option for appending the data.
    c. Select Auction as the table.
    d. In the Import Text File Wizard dialog boxes, choose the options to import delimited data, to use a comma delimiter, and to import the data into the Auction table. Do not save the import steps.

14. Open the Auction table in Datasheet view, and resize all columns to their best fit.

15. Display the Auction table in Design view. Move the DonationID field to make it the second field in the table, and enter the description **Foreign key** for the DonationID field. Save the modified Auction table design.

16. Switch to Datasheet view, and then add the records shown in Figure 2-57 to the Auction table. (*Hint:* Use the New (blank) record button in the navigation buttons to add a new record.) Close the table when finished.

Figure 2-57   **Records for the Auction table**

AuctionID	DonationID	AuctionDate	MinPrice	ItemSold
205	5132	8/12/2017	200	No
235	5217	10/14/2017	150	No

17. Define the one-to-many relationships between the database tables as follows: between the primary Patron table and the related Donation table, and between the primary Donation table and the related Auction table. Resize any field lists so that all field names are visible. Select the referential integrity option and the cascade updates option for each relationship.

18. Save the changes to the Relationships window and close it, compact and repair the Center database, and then close the database.

Case Problem 4

Data Files needed for this Case Problem: Appalachia.accdb *(cont. from Module 1)*, Travel.accdb, and Bookings.txt

Hike Appalachia   Molly and Bailey Johnson use the Appalachia database to track the data about the hikers and tours offered through their business. They ask you to help them maintain this database. Complete the following:

1. Open the **Appalachia** database you created in the previous module, open the **Hiker** table in Design view, and then change the following field properties:
   a. HikerID: Enter **Primary key** for the description, change the field size to **3**, and enter **Hiker ID** for the caption.
   b. HikerFirst: Change the field size to **20**, and enter **Hiker First Name** for the caption.
   c. HikerLast: Change the field size to **25**, and enter **Hiker Last Name** for the caption.
   d. Address: Change the field size to **35**.
   e. City: Change the field size to **25**.
   f. State: Change the field size to **2**.
   g. Zip: Change the field size to **10**.
   h. Phone: Change the field size to **14**.

2. Save the Hiker table, click the Yes button when a message appears, indicating some data might be lost, resize the Hiker First Name and Hiker Last Name columns in Datasheet view to their best fit, and then save and close the table.
   a. Import the **Trip** table structure and data from the **Travel** database into a new table in the **Appalachia** database. As the source of the data, specify the Travel database, which is located in the Access1 > Case4 folder provided with your Data Files; select the option button to import tables, queries, forms, reports, macros, and modules into the current database; and in the Import Objects dialog box, select the **Trip** table, click the **Options** button, and then make sure that the correct option is selected to import the table's data and structure (definition).
   b. Do not save your import steps.

CHALLENGE

⊕ **Explore** 3. Using a shortcut menu in the Navigation Pane, rename the Trip table as **Tour** to give this name to the new table in the Appalachia database.

4. Open the **Tour** table in Design view, and then delete the VIPDiscount field.

5. Change the following properties:

   a. TourID: Enter the description **Primary key**, change the field size to **3**, and enter **Tour ID** for the caption.

   b. TourName: Enter **Tour Name** for the caption, and change the field size to **35**.

   c. TourType: Enter **Tour Type** for the caption, and change the field size to **15**.

   d. PricePerPerson: Enter **Price Per Person** for the caption.

6. Save the modified table, click the Yes button when a message appears, indicating some data might be lost, and then display the table in Datasheet view. Resize all datasheet columns to their best fit, and then save and close the table.

7. In Design view, create a table using the table design shown in Figure 2-58.

Figure 2-58 **Design for the Reservation table**

Field Name	Data Type	Description	Field Size	Other
ReservationID	Short Text	Primary key	4	Caption = Reservation ID
HikerID	Short Text	Foreign key	3	Caption = Hiker ID
TourID	Short Text	Foreign key	3	Caption = Tour ID
TourDate	Date/Time			Caption = Tour Date
People	Number		Integer	Decimal Places = 0
				Default Value = [no entry]

8. Specify **ReservationID** as the primary key, and then save the table as **Reservation**.

⊕ **Explore** 9. Refer back to Figure 2-11 to review the custom date formats. Change the Format property of the TourDate field to a custom format that displays dates in a format similar to 02/15/17. Save and close the Reservation table.

10. Use the Import Text File Wizard to add data to the Reservation table. The data you need to import is contained in the Bookings text file, which is located in the Access1 > Case4 folder provided with your Data Files.

    a. Specify the Bookings text file as the source of the data.

    b. Select the option for appending the data.

    c. Select Reservation as the table.

    d. In the Import Text File Wizard dialog boxes, choose the options to import delimited data, to use a comma delimiter, and to import the data into the Reservation table. Do not save the import steps.

11. Open the **Reservation** table, and then resize columns in the table datasheet to their best fit (as necessary), verify that the date values in the StartDate field are displayed correctly according to the custom format, and then save and close the table.

12. Define the one-to-many relationships between the database tables as follows: between the primary Hiker table and the related Reservation table, and between the primary Tour table and the related Reservation table. (*Hint:* Place the Reservation table as the middle table in the Relationships window to make it easier to join the tables.) Resize the Hiker field list so that all field names are visible. Select the referential integrity option and the cascade updates option for each relationship.

13. Save the changes to the Relationships window and close it, compact and repair the Appalachia database, and then close the database.

OBJECTIVES

Session 3.1
- Find, modify, and delete records in a table
- Hide and unhide fields in a datasheet
- Work in the Query window in Design view
- Create, run, and save queries
- Update data using a query datasheet
- Create a query based on multiple tables
- Sort data in a query
- Filter data in a query

Session 3.2
- Specify an exact match condition in a query
- Use a comparison operator in a query to match a range of values
- Use the And and Or logical operators in queries
- Change the font size and alternate row color in a datasheet
- Create and format a calculated field in a query
- Perform calculations in a query using aggregate functions and record group calculations
- Change the display of database objects in the Navigation Pane

Maintaining and Querying a Database

Updating Tables and Retrieving Care Center Information

Case | *Riverview Veterinary Care Center*

At a recent meeting, Kimberly Johnson and her staff discussed the importance of maintaining accurate information about the animals seen by Riverview Veterinary Care Center, as well as the owners, visits, and invoices, and regularly monitoring the business activities of the care center. For example, Kelly Flannagan, Kimberly's assistant, needs to make sure she has up-to-date contact information, such as phone numbers and email addresses, for the owners of all the animals seen by the care center. The office staff also must monitor billing activity to ensure that invoices are paid on time and in full. In addition, the staff handles marketing efforts for the care center and tracks services provided to develop new strategies for promoting these services. Kimberly is also interested in analyzing other aspects of the business related to animal visits and finances. You can satisfy all these informational needs for Riverview Veterinary Care Center by updating data in the Riverview database and by creating and using queries that retrieve information from the database.

STARTING DATA FILES

Access1 → Module
Riverview.accdb (*cont.*)

Review
Vendor.accdb (*cont.*)

Case1
Beauty.accdb (*cont.*)

Case2
Programming.accdb (*cont.*)

Case3
Center.accdb (*cont.*)

Case4
Appalachia.accdb (*cont.*)
HikeApp.accdb

Session 3.1 Visual Overview:

When you are constructing a query, you can see the results at any time by clicking the View button or the Run button. In response, Access displays the query datasheet, which contains the set of fields and records that results from answering, or **running**, the query.

In the Query Type group, the active Select button indicates that you are creating a select query, which is the default type of query. A **select query** is one in which you specify the fields and records you want Access to select.

The top portion of the Query window in Design view contains the field list (or lists) for the table(s) used in the query.

Each **field list** contains the fields for the table(s) you are querying. The table name appears at the top of the field list, and the fields are listed in the order in which they appear in the table. Notice that the primary key for the table is identified by the key symbol.

The default query name, Query1, is displayed on the tab for the query. You change the default query name to a more meaningful one when you save the query.

The bottom portion of the Query window in Design view contains the design grid. In the **design grid**, you include the fields and record selection criteria for the information you want to see.

Query Window in Design View

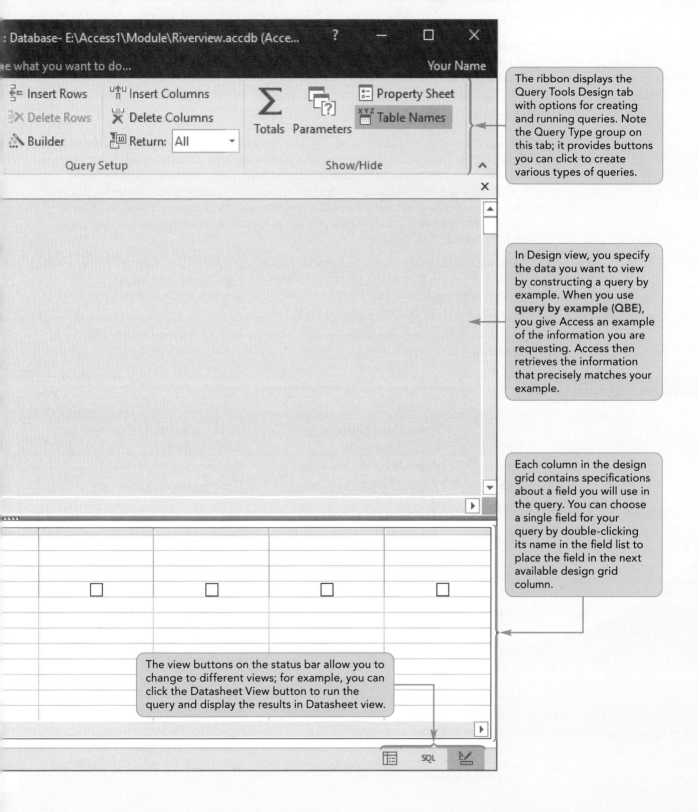

The ribbon displays the Query Tools Design tab with options for creating and running queries. Note the Query Type group on this tab; it provides buttons you can click to create various types of queries.

In Design view, you specify the data you want to view by constructing a query by example. When you use **query by example (QBE)**, you give Access an example of the information you are requesting. Access then retrieves the information that precisely matches your example.

Each column in the design grid contains specifications about a field you will use in the query. You can choose a single field for your query by double-clicking its name in the field list to place the field in the next available design grid column.

The view buttons on the status bar allow you to change to different views; for example, you can click the Datasheet View button to run the query and display the results in Datasheet view.

Updating a Database

Updating, or **maintaining**, a database is the process of adding, modifying, and deleting records in database tables to keep them current and accurate. After reviewing the data in the Riverview database, Kelly identified some changes that need to be made to the data. She would like you to update the field values in one record in the Owner table, correct an error in one record in the Visit table, and then delete a record in the Visit table.

Modifying Records

To modify the field values in a record, you must first make the record the current record. Then you position the insertion point in the field value to make minor changes or select the field value to replace it entirely. Earlier you used the mouse with the scroll bars and the navigation buttons to navigate the records in a datasheet. You can also use keyboard shortcuts and the F2 key to navigate a datasheet and to select field values. The **F2 key** is a toggle that you use to switch between navigation mode and editing mode.

- In **navigation mode**, Access selects an entire field value. If you type while you are in navigation mode, your typed entry replaces the highlighted field value.
- In **editing mode**, you can insert or delete characters in a field value based on the location of the insertion point.

Figure 3-1 shows some of the navigation mode and editing mode keyboard shortcuts.

Figure 3-1 Navigation mode and editing mode keyboard shortcuts

Press	To Move the Selection in Navigation Mode	To Move the Insertion Point in Editing Mode
←	Left one field value at a time	Left one character at a time
→	Right one field value at a time	Right one character at a time
Home	Left to the first field value in the record	To the left of the first character in the field value
End	Right to the last field value in the record	To the right of the last character in the field value
↑ or ↓	Up or down one record at a time	Up or down one record at a time and switch to navigation mode
Tab or Enter	Right one field value at a time	Right one field value at a time and switch to navigation mode
Ctrl + Home	To the first field value in the first record	To the left of the first character in the field value
Ctrl + End	To the last field value in the last record	To the right of the last character in the field value

The Owner table record Kelly wants you to change is for Taylor Johnson. This owner recently moved to another location in Cody and also changed her email address, so you need to update the Owner table record with the new street address and email address.

To open the Owner table in the Riverview database:

▶ **1.** Start Access and open the **Riverview** database you created and worked with earlier.

   Trouble? If the security warning is displayed below the ribbon, click the Enable Content button.

▶ **2.** Open the **Owner** table in Datasheet view.

The Owner table contains many fields. Sometimes, when updating data in a table, it can be helpful to remove the display of some fields on the screen.

Hiding and Unhiding Fields

TIP

Hiding a field removes it from the datasheet display only; the field and its contents are still part of the table.

When you are viewing a table or query datasheet in Datasheet view, you might want to temporarily remove certain fields from the displayed datasheet, making it easier to focus on the data you're interested in viewing. The **Hide Fields** command allows you to remove the display of one or more fields, and the **Unhide Fields** command allows you to redisplay any hidden fields.

To make it easier to modify the owner record, you'll first hide a couple of fields in the Owner table.

To hide fields in the Owner table and modify the owner record:

▶ **1.** Right-click the **State** field name to display the shortcut menu, and then click **Hide Fields**. The State column is removed from the datasheet display.

▶ **2.** Right-click the **Zip** field name, and then click **Hide Fields** on the shortcut menu. The Zip column is removed from the datasheet display.

   With the fields hidden, you can now update the owner record. The record you need to modify is near the end of the table and has an OwnerID field value of 2412.

▶ **3.** Scroll the datasheet until you see the last record in the table.

▶ **4.** Click the OwnerID field value **2412**, for Taylor Johnson. The insertion point appears within the field value, indicating you are in editing mode.

▶ **5.** Press the **Tab** key to move to the First Name field value, Taylor. The field value is selected, indicating you are in navigation mode.

▶ **6.** Press the **Tab** key three times to move to the Address field and select its field value, type **458 Rose Ln**, and then press the **Tab** key twice to move to the Email field.

▶ **7.** Type **taylor.johnson@example.net**, and then press the **Tab** key to move to the insertion point to the OwnerID field in the blank record at the bottom of the table. The changes to the record are complete. See Figure 3-2.

Figure 3-2	Table after changing field values in a record

field values changed

Access saves changes to field values when you move to a new field or another record, or when you close the table. You don't have to click the Save button to save changes to field values or records.

8. Press the **Ctrl+Home** keys to move to the first field value in the first record. With the changes to the record complete, you can unhide the hidden fields.

9. Right-click any field name to display the shortcut menu, and then click **Unhide Fields**. The Unhide Columns dialog box opens. See Figure 3-3.

Figure 3-3   Unhide Columns dialog box

All currently displayed fields are checked in this dialog box, and all hidden fields are unchecked. To redisplay them, you simply click their check boxes to select them.

10. In the Unhide Columns dialog box, click the **State** check box to select it, click the **Zip** check box to select it, and then click the **Close** button to close the dialog box. The two hidden fields are now displayed in the datasheet.

11. Close the Owner table, and then click the **No** button in the dialog box that opens, asking if you want to save changes to the layout of the Owner table. This box appears because you hid fields and redisplayed them.

    In this case, you can click either the Yes button or the No button, because no changes were actually made to the table layout or design.

Next you need to correct an error in the Visit table for a visit made by Molly, Animal ID 12312. A staff member incorrectly entered "Vaccinations" as the reason for the visit, when the animal actually came to the care center that day for a wellness exam. Ensuring the accuracy of the data in a database is an important maintenance task.

To correct the record in the Visit table:

1. Open the **Visit** table in Datasheet view. The record containing the error is for Visit ID 1024.

2. Scroll the Visit table as necessary until you locate Visit ID **1024**, and then click at the end of the **Reason/Diagnosis** field value "Vaccinations" for this record. You are in editing mode.

3. Delete **Vaccinations** from the Reason/Diagnosis field, type **Wellness exam**, and then press the **Enter** key twice. The record now contains the correct value in the Reason/Diagnosis field, and this change is automatically saved in the Visit table.

The next update Kelly asks you to make is to delete a record in the Visit table. The owner of Butch, one of the animals seen by the care center, recently notified Taylor that he received an invoice for a neutering visit, but that he had canceled this scheduled appointment. Because this visit did not take place, the record for this visit needs to be deleted from the Visit table. Rather than scrolling through the table to locate the record to delete, you can use the Find command.

Finding Data in a Table

Access provides options you can use to locate specific field values in a table. Instead of scrolling the Visit table datasheet to find the visit that you need to delete—the record for Visit ID 1128—you can use the Find command to find the record. The **Find command** allows you to search a table or query datasheet, or a form, to locate a specific field value or part of a field value. This feature is particularly useful when searching a table that contains a large number of records.

To search for the record in the Visit table:

TIP

You can click any value in the column containing the field you want to search to make the field current.

1. Make sure the VisitID field value **1028** is still selected, and the **Home** tab is selected on the ribbon. You need to search the VisitID field to find the record containing the value 1128, so the insertion point is already correctly positioned in the field you want to search.

2. In the Find group, click the **Find** button. The Find and Replace dialog box opens. See Figure 3-4.

Figure 3-4   **Find and Replace dialog box**

The field value 1028 appears in the Find What box because this value is selected in the table datasheet. You also can choose to search for only part of a field value, such as when you need to find all Visit IDs that start with a certain value. The Search box indicates that all the records in the table will be searched for the value you want to find. You also can choose to search up or down from the currently selected record.

Trouble? Some of the settings in your dialog box might be different from those shown in Figure 3-4 depending on the last search performed on the computer you're using. If so, change the settings so that they match those in the figure.

3. Make sure the value 1028 is selected in the Find What box, type **1128** to replace the selected value, and then click the **Find Next** button. Record 50 appears with the field value you specified selected.

4. Click the **Cancel** button to close the Find and Replace dialog box.

Deleting Records

To delete a record, you need to select the record in Datasheet view and then delete it using the Delete button in the Records group on the Home tab or the Delete Record option on the shortcut menu.

REFERENCE

Deleting a Record

- With the table open in Datasheet view, click the row selector for the record you want to delete.
- In the Records group on the Home tab, click the Delete button (or right-click the row selector for the record, and then click Delete Record on the shortcut menu).
- In the dialog box asking you to confirm the deletion, click the Yes button.

Now that you have found the record with Visit ID 1128, you can delete it. To delete a record, you must first select the entire row for the record.

To delete the record:

1. Click the row selector for the record containing the VisitID field value **1128**, which should still be highlighted. The entire row is selected.

2. On the Home tab, in the Records group, click the **Delete** button. A dialog box opens indicating that you cannot delete the record because the Billing table contains records that are related to VisitID 1128. Recall that you defined a one-to-many relationship between the Visit and Billing tables and you enforced referential integrity. When you try to delete a record in the primary table (Visit), the enforced referential integrity prevents the deletion if matching records exist in the related table (Billing). This protection helps to maintain the integrity of the data in the database.

To delete the record in the Visit table, you first must delete the related records in the Billing table.

3. Click the **OK** button in the dialog box to close it. Notice the plus sign that appears at the beginning of each record in the Visit table. The plus sign, also called the **expand indicator**, indicates that the Visit table is the primary table related to another table—in this case, the Billing table. Clicking the expand indicator displays related records from other tables in the database in a **subdatasheet**.

4. Scroll down the datasheet until the selected record is near the top of the datasheet, so that you have room to view the related records for the visit record.

5. Click the **expand indicator** next to VisitID 1128. Two related records from the Billing table for this visit are displayed in the subdatasheet. See Figure 3-5.

Figure 3-5   **Related records from the Billing table in the subdatasheet**

When the subdatasheet is open, you can navigate and update it, just as you can using a table datasheet. The expand indicator for an open subdatasheet is replaced by a minus sign. Clicking the minus sign, or **collapse indicator**, hides the subdatasheet.

You need to delete the records in the Billing table that are related to Visit ID 1128 before you can delete this visit record. The records are for the invoices that were mistakenly sent to the owner of Butch, who had canceled his dog's neutering visit at the care center. You could open the Billing table and find the related records. However, an easier way is to delete the records right in the subdatasheet. The records will be deleted from the Billing table automatically.

6. In the Billing table subdatasheet, click the row selector for invoice number **42395**, and then drag down one row. The rows are selected for both invoice number 42395 and invoice number 42396.

7. On the Home tab, in the Records group, click the **Delete** button. Because the deletion of records is permanent and cannot be undone, a dialog box opens asking you to confirm the deletion of two records.

8. Click the **Yes** button to confirm the deletion and close the dialog box. The records are removed from the Billing table, and the subdatasheet is now empty.

9. Click the **collapse indicator** next to VisitID 1128 to close the subdatasheet.

Now that you have deleted the related records in the Billing table, you can delete the record for Visit ID 1128. You'll use the shortcut menu to do so.

Be sure to select the correct record before deleting it.

10. Right-click the row selector for the record for Visit ID **1128** to select the record and open the shortcut menu.

11. Click **Delete Record** on the shortcut menu, and then click the **Yes** button in the dialog box to confirm the deletion. The record is deleted from the Visit table.

12. Close the Visit table.

INSIGHT

Process for Deleting Records

When working with more complex databases that are managed by a database administrator, you typically need special permission to delete records from a table. Many companies also follow the practice of archiving records before deleting them so that the information is still available but not part of the active database.

You have finished updating the Riverview database by modifying and deleting records. Next, you'll retrieve specific data from the database to meet various requests for information about Riverview Veterinary Care Center.

Introduction to Queries

As you have learned, a query is a question you ask about data stored in a database. For example, Kimberly might create a query to find records in the Owner table for only those owners located in a specific city. When you create a query, you tell Access which fields you need and what criteria Access should use to select the records. Access provides powerful query capabilities that allow you to do the following:

- Display selected fields and records from a table
- Sort records
- Perform calculations
- Generate data for forms, reports, and other queries
- Update data in the tables in a database
- Find and display data from two or more tables

Most questions about data are generalized queries in which you specify the fields and records you want Access to select. These common requests for information, such as "Which owners are located in Ralston?" or "How many invoices have been paid?" are select queries. The answer to a select query is returned in the form of a datasheet. The result of a query is also referred to as a **recordset** because the query produces a set of records that answers your question.

INSIGHT

Designing Queries vs. Using a Query Wizard

More specialized, technical queries, such as finding duplicate records in a table, are best formulated using a Query Wizard. A **Query Wizard** prompts you for information by asking a series of questions and then creates the appropriate query based on your answers. For example, earlier you used the Simple Query Wizard to display only some of the fields in the Visit table; Access provides other Query Wizards for more complex queries. For common, informational queries, designing your own query is more efficient than using a Query Wizard.

The care center staff is planning an email campaign advertising a microchipping service being offered to animals seen by Riverview Veterinary Care Center. You need to create a query to display the owner ID, last name, first name, city, and email address for each record in the Owner table. You'll open the Query window in Design view to create the query.

To open the Query window in Design view:

▶ **1.** Close the Navigation Pane, and then, on the ribbon, click the **Create** tab.

▶ **2.** In the Queries group, click the **Query Design** button to display the Query window in Design view, with the Show Table dialog box open and the Tables tab selected. See Figure 3-6.

Figure 3-6   Show Table dialog box

tabs for selecting the source of the query

list of tables in the database

The Show Table dialog box lists all the tables in the Riverview database. You can choose to base a query on one or more tables, on other queries, or on a combination of tables and queries. The query you are creating will retrieve data from the Owner table, so you need to add this table to the Query window.

▶ **3.** In the Tables list, click **Owner**, click the **Add** button, and then click the **Close** button to close the Show Table dialog box. The Owner table's field list appears in the Query window. Refer to the Session 3.1 Visual Overview to familiarize yourself with the Query window in Design view.

Trouble? If you add the wrong table to the Query window, right-click the bar at the top of the field list containing the table name, and then click Remove Table on the shortcut menu. To add the correct table to the Query window, repeat Steps 2 and 3.

Now you'll create and run the query to display selected fields from the Owner table.

Creating and Running a Query

The default table datasheet displays all the fields in the table in the same order as they appear in the table. In contrast, a query datasheet can display selected fields from a table, and the order of the fields can be different from that of the table, enabling those viewing the query results to see only the information they need and in the order they want.

You need the OwnerID, LastName, FirstName, City, and Email fields from the Owner table to appear in the query results. You'll add each of these fields to the design grid. First you'll resize the Owner table field list to display all of the fields.

To select the fields for the query, and then run the query:

▶ **1.** Drag the bottom border of the Owner field list to resize the field list so that all the fields in the Owner table are visible.

▶ **2.** In the Owner field list, double-click **OwnerID** to place the field in the design grid's first column Field box. See Figure 3-7.

Figure 3-7   **Field added to the design grid**

field list resized to display all the fields in the table

click the field selector to select a field's column

indicates that the field will appear in the query datasheet

field added from field list to the first column in the design grid

specifies the field is in the Owner table

In the design grid's first column, the field name OwnerID appears in the Field box, the table name Owner appears in the Table box, and the checkmark in the Show check box indicates that the field will be displayed in the datasheet when you run the query. Sometimes you might not want to display a field and its values in the query results. For example, if you are creating a query to list all owners located in Ralston, and you assign the name "RalstonOwners" to the query, you do not need to include the City field value for each record in the query results—the query design lists only owners with the City field value of "Ralston." Even if you choose not to display a field in the query results, you can still use the field as part of the query to select specific records or to specify a particular sequence for the records in the datasheet. You can also add a field to the design grid using the arrow on the Field box; this arrow appears when you click the Field box, and if you click the arrow or the right side of an empty Field box, a menu of available fields opens.

TIP

You can also use the mouse to drag a field from the field list to a column in the design grid.

3. In the design grid, click the right side of the second column's Field box to display a menu listing all the fields in the Owner table, and then click **LastName** to add this field to the second column in the design grid.

4. Add the **FirstName**, **City**, and **Email** fields to the design grid in that order.

Trouble? If you accidentally add the wrong field to the design grid, select the field's column by clicking the pointer ↓ on the field selector, which is the thin bar above the Field box, for the field you want to delete, and then press the Delete key (or in the Query Setup group on the Query Tools Design tab, click the Delete Columns button).

Now that the five fields for the query have been selected, you can run the query.

5. On the Query Tools Design tab, in the Results group, click the **Run** button. Access runs the query and displays the results in Datasheet view. See Figure 3-8.

Figure 3-8   Datasheet displayed after running the query

selected fields displayed

The five fields you added to the design grid appear in the datasheet in the same order as they appear in the design grid. The records are displayed in primary key sequence by OwnerID. The query selected all 25 records from the Owner table for display in the query datasheet. You will save the query as "OwnerEmail" so that you can easily retrieve the same data again.

6. On the Quick Access Toolbar, click the **Save** button 🖫. The Save As dialog box opens.

7. In the Query Name box, type **OwnerEmail** and then press the **Enter** key. The query is saved with the specified name in the Riverview database, and its name appears on the tab for the query.

Decision Making: Comparing Methods for Adding All Fields to the Design Grid

If the query you are creating includes every field from the specified table, you can use one of the following three methods to transfer all the fields from the field list to the design grid:

- Double-click (or click and drag) each field individually from the field list to the design grid. Use this method if you want the fields in your query to appear in an order that is different from the order in the field list.
- Double-click the asterisk at the top of the field list. The table name, followed by a period and an asterisk (as in "Owner.*"), appears in the Field box of the first column in the design grid, which signifies that the order of the fields is the same in the query as it is in the field list. Use this method if you don't need to sort the query or specify conditions based on the fields in the table you added in this way (for example, in a query based on more than one table). The advantage of using this method is that you do not need to change the query if you add or delete fields from the underlying table structure. Such changes are reflected automatically in the query.
- Double-click the field list title bar to select all the fields, and then click and drag one of the selected fields to the first column in the design grid. Each field appears in a separate column, and the fields are arranged in the order in which they appear in the field list. Use this method when you need to sort your query or include record selection criteria.

By choosing the most appropriate method to add all the table fields to the query design grid, you can work more efficiently and ensure that the query produces the results you want.

The record for one of the owners in the query results contains information that is not up to date. This owner, Jimmy Gonzalez, had informed the care center that he now prefers to go by the name James; he also provided a new email address. You need to update the record with the new first name and email address for this owner.

Updating Data Using a Query

A query datasheet is temporary, and its contents are based on the criteria in the query design grid; however, you can still update the data in a table using a query datasheet. In this case, you want to make changes to a record in the Owner table. Instead of making the changes in the table datasheet, you can make them in the OwnerEmail query datasheet because the query is based on the Owner table. The underlying Owner table will be updated with the changes you make.

To update data using the OwnerEmail query datasheet:

1. Locate the record with OwnerID 2330, Jimmy Gonzalez (record 6 in the query datasheet).

2. In the First Name column for this record, double-click **Jimmy** to select the name, and then type **James**.

3. Press the **Tab** key twice to move to the Email column, type **thewholething@ example.com** and then press the **Tab** key.

4. Close the OwnerEmail query, and then open the Navigation Pane. Note that the OwnerEmail query is listed in the Queries section of the Navigation Pane.

Now you'll check the Owner table to verify that the changes you made in the query datasheet are reflected in the Owner table.

5. Open the **Owner** table in Datasheet view, and then close the Navigation Pane.

6. Locate the record for OwnerID 2330 (record 6). Notice that the changes you made in the query datasheet to the First Name and Email field values were made to the record in the Owner table.

7. Close the Owner table.

Kelly also wants to view specific information in the Riverview database. She would like to review the visit data for animals while also viewing certain information about them. So, she needs to see data from both the Animal table and the Visit table at the same time.

Creating a Multitable Query

A multitable query is a query based on more than one table. If you want to create a query that retrieves data from multiple tables, the tables must have a common field. Earlier, you established a relationship between the Animal (primary) and Visit (related) tables based on the common AnimalID field that exists in both tables, so you can now create a query to display data from both tables at the same time. Specifically, Kelly wants to view the values in the AnimalType, AnimalBreed, and AnimalName fields from the Animal table and the VisitDate and Reason fields from the Visit table.

To create the query using the Animal and Visit tables:

1. On the ribbon, click the **Create** tab.

2. In the Queries group, click the **Query Design** button. The Show Table dialog box opens in the Query window. You need to add the Animal and Visit tables to the Query window.

3. Click **Animal** in the Tables list, click the **Add** button, click **Visit**, click the **Add** button, and then click the **Close** button to close the Show Table dialog box. The Animal and Visit field lists appear in the Query window.

4. Resize the Animal and Visit field lists if necessary so that all the fields in each list are displayed.

The one-to-many relationship between the two tables is shown in the Query window in the same way that a relationship between two tables is shown in the Relationships window. Note that the join line is thick at both ends; this signifies that you selected the option to enforce referential integrity. If you had not selected this option, the join line would be thin at both ends, and neither the "1" nor the infinity symbol would appear, even though the tables have a one-to-many relationship.

You need to place the AnimalType, AnimalBreed, and AnimalName fields (in that order) from the Animal field list into the design grid and then place the VisitDate and Reason fields from the Visit field list into the design grid. This is the order in which Taylor wants to view the fields in the query results.

5. In the Animal field list, double-click **AnimalType** to place this field in the design grid's first column Field box.

6. Repeat Step 5 to add the **AnimalBreed** and **AnimalName** fields from the Animal table to the second and third columns of the design grid.

7. Repeat Step 5 to add the **VisitDate** and **Reason** fields (in that order) from the Visit table to the fourth and fifth columns of the design grid. The query specifications are complete, so you can now run the query.

8. In the Results group on the Query Tools Design tab, click the **Run** button. After the query runs, the results are displayed in Datasheet view. See Figure 3-9.

Figure 3-9   **Datasheet for query based on the Animal and Visit tables**

fields from the Animal table

fields from the Visit table

Animal Type	Animal Breed	Animal Name	Date of Visit	Reason/Diagnosis
Dog	Beagle	Bailey	12/2/2016	Vaccinations
Dog	Beagle	Bailey	1/20/2017	Spaying
Cat	Burmese	Whiskers	11/8/2016	Vaccinations
Cat	Burmese	Whiskers	12/14/2016	Grooming
Cat	Burmese	Whiskers	1/11/2017	Grooming
Dog	Border collie	Lady	12/1/2016	Vaccinations
Dog	Australian shepherd	Rustle	11/11/2016	Vaccinations
Dog	Australian shepherd	Rustle	12/16/2016	Vaccinations
Dog	Australian shepherd	Rustle	12/21/2016	Injured paw
Dog	Australian shepherd	Rustle	1/9/2017	Injured paw
Cat	Himalayan	Bushy	11/29/2016	Declawing
Cat	Himalayan	Bushy	1/18/2017	Grooming
Cat	Siberian	Patches	11/28/2016	Grooming
Cat	Siberian	Patches	1/3/2017	Declawing
Dog	Russell terrier	Buddy	11/28/2016	Grooming
Bird	Parakeet	Tweets	12/19/2016	Vaccinations
Bird	Parakeet	Tweets	1/9/2017	Not eating
Dog	Dalmatian	Rosie	11/15/2016	Nail clipping and grooming
Dog	Dalmatian	Rosie	1/13/2017	Injured paw
Dog	Labrador retriever	Molly	11/22/2016	Wellness exam
Dog	Labrador retriever	Molly	1/4/2017	Grooming
Dog	Chihuahua	Silly	12/9/2016	Injured paw
Dog	Chihuahua	Silly	1/23/2017	Not eating
Dog	Bloodhound	Tracker	12/2/2016	Injured paw
Dog	Bloodhound	Tracker	1/13/2017	Not eating

Record: 1 of 74   No Filter   Search

Ready

Only the five selected fields from the Animal and Visit tables appear in the datasheet. The records are displayed in order according to the values in the AnimalID field because it is the primary key field in the primary table, even though this field is not included in the query datasheet.

Kelly plans on frequently tracking the data retrieved by the query, so she asks you to save it as "AnimalVisits."

9. On the Quick Access Toolbar, click the **Save** button 🖫. The Save As dialog box opens.

10. In the Query Name box, type **AnimalVisits** and then press the **Enter** key. The query is saved, and its name appears on the object tab.

Kelly decides she wants the records displayed in alphabetical order by animal type. Because the query displays data in order by the field values in the AnimalID field, which is the primary key for the Animal table, you need to sort the records by the AnimalType field to display the data in the order Kelly wants.

Sorting Data in a Query

Sorting is the process of rearranging records in a specified order or sequence. Sometimes you might need to sort data before displaying or printing it to meet a specific request. For example, Kelly might want to review visit information arranged by the VisitDate field because she needs to know which months are the busiest for Riverview Veterinary Care Center in terms of animal visits. Kimberly might want to view billing information arranged by the InvoiceAmt field because she monitors the finances of the care center.

When you sort data in a query, you do not change the sequence of the records in the underlying tables. Only the records in the query datasheet are rearranged according to your specifications.

To sort records, you must select the **sort field**, which is the field used to determine the order of records in the datasheet. In this case, Kelly wants the data sorted alphabetically by animal type, so you need to specify AnimalType as the sort field. Sort fields can be Short Text, Number, Date/Time, Currency, AutoNumber, or Yes/No fields, but not Long Text, Hyperlink, or Attachment fields. You sort records in either ascending (increasing) or descending (decreasing) order. Figure 3-10 shows the results of each type of sort for these data types.

Figure 3-10   **Sorting results for different data types**

Data Type	Ascending Sort Results	Descending Sort Results
Short Text	A to Z (alphabetical)	Z to A (reverse alphabetical)
Number	lowest to highest numeric value	highest to lowest numeric value
Date/Time	oldest to most recent date	most recent to oldest date
Currency	lowest to highest numeric value	highest to lowest numeric value
AutoNumber	lowest to highest numeric value	highest to lowest numeric value
Yes/No	yes (checkmark in check box) then no values	no then yes values

Access provides several methods for sorting data in a table or query datasheet and in a form. One of the easiest ways is to use the AutoFilter feature for a field.

Using an AutoFilter to Sort Data

TIP

You can also use the Ascending and Descending buttons in the Sort & Filter group on the Home tab to quickly sort records based on the currently selected field in a datasheet.

As you've probably noticed when working in Datasheet view for a table or query, each column heading has an arrow to the right of the field name. This arrow gives you access to the **AutoFilter** feature, which enables you to quickly sort and display field values in various ways. When you click this arrow, a menu opens with options for sorting and displaying field values. The first two options on the menu enable you to sort the values in the current field in ascending or descending order. Unless you save the datasheet or form after you've sorted the records, the rearrangement of records is temporary.

Next, you'll use an AutoFilter to sort the AnimalVisits query results by the AnimalType field.

To sort the records using an AutoFilter:

▶ **1.** Click the **arrow** on the Animal Type column heading to display the AutoFilter menu. See Figure 3-11.

Figure 3-11	Using AutoFilter to sort records in the datasheet

sort buttons on the ribbon

AnimalType field will be sorted

choose this option to specify an ascending sort order

menu displayed with AutoFilter options

Kelly wants the data sorted in ascending (alphabetical) order by the values in the AnimalType field, so you need to select the first option in the menu.

▶ **2.** Click **Sort A to Z**. The records are rearranged in ascending alphabetical order by animal type. A small, upward-pointing arrow appears on the right side of the Animal Type column heading. This arrow indicates that the values in the field have been sorted in ascending order. If you used the same method to sort the field values in descending order, a small downward-pointing arrow would appear there instead.

After viewing the query results, Kelly decides that she would also like to see the records arranged by the values in the VisitDate field, so that the data is presented in chronological order. She still wants the records to be arranged by the AnimalType field values as well. To produce the results Kelly wants, you need to sort using two fields.

Sorting on Multiple Fields in Design View

Sort fields can be unique or nonunique. A sort field is **unique** if the value in the sort field for each record is different. The AnimalID field in the Animal table is an example of a unique sort field because each animal record has a different value in this primary key field. A sort field is **nonunique** if more than one record can have the same value for the sort field. For example, the AnimalType field in the Animal table is a nonunique sort field because more than one record can have the same AnimalType value.

TIP

The primary sort field is not the same as a table's primary key. A table has at most one primary key, which must be unique, whereas any field in a table can serve as a primary sort field.

When the sort field is nonunique, records with the same sort field value are grouped together, but they are not sorted in a specific order within the group. To arrange these grouped records in a specific order, you can specify a **secondary sort field**, which is a second field that determines the order of records that are already sorted by the **primary sort field** (the first sort field specified).

In Access, you can select up to 10 different sort fields. When you use the buttons on the ribbon to sort by more than one field, the sort fields must be in adjacent columns in the datasheet. (Note that you cannot use an AutoFilter to sort on more than one field. This method works for a single field only.) You can specify only one type of sort—either ascending or descending—for the selected columns in the datasheet. You select the adjacent columns, and Access sorts first by the first column and then by each remaining selected column in order from left to right.

Kelly wants the records sorted first by the AnimalType field values, as they currently are, and then by the VisitDate values. The two fields are in the correct left-to-right order in the query datasheet, but they are not adjacent, so you cannot use the Ascending and Descending buttons on the ribbon to sort them. You could move the AnimalType field to the left of the VisitDate field in the query datasheet, but both columns would have to be sorted with the same sort order. This is not what Kelly wants—she wants the AnimalType field values sorted in ascending order so that they are in the correct alphabetical order, for ease of reference; and she wants the VisitDate field values to be sorted in descending order, so that she can focus on the most recent animal visits first. To sort the AnimalType and VisitDate fields with different sort orders, you must specify the sort fields in Design view.

In the Query window in Design view, you must arrange the fields you want to sort from left to right in the design grid, with the primary sort field being the leftmost. In Design view, multiple sort fields do not have to be adjacent to each other, as they do in Datasheet view; however, they must be in the correct left-to-right order.

REFERENCE

Sorting a Query Datasheet

- In the query datasheet, click the arrow on the column heading for the field you want to sort.
- In the menu that opens, click Sort A to Z for an ascending sort, or click Sort Z to A for a descending sort.

or

- In the query datasheet, select the column or adjacent columns on which you want to sort.
- In the Sort & Filter group on the Home tab, click the Ascending button or the Descending button.

or

- In Design view, position the fields serving as sort fields from left to right.
- Click the right side of the Sort box for each field you want to sort, and then click Ascending or Descending for the sort order.

To achieve the results Kelly wants, you need to modify the query in Design view to specify the sort order for the two fields.

To select the two sort fields in Design view:

1. On the Home tab, in the Views group, click the **View** button to open the query in Design view. The fields are currently in the correct left-to-right order in the design grid, so you only need to specify the sort order for the two fields.

First, you need to specify an ascending sort order for the AnimalType field. Even though the records are already sorted by the values in this field, you need to modify the query so that this sort order, and the sort order you will specify for the VisitDate field, are part of the query's design. Any time the query is run, the records will be sorted according to these specifications.

2. Click the right side of the **AnimalType Sort** box to display the arrow and the sort options, and then click **Ascending**. You've selected an ascending sort order for the AnimalType field, which will be the primary sort field. The AnimalType field is a Short Text field, and an ascending sort order will display the field values in alphabetical order.

3. Click the right side of the **VisitDate Sort** box, click **Descending**, and then click in one of the empty text boxes below the VisitDate field to deselect the setting. You've selected a descending sort order for the VisitDate field, which will be the secondary sort field because it appears to the right of the primary sort field (AnimalType) in the design grid. The VisitDate field is a Date/Time field, and a descending sort order will display the field values with the most recent dates first. See Figure 3-12.

Figure 3-12   Selecting two sort fields in Design view

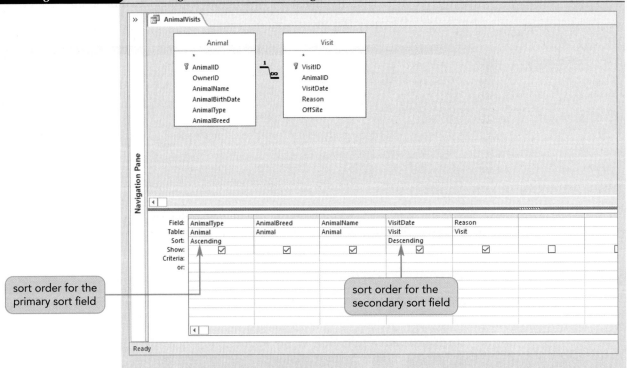

You have finished your query changes, so now you can run the query and then save the modified query with the same name.

4. On the Query Tools Design tab, in the Results group, click the **Run** button. After the query runs, the records appear in the query datasheet in ascending order based on the values in the AnimalType field. Within groups of records with the same AnimalType field value, the records appear in descending order by the values of the VisitDate field. See Figure 3-13.

| Figure 3-13 | Datasheet sorted on two fields |

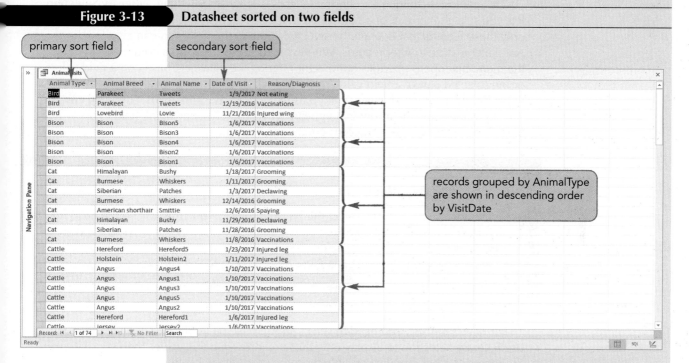

When you save the query, all of your design changes—including the selection of the sort fields—are saved with the query. The next time Kelly runs the query, the records will appear sorted by the primary and secondary sort fields.

5. On the Quick Access Toolbar, click the **Save** button to save the revised AnimalVisits query.

Kelly knows that Riverview Veterinary Care Center has seen an increase in the number of dogs receiving care. She would like to focus briefly on the information for that animal type only. Also, she is interested in knowing how many dogs have had recent vaccinations. She is concerned that, although more dogs are being brought to the care center, not enough of them are receiving regular vaccinations. Selecting only the records with an AnimalType field value of "Dog" and a Reason field value beginning with "Vaccination" is a temporary change that Kelly wants in the query datasheet, so you do not need to switch to Design view and change the query. Instead, you can apply a filter.

Filtering Data

A **filter** is a set of restrictions you place on the records in an open datasheet or form to *temporarily* isolate a subset of the records. A filter lets you view different subsets of displayed records so that you can focus on only the data you need. Unless you save a query or form with a filter applied, an applied filter is not available the next time you run the query or open the form.

The simplest technique for filtering records is Filter By Selection. **Filter By Selection** lets you select all or part of a field value in a datasheet or form and then display only those records that contain the selected value in the field. You can also use the AutoFilter feature to filter records. When you click the arrow on a column heading, the menu that opens provides options for filtering the datasheet based on a field value or the selected part of a field value. Another technique for filtering records is to use **Filter By Form**, which changes your datasheet to display blank fields. Then you can select a value using the arrow that appears when you click any blank field to apply a filter that selects only those records containing that value.

Using Filter By Selection

- In the datasheet or form, select the part of the field value that will be the basis for the filter; or, if the filter will be based on the entire field value, click anywhere within the field value.
- On the Home tab, in the Sort & Filter group, click the Selection button.
- Click the type of filter you want to apply.

For Kelly's request, you need to select an AnimalType field value of Dog and then use Filter By Selection to display only those records with this value. Then you will filter the records further by selecting only those records with a Reason value that begins with "Vaccination" (for visits that include a single vaccination or multiple vaccinations).

To display the records using Filter By Selection:

1. In the query datasheet, locate the first occurrence of an AnimalType field containing the value **Dog**, and then click anywhere within that field value.

2. On the Home tab, in the Sort & Filter group, click the **Selection** button. A menu opens with options for the type of filter to apply. See Figure 3-14.

Figure 3-14   **Using Filter By Selection**

options for the
type of filter to
apply

current field is the
basis for the filter

The menu provides options for displaying only those records with an
AnimalType field value that equals the selected value (in this case,
Dog); does not equal the value; contains the value somewhere within the field; or
does not contain the value somewhere within the field. You want to display
all the records whose AnimalType field value equals Dog.

3. In the Selection menu, click **Equals "Dog"**. Only the 25 records that have an
AnimalType field value of Dog appear in the datasheet. See Figure 3-15.

Figure 3-15 Datasheet after applying the filter

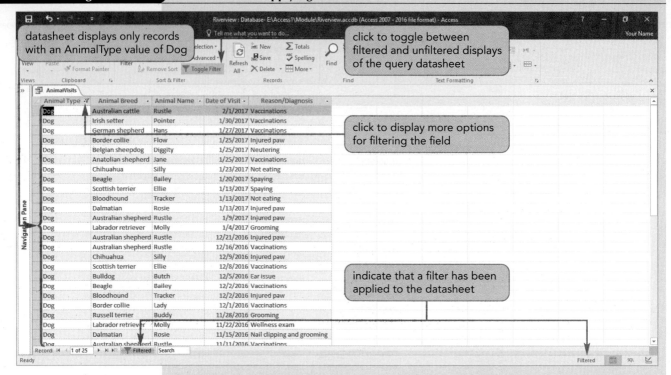

Next, Kelly wants to view only those records with a Reason field value beginning with the word "Vaccination" so she can view the records for visits that involved one or more vaccinations. You need to apply an additional filter to the datasheet.

4. In any Reason field value beginning with the word "Vaccination," select only the text **Vaccination**.

5. In the Sort & Filter group, click the **Selection** button. The same four filter types are available for this selection as when you filtered the AnimalType field.

6. On the Selection menu, click **Begins With "Vaccination"**. The first filter is applied to the query datasheet, which now shows only the nine records for dogs who have had one or more vaccinations at the care center.

   Trouble? If you do not see the Begins With "Vaccination" option, click anywhere in the datasheet to close the Selection menu, and then repeat Steps 4–6, being sure not to select the letter "s" at the end of the word "Vaccination."

   Now you can redisplay all the query records by clicking the Toggle Filter button, which you use to switch between the filtered and unfiltered displays.

TIP

The ScreenTip for this button is Remove Filter.

7. In the Sort & Filter group, click the **Toggle Filter** button. The filter is removed, and all 74 records appear in the query datasheet.

8. Close the AnimalVisits query. A dialog box opens, asking if you want to save your changes to the design of the query—in this case, the filtered display, which is still available through the Toggle Filter button. Kelly does not want the query saved with the filter because she doesn't need to view the filtered information on a regular basis.

9. Click the **No** button to close the query without saving the changes.

10. If you are not continuing to Session 3.2, click the **File** tab, and then click **Close** in the navigation bar to close the Riverview database.

REVIEW

Session 3.1 Quick Check

1. In Datasheet view, what is the difference between navigation mode and editing mode?
2. What command can you use in Datasheet view to remove the display of one or more fields from the datasheet?
3. What is a select query?
4. Describe the field list and the design grid in the Query window in Design view.
5. How are a table datasheet and a query datasheet similar? How are they different?
6. For a Date/Time field, how do the records appear when sorted in ascending order?
7. When you define multiple sort fields in Design view, describe how the sort fields must be positioned in the design grid.
8. A(n) _____ is a set of restrictions you place on the records in an open datasheet or form to isolate a subset of records temporarily.

Session 3.2 Visual Overview:

When creating queries in Design view, you can enter criteria so that only selected records are displayed in the query results.

Field:	AnimalName	AnimalBirthDate	AnimalType	VisitDate	Reason
Table:	Animal	Animal	Animal	Visit	Visit
Sort:					
Show:	☑	☑	☑	☑	☑
Criteria:			"Bird"		
or:					

To define a condition for a field, you place the condition in the field's Criteria box in the design grid.

To indicate which records you want to select, you must specify a condition as part of the query. A **condition** is a criterion, or rule, that determines which records are selected.

Field:	InvoiceNum	InvoiceDate	InvoiceAmt	
Table:	Billing	Billing	Billing	
Sort:				
Show:	☑	☑	☑	☐
Criteria:			> 100	
or:				

A condition usually consists of an operator, often a comparison operator, and a value. A **comparison operator** compares the value in a field to the condition value and selects all the records for which the condition is true.

Field:	VisitID	AnimalID	VisitDate	Reason
Table:	Visit	Visit	Visit	Visit
Sort:				
Show:	☑	☑	☑	☑
Criteria:			Between #1/1/2017# And #1/15/2017#	
or:				

Most comparison operators (such as Between…And…) select records that match a range of values for the condition—in this case, all records with dates that fall within the range shown.

Selection Criteria in Queries

The results of a query containing selection criteria include only the records that meet the specified criteria.

BirdAnimalType

Animal Name	Animal Birth Date	Animal Type	Date of Visit
Tweets	11/12/2010	Bird	12/19/2016
Tweets	11/12/2010	Bird	1/9/2017
Lovie	02/03/2002	Bird	11/21/2016
*			

The results of this query show only birds because the condition "Bird" in the AnimalType field's Criteria box specifies that the query should select records only with AnimalType field values of bird. This type of condition is called an **exact match** because the value in the specified field must match the condition exactly in order for the record to be included in the query results.

LargeInvoiceAmts

Invoice Num	Invoice Date	Invoice Amt
42145	11/22/2016	$275.00
42182	11/30/2016	$225.00
42320	01/04/2017	$225.00
42435	01/16/2017	$125.00
42525	01/26/2017	$125.00
*		$0.00

The results of this query show only those invoices with amounts greater than $100 because the condition >100, which uses the greater than comparison operator, specifies that query should select records only with InvoiceAmt field values over $100.

EarlyJanuaryVisits

Visit ID	Animal ID	Date of Visit	Reason/Diagnosis
1098	12296	1/3/2017	Declawing
1101	12312	1/4/2017	Grooming
1120	12304	1/9/2017	Not eating
1124	12290	1/9/2017	Injured paw
1140	12282	1/11/2017	Grooming
1148	12308	1/13/2017	Injured paw
1152	12318	1/13/2017	Not eating
1156	12322	1/13/2017	Spaying
*			

The results of this query show only those visits that took place in the first half of January 2017 because the condition in the VisitDate Criteria box specifies that the query should select records only with a visit date between 1/1/2017 and 1/15/2017.

Defining Record Selection Criteria for Queries

Kimberly is considering offering a workshop on dog care at the care center, with a special emphasis on the needs of older dogs. To prepare for this, she is interested in knowing more about the level of care provided to the dogs that have visited the care center, as well as where these dogs live. For this request, you could create a query to select the correct fields and all records in the Owner, Animal, and Visit tables, select an AnimalType field value of Dog in the query datasheet, and then click the Selection button and choose the appropriate filter option to display the information for only those animals that are dogs. However, a faster way of accessing the data Kimberly needs is to create a query that displays the selected fields and only those records in the Owner, Animal, and Visit tables that satisfy a condition.

Just as you can display selected fields from a database in a query datasheet, you can display selected records. To identify which records you want to select, you must specify a condition as part of the query, as illustrated in the Session 3.2 Visual Overview. A condition usually includes one of the comparison operators shown in Figure 3-16.

Figure 3-16	Access comparison operators

Operator	Meaning	Example
=	equal to (optional; default operator)	="Hall"
<>	not equal to	<>"Hall"
<	less than	<#1/1/99#
<=	less than or equal to	<=100
>	greater than	>"C400"
>=	greater than or equal to	>=18.75
Between ... And ...	between two values (inclusive)	Between 50 And 325
In ()	in a list of values	In ("Hall", "Seeger")
Like	matches a pattern that includes wildcards	Like "706*"

Specifying an Exact Match

For Kimberly's request, you need to first create a query that will display only those records in the Animal table with the value Dog in the AnimalType field. This type of condition is an exact match because the value in the specified field must match the condition exactly in order for the record to be included in the query results. You'll create the query in Design view.

To create the query in Design view:

1. If you took a break after the previous session, make sure that the Riverview database is open and the Navigation Pane is closed, and then on the ribbon, click the **Create** tab.

2. In the Queries group, click the **Query Design** button. The Show Table dialog box opens. You need to add the Owner, Animal, and Visit tables to the Query window.

3. Click **Owner** in the Tables list, click the **Add** button, click **Animal**, click the **Add** button, click **Visit**, click the **Add** button, and then click the **Close** button. The field lists for the Owner, Animal, and Visit tables appear in the top portion of the window, and join lines indicating one-to-many relationships connect the tables.

4. Resize all three field lists so that all the fields are displayed.

5. Add the following fields from the Animal table to the design grid in this order: **AnimalName**, **AnimalBirthDate**, and **AnimalType**.

   Kimberly also wants information from the Visit table and the Owner table included in the query results.

6. Add the following fields from the Visit table to the design grid in this order: **VisitDate** and **Reason**.

7. Add the following fields from the Owner table to the design grid in this order: **FirstName**, **LastName**, **Phone**, and **Email**. All the fields needed for the query appear in the design grid. See Figure 3-17.

| Figure 3-17 | Design grid after adding fields from both tables |

To display the information Kimberly wants, you need to enter the condition for the AnimalType field in its Criteria box, as shown in Figure 3-17. Kimberly wants to display only those records with an AnimalType field value of Dog.

To enter the exact match condition, and then save and run the query:

1. Click the **AnimalType Criteria** box, type **Dog**, and then press the **Enter** key. The condition changes to "Dog".

   Access automatically enclosed the condition you typed in quotation marks. You must enclose text values in quotation marks when using them as selection criteria. If you omit the quotation marks, however, Access will include them automatically in most cases. Some words—including "in" and "select"—are special keywords in Access that are reserved for functions and commands. If you want to enter one of these keywords as the condition, you must type the quotation marks around the text or an error message will appear indicating the condition cannot be entered.

2. Save the query with the name **DogAnimalType**. The query is saved, and its name is displayed on the object tab.

3. Run the query. After the query runs, the selected field values for only those records with an AnimalType field value of Dog are shown. A total of 25 records is selected and displayed in the datasheet. See Figure 3-18.

Figure 3-18   **Datasheet displaying selected fields and records**

Kimberly realizes that it's not necessary to include the AnimalType field values in the query results. The name of the query, DogAnimalType, indicates that the query design includes all animals with an AnimalType of Dog, so the AnimalType field values are unnecessary and repetitive in the query results. Also, she decides that she would prefer the query datasheet to show the fields from the Owner table first, followed by the Animal table fields and then the Visit table fields. You need to modify the query to produce the results Kimberly wants.

Modifying a Query

After you create a query and view the results, you might need to make changes to the query if the results are not what you expected or require. First, Kimberly asks you to modify the DogAnimalType query so that it does not display the AnimalType field values in the query results.

To remove the display of the AnimalType field values:

1. On the Home tab, in the Views group, click the **View** button. The DogAnimalType query opens in Design view.

   You need to keep the AnimalType field as part of the query design because it contains the defined condition for the query. You only need to remove the display of the field's values from the query results.

2. Click the **AnimalType Show** check box to remove the checkmark. The query will still find only those records with the value Dog in the AnimalType field, but the query results will not display these field values.

Next, you need to change the order of the fields in the query so that the owner information is listed first.

To move the Owner table fields to precede the Animal and Visit table fields:

▶ **1.** Position the pointer on the FirstName field selector until the pointer changes to ↓, and then click to select the field. See Figure 3-19.

Figure 3-19	Selected FirstName field

Show check box is cleared

FirstName field selector

entire column is selected

▶ **2.** Position the pointer on the FirstName field selector, and then press and hold the mouse button; notice that the pointer changes to ↖, and a black vertical line appears to the left of the selected field. This line represents the selected field when you drag the mouse to move it.

▶ **3.** Drag the pointer to the left until the vertical line representing the selected field is positioned to the left of the AnimalName field. See Figure 3-20.

Figure 3-20	Dragging the field in the design grid

line representing selected field

drag pointer to here

selected field being moved

TIP

Instead of moving a field by dragging, you can also delete the field and then add it back to the design grid in the location you want.

▶ **4.** Release the mouse button. The FirstName field moves to the left of the AnimalName field.

You can also select and move multiple fields at once. You need to select and move the LastName, Phone, and Email fields so that they appear directly after the FirstName field in the query design. To select multiple fields, you click and drag the mouse over the field selectors for the fields you want.

▶ **5.** Point to the LastName field selector. When the pointer changes to ↓, press and hold the mouse button, drag to the right to select the Phone and Email fields, and then release the mouse button. All three fields are now selected. See Figure 3-21.

Figure 3-21 Multiple fields selected to be moved

selected fields
highlighted in black

6. Position the pointer on the field selector for any of the three selected fields, press and hold the mouse button, and then drag to the left until the vertical line representing the selected fields is positioned to the left of the AnimalName field.

7. Release the mouse button. The four fields from the Owner table are now the first four fields in the query design.

You have finished making the modifications to the query Kimberly requested, so you can now run the query.

8. Run the query. The results of the modified query are displayed. See Figure 3-22.

Figure 3-22 Results of the modified query

fields from the Owner table are now
listed first in the query datasheet

AnimalType field values
are no longer displayed

Note that the AnimalType field values are no longer displayed in the query results.

9. Save and close the DogAnimalType query.

Kimberly asks you to create a new query. She is interested to know which animals of all animal types that have not been to the care center recently, so that her staff can follow up with their owners by sending them reminder notes or emails. To create the query that will produce the results Kimberly wants, you need to use a comparison operator to match a range of values—in this case, any VisitDate value less than 1/1/2017. Because this new query will include information from several of the same fields as the DogAnimalType query, you can use that query as a starting point in designing this new query.

Using a Comparison Operator to Match a Range of Values

As you know, after you create and save a query, you can double-click the query name in the Navigation Pane to run the query again. You can then click the View button to change its design. You can also use an existing query as the basis for creating another query. Because the design of the query you need to create next is similar to the DogAnimalType query, you will copy, paste, and rename this query to create the new query. Using this approach keeps the DogAnimalType query intact.

To create the new query by copying the DogAnimalType query:

▶ **1.** Open the Navigation Pane. Note that the DogAnimalType query is listed in the Queries section.

   You need to use the shortcut menu to copy the DogAnimalType query and paste it in the Navigation Pane; then you'll give the copied query a different name.

▶ **2.** In the Queries section of the Navigation Pane, right-click **DogAnimalType** to select it and display the shortcut menu.

▶ **3.** Click **Copy** on the shortcut menu.

▶ **4.** Right-click the empty area near the bottom of the Navigation Pane, and then click **Paste** on the shortcut menu. The Paste As dialog box opens with the text "Copy Of DogAnimalType" in the Query Name box. Because Kimberly wants the new query to show data for animals that have not visited the care center recently, you'll name the new query "EarlierVisits."

▶ **5.** In the Query Name box, type **EarlierVisits** and then press the **Enter** key. The new query appears in the Queries section of the Navigation Pane.

▶ **6.** Double-click the **EarlierVisits** query to open, or run, the query. The design of this query is currently the same as the original DogAnimalType query.

▶ **7.** Close the Navigation Pane.

Next, you need to open the query in Design view and modify its design to produce the results Kimberly wants—to display records for all animals and only those records with VisitDate field values that are earlier than, or less than, 1/1/2017.

To modify the design of the new query:

 1. Display the query in Design view.

 2. Click the **VisitDate Criteria** box, type **<1/1/2017** and then press the **Tab** key. Note that Access automatically encloses the date criteria with number signs. The condition specifies that a record will be selected only if its VisitDate field value is less than (earlier than) 1/1/2017. See Figure 3-23.

Figure 3-23   Criteria entered for the VisitDate field

new condition entered

original condition needs to be deleted

Before you run the query, you need to delete the condition for the AnimalType field. Recall that the AnimalType field is part of the query, but its values are not displayed in the query results. When you modified the query to remove the AnimalType field values from the query results, Access moved the field to the end of the design grid. You need to delete the AnimalType field's condition, specify that the AnimalType field values should be included in the query results, and then move the field back to its original position following the AnimalBirthDate field.

 3. Press the **Tab** key to select the condition for the AnimalType field, and then press the **Delete** key. The condition for the AnimalType field is removed.

 4. Click the **Show** check box for the AnimalType field to insert a checkmark so that the field values will be displayed in the query results.

 5. Use the pointer to select the AnimalType field, drag the selected field to position it to the left of the VisitDate field, and then click in an empty box to deselect the AnimalType field. See Figure 3-24.

Figure 3-24   Design grid after moving the AnimalType field

Show check box is selected

AnimalType field moved back to its original location

condition removed from AnimalType Criteria box

 6. Run the query. The query datasheet displays the selected fields for only those records with a VisitDate field value less than 1/1/2017, a total of 34 records. See Figure 3-25.

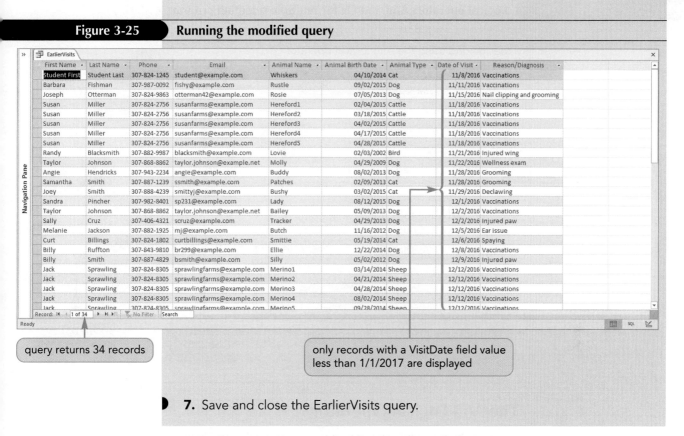

| Figure 3-25 | Running the modified query |

only records with a VisitDate field value less than 1/1/2017 are displayed

query returns 34 records

7. Save and close the EarlierVisits query.

Kimberly continues to analyze animal visits to Riverview Veterinary Care Center. Although the care center offers payment plans and pet insurance options, she realizes that owners of younger animals seen off-site might not see the literature about these options that is available in the care center's waiting room. With this in mind, she would like to see a list of all animals that are less than a year old and that the care center has visited off-site. She wants to track these animals in particular so that her staff can contact their owners to review payment plans and pet insurance options. To produce this list, you need to create a query containing two conditions—one for the animal's date of birth and another for whether each visit was off-site.

Defining Multiple Selection Criteria for Queries

Multiple conditions require you to use **logical operators** to combine two or more conditions. When you want a record selected only if two or more conditions are met, you need to use the **And logical operator**. In this case, Kimberly wants to see only those records with an AnimalBirthDate field value greater than or equal to 7/1/2015 *and* an OffSite field value of "Yes" (indicating a checked box). If you place conditions in separate fields in the *same* Criteria row of the design grid, all conditions in that row must be met in order for a record to be included in the query results. However, if you place conditions in *different* Criteria rows, a record will be selected if at least one of the conditions is met. If none of the conditions are met, Access does not select the record. When you place conditions in different Criteria rows, you are using the **Or logical operator**. Figure 3-26 illustrates the difference between the And and Or logical operators.

Figure 3-26   **Logical operators And and Or for multiple selection criteria**

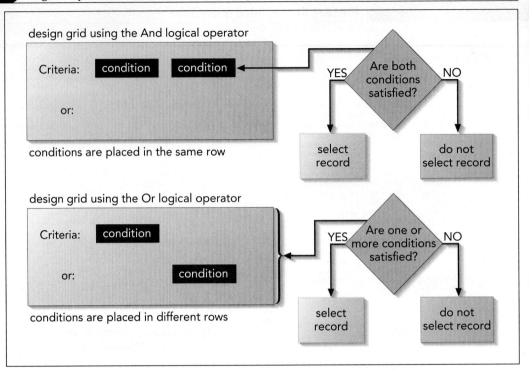

The And Logical Operator

To create the query for Kimberly, you need to use the And logical operator to show only the records for animals that were born on or after 7/1/2015 *and* who have had an off-site visit. You'll create a new query based on the Owner, Animal, and Visit tables to produce the necessary results. In the query design, both conditions you specify will appear in the same Criteria row; therefore, the query will select records only if both conditions are met.

To create a new query using the And logical operator:

▶ **1.** On the ribbon, click the **Create** tab.

▶ **2.** In the Queries group, click the **Query Design** button.

▶ **3.** Add the **Owner, Animal,** and **Visit** tables to the Query window in that order, and then close the Show Table dialog box. Resize all three field lists to display all the field names.

▶ **4.** Add the **AnimalName** and **AnimalBirthDate** fields from the Animal table to the design grid.

▶ **5.** Add the **FirstName, LastName,** and **Phone** fields from the Owner field list to the design grid.

▶ **6.** Add the **VisitDate** and **OffSite** fields from the Visit table to the design grid.

Now you need to enter the two conditions for the query.

▶ **7.** Click the **AnimalBirthDate Criteria** box, and then type **>=7/1/2015**.

▶ **8.** Press the **Tab** key five times to move to the **OffSite** box, type **Yes**, and then press the **Tab** key. Notice that for a Yes/No field such as OffSite, the criteria value is not automatically enclosed in quotes. See Figure 3-27.

| Figure 3-27 | Query to find younger animals who have had off-site visits |

And logical operator with conditions entered in the same row

9. Run the query. The query displays only those records that meet both conditions: an AnimalBirthDate field value greater than or equal to 7/1/2015 *and* an OffSite field value of Yes. 14 records are displayed for 14 different animals. See Figure 3-28.

| Figure 3-28 | Results of query using the And logical operator |

10. On the Quick Access Toolbar, click the **Save** button 🖫, and then save the query as **YoungerAndOffsiteAnimals**.

11. Close the query.

Kimberly meets with staff members to discuss the issue of owners with younger animals being informed of the care center's payment plans and insurance options. After viewing the results of the YoungerAndOffsiteAnimals query, the group agrees that the care center should reach out to the owners of all younger animals regarding these services, because first-time owners are more likely to be unaware of the care center's options. In addition, the care center should contact the owner of any animal that has received an off-site visit, because these owners are less likely to have seen the care center's waiting room literature on these payment options. To help with their planning, Kimberly asks you to produce a list of all animals that were born on or after 7/1/2015 or that received an off-site visit. To create this query, you need to use the Or logical operator.

The Or Logical Operator

To create the query that Kimberly requested, your query must select a record when either one of two conditions is satisfied or when both conditions are satisfied. That is, a record is selected if the AnimalBirthDate field value is greater than or equal to 7/1/2015 *or* if the OffSite field value is Yes *or* if both conditions are met. You will enter the condition for the AnimalBirthDate field in the Criteria row and the condition for the OffSite field in the "or" criteria row, thereby using the Or logical operator.

To display the information, you'll create a new query based on the existing YoungerAndOffsiteAnimals query, since it already contains the necessary fields. Then you'll specify the conditions using the Or logical operator.

To create a new query using the Or logical operator:

1. Open the Navigation Pane. You'll use the shortcut menu to copy and paste the YoungerAndOffsiteAnimals query to create the new query.

2. In the Queries section of the Navigation Pane, right-click **YoungerAndOffsiteAnimals**, and then click **Copy** on the shortcut menu.

3. Right-click the empty area near the bottom of the Navigation Pane, and then click **Paste** on the shortcut menu. The Paste As dialog box opens with the text "Copy Of YoungerAndOffsiteAnimals" in the Query Name box. You'll name the new query "YoungerOrOffsiteAnimals."

4. In the Query Name box, type **YoungerOrOffsiteAnimals** and then press the **Enter** key. The new query appears in the Queries section of the Navigation Pane.

5. In the Navigation Pane, right-click the **YoungerOrOffsiteAnimals** query, click **Design View** on the shortcut menu to open the query in Design view, and then close the Navigation Pane.

   The query already contains all the fields Kimberly wants to view, as well as the first condition—a BirthDate field value greater than or equal to 7/1/2015. Because you want records selected if either the condition for the BirthDate field or the condition for the OffSite field is satisfied, you must delete the existing condition for the OffSite field in the Criteria row and then enter this same condition in the "or" row of the design grid for the OffSite field.

6. In the design grid, delete **Yes** in the OffSite Criteria box.

7. Press the ↓ key to move to the "or" row for the OffSite field, type **Yes**, and then press the **Tab** key. See Figure 3-29.

Figure 3-29	Query window with the Or logical operator

Or logical operator with conditions entered in different rows

To better analyze the data, Kimberly wants the list displayed in descending order by AnimalBirthDate.

▶ **8.** Click the right side of the **AnimalBirthDate Sort** box, and then click **Descending**.

▶ **9.** Run the query. The query datasheet displays only those records that meet either condition: a BirthDate field value greater than or equal to 7/1/2015 *or* an OffSite field value of Yes. The query also returns records that meet both conditions. The query displays a total of 43 records. The records in the query datasheet appear in descending order based on the values in the AnimalBirthDate field. See Figure 3-30.

Figure 3-30   Results of query using the Or logical operator

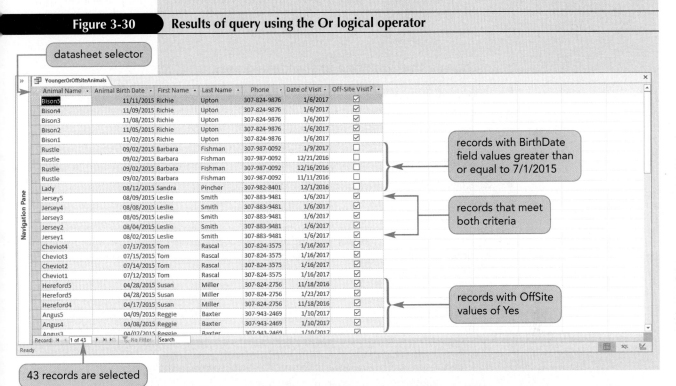

datasheet selector

43 records are selected

records with BirthDate field values greater than or equal to 7/1/2015

records that meet both criteria

records with OffSite values of Yes

INSIGHT

Understanding the Results of Using And vs. Or

When you use the And logical operator to define multiple selection criteria in a query, you *narrow* the results produced by the query because a record must meet more than one condition to be included in the results. For example, the YoungerAndOffsiteAnimals query you created resulted in only 14 records. When you use the Or logical operator, you *broaden* the results produced by the query because a record must meet only one of the conditions to be included in the results. For example, the YoungerOrOffsiteAnimals query you created resulted in 43 records. This is an important distinction to keep in mind when you include multiple selection criteria in queries, so that the queries you create will produce the results you want.

Kimberly would like to spend some time reviewing the results of the YoungerOrOffsiteAnimals query. To make this task easier, she asks you to change how the datasheet is displayed.

Changing a Datasheet's Appearance

You can make many formatting changes to a datasheet to improve its appearance or readability. Many of these modifications are familiar types of changes you can also make in Word documents or Excel spreadsheets, such as modifying the font type, size, color, and the alignment of text. You can also apply different colors to the rows and columns in a datasheet to enhance its appearance.

Modifying the Font Size

Depending on the size of the monitor you are using or the screen resolution, you might need to increase or decrease the size of the font in a datasheet to view more or fewer columns of data. Kimberly asks you to change the font size in the query datasheet from the default 11 points to 14 points so that she can read the text more easily.

To change the font size in the datasheet:

▶ **1.** On the Home tab, in the Text Formatting group, click the **Font Size** arrow, and then click **14**. The font size for the entire datasheet increases to 14 points.

Next, you need to resize the columns to their best fit, so that all field values are displayed. Instead of resizing each column individually, you'll use the datasheet selector to select all the columns and resize them at the same time.

▶ **2.** Click the **datasheet selector**. All the columns in the datasheet are selected.

▶ **3.** Move the pointer to one of the vertical lines separating two columns in the datasheet until the pointer changes to ✛, and then double-click the vertical line. All the columns visible on the screen are resized to their best fit. Scroll down and repeat the resizing, as necessary, to make sure that all field values are fully displayed.

Trouble? If all the columns are not visible on your screen, you need to scroll the datasheet to the right to make sure all field values for all columns are fully displayed. If you need to resize any columns, click a field value first to deselect the columns before resizing an individual column.

▶ **4.** Click any value in the Animal Name column to make it the current field and to deselect the columns in the datasheet.

Changing the Alternate Row Color in a Datasheet

TIP

When choosing a row color, be sure not to select a color that is too dark because it might obscure the data rather than enhance it.

Access uses themes to format the objects in a database. A **theme** is a predefined set of formats including colors, fonts, and other effects that enhance an object's appearance and usability. When you create a database, Access applies the Office theme to objects as you create them. By default, the Office theme formats every other row in a datasheet with a gray background color to distinguish one row from another, making it easier to view and read the contents of a datasheet. The gray alternate row color provides a subtle difference compared to the rows that have the default white color. You can change the alternate row color in a datasheet to something more noticeable using the Alternate Row Color button in the Text Formatting group on the Home tab. Kimberly suggests that you change the alternate row color in the datasheet to see the effect of using this feature.

To change the alternate row color in the datasheet:

1. On the Home tab, in the Text Formatting group, click the **Alternate Row Color button arrow** ⊞ ▾ to display the gallery of color choices. See Figure 3-31.

Figure 3-31   Gallery of color choices for alternate row color

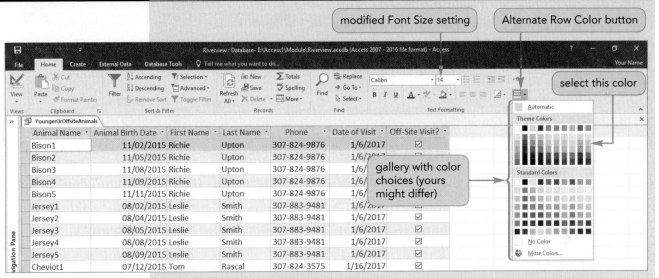

TIP

The name of the color appears in a ScreenTip when you point to a color in the gallery.

The Theme Colors section provides colors from the default Office theme, so that your datasheet's color scheme matches the one in use for the database. The Standard Colors section provides many standard color choices. You might also see a Recent Colors section, with colors that you have recently used in a datasheet. The No Color option, which appears at the bottom of the gallery, sets each row's background color to white. If you want to create a custom color, you can do so using the More Colors option. You'll use one of the theme colors.

2. In the Theme Colors section, click the **Green, Accent 6, Lighter 60%** color (third row, tenth color). The alternate row color is applied to the query datasheet. See Figure 3-32.

Figure 3-32   Datasheet formatted with alternate row color

Every other row in the datasheet uses the selected theme color. Kimberly likes how the datasheet looks with this color scheme, so she asks you to save the query.

3. Save and close the YoungerOrOffsiteAnimals query. The query is saved with both the increased font size and the green alternate row color.

Next, Kimberly turns her attention to some financial aspects of operating the care center. She wants to use the Riverview database to perform calculations. She is considering imposing a 2% late fee on unpaid invoices and wants to know exactly what the late fee charges would be, should she decide to institute such a policy in the future. To produce the information for Kimberly, you need to create a calculated field.

Creating a Calculated Field

In addition to using queries to retrieve, sort, and filter data in a database, you can use a query to perform calculations. To perform a calculation, you define an **expression** containing a combination of database fields, constants, and operators. For numeric expressions, the data types of the database fields must be Number, Currency, or Date/Time; the constants are numbers such as .02 (for the 2% late fee); and the operators can be arithmetic operators (+ − * /) or other specialized operators. In complex expressions, you can enclose calculations in parentheses to indicate which one should be performed first; any calculation within parentheses is completed before calculations outside the parentheses. In expressions without parentheses, Access performs basic calculations using the following order of precedence: multiplication and division before addition and subtraction. When operators have equal precedence, Access calculates them in order from left to right.

To perform a calculation in a query, you add a calculated field to the query. A **calculated field** is a field that displays the results of an expression. A calculated field that you create with an expression appears in a query datasheet or in a form or report; however, it does not exist in a database. When you run a query that contains a calculated field, Access evaluates the expression defined by the calculated field and displays the resulting value in the query datasheet, form, or report.

To enter an expression for a calculated field, you can type it directly in a Field box in the design grid. Alternately, you can open the Zoom box or Expression Builder and use either one to enter the expression. The **Zoom box** is a dialog box that you can use to enter text, expressions, or other values. To use the Zoom box, however, you must know all the parts of the expression you want to create. **Expression Builder** is an Access tool that makes it easy for you to create an expression; it contains a box for entering the expression, an option for displaying and choosing common operators, and one or more lists of expression elements, such as table and field names. Unlike a Field box, which is too narrow to show an entire expression at one time, the Zoom box and Expression Builder are large enough to display longer expressions. In most cases, Expression Builder provides the easiest way to enter expressions because you don't have to know all the parts of the expression; you can choose the necessary elements from the Expression Builder dialog box, which also helps to prevent typing errors.

REFERENCE

Creating a Calculated Field Using Expression Builder

- Create and save the query in which you want to include a calculated field.
- Open the query in Design view.
- In the design grid, click the Field box in which you want to create an expression.
- In the Query Setup group on the Query Tools Design tab, click the Builder button.
- Use the expression elements and common operators to build the expression, or type the expression directly in the expression box.
- Click the OK button.

To produce the information Kimberly wants, you need to create a new query based on the Billing and Visit tables and, in the query, create a calculated field that will multiply each InvoiceAmt field value by .02 to calculate the proposed 2% late fee.

To create the new query:

▶ 1. On the ribbon, click the **Create** tab.

▶ 2. In the Queries group, click the **Query Design** button. The Show Table dialog box opens.

Kimberly wants to see data from both the Visit and Billing tables, so you need to add these two tables to the Query window.

▶ 3. Add the **Visit** and **Billing** tables to the Query window, and resize the field lists as necessary so that all the field names are visible. The field lists appear in the Query window, and the one-to-many relationship between the Visit (primary) and Billing (related) tables is displayed.

▶ 4. Add the following fields to the design grid in the order given: **VisitID**, **AnimalID**, and **VisitDate** from the Visit table; and **InvoiceItem**, **InvoicePaid**, and **InvoiceAmt** from the Billing table.

Kimberly is interested in viewing data only for unpaid invoices because a late fee would apply only to them, so you need to enter the necessary condition for the InvoicePaid field. Recall that InvoicePaid is a Yes/No field. The condition you need to enter is the word "No" in the Criteria box for this field, so that Access will retrieve the records for unpaid invoices only.

▶ 5. In the **InvoicePaid Criteria box**, type **No**. As soon as you type the letter "N," a menu appears with options for entering various functions for the criteria. You don't need to enter a function, so you can close this menu.

▶ 6. Press the **Esc** key to close the menu.

You must close the menu or you'll enter a function, which will cause an error.

▶ 7. Press the **Tab** key. The query name you'll use will indicate that the data is for unpaid invoices, so you don't need to include the InvoicePaid values in the query results.

▶ 8. Click the **InvoicePaid Show** check box to remove the checkmark.

▶ 9. Save the query with the name **UnpaidInvoiceLateFee**.

Now you can use Expression Builder to create the calculated field for the InvoiceAmt field.

To create the calculated field:

1. Click the blank Field box to the right of the InvoiceAmt field. This field will contain the expression.

2. On the Query Tools Design tab, in the Query Setup group, click the **Builder** button. The Expression Builder dialog box opens.

The insertion point is positioned in the large box at the top of the dialog box, ready for you to enter the expression. The Expression Categories section of the dialog box lists the fields from the query so you can include them in the expression. The Expression Elements section contains options for including other elements in the expression, including functions, constants, and operators. If the expression you're entering is a simple one, you can type it in the box; if it's more complex, you can use the options in the Expression Elements section to help you build the expression.

The expression for the calculated field will multiply the InvoiceAmt field values by the numeric constant .02 (which represents a 2% late fee).

3. In the Expression Categories section of the dialog box, double-click **InvoiceAmt**. The field name is added to the expression box, within brackets and with a space following it. In an expression, all field names must be enclosed in brackets.

Next you need to enter the multiplication operator, which is the asterisk (*), followed by the constant.

4. Type * (an asterisk) and then type **.02**. You have finished entering the expression. See Figure 3-33.

TIP

You must first save and name a query in order for its fields to be listed in the Expression Categories section.

Figure 3-33   Completed expression for the calculated field

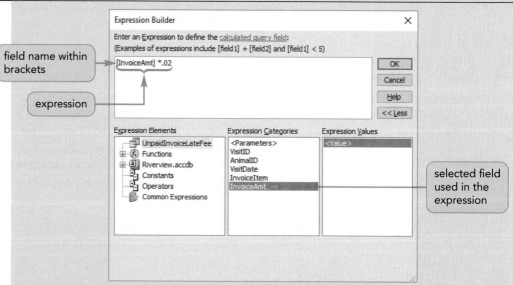

If you're not sure which operator to use, you can click Operators in the Expression Elements section to display a list of available operators in the center section of the dialog box.

5. Click the **OK** button. The Expression Builder dialog box closes, and the expression is added to the design grid in the Field box for the calculated field.

When you create a calculated field, Access uses the default name "Expr1" for the field. You need to specify a more meaningful field name so it will appear in the query results. You'll enter the name "LateFee," which better describes the field's contents.

6. Click to the left of the text "Expr1:" at the beginning of the expression, and then press the **Delete** key five times to delete the text **Expr1**. *Do not delete the colon*; it is needed to separate the calculated field name from the expression.

7. Type **LateFee**. Next, you'll set this field's Caption property so that the field name will appear as "Late Fee" in the query datasheet.

8. On the Query Tools Design tab, in the Show/Hide group, click the **Property Sheet** button. The Property Sheet for the current field, LateFee, opens on the right side of the window. See Figure 3-34.

| Figure 3-34 | Property Sheet for the calculated field |

9. In the Property sheet, click in the Caption box, type **Late Fee** and then close the Property Sheet.

10. Run the query. The query datasheet is displayed and contains the specified fields and the calculated field with the caption "Late Fee." See Figure 3-35.

Figure 3-35   **Datasheet displaying the calculated field**

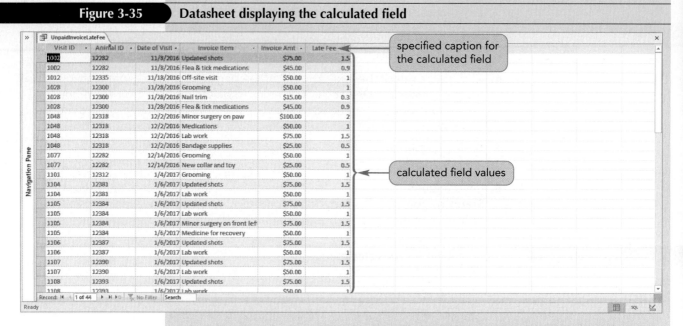

Trouble? If a dialog box opens noting that the expression contains invalid syntax, you might not have included the required colon in the expression. Click the OK button to close the dialog box, resize the column in the design grid that contains the calculated field to its best fit, change your expression to LateFee: [InvoiceAmt]*0.02 and then repeat Step 10.

The LateFee field values are currently displayed without dollar signs and decimal places. Kimberly wants these values to be displayed in the same format as the InvoiceAmt field values for consistency.

Formatting a Calculated Field

You can specify a particular format for a calculated field, just as you can for any field, by modifying its properties. Next, you'll change the format of the LateFee calculated field so that all values appear in the Currency format.

To format the calculated field:

1. Switch to Design view.

2. In the design grid, click in the **LateFee** calculated field to make it the current field, if necessary.

3. On the Query Tools Design tab, in the Show/Hide group, click the **Property Sheet** button to open the Property Sheet for the calculated field.

   You need to change the Format property to Currency, which displays values with a dollar sign and two decimal places.

4. In the Property Sheet, click the right side of the **Format** box to display the list of formats, and then click **Currency**.

5. Close the Property Sheet, and then run the query. The amounts in the LateFee calculated field are now displayed with dollar signs and two decimal places.

6. Save and close the UnpaidInvoiceLateFee query.

PROSKILLS

Problem Solving: Creating a Calculated Field vs. Using the Calculated Field Data Type

You can also create a calculated field using the Calculated Field data type, which lets you store the result of an expression as a field in a table. However, database experts caution users against storing calculations in a table for several reasons. First, storing calculated data in a table consumes valuable space and increases the size of the database. The preferred approach is to use a calculated field in a query; with this approach, the result of the calculation is not stored in the database—it is produced only when you run the query—and it is always current. Second, the Calculated Field data type provides limited options for creating a calculation, whereas a calculated field in a query provides more functions and options for creating expressions. Third, including a field in a table using the Calculated Field data type limits your options if you need to upgrade the database at some point to a more robust DBMS, such as Oracle or SQL Server, that doesn't support this data type; you would need to redesign your database to eliminate this data type. Finally, most database experts agree that including a field in a table whose value is dependent on other fields in the table violates database design principles. To avoid such problems, it's best to create a query that includes a calculated field to perform the calculation you want, instead of creating a field in a table that uses the Calculated Field data type.

To better analyze costs at Riverview Veterinary Care Center, Kimberly wants to view more detailed information about invoices for animal care. Specifically, she would like to know the minimum, average, and maximum invoice amounts. She asks you to determine these statistics from data in the Billing table.

Using Aggregate Functions

You can calculate statistical information, such as totals and averages, on the records displayed in a table datasheet or selected by a query. To do this, you use the Access aggregate functions. **Aggregate functions** perform arithmetic operations on selected records in a database. Figure 3-36 lists the most frequently used aggregate functions.

Figure 3-36   Frequently used aggregate functions

Aggregate Function	Determines	Data Types Supported
Average	Average of the field values for the selected records	AutoNumber, Currency, Date/Time, Number
Count	Number of records selected	AutoNumber, Currency, Date/Time, Long Text, Number, OLE Object, Short Text, Yes/No
Maximum	Highest field value for the selected records	AutoNumber, Currency, Date/Time, Number, Short Text
Minimum	Lowest field value for the selected records	AutoNumber, Currency, Date/Time, Number, Short Text
Sum	Total of the field values for the selected records	AutoNumber, Currency, Date/Time, Number

Working with Aggregate Functions Using the Total Row

If you want to quickly perform a calculation using an aggregate function in a table or query datasheet, you can use the Totals button in the Records group on the Home tab. When you click this button, a row labeled "Total" appears at the bottom of the datasheet. You can then choose one of the aggregate functions for a field in the datasheet, and the results of the calculation will be displayed in the Total row for that field.

Kimberly wants to know the total amount of all invoices for the care center. You can quickly display this amount using the Sum function in the Total row in the Billing table datasheet.

To display the total amount of all invoices in the Billing table:

▶ **1.** Open the Navigation Pane, open the **Billing** table in Datasheet view, and then close the Navigation Pane.

▶ **2.** Make sure the Home tab is displayed.

▶ **3.** In the Records group, click the **Totals** button. A row with the label "Total" is added to the bottom of the datasheet.

▶ **4.** Scroll to the bottom of the datasheet to view the Total row. You want to display the sum of all the values in the Invoice Amt column.

▶ **5.** In the Total row, click the **Invoice Amt** field. An arrow appears on the left side of the field.

▶ **6.** Click the **arrow** to display the menu of aggregate functions. The functions displayed depend on the data type of the current field; in this case, the menu provides functions for a Currency field. See Figure 3-37.

| Figure 3-37 | Using aggregate functions in the Total row |

▶ **7.** Click **Sum** in the menu. All the values in the Invoice Amt column are added, and the total $12,015.00 appears in the Total row for the column.

Kimberly doesn't want to change the Billing table to always display this total. You can remove the Total row by clicking the Totals button again; this button works as a toggle to switch between the display of the Total row with the results of any calculations in the row, and the display of the datasheet without this row.

▶ **8.** In the Records group, click the **Totals** button. The Total row is removed from the datasheet.

▶ **9.** Close the Billing table without saving the changes.

Kimberly wants to know the minimum, average, and maximum invoice amounts for Riverview Veterinary Care Center. To produce this information for Kimberly, you need to use aggregate functions in a query.

Creating Queries with Aggregate Functions

Aggregate functions operate on the records that meet a query's selection criteria. You specify an aggregate function for a specific field, and the appropriate operation applies to that field's values for the selected records.

To display the minimum, average, and maximum of all the invoice amounts in the Billing table, you will use the Minimum, Average, and Maximum aggregate functions for the InvoiceAmt field.

To calculate the minimum of all invoice amounts:

▶ **1.** Create a new query in Design view, add the **Billing** table to the Query window, and then resize the Billing field list to display all fields.

To perform the three calculations on the InvoiceAmt field, you need to add the field to the design grid three times.

▶ **2.** In the Billing field list, double-click **InvoiceAmt** three times to add three copies of the field to the design grid.

You need to select an aggregate function for each InvoiceAmt field. When you click the Totals button in the Show/Hide group on the Design tab, a row labeled "Total" is added to the design grid. The Total row provides a list of the aggregate functions that you can select.

▶ **3.** On the Query Tools Design tab, in the Show/Hide group, click the **Totals** button. A new row labeled "Total" appears between the Table and Sort rows in the design grid. The default entry for each field in the Total row is the Group By operator, which you will learn about later in this module. See Figure 3-38.

Figure 3-38 **Total row inserted in the design grid**

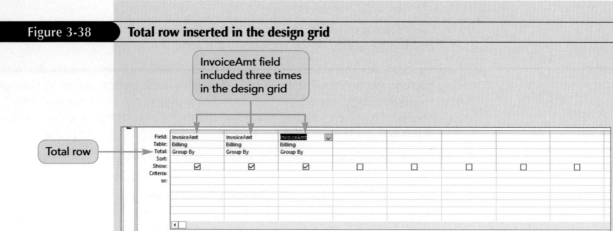

InvoiceAmt field
included three times
in the design grid

Total row

In the Total row, you specify the aggregate function you want to use for a field.

4. Click the right side of the first column's **Total** box, and then click **Min**.
This field will calculate the minimum amount of all the InvoiceAmt field values.

When you run the query, Access automatically will assign a datasheet column
name of "MinOfInvoiceAmt" for this field. You can change the datasheet
column name to a more descriptive or readable name by entering the name you
want in the Field box. However, you must also keep the InvoiceAmt field name
in the Field box because it identifies the field to use in the calculation. The Field
box will contain the datasheet column name you specify followed by the field
name (InvoiceAmt) with a colon separating the two names.

5. In the first column's Field box, click to the left of InvoiceAmt, and then type
MinimumInvoiceAmt: (including the colon).

Be sure to type the colon following the name or the query will not work correctly.

6. Resize the column so that you can see the complete field name,
MinimumInvoiceAmt:InvoiceAmt.

Next, you need to set the Caption property for this field so that the field
name appears with spaces between words in the query datatsheet.

7. On the Query Tools Design tab, in the Show/Hide group, click the **Property
Sheet** button to open the Property Sheet for the current field.

8. In the Caption box, type **Minimum Invoice Amt**, and then close the
Property Sheet.

You'll follow the same process to complete the query by calculating the average and
maximum invoice amounts.

To calculate the average and maximum of all invoice amounts:

1. Click the right side of the second column's **Total** box, and then click **Avg**.
This field will calculate the average of all the InvoiceAmt field values.

2. In the second column's Field box, click to the left of InvoiceAmt, and then
type **AverageInvoiceAmt:**.

3. Resize the second column to fully display the field name,
AverageInvoiceAmt:InvoiceAmt.

4. Open the Property Sheet for the current field, and then set its Caption property to **Average Invoice Amt**.

5. Click the right side of the third column's **Total** box, and then click **Max**. This field will calculate the maximum amount of all the InvoiceAmt field values.

6. In the third column's Field box, click to the left of InvoiceAmt, and then type **MaximumInvoiceAmt:**.

7. Resize the third column to fully display the field name, MaximumInvoiceAmt:InvoiceAmt.

8. In the Property Sheet, set the Caption property to **Maximum Invoice Amt**, and then close the Property Sheet. See Figure 3-39.

Figure 3-39	Query with aggregate functions entered

functions entered and columns resized

Trouble? Carefully compare your field names to those shown in the figure to make sure they match exactly; otherwise the query will not work correctly.

9. Run the query. One record displays containing the three aggregate function results. The single row of summary statistics represents calculations based on all the records selected for the query—in this case, all 202 records in the Billing table.

10. Resize all columns to their best fit so that the column names are fully displayed, and then click the field value in the first column to deselect the value and view the results. See Figure 3-40.

Figure 3-40	Result of the query using aggregate functions

11. Save the query as **InvoiceAmtStatistics**.

Kimberly would like to view the same invoice amount statistics (minimum, average, and maximum) as they relate to both appointments at the care center and off-site visits.

Using Record Group Calculations

In addition to calculating statistical information on all or selected records in selected tables, you can calculate statistics for groups of records. The **Group By operator** divides the selected records into groups based on the values in the specified field. Those records with the same value for the field are grouped together, and the datasheet displays one record for each group. Aggregate functions, which appear in the other columns of the design grid, provide statistical information for each group.

To create a query for Kimberly's latest request, you will modify the current query by adding the OffSite field and assigning the Group By operator to it. The Group By operator will display the statistical information grouped by the values of the OffSite field for all the records in the query datasheet. To create the new query, you will save the InvoiceAmtStatistics query with a new name, keeping the original query intact, and then modify the new query.

To create a new query with the Group By operator:

1. Display the InvoiceAmtStatistics query in Design view. Because the query is open, you can use Backstage view to save it with a new name, keeping the original query intact.

2. Click the **File** tab to display Backstage view, and then click **Save As** in the navigation bar. The Save As screen opens.

3. In the File Types section on the left, click **Save Object As**. The right side of the screen changes to display options for saving the current database object as a new object.

4. Click the **Save As** button. The Save As dialog box opens, indicating that you are saving a copy of the InvoiceAmtStatistics query.

5. Type **InvoiceAmtStatisticsByOffsite** to replace the selected name, and then press the **Enter** key. The new query is saved with the name you specified and appears in Design view.

   You need to add the OffSite field to the query. This field is in the Visit table. To include another table in an existing query, you open the Show Table dialog box.

TIP

You could also open the Navigation Pane and drag the Visit table from the pane to the Query window.

6. On the Query Tools Design tab, in the Query Setup group, click the **Show Table** button to open the Show Table dialog box.

7. Add the **Visit** table to the Query window, and then resize the Visit field list if necessary.

8. Drag the **OffSite** field from the Visit field list to the first column in the design grid. When you release the mouse button, the OffSite field appears in the design grid's first column, and the existing fields shift to the right. Group By, the default option in the Total row, appears for the OffSite field.

9. Run the query. The query displays two records—one for each OffSite group, Yes and No. Each record contains the OffSite field value for the group and the three aggregate function values. The summary statistics represent calculations based on the 202 records in the Billing table. See Figure 3-41.

Figure 3-41   **Aggregate functions grouped by OffSite**

record groups

aggregate function
results

Kimberly notes that the minimum and average invoice amounts for off-site
visits are slightly higher than those for visits to the care center, while the
maximum amount is higher for visits to the care center.

▶ **10.** Save and close the query.

▶ **11.** Open the Navigation Pane.

You have created and saved many queries in the Riverview database. The Navigation
Pane provides options for opening and managing the queries you've created, as well as
the other objects in the database, such as tables, forms, and reports.

Working with the Navigation Pane

As noted earlier, the Navigation Pane is the main area for working with the objects
in a database. As you continue to create objects in your database, you might want to
display and work with them in different ways. The Navigation Pane provides options
for grouping database objects in various ways to suit your needs. For example, you
might want to view only the queries created for a certain table or all the query objects
in the database.

TIP

You can hide the display
of a group's objects by
clicking the button to the
right of the group name;
click the button again to
expand the group and
display its objects.

As you know, the Navigation Pane divides database objects into categories. Each
category contains groups, and each group contains one or more objects. The default
category is **Object Type**, which arranges objects by type—tables, queries, forms, and
reports. The default group is **All Access Objects**, which displays all objects in the
database. You can also choose to display only one type of object, such as tables.

The default group name, All Access Objects, appears at the top of the Navigation
Pane. Currently, each object type—Tables, Queries, Forms, and Reports—is displayed
as a heading, and the objects related to each type are listed below the heading.
To group objects differently, you can select another category by using the Navigation
Pane menu. You'll try this next.

To group objects differently in the Navigation Pane:

▶ **1.** At the top of the Navigation Pane, click the **All Access Objects** button ⊙.
A menu opens with options for choosing different categories and groups.
See Figure 3-42.

Figure 3-42   Navigation Pane menu

default category
selected

category options

default group
selected

group options

The top section of the menu provides the options for choosing a different
category. The Object Type category has a checkmark next to it, signifying
that it is the currently selected category. The lower section of the menu
provides options for choosing a different group; these options might change
depending on the selected category.

2. In the Navigate To Category section, click **Tables and Related Views**.
   The Navigation Pane is now grouped into categories of tables, and each
   table in the database—Visit, Billing, Owner, and Animal—is its own group.
   All database objects related to a table are listed below the table's name.
   Notice the UnpaidInvoiceLateFee query is based on both the Visit and Billing
   tables, so it is listed in the group for both tables. See Figure 3-43.

Figure 3-43   Database objects grouped by table in the Navigation Pane

You can also choose to display the objects for only one table to better focus on that table.

3. At the top of the Navigation Pane, click the **All Tables** button to display the Navigation Pane menu, and then click **Owner**. The Navigation Pane now shows only the objects related to the Owner table—the table itself plus the five queries you created that include fields from the Owner table.

4. At the top of the Navigation Pane, click the **Owner** button, and then click **Object Type** to return to the default display of the Navigation Pane.

5. Compact and repair the Riverview database, and then close the database.

   Trouble? If a dialog box opens and warns that this action will cause Microsoft Access to empty the Clipboard, click the Yes button to continue.

The default All Access Objects category is a predefined category. You can also create custom categories to group objects in the way that best suits how you want to manage your database objects. As you continue to build a database and the list of objects grows, creating a custom category can help you to work more efficiently with the objects in the database.

The queries you've created and saved will help Kimberly and her staff to monitor and analyze the business activity of Riverview Veterinary Care Center and its patients. Now any staff member can run the queries at any time, modify them as needed, or use them as the basis for designing new queries to meet additional information requirements.

REVIEW

Session 3.2 Quick Check

1. A(n) _____ is a criterion, or rule, that determines which records are selected for a query datasheet.

2. In the design grid, where do you place the conditions for two different fields when you use the And logical operator, and where do you place them when you use the Or logical operator?

3. To perform a calculation in a query, you define a(n) _____ containing a combination of database fields, constants, and operators.

4. Which Access tool do you use to create an expression for a calculated field in a query?

5. What is an aggregate function?

6. The _____ operator divides selected records into groups based on the values in a field.

7. What is the default category for the display of objects in the Navigation Pane?

Review Assignments

PRACTICE

Data File needed for the Review Assignments: Vendor.accdb *(cont. from Module 2)*

Kimberly asks you to update some information in the Vendor database and also to retrieve specific information from the database. Complete the following:

1. Open the **Vendor** database you created and worked with in previous modules, and then click the Enable Content button next to the security warning, if necessary.

2. Open the **Supplier** table in Datasheet view, and then change the following field values for the record with the Supplier ID GGF099: Address to **738 26th St**, Contact Phone to **321-296-1958**, Contact First Name to **Carmela**, and Contact Last Name to **Montoya**. Close the table.

3. Create a query based on the Supplier table. Include the following fields in the query, in the order shown: Company, Category, ContactFirst, ContactLast, Phone, and City. Sort the query in ascending order based on the Category field values. Save the query as **ContactList**, and then run the query.

4. Use the ContactList query datasheet to update the Supplier table by changing the Phone field value for A+ Labs to **402-495-3957**.

5. Change the size of the font in the ContactList query datasheet to 12 points. Resize columns, as necessary, so that all field values and column headings are visible.

6. Change the alternate row color in the ContactList query datasheet to the Theme Color named Gold, Accent 4, Lighter 60%, and then save and close the query.

7. Create a query based on the Supplier and Product tables. Select the Company, Category, and State fields from the Supplier table, and the ProductName, Price, Units, and Weight fields from the Product table. Sort the query results in descending order based on price. Select only those records with a Category field value of Supplies, but do not display the Category field values in the query results. Save the query as **SupplyProducts**, run the query, and then close it.

8. Create a query that lists all products that cost more than $50 and are temperature controlled. Display the following fields from the Product table in the query results: ProductID, ProductName, Price, Units, and Sterile. (*Hint*: The TempControl field is a Yes/No field that should not appear in the query results.) Save the query as **HighPriceAndTempControl**, run the query, and then close it.

9. Create a query that lists information about suppliers who sell equipment or sterile products. Include the Company, Category, ContactFirst, and ContactLast fields from the Supplier table; and the ProductName, Price, TempControl, and Sterile fields from the Product table. Save the query as **EquipmentOrSterile**, run the query, and then close it.

10. Create a query that lists all resale products, along with a 10% markup amount based on the price of the product. Include the Company field from the Supplier table and the following fields from the Product table in the query: ProductID, ProductName, and Price. Save the query as **ResaleProductsWithMarkup**. Display the discount in a calculated field named **Markup** that determines a 10% markup based on the Price field values. Set the Caption property **Markup** for the calculated field. Display the query results in descending order by Price. Save and run the query.

11. Modify the format of the Markup field in the ResaleProductsWithMarkup query so that it uses the Standard format and two decimal places. Run the query, resize all columns in the datasheet to their best fit, and then save and close the query.

12. Create a query that calculates the lowest, highest, and average prices for all products using the field names **MinimumPrice**, **MaximumPrice**, and **AveragePrice**, respectively. Set the Caption property for each field to include a space between the two words in the field name. Run the query, resize all columns in the datasheet to their best fit, save the query as **PriceStatistics**, and then close it.

13. In the Navigation Pane, copy the PriceStatistics query, and then rename the copied query as **PriceStatisticsBySupplier**.

14. Modify the PriceStatisticsBySupplier query so that the records are grouped by the Company field in the Supplier table. The Company field should appear first in the query datasheet. Save and run the query, and then close it.

15. Compact and repair the Vendor database, and then close it.

Case Problem 1

APPLY

Data File needed for this Case Problem: Beauty.accdb *(cont. from Module 2)*

Beauty To Go Sue Miller needs to modify a few records in the Beauty database and analyze the data for customers that subscribe to her business. To help Sue, you'll update the Beauty database and create queries to answer her questions. Complete the following:

1. Open the **Beauty** database you created and worked with in previous modules, and then click the Enable Content button next to the security warning, if necessary.

2. In the **Member** table, find the record for MemberID 2163, and then change the Street value to **844 Sanford Ln** and the Zip to **32804**.

3. In the **Member** table, find the record for MemberID 2169, and then delete the record. Close the Member table.

4. Create a query that lists customers who did not have to pay a fee when they signed up for their current option. In the query results, display the FirstName, LastName, and OptionBegin fields from the Member table, and the OptionCost field from the Option table. Sort the records in ascending order by the option start date. Select records only for customers whose fees were waived. (*Hint*: The FeeWaived field is a Yes/No field that should not appear in the query results.) Save the query as **NoFees**, and then run the query.

5. Use the NoFees query datasheet to update the Member table by changing the Last Name value for Gilda Packson to **Washington**.

6. Use the NoFees query datasheet to display the total Option Cost for the selected members. Save and close the query.

7. Create a query that lists the MemberID, FirstName, LastName, OptionBegin, OptionDescription, and OptionCost fields for customers who signed up with Beauty To Go between January 1, 2017 and January 31, 2017. Save the query as **JanuaryOptions**, run the query, and then close it.

8. Create a query that lists all customers who live in Celebration and whose options end on or after 4/1/2017. Display the following fields from the Member table in the query results: MemberID, FirstName, LastName, Phone, and OptionEnd. (*Hint*: The City field values should not appear in the query results.) Sort the query results in ascending order by last name. Save the query as **CelebrationAndEndDate**, run the query, and then close it.

9. Copy and paste the CelebrationAndEndDate query to create a new query named **CelebrationOrEndDate**. Modify the new query so that it lists all members who live in Celebration or whose memberships expire on or after 4/1/2017. Display the City field values in the query results following the Phone field values, and sort the query results in ascending order by city (this should be the only sort in the query). Save and run the query.

10. Change the size of the font in the CelebrationOrEndDate query datasheet to 14 points. Resize columns, as necessary, so that all field values and column headings are visible.

11. Change the alternate row color in the CelebrationOrEndDate query datasheet to the Theme Color named Green, Accent 6, Lighter 80%, and then save and close the query.

12. Create a query that calculates the lowest, highest, and average cost for all options using the field names **LowestCost**, **HighestCost**, and **AverageCost**, respectively. Set the Caption property for each field to include a space between the two words in the field name. Run the query, resize all columns in the datasheet to their best fit, save the query as **CostStatistics**, and then close it.

13. Copy and paste the CostStatistics query to create a new query named **CostStatisticsByZip**.

14. Modify the CostStatisticsByZip query to display the same statistics grouped by Zip, with Zip appearing as the first field. (*Hint*: Add the Member table to the query.) Run the query, and then save and close it.

15. Compact and repair the Beauty database, and then close it.

Case Problem 2

Data File needed for this Case Problem: Programming.accdb (*cont. from Module 2*)

Programming Pros   After reviewing the Programming database, Brent Hovis wants to modify some records and then view specific information about the students, tutors, and contracts for his tutoring services company. He asks you to update and query the Programming database to perform these tasks. Complete the following:

1. Open the **Programming** database you created and worked with in previous modules, and then click the Enable Content button next to the security warning, if necessary.

2. In the **Tutor** table, change the following information for the record with TutorID 1048: Major is **Computer Science** and Year In School is **Graduate**. Close the table.

3. In the **Student** table, find the record with the StudentID RAM4025, and then delete the related record in the subdatasheet for this student. Delete the record for StudentID RAM4025, and then close the Student table.

4. Create a query based on the Student table that includes the LastName, FirstName, and CellPhone fields, in that order. Save the query as **StudentCellList**, and then run the query.

5. In the results of the StudentCellList query, change the cell phone number for Hidalgo Hickman to **919-301-2209**. Close the query.

6. Create a query based on the Tutor and Contract tables. Display the LastName field from the Tutor table, and the StudentID, ContractDate, SessionType, Length, and Cost fields, in that order, from the Contract table. Sort first in ascending order by the tutor's last name, and then in ascending order by the StudentID. Save the query as **SessionsByTutor**, run the query, and then close it.

7. Copy and paste the SessionsByTutor query to create a new query named **GroupSessions**. Modify the new query so that it displays the same information for records with a Group session type only. Do not display the SessionType field values in the query results. Save and run the query, and then close it.

8. Create and save a query that produces the results shown in Figure 3-44. Close the query when you are finished.

Figure 3-44 **RaleighPrivate query results**

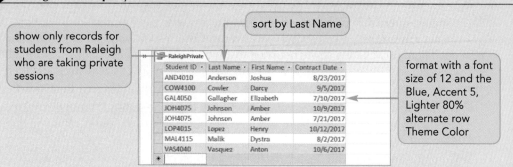

show only records for students from Raleigh who are taking private sessions

sort by Last Name

format with a font size of 12 and the Blue, Accent 5, Lighter 80% alternate row Theme Color

9. Create and save a query that produces the results shown in Figure 3-45. Close the query when you are finished.

Figure 3-45 **CaryOrSemi query results**

show only records for students from Cary or students taking semi-private sessions

sort in descending order by Contract Date

Total row shows the sum of the Cost values

10. Create and save a query to display statistics for the Cost field, as shown in Figure 3-46. Close the query when you are finished.

Figure 3-46 **CostStatistics query results**

set captions to include spaces between words

format values as Standard with two decimal places

11. Copy and paste the CostStatistics query to create a new query named **CostStatisticsByCity**.

12. Modify the CostStatisticsByCity query to display the same statistics grouped by City, with City appearing as the first field. (*Hint*: Add the Student table to the query.) Run the query, and then save and close it.

13. Compact and repair the Programming database, and then close it.

Case Problem 3

Data File needed for this Case Problem: Center.accdb (*cont. from Module 2*)

Diane's Community Center   Diane Coleman needs to modify some records in the Center database, and then she wants to find specific information about the patrons, donations, and auction items for her not-for-profit community center. Diane asks you to help her update the database and create queries to find the information she needs. Complete the following:

1. Open the **Center** database you created and worked with in previous modules, and then click the Enable Content button next to the security warning, if necessary.

2. In the **Patron** table, delete the record with PatronID 3024. (*Hint*: Delete the related records in the Donation subdatasheet first.) Close the Patron table without saving changes to the table layout.

3. Create a query based on the Auction and Donation tables that includes the AuctionID, DonationID, DonationDate, and Description fields, in that order. Save the query as **AuctionItemsByDate**, and then run it.

4. Modify the AuctionItemsByDate query design so that it sorts records in ascending order first by DonationDate and then by Description. Save and run the query.

5. In the AuctionItemsByDate query datasheet, find the record for the auction item with Auction ID 250, and then change the description for this item to **New scooter**. Close the query.

6. Create a query that displays the PatronID, FirstName, and LastName fields from the Patron table, and the Description and DonationValue fields from the Donation table for all donations over $150. Sort the query in ascending order by donation value. Save the query as **LargeDonations**, run the query, and then close it.

7. Copy and paste the LargeDonations query to create a new query named **LargeCashDonations**.

⊕ **Explore** 8. Modify the LargeCashDonations query to display only those records with donations valued at more than $150 in cash. Do not include the Description field values in the query results. Use the query datasheet to calculate the average cash donation. Save and close the query.

9. Create a query that displays the PatronID, FirstName, and LastName fields from the Patron table, and the AuctionID, AuctionDate, and MinPrice fields from the Auction table. Specify that the results show records for only those items with a minimum price greater than $150. Save the query as **ExpensiveAuctionItems**, and then run the query.

10. Filter the results of the ExpensiveAuctionItems query datasheet to display records with an auction date of 10/14/2017 only.

⊕ **Explore** 11. Format the datasheet of the ExpensiveAuctionItems query so that it does not display gridlines, uses an alternate row Standard Color of Maroon 2, and displays a font size of 12. (*Hint*: Use the Gridlines button in the Text Formatting group on the Home tab to select the appropriate gridlines option.) Resize the columns to display the complete field names and values, if necessary. Save and close the query.

⊕ **Explore** 12. Create a query that displays the PatronID, FirstName, and LastName fields from the Patron table, and the Description, DonationDate, and DonationValue fields from the Donation table. Specify that the query include records for noncash donations only or for donations made in the month of September 2017. Sort the records first in ascending order by the patron's last name, and then in descending order by the donation value. Save the query as **NonCashOrSeptemberDonations**, run the query, and then close it.

13. Copy and paste the NonCashOrSeptemberDonations query to create a new query named **DonationsAfterStorageCharge**.

⊕ **Explore** 14. Modify the DonationsAfterStorageCharge query so that it displays records for noncash donations made on all dates. Create a calculated field named **NetDonation** that displays the results of subtracting $3.50 from the DonationValue field values to account for the cost of storing each noncash donated item. Set the Caption property **Net Donation** for the calculated field. Display the results in ascending order by donation value and not sorted on any other field. Run the query, and then modify it to format both the DonationValue field and the calculated field as Currency with two decimal places. Run the query again, and resize the columns in the datasheet to their best fit, as necessary. Save and close the query.

⊕ **Explore** 15. Create a query based on the **Donation** table that displays the sum, average, and count of the DonationValue field for all donations. Then complete the following:

a. Specify field names of **TotalDonations**, **AverageDonation**, and **NumberOfDonations**. Then specify captions to include spaces between words.

b. Save the query as **DonationStatistics**, and then run it. Resize the query datasheet columns to their best fit.

c. Modify the field properties so that the values in the Total Donations and Average Donation columns display two decimal places and the Standard format. Run the query again, and then save and close the query.

d. Copy and paste the DonationStatistics query to create a new query named **DonationStatisticsByDescription**.

e. Modify the DonationStatisticsByDescription query to display the sum, average, and count of the DonationValue field for all donations grouped by Description, with Description appearing as the first field. Sort the records in descending order by Total Donations. Save, run, and then close the query.

16. Compact and repair the Center database, and then close it.

Case Problem 4

Data Files needed for this Case Problem: Appalachia.accdb *(cont. from Module 2)* and HikeApp.accdb

Hike Appalachia   Molly and Bailey Johnson need your help to maintain and analyze data about the hikers, reservations, and tours for their hiking tour business. Additionally, you'll troubleshoot some problems in another database containing tour information. Complete the following:

1. Open the **Appalachia** database you created and worked with in previous modules, and then click the Enable Content button next to the security warning, if necessary.

2. In the **Hiker** table, change the phone number for Wilbur Sanders to **828-910-2058**, and then close the table.

3. Create a query based on the Tour table that includes the TourName, Hours, PricePerPerson, and TourType fields, in that order. Sort in ascending order based on the PricePerPerson field values. Save the query as **ToursByPrice**, and then run the query.

TROUBLESHOOT

4. Use the ToursByPrice query datasheet to display the total Price Per Person for the tours. Save and close the query.

5. Create a query that displays the HikerLast, City, and State fields from the Hiker table, and the ReservationID, TourDate, and People fields from the Reservation table. Save the query as **HikerTourDates**, and then run the query. Change the alternate row color in the query datasheet to the Theme Color Blue, Accent 1, Lighter 80%. In Datasheet view, use an AutoFilter to sort the query results from oldest to newest Tour Date. Save and close the query.

6. Create a query that displays the HikerFirst, HikerLast, City, ReservationID, TourID, and TourDate fields for all guests from North Carolina (NC). Do not include the State field in the query results. Sort the query in ascending order by the guest's last name. Save the query as **NorthCarolinaHikers** and then run it. Close the query.

7. Create a query that displays data from all three tables in the database as follows: the HikerLast, City, and State fields from the Hiker table; the TourDate field from the Reservation table; and the TourName and TourType fields from the Tour table. Specify that the query select only those records for guests from West Virginia (WV) or guests who are taking climbing tours. Sort the query in ascending order by Tour Name. Save the query as **WestVirginiaOrClimbing** and then run the query. Resize datasheet columns to their best fit, as necessary, and then save and close the query.

8. Copy and paste the **WestVirginiaOrClimbing** query to create a new query named **SouthCarolinaAndSeptember**.

9. Modify the **SouthCarolinaAndSeptember** query to select all guests from South Carolina (SC) who are taking a tour starting sometime in the month of September 2017. Do not include the State field values in the query results. Run the query. Resize datasheet columns to their best fit, as necessary, and then save and close the query.

10. Create a query that displays the ReservationID, TourDate, and People fields from the Reservation table, and the TourName and PricePerPerson fields from the Tour table for all reservations with a People field value greater than 1. Save the query as **ReservationCosts**. Add a field to the query named **TotalCost** that displays the results of multiplying the People field values by the PricePerPerson field values. Set the Caption property **Total Cost** for the calculated field. Display the results in descending order by TotalCost. Run the query. Modify the query by formatting the TotalCost field to show 0 decimal places. Run the query, resize datasheet columns to their best fit, as necessary, and then save and close the query.

11. Create a query based on the Tour table that determines the minimum, average, and maximum price per person for all tours. Then complete the following:

    a. Specify field names of **LowestPrice**, **AveragePrice**, and **HighestPrice**.

    b. Set the Caption property for each field to include a space between the two words in the field name.

    c. Save the query as **PriceStatistics**, and then run the query.

    d. In Design view, specify the Standard format and two decimal places for each column.

    e. Run the query, resize all the datasheet columns to their best fit, save your changes, and then close the query.

    f. Create a copy of the PriceStatistics query named **PriceStatisticsByTourType**.

    g. Modify the PriceStatisticsByTourType query to display the price statistics grouped by TourType, with TourType appearing as the first field. Save your changes, and then run and close the query.

    h. Compact and repair the Appalachia database, and then close it.

⚙ **Troubleshoot** 12. Open the **HikeApp** database located in the Access1 > Case4 folder provided with your Data Files, and then click the Enable Content button next to the security warning, if necessary. Run the ReservationByDateAndState query in the HikeApp database. The query is not producing the desired results. Fix the query so that the data from the Reservation table is listed first and the data is sorted only by TourDate in ascending order. Save and close the corrected query.

⚙ **Troubleshoot** 13. Run the NCGuestsFewerPeople query, which displays no records in the results. This query is supposed to show data for guests from North Carolina (NC) with fewer than four people in their booking. Find and correct the errors in the query design, run the query, and then close it.

⚙ **Troubleshoot** 14. Run the GeorgiaOrOctStart query. This query should display the records for all guests who are from Georgia (GA) or whose tour date is on or after 10/1/2017. Find and correct the errors in the query design, run the query, and then close it.

15. Compact and repair the HikeApp database, and then close it.

Creating Forms and Reports

Using Forms and Reports to Display Owner, Animal, and Visit Data

ACCESS

Case | *Riverview Veterinary Care Center*

Kimberly Johnson wants to continue enhancing the Riverview database to make it easier for her staff to enter, locate, and maintain data. In particular, she wants the database to include a form based on the Owner table that staff can use to enter and change data about the owners of the animals that the care center sees. She also wants the database to include a form that shows data from both the Owner and Animal tables at the same time. This form will show the basic information for each owner along with the corresponding animal data, providing a complete picture of Riverview Veterinary Care Center clients and their animals.

In addition, she would like the database to include a report of owner and visit data so that she and other staff members will have printed output when completing analyses of the owners who are clients of the care center and planning strategies for making additional veterinary services available to them. She wants the report to be formatted professionally and easy to use.

In this module, you will create the forms and reports in the Riverview database for Kimberly and her staff.

STARTING DATA FILES

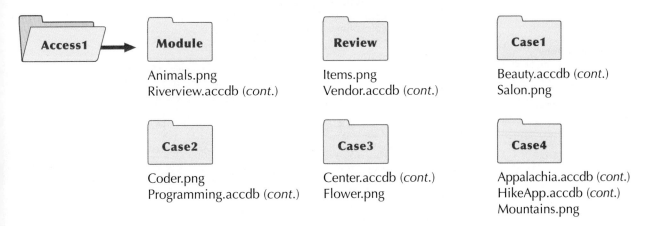

Access1 →

Module
Animals.png
Riverview.accdb (*cont.*)

Review
Items.png
Vendor.accdb (*cont.*)

Case1
Beauty.accdb (*cont.*)
Salon.png

Case2
Coder.png
Programming.accdb (*cont.*)

Case3
Center.accdb (*cont.*)
Flower.png

Case4
Appalachia.accdb (*cont.*)
HikeApp.accdb (*cont.*)
Mountains.png

Session 4.1 Visual Overview:

The form object's name is displayed on the tab for the form.

The form title appears at the top of the form. By default, the form object name is used as the form title, but you can edit the title to display the text you want, as done here—a space was added between the two words for readability.

With the Columnar form layout, the field captions appear in a column on the left side of the form. If captions had not been specified for the fields, the field names would appear here instead.

You can add graphic elements, such as a picture, to a form to improve its appearance or add visual appeal.

The Columnar form layout displays the corresponding field values in boxes to the right of the field captions (or field names).

The navigation buttons allow you to display the first, last, next, or previous record in the form, enter a specific record number and move to that record, and create a new record.

You can use the Search box to find and display a record containing the text you enter.

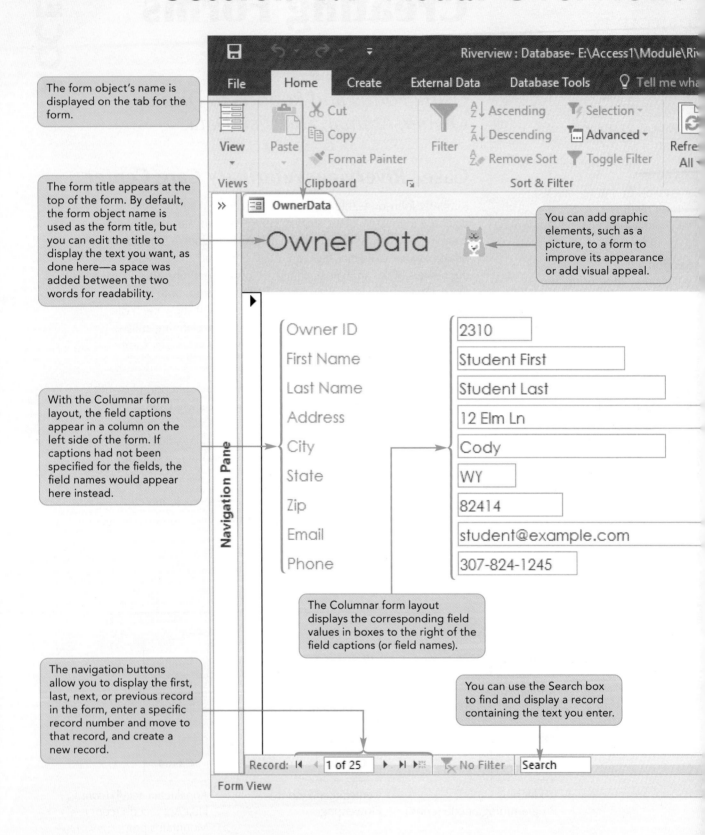

Riverview : Database- E:\Access1\Module\Ri

File　Home　Create　External Data　Database Tools　♀ Tell me wha

View　Paste　✂ Cut　🖺 Copy　✎ Format Painter　Filter　A↓ Ascending　Z↓ Descending　A↓Z Remove Sort　▼ Selection ▾　🖾 Advanced ▾　▼ Toggle Filter　Refre All ▾

Views　Clipboard　Sort & Filter

OwnerData

Owner Data

Owner ID　2310
First Name　Student First
Last Name　Student Last
Address　12 Elm Ln
City　Cody
State　WY
Zip　82414
Email　student@example.com
Phone　307-824-1245

Navigation Pane

Record: ◄ ◄ 1 of 25 ► ►► ►⊞　🖾 No Filter　Search

Form View

Form Displayed in Form View

You use the Find button to display the Find and Replace dialog box, which lets you search for specific data in the form.

You can apply a theme to a form, as done here with the OwnerData form. A theme is a predefined set of formats including colors, fonts, and other effects that enhance a form's appearance and usability.

The OwnerData form was created using the Form Wizard, which allows you to choose some or all of the fields in the table or query used as the basis for the form, choose fields from other tables and queries, and display the selected fields in any order on the form.

This selected button indicates the form is displayed in Form view, which you use to view, enter, and maintain data in the table on which the form is based.

You can click this button to display the form in Layout view, which allows you to modify many aspects of a form's layout and design.

Creating a Form Using the Form Wizard

As you learned earlier, a form is an object you use to enter, edit, and view records in a database. You can design your own forms or use tools in Access to create them automatically. You have already used the Form tool to create the VisitData form in the Riverview database. Recall that the Form tool creates a form automatically, using all the fields in the selected table or query.

Kimberly asks you to create a new form that her staff can use to view and maintain data in the Owner table. To create the form for the Owner table, you'll use the Form Wizard, which guides you through the process.

To open the Riverview database and start the Form Wizard:

▶ **1.** Start Access and open the **Riverview** database you created and worked with in the previous modules.

Trouble? If the security warning is displayed below the ribbon, click the Enable Content button.

▶ **2.** Open the Navigation Pane, if necessary. To create a form based on a table or query, you can select the table or query in the Navigation Pane first, or you can select it using the Form Wizard.

▶ **3.** In the Tables section of the Navigation Pane, click **Owner** to select the Owner table as the basis for the new form.

▶ **4.** On the ribbon, click the **Create** tab. The Forms group on the Create tab provides options for creating various types of forms and designing your own forms.

▶ **5.** In the Forms group, click the **Form Wizard** button. The first Form Wizard dialog box opens. See Figure 4-1.

Figure 4-1 **First Form Wizard dialog box**

selected table

scrollable list of fields in the selected table

Because you selected the Owner table in the Navigation Pane before starting the Form Wizard, this table is selected in the Tables/Queries box, and the fields for the Owner table are listed in the Available Fields box.

Kimberly wants the form to display all the fields in the Owner table, but in a different order. She would like the Phone field to appear at the bottom of the form so that it stands out, making it easier for someone who needs to call an animal's owner to use the form to quickly locate the phone number.

To create the form using the Form Wizard:

▶ **1.** Click the >> button to move all the fields to the Selected Fields box. Next, you need to position the Phone field so it will appear as the bottom-most field on the form. To accomplish this, you will first remove the Phone field and then add it back as the last selected field.

▶ **2.** In the Selected Fields box, click the **Phone** field, and then click the < button to move the field back to the Available Fields box.

Because a new field is always added after the selected field in the Selected Fields box, you need to first select the last field in the list and then move the Phone field back to the Selected Fields box so it will be the last field on the form.

▶ **3.** In the Selected Fields box, click the **Email** field.

▶ **4.** With the Phone field selected in the Available Fields box, click the > button to move the Phone field to the end of the list in the Selected Fields box.

▶ **5.** Click the **Next** button to display the second Form Wizard dialog box, in which you select a layout for the form. See Figure 4-2.

Figure 4-2   **Choosing a layout for the form**

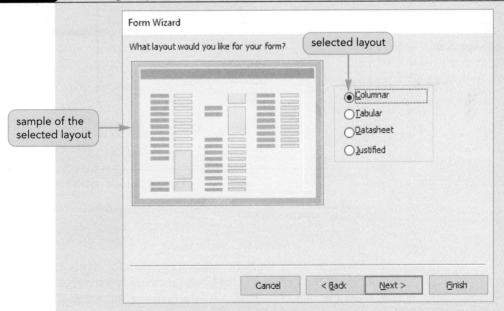

The layout choices are Columnar, Tabular, Datasheet, and Justified. A sample of the selected layout appears on the left side of the dialog box.

▶ **6.** Click each of the option buttons and review the corresponding sample layout.

The Tabular and Datasheet layouts display the fields from multiple records at one time, whereas the Columnar and Justified layouts display the fields from one record at a time. Kimberly thinks the Columnar layout is the appropriate arrangement for displaying and updating data in the table, so that anyone using the form can focus on just one owner record at a time.

7. Click the **Columnar** option button (if necessary), and then click the **Next** button.

The third and final Form Wizard dialog box shows the Owner table's name as the default form name. "Owner" is also the default title that will appear on the tab for the form.

You'll use "OwnerData" as the form name, and, because you don't need to change the form's design at this point, you'll display the form.

8. Click to position the insertion point to the right of Owner in the box, type **Data**, and then click the **Finish** button.

Close the Navigation Pane to display only the Form window. The completed form is displayed in Form view, displaying the values for the first record in the Owner table. The Columnar layout you selected places the field captions in labels on the left and the corresponding field values in boxes on the right, which vary in width depending on the size of the field. See Figure 4-3.

Figure 4-3	OwnerData form in Form view

After viewing the form, Kimberly makes suggestions for improving the form's readability and appearance. The font used in the labels on the left is somewhat light in color and small, making them a bit difficult to read. Also, she thinks inserting a graphic on the form would add visual interest, and modifying other form elements—such as the color of the title text—would improve the look of the form. You can make all of these changes working with the form in Layout view.

Modifying a Form's Design in Layout View

After you create a form, you might need to modify its design to improve its appearance or to make the form easier to use. You cannot make any design changes in Form view. However, Layout view displays the form as it appears in Form view while allowing you to modify the form's design. Because you can see the form and its data while you are modifying the form, Layout view makes it easy for you to see the results of any design changes you make.

The first modification you'll make to the OwnerData form is to change its appearance by applying a theme.

Applying a Theme to a Database Object

By default, the objects you create in a database are formatted with the Office theme. A theme provides a design scheme for the colors and fonts used in the database objects. Access, like other Microsoft Office programs, provides many built-in themes, including the Office theme, making it easy for you to create objects with a unified look. You can also create a customized theme if none of the built-in themes suit your needs.

Sometimes a theme works well for one database object but is not as suitable for other objects in that database. Therefore, when applying a theme to an object, you can choose to apply the theme just to the open object or to objects of a particular type, or you can choose to apply the theme to all the existing objects in the database and set it as the default theme for any new objects that might be created.

To change a form's appearance, you can easily apply a new theme to it.

REFERENCE

Applying a Theme to Database Objects

- Display the object in Layout view.
- In the Themes group on the Form Layout Tools Design tab or Report Layout Tools Design tab, click the Themes button.
- In the Themes gallery, click the theme you want to apply to all objects; or, right-click the theme to display the shortcut menu, and then choose to apply the theme to the current object only or to all matching objects.

Kimberly would like to see if the OwnerData form's appearance can be improved with a different theme. To apply a theme, you first need to switch to Layout view.

To apply a theme to the OwnerData form:

1. On the ribbon, make sure the Home tab is displayed.

2. In the Views group, click the **View** button. The form is displayed in Layout view. See Figure 4-4.

Figure 4-4   **Form displayed in Layout view**

Themes button

Format Layout Tools Design tab displays options for changing the form's appearance

OwnerData

Owner ID	2310	← orange border indicates the selected field value
First Name	Student First	
Last Name	Student Last	
Address	12 Elm Ln	
City	Cody	
State	WY	
Zip	82414	
Email	student@example.com	
Phone	307-824-1245	

Trouble? If the Field List or Property Sheet opens on the right side of the program window, close it before continuing.

In Layout view, an orange border identifies the currently selected element on the form. In this case, the field value for the OwnerID field, 2310, is selected. You need to apply a theme to the OwnerData form.

3. On the Form Layout Tools Design tab, in the Themes group, click the **Themes** button. A gallery opens showing the available themes for the form. See Figure 4-5.

Figure 4-5   **Themes gallery**

Figure 4-5

The Office theme, the default theme currently applied in the database, is listed in the "In this Database" section and is also the first theme listed in the section containing other themes. You can point to each theme in the gallery to see its name in a ScreenTip. Also, when you point to a theme, the Live Preview feature shows the effect of applying the theme to the open object.

TIP

Themes other than the Office theme are listed in alphabetical order in the gallery.

4. In the gallery, point to each of the themes to see how they would format the OwnerData form. Notice the changes in color and font type of the text, for example.

Kimberly likes the Wisp theme because of its light gray color in the title area at the top and its larger font size, which makes the text in the form easier to read.

5. Right-click the **Wisp** theme. A shortcut menu opens with options for applying the theme. See Figure 4-6.

Figure 4-6	Shortcut menu for applying the theme

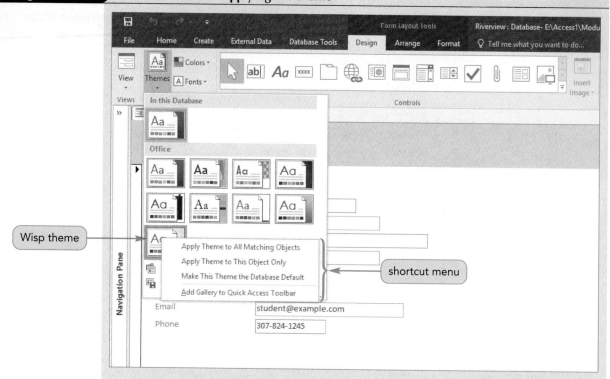

Wisp theme

shortcut menu

The menu provides options for applying the theme to all matching objects—for example, all the forms in the database—or to the current object only. You can also choose to make the theme the default theme in the database, which means any new objects you create will be formatted with the selected theme. Because Kimberly is not sure if all forms in the Riverview database will look better with the Wisp theme, she asks you to apply it only to the OwnerData form.

Choose this option to avoid applying the theme to other forms in the database.

6. On the shortcut menu, click **Apply Theme to This Object Only**.

The gallery closes, and the Wisp theme's colors and fonts are applied to the form.

Trouble? If you choose the wrong option by mistake, you might have applied the selected theme to other forms and/or reports in the database. Repeat Steps 3 through 6 to apply the Wisp theme to the OwnerData form. You can also follow the same process to reapply the default Office theme to the other forms and reports in the Riverview database, as directed by your instructor.

INSIGHT

Working with Themes

Themes provide a quick and easy way for you to format the objects in a database with a consistent look, which is a good design principle to follow. In general, all objects of a type in a database—for example, all forms—should have a consistent design. However, keep in mind that when you select a theme in the Themes gallery and choose the option to apply the theme to all matching objects or to make the theme the default for the database, it might be applied to all the existing forms and reports in the database as well as to new forms and reports you create. Although this approach ensures a consistent design, it can cause problems. For example, if you have already created a form or report and its design is suitable, applying a theme that includes a larger font size could cause the text in labels and field value boxes to be cut off or to extend into other objects on the form or report. The colors applied by the theme could also interfere with elements on existing forms and reports. To handle these unintended results, you would have to spend time checking the existing forms and reports and fixing any problems introduced by applying the theme. A better approach is to select the option "Apply Theme to This Object Only," available on the shortcut menu for a theme in the Themes gallery, for each existing form and report. If the newly applied theme causes problems for any individual form or report, you can then reapply the original theme to return the object to its original design.

Next, you will add a picture to the form for visual interest. The picture, which is included on various flyers and other owner correspondence for Riverview Veterinary Care Center, is a small graphic of a dog and a cat.

Adding a Picture to a Form

A picture is one of many controls you can add and modify on a form. A **control** is an item on a form, report, or other database object that you can manipulate to modify the object's appearance. The controls you can add and modify in Layout view for a form are available in the Controls group and the Header/Footer group on the Form Layout Tools Design tab. The picture you need to add is contained in a file named Animals.png, which is located in the Access1 > Module folder provided with your Data Files.

To add the picture to the form:

▸ 1. Make sure the form is still displayed in Layout view and that the Form Layout Tools Design tab is active.

▸ 2. In the Header/Footer group, click the **Logo** button. The Insert Picture dialog box opens.

▸ 3. Navigate to the **Access1 > Module** folder provided with your Data Files, click the **Animals** file, and then click the **OK** button. The picture appears on top of the form's title. See Figure 4-7.

Figure 4-7   **Form with picture added**

A solid orange border surrounds the picture, indicating it is selected. The picture is placed in a **control layout**, which is a set of controls grouped together in a form or report so that you can manipulate the set as a single control. The dotted blue outline indicates the control layout. The easiest way to move the picture off the form title is to first remove it from the control layout. Doing so allows you to move the picture independently.

4. Right-click the picture to open the shortcut menu, point to **Layout**, and then click **Remove Layout**. The dotted blue outline no longer appears, and the picture is removed from the control layout. Now you can move the picture to the right of the form title.

5. Position the pointer ⊹ on the picture, and then drag to the right of the form title. Although the image may not be visible while dragging, you can use the position of the pointer as a guide to where the image will be placed.

TIP

You can resize a selected image by dragging a corner of the orange selection border.

6. When the pointer is roughly one-half inch to the right of the form's title, release the mouse button. The picture is positioned to the right of the form title.

7. Click in a blank area to the right of the field values in the form to deselect the picture. See Figure 4-8.

Trouble? Don't be concerned if the picture is not in the exact location as the one shown in Figure 4-8. Just make sure the picture is not blocking any part of the form title and that it appears to the right of the form title and within the gray shaded area at the top of the form.

Figure 4-8 | **Form with theme applied and picture repositioned**

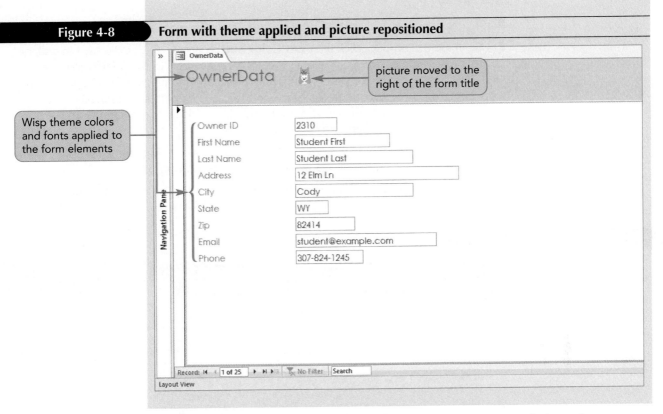

Next, Kimberly asks you to change the color of the form title to a darker color so that it will stand out more on the form.

Changing the Color of Text on a Form

The Font group on the Form Layout Tools Format tab provides many options you can use to change the appearance of text on a form. For example, you can bold, italicize, and underline text; change the font, font color, and font size; and change the alignment of text. Before you change the color of the "OwnerData" title on the form, you'll change the title to two words so it is easier to read.

To change the form title's text and color:

1. Click the **OwnerData** form title. An orange border surrounds the title, indicating it is selected.

2. Click between the letters "r" and "D" to position the insertion point, and then press the **spacebar**. The title on the form is now "Owner Data," but the added space caused the words to appear on two lines. You can fix this by resizing the box containing the title.

3. Position the pointer on the right edge of the box containing the form title until the pointer changes to ↔, and then drag to the right until the word "Data" appears on the same line as the word "Owner."

   Trouble? You might need to repeat Step 3 until the title appears on one line. Also, you might have to move the picture further to the right to make room for the title.

   Next you will change the title's font color.

TIP

Changing the form's title does not affect the form object name; it is still OwnerData, as shown on the object tab.

> **4.** On the ribbon, click the **Form Layout Tools Format** tab.

> **5.** In the Font group, click the **Font Color button arrow** ![A] to display the gallery of available colors. The gallery provides theme colors and standard colors, as well as an option for creating a custom color. The theme colors available depend on the theme applied to the form—in this case, the colors are related to the Wisp theme. The current color of the title text—Black, Text 1, Lighter 50%—is outlined in the gallery, indicating it is the currently applied font color.

> **6.** In the Theme Colors palette, click the **Black, Text 1, Lighter 25%** color, which is the fourth color down in the second column.

> **7.** Click a blank area of the form to deselect the title. The darker black color is applied to the form title text, making it stand out more. See Figure 4-9.

Figure 4-9 | **Form title with new color applied**

form title in a darker black font and edited with a space between words

> **8.** On the Quick Access Toolbar, click the **Save** button ![save] to save the modified form.

> **9.** On the status bar, click the **Form View** button ![form view] to display the form in Form view.

Kimberly is pleased with the modified appearance of the form. Later, she plans to revise the existing VisitData form and make the same changes to it, so that it matches the appearance of the OwnerData form.

PROSKILLS

Written Communication: Understanding the Importance of Form Design

Similar to any document, a form must convey written information clearly and effectively. When you create a form, it's important to consider how the form will be used, so that its design will accommodate the needs of people using the form to view, enter, and maintain data. For example, if a form in a database is meant to mimic a paper form that users will enter data from, the form in the database should have the same fields in the same order as on the paper form. This will enable users to easily tab from one field to the next in the database form to enter the necessary information from the paper form. Also, it's important to include a meaningful title on the form to identify its purpose and to enhance the appearance of the form. A form that is visually appealing makes working with the database more user-friendly and can improve the readability of the form, thereby helping to prevent errors in data entry. Also, be sure to use a consistent design for the forms in your database whenever possible. Users will expect to see similar elements—titles, pictures, fonts, and so on—in each form contained in a database. A mix of form styles and elements among the forms in a database could lead to problems when working with the forms. Finally, make sure the text on your form does not contain any spelling or grammatical errors. By producing a well-designed and well-written form, you can help to ensure that users will be able to work with the form in a productive and efficient manner.

Navigating a Form

To view, navigate, and change data using a form, you need to display the form in Form view. As you learned earlier, you navigate a form in the same way that you navigate a table datasheet. Also, the same navigation mode and editing mode keyboard shortcuts you have used working with datasheets can also be used when working with a form.

Kimberly wants to view data in the Owner table. Before using the OwnerData form to display the specific information Kimberly wants to view, you will practice navigating between the fields in a record and navigating between records in the form. The OwnerData form is already displayed in Form view, so you can use it to navigate through the fields and records of the Owner table.

To navigate the OwnerData form:

1. If necessary, click in the **Owner ID** field value box to make it current.

2. Press the **Tab** key twice to move to the Last Name field value box, and then press the **End** key to move to the Phone field value box.

3. Press the **Home** key to move back to the Owner ID field value box. The first record in the Owner table still appears in the form.

4. Press the **Ctrl+End** keys to move to the Phone field value box for record 25, which is the last record in the table. The record number for the current record appears in the Current Record box between the navigation buttons at the bottom of the form.

5. Click the **Previous record** button ◀ to move to the Phone field value box in record 24.

6. Press the ↑ key twice to move to the Zip field value box in record 24.

▶ **7.** Click to position the insertion point within the word "Rascal" in the Address field value to switch to editing mode, press the **Home** key to move the insertion point to the beginning of the field value, and then press the **End** key to move the insertion point to the end of the field value.

▶ **8.** Click the **First record** button ◄ to move to the Address field value box in the first record. The entire field value is highlighted because you switched from editing mode to navigation mode.

▶ **9.** Click the **Next record** button ▶ to move to the Address field value box in record 2, the next record.

Kimberly wants to find the record for an owner named Thomas. The paper form containing all the original contact information for this owner was damaged. Other than the owner's first name, Kimberly knows only the street the owner lives on. You will use the OwnerData form to locate and view the complete record for this owner.

Finding Data Using a Form

As you learned earlier, the Find command lets you search for data in a datasheet so you can display only those records you want to view. You can also use the Find command to search for data in a form. You first choose a field to serve as the basis for the search by making that field the current field, and then you enter the value you want Access to match in the Find and Replace dialog box.

REFERENCE

Finding Data in a Form or Datasheet

• Open the form or datasheet, and then make the field you want to search the current field.
• On the Home tab, in the Find group, click the Find button to open the Find and Replace dialog box.
• In the Find What box, type the field value you want to find.
• Complete the remaining options, as necessary, to specify the type of search to conduct.
• Click the Find Next button to begin the search.
• Click the Find Next button to continue searching for the next match.
• Click the Cancel button to stop the search operation.

You need to find the record for the owner Kimberly wants to contact. The owner whose record she needs to find is named Thomas and he lives on Bobcat Trail. You'll search for this record using the Address field.

To find the record using the OwnerData form:

▶ **1.** Make sure the Address field value is still selected for the current record. This is the field you need to search.

You can search for a record that contains part of the address anywhere in the Address field value. Performing a partial search such as this is often easier than matching the entire field value and is useful when you don't know or can't remember the entire field value.

▶ **2.** On the Home tab, in the Find group, click the **Find** button. The Find and Replace dialog box opens. The Look In box indicates that the current field (in this case, Address) will be searched. You'll search for records that contain the word "bobcat" in the address.

▶ **3.** In the Find What box, type **bobcat**. Note that you do not have to enter the word as "Bobcat" with a capital letter "B" because the Match Case check box is not selected in the Find and Replace dialog box. The search will find any record containing the word "bobcat" with any combination of uppercase and lowercase letters.

▶ **4.** Click the **Match** arrow to display the list of matching options, and then click **Any Part of Field**. The search will find any record that contains the word "bobcat" in any part of the Address field. See Figure 4-10.

Figure 4-10	Completed Find and Replace dialog box

▶ **5.** Click the **Find Next** button. The Find and Replace dialog box remains open, and the OwnerData form now displays record 13, which is the record for Thomas Jones (OwnerID 2362). The word "Bobcat" is selected in the Address field value box because you searched for this word.

The search value you enter can be an exact value or it can include wildcard characters. A **wildcard character** is a placeholder you use when you know only part of a value or when you want to start or end with a specific character or match a certain pattern. Figure 4-11 shows the wildcard characters you can use when searching for data.

Figure 4-11	Wildcard characters

Wildcard Character	Purpose	Example
*	Match any number of characters it can be used as the first and/or last character in the character string	th* finds the, that, this, therefore, and so on
?	Match any single alphabetic character	a?t finds act, aft, ant, apt, and art
[]	Match any single character within the brackets	a[fr]t finds aft and art but not act, ant, or apt
!	Match any character not within brackets	a[!fr]t finds act, ant, and apt but not aft or art
-	Match any one of a range of characters the range must be in ascending order (a to z, not z to a)	a[d-p]t finds aft, ant, and apt but not act or art
#	Match any single numeric character	#72 finds 072, 172, 272, 372, and so on

Next, to see how a wildcard works, you'll view the records for any owners with phone numbers that contain the exchange 824 as part of the phone number. The exchange consists of the three digits that follow the area code in the phone number. You could search for any record containing the digits 824 in any part of the Phone field, but this search would also find records with the digits 824 in any part of the phone number. To find only those records with the digits 824 as the exchange, you'll use the * wildcard character.

To find the records using the * wildcard character:

▶ **1.** Make sure the Find and Replace dialog box is still open.

▶ **2.** Click anywhere in the OwnerData form to make it active, and then press the **Tab** key until you reach the Phone field value box. This is the field you want to search.

▶ **3.** Click the title bar of the Find and Replace dialog box to make it active, and then drag the Find and Replace dialog box to the right so you can see the Phone field on the form, if necessary. "Current field" is still selected in the Look In box, meaning now the Phone field is the field that will be searched.

▶ **4.** Double-click **bobcat** in the Find What box to select the entire value, and then type **307-824***.

▶ **5.** Click the **Match** arrow, and then click **Whole Field**. Because you're using a wildcard character in the search value, you want the whole field to be searched.

With the settings you've entered, the search will find records in which any field value in the Phone field begins with the area code 307 followed by a hyphen and the exchange 824.

▶ **6.** Click the **Find Next** button. Record 15 displays in the form, which is the first record found for a customer with the exchange 824. Notice that the search process started from the point of the previously displayed record in the form, which was record 13.

▶ **7.** Click the **Find Next** button. Record 16 displays in the form, which is the next record found for a customer with the exchange 824.

▶ **8.** Click the **Find Next** button to display record 18, and then click the **Find Next** button again. Record 19 displays, the fourth record found.

▶ **9.** Click the **Find Next** button two more times to display records 21 and 24.

▶ **10.** Click the **Find Next** button again. Record 1 displays. Notice that the search process cycles back through the beginning of the records in the underlying table.

▶ **11.** Click the **Find Next** button. A dialog box opens, informing you that the search is finished.

▶ **12.** Click the **OK** button to close the dialog box, and then click the **Cancel** button to close the Find and Replace dialog box.

Kimberly has identified some owner updates she wants you to make. You'll use the OwnerData form to update the data in the Owner table.

Maintaining Table Data Using a Form

Maintaining data using a form is often easier than using a datasheet because you can focus on all the changes for a single record at one time. In Form view, you can edit the field values for a record, delete a record from the underlying table, or add a new record to the table.

Now you'll use the OwnerData form to make the changes Kimberly wants to the Owner table. First, you'll update the record for owner Sandra Pincher, who recently moved from Cody to Powell and provided a new mailing address. In addition to using the Find and Replace dialog box to locate a specific record, you can use the Search box to the right of the navigation buttons. You'll use the Search box to search for the owner's last name, Pincher, and display the owner record in the form.

To change the record using the OwnerData form:

1. To the right of the navigation buttons, click the **Search** box and then type **Pincher**. As soon as you start to type, Access begins searching through all fields in the records to match your entry. Record 3 (Sandra Pincher) is now current.

   You will first update the address in this record.

2. Select the current entry in the Address field value box, and then type **53 Verde Ln** to replace it.

3. Press the **Tab** key to select the city in the City field value box, and then type **Powell**.

4. Press the **Tab** key twice to move to and select the Zip field value, and then type **82440**. The updates to the record are complete. See Figure 4-12.

TIP

The pencil symbol appears in the upper-left corner of the form when the form is in editing mode.

Figure 4-12   **Owner record after changing field values**

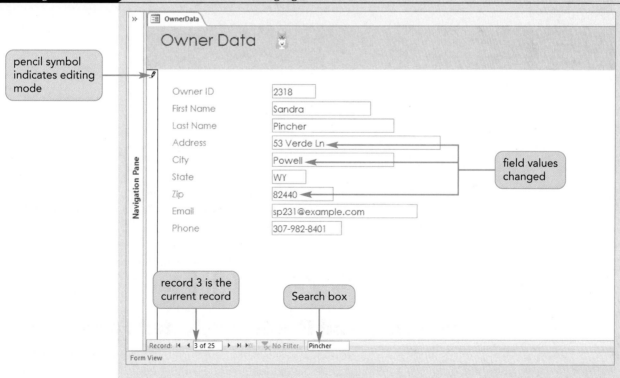

pencil symbol indicates editing mode

Owner Data

Owner ID	2318
First Name	Sandra
Last Name	Pincher
Address	53 Verde Ln
City	Powell
State	WY
Zip	82440
Email	sp231@example.com
Phone	307-982-8401

field values changed

record 3 is the current record

Search box

Record: ⏮ ◀ 3 of 25 ▶ ▶▶ ▶✱   🔽 No Filter   Pincher

Form View

Next, Kimberly asks you to add a record for a new owner. This person indicated plans to bring a pet to the care center at a recent adoption fair in which Riverview Veterinary Care Center participated, but the owner has not yet provided information about the animal or scheduled an appointment. You'll use the OwnerData form to add the new record.

To add the new record using the OwnerData form:

▶ **1.** On the Home tab, in the Records group, click the **New** button. Record 26, the next available new record, becomes the current record. All field value boxes are empty (except the State field, which displays the default value of WY), and the insertion point is positioned in the Owner ID field value box.

▶ **2.** Refer to Figure 4-13 and enter the value shown for each field, pressing the **Tab** key to move from field to field.

Figure 4-13 Completed form for the new record

»	OwnerData	
	Owner Data 🦉	

	Owner ID	2416
	First Name	Mei
	Last Name	Kostas
	Address	812 Playa Hwy
	City	Elk Butte
	State	WY
	Zip	82433
	Email	meowmeow@example.com
	Phone	307-824-5873

Record: I◀ ◀ 26 of 26 ▶ ▶I ▶□ No Filter   Search

Form View

▶ **3.** After entering the Phone field value, press the **Tab** key. Record 27, the next available new record, becomes the current record, and the record for OwnerID 2416 is saved in the Owner table.

Kimberly would like a printed copy of the OwnerData form to show to her staff members. She asks you to print one form record.

Previewing and Printing Selected Form Records

You can print as many form records as can fit on a printed page. If only part of a form record fits on the bottom of a page, the remainder of the record prints on the next page. You can print all pages or a range of pages. In addition, you can print just the currently selected form record.

Kimberly asks you to use the OwnerData form to print the first record in the Owner table. Before you do, you'll preview the form record to see how it will look when printed.

To preview the form and print the data for record 1:

▶ 1. Click the **First record** button |◄ to display record 1 in the form. This is the record in which you have entered your first and last names.

▶ 2. Click the **File** tab to open Backstage view, click **Print** in the navigation bar, and then click **Print Preview**. The Print Preview window opens, showing the form records for the Owner table. Notice that each record appears in its own form and that shading is used to distinguish one record from another. See Figure 4-14.

Figure 4-14   **Form records displayed in Print Preview**

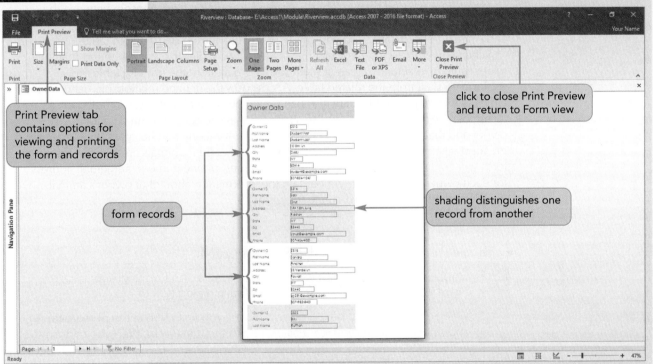

Print Preview tab contains options for viewing and printing the form and records

click to close Print Preview and return to Form view

form records

shading distinguishes one record from another

To print one selected record on a page by itself, you need to use the Print dialog box.

▶ 3. On the Print Preview tab, in the Close Preview group, click the **Close Print Preview** button. You return to Form view with the first record still displayed.

▶ 4. Click the **File** tab to open Backstage view again, click **Print** in the navigation bar, and then click **Print**. The **Print** dialog box opens.

▶ 5. Click the **Selected Record(s)** option button to print the current form record (record 1).

Trouble? Check with your instructor to be sure you should print the form, then continue to the next step. If you should not print the form, click the Cancel button, and then skip to Step 7.

▶ **6.** Click the **OK** button to close the dialog box and print the selected record.

▶ **7.** Close the OwnerData form.

After reviewing the printed OwnerData form with her staff, Kimberly realizes that it would be helpful for staff members to also have a form showing information about both owners and their animals. Because this form will need to display information from two different tables, the type of form you need to create will include a main form and a subform.

Creating a Form with a Main Form and a Subform

To create a form based on two tables, you must first define a relationship between the two tables. Earlier, you defined a one-to-many relationship between the Owner (primary) and Animal (related) tables, so you can now create a form based on both tables.

When you create a form containing data from two tables that have a one-to-many relationship, you actually create a **main form** for data from the primary table and a **subform** for data from the related table. Access uses the defined relationship between the tables to join them automatically through the common field that exists in both tables.

Kimberly would like you to create a form so that she can view the data for each owner and that owner's animals at the same time. Kimberly and her staff will then use the form when contacting the owners about care that their animals are due for. The main form will contain the owner ID, first and last names, phone number, and email address for each owner. The subform will contain the information about that owner's animals. You'll use the Form Wizard to create the form.

To create the form using the Form Wizard:

▶ **1.** On the ribbon, click the **Create** tab, and then in the Forms group, click the **Form Wizard** button. The first Form Wizard dialog box opens.

When creating a form based on two tables, you first choose the primary table and select the fields you want to include in the main form; then you choose the related table and select fields from it for the subform. In this case, the correct primary table, Table: Owner, is already selected in the Tables/Queries box.

Trouble? If Table: Owner is not currently selected in the Tables/Queries box, click the Tables/Queries arrow, and then click Table: Owner.

The form needs to include only the OwnerID, FirstName, LastName, Phone, and Email fields from the Owner table.

▶ **2.** Click **OwnerID** in the Available Fields box if necessary, and then click the ❘ > ❘ button to move the field to the Selected Fields box.

▶ **3.** Repeat Step 2 for the **FirstName, LastName, Phone,** and **Email** fields.

The subform needs to include all the fields from the Animal table, with the exception of the OwnerID field, as that field has been added already for the main form.

▶ **4.** Click the **Tables/Queries** arrow, and then click **Table: Animal.** The fields from the Animal table appear in the Available Fields box. The quickest way to add the fields you want to include is to move all the fields to the Selected Fields box, and then remove the only field you don't want to include (OwnerID).

TIP

The table name (Animal) is included in the OwnerID field name to distinguish it from the same field in the Owner table.

5. Click the >> button to move all the fields in the Animal table to the Selected Fields box.

6. Click **Animal.OwnerID** in the Selected Fields box, and then click the < button to move the field back to the Available Fields box.

7. Click the **Next** button. The next Form Wizard dialog box opens. See Figure 4-15.

| Figure 4-15 | Choosing a format for the main form and subform |

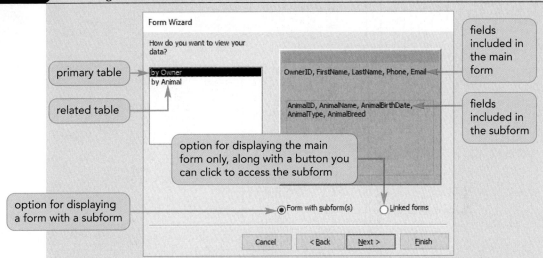

In this dialog box, the section on the left shows the order in which you will view the selected data: first by data from the primary Owner table, and then by data from the related Animal table. The form will be displayed as shown on the right side of the dialog box, with the fields from the Owner table at the top in the main form, and the fields from the Animal table at the bottom in the subform.

8. Click the **Next** button. The next Form Wizard dialog box opens, in which you choose the subform layout.

The Tabular layout displays subform fields as a table, whereas the Datasheet layout displays subform fields as a table datasheet. The layout choice is a matter of personal preference. You'll use the Datasheet layout.

9. Click the **Datasheet** option button to select it if necessary, and then click the **Next** button. The next Form Wizard dialog box opens, in which you specify titles for the main form and the subform. You'll use the title "OwnerAnimals" for the main form and the title "AnimalSubform" for the subform. These titles will also be the names for the form objects.

10. In the Form box, click to position the insertion point to the right of the last letter, and then type **Animals**. The main form name is now OwnerAnimals.

11. In the Subform box, delete the space between the two words so that the subform name appears as **AnimalSubform**, and then click the **Finish** button. The completed form opens in Form view. See Figure 4-16.

| Figure 4-16 | Main form with subform in Form view |

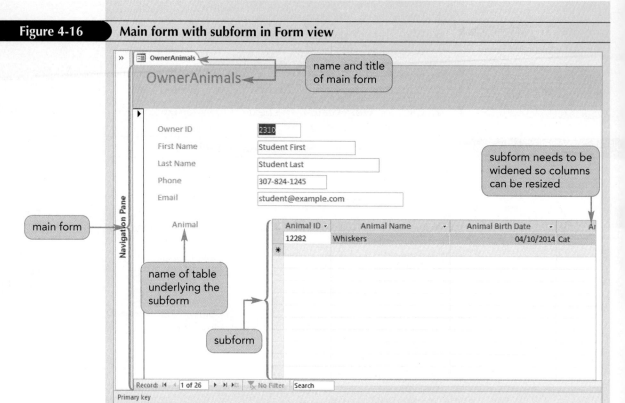

The main form displays the fields from the first record in the Owner table in a columnar format. The records in the main form appear in primary key order by OwnerID. OwnerID 2310 has one related record in the Animal table; this record, for AnimalID 12282, is shown in the subform, which uses the datasheet format. The main form name, "OwnerAnimals," appears on the object tab and as the form title. The name of the table "Animal" appears to the left of the subform indicating the underlying table for the subform. Note that only the word "Animal" and not the complete name "AnimalSubform" appears on the form. Only the table name is displayed for the subform itself, but the complete name of the object, "AnimalSubform," is displayed when you view and work with objects in the Navigation Pane. The subform designation is necessary in a list of database objects so that you can distinguish the Animal subform from other objects, such as the Animal table, but the subform designation is not needed in the OwnerAnimals form. Only the table name is required to identify the table containing the records in the subform.

Next, you need to make some changes to the form. First, you'll edit the form title to add a space between the words so that it appears as "Owner Animals." Then, you'll resize the subform so that it is wide enough to allow for all the columns to be fully displayed. To make these changes, you need to switch to Layout view.

To modify the OwnerAnimals form in Layout view:

▸ **1.** Switch to Layout view.

▸ **2.** Click **OwnerAnimals** in the gray area at the top of the form. The form title is selected.

▶ **3.** Click between the letters "r" and "A" to place the insertion point, and then press the **spacebar**. The title on the form is now "Owner Animals."

▶ **4.** Click in a blank area of the form to the right of the field value boxes to deselect the title. Next, you'll increase the width of the subform.

▶ **5.** Click the **subform**. An orange border surrounds the subform, indicating it is selected.

▶ **6.** Position the pointer on the right border of the selected subform until the pointer changes to ↔, and then drag to the right approximately three inches. The wider subform makes all the columns visible. See Figure 4-17.

Figure 4-17	Modified form in Layout view

▶ **7.** On the Quick Access Toolbar, click the **Save** button 🖫 to save both the main form and the subform.

▶ **8.** Switch to Form view, and then if necessary, scroll up to view all the fields in the main form.

The form includes two sets of navigation buttons. You use the set of navigation buttons at the bottom of the Form window to select records from the primary table in the main form (see Figure 4-17). The second set of navigation buttons is currently not visible; you need to scroll down the main form to see these buttons, which appear at the bottom of the subform. You use the subform navigation buttons to select records from the related table in the subform.

You'll use the navigation buttons to view different records.

To navigate to different main form and subform records:

▶ **1.** In the main form, click the **Next record** button ▶ six times. Record 7 of 26 total records in the Owner table (for Joey Smith) becomes the current record in the main form. The subform shows that this owner has one animal, a cat. Note that the Animal Name, Animal Birth Date, and Animal Type columns are much wider than necessary for the information displayed.

2. Double-click the ✛ pointer on the right column divider of the Animal Name column in the subform to resize this field to its best fit.

3. Repeat Step 2 to resize the Animal Birth Date and Animal Type columns in the subform.

4. Use the main form navigation buttons to view each record, resizing any subform column to fully display any field values that are not completely visible.

5. In the main form, click the **Last record** button ▶|. Record 26 in the Owner table (for Mei Kostas) becomes the current record in the main form. The subform shows that this owner currently has no animals; recall that you just entered this record using the OwnerData form. Kimberly could use the subform to enter the information on this owner's animal(s), and that information will be updated in the Animal table.

6. In the main form, click the **Previous record** button ◀. Record 25 in the Owner table (for Taylor Johnson) becomes the current record in the main form. The subform shows that this owner has two animals. If you know the number of the record you want to view, you can enter the number in the Current Record box to move to that record.

7. In the main form, select **25** in the Current Record box, type **18**, and then press the **Enter** key. Record 18 in the Owner table (for Susan Miller) becomes the current record in the main form. The subform shows that this owner has six animals that are seen by the care center.

8. If necessary, use the vertical scroll bar for the main form to scroll down and view the bottom of the subform. Note the navigation buttons for the subform.

9. At the bottom of the subform, click the **Last record** button ▶|. Record 6 in the Animal subform, for Animal ID 12440, becomes the current record.

10. Save and close the OwnerAnimals form.

11. If you are not continuing to Session 4.2, click the **File** tab, and then click **Close** in the navigation bar to close the Riverview database.

Both the OwnerData form and the OwnerAnimals form you created will enable Kimberly and her staff to view, enter, and maintain data easily in the Owner and Animal tables in the Riverview database.

Session 4.1 Quick Check

1. Describe the difference between creating a form using the Form tool and creating a form using the Form Wizard.

2. What is a theme, and how do you apply one to an existing form?

3. A(n) _____ is an item on a form, report, or other database object that you can manipulate to modify the object's appearance.

4. Which table record is displayed in a form when you press the Ctrl+End keys while you are in navigation mode?

5. Which wildcard character matches any single alphabetic character?

6. To print only the current record displayed in a form, you need to select the _____ option button in the Print dialog box.

7. In a form that contains a main form and a subform, what data is displayed in the main form and what data is displayed in the subform?

Session 4.2 Visual Overview:

The report object's name is displayed on the tab for the report.

The report title appears at the top of the report. By default, the report object name is used as the report title, but you can edit the title to display the text you want, as done here, with spaces added between words for readability.

Fields from the primary Owner table appear first in the report.

Fields from the related Visit Table appear below the fields from the primary table.

For a **grouped report**, the data from a record in the primary table (the Owner table in this report) appears as a group, followed on subsequent lines of the report by the joined records from the related table (the Visit table in this report).

The navigation buttons allow you to display the first, last, next, or previous page in the report, or to enter a specific page number and move to that page.

Report Displayed in Print Preview

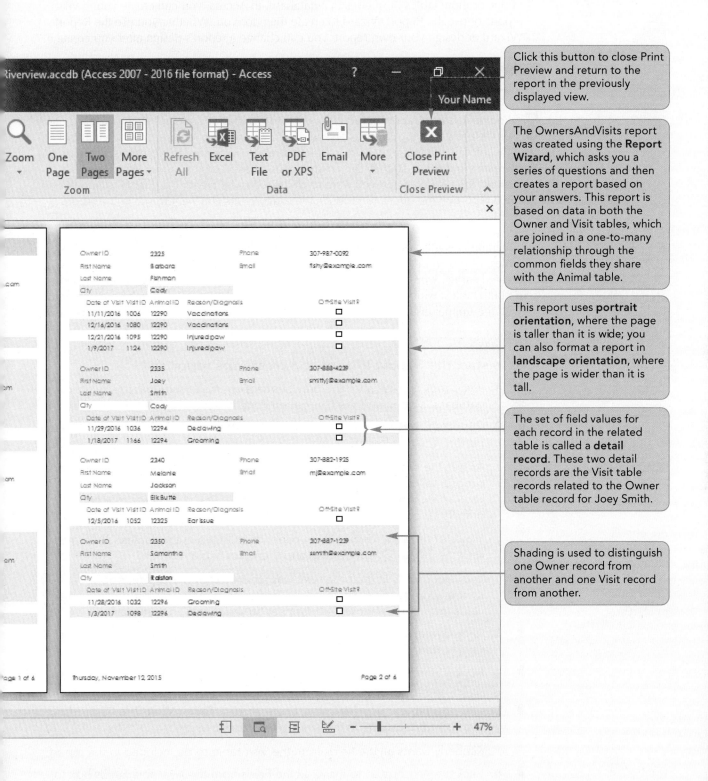

Click this button to close Print Preview and return to the report in the previously displayed view.

The OwnersAndVisits report was created using the **Report Wizard**, which asks you a series of questions and then creates a report based on your answers. This report is based on data in both the Owner and Visit tables, which are joined in a one-to-many relationship through the common fields they share with the Animal table.

This report uses **portrait orientation**, where the page is taller than it is wide; you can also format a report in **landscape orientation**, where the page is wider than it is tall.

The set of field values for each record in the related table is called a **detail record**. These two detail records are the Visit table records related to the Owner table record for Joey Smith.

Shading is used to distinguish one Owner record from another and one Visit record from another.

Creating a Report Using the Report Wizard

As you learned earlier, a report is a formatted printout or screen display of the contents of one or more tables or queries in a database. In Access, you can create your own reports or use the Report Wizard to create them for you. Whether you use the Report Wizard or design your own report, you can change a report's design after you create it.

INSIGHT

Creating a Report Based on a Query

You can create a report based on one or more tables or queries. When you use a query as the basis for a report, you can use criteria and other query features to retrieve only the information you want to display in the report. Experienced Access users often create a query just so they can create a report based on that query. When thinking about the type of report you want to create, consider creating a query first and basing the report on the query, to produce the exact results you want to see in the report.

Kimberly wants you to create a report that includes data from the Owner and Visit tables, as shown in the Session 4.2 Visual Overview. Like the OwnerAnimals form you created earlier, which includes a main form and a subform, the report will be based on both tables, which are joined in a one-to-many relationship through common fields with the Animal table. You'll use the Report Wizard to create the report for Kimberly.

To start the Report Wizard and create the report:

▶ **1.** If you took a break after the previous session, make sure that the Riverview database is open and the Navigation Pane is closed.

▶ **2.** Click the **Create** tab, and then in the Reports group, click the **Report Wizard** button. The first Report Wizard dialog box opens.

As was the case when you created the form with a subform, initially you can choose only one table or query to be the data source for the report. Then you can include data from other tables or queries. In this case, the correct primary table, Table: Owner, is already selected in the Tables/Queries box.

Trouble? If Table: Owner is not currently selected in the Tables/Queries box, click the Tables/Queries arrow, and then click Table: Owner.

You select fields in the order you want them to appear on the report. Kimberly wants the OwnerID, FirstName, LastName, City, Phone, and Email fields from the Owner table to appear on the report, in that order.

▶ **3.** Click **OwnerID** in the Available Fields box (if necessary), and then click the > button. The field moves to the Selected Fields box.

▶ **4.** Repeat Step 3 to add the **FirstName**, **LastName**, **City**, **Phone**, and **Email** fields to the report.

▶ **5.** Click the **Tables/Queries** arrow, and then click **Table: Visit**. The fields from the Visit table appear in the Available Fields box.

Kimberly wants all the fields from the Visit table to be included in the report.

▶ **6.** Click the >> button to move all the fields from the Available Fields box to the Selected Fields box, and then click the **Next** button. The second Report Wizard dialog box opens. See Figure 4-18.

Figure 4-18	Choosing a grouped or ungrouped report

- data grouped by table
- click to display tips, examples, and instructions for creating an ungrouped report

You can choose to arrange the selected data grouped by table, which is the default, or ungrouped. You're creating a grouped report; the data from each record in the Owner table will appear in a group, followed by the related records for that owner from the Visit table.

7. Click the **Next** button. The next Report Wizard dialog box opens, in which you choose additional grouping levels.

Currently the report contains only one grouping level, which is for the owner's data. Grouping levels are useful for reports with multiple levels, such as those containing monthly, quarterly, and annual totals, or for those containing city and country groups. The report requires no further grouping levels, so you can accept the default options.

8. Click the **Next** button. The next Report Wizard dialog box opens, in which you choose the sort order for the detail records. See Figure 4-19.

Figure 4-19	Choosing the sort order for detail records

- click to display a list of the fields in the related table
- options for sorting on multiple fields
- ascending sort order selected; click to change to descending sort order

The records from the Visit table for an owner represent the detail records for Kimberly's report. She wants these records to appear in ascending order by the value in the VisitDate field, so that the visits will be shown in chronological order. The Ascending option is already selected by default. To change to descending order, you click this same button, which acts as a toggle between the two sort orders. Also, you can sort on multiple fields, as you can with queries.

▶ **9.** Click the **arrow** on the first box, click **VisitDate**, and then click the **Next** button. The next Report Wizard dialog box opens, in which you choose a layout and page orientation for the report. See Figure 4-20.

Figure 4-20   **Choosing the report layout**

▶ **10.** Click each layout option to view each sample that appears, and then click the **Outline** option button to select that layout for the report.

Because most of the fields in both the Owner and Visit tables contain relatively short field values, the portrait page orientation should provide enough space across the page to display all the field values.

▶ **11.** Click the **Next** button. The final Report Wizard dialog box opens, in which you choose a report title, which also serves as the name for the report object in the database.

Kimberly wants the report title "Owners and Visits" at the top of the report. Because the name you enter in this dialog box is also the name of the report object, you'll enter the report name as one word and edit the title on the report later.

▶ **12.** In the box for the title, enter **OwnersAndVisits** and then click the **Finish** button.

The Report Wizard creates the report based on your answers, saves it as an object in the Riverview database, and opens the report in Print Preview.

After you create a report, you should view it in Print Preview to see if you need to make any formatting or design changes. To view the entire page, you need to change the Zoom setting.

To view the report in Print Preview:

▶ **1.** On the Print Preview tab, in the Zoom group, click the **Zoom button arrow**, and then click **Fit to Window**. The first page of the report is displayed in Print Preview.

▶ **2.** At the bottom of the window, click the **Next Page** button ▶ to display the second page of the report.

When a report is displayed in Print Preview, you can zoom in for a close-up view of a section of the report.

▶ **3.** Move the pointer to the center of the report, and then click the 🔍 pointer at the center of the report. The display changes to show a close-up view of the report. See Figure 4-21.

Figure 4-21	Close-up view of the report

shading distinguishes one Owner record from another

Visit records listed in ascending order by VisitDate

shading distinguishes one Visit record from another

TIP

Clicking a report in Print Preview toggles between a full-page display and a close-up display of the report.

Shading is used to distinguish both one Owner record from another and, within a group of each owner's Visit records, one Visit record from another.

Trouble? Depending on your computer settings, the shading and colors used in your report might look different. This difference should not cause any problems.

The detail records for the Visit table fields appear in ascending order based on the values in the VisitDate field. Because the VisitDate field is used as the basis for sorting records, it appears as the first field in this section, even though you selected the fields in the order in which they appear in the Visit table.

▶ **4.** Scroll to the bottom of the second page, checking the text in the report as you scroll. Notice the current date and page number at the bottom of the page; the Report Wizard included these elements as part of the report's design.

▶ **5.** Move the pointer onto the report, click the 🔍 pointer to zoom back out, and then click the **Next Page** navigation button ▶ to move to page 3 of the report.

▶ **6.** Continue to move through the pages of the report, and then click the **First Page** button ◀ to return to the first page.

INSIGHT

Changing a Report's Page Orientation and Margins

When you display a report in Print Preview, you can easily change the report layout using options on the Print Preview tab (refer to the Session 4.2 Visual Overview). For example, sometimes fields with longer values cause the report content to overflow onto the next page. You can fix this problem by clicking the Landscape button in the Page Layout group on the Print Preview tab to switch the report orientation to landscape, where the page is wider than it is tall. Landscape orientation allows more space for content to fit across the width of the report page. You can also use the Margins button in the Page Size group to change the margins of the report, choosing from commonly used margin formats or creating your own custom margins. Simply click the Margins button arrow to display the menu of available margin options and select the one that works best for your report.

When you created the OwnerData form, you applied the Wisp theme. Kimberly would like the OwnersAndVisits report to be formatted with the same theme. You need to switch to Layout view to make this change. You'll also make other modifications to improve the report's design.

Modifying a Report's Design in Layout View

Similar to Layout view for forms, Layout view for reports enables you to make modifications to the report's design. Many of the same options—such as those for applying a theme and changing the color of text—are provided in Layout view for reports.

Applying a Theme to a Report

The same themes available for forms are also available for reports. You can choose to apply a theme to the current report object only, or to all reports in the database. In this case, you'll apply the Wisp theme only to the OwnersAndVisits report because Kimberly isn't certain if it is the appropriate theme for other reports in the Riverview database.

To apply the Wisp theme to the report and edit the report name:

▶ **1.** On the status bar, click the **Layout View** button ▣. The report is displayed in Layout view and the Report Layout Tools Design tab is the active tab on the ribbon.

▶ **2.** In the Themes group, click the **Themes** button. The "In this Database" section at the top of the gallery shows both the default Office theme and the Wisp theme. The Wisp theme is included here because you applied it earlier to the OwnerData form.

▶ **3.** At the top of the gallery, right-click the **Wisp** theme to display the shortcut menu, and then click **Apply Theme to This Object Only**. The gallery closes and the theme is applied to the report.

The larger font used by the Wisp theme has caused the report title text to be cut off on the right. You'll fix this problem and edit the title text as well.

Trouble? After you apply the theme, some VisitDate values may be displayed as a series of # symbols rather than actual date values. You'll fix this later in the session.

▶ **4.** Click the **OwnersAndVisits** title at the top of the report to select it.

▶ **5.** Position the pointer on the right border of the title's selection box until it changes to ↔, and then drag to the right until the title is fully displayed.

▶ **6.** Click between the letters "s" and "A" in the title, press the **spacebar**, change the capital letter "A" to **a**, place the insertion point between the letters "d" and "V," and then press the **spacebar**. The title is now "Owners and Visits."

▶ **7.** Click to the right of the report title in the shaded area to deselect the title.

Kimberly views the report and notices some other formatting changes she would like you to make. First, she doesn't like how the VisitDate field values are aligned compared to the other field values from the Visit table. You'll fix this next.

Changing the Alignment of Field Values

The Report Layout Tools Format tab provides options for you to easily modify the format of various report objects. For example, you can change the alignment of the text in a field value. Recall that Date/Time fields, like VisitDate, automatically right-align their field values, whereas Short Text fields, like VisitID, automatically left-align their field values. Kimberly asks you to change the alignment of the VisitDate field so its values appear left-aligned, which will improve the format of the report.

To change the alignment of the VisitDate field values:

1. On the ribbon, click the **Report Layout Tools Format** tab. The ribbon changes to display options for formatting the report. The options for modifying the format of a report are the same as those available for forms.

2. In the report, click the **first VisitDate** field value box, which contains the date 11/8/2016. The field value box has an orange border, indicating it is selected. Note that the other VisitDate field value boxes have a lighter orange border, indicating they are selected as well. Any changes you make will be applied to all VisitDate field values throughout the report.

3. On the Report Layout Tools Format tab, in the Font group, click the **Align Left** button ⊟. The text in the VisitDate field value boxes is now left-aligned. See Figure 4-22.

| Figure 4-22 | Report after applying a theme and changing field alignment |

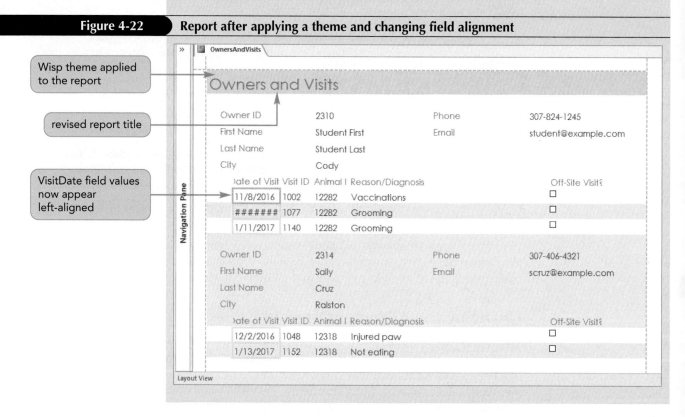

Moving and Resizing Fields on a Report

Working in Layout view, you can resize and reposition fields and field value boxes to improve the appearance and readability of a report. You resize field value boxes by dragging their borders to the desired size. You can also move field labels and field value boxes by selecting one or more of them and then dragging them to a new location; or, for more precise control over the move, you can use the keyboard arrow keys to move selected objects.

In the OwnersAndVisits report, you need to move and resize the VisitDate, VisitID, and OffSite field labels so that the complete caption is displayed for each. Also, some of the VisitDate field values are not displayed on the report but are instead represented by a series of # symbols. This occurs when a field value box is not wide enough for its content. To fix this, you'll widen the VisitDate field value box. Before addressing these issues, you will move the OffSite field label so it appears centered over its check box.

To move and resize the OffSite field label:

▶ **1.** In the report, click the first occurrence of the **Off-Site Visit?** field label. All instances of the label are selected throughout the report.

▶ **2.** Press the ← key repeatedly until the label is centered (roughly) over its check box.

▶ **3.** Position the pointer on the right border of the field label's selection box until the pointer changes to ↔, and then drag to the right until the label text is fully displayed.

Next, you need to move the field label and field value box for the Reason and OffSite fields to the right, to make room to widen the Animal ID field label. You also need to make adjustments to the field label and field value box for the VisitDate field.

To resize and move field labels and field value boxes in the report:

▶ **1.** In the report, click the first occurrence of the **Reason/Diagnosis** field label, press and hold the **Shift** key, click the first occurrence of the **Reason** field value box, which contains the text "Vaccinations," click the first occurrence of the **Off-Site Visit?** field label, and then click the first occurrence of the **OffSite** field value box. Both field labels and their associated field value boxes are selected and can be moved. See Figure 4-23.

Figure 4-23   **Report after selecting field labels and field value boxes**

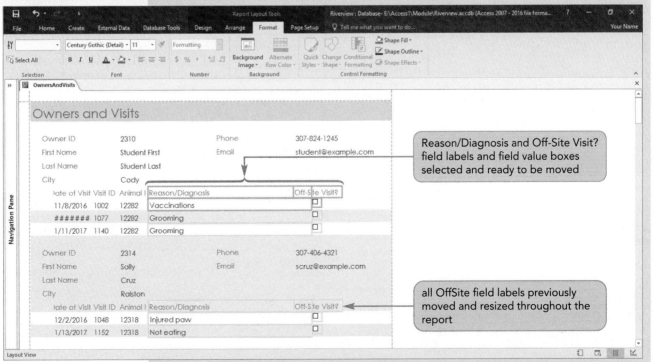

▶ **2.** Press the → key six times to move the field labels and field value boxes to the right.

   Trouble? Once you press the right arrow key, the report might jump to display the end of the report. Just continue to press the right arrow key to move the labels and values. Then scroll the window back up to display the beginning of the report.

▶ **3.** Click the **Animal ID** field label to select it and deselect the moved field labels and field value boxes.

▶ **4.** Position the pointer on the right border of the Animal ID field label's selection box until it changes to ↔, and then drag to the right until the Animal ID label is fully displayed.

   Now you need to modify the VisitDate field so that the # symbols that currently appear are replaced with the actual field values. You'll resize the VisitDate field value boxes to fix this problem.

▶ **5.** Scroll to the top of the report if necessary to display the first record in the report, and then click the **#######** symbols that appear in the second VisitDate field value in the first record.

▶ **6.** Using the ↔ pointer, drag the left border of VisitDate field value's selection box to the left until the date value is fully displayed.

▶ **7.** Scroll through the report, resizing the VisitDate field values as necessary until all values are fully displayed, and then scroll back up to display the top of the report.

▶ **8.** Click the **Date of Visit** field label to select it, and then drag the left border of the selection box to the left until the label text is fully displayed.

▶ **9.** Click to the right of the report title in the shaded area to deselect the field label.

▶ **10.** On the Quick Access Toolbar, click the **Save** button 🖫 to save the modified report.

Next, Kimberly asks you to enhance the report's appearance to make it more consistent with the OwnerData form.

Changing the Font Color and Inserting a Picture in a Report

You can change the color of text on a report to enhance its appearance. You can also add a picture to a report for visual interest or to identify a particular section of the report.

Before you print the report for Kimberly, she asks you to change the report title color to the darker black you applied earlier to the OwnerData form and to include the Animals picture to the right of the report title.

To change the color of the report title and insert the picture:

> **1.** At the top of the report, click the **Owners and Visits** title to select it.

> **2.** Make sure the Report Layout Tools Format tab is still active on the ribbon.

Make sure the title is selected so the picture is inserted in the correct location.

> **3.** In the Font group, click the **Font Color button arrow** [A], and then in the Theme Colors section, click the **Black, Text 1, Lighter 25%** color (fourth color in the second column). The color is applied to the report title.

Now you'll insert the picture to the right of the report title text.

> **4.** On the ribbon, click the **Report Layout Tools Design** tab. The options provided on this tab for reports are the same as those you worked with for forms.

> **5.** In the Header/Footer group, click the **Logo** button.

> **6.** Navigate to the **Access1 > Module** folder provided with your Data Files, and then double-click the **Animals** file. The picture is inserted in the top-left corner of the report, partially covering the report title.

> **7.** Position the ⬚ pointer on the selected picture, and then drag it to the right of the report title.

> **8.** Click in a blank area of the shaded bar to deselect the picture. See Figure 4-24.

Figure 4-24   **Report after changing the title font color and inserting the picture**

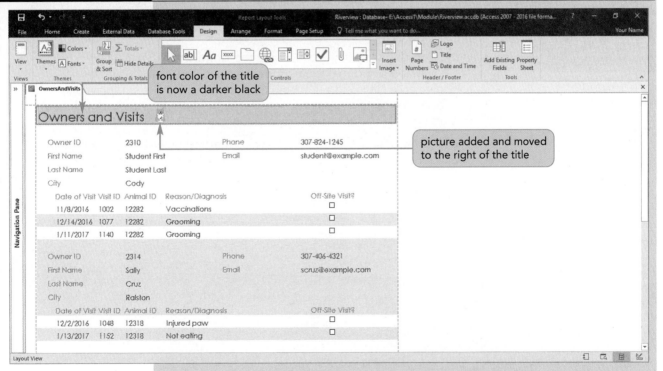

> **Trouble?** Don't be concerned if the picture in your report is not in the exact same location as the one shown in the figure. Just make sure it is to the right of the title text and within the shaded area.

Riverview Veterinary Care Center is planning a mobile clinic day in Ralston. Kimberly would like to make it easier to locate the records in the report for owners who live in Ralston by applying unique formatting to their city names. Because you don't need to apply this formatting to the city names in all the records in the report, you will use conditional formatting.

Using Conditional Formatting in a Report

Conditional formatting in a report (or form) is special formatting applied to certain field values depending on one or more conditions—similar to criteria you establish for queries. If a field value meets the condition or conditions you specify, the formatting is applied to the value.

Kimberly would like the OwnersAndVisits report to show a city name of Ralston in a bold, dark red font. This formatting will help to highlight the owner records for owners who live in this location.

To apply conditional formatting to the City field in the report:

1. Make sure the report is still displayed in Layout view, and then click the **Report Layout Tools Format** tab on the ribbon.

   To apply conditional formatting to a field, you must first make it the active field by clicking any field value in the field's column.

TIP
You must select a field value box, and not the field label, before applying a conditional format.

2. Click the first City field value, **Cody**, for OwnerID 2310 to select the City field values in the report. The conditional formatting you specify will affect all the values for the field.

3. In the Control Formatting group, click the **Conditional Formatting** button. The Conditional Formatting Rules Manager dialog box opens. Because you selected a City field value box, the name of this field is displayed in the "Show formatting rules for" box. Currently, there are no conditional formatting rules set for the selected field. You need to create a new rule.

4. Click the **New Rule** button. The New Formatting Rule dialog box opens. See Figure 4-25.

Figure 4-25 · New Formatting Rule dialog box

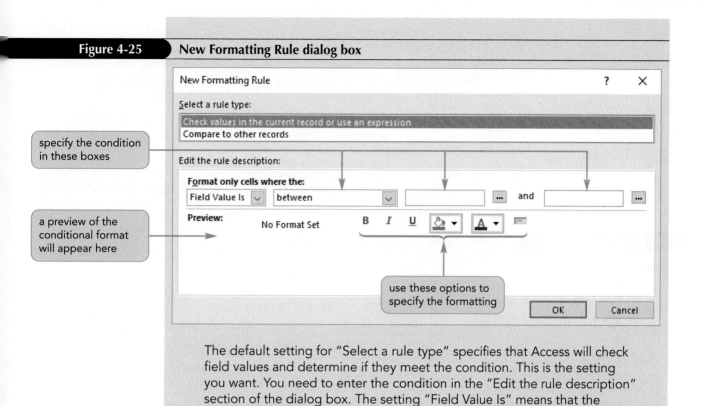

specify the condition in these boxes

a preview of the conditional format will appear here

use these options to specify the formatting

The default setting for "Select a rule type" specifies that Access will check field values and determine if they meet the condition. This is the setting you want. You need to enter the condition in the "Edit the rule description" section of the dialog box. The setting "Field Value Is" means that the conditional format you specify will be applied only when the value for the selected field, City, meets the condition.

▶ **5.** Click the **arrow** for the box containing the word "between," and then click **equal to**. You want only the city name Ralston to be formatted.

▶ **6.** Click in the next box, and then type **Ralston**.

▶ **7.** In the Preview section, click the **Font color button arrow** [A▾], and then click the **Dark Red** color (first color in the last row in the Standard Colors section).

▶ **8.** In the Preview section, click the **Bold** button [B]. The specifications for the conditional formatting are complete. See Figure 4-26.

Figure 4-26 · Conditional formatting set for the City field

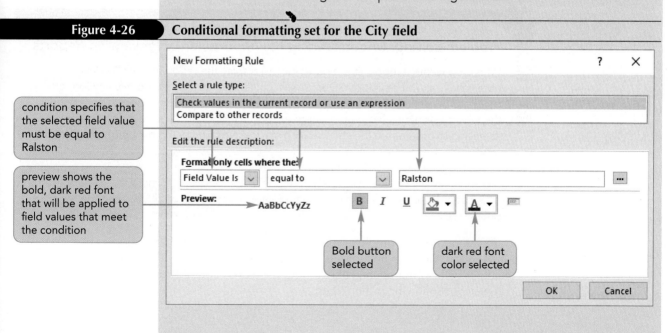

condition specifies that the selected field value must be equal to Ralston

preview shows the bold, dark red font that will be applied to field values that meet the condition

Bold button selected

dark red font color selected

9. Click the **OK** button. The new rule you specified appears in the Rule section of the Conditional Formatting Rules Manager dialog box as Value = "Ralston"; the Format section on the right shows the conditional formatting (dark red, bold font) that will be applied based on this rule.

10. Click the **OK** button. The conditional format is applied to the City field values. To get a better view of the report and the formatting, you'll switch to Print Preview.

11. On the status bar, click the **Print Preview** button. Notice that the conditional formatting is applied only to City field values equal to Ralston. See Figure 4-27.

Figure 4-27   **Viewing the finished report in Print Preview**

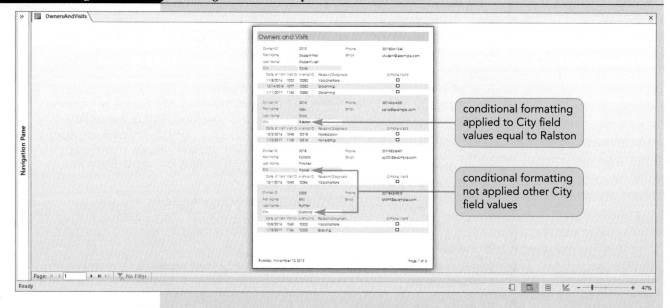

conditional formatting applied to City field values equal to Ralston

conditional formatting not applied other City field values

Problem Solving: Understanding the Importance of Previewing Reports

When you create a report, it is a good idea to display the report in Print Preview occasionally as you develop it. Doing so will give you a chance to identify any formatting problems or other issues so that you can make any necessary corrections before printing the report. It is particularly important to preview a report after you've made changes to its design to ensure that the changes you made have not created new problems with the report's format. Before printing any report, you should preview it so you can determine where the pages will break and make any necessary adjustments. Following this problem-solving approach not only will ensure that the final report looks exactly the way you want it to, but will also save you time and help to avoid wasting paper if you print the report.

The report is now complete. You'll print just the first page of the report so that Kimberly can view the final results and share the report design with other staff members before printing the entire report. (*Note*: Ask your instructor if you should complete the following printing steps.)

To print page 1 of the report:

▶ **1.** On the Print Preview tab, in the Print group, click the **Print** button. The Print dialog box opens.

▶ **2.** In the Print Range section, click the **Pages** option button. The insertion point now appears in the From box so that you can specify the range of pages to print.

▶ **3.** Type **1** in the From box, press the **Tab** key to move to the To box, and then type **1**. These settings specify that only page 1 of the report will be printed.

▶ **4.** Click the **OK** button. The Print dialog box closes, and the first page of the report is printed.

▶ **5.** Save and close the OwnersAndVisits report.

You've created many different objects in the Riverview database. Before you close it, you'll open the Navigation Pane to view all the objects in the database.

To view the Riverview database objects in the Navigation Pane:

▶ **1.** Open the **Navigation Pane** and scroll down, if necessary, to display the bottom of the pane.

The Navigation Pane now includes the OwnersAndVisits report in the Reports section of the pane. Also notice the OwnerAnimals form in the Forms section. This is the form you created containing a main form based on the Owner table and a subform based on the Animal table. The AnimalSubform object is also listed; you can open it separately from the main form. See Figure 4-28.

Figure 4-28 Riverview database objects in the Navigation Pane

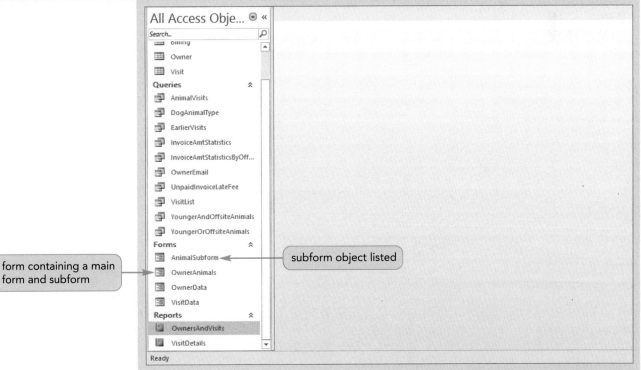

form containing a main form and subform

subform object listed

▶ **2.** Compact and repair the Riverview database, and then close the database.

Kimberly is satisfied that the forms you created—the OwnerData form and the OwnerAnimals form—will make it easier to enter, view, and update data in the Riverview database. The OwnersAndVisits report presents important information about the owners of the animals that the care center treats in an attractive and professional format, which will help Kimberly and other staff members in their work.

REVIEW

Session 4.2 Quick Check

1. In a(n) _____ report, the data from a record in the primary table appears together, followed on subsequent lines by the joined records from the related table.

2. When you create a report based on two tables that are joined in a one-to-many relationship, the field values for the records from the related table are called the _____ records.

3. Identify three types of modifications you can make to a report in Layout view.

4. Describe the process for moving a control to another location on a report in Layout view.

5. When working in Layout view for a report, which key do you press and hold down so that you can click to select multiple controls (field labels, field value boxes, and so on)?

6. _____ in a report (or form) is special formatting applied to certain field values depending on one or more conditions.

Review Assignments

Data Files needed for the Review Assignments: Items.png and Vendor.accdb *(cont. from Module 3)*

Kimberly asks you to enhance the Vendor database with forms and reports. Complete the following steps:

1. Open the **Vendor** database you created and worked with in previous modules, and then click the Enable Content button next to the security warning, if necessary.
2. Use the Form Wizard to create a form based on the Product table. Select all fields for the form and the Columnar layout; specify the title **ProductData** for the form.
3. Apply the Ion theme to the ProductData form *only*.
4. Insert the **Items** picture, which is located in the Access1 > Review folder provided with your Data Files, in the ProductData form. Remove the picture from the control layout, and then move the picture to the right of the form title.
5. Edit the form title so that it appears as "Product Data" (two words), resize the title box as necessary so the title appears on a single line, and then change the font color of the form title to the Gray-25%, Background 2, Darker 75% theme color.
6. Resize the Weight in Lbs field value box so it is the same width (approximately) as the Units/Case field value box above it.
7. Change the alignment of the Price, Units/Case, and Weight in Lbs fields so that their values appear left-aligned in the field value boxes.
8. Save your changes to the form design.
9. Use the ProductData form to update the Product table as follows:
   a. Use the Find command to search for the word "premium" anywhere in the ProductName field, and then display the record for the Premium puppy food (ProductID PF200). Change the Price in this record to **44.00**.
   b. Add a new record with the following field values:
      Product ID: **CT200**
      Supplier ID: **KLS321**
      Product Name: **Cloth tape roll**
      Price: **24.00**
      Units/Case: **10**
      Weight in Lbs: **4**
      Temp Controlled?: **no**
      Sterile?: **no**
   c. Use the form to view each record with a ProductID value that starts with "CT".
   d. Save and close the form.
10. Use the Form Wizard to create a form containing a main form and a subform. Select all fields from the Supplier table for the main form, and select ProductID, ProductName, Price, TempControl, and Sterile—in that order—from the Product table for the subform. Use the Datasheet layout. Specify the title **SuppliersAndProducts** for the main form and **ProductSubform** for the subform.
11. Change the form title text to **Suppliers and Products**.
12. Resize the subform by widening it from its right side, increasing its width by approximately one inch, and then resize all columns in the subform to their best fit, working left to right. Navigate through each record in the main form to make sure all the field values in the subform are completely displayed, resizing subform columns and the subform itself, as necessary. Save and close the SuppliersAndProducts form.

13. Use the Report Wizard to create a report based on the primary Supplier table and the related Product table. Select the SupplierID, Company, City, Category, ContactFirst, ContactLast, and Phone fields—in that order—from the Supplier table, and the ProductID, ProductName, Price, and Units fields from the Product table. Do not specify any additional grouping levels, and sort the detail records in ascending order by ProductID. Choose the Outline layout and Portrait orientation. Specify the title **ProductsBySupplier** for the report.

14. Change the report title text to **Products by Supplier**.

15. Apply the Ion theme to the ProductsBySupplier report *only*.

16. Resize and reposition the following objects in the report in Layout view, and then scroll through the report to make sure all field labels and field values are fully displayed:

    a. Resize the report title so that the text of the title, Products by Supplier, is fully displayed.

    b. Move the ProductName field label and field value box to the right a bit (be sure not to move them too far so that the longest product name will still be completely visible).

    c. Resize the Product ID field label from its right side, increasing its width slightly so the label is fully displayed.

    d. Move the Price field label to the left a bit so the right side of the field label aligns with the right side of the field value below it.

    e. Move the Units/Case field label and field value box to the right a bit; then resize the label on its left side, increasing its width slightly so the label is fully displayed.

    f. Select the field value boxes *only* (not the field labels) for the following four fields: SupplierID, Company, City, and Category. Then move the four field value boxes to the left until their left edges align (roughly) with the "S" in "Supplier" in the report title.

17. Change the color of the report title text to the Gray-25%, Background 2, Darker 75% theme color.

18. Insert the **Items** picture, which is located in the Access1 > Review folder provided with your Data Files, in the report. Move the picture to the right of the report title.

19. Apply conditional formatting so that the Category field values equal to Supplies appear as dark red and bold.

20. Preview each page of the report, verifying that all the fields fit on the page. If necessary, return to Layout view and make changes so the report prints within the margins of the page and so that all field names and values are completely displayed.

21. Save the report, print its first page (only if asked by your instructor to do so), and then close the report.

22. Compact and repair the Vendor database, and then close it.

Case Problem 1

Data Files needed for this Case Problem: Beauty.accdb *(cont. from Module 3)* **and Salon.png**

Beauty To Go   Sue Miller uses the Beauty database to track and view information about the services her business offers. She asks you to create the necessary forms and a report to help her work with this data more efficiently. Complete the following:

1. Open the **Beauty** database you created and worked with in previous modules, and then click the Enable Content button next to the security warning, if necessary.
2. Use the Form Wizard to create a form based on the Member table. Select all the fields for the form and the Columnar layout. Specify the title **MemberData** for the form.
3. Apply the Slice theme to the MemberData form *only*.
4. Edit the form title so that it appears as "Member Data" (two words); resize the title so that both words fit on the same line; and then change the font color of the form title to the Orange, Accent 5, Darker 25% theme color.
5. Use the Find command to display the record for Maita Rios, and then change the OptionEnds field value for this record to **9/3/2017**.
6. Use the MemberData form to add a new record to the Member table with the following field values:
   Member ID: **2180**
   Option ID: **135**
   First Name: **Risa**
   Last Name: **Kaplan**
   Street: **122 Bolcher Ave**
   City: **Orlando**
   State: **FL**
   Zip: **32805**
   Phone: **212-858-4007**
   Option Begins: **11/11/2017**
   Option Ends: **5/11/2018**
7. Save and close the MemberData form.
8. Use the Form Wizard to create a form containing a main form and a subform. Select all the fields from the Option table for the main form, and select the MemberID, FirstName, LastName, OptionEnd, and Phone fields from the Member table for the subform. Use the Datasheet layout. Specify the title **MembersByOption** for the main form and the title **MemberSubform** for the subform.
9. Change the form title text for the main form to **Members by Option**.
10. Resize all columns in the subform to their best fit, working from left to right; then move through all the records in the main form and check to make sure that all subform field values are fully displayed, resizing the columns as necessary.
11. Save and close the MembersByOption form.
12. Use the Report Wizard to create a report based on the primary Option table and the related Member table. Select all the fields from the Option table, and then select the MemberID, FirstName, LastName, City, Phone, OptionBegin, and OptionEnd fields from the Member table. Do not select any additional grouping levels, and sort the detail records in ascending order by MemberID. Choose the Outline layout and Landscape orientation. Specify the title **MemberOptions** for the report.

13. Apply the Slice theme to the MemberOptions report *only*.

14. Resize the report title so that the text is fully displayed; edit the report title so that it appears as "Member Options" (two words); and change the font color of the title to the Orange, Accent 5, Darker 25% theme color.

15. Change the alignment of the Option Cost field so that its values appear left-aligned in the field value boxes.

16. Resize and reposition the following objects in the report in Layout view, and then scroll through the report to make sure all field labels and field values are fully displayed:

    a. Move the FirstName label and field value box to the right a bit (be sure not to move them too far so that the longest first name will still be completely visible).

    b. Resize the MemberID field label on its right side, increasing its width until the label is fully displayed.

    c. Move the Phone label and field value box to the left; then resize the Option Begins label on its left side, increasing its width until the label is fully displayed.

    d. Scroll to the bottom of the report; note that the page number might not be completely within the page border (the dotted vertical line). If necessary, select and move the box containing the text "Page 1 of 1" until the entire text is positioned to the left of the dotted vertical line marking the right page border.

17. Insert the **Salon** picture, which is located in the Access1 > Case1 folder provided with your Data Files, in the report. Move the picture to the right of the report title.

18. Apply conditional formatting so that any OptionEnds field value less than 3/15/2017 appears as bold and with the Red color applied.

19. Preview the entire report to confirm that it is formatted correctly. If necessary, return to Layout view and make changes so that all field labels and field values are completely displayed.

20. Save the report, print its first page (only if asked by your instructor to do so), and then close the report.

21. Compact and repair the Beauty database, and then close it.

Case Problem 2

CREATE

Data Files needed for this Case Problem: Coder.png and Programming.accdb *(cont. from Module 3)*

Programming Pros   Brent Hovis is using the Programming database to track and analyze the business activity of his tutoring services company. To make his work easier, you'll create a form and a report in the Programming database. Complete the following:

1. Open the **Programming** database you created and worked with in previous modules, and then click the Enable Content button next to the security warning, if necessary.
2. Create the form shown in Figure 4-29.

Figure 4-29	Completed ContractsByTutor form

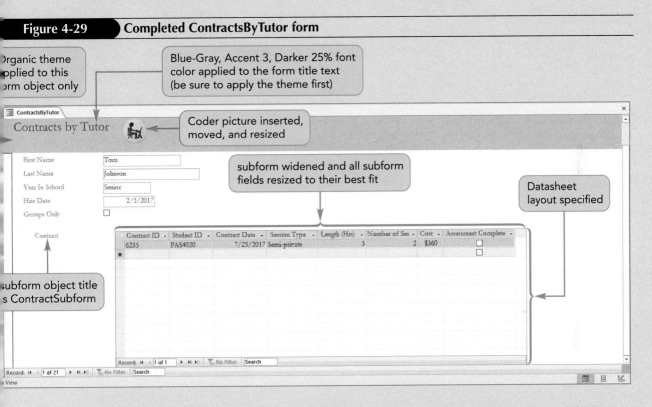

3. Using the form you just created, navigate to the second record in the subform for the eighth main record, and then change the Assessment Complete field value to **yes**.
4. Use the Find command to move to the record for Gail Fordham, and then change the value in the Year In School field to **Senior**.

5. Use the appropriate wildcard character to find all records with a Hire Date field value that begins with the month of February (2). Change the Hire Date field value for Ian Rodriguez (Tutor ID 1020) to **1/17/2017**. Save and close the form.

6. Create the report shown in Figure 4-30.

Figure 4-30   **Completed TutorsAndContracts report**

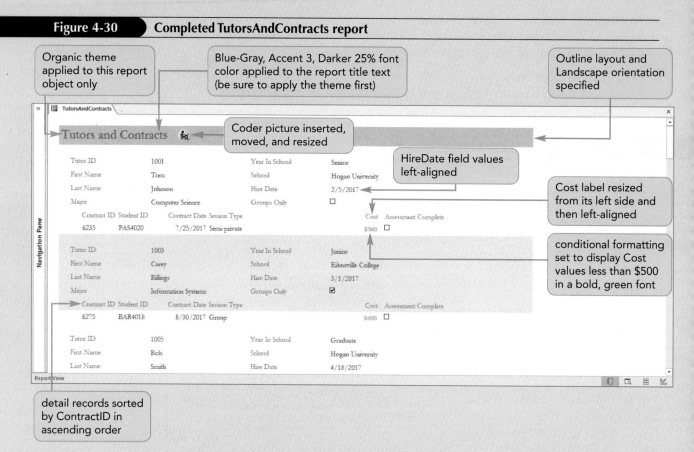

Organic theme applied to this report object only

Blue-Gray, Accent 3, Darker 25% font color applied to the report title text (be sure to apply the theme first)

Outline layout and Landscape orientation specified

Coder picture inserted, moved, and resized

HireDate field values left-aligned

Cost label resized from its left side and then left-aligned

conditional formatting set to display Cost values less than $500 in a bold, green font

detail records sorted by ContractID in ascending order

7. Scroll to the bottom of the report; note that the page number might not be completely within the page border (the dotted vertical line). If necessary, select and move the box containing the text "Page 1 of 1" until the entire text is positioned to the left of the dotted vertical line marking the right page border.

8. Preview each page of the report, verifying that all the fields fit on the page. If necessary, return to Layout view and make changes so the report prints within the margins of the page and all field names and values are completely displayed.

9. Save the report, print its first page (only if asked by your instructor to do so), and then close the report.

10. Compact and repair the Programming database, and then close it.

Case Problem 3

Data Files needed for this Case Problem: Center.accdb *(cont. from Module 3)* and Flower.png

CHALLENGE

Diane's Community Center   Diane Coleman uses the Center database to track, maintain, and analyze data about the patrons, donations, and auction items for her not-for-profit community center. You'll help Diane by creating a form and a report based on this data. Complete the following:

1. Open the **Center** database you created and worked with in previous modules, and then click the Enable Content button next to the security warning, if necessary.

2. Use the Form Wizard to create a form based on the Auction table. Select all the fields for the form and the Columnar layout. Specify the title **AuctionInfo** for the form.

3. Apply the Retrospect theme to the AuctionInfo form *only*.

4. Edit the form title so that it appears as "Auction Info" (two words), and change the font color of the form title to the Brown, Accent 3, Darker 25% theme color.

⊕ **Explore** 5. Use the appropriate button in the Font group on the Form Layout Tools Format tab to italicize the form title. Save the form.

6. Use the AuctionInfo form to update the Auction table as follows:

   a. Use the Find command to search for the record that contains the value "240" for the AuctionID field, and then change the MinimumSalesPrice field value for this record to **275**.

   b. Add a new record with the following values:

   Auction ID: **260**

   Donation ID: **5265**

   Date of Auction: **11/11/2017**

   Minimum Sales Price: **125**

   Item Sold at Auction?: [leave blank]

   ⊕ **Explore** c. Find the record with AuctionID 245, and then delete the record. (*Hint*: After displaying the record in the form, you need to select it by clicking the right-pointing triangle in the bar to the left of the field labels. Then use the appropriate button on the Home tab in the Records group to delete the record. When asked to confirm the deletion, click the Yes button.) Close the form.

7. Use the Form Wizard to create a form containing a main form and a subform. Select all the fields from the Patron table for the main form, and select all fields except PatronID from the Donation table for the subform. Use the Datasheet layout. Specify the name **PatronsAndDonations** for the main form and the title **DonationSubform** for the subform.

8. Apply the Retrospect theme to the PatronsAndDonations form *only*.

9. Edit the form title so that it appears as "Patrons and Donations." Resize the form title so that the text fits on one line. Change the font color of the title to the Brown, Accent 3, Darker 25% theme color.

10. Insert the **Flower** picture, which is located in the Access1 > Case3 folder provided with your Data Files, in the PatronsAndDonations form. Remove the picture from the control layout, and then move the picture to the right of the form title. Resize the picture so it is approximately double the original size.

⊕ **Explore** 11. Use the appropriate button in the Font group on the Form Layout Tools Format tab to apply the theme color Tan, Accent 5, Lighter 80% as a background color for all the field value boxes in the main form. Then use the appropriate button in the Control Formatting group to change the outline of all the main form field value boxes to have a line thickness of 1 pt. (*Hint*: Select all the field value boxes before making these changes.)

12. Resize the subform by extending it to the right, and then resize all columns in the subform to their best fit. Navigate through the records in the main form to make sure all the field values in the subform are completely displayed, resizing subform columns as necessary. Save and close the form.

13. Use the Report Wizard to create a report based on the primary Patron table and the related Donation table. Select all the fields from the Patron table, and select all fields except PatronID from the Donation table. Sort the detail records in *descending* order by DonationValue. Choose the Outline layout and Portrait orientation. Specify the name **PatronsAndDonations** for the report.

14. Apply the Retrospect theme to the PatronsAndDonations report *only*.

15. Resize the report title so that the text is fully displayed; edit the report title so that it appears as "Patrons and Donations"; and change the font color of the title to the Brown, Accent 3, Darker 25% theme color.

16. Move the Donation Value field label and its field value box to the left a bit. Then resize the Donation ID field label on the right to fully display the label. Move the Donation ID field label and its field value box to the left to provide space between the Donation ID and Donation Date fields, and then move the Description field label and its field value box to the right a bit, to provide more space between the Donation Date and Description fields. Widen the Cash Donation? field label so all the text is displayed, and then reposition the field label so it is centered over the CashDonation check boxes below it. Move the AuctionItem check boxes to the right so they are centered below the Possible Auction Item? field label. Finally, resize the Phone and Email field labels from their left sides to reduce the width of the label boxes, moving the words "Phone" and "Email" closer to the field value boxes. Save the report.

17. Insert the **Flower** picture, which is located in the Access1 > Case3 folder provided with your Data Files, in the PatronsAndDonations report. Move the picture to the right of the report title.

⊕ **Explore** 18. Use the appropriate button on the Report Layout Tools Format tab in the Background group to apply the theme color Tan, Accent 5, Lighter 60% as the alternate row color for the fields from the Patron table; then apply the theme color Tan, Accent 5, Lighter 80% as the alternate row color for the fields from the Donation table. (*Hint*: You must first select an entire row with no background color for the appropriate fields before applying each alternate row color.) Scroll through the report to find a patron record with multiple donations so you can verify the effect of applying the alternate row color to the Donation fields.

19. Apply conditional formatting so that any DonationValue greater than or equal to 250 is formatted as bold and with the Brown 5 font color.

⊕ **Explore** 20. Preview the report so you can see two pages at once. (*Hint*: Use a button on the Print Preview tab.) Check the report to confirm that it is formatted correctly and all field labels and field values are fully displayed. Save the report, print its first page (only if asked by your instructor to do so), and then close the report.

21. Compact and repair the Center database, and then close it.

Case Problem 4

TROUBLESHOOT

Data Files needed for this Case Problem: Appalachia.accdb *(cont. from Module 3)*, **HikeApp.accdb, and Mountains.png**

Hike Appalachia Molly and Bailey Johnson use the Appalachia database to maintain and analyze data about the hikers, reservations, and tours for their hiking tour business. You'll help them by creating a form and a report in the Appalachia database. Additionally, you'll troubleshoot some problems in another database containing tour information. Complete the following:

1. Open the **Appalachia** database you created and worked with in previous modules, and then click the Enable Content button next to the security warning, if necessary.

2. Use the Form Wizard to create a form containing a main form and a subform. Select all the fields from the Hiker table for the main form, and select all the fields except HikerID from the Reservation table for the subform. Use the Datasheet layout. Specify the title **HikerReservations** for the main form and the title **ReservationSubform** for the subform.

3. Apply the Integral theme to the HikerReservations form *only*.

4. Edit the form title so that it appears with a space between the two words. Change the font color of the title to the Dark Teal, Text 2, Darker 25% theme color.

5. Insert the **Mountains** picture, which is located in the Access1 > Case4 folder provided with your Data Files, in the HikerReservations form. Remove the picture from the control layout, and then move the picture to the right of the form title. Resize the picture so it is approximately double the original size.

6. Resize all columns in the subform to their best fit so that the subform column titles are fully displayed. Save the form.

7. Use the Find command to search for records that contain "WV" in the State field. Display the record for Sarah Peeler (HikerID 509), and then change the Phone field value for this record to **703-599-2043**. Close the form.

8. Use the Report Wizard to create a report based on the primary Hiker table and the related Reservation table. Select all the fields from the Hiker table, and then select all the fields except HikerID from the Reservation table. Do not select any additional grouping levels, and sort the detail records in ascending order by ReservationID. Choose the Outline layout and Portrait orientation. Specify the title **HikersAndReservations** for the report.

9. Apply the Integral theme to the HikersAndReservations report *only*.

10. Edit the report title so that it appears as "Hikers and Reservations"; then change the font color of the title to the Dark Teal, Text 2, Darker 25% theme color.

11. Left-align the Tour Date field label and field value box, then move the People field label and field value box to the left, to reduce the space between the Tour Date and People columns.

12. Insert the **Mountains** picture, which is located in the Access1 > Case4 folder provided with your Data Files, in the HikersAndReservations report. Move the picture to the right of the report title.

13. Apply conditional formatting so that any People field value greater than or equal to 3 appears as bold and with the Red color applied.

14. Preview the entire report to confirm that it is formatted correctly. If necessary, return to Layout view and make changes so that all field labels and field values are completely displayed.

15. Save the report, print its first page (only if asked by your instructor to do so), and then close the report.

16. Compact and repair the Appalachia database, and then close it.

⚙ **Troubleshoot** 17. Open the **HikeApp** database located in the Access1 > Case4 folder provided with your Data Files. Open the HikerData form in the HikeApp database. The form is not formatted correctly; it should be formatted with the Ion Boardroom theme and the theme color Plum, Accent 1, Darker 50% applied to the title. There are other problems with the form title's format as well. Additionally, some of the field labels are not properly formatted with regard to spacing between words. Identify and fix the problems with the form's format. (*Hint*: To fix the spacing between words in the necessary field labels, use the same procedure you use to fix the spacing between words in the form title text.) Save and close the corrected form.

⚙ **Troubleshoot** 18. Open the **HikerReservations** form, which is also not formatted correctly. Modify the form so that it matches the corrected format of the HikerData form and has a consistent design, including the correctly placing the logo image and resizing it to approximately double its original size. Fix the formatting problems with the subform as well, and then save and close the corrected form with subform.

⚙ **Troubleshoot** 19. Open the **HikersAndReservations** report. This report should have a consistent format in terms of theme, color, and so on as the two forms. Additionally, some of the field labels are not properly formatted with regard to spacing between words. (*Hint*: To fix the spacing between words in the necessary field labels, use the same procedure you use to fix the spacing between words in the report title text.) Find and fix these formatting errors. The report also has several problems with field labels and field value boxes, where the labels and values are not fully displayed. Locate and correct all of these problems, being sure to scroll through the entire report. Also, the conditional formatting applied to the People field is supposed to use a bold Red font. Edit the rule to correct the conditional formatting. Save the corrected report, and then preview it to identify and correct any remaining formatting problems.

20. Compact and repair the HikeApp database, and then close it.

OBJECTIVES

Session 5.1
- Review object naming standards
- Use the Like, In, Not, and & operators in queries
- Filter data using an AutoFilter
- Use the IIf function to assign a conditional value to a calculated field in a query
- Create a parameter query

Session 5.2
- Use query wizards to create a crosstab query, a find duplicates query, and a find unmatched query
- Create a top values query

Session 5.3
- Modify table designs using lookup fields, input masks, and data validation rules
- Identify object dependencies
- Review a Long Text field's properties
- Designate a trusted folder

Creating Advanced Queries and Enhancing Table Design

Making the CareCenter Database Easier to Use

ACCESS

Case | *Riverview Veterinary Care Center*

Riverview Veterinary Care Center, a veterinary care center in Cody, Wyoming, provides a range of medical services for pets and livestock in the greater Cody area. In addition to caring for household pets, such as dogs and cats, the center specializes in serving the needs of livestock on ranches in the surrounding area. Kimberly Johnson, the office manager for Riverview Veterinary Care Center, oversees a small staff and is responsible for maintaining the medical records for all of the animals the care center serves.

Kimberly and her staff rely on Microsoft Access 2016 to manage electronic medical records for owner and animal information, billing, inventory control, purchasing, and accounts payable. The Riverview staff developed the CareCenter database, which contains tables, queries, forms, and reports that Kimberly and other staff members use to track animal, owner, visit, and billing information.

Kimberly is interested in taking better advantage of the power of Access to make the database easier to use and to create more sophisticated queries. For example, Kimberly wants to obtain lists of owners in certain cities. She also needs a summarized list of invoice amounts by city. In this module, you'll modify and customize the CareCenter database to satisfy these and other requirements.

STARTING DATA FILES

Access2 → Module
CareCenter.accdb

Review
Supplier.accdb

Case1
MoreBeauty.accdb

Case2
Tutoring.accdb

Case3
Community.accdb

Case4
AppTrail.accdb

Session 5.1 Visual Overview:

A Select query selects the records in the fields that satisfy the criteria.

The tbl prefix tag identifies a table object.

The qry prefix tag identifies a query object.

The frm prefix tag identifies a form object.

The rpt prefix tag identifies a report object.

A calculated field contains an expression that calculates the values of the data in the field.

The design grid contains the fields and criteria that will be used in the query.

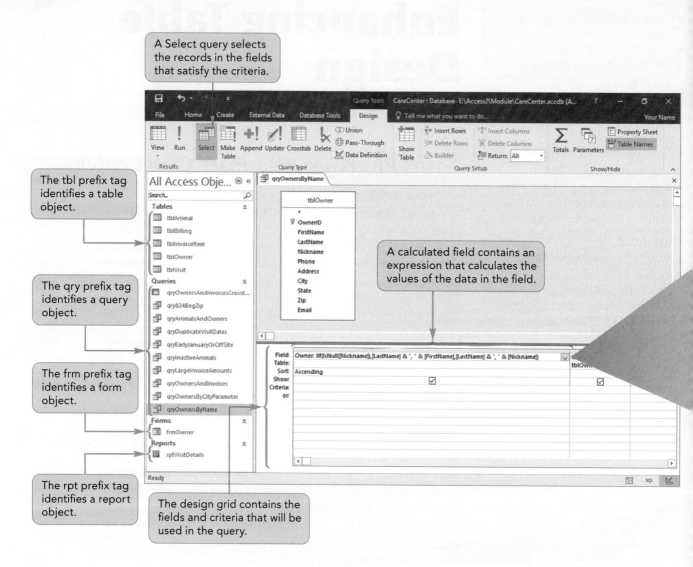

Calculated Field

The name of the new calculated field is placed to the left of the expression, separated with a colon.

The **IIf function** tests a condition and returns one of two values. The function returns the first value if the condition is true and the second value if the condition is false.

The Expression Builder can be used to create an expression for a calculated field.

The falsepart of this IIf function will concatenate the data in the LastName field to a string with a comma and space. It will then concatenate the result to the data in the Nickname field.

The truepart of this IIf function will concatenate the data in the LastName field to a string with a comma and space. It will then concatenate the result to the data in the FirstName field.

The **IsNull function** will return a value of true if the field is empty and will return a value of false if the field is not empty.

Reviewing the CareCenter Database

Kimberly and her staff had no previous database experience when they created the CareCenter database; they simply used the wizards and other easy-to-use Access tools. As business continued to grow at Riverview Veterinary Care Center, Kimberly realized she needed a database expert to further enhance the CareCenter database. She hired Daksha Yatawara, who has a business information systems degree and nine years of experience developing database systems. Daksha spent a few days reviewing the CareCenter database, making sure the database adhered to simple naming standards for the objects and field names to make his future work easier.

Before implementing the enhancements for Kimberly, you'll review the naming conventions for the object names in the CareCenter database.

To review the object naming conventions in the CareCenter database:

▶ **1.** Make sure you have the Access starting Data Files on your computer.

   Trouble? If you don't have the Access Data Files, you need to get them before you can proceed. Your instructor will either give you the Data Files or ask you to obtain them from a specified location (such as a network drive). If you have any questions about the Data Files, see your instructor or technical support person for assistance.

▶ **2.** Start Access, and then open the **CareCenter** database from the Access2 > Module folder where your starting Data Files are stored.

   Trouble? If the security warning is displayed below the ribbon, click the Enable Content button.

As shown in Visual Overview 5.1, the Navigation Pane displays the objects grouped by object type. Each object name has a prefix tag—a tbl prefix tag for tables, a qry prefix tag for queries, a frm prefix tag for forms, and a rpt prefix tag for reports. All three characters in each prefix tag are lowercase. The word immediately after the three-character prefix begins with an uppercase letter. Using object prefix tags, you can readily identify the object type, even when the objects have the same base name—for instance, tblOwner, frmOwner, and rptOwnersAndVisits. In addition, object names have no spaces, because other database management systems, such as SQL Server and Oracle, do not permit spaces in object and field names. It is important to adhere to industry standard naming conventions, both to make it easier to convert your database to another DBMS in the future, if necessary, and to develop personal habits that enable you to work seamlessly with other major DBMSs. If Riverview Veterinary Care Center needs to upscale to one of these other systems in the future, using standard naming conventions means that Daksha will have to do less work to make the transition.

Teamwork: Following Naming Conventions

Most Access databases have hundreds of fields, objects, and controls. You'll find it easier to identify the type and purpose of these database items when you use a naming convention or standard. Most companies adopt a standard naming convention, such as the one used for the CareCenter database, so that multiple people can develop a database, troubleshoot database problems, and enhance and improve existing databases. When working on a database, a team's tasks are difficult, if not impossible, to perform if a standard naming convention isn't used. In addition, most databases and database samples on websites and in training books use standard naming conventions that are similar to the ones used for the CareCenter database. By following the standard naming convention established by your company or organization, you'll help to ensure smooth collaboration among all team members.

Now you'll create the queries that Kimberly needs.

Using a Pattern Match in a Query

You are already familiar with queries that use an exact match or a range of values (for example, queries that use the > or < comparison operators) to select records. Many other operators are available for creating select queries. These operators let you build more complicated queries that are difficult or impossible to create with exact-match or range-of-values selection criteria.

Kimberly created a list of questions she wants to answer using the CareCenter database:

- Which owners have a zip code beginning with 824?
- What is the owner information for owners located in Cody, Ralston, or Powell?
- What is the owner information for all owners except those located in Cody, Ralston, or Powell?
- What is the owner and visit information for owners in Cody or Powell whose animals were seen offsite or visited during early January?
- What are the first and last names of Riverview Veterinary Care Center owners? Nicknames should be used where listed.
- What is the owner information for owners in a particular city? This query needs to be flexible to allow the user to specify the city.

Next, you will create the queries necessary to answer these questions. Kimberly wants to view the records for all owners whose zip code begins with 824. To answer Kimberly's question, you can create a query that uses a pattern match. A **pattern match** selects records with a value for the designated field that matches the pattern of a simple condition value—in this case, owners with a zip code beginning with 824. You do this using the Like comparison operator.

The **Like comparison operator** selects records by matching field values to a specific pattern that includes one or more of these wildcard characters: asterisk (*), question mark (?), and number symbol (#). The asterisk represents any string of characters, the question mark represents any single character, and the number symbol represents any single digit. Using a pattern match is similar to using an exact match, except that a pattern match includes wildcard characters.

To create the new query, you must first place the tblOwner table field list in the Query window in Design view.

To create the new query in Design view:

▶ 1. If necessary, click the **Shutter Bar Open/Close Button** « at the top of the Navigation Pane to close it.

▶ 2. On the ribbon, click the **Create** tab.

▶ 3. In the Queries group, click the **Query Design** button. The Show Table dialog box opens in front of the Query window in Design view.

▶ 4. Click **tblOwner** in the Tables box, click the **Add** button, and then click the **Close** button. The tblOwner table field list is added to the Query window, and the Show Table dialog box closes.

▶ 5. Drag the bottom border of the tblOwner window down until you can see the full list of fields.

▶ 6. Double-click the **title bar** of the tblOwner field list to highlight all the fields, and then drag the highlighted fields to the first column's Field box in the design grid. Each field is placed in a separate column in the design grid, in the same order that the fields appear in the table. See Figure 5-1.

> **TIP**
>
> You can also double-click a table name to add the table's field list to the Query window.

| Figure 5-1 | Adding the fields for the pattern match query |

Trouble? If tblOwner.* appears in the first column's Field box, you dragged the * from the field list instead of the highlighted fields. Press the Delete key, and then repeat Step 6.

Now you will enter the pattern match condition Like "824*" for the Zip field. The query will select records with a Zip field value of 824 in positions one through three. The asterisk wildcard character specifies that any characters can appear in the remaining positions of the field value.

To specify records that match the indicated pattern:

TIP

If you omit the Like operator, it is automatically added when you run the query.

1. Click the **Zip Criteria** box, and then type **L**. The Formula AutoComplete menu displays a list of functions beginning with the letter L, but the Like operator is not one of the choices in the list. You'll finish typing the condition.

2. Type **ike "824*"**. See Figure 5-2.

Figure 5-2	Record selection based on matching a specific pattern

pattern match selection criterion

3. Click the **Save** button 💾 on the Quick Access Toolbar to open the Save As dialog box.

4. Type **qry824BegZip** in the Query Name box, and then press the **Enter** key. The query is saved, and the name is displayed on the object tab.

5. On the Query Tools Design tab, in the Results group, click the **Run** button. The query results are displayed in the query window. Twenty-three records have zip codes beginning with 824. See Figure 5-3.

Figure 5-3	tblOwner table records for zip codes starting with 824

Note that Daksha removed the hyphens from the Phone field values; for example, 3078241245 in the first record used to be 307-824-1245. You'll modify the Phone field later in this module to format its values with hyphens.

6. Change the first record in the table, with Owner ID 2310, so the Last Name and First Name columns contain your last and first names, respectively.

7. Close the qry824BegZip query.

Next, Kimberly asks you to create a query that displays information about owners who live in Cody, Ralston, or Powell. To produce the results Kimberly wants, you'll create a query using a list-of-values match.

Using a List-of-Values Match in a Query

A **list-of-values match** selects records whose value for the designated field matches one of two or more simple condition values. You could accomplish this by including several Or conditions in the design grid, but the In comparison operator provides an easier and clearer way to do this. The **In comparison operator** lets you define a condition with a list of two or more values for a field. If a record's field value matches one value from the list of defined values, then that record is selected and included in the query results.

To display the information Kimberly requested, you want to select records if their City field value equals Cody, Ralston, or Powell. These are the values you will use with the In comparison operator. Kimberly wants the query to contain the same fields as the qry824BegZip query, so you'll make a copy of that query and modify it.

To create the query using a list-of-values match:

▶ **1.** Open the Navigation Pane.

▶ **2.** In the Queries group on the Navigation Pane, right-click **qry824BegZip**, and then click **Copy** on the shortcut menu.

Trouble? If you don't see the qry824BegZip query in the Queries group, press the F5 function key to refresh the object listings in the Navigation pane.

▶ **3.** Right-click in the empty area in the Navigation Pane below the report and then click **Paste**.

▶ **4.** In the Query Name box, type **qryCodyRalstonPowellOwners**, and then press the **Enter** key.

To modify the copied query, you need to open it in Design view.

▶ **5.** In the Queries group on the Navigation Pane, right-click **qryCodyRalstonPowellOwners** to select it and display the shortcut menu.

▶ **6.** Click **Design View** on the shortcut menu to open the query in Design view, and then close the Navigation Pane.

You need to delete the existing condition from the Phone field.

▶ **7.** Click the **Zip Criteria** box, press the **F2** key to highlight the entire condition, and then press the **Delete** key to remove the condition.

Now you can enter the criterion for the new query using the In comparison operator. When you use this operator, you must enclose the list of values you want to match within parentheses and separate the values with commas. In addition, for fields defined using the Short Text data type, you enclose each value in quotation marks, although the quotation marks are automatically added if you omit them. For fields defined using the Number or Currency data type, you don't enclose the values in quotation marks.

8. Right-click the **City Criteria** box to open the shortcut menu, click **Zoom** to open the Zoom dialog box, and then type **In ("Cody","Ralston","Powell")**, as shown in Figure 5-4.

| Figure 5-4 | Record selection based on matching field values to a list of values |

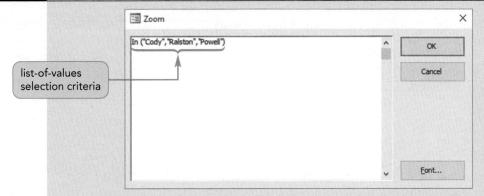

list-of-values
selection criteria

TIP

After clicking in a box, you can also open its Zoom dialog box by holding down the Shift key and pressing the F2 key.

9. Click the **OK** button to close the Zoom dialog box, and then save and run the query. The recordset is displayed, which shows the 17 records with Cody, Ralston, or Powell in the City field.

10. Close the query.

Kimberly would also like a list of owners who do not live in Cody, Ralston, or Powell. You can provide Kimberly with this information by creating a query with the Not logical operator.

Using the Not Logical Operator in a Query

The **Not logical operator** negates a criterion or selects records for which the designated field does not match the criterion. For example, if you enter *Not "Cody"* in the Criteria box for the City field, the query results show records that do not have the City field value Cody—that is, records of all owners not located in Cody.

To create Kimberly's query, you will combine the Not logical operator with the In comparison operator to select owners whose City field value is not in the list *("Cody","Ralston","Powell")*. The qryCodyRalstonPowellOwners query has the fields that Kimberly needs to see in the query results. Kimberly doesn't need to keep the qryCodyRalstonPowellOwners query, so you'll rename and then modify the query.

To create the query using the Not logical operator:

1. Open the Navigation Pane.

TIP

You can rename any type of object, including a table, in the Navigation Pane using the Rename command on the shortcut menu.

2. In the Queries group, right-click **qryCodyRalstonPowellOwners**, and then on the shortcut menu click **Rename**.

3. Position the insertion point after "qry," type **Non**, and then press the **Enter** key. The query name is now qryNonCodyRalstonPowellOwners.

4. Open the **qryNonCodyRalstonPowellOwners** query in Design view, and then close the Navigation Pane.

You need to change the existing condition in the City field to add the Not logical operator.

▶ **5.** Click the **City Criteria** box, open the Zoom dialog box, click at the beginning of the expression, type **Not**, and then press the **spacebar**. See Figure 5-5.

Figure 5-5	Record selection based on not matching a list of values

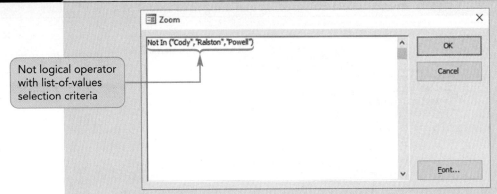

Not logical operator with list-of-values selection criteria

▶ **6.** Click the **OK** button, and then save and run the query. The recordset displays only those records with a City field value that is not Cody, Ralston, or Powell. The recordset includes a total of nine owner records.

▶ **7.** Scroll down the datasheet if necessary to make sure that no Cody, Ralston, or Powell owners appear in your results.

Now you can close and delete the query, because Kimberly does not need to run this query again.

▶ **8.** Close the query, and then open the Navigation Pane.

TIP

You can delete any type of object, including a table, in the Navigation Pane using the Delete command on the shortcut menu.

▶ **9.** Right-click **qryNonCodyRalstonPowellOwners**, click **Delete** on the shortcut menu, and then click **Yes** in the dialog box warning that deleting this object will remove it from all groups.

You now are ready to answer Kimberly's question about owners in Cody or Powell who have invoice amounts for less than $75 or who visited during the first week of January.

Using an AutoFilter to Filter Data

Kimberly wants to view the owner first and last names, cities, animal names, visit dates, offsite statuses, and visit reasons for owners in Cody or Powell whose animals either were seen offsite or visited during the first week in January. The qryEarlyJanuaryOrOffSite query contains the same fields Kimberly wants to view. This query also uses the Or logical operator to select records if the OffSite field has a value of true or if the VisitDate field value is between 1/1/2017 and 1/7/2017. These are two of the conditions needed to answer Kimberly's question. You could modify the qryEarlyJanuaryOrOffSite query in Design view to further restrict the records selected to Owners located only in Cody or Powell. However, you can use the AutoFilter feature to choose the city restrictions faster and with more flexibility. You previously used the AutoFilter feature to sort records, and you previously used Filter By Selection to filter records. Now you'll use the AutoFilter feature to filter records.

To filter the records using an AutoFilter:

▶ **1.** Open the **qryEarlyJanuaryOrOffSite** query in Design view, and then close the Navigation Pane.

The true condition for the OffSite field selects records for owners whose animals were seen offsite, and the Between #1/1/2017# And #1/7/2017# condition for the VisitDate field selects records for animals whose visit date was in the first week of January 2017. Although the OffSite field is a yes/no field, these values are represented by true (yes) and false (no). Because the conditions are in two different rows, the query uses the Or logical operator. If you wanted to answer Kimberly's question in Design view, you would add a condition for the City field, using either the Or logical operator—"Cody" Or "Powell"—or the In comparison operator—In ("Cody","Powell"). You'd place the condition for the City field in both the Criteria row and in the Or row. The query recordset would include a record only if both conditions in either row are satisfied. Instead of changing the conditions in Design view, though, you'll choose the information Kimberly wants using an AutoFilter.

▶ **2.** Run the query, and then click the **arrow** on the City column heading to display the AutoFilter menu. See Figure 5-6.

Figure 5-6   **Using an AutoFilter to filter records in the query recordset**

The AutoFilter menu lists all City field values that appear in the recordset. A checkmark next to an entry indicates that records with that City field value appear in the recordset. To filter for selected City field values, you uncheck the cities you don't want selected and leave checked the cities you do want selected. You can click the "(Select All)" check box to select or deselect all field values. The "(Blanks)" option includes null values when checked and excludes null values when unchecked. (Recall that a null field value is the absence of a value for the field.)

▶ **3.** Click the **(Select All)** check box to deselect all check boxes, click the **Cody** check box, and then click the **Powell** check box.

The two check boxes indicate that the AutoFilter will include only Cody and Powell City field values.

▶ **4.** Click the **OK** button. The AutoFilter displays the 28 records for owners in Cody and Powell whose animals were seen offsite or who had a visit in the first week in January. See Figure 5-7.

Figure 5-7   **Recordset showing results of an AutoFilter**

You click the Toggle Filter button in the Sort & Filter group on the Home tab to remove the current filter and display all records in the query. If you click the Toggle Filter button a second time, you reapply the filter.

▶ **5.** On the Home tab, in the Sort & Filter group, click the **Toggle Filter** button. The filter is removed, and all 40 records appear in the recordset.

▶ **6.** Click the **Toggle Filter** button. The City filter is applied, displaying the 28 records for owners in Cody and Powell.

▶ **7.** Save the query and close it.

Next, Kimberly wants to view all fields from the tblOwner table, along with the owner name. If a nickname is available, she would like it to be used in place of the proper first name of the owner.

Assigning a Conditional Value to a Calculated Field

If a field in a record does not contain any information at all, it has a null value. Such a field is also referred to as a null field. A field in a record that contains any data at all—even a single space—is nonnull. Records for owners have nonnull FirstName and LastName field values in the tblOwner table. If an owner does not have a requested nickname, the owner has a null Nickname field value. Kimberly wants to view records from the tblOwner table in order by last name. She wants the owner's nickname to be shown in place of the first name if the Nickname field is nonnull; otherwise, if the Nickname field is null, she wants the FirstName field value to be shown. To produce this information for Kimberly, you need to create a query that includes all fields from the tblOwner table and then add a calculated field that will display the owner name, including either the Nickname field value, if present, or the FirstName field value. The LastName field and either the Nickname or FirstName fields will be separated by a comma and a space.

To combine the LastName and FirstName fields, you'll use the expression *LastName & ", " & FirstName*. The **& (ampersand) operator** is a concatenation operator that joins text expressions. **Concatenation** refers to joining two or more text fields or characters encapsulated in quotes. When you join the LastName field value to the string that contains the comma and space, you are concatenating these two strings. If the LastName field value is Vasquez and the FirstName field value is Katrina, for example, the result of the expression *LastName & ", " & FirstName* is *Vasquez & ", " & Katrina* which results in *Vasquez, Katrina*.

To display the correct owner value, you'll use the IIf function. The **IIf (Immediate If)** function assigns one value to a calculated field or control if a condition is true and a second value if the condition is false. The IIf function has three parts: a condition that is true or false, the result when the condition is true, and the result when the condition is false. Each part of the IIf function is separated by a comma. The condition you'll use is *IsNull(Nickname)*. The IsNull function tests a field value or an expression for a null value; if the field value or expression is null, the result is true; otherwise, the result is false. The expression *IsNull(Nickname)* is true when the Nickname field value is null and is false when the Nickname field value is not null.

For the calculated field, you'll enter *IIf(IsNull(Nickname),LastName & ", " & FirstName,LastName & ", " & Nickname)*. You interpret this expression as follows: If the Nickname field value is null, then set the calculated field value to the concatenation of the LastName field value and the text string ", " and the FirstName field value. If the Nickname field value is not null, then set the calculated field value to the concatenation of the LastName field value and the text string ", " and the Nickname field value.

Now you're ready to create Kimberly's query to display the owner name.

To create the query to display the owner name:

▶ **1.** Click the **Create** tab, and then in the Queries group, click the **Query Design** button. The Show Table dialog box opens on top of the Query window in Design View.

▶ **2.** Click **tblOwner** in the Tables box, click the **Add** button, and then click the **Close** button. The tblOwner table field list is placed in the Query window, and the Show Table dialog box closes.

Kimberly wants all fields from the tblOwner table to appear in the query recordset, with the new calculated field in the first column.

▶ **3.** Drag the bottom border of the tblOwner field list down until all fields are visible, double-click the title bar of the tblOwner field list to highlight all the fields, and then drag the highlighted fields to the second column's Field box in the design grid. Each field is placed in a separate column in the design grid starting with the second column, in the same order that the fields appear in the table.

Trouble? If you accidentally drag the highlighted fields to the first column in the design grid, click the OwnerID Field box, and then in the Query Setup group, click the Insert Columns button. Continue with Step 4.

TIP

After clicking in a box, you can also open its Expression Builder dialog box by holding down the Ctrl key and pressing the F2 key.

▶ **4.** Right-click the blank Field box to the left of the OwnerID field, and then click **Build** on the shortcut menu. The Expression Builder dialog box opens.

Kimberly wants to use "Owner" as the name of the calculated field, so you'll type that name, followed by a colon, and then you'll choose the IIf function.

▶ **5.** Type **Owner:** and then press the **spacebar**.

▶ **6.** Double-click **Functions** in the Expression Elements (left) column, and then click **Built-In Functions**.

Make sure you double-click instead of single-click the IIf function.

▶ **7.** Scroll down the Expression Categories (middle) column, click **Program Flow**, and then in the Expression Values (right) column, double-click **IIf**. The IIf function is added with four placeholders to the right of the calculated field name in the expression box. See Figure 5-8.

Figure 5-8   **IIf function inserted for the calculated field**

The expression you will create does not need the leftmost placeholder (<<Expr>>), so you'll delete it. You'll replace the second placeholder (<<expression>>) with the condition using the IsNull function, the third placeholder (<<truepart>>) with the expression using the & operator and the FirstName and LastName fields, and the fourth placeholder (<<falsepart>>) with the expression using the & operator and the Nickname and LastName fields.

▶ 8. Click **<<Expr>>** in the expression box, and then press the **Delete** key. The first placeholder is deleted.

▶ 9. Click **<<expression>>** in the expression box, and then click **Inspection** in the Expression Categories (middle) column.

▶ 10. Double-click **IsNull** in the Expression Values (right) column, click **<<expression>>** in the expression box, and then type **Nickname**. You've completed the entry of the condition in the IIf function. See Figure 5-9.

Figure 5-9   After entering the condition for the calculated field's IIf function

After you typed the first letter of "Nickname," the Formula AutoComplete box displayed a list of functions beginning with the letter N, and a ScreenTip for the IsNull function was displayed above the box. The box closed after you typed the third letter, but the ScreenTip remains on the screen.

Instead of typing the field name of Nickname in the previous step, you could have double-clicked CareCenter.accdb in the Expression Elements column, double-clicked Tables in the Expression Elements column, clicked tblOwner in the Expression Elements column, and then double-clicked Nickname in the Expression Categories column.

Now you'll replace the third placeholder and then the fourth placeholder.

▶ 11. Click **<<truepart>>**, and then type **LastName & ", " & FirstName**. Be sure you type a space after the comma within the quotation marks.

▶ 12. Click **<<falsepart>>**, and then type **LastName & ", " & Nickname**. Be sure you type a space after the comma within the quotation marks. See Figure 5-10.

Figure 5-10 | **Completed calculated field**

truepart expression

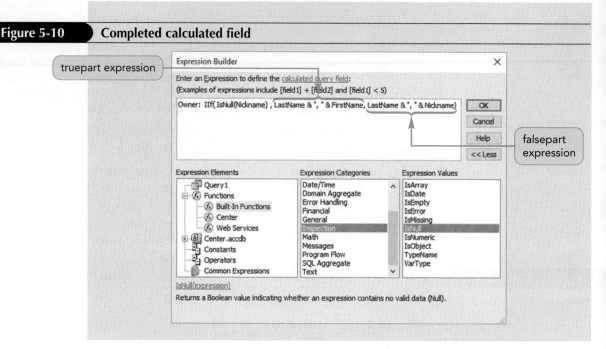

falsepart expression

Kimberly wants the query to sort records in ascending order by the Owner calculated field.

To sort, save, and run the query:

▶ **1.** Click the **OK** button in the Expression Builder dialog box to close it.

▶ **2.** Click the right side of the Owner Sort box to display the sort order options, and then click **Ascending**. The query will display the records in alphabetical order based on the Owner field values.

The calculated field name of Owner consists of a single word, so you do not need to set the Caption property for it. However, you'll review the properties for the calculated field by opening its property sheet.

▶ **3.** On the Query Tools Design tab, in the Show/Hide group, click the **Property Sheet** button. The property sheet opens and displays the properties for the Owner calculated field. See Figure 5-11.

Figure 5-11 | **Property sheet for the Owner calculated field**

properties for the calculated field

calculated field is the current field

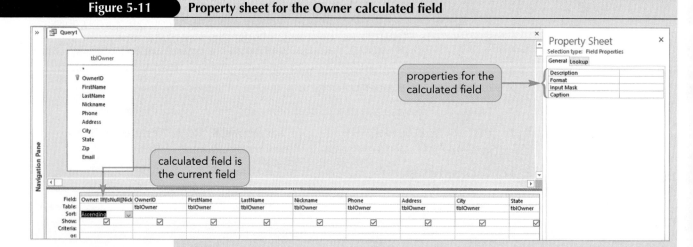

Among the properties for the calculated field, which is the current field, is the Caption property. Leaving the Caption property set to null means that the column name for the calculated field in the query recordset will be Owner, which is the calculated field name. The Property Sheet button is a toggle, so you'll click it again to close the property sheet.

4. Click the **Property Sheet** button again to close the property sheet.

5. Save the query as **qryOwnersByName**, run the query, and then resize the Owner column to its best fit. All records from the tblOwner table are displayed in alphabetical order by the Owner field. See Figure 5-12.

Figure 5-12	Completed query displaying the Owner calculated field

qryOwnersByName

Owner	Owner ID	First Name	Last Name	Nickname	Phone	Address
Baxter, Reg	2404	Reggie	Baxter	Reg	3079432469	880 Powell-Cody Rd
Billings, Curt	2370	Curt	Billings		4066124711	10 Ridgewood Ln
Blacksmith, Wilbur	2354	Randy	Blacksmith	Wilbur	3078829987	245 18th Ave
Cruz, Sally	2314	Sally	Cruz		3074064321	199 18th Ave
Fishman, Barbara	2325	Barbara	Fishman		4067921410	21 Mountain Ln
Gonzalez, James	2330	James	Gonzalez		3079870334	16 Rockway Rd
Hendricks, Angie	2358	Angie	Hendricks		3079432234	27 Locklear Ln
Jackson, Aaron	2366	Aaron	Jackson		4068172392	417 Rocky Rd
Jackson, Elmer	2392	Elmer	Jackson		3078438472	22 Jackson Farm Rd
Jackson, Melanie	2340	Melanie	Jackson		3078821925	42 Blackwater Way
Johnson, Taylor	2412	Taylor	Johnson		3078688862	458 Rose Ln
Jones, Thomas	2362	Thomas	Jones		3079859981	622 Bobcat Tr
Kostas, Mei	2416	Mei	Kostas		3078245873	812 Playa Hwy
Miller, Susan	2384	Susan	Miller		3078242756	1283 Old Roundabout Rd
Otterman, Zack	2375	Joseph	Otterman	Zack	3078249863	42 Rock Ln
Pincher, Sandra	2318	Sandra	Pincher		3079828401	53 Verde Ln
Poleman, Dan	2345	Dan	Poleman		3078878873	75 Stream Rd
Rascal, Tom	2408	Tom	Rascal		3078243575	1 Rascal Farm Rd

owner names are the concatenation for LastName, FirstName for null Nickname values

owner names are the concatenation for LastName, Nickname for nonnull Nickname values

6. Save and close the query.

You're now ready to create the query to satisfy Kimberly's request for information about owners in a particular city.

Creating a Parameter Query

Kimberly's next request is for records in the qryOwnersByName query for owners in a particular city. For this query, she wants to specify a city, such as Cody or Garland, each time she runs the query.

To create this query, you will copy, rename, and modify the qryOwnersByName query. You could create a simple condition using an exact match for the City field, but you would need to change it in Design view every time you run the query. Alternatively, Kimberly or a member of her staff could filter the qryOwnersByName query for the city records they want to view. Instead, you will create a parameter query. A **parameter query** displays a dialog box that prompts the user to enter one or more criteria values when the query is run. In this case, you want to create a query that prompts for the city and selects only those owner records with that City field value from the table. You will enter the prompt in the Criteria box for the City field. When the query runs, it will open a dialog box and prompt you to enter the city. The query results will then be created, just as if you had changed the criteria in Design view.

Creating a Parameter Query

- Create a select query that includes all fields to appear in the query results.
- Choose the sort fields, and set the criteria that do not change when you run the query.
- Decide which fields to use as prompts when the query runs. In the Criteria box for each of these fields, type the prompt you want to appear in a dialog box when you run the query, and enclose the prompt in brackets.

You'll copy and rename the qryOwnersByName query now, and then you'll change its design to create the parameter query.

To create the parameter query based on an existing query:

1. Open the Navigation Pane, copy and paste the qryOwnersByName query, and then name the new copy **qryOwnersByCityParameter**.

2. Open the **qryOwnersByCityParameter** query in Design view, and then close the Navigation Pane.

   Next, you must enter the criterion for the parameter query. In this case, Kimberly wants the query to prompt users to enter the city for the owner records they want to view. You need to enter the prompt in the Criteria box for the City field. Brackets must enclose the text of the prompt.

3. Click the **City Criteria** box, type **[Type the city:]** and then press the **Enter** key. See Figure 5-13.

Figure 5-13   **Specifying the prompt for the parameter query**

4. Save and run the query. A dialog box is displayed, prompting you for the name of the city. See Figure 5-14.

Figure 5-14   **Enter Parameter Value dialog box**

TIP

You must enter a value
that matches the spelling
of a City field value,
but you can use either
lowercase or uppercase
letters.

The bracketed text you specified in the Criteria box of the City field appears above a box, in which you must type a City field value. Kimberly wants to see all owners in Cody.

▶ **5.** Type **Cody**, press the **Enter** key, and then scroll the datasheet to the right, if necessary, to display the City field values. The recordset displays the data for the 10 owners in Cody. See Figure 5-15.

Figure 5-15   **Results of the parameter query**

Kimberly asks what happens if she doesn't enter a value in the dialog box when she runs the qryOwnersByCityParameter query. You can run the query again to show Kimberly the answer to her question.

▶ **6.** Switch to Design view, and then run the query. The Enter Parameter Value dialog box opens.

If you click the OK button or press the Enter key, you'll run the parameter query without entering a value for the City field criterion.

▶ **7.** Click the **OK** button. No records are displayed in the query results.

When you run the parameter query and enter "Cody" in the dialog box, the query runs just as if you had entered "Cody" in the City Criteria box in the design grid and displays all Cody owner records. When you do not enter a value in the dialog box, the query runs as if you had entered "null" in the City Criteria box. Because none of the records has a null City field value, no records are displayed. Kimberly asks if there's a way to display records for a selected City field value when she enters its value in the dialog box and to display all records when she doesn't enter a value.

Creating a More Flexible Parameter Query

Most users want a parameter query to display the records that match the parameter value the user enters or to display all records when the user doesn't enter a parameter value. To provide this functionality, you can change the value in the Criteria box in the design grid for the specified column. For example, you could change an entry for a City field from *[Type the city:]* to *Like [Type the city:] & "*".* That is, you can prefix the Like operator to the original criterion and concatenate the criterion to a wildcard character. When you run the parameter query with this new entry, one of the following recordsets will be displayed:

- If you enter a specific City field value in the dialog box, such as *Belfry*, the entry is the same as *Like "Belfry" & "*",* which becomes *Like "Belfry*"* after the concatenation operation. That is, all records are selected whose City field values have Belfry in the first six positions and any characters in the remaining positions. If the table on which the query is based contains records with City field values of Belfry, only those records are displayed. However, if the table on which the query is based also contains records with City field values of Belfry City, then both the Belfry and the Belfry City records would be displayed.
- If you enter a letter in the dialog box, such as *B*, the entry is the same as *Like "B*",* and the recordset displays all records with City field values that begin with the letter B, which would include Belfry and Bearcreek.
- If you enter no value in the dialog box, the entry is the same as *Like Null & "*",* which becomes *Like "*"* after the concatenation operation, and the recordset displays all records.

Now you'll modify the parameter query to satisfy Kimberly's request, and you'll test the new version of the query.

To modify and test the parameter query:

1. Switch to Design view.

2. Click the **City Criteria** box, and then open the **Zoom** dialog box.

   You'll use the Zoom dialog box to modify the value in the City Criteria box.

3. Click to the left of the expression in the Zoom dialog box, type **Like**, press the **spacebar**, and then press the **End** key.

4. Press the **spacebar**, type **&**, press the **spacebar**, and then type **"*"** as shown in Figure 5-16.

   Be sure you type **"*"** at the end of the expression.

Figure 5-16   Modified City Criteria value in the Zoom dialog box

Now you can test the modified parameter query.

▶ **5.** Click the **OK** button to close the Zoom dialog box, save your query design changes, and then run the query.

First, you'll test the query to display owners in Powell.

▶ **6.** Type **Powell**, and then press the **Enter** key. The recordset displays the data for the three owners in Powell.

Now you'll test the query without entering a value when prompted.

▶ **7.** Switch to Design view, run the query, and then click the **OK** button. The recordset displays all 26 original records from the tblOwner table.

Finally, you'll test how the query performs when you enter B in the dialog box.

▶ **8.** On the Home tab, in the Records group, click the **Refresh All** button to open the Enter Parameter Value dialog box.

▶ **9.** Type **B**, press the **Enter** key, and then scroll to the right, if necessary, to display the City field values. The recordset displays the two records for owners in Belfry and Bearcreek.

▶ **10.** Close the query.

▶ **11.** If you are not continuing on to the next session, close the CareCenter database, and then click the **Yes** button if necessary to empty the Clipboard.

The queries you created will make the CareCenter database easier to use. In the next session, you'll use query wizards to create three different types of queries, and you'll use Design view to create a top values query.

Session 5.1 Quick Check

REVIEW

1. According to the naming conventions used in this session, you use the _____ prefix tag to identify queries.
2. Which comparison operator selects records based on a specific pattern?
3. What is the purpose of the asterisk (*) in a pattern match query?
4. When do you use the In comparison operator?
5. How do you negate a selection criterion?
6. The _____ function returns one of two values based on whether the condition being tested is true or false.
7. When do you use a parameter query?

Session 5.2 Visual Overview:

A **crosstab query** uses aggregate functions such as Sum and Count to perform arithmetic operations on selected records.

A simple query selects records from one or more tables that satisfy criteria.

A **find duplicates query** is a select query that finds duplicate records in a table or query.

A **find unmatched query** is a select query that finds all records in a table or query that have no related records in a second table or query.

Each column and row intersection will display the sum of the InvoiceAmt values.

The selected field (InvoiceAmt) is used in the calculations for each column and row intersection.

This option determines whether to display an overall totals column in the crosstab query.

The crosstab query will display one column for the paid invoices and a second column for the unpaid invoices.

The crosstab query will display one row for each unique City field value.

Advanced Query Wizards

Creating a Crosstab Query

Kimberly wants to analyze the Riverview Veterinary Care Center invoices by city, so she can view the paid and unpaid invoice amounts for all owners located in each city. Crosstab queries use the aggregate functions shown in Figure 5-17 to perform arithmetic operations on selected records. A crosstab query can also display one additional aggregate function value that summarizes the set of values in each row. The crosstab query uses one or more fields for the row headings on the left and one field for the column headings at the top.

Figure 5-17 Aggregate functions used in crosstab queries

Aggregate Function	Definition
Avg	Average of the field values
Count	Number of the nonnull field values
First	First field value
Last	Last field value
Max	Highest field value
Min	Lowest field value
StDev	Standard deviation of the field values
Sum	Total of the field values
Var	Variance of the field values

Figure 5-18 shows two query recordsets—the first recordset (qryOwnersAndInvoices) is from a select query, and the second recordset (qryOwnersAndInvoicesCrosstab) is from a crosstab query based on the select query.

| Figure 5-18 | Comparing a select query to a crosstab query |

The qryOwnersAndInvoices query, a select query, joins the tblOwner, tblVisit, and tblBilling tables to display selected data from those tables for all invoices. The qryOwnersAndInvoicesCrosstab query, a crosstab query, uses the qryOwnersAndInvoices query as its source query and displays one row for each unique City field value. The City column in the crosstab query identifies each row. The crosstab query uses the Sum aggregate function on the InvoiceAmt field to produce the displayed values in the Paid and Unpaid columns for each City row. An entry in the Total Of InvoiceAmt column represents the sum of the Paid and Unpaid values for the City field value in that row.

Decision Making: Using Both Select Queries and Crosstab Queries

Companies use both select queries and crosstab queries in their decision making. A select query displays several records—one for each row selected by the select query—while a crosstab query displays only one summarized record for each unique field value. When managers want to analyze data at a high level to see the big picture, they might start with a crosstab query, identify which field values to analyze further, and then look in detail at specific field values using select queries. Both select and crosstab queries serve as valuable tools in tracking and analyzing a company's business, and companies use both types of queries in the appropriate situations. By understanding how managers and other employees use the information in a database to make decisions, you can create the correct type of query to provide the information they need.

The quickest way to create a crosstab query is to use the **Crosstab Query Wizard**, which guides you through the steps for creating one. You could also change a select query to a crosstab query in Design view using the Crosstab button in the Query Type group on the Query Tools Design tab.

Using the Crosstab Query Wizard

- On the Create tab, in the Queries group, click the Query Wizard button.
- In the New Query dialog box, click Crosstab Query Wizard, and then click the OK button.
- Complete the Wizard dialog boxes to select the table or query on which to base the crosstab query, select the row heading field (or fields), select the column heading field, select the calculation field and its aggregate function, and enter a name for the crosstab query.

The crosstab query you will create, which is similar to the one shown in Figure 5-18, has the following characteristics:

- The qryOwnersAndInvoices query in the CareCenter database is the basis for the new crosstab query. The base query includes the LastName, FirstName, City, InvoiceAmt, and InvoicePaid fields.
- The City field is the leftmost column in the crosstab query and identifies each crosstab query row.
- The values from the InvoicePaid field, which is a Yes/No field, identify the rightmost columns of the crosstab query.
- The crosstab query applies the Sum aggregate function to the InvoiceAmt field values and displays the resulting total values in the Paid and Unpaid columns of the query results.
- The grand total of the InvoiceAmt field values appears for each row in a column with the heading Total Of InvoiceAmt.

Next you will create the crosstab query based on the qryOwnersAndInvoices query.

To start the Crosstab Query Wizard:

1. If you took a break after the previous session, make sure that the CareCenter database is open and the Navigation Pane is closed.

   Trouble? If the security warning is displayed below the ribbon, click the Enable Content button next to the security warning.

2. Click the **Create** tab on the ribbon.

3. In the Queries group, click the **Query Wizard** button. The New Query dialog box opens.

4. Click **Crosstab Query Wizard**, and then click the **OK** button. The first Crosstab Query Wizard dialog box opens.

You'll now use the Crosstab Query Wizard to create the crosstab query for Kimberly.

To finish the Crosstab Query Wizard:

1. In the View section, click the **Queries** option button to display the list of queries in the CareCenter database, and then click **Query: qryOwnersAndInvoices**. See Figure 5-19.

Figure 5-19   Choosing the query for the crosstab query

qryOwnersAndInvoices query selected

Queries option button selected

2. Click the **Next** button to open the next Crosstab Query Wizard dialog box. This is the dialog box where you choose the field (or fields) for the *row* headings. Because Kimberly wants the crosstab query to display one row for each unique City field value, you will select that field for the row headings.

TIP

When you select a field, the sample crosstab query in the dialog box changes to illustrate your choice.

3. In the Available Fields box, click **City**, and then click the ⟩ button to move the City field to the Selected Fields box.

4. Click the **Next** button to open the next Crosstab Query Wizard dialog box, in which you select the field values that will serve as column headings. Kimberly wants to see the paid and unpaid total invoice amounts, so you need to select the InvoicePaid field for the column headings.

5. Click **InvoicePaid** in the box, and then click the **Next** button.

In the next Crosstab Query Wizard dialog box, you choose the field that will be calculated for each row and column intersection and the function to use for the calculation. The results of the calculation will appear in the row and column intersections in the query results. Kimberly needs to calculate the sum of the InvoiceAmt field value for each row and column intersection.

6. Click **InvoiceAmt** in the Fields box, click **Sum** in the Functions box, and then make sure that the "Yes, include row sums" check box is checked. The "Yes, include row sums" option creates a column showing the overall totals for the values in each row of the query recordset. See Figure 5-20.

Figure 5-20 **Completed crosstab query design**

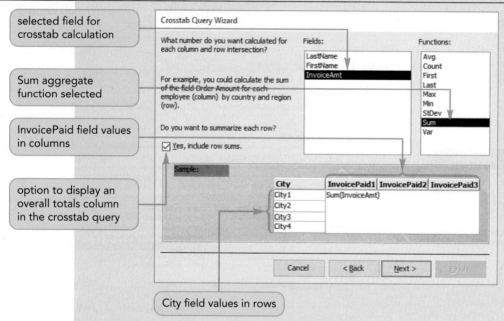

selected field for crosstab calculation

Sum aggregate function selected

InvoicePaid field values in columns

option to display an overall totals column in the crosstab query

City field values in rows

7. Click the **Next** button to open the final Crosstab Query Wizard dialog box, in which you choose the query name.

8. Click in the box, delete the underscore character so that the query name is qryOwnersAndInvoicesCrosstab, be sure the option button for viewing the query is selected, and then click the **Finish** button. The crosstab query is saved, and then the query recordset is displayed.

9. Resize all the columns in the query recordset to their best fit, and then click the City field value in the first row (**Bearcreek**). See Figure 5-21.

Figure 5-21   Crosstab query recordset

unpaid invoices by city

paid invoices by city

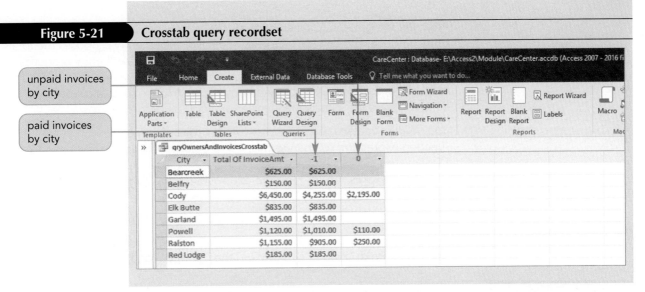

The query recordset contains only one row for each City field value. The Total Of InvoiceAmt column shows the total invoice amount for the owners in each city. The columns labeled -1 and 0 show the sum total paid (-1 column) and sum total unpaid (0 column) invoice amounts for owners in each city. Because the InvoicePaid field is a Yes/No field, by default, field values in datasheets, forms, and reports are displayed in a check box (either checked or unchecked), but a checked value is stored in the database as a -1 and an unchecked value as a 0. Instead of displaying check boxes, the crosstab query displays the stored values as column headings.

Kimberly wants you to change the column headings of -1 to Paid and 0 to Unpaid. You'll use the IIf function to change the column headings, using the expression *IIf (InvoicePaid, "Paid", "Unpaid")*—if the InvoicePaid field value is true (because it's a Yes/No field or a True/False field), or is checked, use "Paid" as the column heading; otherwise, use "Unpaid" as the column heading. Because the InvoicePaid field is a Yes/No field, the condition *InvoicePaid* is the same as the condition *InvoicePaid = -1*, which uses a comparison operator and a value. For all data types except Yes/No fields, you must use a comparison operator in a condition.

To change the crosstab query column headings:

▸ **1.** Click the **Home** tab on the ribbon, and then switch to Design view. The design grid has four entries. See Figure 5-22.

Figure 5-22   Crosstab query in the design grid

produces row headings

produces column headings

produces total values

produces grand total column heading and values

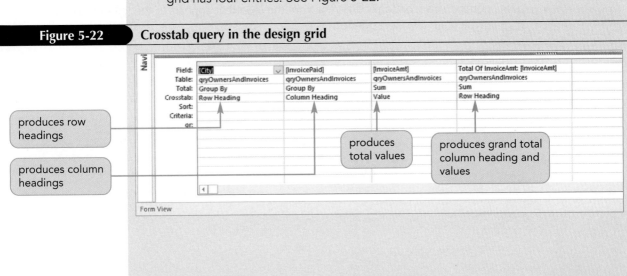

From left to right, the [City] entry produces the row headings, the [InvoicePaid] entry produces the column headings, the [InvoiceAmt] entry produces the totals in each row/column intersection, and the Total Of InvoiceAmt entry produces the row total column heading and total values. The field names are enclosed in brackets; the Total Of InvoiceAmt entry is the name of this calculated field, which displays the sum of the InvoiceAmt field values for each row.

You need to replace the Field box value in the second column with the IIf function expression to change the -1 and 0 column headings to Paid and Unpaid. You can type the expression in the box, use Expression Builder to create the expression, or type the expression in the Zoom dialog box. You'll use the last method.

▶ **2.** Right-click the **InvoicePaid Field** box, and then open the Zoom dialog box.

▶ **3.** Delete the InvoicePaid expression, and then type **IIf (InvoicePaid,"Paid","Unpaid")** in the Zoom dialog box. See Figure 5-23.

| Figure 5-23 | IIf function for the crosstab query column headings |

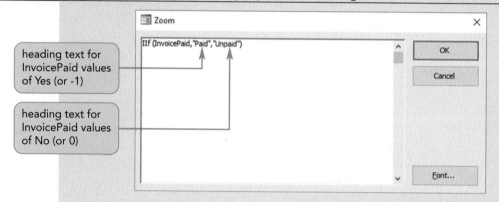

heading text for InvoicePaid values of Yes (or -1)

heading text for InvoicePaid values of No (or 0)

▶ **4.** Click the **OK** button, and then save and run the query. The completed crosstab query is displayed with Paid and Unpaid as the last two column headings, in alphabetical order, as shown in Figure 5-18.

▶ **5.** Close the query, and then open the Navigation Pane.

TIP

Point to an object in the Navigation Pane to display the full object name in a ScreenTip.

In the Navigation Pane, unique icons represent different types of queries. The crosstab query icon appears in the Queries list to the left of the qryOwnersAndInvoicesCrosstab query. This icon looks different from the icon that appears to the left of the other queries, which are all select queries.

Using Special Database Features Cautiously

When you create a query in Design view or with a wizard, an equivalent SQL statement is constructed, and only the SQL statement version of the query is saved. **SQL (Structured Query Language)** is a standard language used in querying, updating, and managing relational databases. If you learn SQL for one relational DBMS, it's a relatively easy task to begin using SQL for other relational DBMSs. However, differences exist between DBMSs in their versions of SQL—somewhat like having different dialects in English—and in what additions they make to SQL. The SQL-equivalent statement created for a crosstab query in Access is one such SQL-language addition. If you need to convert an Access database to SQL Server, Oracle, or another DBMS, crosstab queries created in Access will not work in these other DBMSs. You'd have to construct a set of SQL statements in the other DBMS to replace the SQL statement automatically created by Access. Constructing this replacement set of statements is a highly technical process that only an experienced programmer can complete, so you should use special features of a DBMS judiciously.

Next, Kimberly wants to identify any visit dates that have the same visit dates as other owners because these are the ones that might have potential scheduling difficulties. To find the information Kimberly needs, you'll create a find duplicates query.

Creating a Find Duplicates Query

A find duplicates query is a select query that finds duplicate records in a table or query. You can create this type of query using the **Find Duplicates Query Wizard**. A find duplicates query searches for duplicate values based on the fields you select when answering the Wizard's questions. For example, you might want to display all employers that have the same name, all students who have the same phone number, or all products that have the same description. Using this type of query, you can locate duplicates to avert potential problems (for example, you might have inadvertently assigned two different numbers to the same product), or you can eliminate duplicates that cost money (for example, you could send just one advertising brochure to all owners having the same address).

Using the Find Duplicates Query Wizard

- On the Create tab, in the Queries group, click the Query Wizard button.
- In the New Query dialog box, click Find Duplicates Query Wizard, and then click the OK button.
- Complete the Wizard dialog boxes to select the table or query on which to base the query, select the field (or fields) to check for duplicate values, select the additional fields to include in the query results, enter a name for the query, and then click the Finish button.

You'll use the Find Duplicates Query Wizard to create and run a new query to display duplicate visit dates in the tblVisit table.

To create the query using the Find Duplicates Query Wizard:

1. Close the Navigation Pane, click the **Create** tab on the ribbon, and then, in the Queries group, click the **Query Wizard** button to open the New Query dialog box.

2. Click **Find Duplicates Query Wizard**, and then click the **OK** button. The first Find Duplicates Query Wizard dialog box opens. In this dialog box, you select the table or query on which to base the new query. You'll use the tblVisit table.

3. Click **Table: tblVisit** (if necessary), and then click the **Next** button. The next Find Duplicates Query Wizard dialog box opens, in which you choose the fields you want to check for duplicate values.

4. In the Available fields box, click **VisitDate**, click the ⟩ button to select the VisitDate field as the field to check for duplicate values, and then click the **Next** button. In the next Find Duplicates Query Wizard dialog box, you select the additional fields you want displayed in the query results.

   Kimberly wants all remaining fields to be included in the query results.

5. Click the ⟩⟩ button to move all fields from the Available fields box to the Additional query fields box, and then click the **Next** button. The final Find Duplicates Query Wizard dialog box opens, in which you enter a name for the query. You'll use qryDuplicateVisitDates as the query name.

6. Type **qryDuplicateVisitDates** in the box, be sure the option button for viewing the results is selected, and then click the **Finish** button. The query is saved, and then the 51 records for visits with duplicate visit dates are displayed. See Figure 5-24.

Figure 5-24   **Query recordset for duplicate visit dates**

all records returned by the query share a visit date with other records

Date of Visit	Visit ID	Animal ID	Reason/Diagnosis	Off-Site Visit?
11/18/2016	1013	12337	Vaccinations	☑
11/18/2016	1014	12340	Vaccinations	☑
11/18/2016	1015	12343	Vaccinations	☑
11/18/2016	1016	12345	Vaccinations	☑
11/18/2016	1012	12335	Vaccinations	☑
11/28/2016	1028	12300	Grooming	☐
11/28/2016	1032	12296	Grooming	☐
12/2/2016	1044	12278	Vaccinations	☐
12/2/2016	1048	12318	Injured paw	☐
12/12/2016	1072	12356	Vaccinations	☑
12/12/2016	1073	12359	Vaccinations	☑
12/12/2016	1071	12353	Vaccinations	☑
12/12/2016	1070	12350	Vaccinations	☑
12/12/2016	1074	12362	Vaccinations	☑
12/20/2016	1087	12365	Vaccinations	☑
12/20/2016	1088	12368	Vaccinations	☑
12/20/2016	1089	12372	Vaccinations	☑
12/20/2016	1090	12375	Vaccinations	☑
12/20/2016	1091	12378	Vaccinations	☑
1/6/2017	1114	12404	Vaccinations	☑
1/6/2017	1104	12381	Vaccinations	☑
1/6/2017	1105	12384	Vaccinations	☑
1/6/2017	1106	12387	Vaccinations	☑
1/6/2017	1107	12390	Vaccinations	☑
1/6/2017	1108	12393	Vaccinations	☑

Record: 1 of 51   No Filter   Search

Datasheet View

7. Close the query.

Kimberly now asks you to find the records for animals with no visits. These are animals whose owners have contacted the center and have given the center information about themselves and their animals; however, the animals have not had a first visit. Kimberly wants to contact the owners of these animals to see if they would like to book initial appointments. To provide Kimberly with this information, you need to create a find unmatched query.

Creating a Find Unmatched Query

A find unmatched query is a select query that finds all records in a table or query that have no related records in a second table or query. For example, you could display all owners who have had an appointment but have never been invoiced or all students who are not currently enrolled in classes. Such a query provides information for a veterinary care center to ensure all owners who have received services have also been billed for those services and for a school administrator to contact the students to find out their future educational plans. You can use the **Find Unmatched Query Wizard** to create this type of query.

Kimberly wants to know which animals have no visits. She will contact their owners to determine if they will be visiting Riverview Veterinary Care Center or whether they are receiving their veterinary care elsewhere. To create a list of animals who have not had a visit to the Center, you'll use the Find Unmatched Query Wizard to display only those records from the tblAnimal table with no matching AnimalID field value in the related tblVisit table.

To create the query using the Find Unmatched Query Wizard:

1. On the Create tab, in the Queries group, click the **Query Wizard** button to open the New Query dialog box.

2. Click **Find Unmatched Query Wizard**, and then click the **OK** button. The first Find Unmatched Query Wizard dialog box opens. In this dialog box, you select the table or query on which to base the new query. You'll use the qryAnimalsAndOwners query.

3. In the View section, click the **Queries** option button to display the list of queries, click **Query: qryAnimalsAndOwners** in the box to select this query, and then click the **Next** button. The next Find Unmatched Query Wizard dialog box opens, in which you choose the table that contains the related records. You'll select the tblVisit table.

4. Click **Table: tblVisit** in the box (if necessary), and then click the **Next** button. The next dialog box opens, in which you choose the common field for both tables. See Figure 5-25.

Figure 5-25	Selecting the common field

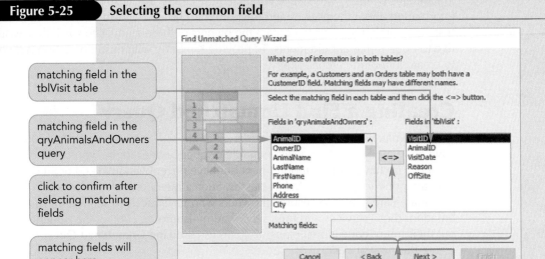

matching field in the tblVisit table

matching field in the qryAnimalsAndOwners query

click to confirm after selecting matching fields

matching fields will appear here

The common field between the query and the table is the AnimalID field. You need to click the common field in each box and then click the <=> button between the two boxes to join the two objects. The Matching fields box then will display AnimalID <=> AnimalID to indicate the joining of the two matching fields. If the two selected objects already have a one-to-many relationship defined in the Relationships window, the Matching fields box will join the correct fields automatically.

Be sure you click the AnimalID field in both boxes.

5. In the Fields in 'qryAnimalsAndOwners' box click **AnimalID**, in the Fields in 'tblVisit' box click **AnimalID**, click the <=> button to connect the two selected fields, and then click the **Next** button. The next Find Unmatched Query Wizard dialog box opens, in which you choose the fields you want to see in the query recordset. Kimberly wants the query recordset to display all available fields.

6. Click the >> button to move all fields from the Available fields box to the Selected fields box, and then click the **Next** button. The final dialog box opens, in which you enter the query name.

7. Type **qryInactiveAnimals**, be sure the option button for viewing the results is selected, and then click the **Finish** button. The query is saved, and then two records are displayed in the query recordset. See Figure 5-26.

Figure 5-26	Query recordset displaying two animals without visits

records for animals without visits

8. Close the query.

Next, Kimberly wants to contact those owners who have the highest invoice amounts to make sure that Riverview Veterinary Care Center is providing satisfactory service. To display the information Kimberly needs, you will create a top values query.

Creating a Top Values Query

Whenever a query displays a large group of records, you might want to limit the number to a more manageable size by displaying, for example, just the first 10 records. The **Top Values property** for a query lets you limit the number of records in the query results. To find a limited number of records using the Top Values property, you can click one of the preset values from a list or enter either an integer (such as 15, to display the first 15 records) or a percentage (such as 20%, to display the first fifth of the records).

For instance, suppose you have a select query that displays 45 records. If you want the query recordset to show only the first five records, you can change the query by entering a Top Values property value of either 5 or 10%. If the query contains a sort, and the last record that can be displayed is one of two or more records with the same value for the primary sort field, all records with that matching key value are displayed.

Kimberly wants to view the same data that appears in the qryLargeInvoiceAmounts query for owners with the highest 25 percent invoice amounts. Based on the number or percentage you enter, a top values query selects that number or percentage of records starting from the top of the recordset. Thus, you usually include a sort in a top values query to display the records with the highest or lowest values for the sorted field. You will modify the query and then use the Top Values property to produce this information for Kimberly.

To set the Top Values property for the query:

▶ **1.** Open the Navigation Pane, open the **qryLargeInvoiceAmounts** query in Datasheet view, and then close the Navigation Pane. Ten records are displayed, all with InvoiceAmt field values greater than $75, in descending order by InvoiceAmt.

▶ **2.** Switch to Design view.

▶ **3.** On the Query Tools Design tab, in the Query Setup group, click the **Return** arrow (with the ScreenTip "Top Values"), and then click **25%**. See Figure 5-27.

Figure 5-27 Creating the top values query

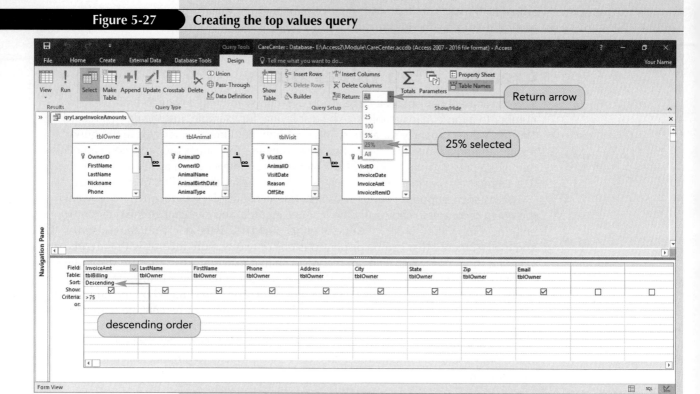

If the number or percentage of records you want to select, such as 15 or 20%, doesn't appear in the Top Values list, you can type the number or percentage in the Return box.

4. Run the query. Three records are displayed in the query recordset; these records represent the owners with the highest 25 percent of the invoice amounts (25 percent of the original 10 records). See Figure 5-28.

Figure 5-28   Top values query recordset

5. Save and close the query.

6. If you are not continuing on to the next session, close the CareCenter database.

Kimberly will use the information provided by the queries you created to analyze the Riverview Veterinary Care Center business and to contact owners. In the next session, you will enhance the tblOwner and tblVisit tables.

Session 5.2 Quick Check

REVIEW

1. What is the purpose of a crosstab query?

2. What are the four query wizards you can use to create a new query?

3. What is a find duplicates query?

4. What does a find unmatched query do?

5. What happens when you set a query's Top Values property?

6. What happens if you set a query's Top Values property to 2, and the first five records have the same value for the primary sort field?

Session 5.3 Visual Overview:

The tblInvoiceItem table supplies the field values for the lookup field in the tblBilling table. A **lookup field** lets the user select a value from a list of possible values to enter data into the field.

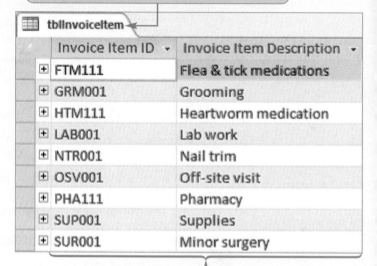

tblInvoiceItem

Invoice Item ID ▾	Invoice Item Description ▾
⊞ FTM111	Flea & tick medications
⊞ GRM001	Grooming
⊞ HTM111	Heartworm medication
⊞ LAB001	Lab work
⊞ NTR001	Nail trim
⊞ OSV001	Off-site visit
⊞ PHA111	Pharmacy
⊞ SUP001	Supplies
⊞ SUR001	Minor surgery

The InvoiceItemID and InvoiceItemDesc fields from the tblInvoiceItem table are used to look up InvoiceItemID values in the tblBilling table.

The tblBilling table contains the lookup field.

tblBilling

Invoice Num ▾	Visit ID ▾	Invoice Date ▾	Invoice Amt ▾	Invoice Item ID ▾	Invoice Paid ▾
42098	1002	11/09/2016	$50.00	Lab work ⌄	☑
42099	1002	11/09/2016	$75.00	Flea & tick medicati FTM111	☐
42100	1002	11/09/2016	$45.00	Grooming GRM001	☐
42110	1006	11/14/2016	$35.00	Heartworm medicat HTM111	☐
42111	1006	11/14/2016	$65.00	Lab work LAB001	☐
42112	1006	11/14/2016	$50.00	Nail trim NTR001	☐
42118	1009	11/16/2016	$50.00	Off-site visit OSV001	☐
42119	1009	11/16/2016	$15.00	Pharmacy PHA111	☐
42125	1012	11/21/2016	$50.00	Supplies SUP001	☐
42126	1012	11/21/2016	$75.00	Minor surgery SUR001	☐
42127	1012	11/21/2016	$75.00	Major surgery SUR002	☐
42128	1013	11/21/2016	$75.00	Spaying - surgery SUR111	☐
42129	1013	11/21/2016	$75.00	Neutering - surgery SUR222	☐
42130	1014	11/21/2016	$75.00	Declawing - surgery SUR333	☐
42131	1014	11/21/2016	$75.00	Vaccinations VAC111	☑
42132	1015	11/21/2016	$75.00	Vaccinations	☑

Values in the lookup field appear in alphabetical order, sorted by Invoice Item ID.

Only the InvoiceItemID values are stored in the InvoiceItemID field in the tblBilling table even though the user also sees the InvoiceItemDesc values in the datasheet.

Lookup Fields and Input Masks

The tblOwner table contains the field that displays values with an input mask. An **input mask** is a predefined format that is used to enter and display data in a field.

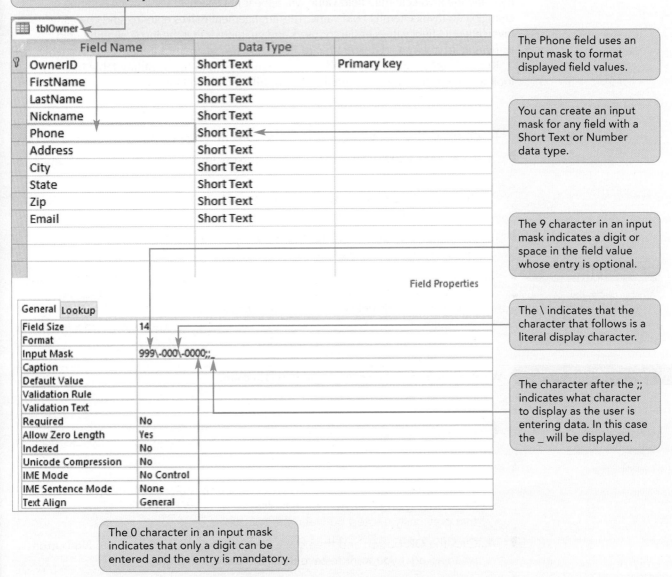

The Phone field uses an input mask to format displayed field values.

You can create an input mask for any field with a Short Text or Number data type.

The 9 character in an input mask indicates a digit or space in the field value whose entry is optional.

The \ indicates that the character that follows is a literal display character.

The character after the ;; indicates what character to display as the user is entering data. In this case the _ will be displayed.

The 0 character in an input mask indicates that only a digit can be entered and the entry is mandatory.

tblOwner

Field Name	Data Type	
OwnerID	Short Text	Primary key
FirstName	Short Text	
LastName	Short Text	
Nickname	Short Text	
Phone	Short Text	
Address	Short Text	
City	Short Text	
State	Short Text	
Zip	Short Text	
Email	Short Text	

Field Properties

General Lookup

Field Size	14
Format	
Input Mask	999\-000\-0000;;
Caption	
Default Value	
Validation Rule	
Validation Text	
Required	No
Allow Zero Length	Yes
Indexed	No
Unicode Compression	No
IME Mode	No Control
IME Sentence Mode	None
Text Align	General

Creating a Lookup Field

The tblBilling table in the CareCenter database contains information about owner invoices. Kimberly wants to make entering data in the table easier for her staff. In particular, data entry is easier if they do not need to remember the correct InvoiceItemID field value for each treatment. Because the tblInvoiceItem and tblBilling tables have a one-to-many relationship, Kimberly asks you to change the tblBilling table's InvoiceItemID field, which is a foreign key to the tblInvoiceItem table, to a lookup field. A lookup field lets the user select a value from a list of possible values. For the InvoiceItemID field, a user will be able to select an invoice item's ID number from the list of invoice item names in the tblBilling table rather than having to remember the correct InvoiceItemID field value. The InvoiceItemID field value will be stored in the tblBilling table, but both the invoice item and the InvoiceItemID field value will appear in Datasheet view when entering or changing an InvoiceItemID field value. This arrangement makes entering and changing InvoiceItemID field values easier for users and guarantees that the InvoiceItemID field value is valid. You use a **Lookup Wizard field** in Access to create a lookup field in a table.

Kimberly asks you to change the InvoiceItemID field in the tblBilling table to a lookup field. You'll begin by opening the tblBilling table in Design view.

To change the InvoiceItemID field to a lookup field:

1. If you took a break after the previous session, make sure that the CareCenter database is open.

   Trouble? If the security warning is displayed below the ribbon, click the Enable Content button next to the warning.

2. If necessary, open the Navigation Pane, open the **tblBilling** table in Design view, and then close the Navigation Pane.

TIP

You can display the arrow and the menu simultaneously if you click the box near its right side.

3. Click the **Data Type** box for the InvoiceItemID field, click the drop-down arrow to display the list of data types, and then click **Lookup Wizard**. A message box appears, instructing you to delete the relationship between the tblBilling and tblInvoiceItem tables if you want to make the InvoiceItemID field a lookup field. See Figure 5-29.

Figure 5-29 | Warning message for an existing table relationship

Lookup Wizard   ×

You can't change the data type or field size of this field; it is part of one or more relationships. If you want to change the data type of this field, first delete its relationships in the Relationships window.

OK

The lookup field will be used to form the one-to-many relationship between the tblBilling and tblInvoiceItem tables, so you don't need the relationship that previously existed between the two tables.

4. Click the **OK** button and then close the tblBilling table, clicking the **No** button when asked if you want to save the table design changes.

5. Click the **Database Tools** tab on the ribbon, and then in the Relationships group, click the **Relationships** button to open the Relationships window.

6. Right-click the join line between the tblBilling and tblInvoiceItem tables, click **Delete**, and then click the **Yes** button to confirm the deletion.

   Trouble? If the Delete command does not appear on the shortcut menu, click a blank area in the Relationships window to close the shortcut menu, and then repeat Step 6, ensuring you right-click on the relationship line.

7. Close the Relationships window.

Now you can resume changing the InvoiceItemID field to a lookup field.

To finish changing the InvoiceItemID field to a lookup field:

1. Open the **tblBilling** table in Design view, and then close the Navigation Pane.

2. Click the right side of the **Data Type** box for the InvoiceItemID field, if necessary click the drop-down arrow, and then click **Lookup Wizard**. The first Lookup Wizard dialog box opens.

This dialog box lets you specify a list of allowed values for the InvoiceItemID field in a record in the tblBilling table. You can specify a table or query from which users select the value, or you can enter a new list of values. You want the InvoiceItemID values to come from the tblInvoiceItem table.

3. Make sure the option for "I want the lookup field to get the values from another table or query" is selected, and then click the **Next** button to display the next Lookup Wizard dialog box.

4. In the View section, click the **Tables** option button, if necessary, to display the list of tables, click **Table: tblInvoiceItem**, and then click the **Next** button to display the next Lookup Wizard dialog box. See Figure 5-30.

| Figure 5-30 | Selecting the lookup fields |

This dialog box lets you select the lookup fields from the tblInvoiceItem table. You need to select the InvoiceItemID field because it's the common field that links the tblInvoiceItem table and the tblBilling table. You must also select the InvoiceItemDesc field because Kimberly wants the user to be able to select from a list of invoice item names when entering a new contract record or changing an existing InvoiceItemID field value.

5. Click the **>>** button to move the InvoiceItemID and InvoiceItemDesc fields to the Selected Fields box, and then click the **Next** button to display the next Lookup Wizard dialog box. This dialog box lets you choose a sort order for the box entries. Kimberly wants the entries to appear in ascending Invoice Item Description order. Note that ascending is the default sort order.

▶ **6.** Click the **arrow** for the first box, click **InvoiceItemDesc**, and then click the **Next** button to open the next dialog box.

In this dialog box, you can adjust the widths of the lookup columns. Note that when you resize a column to its best fit, the column is resized so that the widest column heading and the visible field values fit the column width. However, some field values that aren't visible in this dialog box might be wider than the column width, so you must scroll down the column to make sure you don't have to repeat the column resizing.

▶ **7.** Click the **Hide key column** check box to remove the checkmark and display the InvoiceItemID field.

▶ **8.** Click the Invoice Item ID column heading to select it. With the mouse pointer on the Invoice Item ID heading, drag it to the right of the Invoice Item Description column to reposition it.

▶ **9.** Place the pointer on the right edge of the Invoice Item Description field column heading, and then when the pointer changes to ↔, double-click to resize the column to its best fit.

▶ **10.** Scroll down the columns, and repeat Step 9 as necessary until the Invoice Item Description column accommodates all contents, and then press **Ctrl + Home** to scroll back to the top of the columns. See Figure 5-31.

Figure 5-31	Adjusting the width of the lookup column

11. Click the **Next** button.

In the next dialog box, you select the field you want to store in the table. You'll store the InvoiceItemID field in the tblBilling table because it's the foreign key to the tblInvoiceItem table.

▶ **12.** Click **InvoiceItemID** in the Available Fields box if it's not already selected, and then click the **Next** button.

In the next dialog box, you specify the field name for the lookup field. Because you'll be storing the InvoiceItemID field in the table, you'll accept the default field name, InvoiceItemID.

▶ **13.** Click the **Finish** button, and then click **Yes** to save the table.

The Data Type value for the InvoiceItemID field is still Short Text because this field contains text data. However, when you update the field, the InvoiceItemID field value will be used to look up and display in the tblBilling table datasheet both the InvoiceItemDesc and InvoiceItemID field values from the tblInvoiceItem table.

In reviewing animal visits recently, Kimberly noticed that the InvoiceItemID field value stored in the tblBilling table for visit number 42112 is incorrect. She asks you to test the new lookup field to select the correct field value. To do so, you need to switch to Datasheet view.

To change the InvoiceItemID field value:

1. Switch to Datasheet view, and then resize the Invoice Item ID column to its best fit.

   Notice that the Invoice Item ID column displays InvoiceItem field values, even though the InvoiceItemID field values are stored in the table.

2. For Invoice Num 42112, click **Lab work** in the Invoice Item ID column, and then click the **arrow** to display the list of InvoiceItemDesc and InvoiceItemID field values from the tblInvoiceItems table. See Figure 5-32.

| Figure 5-32 | List of InvoiceItemDesc and InvoiceItemID field values |

scrollable list of values for the lookup table

Note that the column displaying InvoiceItemDesc values in your list may be narrower than the values themselves, even though you resized the column. This bug should be fixed in a future version of Access.

The invoice item for visit 42112 should be Pharmacy, so you need to select this entry in the list to change the InvoiceItemID field value.

3. Scroll through the list if necessary, and then click **Pharmacy** to select that value to display in the datasheet and to store the InvoiceItemID field value of PHA111 in the table. The list closes, and "Pharmacy" appears in the Invoice Item ID column.

4. Save and close the tblBilling table.

Next, Kimberly asks you to change the appearance of the Phone field in the tblOwner table to a standard telephone number format.

Using the Input Mask Wizard

The Phone field in the tblOwner table is a 10-digit number that's difficult to read because it appears with none of the special formatting characters usually associated with a telephone number. For example, the Phone field value for Sally Cruz, which appears as 3074064321, would be more readable in any of the following formats: 307-406-4321, 307.406.4321, 307/406-4321, or (307) 406-4321. Kimberly asks you to use the (307) 406-4321 style for the Phone field.

Kimberly wants the parentheses and hyphens to appear as literal display characters whenever users enter Phone field values. A literal display character is a special character that automatically appears in specific positions of a field value; users don't need to type literal display characters. To include these characters, you need to create an input mask, which is a predefined format used to enter and display data in a field. An easy way to create an input mask is to use the **Input Mask Wizard**, an Access tool that guides you in creating a predefined format for a field. You must be in Design view to use the Input Mask Wizard.

To use the Input Mask Wizard for the Phone field:

▶ 1. Open the **tblOwner** table, close the Navigation Pane, and then, if necessary, switch to Design view.

▶ 2. Click the **Phone Field Name** box to make that row the current row and to display its Field Properties options.

▶ 3. Click the **Input Mask** box in the Field Properties pane. The Build button […] appears at the right edge of the Input Mask box.

▶ 4. Click the **Build** button […] in the Input Mask box. The first Input Mask Wizard dialog box opens. See Figure 5-33.

| Figure 5-33 | Input Mask Wizard dialog box |

You can scroll the Input Mask box, select the input mask you want, and then enter representative values to practice using the input mask.

▶ 5. If necessary, click **Phone Number** in the Input Mask box to select it.

6. Click the far left side of the **Try It** box. (___) ___-____ appears in the Try It box. As you type a phone number, the underscores, which are placeholder characters, are replaced.

    Trouble? If your insertion point is not immediately to the right of the left parenthesis, press the ← key until it is.

7. Type **3074064321** to practice entering a sample phone number. The input mask formats the typed value as (307) 406-4321.

8. Click the **Next** button. The next Input Mask Wizard dialog box opens. In it, you can change the input mask and the placeholder character. Because you can change an input mask easily after the Input Mask Wizard finishes, you'll accept all wizard defaults.

9. Click the **Finish** button, and then click to the right of the value in the Input Mask box to deselect the characters. The Input Mask Wizard creates the phone number input mask, placing it in the Input Mask box for the Phone field. See Figure 5-34.

Figure 5-34	Phone number input mask created by the Input Mask Wizard

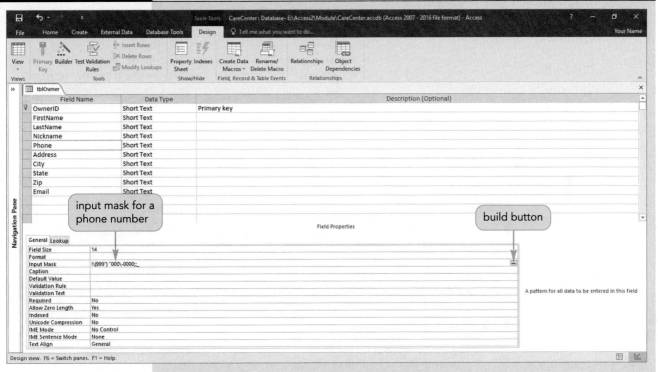

The characters used in a field's input mask restrict the data you can enter in the field, as shown in Figure 5-35. Other characters that appear in an input mask, such as the left and right parentheses in the phone number input mask, are literal display characters.

Figure 5-35   Input mask characters

Input Mask Character	Description
0	Digit only must be entered. Entry is required.
9	Digit or space can be entered. Entry is optional.
#	Digit, space, or a plus or minus sign can be entered. Entry is optional.
L	Letter only must be entered. Entry is required.
?	Letter only can be entered. Entry is optional.
A	Letter or digit must be entered. Entry is required.
a	Letter or digit can be entered. Entry is optional.
&	Any character or a space must be entered. Entry is required.
C	Any character or a space can be entered. Entry is optional.
>	All characters that follow are displayed in uppercase.
<	All characters that follow are displayed in lowercase.
"	Enclosed characters treated as literal display characters.
\	Following character treated as a literal display character. This is the same as enclosing a single character in quotation marks.
!	Input mask is displayed from right to left, rather than the default of left to right. Characters typed into the mask always fill in from left to right.
;;	The character between the first and second semicolons determines whether to store the literal display characters in the database. If the value is 1 or if no value is provided, the literal display characters are not stored. If the value is 0, the literal display characters are stored. The character following the second semicolon is the placeholder character that appears in the displayed input mask.

Kimberly wants to view the Phone field with the default input mask.

To view and change the input mask for the Phone field:

1. Save the table, and then switch to Datasheet view. The Phone field values now have the format specified by the input mask.

   Kimberly decides that she would prefer to omit the parentheses around the area codes and use only hyphens as separators in the displayed Phone field values, so you'll change the input mask in Design view.

2. Switch to Design view.

   The input mask is set to !\(999") "000\-0000;;_. The backslash character (\) causes the character that follows it to appear as a literal display character. Characters enclosed in quotation marks also appear as literal display characters. (See Figure 5-35.) The exclamation mark (!) forces the existing data to fill the input mask from right to left instead of left to right. This does not affect new data. This applies only to the situation when data already exists in the table and a new input mask is applied. For instance, if the existing data is 5551234 and the input mask fills from left to right, the data with the input mask would look like (555) 123-4. If the input mask fills from right to left, the data with the input mask applied would look like ( ) 555-1234.

   If you omit the backslashes preceding the hyphens, they will automatically be inserted when you press the Tab key. However, backslashes are not added automatically for other literal display characters, such as periods and slashes, so it's best to always type the backslashes. Since all of the existing data includes the area code, it will not make a difference whether the input mask applied to the data fills the data from left to right or from right to left, so you'll omit the ! symbol.

3. In the Input Mask box for the Phone field, change the input mask to **999\-000\-0000;;_** and then press the **Tab** key.

   Because you've modified a field property, the Property Update Options button 📝 appears to the left of the Input Mask property.

4. Click the **Property Update Options** button 📝. A menu opens below the button, as shown in Figure 5-36.

Figure 5-36 **Property Update Options button menu**

Property Update Options button

---

5. Click **Update Input Mask everywhere Phone is used**. The Update Properties dialog box opens. See Figure 5-37.

Figure 5-37 **Update Properties dialog box**

object dependent on Phone field

Because the frmOwner form displays the Phone field values from the tblOwner table, the Phone field's Input Mask property in this object will automatically be changed to your new input mask. If other form objects included the Phone field from the tblOwner table, they would be included in this dialog box as well. This capability to update field properties in objects automatically when you modify a table field property is called **property propagation**. Although the Update Properties dialog box displays no queries, property propagation also occurs with queries automatically. Property propagation is limited to field properties such as the Decimal Places, Description, Format, and Input Mask properties.

6. Click the **Yes** button, save the table, switch to Datasheet view, and then resize the Phone column to its best fit. The Phone field values now have the format Kimberly requested. See Figure 5-38.

Figure 5-38   **After changing the Phone field input mask**

Because Kimberly wants her staff to store only standard 10-digit U.S. phone numbers for owners, the input mask you've created will enforce the standard entry and display format that Kimberly desires.

Understanding When to Use Input Masks

INSIGHT

An input mask is appropriate for a field only if all field values have a consistent format. For example, you can use an input mask with hyphens as literal display characters to store U.S. phone numbers in a consistent format of 987-654-3210. However, a multinational company would not be able to use an input mask to store phone numbers from all countries because international phone numbers do not have a consistent format. In the same way, U.S. zip codes have a consistent format, and you could use an input mask of 00000#9999 to enter and display U.S. zip codes such as 98765 and 98765-4321, but you could not use an input mask if you need to store and display foreign postal codes in the same field. If you need to store and display phone numbers, zip/postal codes, and other fields in a variety of formats, it's best to define them as Short Text fields without an input mask so users can enter the correct literal display characters.

After you changed the Phone field's input mask, you had the option to update, selectively and automatically, the Phone field's Input Mask property in other objects in the database. Kimberly is thinking about making significant changes to the way data is stored in the tblOwner table and wants to understand which other elements those changes might impact. To determine the dependencies among objects in an Access database, you'll open the Object Dependencies pane.

Identifying Object Dependencies

An **object dependency** exists between two objects when a change to the properties of data in one object affects the properties of data in the other object. Dependencies between Access objects, such as tables, queries, and forms, can occur in various ways. For example, the tblVisit and tblBilling tables are dependent on each other because they have a one-to-many relationship. In the same way, the tblOwner table uses the qryOwnersByName query to obtain the Owner field to display along with the OwnerID field, and this creates a dependency between these two objects. Any query, form, or other object that uses fields from a given table is dependent on that table. Any form or report that uses fields from a query is directly dependent on the query and is indirectly dependent on the tables that provide the data to the query. Large databases contain hundreds of objects, so it is useful to have a way to easily view the dependencies among objects before you attempt to delete or modify an object. The **Object Dependencies pane** displays a collapsible list of the dependencies among the objects in an Access database; you click the list's expand indicators to show or hide different levels of dependencies. Next, you'll open the Object Dependencies pane to examine the object dependencies in the CareCenter database.

To open and use the Object Dependencies pane:

1. Click the **Database Tools** tab on the ribbon.

2. In the Relationships group, click the **Object Dependencies** button to open the Object Dependencies pane, and then drag the left edge of the pane to the left until none of the items in the list are cut off.

3. If necessary, click the **Objects that depend on me** option button to select it, then click the **Refresh** link to display the list of objects. See Figure 5-39.

Figure 5-39	After opening the Object Dependencies pane

The Object Dependencies pane displays the objects that depend on the tblOwner table, the object name that appears at the top of the pane. If you change the design of the tblOwner table, the change might affect objects in the pane. Changing a property for a field in the tblOwner table that's also used by a listed object affects that listed object. If a listed object does not use the field you are changing, that listed object is not affected.

Objects listed in the Ignored Objects section of the box might have an object dependency with the tblOwner table, and you'd have to review them individually to determine if a dependency exists. The Help section at the bottom of the pane displays links for further information about object dependencies.

▶ 4. Click the **frmOwner** link in the Object Dependencies pane. The frmOwner form opens in Design view. All the fields in the form are fields from the tblOwner table, which is why the form has an object dependency with the table.

▶ 5. Switch to Form view for the frmOwner form. Note that the Phone field value is displayed using the input mask you applied to the field in the tblOwner table. This change was propagated from the table to the form.

▶ 6. Close the frmOwner form, open the Navigation Pane, open the **tblAnimal** table in Datasheet view, and then click the **Refresh** link near the top of the Object Dependencies pane. The Object Dependencies box now displays the objects that depend on the tblAnimal table.

▶ 7. Click the **Objects that I depend on** option button near the top of the pane to view the objects that affect the tblAnimal table.

▶ 8. Click the **Objects that depend on me** option button, and then click the **expand indicator** ▷ for the qryAnimalsAndOwners query in the Object Dependencies pane. The list expands to display the qryInactiveAnimals query, which is another query that the qryAnimalsAndOwners query depends upon.

▶ 9. Close the tblAnimal table, close the Object Dependencies pane, and then save and close the tblOwner table.

You let Kimberly know about the object dependencies for the tblOwner table. She decides to leave the tblOwner table the way it is for the moment to avoid making changes to forms and/or queries.

Defining Data Validation Rules

Kimberly wants to minimize the amount of incorrect data in the database caused by typing errors. To do so, she wants to limit the entry of InvoiceAmt field values in the tblBilling table to values greater than $5 because Riverview Veterinary Care Center does not invoice owners for balances of $5 or less. In addition, she wants to make sure that the Insurance field value entered in each tblBilling table record is either the same or less than the InvoiceAmt field value. The InvoiceAmt value represents the total price for the visit or procedure, and the Insurance value is the amount covered by the owner's pet insurance. The Insurance value may be equal to or less than the InvoiceAmt value, but it will never be more, so comparing these numbers is an additional test to ensure the data entered in a record makes sense. To provide these checks on entered data, you'll set field validation properties for the InvoiceAmt field in the tblBilling table and set table validation properties in the tblBilling table.

Defining Field Validation Rules

To prevent a user from entering an unacceptable value in the InvoiceAmt field, you can create a **field validation rule** that verifies a field value by comparing it to a constant or to a set of constants. You create a field validation rule by setting the Validation Rule and the Validation Text field properties. The **Validation Rule property** value specifies the valid values that users can enter in a field. The **Validation Text property** value will be displayed in a dialog box if a user enters an invalid value (in this case, an InvoiceAmt field value of $5 or less). After you set these two InvoiceAmt field properties in the tblBilling table, users will be prevented from entering an invalid InvoiceAmt field value in the tblBilling table and in all current and future queries and future forms that include the InvoiceAmt field.

You'll now set the Validation Rule and Validation Text properties for the InvoiceAmt field in the tblBilling table.

To create and test a field validation rule for the InvoiceAmt field:

▶ **1.** Open the **tblBilling** table in Design view, close the Navigation Pane, and then click the **InvoiceAmt Field Name** box to make that row the current row.

To make sure that all values entered in the InvoiceAmt field are greater than 5, you'll use the > comparison operator in the Validation Rule box.

▶ **2.** In the Field Properties pane, click the **Validation Rule** box, type **>5**, and then press the **Tab** key.

You can set the Validation Text property to a value that appears in a dialog box that opens if a user enters a value not listed in the Validation Rule box.

▶ **3.** In the Validation Text box, type **Invoice amounts must be greater than 5.** See Figure 5-40.

Figure 5-40   **Validation properties for the InvoiceAmt field**

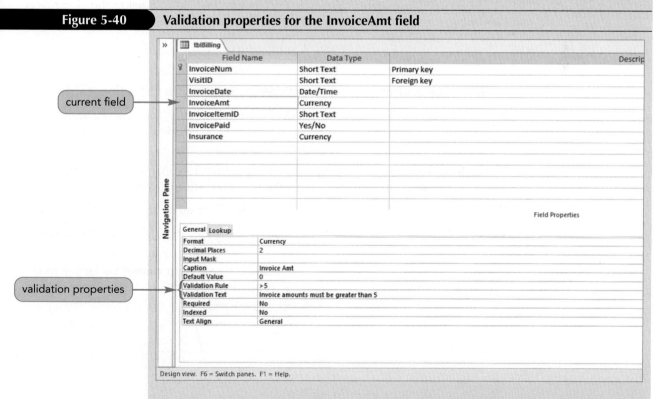

current field

validation properties

You can now save the table design changes and then test the validation properties.

▶ **4.** Save the table, and then click the **Yes** button when asked if you want to test the existing InvoiceAmt field values in the tblBilling table against the new validation rule.

The existing records in the tblBilling table are tested against the validation rule. If any existing record violated the rule, you would be prompted to continue testing or to revert to the previous Validation Rule property setting. Next, you'll test the validation rule.

▶ **5.** Switch to Datasheet view, select **$50.00** in the first row's InvoiceAmt field box, type **3**, and then press the **Tab** key. A dialog box opens containing the message "Invoice amounts must be greater than 5," which is the Validation Text property setting you created in Step 3.

▶ **6.** Click the **OK** button, and then press the **Esc** key. The first row's InvoiceAmt field reverts to its original value, $50.00.

▶ **7.** Close the tblBilling table.

Now that you've finished entering the field validation rule for the InvoiceAmt field in the tblBilling table, you'll enter the table validation rule for the date fields in the tblVisit table.

Defining Table Validation Rules

To make sure that the Insurance field value that a user enters in the tblBilling table is not larger than the InvoiceAmt field value, you can create a **table validation rule**. Once again, you'll use the Validation Rule and Validation Text properties, but this time you'll set these properties for the table instead of for an individual field. You'll use a table validation rule because this validation involves multiple fields. A field validation rule is used when the validation involves a restriction for only the selected field and does not depend on other fields.

To create and test a table validation rule in the tblBilling table:

> Be sure "Table Properties" is listed as the selection type in the property sheet.

▶ **1.** Open the **tblBilling** table in Design view, close the Navigation Pane, and then on the Table Tools Design tab, in the Show/Hide group, click the **Property Sheet** button to open the property sheet for the table.

To make sure that each Insurance field value is less than or equal to the InvoiceAmt field value, you use the Validation Rule box for the table.

▶ **2.** In the property sheet, click the **Validation Rule** box.

▶ **3.** Type **Insur**, press the **Tab** key to select Insurance in the AutoComplete box, type **<= InvoiceAm**, and then press the **Tab** key.

▶ **4.** In the Validation Text box, type **Insurance coverage cannot be larger than the invoice amount** and then, if necessary, widen the Property Sheet so the Validation Rule text is visible. See Figure 5-41.

Figure 5-41   **Setting table validation properties**

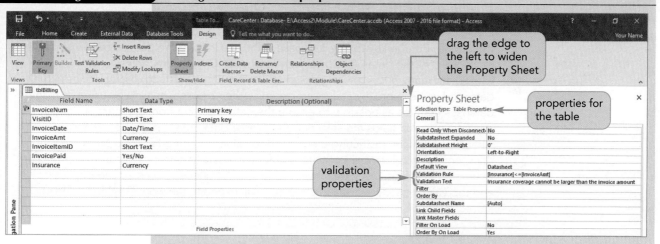

You can now test the validation properties.

5. Close the property sheet, save the table, and then click the **Yes** button when asked if you want to test the existing dates in the tblBilling table against the new validation rule.

6. Switch to Datasheet view, and then click the Insurance column value in the first record.

7. Edit the Insurance value to change it to $150.00, and then press the **Tab** key to complete your changes to the record. A dialog box opens containing the message "Insurance coverage cannot be larger than the invoice amount," which is the Validation Text property setting you entered in Step 4.

Unlike field validation rule violations, which are detected immediately after you finish a field entry and advance to another field, table validation rule violations are detected only when you finish all changes to the current record and advance to another record.

8. Click the **OK** button, and then press the **Esc** key to undo your change to the Insurance column value.

9. Close the tblBilling table.

PROSKILLS

Problem Solving: Perfecting Data Quality

It's important that you design useful queries, forms, and reports and that you test them thoroughly. But the key to any database is the accuracy of the data stored in its tables. It's critical that the data be as error-free as possible. Most companies employ people who spend many hours tracking down and correcting errors and discrepancies in their data, and you can greatly assist and minimize their problem solving by using as many database features as possible to ensure the data is correct from the start. Among these features for fields are selecting the proper data type, setting default values whenever possible, restricting the permitted values by using field and table validation rules, enforcing referential integrity, and forcing users to select values from lists instead of typing the values. Likewise, having an arsenal of queries—such as find duplicates and top values queries—available to users will expedite the work they do to find and correct data errors.

Based on a request from Kimberly, Daksha added a Long Text field to the tblVisit table. Next you'll review Daksha's work.

Working with Long Text Fields

You use a Long Text field to store long comments and explanations. Short Text fields are limited to 255 characters, but Long Text fields can hold up to 65,535 characters. In addition, Short Text fields limit you to plain text with no special formatting, but you can define Long Text fields to store plain text similar to Short Text fields or to store rich text, which you can selectively format with options such as bold, italic, and different fonts and colors.

You'll review the Long Text field, named Comments, that Daksha added to the tblVisit table.

To review the Long Text field in the tblVisit table:

▶ **1.** Open the Navigation Pane, open the **tblVisit** table in Datasheet view, and then close the Navigation Pane.

▶ **2.** Increase the width of the Comments field so most of the comments fit in the column.

Although everything fits on the screen when using a screen of average size and resolution, on some computer systems freezing panes is necessary to be able to view everything at once. On a smaller screen, if you scroll to the right to view the Comments field, you'll no longer be able to identify which animal applies to a row because the Animal ID column will be hidden. You may also see this effect if you shrink the size of the Access window. You'll freeze the Visit ID, Animal ID, and Date of Visit columns so they remain visible in the datasheet as you scroll to the right.

▶ **3.** Click the **Visit ID column** selector, press and hold down the **Shift** key, click the **Date of Visit** column selector, and then release the **Shift** key. The Visit ID, Animal ID, and Date of Visit columns are selected.

▶ **4.** On the Home tab, in the Records group, click the **More** button, and then click **Freeze Fields**.

5. If necessary, reduce the size of the Access window so not all columns are visible, and then scroll to the right until you see the Comments column. Notice that the Visit ID, Animal ID, and Date of Visit columns, the three leftmost columns, remain visible when you scroll. See Figure 5-42.

Figure 5-42 **Freezing three datasheet columns**

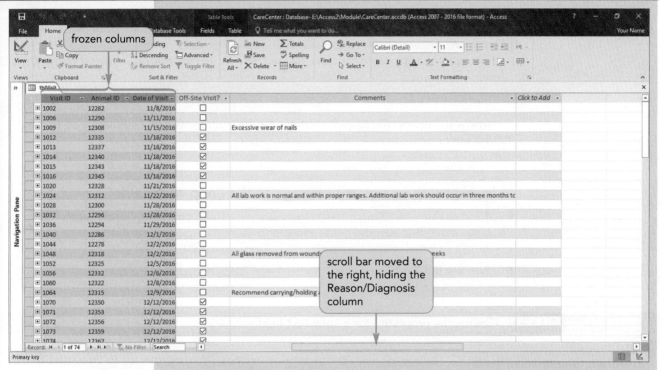

The Comments column is a Long Text field that Riverview Veterinary Care Center clinicians use to store observations and other commentary about each animal visit. Note that the Comment for Visit ID 1048 displays rich text using a bold and red font. Comments field values are partially hidden because the datasheet column is not wide enough. You'll view a record's Comments field value in the Zoom dialog box.

6. Click the **Comments** box for the record for Visit ID 1024, hold down the **Shift** key, press the **F2** key, and then release the **Shift** key. The Zoom dialog box displays the entire Comments field value.

7. Click the **OK** button to close the Zoom dialog box.

INSIGHT

Viewing Long Text Fields with Large Contents in Datasheet View

For a Long Text field that contains many characters, you can widen the field's column to view more of its contents by dragging the right edge of the field's column selector to the right or by using the Field Width command when you click the More button in the Records group on the Home tab. However, increasing the column width reduces the number of other columns you can view at the same time. Further, for Long Text fields containing thousands of characters, you can't widen the column enough to be able to view the entire contents of the field at one time across the width of the screen. Therefore, increasing the column width of a Long Text field isn't necessarily the best strategy for viewing table contents. Instead, you should use the Zoom dialog box in a datasheet or use a large scrollable box on a form.

Now you'll review the property settings for the Comments field Daksha added to the tblVisit table.

To review the property settings of the Long Text field:

1. Save the table, switch to Design view, click the **Comments Field Name** box to make that row the current row, and then, if necessary, scroll to the bottom of the list of properties in the Field Properties pane.

2. Click the **Text Format** box in the Field Properties pane, and then click its arrow. The list of available text formats appears in the box. See Figure 5-43.

Figure 5-43	Viewing the properties for a Long Text field

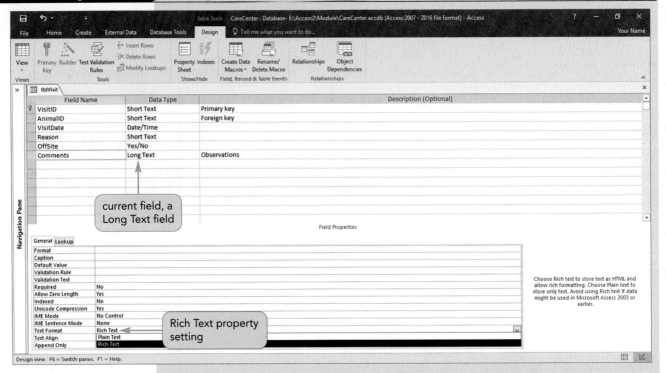

Daksha set the **Text Format property** for the Comments field to Rich Text, which lets you format the field contents using the options in the Font group on the Home tab. The default Text Format property setting for a Long Text field is Plain Text, which doesn't allow text formatting.

▶ **3.** Click the **arrow** on the Text Format box to close the list, and then click the **Append Only** box.

The **Append Only property**, which appears at the bottom of the list of properties, enables you to track the changes that you make to a Long Text field. Setting this property to Yes causes a historical record of all versions of the Long Text field value to be maintained. You can view each version of the field value, along with a date and time stamp of when each version change occurred.

You've finished your review of the Long Text field, so you can close the table.

▶ **4.** Close the tblVisit table.

When employees at Riverview Veterinary Care Center open the CareCenter database, a security warning might appear below the ribbon, and they must enable the content of the database before beginning their work. Kimberly asks if you can eliminate this extra step when employees open the database.

Designating a Trusted Folder

A database is a file, and files can contain malicious instructions that can damage other files on your computer or files on other computers on your network. Unless you take special steps, every database is treated as a potential threat to your computer. One special step that you can take is to designate a folder as a trusted folder. A **trusted folder** is a folder on a drive or network that you designate as trusted and where you place databases you know are safe. When you open a database located in a trusted folder, it is treated as a safe file, and a security warning is no longer displayed. You can also place files used with other Microsoft Office programs, such as Word documents and Excel workbooks, in a trusted folder to eliminate warnings when you open them.

Because the CareCenter database is from a trusted source, you'll specify its location as a trusted folder to eliminate the security warning when a user opens the database.

To designate a trusted folder:

▶ **1.** Click the **File** tab, and then click **Options** in the navigation bar. The Access Options dialog box opens.

▶ **2.** In the left section of the dialog box, click **Trust Center**. The Trust Center options are displayed in the dialog box.

▶ **3.** In the right section of the dialog box, click the **Trust Center Settings** button to open the Trust Center dialog box.

▶ **4.** In the left section of the Trust Center dialog box, click **Trusted Locations**. The trusted locations for your installation of Access and other trust options are displayed on the right. See Figure 5-44.

Figure 5-44   **Designating a trusted folder**

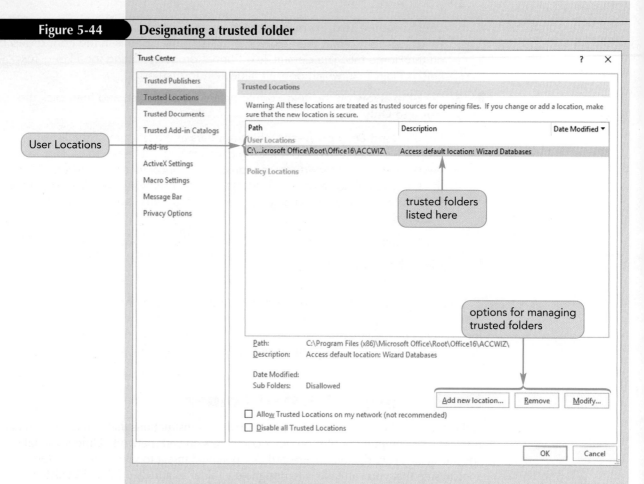

Existing trusted locations appear in the list at the top, and options to add, remove, and modify trusted locations appear at the bottom.

Trouble? Check with your instructor before adding a new trusted location. If your instructor tells you not to create a new trusted location, skip to Step 8.

5. Click the **Add new location** button to open the Microsoft Office Trusted Location dialog box.

6. In the Microsoft Office Trusted Location dialog box, click the **Browse** button, navigate to the Access2 > Module folder where your Data Files are stored, and then click the **OK** button.

You can also choose to designate subfolders of the selected location as trusted locations, but you won't select this option. By default, files in subfolders are not trusted.

7. Click the **OK** button. The Access2 > Module folder is added to the list of trusted locations.

8. Click the **OK** button to close the Trust Center dialog box, and then click the **OK** button to close the Access Options dialog box.

You've created several queries and completed several table design changes, so you should compact and repair the CareCenter database. Daksha doesn't use the Compact on Close option with the CareCenter database because it's possible to lose the database if there's a computer malfunction when the Compact on Close operation runs.

As a precaution, you'll make a backup copy of the database before you compact and repair it. Making frequent backup copies of your critical files safeguards your data from hardware and software malfunctions, which can occur at any time.

To back up, compact, and repair the CareCenter database:

▶ **1.** Click the **File** tab on the ribbon, and then click the **Save As** menu item.

▶ **2.** Click the **Back Up Database** option, and then click the **Save As** button. The Save As dialog box opens with a suggested filename of CareCenter_date in the File name box, where date is the current date in the format year-month-day. For instance, if you made a backup on February 15, 2017, the suggested filename would be CareCenter_2017-02-15.

▶ **3.** Navigate to the location of a USB drive or other external medium, if available, and then click the **Save** button to save the backup file.

Next, you'll verify that the trusted location is working.

▶ **4.** Click the **File** tab on the ribbon, and then click the **Close** command to close the CareCenter database.

▶ **5.** Click the **File** tab on the ribbon, click **Open** on the navigation bar, and then click **CareCenter.accdb** in the Recent list. The database opens, and no security warning appears below the ribbon because the database is located in the trusted location you designated.

Next, you'll compact and repair the database.

▶ **6.** Click the **File** tab on the ribbon, and then click the **Compact & Repair Database** button.

▶ **7.** Close the CareCenter database.

You've completed the table design changes to the CareCenter database, which will make working with it easier and more accurate.

Session 5.3 Quick Check

REVIEW

1. What is a lookup field?

2. A(n) _____ is a predefined format you use to enter and display data in a field.

3. What is property propagation?

4. Define the Validation Rule property, and give an example of when you would use it.

5. Define the Validation Text property, and give an example of when you would use it.

6. Setting a Long Text field's Text Format property to _____ lets you format its contents.

7. A(n) _____ folder is a location where you can place databases that you know are safe.

PRACTICE

Review Assignments

Data File needed for the Review Assignments: Supplier.accdb

Kimberly asks you to create several new queries and enhance the table design for the Vendor database. This database contains information about the vendors that Riverview Veterinary Care Center works with to obtain medical supplies and equipment for the center, as well as the vendors who service and maintain the equipment. Complete the following steps:

1. Open the **Supplier** database located in the Access2 > Review folder provided with your Data Files.

2. Modify the first record in the **tblSupplier** table datasheet by changing the Contact First Name and Contact Last Name field values to your first and last names. Close the table.

3. Create a query called **qrySupplierNameAndAddress** that lists the following fields from the tblSupplier table: SupplierID, Company, City, State, and Zip. After you have created the query, use the Autofilter feature of Access to list on the suppliers in NC, SC, and VA only. Use the Toggle Filter button to remove and reapply the filter. Save and close the query.

4. Create a query to find all records in the tblSupplier table in which the City field value starts with the letter A. Display all fields in the query recordset, and sort in ascending order by the Company Name. Save the query as **qryASelectedCities**, run the query, and then close it.

5. Make a copy of the qryASelectedCities query using the new name **qryOtherSelectedCities**. Modify the new query to find all records in the tblSupplier table in which the City field values are not Boston, Charlotte, or Billings. Save and run the query, and then close it.

6. Create a query to find all records from the tblSupplier table in which the State value is GA, MA, or NC. Use a list-of-values match for the selection criteria. Display all fields in the query recordset, and sort in descending order by the company name. Save the query as **qrySelectedStates**, run the query, and then close it.

7. Create a query to display all records from the tblSupplier table, selecting the Company, City, and Phone fields, and sorting in ascending order by Company. Add a calculated field named **ContactName** as the last column that concatenates the ContactFirst value, a space, and the ContactLast value. If the contact has a nickname, use the nickname in place of the first name in the calculated field. Set the Caption property for the ContactName field to **Contact Name**. Save the query as **qryCompanyContacts**, run the query, resize the Contact Name column to its best fit, and then save and close the query.

8. Create a parameter query to select the tblSupplier table records for a State field value that the user specifies. If the user doesn't enter a State field value, select all records from the table. Display the Company, Category, City, State, ContactFirst, ContactLast, and Phone fields in the query recordset, sorting in ascending order by City. Save the query as **qryStateParameter**. Run the query and enter no value as the State field value, and then run the query again and enter **NC** as the State field value. Close the query.

9. Create a find duplicates query based on the tblProduct table. Select ProductName as the field that might contain duplicates, and select the ProductID, SupplierID, Price, and Units fields as additional fields in the query recordset. Save the query as **qryDuplicateProductTypes**, run the query, and then close it. Because the tblProduct table does not have any duplicate ProductName values, running this query should show that no duplicate records are found.

10. Create a find unmatched query that finds all records in the tblSupplier table for which there is no matching record in the tblProduct table. Display the SupplierID, Company, City, State, Phone, ContactFirst, and ContactLast fields from the tblSupplier table in the query recordset. Save the query as **qrySuppliersWithoutMatchingProducts**, run the query, and then close it. Because the tblSupplier and tblProduct tables do not have unmatched records, running this query should show that no unmatched records are found.

11. Create a query to display all records from the tblProduct table, selecting the ProductID, SupplierID, ProductName, and Price fields, and sorting in descending order by Price. Use the Top Values property to select the top 25 percent of records. Save the query as **qryTop25Price**, run the query, and then close it.

12. In the tblProduct table, change the SupplierID field to a lookup field. Select the Company field and then the SupplierID field from the tblSupplier table. Sort in ascending order by the Company field, do not hide the key column, make sure the Company Name column is the leftmost column, resize the lookup columns to their best fit, select SupplierID as the field to store in the table, and accept the default label for the lookup column. View the tblProduct table datasheet, resize the Supplier ID column to its best fit, test the lookup field without changing a value permanently, and then save and close the table.

13. Use the Input Mask Wizard to add an input mask to the Phone field in the tblSupplier table. The ending input mask should use periods as separators, as in 987.654.3210 with only the last seven digits required; do not store the literal display characters, if you are asked to do so. Update the Input Mask property everywhere the Phone field is used. Resize all columns in the datasheet to their best fit, and then test the input mask by typing over an existing Phone field value, being sure not to change the value by pressing the Esc key after you type the last digit in the Phone field.

14. Create a crosstab query based on the tblSupplier table. Use the Category field values for the row headings, the SupplierID field values for the column headings, and the count of the Company field values as the summarized value, and include row sums. Save the query as **qrySupplierCategoryCrosstab**. Change the column heading for the total of each category to **Total of Companies**. Resize the Total of Companies column in the query recordset to its best fit, and then save and close the query.

15. Open the tblProduct table, and then open the Object Dependencies pane for the tblProduct object. Click on the Objects that depend on me option button, then click the Refresh link if necessary to see the list of objects that depend upon the tblProduct table. Verify that the following objects depend upon the tblProduct table: tblSupplier table, qrySuppliersWithoutMatchingProducts query, and qryTop25Price query. Close the Object Dependencies pane.

16. Set a field validation rule on the Price field in the tblProduct table. Ensure that each product entered will have a price greater than zero. Should a user attempt to enter a value of zero, or less than zero, the following message should be displayed: "All prices must be greater than zero." Test the field validation rule by modifying the price of the first item in the recordset to 0, and verify that the error message is displayed. Reset the value of the record to its original value. Save and close the tblProduct table.

17. Open the tblSupplier table, and then set a table validation rule on the tblSupplier table to ensure the initial contact date is prior to, or equal to, the latest contact date. If an invalid value is entered, the following message should be displayed: "Latest contact date cannot be prior to the initial contact date." Test the table validation rule by changing the latest contact date prior to the initial contact date in the first record. Advance to the next record, then verify that the error message is displayed. Reset the values of the first record to their original values. Save your changes to the tblSupplier table.

18. In the tblSupplier table, examine the field properties pane for the Notes field. Verify that the Text Format property is set to Rich Text, and that the Append Only property is set to Yes. Close the tblSupplier table without saving changes.

19. Designate the Access2 > Review folder as a trusted folder. (*Note:* Check with your instructor before adding a new trusted location.)

20. Make a backup copy of the database, compact and repair the database, and then close it.

Case Problem 1

Data File needed for this Case Problem: MoreBeauty.accdb

Beauty To Go   Sue Miller, an owner of a nail and hair salon in Orlando, Florida, regularly checks in on her grandmother, who resides in a retirement community. On some of her visits, Sue does her grandmother's hair and nails. Her grandmother told Sue that some of her friends would be glad to pay her and have regularly scheduled services if she could do their hair and nails also. Sue expanded her business to include the services to friends of her grandmother in local retirement communities to meet the needs of these ladies. Sue created an Access database named MoreBeauty to store data about members, plans, and contracts. She wants to create several new queries and make design changes to the tables. Complete the following steps:

1. Open the **MoreBeauty** database located in the Access2 > Case1 folder provided with your Data Files.

2. Modify the first record in the tblMember table datasheet by changing the First Name and Last Name column values to your first and last names. Close the table.

3. Create a query to find all records in the tblOption table in which the OptionCost field is 70, 125, 140, or 250. Use a list-of-values match for the selection criterion, and include all fields from the table in the query recordset. Sort the query in descending order by the OptionID field. Save the query as **qryLowVolumePlans**, run the query, and then close it.

4. Make a copy of the qryLowVolumePlans query using the new name **qryHighVolumePlans**. Modify the new query to find all records in the tblPlan table in which the PlanCost field is not 70, 125, 140, or 250. Save and run the query, and then close it.

5. Create a query to display all records from the tblMember table, selecting the LastName, FirstName, Street, and Phone fields, and sorting in ascending order by LastName and then in ascending order by FirstName. Add a calculated field named **MemberName** as the first column that concatenates FirstName, a space, and LastName. Set the Caption property for the MemberName field to **Member Name**. Do not display the LastName and FirstName fields in the query recordset. Create a second calculated field named **CityLine**, inserting it between the Street and Phone fields. The CityLine field concatenates City, a space, State, two spaces, and Zip. Set the Caption property for the CityLine field to **City Line**. Save the query as **qryMemberNames**, run the query, resize all columns to their best fit, and then save and close the query.

6. Create a query to display all matching records from the tblOption and tblMember tables, selecting the LastName and FirstName fields from the tblMember table and the OptionDescription and OptionCost fields from the tblOption table. Add a calculated field named **FeeStatus** as the last column that equals *Fee Waived* if the FeeWaived field is equal to *yes*, and that equals *Fee Not Waived* otherwise. Set the Caption property for the calculated field to **Fee Status**. Sort the list in ascending order on the LastName field. Save the query as **qryFeeStatus**, run the query, resize all columns to their best fit, and then save and close the query.

7. Create a query based on the tblOption and tblMember tables, selecting the LastName, FirstName, and City fields from the tblMember table and the FeeWaived, OptionDescription, and OptionCost fields from the tblOption table. The query should find the records in which the City field value is Orlando or Celebration and the FeeWaived field value is *Yes*. Save the query as **qryOrlandoAndCelebrationFeeWaived**. Save and run the query, and then close the query.

8. Create a parameter query to select the tblMember table records for a City field value that the user specifies. If the user doesn't enter a City field value, select all records from the table. Display all fields from the tblMember table in the query recordset. Save the query as **qryMemberCityParameter**. Run the query and enter no value as the City field value, and then run the query again and enter **Celebration** as the City field value. Close the query.

9. Create a find duplicates query based on the tblMember table. Select OptionEnd as the field that might contain duplicates, and select all other fields in the table as additional fields in the query recordset. Save the query as **qryDuplicateMemberExpirationDates**, run the query, and then close it.

10. Create a find unmatched query that finds all records in the tblMember table for which there is no matching record in the tblOption table. Select FirstName, LastName, and Phone fields from the tblMembers table. Save the query as **qryMembersWithoutPlans**, run the query, and then close it. Because the tblMember and tblOption tables do not have unmatched records, running this query should show that no unmatched records are found.

11. Create a new query based on the tblMember table. Display the FirstName, LastName, Phone, OptionEnd, and OptionID fields, in this order, in the query recordset. Sort in ascending order by the OptionEnd field, and then use the Top Values property to select the top 25 percent of records. Save the query as **qryUpcomingExpirations**, run the query, and then close it.

12. Use the Input Mask Wizard to add an input mask to the Phone field in the tblMember table. Create the input mask such that the phone number is displayed with a dot separating each part of the phone number. For instance, if the phone number is (303) 123-4567 it should be displayed as 303.123.4567 for new entries. Test the input mask by typing over an existing Phone column value, being certain not to change the value by pressing the Esc key after you type the last digit in the Phone column, and then save and close the table.

13. Define a field validation rule for the OptionCost field in the tblOption table. Acceptable field values for the OptionCost field are values greater than or equal to 70. Enter the message **Value must be greater than or equal to 70** so it appears if a user enters an invalid OptionCost field value. Save your table changes, and then test the field validation rule for the OptionCost field; be certain the field values are the same as they were before your testing, and then close the table.

14. Define a table validation rule for the tblMember table to verify that OptionBegin field values precede OptionEnd field values in time. Use an appropriate validation message. Save your table changes, and then test the table validation rule, making sure any tested field values are the same as they were before your testing.

15. Add a Long Text field named **MemberComments** as the last field in the tblMember table. Set the Caption property to **Member Comments** and the Text Format property to Rich Text. In the table datasheet, resize the new column to its best fit, and then add a comment in the Member Comments column in the first record about special instructions for this member, formatting part of the text with blue, italic font. Save your table changes, and then close the table.

16. Designate the Access2 > Case1 folder as a trusted folder. (*Note:* Check with your instructor before adding a new trusted location.)

17. Make a backup copy of the database, compact and repair the database, and then close it.

Case Problem 2

Data File needed for this Case Problem: Tutoring.accdb

Programming Pros   While in college obtaining his bachelor's degree in Raleigh, North Carolina, Brent Hovis majored in computer science. Prior to graduating, Brent began tutoring freshman and sophomore students in programming to make some extra money. When Brent entered graduate school, he started Programming Pros, a company offering expanded tutoring services for high school and college students through group, private, and semiprivate tutoring sessions. Brent created an Access database to maintain information about the tutors who work for him, the students who sign up for tutoring, and the contracts they sign. To make the database easier to use, Brent wants you to create several queries and modify its table design. Complete the following steps:

1. Open the **Tutoring** database located in the Access2 > Case2 folder provided with your Data Files.

2. Change the last record in the tblTutor table datasheet so the FirstName and LastName field values contain your first and last names. Close the table.

3. Create a query to find all records in the tblStudent table in which the LastName field value begins with L. Display the FirstName, LastName, City, and HomePhone fields in the query recordset, and sort in ascending order by LastName. Save the query as **qryLastNameL**, run the query, and then close it.

4. Create a query that finds all records in the tblTutor table in which the YearInSchool field value is either Senior or Graduate. Use a list-of-values criterion, and include the fields First Name, Last Name, and YearInSchool in the recordset, sorted in ascending order on the LastName field. Save the query using the name **qrySelectedYearInSchool**. Run the query, and then close it.

5. Create a query to find all records in the tblStudent table in which the City field value is not equal to Raleigh. Display the FirstName, LastName, City, and HomePhone fields in the query recordset, and sort in ascending order by City. Save the query as **qryNonRaleigh**, run the query, and then close it.

6. Create a query to display all records from the tblTutor table, selecting all fields, and sorting in ascending order by LastName and then in ascending order by FirstName. Add a calculated field named **TutorName** as the second column that concatenates FirstName, a space, and LastName for each teacher. Set the Caption property for the TutorName field to **Tutor Name**. Do not display the FirstName and LastName fields in the query recordset. Save the query as **qryTutorNames**, run the query, resize the Tutor Name column to its best fit, and then save and close the query.

7. Create a parameter query to select the tblContract table records for a SessionType field value that the user specifies. If the user doesn't enter a SessionType field value, select all records from the table. Include all fields from the tblContract table in the query recordset. Save the query as **qrySessionTypeParameter**. Run the query and enter no value as the SessionType field value, and then run the query again and enter **Group** as the SessionType field value. Close the query.

8. Create a crosstab query based on the tblContract table. Use the SessionType field values for the row headings, the Length field values for the column headings, and the count of the ContractID field values as the summarized value, and include row sums. Save the query as **qrySessionTypeCrosstab**. Change the column heading for the row sum column, which represents the total of each type of session, to **Total Number of Sessions**. Resize the columns in the query recordset to their best fit, and then save and close the query.

9. Create a find duplicates query based on the tblContract table. Select StudentID and SessionType as the fields that might contain duplicates, and select all other fields in the table as additional fields in the query recordset. Save the query as **qryMultipleSessionsForStudents**, run the query, and then close it.

10. Create a find unmatched query that finds all records in the tblStudent table for which there is no matching record in the tblContract table. Display all fields from the tblStudent table in the query recordset. Save the query as **qryStudentsWithoutContracts**, run the query, and then close it.

11. In the tblContract table, change the TutorID field data type to Lookup Wizard. Select the FirstName, LastName, and TutorID fields from the tblTutor table, sort in ascending order by LastName, resize the lookup columns to their best fit, select TutorID as the field to store in the table, and accept the default label for the lookup column. In datasheet view, change the TutorID value for the first record to verify that the lookup functions correctly, then restore the original TutorID value for the first record. Save and close the table.

12. Use the Input Mask Wizard to add an input mask to the HomePhone and CellPhone fields in the tblStudent table. The ending input mask should use periods as separators, as in 987.654.3210, with only the last seven digits required; do not store the literal display characters, if you are asked to do so. Resize the Home Phone and Cell Phone columns to their best fit, and then test the input mask by typing over an existing Phone field value, being sure not to change the value permanently by pressing the Esc key after you type the last digit in the Phone field.

13. Define a field validation rule for the Gender field in the tblStudent table. Acceptable field values for the Gender field are F or M. Use the message "Gender value must be F or M" to notify a user who enters an invalid Gender field value. Save your table changes, test the field validation rule for the Gender field, making sure any tested field values are the same as they were before your testing, and then close the table.

14. Designate the Access2 > Case2 folder as a trusted folder. (*Note:* Check with your instructor before adding a new trusted location.)

15. Make a backup copy of the database, compact and repair the database, and then close it.

CHALLENGE

Case Problem 3

Data File needed for this Case Problem: Community.accdb

Diane's Community Center   Diane Coleman is a successful businesswoman in Dallas, Georgia, but things were not always that way. Diane experienced trying times and fortunately had people in the community come into her life to assist her and her children when times were difficult. To give back to her community and support those in need, Diane has created a community center in Dallas where those in need can come in for goods and services. She has also opened a thrift store to sell and auction donated items to support the center. Diane has created an Access database to manage information about the center's patrons and donations. Diane now wants to create several queries and to make changes to the table design of the database. You'll help Diane by completing the following steps:

1. Open the **Community** database located in the Access2 > Case3 folder provided with your Data Files.

2. Modify the first record in the tblPatron table datasheet by changing the Title, FirstName, and LastName column values to your title and name. Close the table.

3. Create a query to find all records in the tblDonation table that were cash donations. Display the DonationID, PatronID, DonationDate, and DonationValue fields in the query recordset. Sort by descending order by DonationValue. Save the query as **qryCashDonations**, run the query, and then close it.

4. Create a query to find all records in the tblDonation table in which the item donated is a potential auction item. Display the DonationID, PatronID, DonationDate, Description, and DonationValue fields from the tblDonation table. Sort in ascending order by DonationDate. Save the query as **qryPotentialAuctionItems**, run the query, and then close it.

5. Create a query called **qryDonationsSeptemberOrLater** that will contain all fields from the tblDonation and tblPatron tables except for PatronID and DonationID, for all donations that are on or after September 1, 2017. Sort this query by DonationValue in descending order. Save and run the query, and then close it.

6. Create a query to display all records from the tblPatron table, selecting the Title and Phone fields. Add a calculated field named **PatronName** that concatenates FirstName, a space, and LastName. Position this column as the second column, and sort the recordset in ascending order by LastName. Set the Caption property for the PatronName field to **Patron Name**. Save the query as **qryPatronNames**, run the query, resize the new column to its best fit, and then save and close the query.

7. Create a parameter query to select the tblDonation table records for a Description field value that contains a phrase the user specifies. If the user doesn't enter a Description field phrase value, select all records from the table. Display all fields from the tblDonation table in the query recordset, and sort in ascending order by Description. Save the query as **qryDonationParameter**. Run the query and enter no value as the Description phrase field value, and then run the query again and enter **clothes** as the Description field phrase value. Close the query.

⊕ **Explore** 8. Create a crosstab query based on the qryDonationsSeptemberOrLater query. Use the DonationDate field values for the row headings, the CashDonation field values for the column headings, and the sum of the DonationValue field values as the summarized value, and include row sums. Save the query as **qryDonationsSeptemberOrLaterCrosstab**. Change the format of the displayed values to Fixed. Change the column headings to Cash and NonCash. Resize the columns in the query recordset to their best fit, and then save and close the query.

⊕ **Explore** 9. Create a find duplicates query based on the qryDonationsSeptemberOrLater query. Select FirstName and LastName as the fields that might contain duplicates, and select the CashDonation and DonationValue fields in the query as additional fields in the query recordset. Save the query as **qryMultipleDonorDonations**, run the query, and then close it.

10. Create a find unmatched query that finds all records in the tblPatron table for which there is no matching record in the tblDonation table. Include all fields from the tblPatron table, except for PatronID, in the query recordset. Save the query as **qryPatronsWithoutDonations**, run the query, and then close it.

⊕ **Explore** 11. Make a copy of the qryDonationsSeptemberOrLater query using the new name **qryTopDonations**. (*Hint:* Be sure to copy the correct query and not the qryDonationsSeptemberOrLaterCrosstab query.) Modify the new query by using the Top Values property to select the top 40 percent of the records. Save and run the query, and then close the query.

12. Use the Input Mask Wizard to add an input mask to the Phone field in the tblPatron table. The ending input mask should use hyphens as separators, as in 987-654-3210, with only the last seven digits required; do not store the literal display characters, if you are asked to do so. Test the input mask by typing over an existing Phone field value, being sure not to change the value permanently by pressing the Esc key after you type the last digit in the Phone field. Close the table.

13. Designate the Access2 > Case3 folder as a trusted folder. (*Note:* Check with your instructor before adding a new trusted location.)

14. Make a backup copy of the database, compact and repair the database, and then close it.

CHALLENGE

Case Problem 4

Data File needed for this Case Problem: AppTrail.accdb

Hike Appalachia   Molly and Bailey Johnson own Hike Appalachia, a business in which they guide clients on hikes in the Blue Ridge Mountains of North Carolina. They advertise in local and regional outdoor magazines and field requests from people all around the region. Molly and Bailey have created an Access database for their business and now want you to create several queries and modify the table design. To do so, you'll complete the following steps:

1. Open the **AppTrail** database located in the Access2 > Case4 folder provided with your Data Files.

2. Modify the first record in the tblHiker table datasheet by changing the Hiker First Name and Hiker Last Name column values to your first and last names, and then close the table.

3. Create a query to find all records in the tbHiker table in which the HikerLast field value starts with the letter S, sorted in ascending order by HikerLast. Display all fields except the HikerID field in the query recordset. Save the query as **qryHikerLastNameS**, run the query, and then close it.

4. Create a query to find all records in the tblTour table where the tour type is not hiking. Name this query **qryNonHikingTours**. Display all fields, sorting by TourName. Save and run the query, and then close it.

5. Create a query to find all records in the tblHiker table in which the State field value is NC, SC, or GA and display all fields from the tblHiker table in the query recordset, sorted by HikerLast in ascending order. Save the query as **qrySelectedStates**, run the query, and then close it.

6. Create a query to select all records from the tblTour table with a price per person of $100 or less, where the TourType is Hiking. Display all fields in the query recordset, sorted by PricePerPerson in descending order. Save the query as **qryInexpensiveHikingTours**, run the query, and then close it.

7. Create a parameter query to select the tblTour table records for a TourType field phrase value that the user specifies. If the user doesn't enter a phrase field value, select all records from the table. Display all fields from the tblTour table in the query recordset, and sort in ascending order by TourName. Save the query as **qryTourParameter**. Run the query and enter no value as the phrase field value, and then run the query again and enter **Van** as the TourType phrase field value. Close the query.

8. Create a query that contains all records from the tblHiker table and all matching records from the tblReservation table. Display all fields from the tblHiker table and all fields except HikerID from the tblReservation table. Save the query as **qryHikersAndReservations**, run the query, and then close it.

⊕ **Explore** 9. Create a crosstab query based on the qryHikersAndReservations query. Use the TourID field values for the row headings, the HikerID field values for the column headings, and the sum of the People field as the summarized value, and include row sums. Save the query as **qryReservationsCrosstab**, resize the columns in the query recordset to their best fit, and then save and close the query.

⊕ **Explore** 10. Create a find duplicates query based on the qryHikersAndReservations query. Select HikerID as the field that might contain duplicates, and select the fields HikerFirst, HikerLast, TourID, TourDate, and People in the table as additional fields in the query recordset. Save the query as **qryMultipleReservations**, run the query, and then close it.

11. Create a find unmatched query that finds all records in the tblHiker table for which there is no matching record in the tblReservation table. Display the HikerFirst, HikerLast, City, State, and Phone fields from the tblHiker table in the query recordset. Save the query as **qryHikersWithoutReservations**, run the query, and then close it.

12. Copy the qryInexpensiveHikingTours query, and save it as **qryTopInexpensiveHikingTours**. Use the Top Values property to select the top 50 percent of the records. Save and run the query, and then close it.

13. In the tblReservation table, change the TourID field data type to Lookup Wizard. Select all of the fields from the tblTour table, sort in ascending order by TourName, do not show the key column, resize the lookup columns to their best fit, select TourID as the field to store in the table, and accept the default label for the lookup column. View the tblReservation datasheet, resize the TourID column to its best fit, test the lookup field without changing a field value permanently, and then close the table.

14. Define a field validation rule for the People field in the tblReservation table. Acceptable field values for the People field are values less than or equal to 6. Display the message **Please book a custom tour for large groups.** when a user enters an invalid People field value. Save your table changes, and then test the field validation rule for the People field; be certain the field values are the same as they were before your testing.

15. Designate the Access2 > Case4 folder as a trusted folder. (*Note:* Check with your instructor before adding a new trusted location.)

16. Make a backup copy of the database, compact and repair the database, and then close it.

ACCESS

Using Form Tools and Creating Custom Forms

Creating Forms for Riverview Veterinary Care Center

Case | *Riverview Veterinary Care Center*

Kimberly Johnson hired Daksha Yatawara to enhance the CareCenter database, and he initially concentrated on standardizing the table design and creating queries for Riverview Veterinary Care Center. Kimberly and her staff created a few forms before Daksha came onboard, and Daksha's next priority is to work with Kimberly to create new forms that will be more functional and easier to use.

In this module, you will create new forms for Riverview Veterinary Care Center. In creating the forms, you will use many Access form customization features, such as adding controls and a subform to a form, using combo boxes and calculated controls, and adding color and special effects. These features make it easier for database users like Kimberly and her staff to interact with a database.

STARTING DATA FILES

Access2 →	Module	Review	Case1
	CareCenter.accdb (cont.)	Supplier.accdb (cont.)	MoreBeauty.accdb (cont.)
	Case2	Case3	Case4
	Tutoring.accdb (cont.)	Community.accdb (cont.)	AppTrail.accdb (cont.)

Session 6.1 Visual Overview:

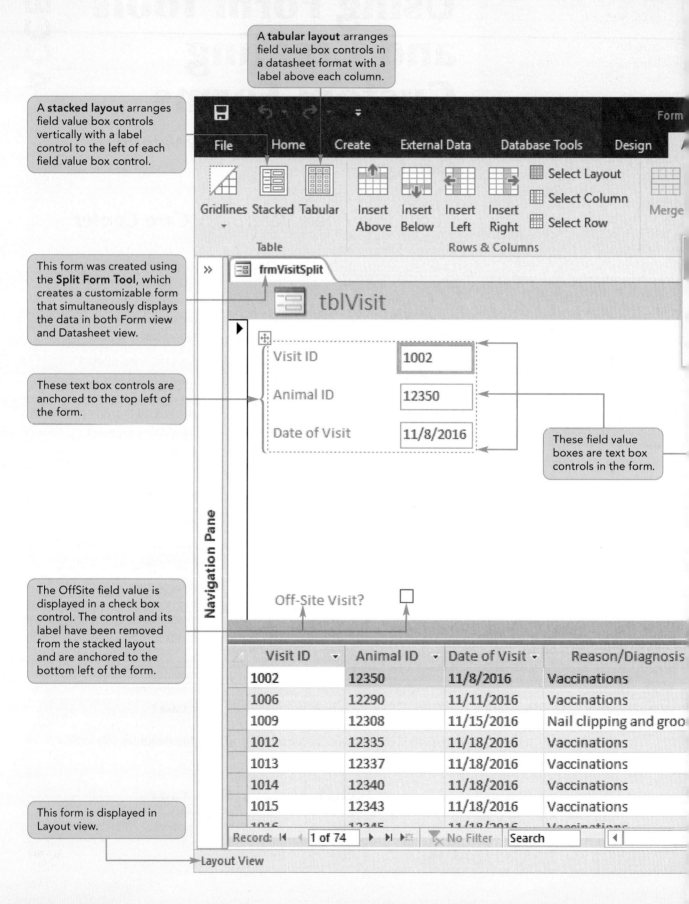

A **tabular layout** arranges field value box controls in a datasheet format with a label above each column.

A **stacked layout** arranges field value box controls vertically with a label control to the left of each field value box control.

This form was created using the **Split Form Tool**, which creates a customizable form that simultaneously displays the data in both Form view and Datasheet view.

These text box controls are anchored to the top left of the form.

The OffSite field value is displayed in a check box control. The control and its label have been removed from the stacked layout and are anchored to the bottom left of the form.

This form is displayed in Layout view.

These field value boxes are text box controls in the form.

Anchoring Controls

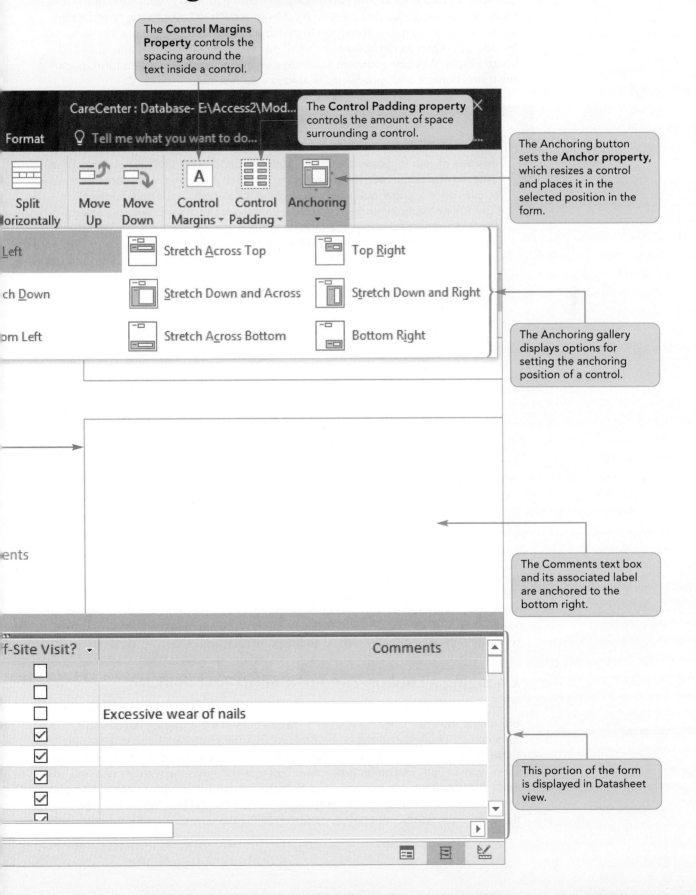

The **Control Margins Property** controls the spacing around the text inside a control.

The **Control Padding property** controls the amount of space surrounding a control.

The Anchoring button sets the **Anchor property**, which resizes a control and places it in the selected position in the form.

The Anchoring gallery displays options for setting the anchoring position of a control.

The Comments text box and its associated label are anchored to the bottom right.

This portion of the form is displayed in Datasheet view.

Designing Forms

To create a **custom form**, you can modify an existing form in Layout view or in Design view, or you can design and create a form from scratch in Layout view or in Design view. You can design a custom form to match a paper form, to display some fields side by side and others top to bottom, to highlight certain sections with color, or to add visual effects. Whether you want to create a simple or complex custom form, planning the form's content and appearance is always your first step.

Form Design Guidelines

The users of your database should use forms to perform all database updates because forms provide better readability and control than do table and query recordsets. When you plan a form, you should keep in mind the following form design guidelines:

- Determine the fields and record source needed for each form. A form's **Record Source property** specifies the table or query that provides the fields for the form.
- Group related fields and position them in a meaningful, logical order.
- If users will refer to a source document while working with the form, design the form to closely match the source document.
- Identify each field value with a label that names the field, and align field values and labels for readability.
- Set the width of each field value box to fully display the values it contains and also to provide a visual cue to users about the length of those values.
- Display calculated fields in a distinctive way, and prevent users from changing and updating them.
- Use default values, list boxes, and other form controls whenever possible to reduce user errors by minimizing keystrokes and limiting entries. A control is an item, such as a text box or command button, that you place in a form or report.
- Use colors, fonts, and graphics sparingly to keep the form uncluttered and to keep the focus on the data. Use white space to separate the form controls so that they are easier to find and read.
- Use a consistent style for all forms in a database. When forms are formatted differently, with form controls in different locations from one form to another, users must spend extra time looking for the form controls.

Kimberly and her staff had created a few forms and made table design changes before implementing proper database maintenance guidelines. These guidelines recommend performing all database updates using forms. As a result, Riverview Veterinary Care Center won't use table or query datasheets to update the database, and Kimberly asks if she should reconsider any of the table design changes she asked you to make to the CareCenter database in the previous module.

Changing a Lookup Field to a Short Text field

The input mask and validation rule changes are important table design modifications, but setting the InvoiceItemID field to a lookup field in the tblBilling table is an unnecessary change. A form combo box provides the same capability in a clearer, more flexible way. Many default forms use text boxes. A **text box** is a control that lets users type an entry. A **combo box** is a control that combines the features of a text box and a list box; it lets users either choose a value from a list or type an entry. A text box should be used when users must enter data, while a combo box should be used when there is a finite number of choices. Before creating the new forms for Kimberly, you'll change the data type of the InvoiceItemID field in the tblBilling table from a Lookup Wizard field to a Short Text field, so that you can create the relationship with referential integrity between the tblBilling and tblInvoiceItems tables.

To change the data type of the InvoiceItemID field:

1. Start Access, and then open the **CareCenter** database you worked with in the previous module.

   Trouble? If the security warning is displayed below the ribbon, click the Enable Content button.

TIP

You can press the F11 key to open or close the Navigation Pane.

2. Open the Navigation Pane, if necessary, open the **tblBilling table** in Design view, and then close the Navigation Pane.

3. Click the **InvoiceItemID** Field Name box, and then in the Field Properties pane, click the **Lookup** tab. The Field Properties pane displays the lookup properties for the InvoiceItemID field. See Figure 6-1.

Figure 6-1   **Lookup properties for the InvoiceItemID field**

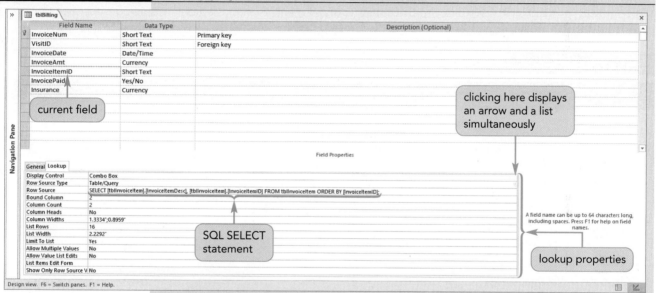

Notice the **Row Source property**, which specifies the data source for a control in a form or report or for a field in a table or query. The Row Source property is usually set to a table name, a query name, or an SQL statement. For the InvoiceItemID field, the Row Source property is set to an SQL SELECT statement. You'll learn more about SQL later in this text.

To remove the lookup feature for the InvoiceItemID field, you need to change the **Display Control property**, which specifies the default control used to display a field, from Combo Box to Text Box.

4. Click the right end of the **Display Control** box, and then click **Text Box** in the list. All the lookup properties in the Field Properties pane disappear, and the InvoiceItemID field changes back to a standard Short Text field without lookup properties.

▶ **5.** Click the **General** tab in the Field Properties pane, and notice that the properties for a Short Text field still apply to the InvoiceItemID field.

▶ **6.** Save the table, switch to Datasheet view, resize the Invoice Item ID column to its best fit, and then click one of the Invoice Item ID boxes. An arrow does not appear in the Invoice Item ID box because the InvoiceItemID field is no longer a lookup field.

▶ **7.** Save the table, and then close the tblBilling table.

Before you could change the InvoiceItemID field in the tblBilling table to a lookup field in the previous module, you had to delete the one-to-many relationship between the tblInvoiceItem and tblBilling tables. Now that you've changed the data type of the InvoiceItemID field back to a Short Text field, you'll view the table relationships to make sure that the tables in the CareCenter database are related correctly.

To view the table relationships in the Relationships window:

▶ **1.** Click the **Database Tools** tab, and then in the Relationships group, click the **Relationships** button to open the Relationships window. See Figure 6-2.

Figure 6-2	CareCenter database tables in Relationships window

Trouble? If the order of the table field lists in your Relationships window do not match Figure 6-2, simply drag the table field lists to rearrange them so that they appear in the same left to right order shown in the figure.

The tblVisit table and the related tblBilling table have a one-to-many relationship with referential integrity enforced. You need to establish a similar one-to-many relationship between the tblInvoiceItem and tblBilling tables.

▶ **2.** Double-click the **relationship line** between the tblBilling and tblInvoiceItem tables to open the Edit Relationships dialog box.

▶ **3.** Click the **Enforce Referential Integrity** check box, click the **Cascade Update Related Fields** check box, and then click the **OK** button to close the dialog box. The join line connecting the tblInvoiceItem and tblBilling tables now indicates a one-to-many relationship with referential integrity enforced.

Kimberly is interested in documenting information on the objects and relationships between objects in the database she and her staff can use as a reference. In Access, you can create a report of the database relationships. You can also give Kimberly information on all the objects in the database using the Documenter.

Creating a Relationship Report and Using the Documenter

From the Relationships window, you can create a Relationship report to document the fields, tables, and relationships in a database. You can also use the **Documenter**, another Access tool, to create detailed documentation of all, or selected, objects in a database. For each selected object, the Documenter lets you print documentation, such as the object's properties and relationships, and the names and properties of fields used by the object. You can use the documentation on an object, referred to as an Object Definition Report, to help you understand an object and to help you plan changes to that object.

PROSKILLS

Written Communication: Satisfying User Documentation Requirements

The Documenter produces object documentation that is useful to the technical designers, analysts, and programmers who develop and maintain Access databases and who need to understand the intricate details of a database's design. However, users who interact with databases generally have little interest in the documentation produced by the Documenter. Users need to know how to enter and maintain data using forms and how to obtain information using forms and reports, so they require special documentation that matches these needs; this documentation isn't produced by the Documenter, though. Many companies assign one or more users the task of creating the documentation needed by users based on the idea that users themselves are the most familiar with their company's procedures and understand most clearly the specific documentation that they and other users require. Databases with dozens of tables and with hundreds of other objects are complicated structures, so be sure you provide documentation that satisfies the needs of users separate from the documentation for database developers.

Next, you will create a Relationship report and use the Documenter to create documentation for the tblVisit table.

To create the Relationship report:

▶ **1.** On the Relationship Tools Design tab, in the Tools group, click the **Relationship Report** button to open the Relationships for CareCenter report in Print Preview.

▶ **2.** In the Page Layout group, click the **Landscape** button to change the report to landscape orientation and display the entire relationship structure. See Figure 6-3.

Figure 6-3 **Relationships for CareCenter report**

relationships for
CareCenter

Trouble? If the order of the table field lists in your Relationships window do not match Figure 6-3, simply drag the table field lists to rearrange them so that they appear in the same left-to-right order shown in the figure.

▶ **3.** Right-click the **Relationships for CareCenter** tab, and then click **Close** to close the tab. A dialog box opens and asks if you want to save the design of the report.

▶ **4.** Click the **Yes** button to save the report, click the **OK** button to use the default report name Relationships for CareCenter, and then close the Relationships window.

Kimberly wants to show her staff a sample of the information the Documenter provides.

REFERENCE

Using the Documenter

- In the Analyze group on the Database Tools tab, click the Database Documenter button.
- In the Documenter dialog box, select the object(s) you want to document.
- If necessary, click the Options button to open the Print Table Definition dialog box, select specific documentation options for the selected object(s), and then click the OK button.
- Click the OK button to close the Documenter dialog box and open the Object Definition window in Print Preview.
- Print the documentation if desired, and then close the Object Definition window.

You will use the Documenter to create an Object Definition Report on the tblVisit table.

To use the Documenter to create, save, and print an Object Definition report:

▶ **1.** On the ribbon, click the **Database Tools** tab.

▶ **2.** In the Analyze group, click the **Database Documenter** button to open the Documenter dialog box, and then click the **Tables** tab (if necessary). See Figure 6-4.

Figure 6-4 Documenter dialog box

click to display all database objects

click to select all objects

click to display more options for the selected object type

3. Click the **tblVisit** check box, and then click the **Options** button. The Print Table Definition dialog box opens. In this dialog box, you select which documentation you want the Documenter to include for the selected table, its fields, and its indexes.

4. Make sure the **Properties**, **Relationships**, and **Permissions by User and Group** check boxes are all checked in the Include for Table section.

5. In the Include for Fields section, click the **Names, Data Types, and Sizes** option button (if necessary), then click the **Names and Fields** option button in the Include for Indexes section (if necessary). See Figure 6-5.

Figure 6-5 Print Table Definition dialog box

table documentation options

field documentation options

index documentation options

TIP

The Print Preview tab in the Print Preview window provides options for setting various printing options, such as page margins, page orientation, and number of columns to print for a form or report.

6. Click the **OK** button to close the Print Table Definition dialog box, and then click the **OK** button to close the Documenter dialog box. The Object Definition report opens in Print Preview.

7. On the Print Preview tab, in the Zoom group, click the **Zoom button arrow**, and then click **Zoom 100%**. To display more of the report, you will collapse the ribbon.

8. On the right end of the ribbon, click the **Collapse the Ribbon** button ⌃, and then scroll down the report and examine its contents. See Figure 6-6.

| Figure 6-6 | Print Preview of the Object Definition report |

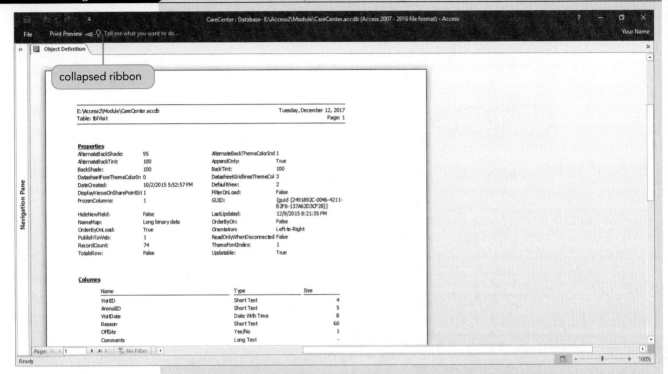

The Object Definition report displays table, field, and relationship documentation for the tblVisit table. Next, you'll export the report and save it as a PDF document.

9. Click the **Print Preview** tab to expand the ribbon, and then in the Data group, click the **PDF or XPS** button. The Publish as PDF or XPS dialog box opens.

10. In the File name box, change the filename to **ClinicDocumenter**, navigate to the location where you are saving your files, click the **Publish** button, and then click the **Close** button in the Export – PDF dialog box to close without saving the steps.

Trouble? If the PDF you created opens automatically during Step 10, close the PDF viewer.

11. Close the Object Definition report. The ribbon is still collapsed.

12. On the ribbon, click the **Home** tab, and then, on the right end of the ribbon, click the **Pin the ribbon** button ⊨ to expand and pin the ribbon again.

> **TIP**
>
> You can also collapse the ribbon by double-clicking any ribbon tab or by right-clicking a blank area of the ribbon and clicking Collapse the Ribbon on the shortcut menu.

The CareCenter database currently contains the frmOwner form. The frmOwner form was created using the Form Wizard with some design changes that were made in Layout view including changing the theme, changing the form title color and line type, adding a picture, and moving a field. Next Kimberly would like you to create a form that allows her and her staff to see and modify the relevant data for animal visits. You will create this form using other form tools.

Creating Forms Using Form Tools

In earlier modules you created forms with and without subforms using the Form Wizard. You can create other types of forms using different form tools, namely the Datasheet tool, the Multiple Items tool, and the Split Form tool.

PROSKILLS

Decision Making: Creating Multiple Forms and Reports

When developing a larger database application, it's not uncommon for the users of the database to be unsure as to what they want with respect to forms and reports. You may obtain some sample data and sample reports during the requirements-gathering phase that give you some ideas, but in the end, it is a good idea to have the users approve the final versions.

While you are actively developing the application, you might design different versions of forms and reports that you think will meet users' needs; later in the process, you might narrow the selection to a few forms and reports. Ultimately, you should ask the users to make the final choices of which forms and reports to incorporate into the database. By involving the users in the planning phase for forms and reports, the database is more likely to meet everyone's needs.

Kimberly has requested a form that her staff can use to work with information from the tblVisit table. Because her requirements at this point are vague, you'll create a selection of form designs for Kimberly to choose from. You'll create two simple forms that show the contents of the tblVisit in a layout that resembles a table, and you'll create a custom form that Kimberly's staff may find a bit more user-friendly. First, you'll create the simple forms for Kimberly and her staff.

Creating a Form Using the Datasheet Tool

You can create a simple form using the Datasheet Tool. The **Datasheet tool** creates a form in a datasheet format that contains all the fields in the source table or query. Kimberly might prefer this if she and her staff are very comfortable entering data in an Access table in Datasheet view. You'll use the Datasheet tool to create a form based on the tblVisit table. When you use the Datasheet tool, the record source (either a table or query) for the form must either be open or selected in the Navigation Pane.

To create the form using the Datasheet tool:

▶ **1.** Open the Navigation Pane, and then click **tblVisit**.

▶ **2.** On the ribbon, click the **Create** tab.

▶ **3.** In the Forms group, click the **More Forms** button, click **Datasheet**, and then, if necessary, close the Property Sheet. The Datasheet tool creates a form showing every field in the tblVisit table in a datasheet format. See Figure 6-7.

Figure 6-7   Form created with the Datasheet tool

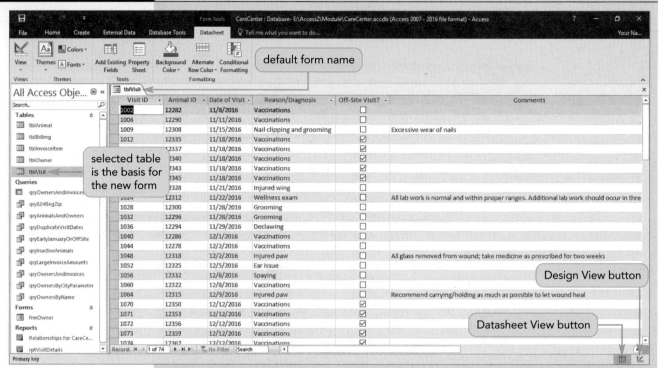

The form resembles the Datasheet view for the table except that it does not include the expand buttons at the beginning of each row. The form name, tblVisit, is the same name as the table used as the basis for the form. Recall that each table and query in a database must have a unique name. Although you could give a form or report the same name as a table or query, doing so would likely cause confusion. Fortunately, using object name prefixes prevents this confusing practice, and you will change the name when you save the form.

As you know, when working with forms, you view and update data in Form view, you view and make simple design changes in Layout view, and you make simple and complex design changes in Design view. However, not all of these views are available for every type of form. For the form created with the Datasheet tool, you'll check the available view options.

4. On the Form Tools Datasheet tab, in the Views group, click the **View button arrow**. See Figure 6-8.

Figure 6-8   View options for a form created with the Datasheet tool

Notice Form view and Layout view are not options on the menu, which means that they are unavailable for this form type. Datasheet view allows you to view and update data, and Design view allows you to modify the form's layout and design. The buttons for accessing these two available views are also on the status bar.

You'll save this form to show Kimberly as one of the options for the forms for animal visits.

▶ **5.** Save the form as **frmVisitDatasheet**, and close the form.

Kimberly might prefer a form created using the Multiple Items tool because it will provide a form with larger text boxes for displaying a record's field values.

Creating a Form Using the Multiple Items Tool

The **Multiple Items tool** creates a customizable form that displays multiple records from a source table or query in a datasheet format. You'll use the Multiple Items tool to create a form based on the tblVisit table.

To create the form using the Multiple Items tool:

▶ **1.** Make sure that the tblVisit table is selected in the Navigation Pane, and then click the **Create** tab.

▶ **2.** In the Forms group, click the **More Forms** button, and then click **Multiple Items**. The Multiple Items tool creates a form showing every field in the tblVisit table and opens the form in Layout view. See Figure 6-9.

| Figure 6-9 | Form created with the Multiple Items tool |

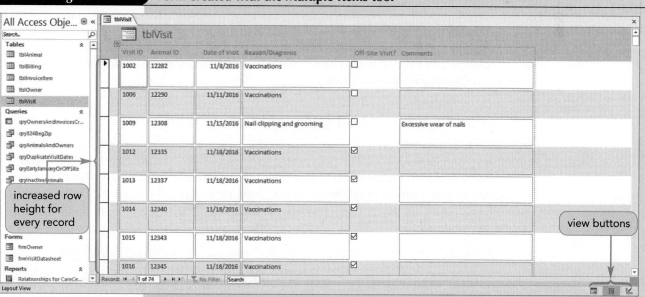

The new form displays all the records and fields from the tblVisit table in a format similar to a datasheet, but the row height for every record is increased compared to a standard datasheet. Unlike a form created with the Datasheet tool, which has only Datasheet view and Design view available, a Multiple Items form is a standard form that can be displayed in Form view, Layout view, and Design view, as indicated by the buttons on the right end of the status bar. You can also access these views for the forms created with the Multiple Items tool from the ribbon.

▶ **3.** On the Form Layout Tools Design tab, in the Views group, click the **View button arrow**. See Figure 6-10.

Figure 6-10 | **Views available for a form created with Multiple Items tool**

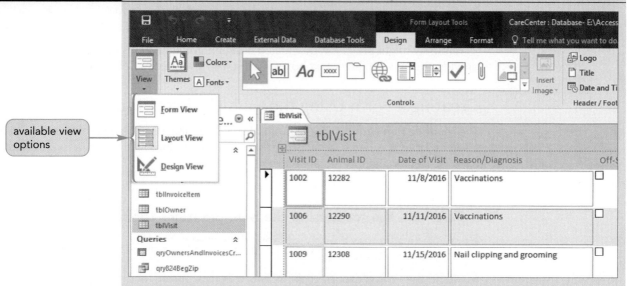

available view options

You'll want to show this form to Kimberly as one of the options, so you'll save it.

▶ **4.** Save the form as **frmVisitMultipleItems**, and then close the form.

The final form you'll create to show Kimberly will include two sections, one providing the standard form inputs of field value boxes and the other section showing the table in datasheet view. She might like this to satisfy both the staff that are more technical and the staff that would like a more user-friendly form. The tool you'll use to create this is the Split Form tool.

Creating a Form Using the Split Form Tool

The Split Form tool creates a customizable form that displays the records in a table in both Form view and Datasheet view at the same time. The two views are synchronized at all times. Selecting a record in one view selects the same record in the other view. You can add, change, or delete data from either view. Typically, you'd use Datasheet view to locate a record and then use Form view to update the record. You'll use the Split Form tool to create a form based on the tblVisit table.

To create the form using the Split Form tool:

▶ **1.** Make sure that the tblVisit table is selected in the Navigation Pane, and then click the **Create** tab.

▶ **2.** In the Forms group, click the **More Forms** button, click **Split Form**, and then close the Navigation Pane. The Split Form tool creates a split form that opens in Layout view and displays a form with the contents of the first record in the tblVisit table in the top section and a datasheet showing the first several records in the tblVisit table in the bottom section. In Layout view, the form on top will present a record's fields either in either a single column or in two columns, depending on the size of the Access window when the form was created. If you have a two-column layout, that won't affect your ability to complete the steps that follow. Figure 6-11 shows the single-column layout.

| Figure 6-11 | Form created with the Split Form tool |

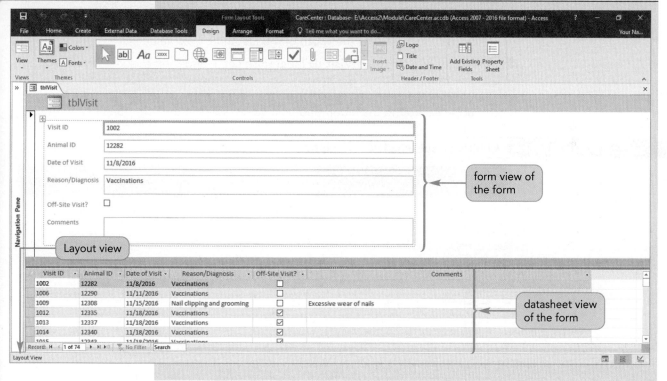

In Layout view, you can make layout and design changes to the form section and layout changes to the datasheet section of the split form.

Modifying a Split Form in Layout View

In previous modules, you've modified forms using options on the Form Layout Tools Format tab. Additional options for modifying forms are available on the Form Layout Tools Arrange tab. When working with a split form, you use the options on the Form Layout Tools Design tab to add controls and make other modifications to the form section but not to the datasheet section. Also in this case, the options on the Arrange tab apply only to the form section and do not apply to the datasheet section.

Kimberly notices that first three field value boxes in the form, Visit ID, Animal ID, and Date of Visit, are much wider than necessary. You will resize these field value boxes, and you will also move and resize the Reason/Diagnosis field label and field value box.

To resize field value boxes in the split form in Layout view:

▶ **1.** On the ribbon, click the **Form Layout Tools Arrange** tab.

The form's field label and field value boxes from the tblVisit table are grouped in a control layout. Recall that a control layout is a set of controls grouped together in a form or report so that you can manipulate the set as a single control. The control layout is a stacked layout, which arranges field value box controls vertically with a label control to the left of each field value box control in one or more vertical columns. You can also choose a tabular layout, which arranges field value box controls in a datasheet format with labels above each column.

As you know, if you reduce the width of any field value box in a control layout, all the value boxes in the control layout are also resized. Kimberly wants you to reduce the width of the first three field value boxes only.

▶ **2.** In the form, click the **Visit ID** label to select it, and then click the **layout selector** ⊞, which is located in the top-left corner of the control layout. An orange selection border, which identifies the controls that you've selected, appears around the labels and field value boxes in the form. See Figure 6-12.

Figure 6-12	Control layout selected in the form

Next, you'll resize the field value boxes in the control layout.

▶ **3.** Click the **VisitDate** field value box (containing the value 11/8/2016) to deselect the control layout and select just the **VisitDate** field value box.

▶ **4.** Position the pointer on the right border of the VisitDate field value box until the pointer changes to ↔, click and drag to the left until the right edge is just to the right of the VisitDate field value, and then release the mouse button. If you have a one-column layout, you've resized all five field value boxes. If you have a two-column layout, you've resized the three field value boxes on the left. Figure 6-13 shows the single-column layout.

Figure 6-13   **Resizing field value boxes in the control layout**

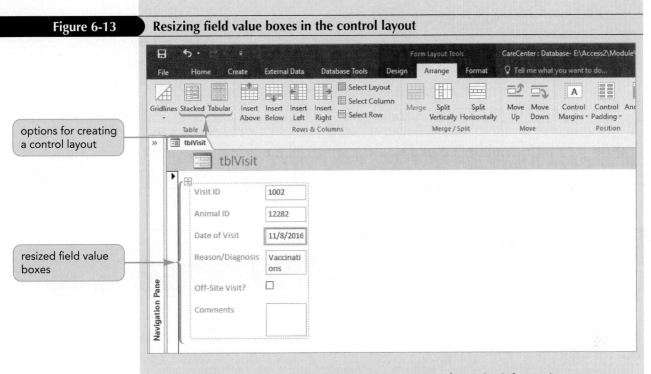

options for creating
a control layout

resized field value
boxes

Trouble? If you resize the field value boxes too far to the left, number signs appear inside the field value boxes, indicating the boxes are too small to display the full values. Repeat Step 4, this time dragging the right border of the field value box to the right until the date values are visible inside the boxes.

With the one-column layout shown in Figure 6-13, the form has too much white space. To better balance the elements in the form, Kimberly suggests you move and resize the Reason/Diagnosis, Off-Site Visit?, and Comments labels and field value boxes to a second column so that they fill this available space. To do this, you first need to remove these items from the stacked layout control.

To remove field value labels and boxes from the layout control, and move, and resize them on the form:

1. Click the **Reason/Diagnosis** label, press and hold the **Ctrl** key, click the **Reason** field value box, click the **Off-Site Visit?** label, click the **OffSite** check box, click the **Comments** label, and then click the **Comments** field value box to select all six controls, and then release the **Ctrl** key.

2. Right-click the **Reason** field value box, point to **Layout** on the shortcut menu, and then click **Remove Layout**. You've removed the six selected controls from the stacked layout.

3. If your form has the single-column layout shown in Figure 6-13, make sure that the six controls are still selected, and then use the ⁺ to drag them up and to the right until the tops of the Reason label and field value box align with the tops of the VisitID label and field value box.

   Trouble? If your form already has a two-column layout, skip Step 3.

4. Click the **Off-Site Visit?** label, press and hold the **Ctrl** key, click the **OffSite** check box, and then release the **Ctrl** key. The Off-Site Visit? label and the OffSite check box are selected.

5. Drag the **Off-Site Visit?** label and **OffSite** check box to the left and position them below the Date of Visit label and VisitDate field value box.

6. Select the **Comments** label and the **Comments** field value box, and then drag the selected controls up until they are top-aligned with the Date of Visit label and VisitDate field value box.

7. Click the **Comments** field value box to select it, and then drag the right border of the control to the right until the field value box is about four inches wide.

8. Click the **Reason** field value box so that it's the only selected control, and then drag the right border of the control to the right until it is the same width as the Comments field value box. Compare your screen with Figure 6-14, making any necessary adjustments.

Figure 6-14	Moved and resized controls in the form

controls in a stacked layout

controls removed from the layout and positioned under the stacked layout controls

resized field value boxes

Trouble? It won't cause any problems if the controls on your screen are in slightly different positions than the ones shown in the figure.

You do not usually need to change the default settings for the Control Margins property, which controls the spacing around the text inside a control, or the Control Padding property, which controls the spacing around the outside of a control. However, you'll explore the effects of changing these properties.

9. In the form, click the **Visit ID** label to select it, and then click the **layout selector** ⊞ to select the six controls that are still grouped in the stacked layout.

10. On the Arrange tab, in the Position group, click the **Control Margins** button, and then click **Medium**. The text inside the stacked layout controls moves down slightly.

11. Click the **Control Margins** button, click **Wide**, and observe the effect of this setting on the text inside the controls.

12. Click the **Control Margins** button again, and then click **Narrow**. Narrow is the default setting for the Control Margins property. Narrow is also the default setting for the Control Padding property.

Now that the form is complete and the controls are sized appropriately, you will save the form.

▶ **13.** Save the form as **frmVisitSplit**.

Next, you'll anchor the controls on the form.

Anchoring Controls in a Form

You can design forms that use the screen dimensions effectively when all the users of a database have the same-sized monitors and use the same screen resolution. How do you design forms when users have a variety of monitor sizes and screen resolutions? If you design a form to fit on large monitors using high screen resolutions, then only a portion of the controls in the form fit on smaller monitors with lower resolutions, forcing users to scroll the form. If you design a form to fit on smaller monitors with low screen resolutions, then the form displays on larger monitors in a small area in the upper-left corner of the screen, making the form look unattractively cramped. As a compromise, you can anchor the controls in the form. As shown in the Visual Overview for this session, as the screen size and resolution change, the Anchor property for a control automatically resizes the control and places it in the same relative position on the screen. Unfortunately, when you use the Anchor property, the control's font size is not scaled to match the screen size and resolution. Sometimes the results of anchoring controls work well, but sometimes the controls are spaced across a large screen, and the form may seem unorganized with controls moved to the corners of the screen.

Next, you'll anchor controls in the frmVisitSplit form. You can't anchor individual controls in a control layout; you can only anchor the entire control layout as a group. You've already removed the Reason/Diagnosis, Off-Site Visit?, and Comments controls from the stacked layout so that you can anchor them separately from the stacked layout. Therefore, you'll have four sets of controls to anchor—the stacked layout is one set, the Reason/Diagnosis controls are the second set, the Comments controls are the third set, and the Off-Site Visit? controls make up the fourth set.

To anchor controls in the form:

▶ **1.** Click the **Off-Site Visit?** label, press and hold the **Ctrl** key, and then click the **OffSite** check box.

▶ **2.** On the Arrange tab, in the Position group, click the **Anchoring** button to open the Anchoring gallery. See Figure 6-15.

| Figure 6-15 | The Anchoring gallery |

selected controls

Anchoring gallery

Four of the nine options in the Anchoring gallery fix the position of the selected controls in the top-left (the default setting), bottom-left, top right, or bottom-right positions in the form. If other controls block the corner positions for controls you're anchoring for the first time, the new controls are positioned in relation to the blocking controls. The other five anchoring options resize (or stretch) and position the selected controls.

You'll anchor the Off-Site Visit? controls in the bottom left, the Reason/Diagnosis controls in the top right, and the Comments controls in the bottom right.

3. Click **Bottom Left** in the Anchoring gallery. The gallery closes, and the Off-Site Visit? label and field value box move to the bottom-left corner of the form.

4. Click the **Reason** field value box, in the Position group, click the **Anchoring** button, and then click **Top Right**. The Reason label and field value box move to the upper-right corner of the form.

5. Anchor the Comments label and field value box to the Bottom Right.

Next, you'll increase the height of the form to simulate the effect of a larger screen for the form.

6. Open the Navigation Pane. The four sets of controls on the left shift to the right because the horizontal dimensions of the form decreased from the left, and these four sets of controls are anchored to the left in the form. The Reason and Comments controls remain in the same position in the form.

7. Position the pointer on the border between the form and the datasheet until the pointer changes to ✛, and then drag down until only the column headings and the first row in the datasheet are visible. The bottom sets of controls shift down, because they are anchored to the bottom of the form, and the two sets of controls at the top remain in the same positions in the form. See Figure 6-16.

Figure 6-16 Anchored controls in a resized form

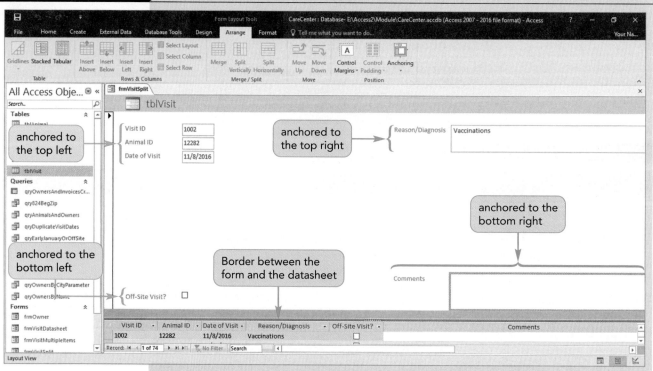

Finally, you'll use another anchoring option to resize the Comments text box as the form dimensions change.

▶ 8. Click the **Comments** field value box (if necessary), in the Position group, click the **Anchoring** button, and then click **Stretch Down and Right**. Because the Comments field value box is already anchored to the bottom right, it can't stretch any more to the right, but it does stretch up while leaving the label in place, to increase the height of the box.

▶ 9. Position the pointer on the border between the form and the datasheet until the pointer changes to ✛, and then drag up to display several rows in the datasheet. The bottom set of controls shifts up, and the bottom edge of the Comments field value box shifts up, and its height is reduced.

Kimberly and her staff have the same computer monitors and screen resolutions, so the controls do not need to be anchored. Therefore, you can close the form without saving the anchoring changes.

▶ 10. Close the form without saving the anchoring changes you've made to the form's design, and then, if you are not continuing on to the next session, close the CareCenter database.

You've used form tools to create forms, and you've modified forms in Layout view. In the next session, you will continue your work with forms.

Session 6.1 Quick Check

REVIEW

1. Which object(s) should you use to perform all database updates?
2. The _____ property specifies the data source for a control in a form or report or for a field in a table or query.
3. What is the Documenter?
4. What is the Multiple Items tool?
5. What is a split form?
6. As the screen's size and resolution change, the _____ property for a control automatically resizes the control.

Session 6.2 Visual Overview:

To move selected controls to the next nearest grid dot, press and hold the Ctrl key, and then press the appropriate arrow key.

The larger handle in a control's upper-left corner is its **move handle**, which you use to move the control.

You can click the **Detail section bar** to select the entire Detail section.

The **grid** is the area with dotted and solid lines that helps you position controls precisely in a form.

The AnimalID field value box is a combo box control.

The Comments field value box is a text box, and a **bound control**, which is a control that is connected, or bound, to a field in the database.

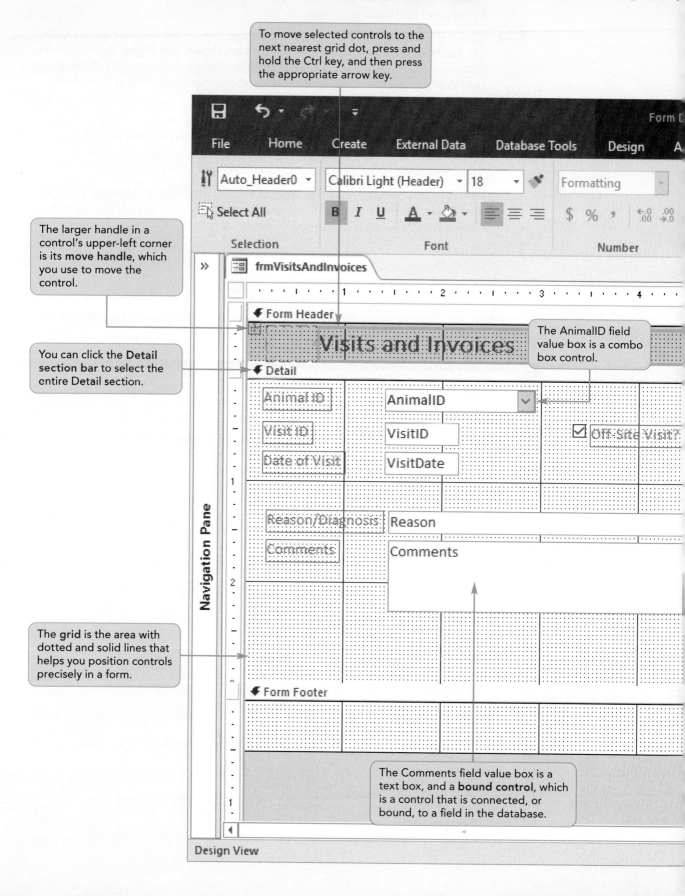

Design View

Custom Form in Design View

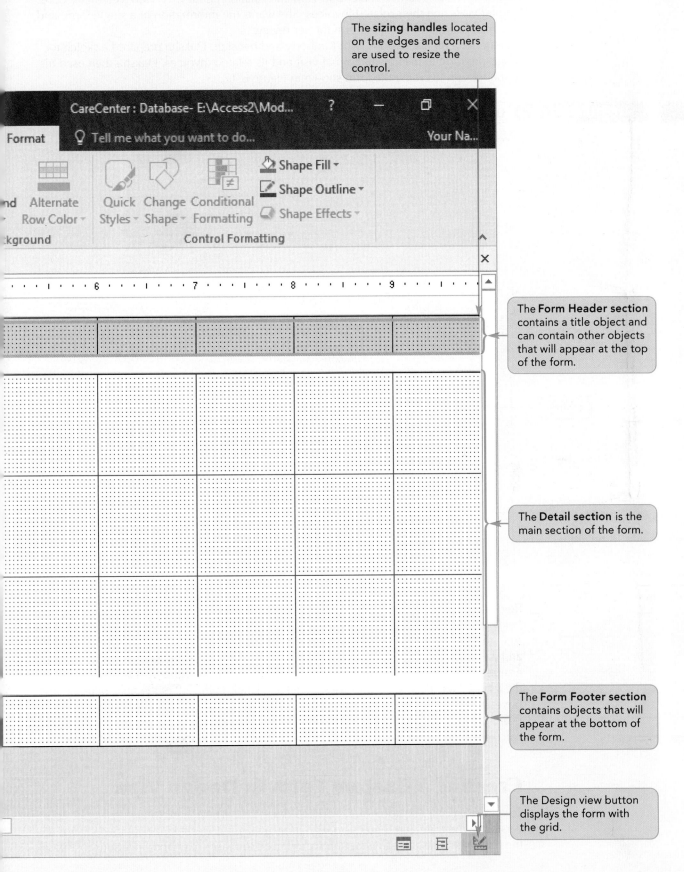

The **sizing handles** located on the edges and corners are used to resize the control.

CareCenter : Database- E:\Access2\Mod...   ?   —   □   ✕

Format   ♀ Tell me what you want to do...   Your Na...

Shape Fill ▾
Shape Outline ▾
Shape Effects ▾

nd   Alternate   Quick   Change   Conditional
Row Color ▾   Styles ▾   Shape ▾   Formatting

:kground   Control Formatting

The **Form Header section** contains a title object and can contain other objects that will appear at the top of the form.

The **Detail section** is the main section of the form.

The **Form Footer section** contains objects that will appear at the bottom of the form.

The Design view button displays the form with the grid.

Planning and Designing a Custom Form

Kimberly needs a form to enter and view information about Riverview Veterinary Care Center visits and their related invoices. She wants the information in a single form, and she asks Daksha to design a form for her review.

After several discussions with Kimberly and her staff, Daksha prepared a sketch for a custom form to display an animal visit and its related invoices. Daksha then used his paper design to create the form shown in Figure 6-17.

Figure 6-17   **Daksha's design for the custom form**

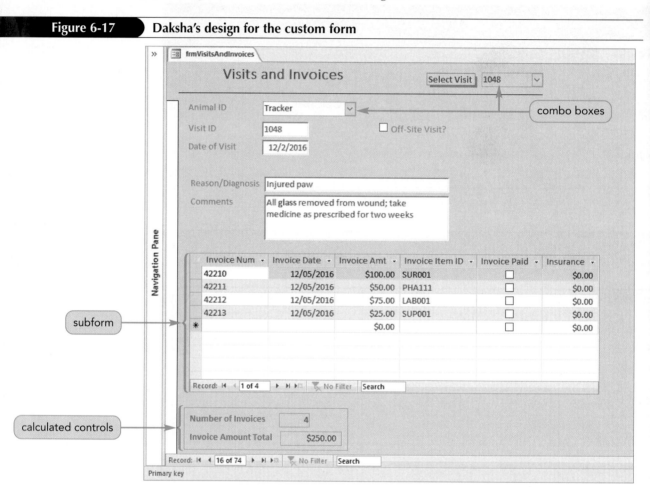

Notice that the top of the form displays a title and a combo box to select a visit record. Below these items are six field values with identifying labels from the tblVisit table; these fields are the AnimalID, VisitID, OffSite, VisitDate, Reason, and Comments fields. The AnimalID field is displayed in a combo box, the OffSite field is displayed as a check box, and the other field values are displayed in text boxes. The tblBilling table fields appear in a subform, which, as you know, is a separate form contained within another form. Unlike the tblVisit table data, which displays identifying labels to the left of the field values in text boxes, the tblBilling table data is displayed in datasheet format with identifying column headings above the field values. Finally, the Number of Invoices and Invoice Amount Total calculated controls in the main form display values based on the content of the subform.

Creating a Custom Form in Design View

To create Daksha's custom form, you could use the Form Wizard to create a basic version of the form and then customize it in Layout and Design views. However, for the form that Daksha designed, you would need to make many modifications to a basic form created by a wizard. You can instead build the form in a more straightforward manner by creating it directly in Design view. Creating forms in Design view allows you more control and precision and provides more options than creating forms in Layout view. You'll also find that you'll create forms more productively if you switch between Design view and Layout view because some design modifications are easier to make in one of the two views than in the other view.

Working in the Form Window in Design View

You can use the Form window in Design view to create and modify forms. To create the custom form based on Daksha's design, you'll create a blank form, add the fields from the tblVisit and tblBilling tables, and then add other controls and make other modifications to the form.

The form you'll create will be a bound form. A **bound form** is a form that has a table or query as its record source. You use bound forms for maintaining and displaying table data. **Unbound forms** are forms that do not have a record source and are usually forms that help users navigate among the objects in a database.

REFERENCE

Creating a Form in Design View

- On the ribbon, click the Create tab.
- In the Forms group, click the Blank Form button to open the Form window in Layout view.
- Click the Design View button on the status bar to switch to Design view.
- Make sure the Field List pane is open, and then add the required fields to the form.
- Add other required controls to the form.
- Modify the size, position, and other properties as necessary for the fields and other controls in the form.
- Save the form.

Now you'll create a blank bound form based on the tblVisit table.

To create a blank bound form in Design view:

1. If you took a break after the previous session, make sure that the CareCenter database is open and the Navigation Pane is open.

2. On the ribbon, click the **Create** tab, and then, in the Forms group, click the **Blank Form** button. The Form window opens in Layout view.

3. Click the **Design View** button on the status bar to switch to Design view, and then close the Navigation Pane. See Figure 6-18.

Figure 6-18 | Blank form in Design view

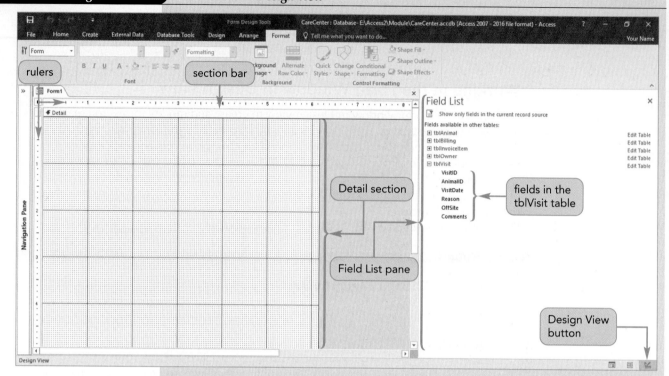

Trouble? If the Field List pane displays the "No fields available to be added to the current view" message, click the "Show all tables" link to display the tables in the CareCenter database, and then click the plus sign next to tblVisit in the Field List pane to display the fields in the tblVisit table.

Trouble? If the tblVisit table in the Field List pane is not expanded to show the fields in the table, click the plus sign next to tblVisit to display the fields.

Design view contains the tools necessary to create a custom form. You create the form by placing controls in the blank form. You can place three kinds of controls in a form:

- A **bound control** is connected, or bound, to a field in the database. The field could be selected from the fields in a table or query that are used as the record source. You use bound controls to display and maintain table field values.
- An **unbound control** is not connected to a field in the database. You use unbound controls to display text, such as a form title or instructions; to display lines, rectangles, and other objects; or to display graphics and pictures created using other software programs. An unbound control that displays text is called a **label**.
- A **calculated control** displays a value that is the result of an expression. The expression usually contains one or more fields, and the calculated control is recalculated each time any value in the expression changes.

To create a bound control, you add fields from the Field List pane to the Form window, and then position the bound controls where you want them to appear in the form. To place other controls in a form or a report, you use the tools in the Controls and Header/Footer groups on the Form Design Tools Design tab. The tools in the Controls group let you add controls such as lines, rectangles, images, buttons, check boxes, and list boxes to a form.

Design view for a form contains a Detail section, which is a rectangular area consisting of a grid with a section bar above the grid. You click the section bar to select the section in preparation for setting properties for the entire section. Some forms use Header, Detail, and Footer sections, but a simple form might have only a Detail section. The grid consists of dotted and solid lines that you use to position controls precisely in a form. In the Detail section, you place bound controls, unbound controls, and calculated controls in your form. You can change the size of the Detail section by dragging its borders. Rulers at the top and left edges of the Detail section define the horizontal and vertical dimensions of the form and serve as guides for placing controls in a form.

Your first task is to add bound controls to the Detail section for the six fields from the tblVisit table.

Adding Fields to a Form

When you add a bound control to a form, Access adds a field value box and, to its left, an attached label. The field value box displays a field value from the record source. The attached label displays either the Caption property value for the field, if the Caption property value has been set, or the field name. To create a bound control, you first display the Field List pane by clicking the Add Existing Fields button in the Tools group on the Form Design Tools Design tab. Then you double-click a field in the Field List pane to add the bound control to the Detail section. You can also drag a field from the Field List pane to the Detail section.

The Field List pane displays the five tables in the CareCenter database and the six fields in the tblVisit table. Next, you'll add bound controls to the Detail section for the tblVisit table's six fields.

To add bound controls from the tblVisit table to the Detail section:

▶ **1.** Double-click **VisitID** in the Field List pane. A bound text box control appears in the Detail section of the form, and the Field List pane lists the tblVisit table in the "Fields available for this view" section and lists the tblAnimal and tblBilling and tables in the "Fields available in related tables" section.

▶ **2.** Repeat Step 1 for the **VisitDate**, **AnimalID**, **Reason**, **Comments**, and **OffSite** fields, in this order, in the Field List pane. Six bound controls—one for each of the six fields in the Field List pane—are added in the Detail section of the form. See Figure 6-19.

Figure 6-19 Bound controls added to the form

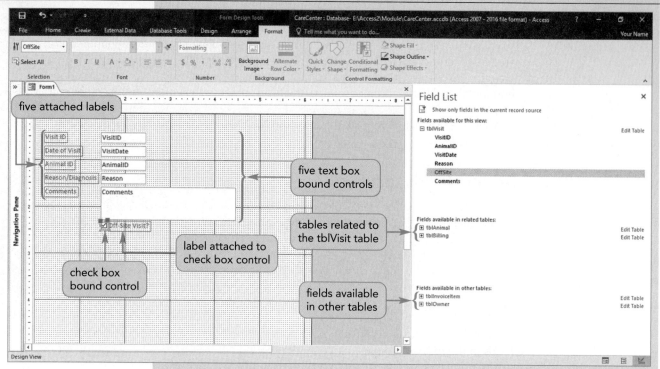

You should periodically save your work as you create a form, so you'll save the form now.

3. Click the **Save** button 🖫 on the Quick Access Toolbar. The Save As dialog box opens.

4. With the default name selected in the Form Name box, type **frmVisitsAndInvoices**, and then press the **Enter** key. The tab for the form now displays the form name, and the form design is saved in the CareCenter database.

You've added the fields you need to the grid, so you can close the Field List pane.

5. Click the **Form Design Tools Design** tab, and then, in the Tools group, click the **Add Existing Fields** button to close the Field List pane.

INSIGHT

Strategies for Building Forms

To help prevent common problems and more easily recover from errors while building forms, you should keep in mind the following suggestions:

- You can click the Undo button one or more times immediately after you make one or more errors or make form adjustments you don't wish to keep.

- You should back up your database frequently, especially before you create new objects or customize existing objects. If you run into difficulty, you can revert to your most recent backup copy of the database.

- You should save your form after you've completed a portion of your work successfully and before you need to perform steps you've never done before. If you're not satisfied with subsequent steps, close the form without saving the changes you made since your last save, and then open the form and perform the steps again.

- You can always close the form, make a copy of the form in the Navigation Pane, and practice with the copy.

- Adding controls, setting properties, and performing other tasks correctly in Access should work all the time with consistent results, but in rare instances, you might find a feature doesn't work properly. If a feature you've previously used successfully suddenly doesn't work, you should save your work, close the database, make a backup copy of the database, open the database, and then compact and repair the database. Performing a compact and repair resolves most of these types of problems.

To make your form's Detail section match Daksha's design (Figure 6-17), you need to move the OffSite bound control up and to the right. To do so, you must start by selecting the bound control.

Selecting, Moving, and Aligning Form Controls

Six field value boxes now appear in the form's Detail section, one below the other. Each field value box is a bound control connected to a field in the underlying table, with an attached label to its left. Each field value box and each label is a control in the form; in addition, each pairing of a field value box and its associated label is itself a control. When you select a control, an orange selection border appears around the control, and eight squares, called handles, appear on the selection border's four corners and at the midpoints of its four edges. The larger handle in a control's upper-left corner is its move handle, which you use to move the control. You use the other seven handles, called sizing handles, to resize the control. When you work in Design view, controls you place in the form do not become part of a control layout, so you can individually select, move, resize, and otherwise manipulate one control without also changing the other controls. However, at any time you can select a group of controls and place them in a control layout—either a stacked layout or a tabular layout.

Based on Daksha's design for the custom form, shown in Figure 6-17, you need to move the OffSite bound control up and to the right in the Detail section. The OffSite bound control consists of a check box and an attached label, displaying the text "Off-Site Visit?" to its right.

You can move a field value box and its attached label together. To move them, you place the pointer anywhere on the selection border of the field value box, but not on a move handle or a sizing handle. When the pointer changes to ⚐, you drag the field value box and its attached label to the new location. As you move a control, an outline of the control moves on the rulers to indicate the current position of the control as you drag it. To move a group of selected controls, point to any selected control until the pointer changes to ⊹⃗, and then drag the group of selected controls to the new position. As you know, you can move controls with more precision by pressing the appropriate arrow key on the keyboard to move the selected control in small increments. To move selected controls to the next nearest grid dot, press and hold the Ctrl key and then press the appropriate arrow key on the keyboard.

You can also move either a field value box or its label individually. If you want to move the field value box but not its label, for example, place the pointer on the field value box's move handle. When the pointer changes to ⊹⃗, drag the field value box to the new location. You use the label's move handle in a similar way to move only the label.

You'll now arrange the controls in the form to match Daksha's design.

To move the OffSite bound control:

▶ **1.** If necessary, click the **Off-Site Visit?** label box to select it. Move handles, which are the larger handles, appear on the upper-left corners of the selected label box and its associated bound control. Sizing handles also appear but only on the label box. See Figure 6-20.

Figure 6-20   **Selected OffSite bound control and label**

▶ **2.** Position the pointer on the Off-Site Visit? label box's orange selection border, but not on a move handle or a sizing handle, until the pointer changes to a ⊹⃗, drag the control up and to the right of the VisitID field value box, as shown in Figure 6-21, and then release the mouse button.

Be sure to position the pointer on one of the edges but not on a move handle or a sizing handle.

| Figure 6-21 | Repositioned Off-Site Visit? label and associated bound control |

selected label and associated bound control moved here

Trouble? If you need to make major adjustments to the placement of the OffSite bound control, click the Undo button 5 on the Quick Access Toolbar one or more times until the bound control is back to its starting position, and then repeat Step 2. If you need to make minor adjustments to the placement of the OffSite bound control, use the arrow keys on the keyboard.

Now you need to top-align the OffSite and VisitID bound controls (meaning their top borders are aligned with one another). When you select a column of controls, you can align the controls along their left or their right borders (left-align or right-align). When you select a row of controls, you can top-align or bottom-align the controls. You can also align To Grid, which aligns the selected controls with the dots in the grid. You access these five alignment options on the Form Design Tools Arrange tab or on the shortcut menu for the selected controls.

You'll use the shortcut menu to align the two bound controls. Then you'll save the modified form and review your work in Form view.

To align the OffSite and VisitID bound controls:

▶ **1.** Make sure the Off-Site Visit? label box is selected.

▶ **2.** Press and hold the **Shift** key, click the **OffSite** check box, click the **VisitID** field value box, click the **Visit ID** label, and then release the **Shift** key. The four controls are selected, and each selected control has an orange selection border.

▶ **3.** Right-click one of the selected controls, point to **Align** on the shortcut menu, and then click **Top**. The four selected controls are top-aligned. See Figure 6-22.

Figure 6-22 Aligned controls in the Detail section

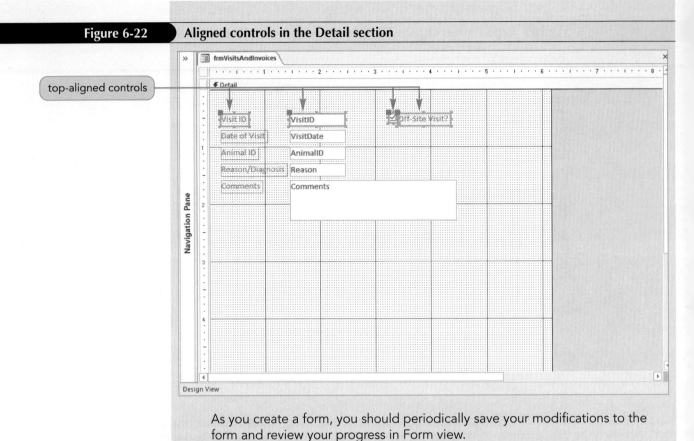

As you create a form, you should periodically save your modifications to the form and review your progress in Form view.

4. Save your form design changes, and then switch to Form view.

5. Click the **Next record** button ▶ twice to display the third record in the dataset (Visit ID #1009) in the form. See Figure 6-23.

Figure 6-23 Form displayed in Form view

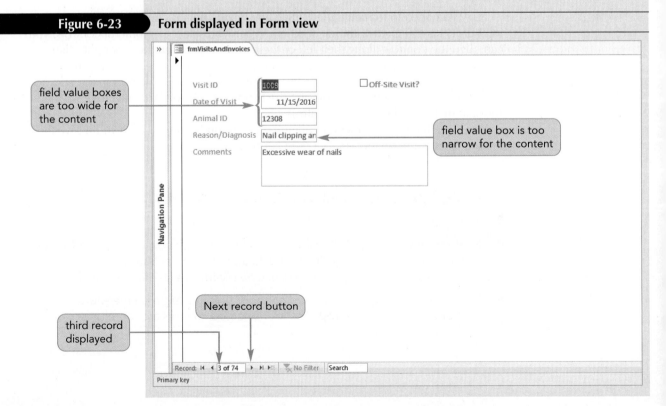

The value in the Reason field value box is not fully displayed, so you need to increase the width of the text box control. The widths of the VisitID and VisitDate text boxes are wider than necessary, so you'll reduce their widths. Also, the AnimalID bound control consists of a label and a text box, but the plan for the form shows a combo box for the AnimalID positioned below the OffSite bound control. You'll delete the AnimalID bound control, and then add it to the form, this time as a combo box.

Resizing and Deleting Controls

As you have seen, a selected control displays seven sizing handles: four at the midpoints on each edge of the control and one at each corner except the upper-left corner. Recall that the upper-left corner displays the move handle. Positioning the pointer over a sizing handle changes the pointer to a two-headed arrow; the directions in which the arrows point indicate in which direction you can resize the selected control. When you drag a sizing handle, you resize the control. As you resize the control, a thin line appears alongside the sizing handle to guide you in completing the task accurately, along with outlines that appear on the horizontal and vertical rulers.

You'll begin by deleting the AnimalD bound control. Then you'll resize the Reason text box, which is too narrow and too short to display Reason field values. Next you'll resize the VisitID and VisitDate text boxes to reduce their widths.

To delete a bound control and resize field value boxes:

1. Switch to Design view, click a blank area of the screen to deselect all controls, and then click the **AnimalID** text box control to select it.

2. Right-click the **AnimalID** text box to open the shortcut menu, and then click **Delete**. The label and the bound text box control for the AnimalID field are deleted.

3. Click the **Reason** text box to select it.

4. Place the pointer on the middle-right handle of the Reason text box until it changes to ↔, drag the right border to the right until it is approximately the same width as the Comments text box. See Figure 6-24.

Figure 6-24 **Resized Reason text box**

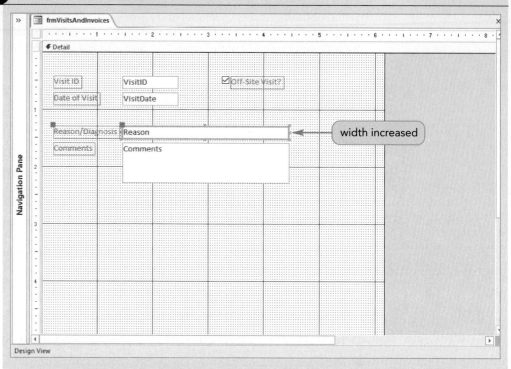

Resizing controls in Design view is a trial-and-error process, in which you resize a control in Design view, switch to Form view to observe the effect of the resizing, switch back to Design view to make further refinements to the control's size, and continue until the control is sized correctly. It's easier to resize controls in Layout view because you can see actual field values while you resize the controls. You'll resize the other two text box controls in Layout view. The sizes of the VisitID and VisitDate controls will look fine if you reduce them to have the same widths, so you'll select both boxes and resize them with one action.

5. Switch to Layout view, and then click the **VisitID** field value box (if necessary) to select it.

6. Press and hold the **Shift** key, click the **VisitDate** field value box (next to the label "Date of Visit") to select it, and then release the mouse button.

7. Position the pointer on the right border of the **VisitID** field value box until the pointer changes to ↔, drag the border to the left until the field box is slightly wider than the field value it contains, and the date in the VisitID field is also visible, and then release the mouse button. See Figure 6-25.

Figure 6-25	Resized field value boxes in Layout view

width of field value
boxes decreased

Trouble? If you resized the field value boxes too far to the left, number signs will be displayed inside the VisitDate field value box. Drag the right border to the right slightly until the date value is visible.

8. Navigate through the first several records to make sure the three field value boxes are sized properly and display the full field values. If any field value box is too small, select it, and then resize it as appropriate.

9. Save your form design changes, switch to Design view, and then deselect all controls by clicking a blank area of the screen.

Making Form Design Modifications

INSIGHT

When you design forms and other objects, you'll find it helpful to switch frequently between Design view and Layout view. Some form modifications are easier to make in Layout view, other form modifications are easier to make in Design view, and still other form modifications can be made only in Design view. You should check your progress frequently in either Layout view or Form view, and you should save your modifications after completing a set of changes successfully.

Recall that you removed the lookup feature from the AnimalID field because a combo box provides the same lookup capability in a form. Next, you'll add a combo box control for the AnimalID field to the custom form.

Adding a Combo Box Control to a Form

The tblAnimal and tblVisit tables are related in a one-to-many relationship. The AnimalID field in the tblVisit table is a foreign key to the tblVisit table, and you can use a combo box control in the custom form to view and maintain AnimalID field values more easily and accurately than using a text box. Recall that a combo box is a control that provides the features of a text box and a list box; you can choose a value from the list or type an entry.

PROSKILLS

Problem Solving: Using Combo Boxes for Foreign Keys

When you design forms, combo box controls are a natural choice for foreign keys because foreign key values must match one of the primary key values in the related primary table. If you do not use a combo box control for a foreign key, you force users to type values in the text box control. When they make typing mistakes, Access rejects the values and displays nonmatching error messages, which can be frustrating and make the form less efficient for users. Combo box controls allow users to select only from a list of valid foreign key values so that nonmatching situations are eliminated. At the same time, combo boxes allow users who are skilled at data entry to more rapidly type the values, instead of using the more time-consuming technique of choosing a value from the list the combo box control provides. Whenever you use an Access feature such as combo boxes for foreign keys, it takes extra time during development to add the feature, but you save users time and improve their accuracy for the many months or years they use the database.

You use the **Combo Box tool** in Design view to add a combo box control to a form. If you want help when adding the combo box, you can select one of the Control Wizards. A **Control Wizard** asks a series of questions and then, based on your answers, creates a control in a form or report. Access offers Control Wizards for the Combo Box, List Box, Option Group, Command Button, Subform/Subreport, and other control tools.

You will use the Combo Box Wizard to add a combo box control to the form for the AnimalID field.

To add a combo box control to the form:

▶ **1.** Click the **Form Design Tools Design** tab, and then in the Controls group, click the **More** button to open the Controls gallery. See Figure 6-26.

Figure 6-26   Controls gallery

The Controls gallery contains tools that allow you to add controls (such as text boxes, lines, charts, and labels) to a form. You drag a control from the Controls gallery and place it in position in the grid. If you want to use the Combo Box Wizard to add a control, you need to select that option below the gallery.

2. In the gallery, make sure the Use Control Wizards option is selected (its icon should appear with an orange background) at the bottom of the Controls gallery, and if it is not selected, click **Use Control Wizards** to select it, and then click the **More** button again to open the Controls gallery.

3. In the Controls gallery, click the **Combo Box** tool ▦. The Controls gallery closes.

Once you select the Combo Box tool (or most other tools in the Controls gallery) and move the mouse pointer into the Detail section of the form, the pointer changes to a shape that is unique for the control with a plus symbol in its upper-left corner. You position the plus symbol in the location where you want to place the upper-left corner of the control.

You'll place the combo box near the top of the form, below the OffSite bound control, and then position it more precisely after you've completed the steps in the wizard.

4. Position the plus symbol of the pointer shape below the OffSite bound control and at the 3.5 inch mark on the horizontal ruler, and then click the mouse button. A combo box control appears in the form, and the first Combo Box Wizard dialog box opens.

You can use an existing table or query as the source for a new combo box or type the values for the combo box. In this case, you'll use the qryAnimalsAndOwners query as the basis for the new combo box.

5. Click the **I want the combo box to get the values from another table or query** option button (if necessary), then click the **Next** button to open the next Combo Box Wizard dialog box, in which you will specify the source of information for the combo box.

6. In the View section of the dialog box, click the **Queries** option button, click **Query: qryAnimalsAndOwners** in the list, and then click the **Next** button. The next dialog box in the Combo Box Wizard lets you select the fields from the query to appear as columns in the combo box. You will select the AnimalName and AnimalID fields, along with the FirstName and LastName fields corresponding to the owner. Having the name of the owner with the Animal Name and Animal ID values might make it easier for users to locate the correct animal in the list.

▶ **7.** In the Available Fields box, double-click **AnimalName** to move this field to the Selected Fields box, double-click **AnimalID**, double-click **FirstName**, double-click **LastName**, and then click the **Next** button. The next dialog box lets you choose a sort order for the combo box entries. Daksha wants the entries to appear in ascending order on the AnimalName field.

▶ **8.** Click the **arrow** in the first box, click **AnimalName**, and then click the **Next** button to open the next Combo Box Wizard dialog box, in which you specify the appropriate width for the columns in the combo box control.

▶ **9.** Scroll the list in the dialog box to ensure all the values are visible, and if any are not, resize the columns as necessary.

▶ **10.** Click the **Next** button to open the next dialog box in the Combo Box Wizard. Here you select the foreign key, which is the AnimalID field.

▶ **11.** In the Available Fields list, click **AnimalID**, and then click the **Next** button.

In this dialog box, you specify the field in the tblVisit table where to store the selected AnimalID value from the combo box. You'll store the value in the AnimalID field in the tblVisit table.

▶ **12.** Click the **Store that value in this field** option button, click the arrow to display a list of fields, click **AnimalID**, and then click the **Next** button.

Trouble? If AnimalID doesn't appear in the list, click the Cancel button, press the Delete key to delete the combo box, click the Add Existing Fields button in the Tools group on the Form Design Tools Design tab, double-click AnimalID in the Field List pane, press the Delete key to delete AnimalID, close the Field List pane, and then repeat Steps 1–12.

In the final Combo Box Wizard dialog box, you specify the name for the combo box control. You'll use the field name of AnimalID.

▶ **13.** With the current text selected in the "What label would you like for your combo box?" box, type **AnimalID** and then click the **Finish** button. The completed AnimalID combo box control appears in the form.

You need to position and resize the combo box control, but first you will change the caption property for the AnimalID combo box label control so that it matches the format used by the other label controls in the form.

Changing a Label's Caption

- Right-click the label to select it and to display the shortcut menu, and then click Properties to display the Property Sheet.
- If necessary, click the All tab to display the All page in the Property Sheet.
- Edit the existing text in the Caption box; or click the Caption box, press the F2 key to select the current value, and then type a new caption.

You want the label control attached to the combo box control to display "Animal ID" instead of "AnimalID". You will change the Caption property for the label control next.

To set the Caption property for the AnimalID combo box's label control:

1. Right-click the **AnimalID** label, which is the control to the left of the AnimalID combo box control, and then click **Properties** on the shortcut menu. The Property Sheet for the AnimalID label control opens.

   Trouble? If the Selection type entry below the Property Sheet title bar is not "Label," then you selected the wrong control in Step 1. Click the AnimalID label in the form to change to the Property Sheet for this control.

2. If necessary, in the Property Sheet, click the **All** tab to display all properties for the selected AnimalID label control.

   The Selection type entry, which appears below the Property Sheet title bar, displays the control type (Label in this case) for the selected control. Below the Selection type entry in the Property Sheet is the Control box, which you can use to select another control in the form and list its properties in the Property Sheet. Alternately, you can simply click a control in the form and modify its properties in the Property Sheet. The first property in the Property Sheet, the **Name property**, specifies the name of a control, section, or object (AnimalID_Label in this case). The Name property value is the same as the value displayed in the Control box, unless the Caption property has been set. For bound controls, the Name property value matches the field name. For unbound controls, an underscore and a suffix of the control type (for example, Label) is added to the Name property setting. For unbound controls, you can set the Name property to another, more meaningful value at any time.

3. In the Caption box, click before "ID", press the **spacebar**, and then press the **Tab** key to move to the next property in the Property Sheet. The Caption property value changes to Animal ID, and the label for the AnimalID bound label control displays Animal ID. See Figure 6-27.

Figure 6-27	AnimalID combo box and updated label added to the form

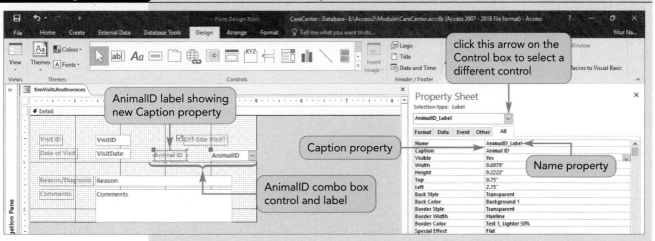

Trouble? Some property values in your Property Sheet, such as the Width and Top property values, might differ if your label's position slightly differs from the label position used as the basis for Figure 6-27. These differences cause no problems.

TIP

You won't see the effects of the new property setting until you select another property, select another control, or close the Property Sheet.

4. Close the Property Sheet, and then save your design changes to the form.

Now that you've added the combo box control to the form, you can position and resize it appropriately. You'll need to view the form in Form view to determine any fine-tuning necessary for the width of the combo box.

To modify the combo box in Design and Layout views:

1. Click the **AnimalID** combo box control, press and hold the **Shift** key, click the **Animal ID** label control, and then release the **Shift** key to select both controls.

First, you'll move the selected controls above the VisitID controls. Then you'll left-align the AnimalID, VisitID, VisitDate, Reason, and Comments labels; left-align the AnimalID combo box control with the VisitID, VisitDate, Reason, and Comments text box controls; and then right-align the OffSite label and check box control with the right edges of the Reason and Comments text box controls.

2. Drag the selected controls to a position above the VisitID controls. Do not try to align them.

3. Click in a blank area of the screen to deselect the selected controls.

4. Press and hold the **Shift** key while you click the **Animal ID** label, the **Visit ID** label, **Date of Visit** label, **Reason/Diagnosis** label, and the **Comments** label, and then release the **Shift** key.

5. Click the **Form Design Tools Arrange** tab, in the Sizing & Ordering group, click the **Align** button, and then click **Left**. The selected controls are left-aligned.

6. Repeat Steps 4 and 5 to left-align the AnimalID combo box, VisitID text box, VisitDate text box, Reason text box, and the Comments text box.

7. Click the **Off-Site Visit?** label, press and hold the **Shift** key, click the **OffSite** check box, the **Reason** text box, and **Comments** text box, and then release the **Shift** key.

8. In the Sizing & Ordering group, click the **Align** button, and then click **Right**. The selected controls are right-aligned.

9. Switch to Form view, and then click the **AnimalID** arrow to open the combo box control's list box. Note that the column is not wide enough to show the full data values. See Figure 6-28.

| Figure 6-28 | AnimalID combo box and updated label in Form view |

AnimalID combo box with arrow

AnimalID list box

You need to widen the AnimalID combo box so that that the widest value in the list is displayed in the combo box. You can widen the combo box in Layout view or in Design view. Because Form view and Layout view display actual data from the table rather than placeholder text in each bound control, these views let you immediately see the effects of your layout changes. You'll use Layout view instead of Design view to make this change because you can determine the proper width more accurately in Layout view.

▶ 10. Switch to Layout view, and then navigate to record 1 (if necessary). Whiskerkitty, which is the animal name for this record, is one of the widest values that is displayed in the combo box. You want to widen the combo box so that it is a little bit wider than the value in record 1.

▶ 11. Make sure that only the combo box is selected, and then drag the right border to widen the combo box until the entire name of the animal is visible. See Figure 6-29.

Figure 6-29   **Resized AnimalID combo box in Layout view**

resized AnimalID
combo box

Now you'll add the title to the top of the form by adding a Form Header section.

Using Form Headers and Form Footers

The **Form Header** and **Form Footer sections** let you add titles, instructions, command buttons, and other controls to the top and bottom of your form, respectively. Controls placed in the Form Header or Form Footer sections remain on the screen whenever the form is displayed in Form view or Layout view; they do not change when the contents of the Detail section change as you navigate from one record to another record.

To add either a form header or footer to your form, you must first add both the Form Header and Form Footer sections as a pair to the form. If your form needs one of these sections but not the other, you can remove a section by setting its height to zero, which is the same method you would use to remove any form section. You can also prevent a section from appearing in Form view or in Print Preview by setting its Visible property to "No." The **Visible property** determines if a control or section appears in Form view, in Print Preview, or when printed. You set the Visible property to Yes to display the control or section, and set the Visible property to No to hide it.

If you've set the Form Footer section's height to zero or set its Visible property to No and a future form design change makes adding controls to the Form Footer section necessary, you can restore the section by using the pointer to drag its bottom border back down or by setting its Visible property to Yes.

In Design view, you can add the Form Header and Form Footer sections as a pair to a form by right-clicking the Detail section selector, and then clicking Form Header/ Footer. You also can click the Logo button, the Title button, or the Date and Time button in the Header/Footer group on the Form Design Tools Design tab or the Form Layout Tools Design tab. Clicking any of these three buttons adds the Form Header and Form Footer sections to the form and places an appropriate control in the Form Header section only. A footer section is added to the form, but with a height set to zero to one-quarter inch.

Daksha's design includes a title at the top of the form. Because the title will not change as you navigate through the form records, you will add the title to the Form Header section in the form.

Adding a Title to a Form

You'll add the title to Daksha's form in Layout view. When you add a title to a form in Layout view, a Form Header section is added to the form and contains the form title. At the same time, a Page Footer section with a height setting of zero is added to the form.

To add a title to the form:

▶ 1. On the Form Layout Tools Design tab, in the Header/Footer group, click the **Title** button. A title consisting of the form name is added to the form and is selected.

    You need to change the title.

▶ 2. Type **Visits and Invoices** to replace the selected default title text. See Figure 6-30.

Figure 6-30   **Title added to the form in the Form Header section**

The title is a larger font size than the font used for the form's labels and field value boxes, but Daksha would like you to apply bold to increase its prominence.

▶ 3. Select the title control, click the **Form Layout Tools Format** tab, and then in the Font group, click the **Bold** button $\boxed{B}$. The title is displayed in 18-point, bold text.

    It is not obvious in Layout view that the title is displayed in the Form Header section, so you'll view the form design in Design view.

▶ 4. Switch to Design view, click a blank area of the screen to deselect all controls. The title is displayed in the Form Header section. See Figure 6-31.

Figure 6-31 **Form Header and Form Footer sections in Design view**

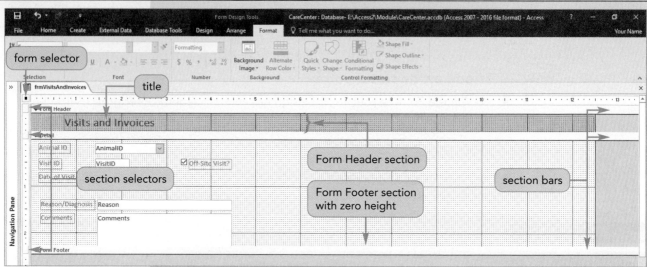

The form now contains a Form Header section that displays the title, a Detail section that displays the bound controls and labels, and a Form Footer section that is set to a height of zero. Each section consists of a **section selector** and a section bar, either of which you can click to select and set properties for the entire section, and a grid or background, which is where you place controls that you want to display in the form. The **form selector** is the selector at the intersection of the horizontal and vertical rulers; you click the form selector when you want to select the entire form and set its properties. The vertical ruler is segmented into sections for the Form Header section, the Detail section, and the Form Footer section.

A form's total height includes the heights of the Form Header, Detail, and Form Footer sections. If you set a form's total height to more than the screen size, users will need to use scroll bars to view the content of your form, which is less productive for users and isn't good form design.

5. Save the design changes to the form, and then, if you are not continuing on to the next session, close the CareCenter database.

So far, you've added controls to the form and modified the controls by selecting, moving, aligning, resizing, and deleting them. You've added and modified a combo box and added a title in the Form Header section. In the next session, you will continue your work with the custom form by adding a combo box control for use in finding records, adding a subform, adding calculated controls, changing form and section properties, and changing control properties.

Session 6.2 Quick Check

REVIEW

1. What is a bound form, and when do you use bound forms?
2. What is the difference between a bound control and an unbound control?
3. The _____ consists of the dotted and solid lines that appear in the Header, Detail, and Footer sections in Design view to help you position controls precisely in a form.
4. The larger handle in a selected object's upper-left corner is the _____ handle.
5. How do you move a selected field value box and its label at the same time?
6. How do you resize a control?
7. A(n) _____ control provides the features of a text box and a list box.
8. How do you change a label's caption?
9. What is the purpose of the Form Header section?

Session 6.3 Visual Overview:

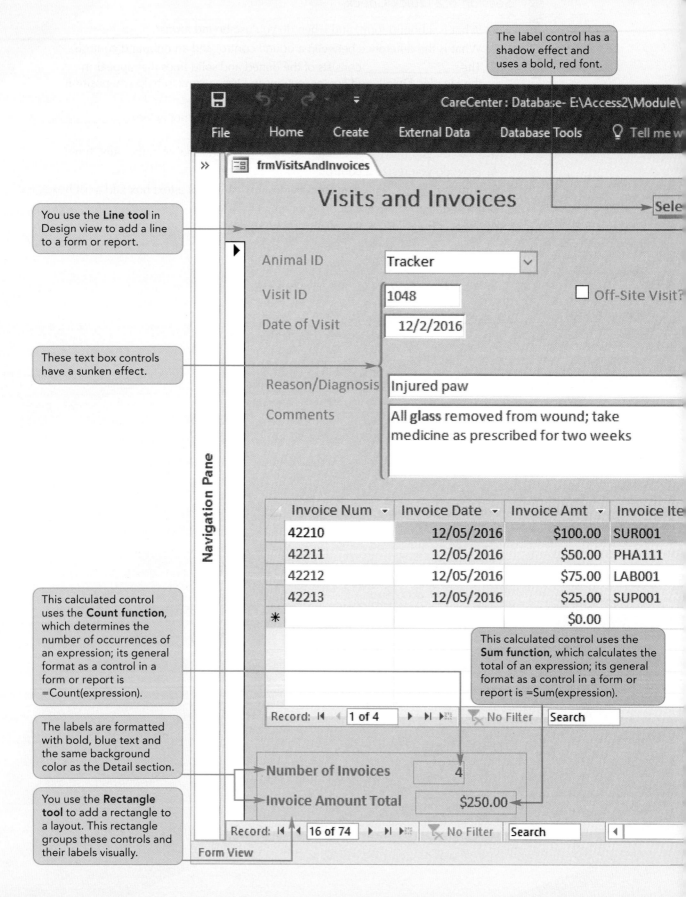

The label control has a shadow effect and uses a bold, red font.

You use the **Line tool** in Design view to add a line to a form or report.

These text box controls have a sunken effect.

This calculated control uses the **Count function**, which determines the number of occurrences of an expression; its general format as a control in a form or report is =Count(expression).

This calculated control uses the **Sum function**, which calculates the total of an expression; its general format as a control in a form or report is =Sum(expression).

The labels are formatted with bold, blue text and the same background color as the Detail section.

You use the **Rectangle tool** to add a rectangle to a layout. This rectangle groups these controls and their labels visually.

CareCenter : Database- E:\Access2\Module\

File   Home   Create   External Data   Database Tools   Tell me w

frmVisitsAndInvoices

Visits and Invoices

Sele

Animal ID   Tracker

Visit ID   1048   Off-Site Visit?

Date of Visit   12/2/2016

Reason/Diagnosis   Injured paw

Comments   All **glass** removed from wound; take medicine as prescribed for two weeks

Invoice Num	Invoice Date	Invoice Amt	Invoice Ite
42210	12/05/2016	$100.00	SUR001
42211	12/05/2016	$50.00	PHA111
42212	12/05/2016	$75.00	LAB001
42213	12/05/2016	$25.00	SUP001
*		$0.00	

Record: 1 of 4   No Filter   Search

Number of Invoices   4

Invoice Amount Total $250.00

Record: 16 of 74   No Filter   Search

Form View

Custom Form in Form View

The combo box control has the same background color as the Header section.

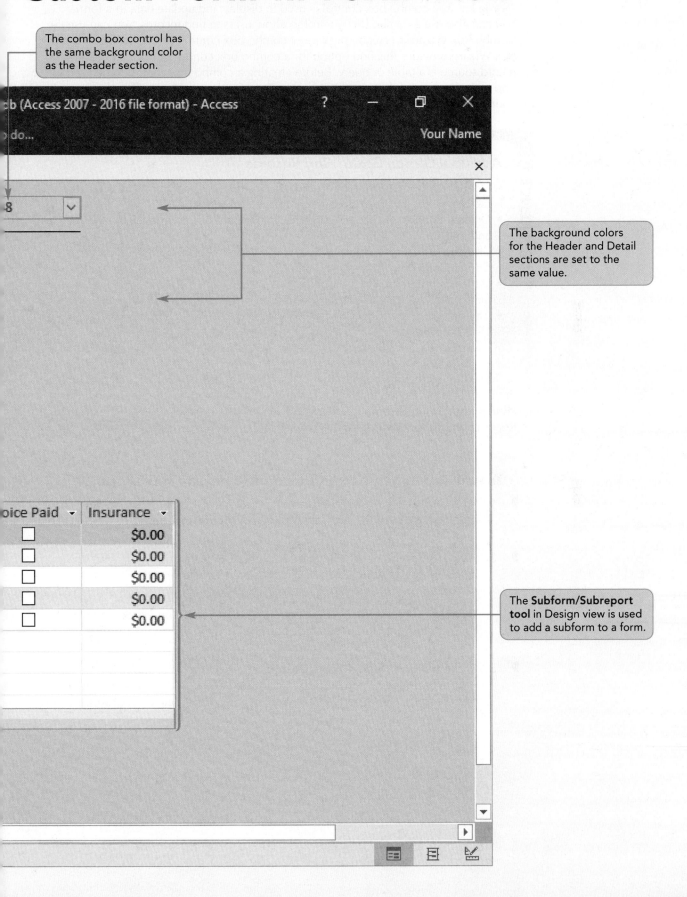

The background colors for the Header and Detail sections are set to the same value.

The **Subform/Subreport tool** in Design view is used to add a subform to a form.

Adding a Combo Box to Find Records

As you know, a combo box control is used to display and update data in a form. You can also use a combo box control to allow users to find records. You can use the Combo Box Wizard to create this type of combo box control. However, the Combo Box Wizard provides this find option for a combo box control only when the form's record source is a table or query. Before creating a combo box control to be used to find records, you should view the Property Sheet for the form to confirm the Record Source property is set to a table or query.

REFERENCE

Adding a Combo Box to Find Records

- Open the Property Sheet for the form in Design view, confirm the record source is a table or query, and then close the Property Sheet.
- On the Form Design Tools Design tab, in the Controls group, click the More button, and then click the Combo Box tool.
- Click the location in the form where you want to place the control, and open the Combo Box Wizard.
- In the first dialog box of the Combo Box Wizard, click the "Find a record on my form based on the value I selected in my combo box" option button.
- Complete the remaining Combo Box Wizard dialog boxes to finish creating the combo box control.

To continue creating the form that Daksha sketched, you will add a combo box to the Form Header section that will allow users to find a specific record in the tblVisit table to display in the form. But first you will view the Property Sheet to make sure the Record Source property is set to the tblVisit table.

To add a combo box to find records to display in the form:

1. If you took a break after the previous session, make sure that the CareCenter database is open, the frmVisitsAndInvoices form is open in Design view, and the Navigation Pane is closed.

2. To the left of the horizontal ruler, click the form selector ⬜ to select the form, if necessary. The form selector changes to ▣, indicating that the form is selected.

   Trouble? If the Form Header section head instead turns black, you might have clicked the header selector button. Click the form selector button, which is just above the header selector button.

3. Click the **Form Design Tools Design** tab, in the Tools group, click the **Property Sheet** button, and then click the **All** tab in the Property Sheet, if necessary. The Property Sheet displays the properties for the form. See Figure 6-32.

Figure 6-32   Property sheet for the form

Figure 6-32   Property sheet for the form

The Record Source property is set to an SQL SELECT statement, which is code that references a table. You need to change the Record Source property to a table or query, or the Combo Box Wizard will not present you with the option to find records in a form. You'll change the Record Source property to the tblVisit table because this table is the record source for all the bound controls you have added to the Detail section of the form.

▶ **4.** In the Record Source box, click the **Record Source** arrow, click **tblVisit** in the list, and then close the Property Sheet.

You'll now use the Combo Box Wizard to add a combo box to the form's Form Header section, which will enable a user to find a record in the tblVisit table to display in the form.

▶ **5.** On the Form Design Tools Design tab, in the Controls group, click the **More** button to open the Controls gallery, and then click the **Combo Box** tool 🔲.

▶ **6.** Position the plus symbol pointer at the top of the Form Header section at the 5-inch mark on the horizontal ruler (see Figure 6-32), and then click the mouse button. A combo box control appears in the Form Header section of the form, and the first Combo Box Wizard dialog box opens.

Trouble? If the Combo Box Wizard dialog box does not open, delete the new controls and try again, ensuring the plus symbol pointer is very near the top of the Form Header grid.

You will recall seeing this dialog box when you used the Combo Box Wizard in the previous session. The first dialog box in the Combo Box Wizard this time displays an additional option than what was available previously. This additional option, "Find a record on my form based on the value I selected in my combo box," is what you need to use for this combo box. (Recall in the last session you selected the first option, "I want the combo box to get the values from another table or query" when you used the Combo Box Wizard to create the AnimalID combo box, allowing the user to select a value from a list of foreign key values from an existing table or query.) You would choose the second option if you wanted users to select a value from a short fixed list of values that don't change. For example, if Riverview Veterinary Care Center wanted to include a field in the tblAnimal table to identify the state in which the animal resides, you could use a combo box with this second option to display a list of states.

7. Click the **Find a record on my form based on the value I selected in my combo box** option button, and then click the **Next** button. The next Combo Box Wizard dialog box lets you select the fields from the tblVisit table to appear as columns in the combo box. You need to include only one column of values, listing the VisitID values.

8. Double-click **VisitID** to move this field to the Selected Fields box, and then click the **Next** button to open the next dialog box in the Combo Box Wizard.

9. In the dialog box, resize the VisitID column to its best fit, and then click the **Next** button.

   In the last dialog box in the Combo Box Wizard, you specify the name for the combo box's label. You'll use "Select Visit" as the label.

10. Type **Select Visit** and then click the **Finish** button. The completed unbound combo box control and its corresponding Select Visit label appear in the form. See Figure 6-33.

Figure 6-33	Unbound combo box added to the form

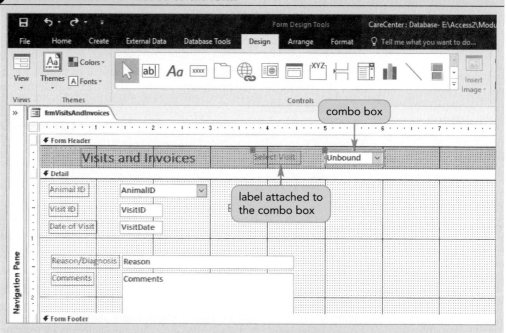

You'll move the attached label closer to the combo box control, and then you'll align the bottoms of the combo box control and its attached label with the bottom of the title in the Form Header section.

11. Click the **Select Visit** label, point to the label's move handle on the upper-left corner of the orange selection border, and then drag the label to the right until its right edge is two grid dots to the left of the combo box.

12. With the Select Visit label still selected, press and hold the **Shift** key, click the **combo box**, and then click the **Visit and Invoices** form title.

13. Right-click the selected controls, point to **Align** on the shortcut menu, and then click **Bottom**. The three selected controls are bottom-aligned. See Figure 6-34.

Figure 6-34   **Aligned combo box control and form title**

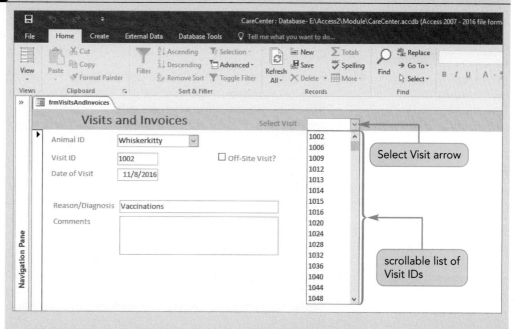

You'll save your form changes and view the new combo box control in Form view.

To save the form and view the Select Visit combo box control:

▶ **1.** Save the form design changes, and then switch to Form view.

▶ **2.** Click the **Select Visit** arrow to display the list of Visit ID numbers. See Figure 6-35.

Figure 6-35   **List of Visit IDs in the combo box**

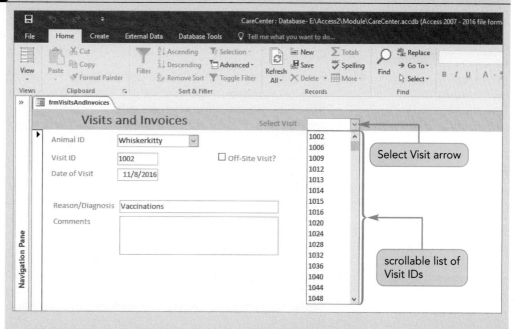

▶ **3.** Scroll down the list, and then click **1048**. The current record changes from record 1 to record 16, which is the record for visit ID 1048.

Trouble? If you see the data for record 1, the navigation combo box is not working correctly. Delete the combo box, check to ensure that you have set the Record Source for the form object correctly, and repeat the previous set of steps to re-create the combo box.

The form design currently is very plain, with no color, formatting effects, or visual contrast among the controls. Before making the form more attractive and useful, though, you'll add the remaining controls: a subform and two calculated controls.

Adding a Subform to a Form

Daksha's plan for the form includes a subform that displays the related invoices for the displayed visit. The form you've been creating is the main form for records from the primary tblVisit table (the "one" side of the one-to-many relationship), and the subform will display records from the related tblBilling table (the "many" side of the one-to-many relationship). You use the Subform/Subreport tool in Design view to add a subform to a form. You can create a subform from scratch, or you can get help adding the subform by using the SubForm Wizard.

You will use the SubForm Wizard to add the subform for displaying tblBilling table records to the bottom of the form. First, you'll increase the height of the Detail section to make room for the subform.

To add the subform to the form:

1. Switch to Design view.

TIP

Drag slightly beyond the desired ending position to expose the vertical ruler measurement, and then decrease the height back to the correct position.

2. Position the pointer on the bottom border of the Detail section until the pointer changes to ╪, and then drag the border down to the 5-inch mark on the vertical ruler.

3. On the Form Design Tools Design tab, in the Controls group, click the **More** button to open the Controls gallery, and then click the **Subform/Subreport** tool ▦.

4. Position the plus symbol of the pointer in the Detail section at the 2.5-inch mark on the vertical ruler and at the 1-inch mark on the horizontal ruler, and then click the mouse button. A subform control appears in the form's Detail section, and the first SubForm Wizard dialog box opens.

   You can use a table, a query, or an existing form as the record source for a subform. In this case, you'll use the related tblBilling table as the record source for the new subform.

5. Make sure the **Use existing Tables and Queries** option button is selected, and then click the **Next** button. The next SubForm Wizard dialog box opens, in which you select a table or query as the record source for the subform and select the fields to use from the selected table or query.

6. Click the **Tables/Queries arrow** to display the list of tables and queries in the CareCenter database, scroll to the top of the list, and then click **Table: tblBilling**. The Available Fields box lists the fields in the tblBilling table.

   Daksha's form design includes all fields from the tblBilling table in the subform, except for the VisitID field, which you already placed in the Detail section of the form from the tblVisit table.

7. Click the >> button to move all available fields to the Selected Fields box, click **VisitID** in the Selected Fields box, click the < button, and then click the **Next** button to open the next SubForm Wizard dialog box. See Figure 6-36.

| Figure 6-36 | Selecting the linking field |

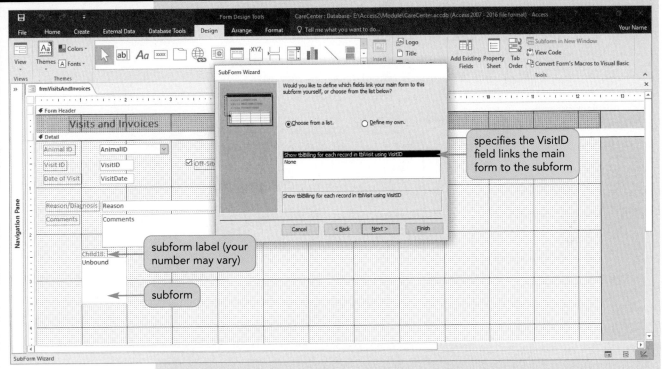

specifies the VisitID field links the main form to the subform

subform label (your number may vary)

subform

In this dialog box, you select the link between the primary tblVisit table and the related tblBilling table. The common field in the two tables, VisitID, links the tables. The form will use the VisitID field to display a record in the main form, which displays data from the primary tblVisit table, and to select and display the related records for that contract in the subform, which displays data from the related tblBilling table.

8. Make sure the **Choose from a list** option button is selected, make sure **"Show tblBilling for each record in tblVisit using VisitID"** is selected in the list, and then click the **Next** button. In the last SubForm Wizard dialog box, you specify a name for the subform.

9. Type **frmBillingSubform** and then click the **Finish** button. The completed subform appears in the Details section of the Form window; its label appears above the subform and displays the subform name.

10. Click a blank area of the screen, and then save the form.

11. Switch to Form view, click the **Select Visit** arrow, and then click **1048**. The subform displays the four invoices related to visit ID 1048. See Figure 6-37.

Figure 6-37

Figure 6-37   **The subform in Form view**

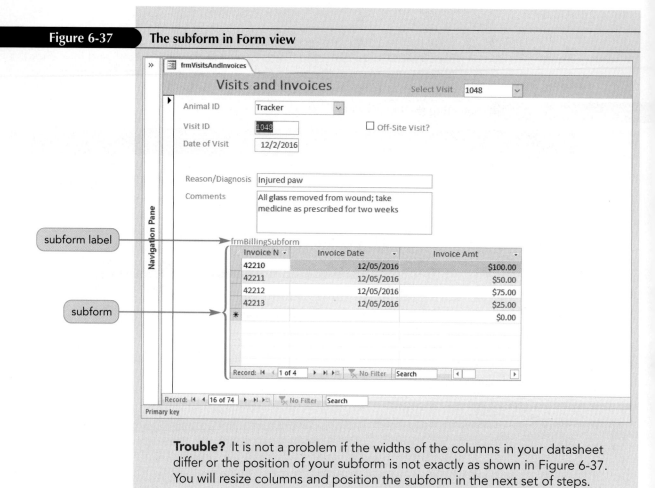

Trouble? It is not a problem if the widths of the columns in your datasheet differ or the position of your subform is not exactly as shown in Figure 6-37. You will resize columns and position the subform in the next set of steps.

After viewing the form, Daksha identifies some modifications he wants you to make. He wants you to resize the subform and its columns so that all columns in the subform are entirely visible and the columns are sized to best fit. Also, he asks you to delete the subform label, because the label is unnecessary for identifying the subform contents. You'll use Design view and Layout view to make these changes.

To modify the subform's design and adjust its position in the form:

1. Switch to Design view. Notice that in Design view, the data in the subform control does not appear in a datasheet format as it does in Form view. That difference causes no problem; you can ignore it.

   First, you'll delete the subform label control.

2. Deselect all controls (if necessary), right-click the **frmBillingSubform** subform label control to open the shortcut menu, and then click **Delete**.

   Next, you'll align the subform control with the Comments label control.

3. Click the border of the subform control to select it, press and hold the **Shift** key, click the **Comments** label control, and then release the **Shift** key. The subform control and the Comments label control are selected. Next you'll left-align the two controls.

4. Right-click the **Comments** label control, point to **Align** on the shortcut menu, and then click **Left**. The two controls are left-aligned. Next, you'll resize the subform control in Layout view so that you can observe the effects of your changes as you make them.

5. Switch to Layout view, click the border of the subform to select it, and then drag the right border of the subform to the right until the Insurance column arrow is fully visible.

   Before resizing the columns in the subform to best fit, you'll display record 16 in the main form. The subform for this record contains the related records in the tblBilling table with one of the longest field values.

6. Use the record navigation bar for the main form (at the bottom left of the form window) to display record 16, for visit number 1048, and then resize each column in the subform to its best fit.

   Next, you'll resize the subform again so that its width matches the width of the five resized columns.

7. Resize the subform so that its right border is aligned with the right border of the Insurance column. See Figure 6-38.

| Figure 6-38 | Moved and resized subform |

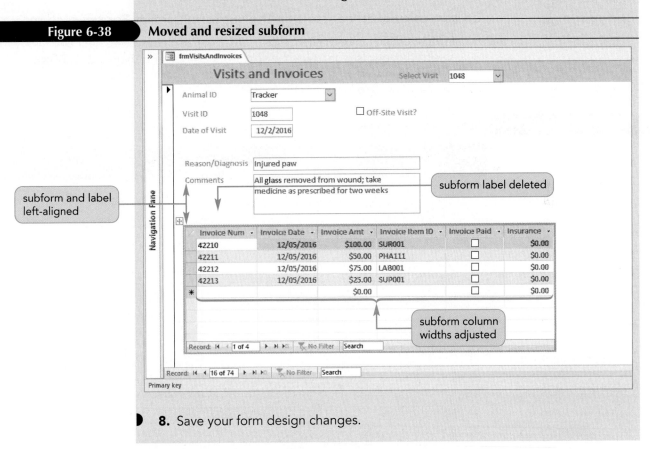

8. Save your form design changes.

You've finished your work with the subform. Now you need to add two calculated controls to the main form.

Displaying a Subform's Calculated Controls in the Main Form

Daksha's form design includes the display of calculated controls in the main form that tally the number of invoices and the total of the invoice amounts for the related records displayed in the subform. To display these calculated controls in a form or report, you use the Count and Sum functions. The Count function determines the number of occurrences of an expression; its general format as a control in a form or report is =Count(*expression*). The Sum function calculates the total of an expression, and its general format as a control in a form or report is =Sum(*expression*). The number of invoices and total of invoice amounts are displayed in the subform's Detail section, so you'll need to place the calculated controls in the subform's Form Footer section.

Adding Calculated Controls to a Subform's Form Footer Section

First, you'll open the subform in Design view in another window and add the calculated controls to the subform's Form Footer section.

To add calculated controls to the subform's Form Footer section:

1. Switch to Design view, click a blank area of the screen to deselect any selected controls, right-click the subform's border, and then click **Subform in New Window** on the shortcut menu. The subform opens in its own tab in Design view. See Figure 6-39.

Figure 6-39	Subform in Design view

The subform's Detail section contains the tblBilling table fields. As a subform in the main form, the fields appear in a datasheet even though the fields do not appear that way in Design view. The heights of the subform's Form

Header and Form Footer sections are zero, meaning that these sections have been removed from the subform. You'll increase the height of the Form Footer section so that you can add the two calculated controls to the section.

▶ **2.** Click the **Form Footer** section bar, position the pointer on the bottom border of the Form Footer section bar until the pointer changes to ╪, and then drag the bottom border of the section down to the 0.5-inch mark on the vertical ruler.

Now you'll add the first calculated control to the Form Footer section. To create the text box for the calculated control, you use the Text Box tool in the Controls group on the Form Design Tools Design tab. Because the Form Footer section is not displayed in a datasheet, you do not need to position the control precisely.

▶ **3.** On the Form Design Tools Design tab, in the Controls group, click the **Text Box** tool ⌨.

▶ **4.** Position the plus symbol of the pointer near the top of the Form Footer section and aligned with the 1-inch mark on the horizontal ruler, and then click the mouse button. A text box control and an attached label control appear in the Form Footer section. The text "Unbound" appears in the text box, indicating it is an unbound control.

Next, you'll set the Name and Control Source properties for the text box. Recall that the Name property specifies the name of an object or control. Later, when you add the calculated control in the main form, you'll reference the subform's calculated control value by using its Name property value. The **Control Source property** specifies the source of the data that appears in the control; the Control Source property setting can be either a field name or an expression.

▶ **5.** Open the Property Sheet for the text box in the Form Footer section, click the **All** tab (if necessary), select the value in the Name box, type **txtInvoiceAmtSum** in the Name box, and then press the **Tab** key to move to the Control Source box.

▶ **6.** In the Control Source box, type **=Sum(Inv**, press the **Tab** key to accept the rest of the field name of InvoiceAmt suggested by Formula AutoComplete, type **)** (a right parenthesis), and then press the **Tab** key. InvoiceAmt is enclosed in brackets in the expression because it's a field name. See Figure 6-40.

Figure 6-40	Setting properties for the subform calculated control

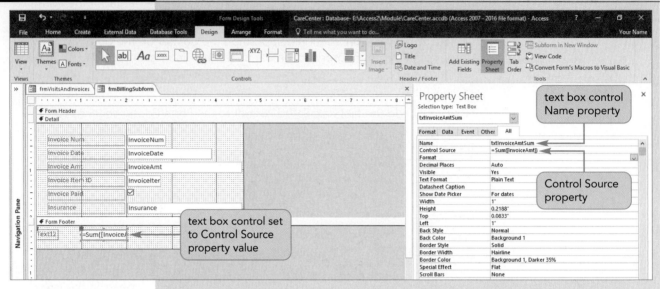

You've finished creating the first calculated control; now you'll create the other calculated control.

TIP

In the Name property, txtInvoiceNumCount, txt identifies the control type (a text box), InvoiceNum is the related field name, and Count identifies the control as a count control.

7. Repeat Steps 3 through 6, positioning the calculated field text box near the top of the Form Footer section aligned to the 3.5-inch mark on the horizontal ruler, setting the Name property value to **txtInvoiceNumCount**, and setting the Control Source property value to **=Count([InvoiceNum])**.

When you use the Count function, you are counting the number of displayed records—in this case, the number of records displayed in the subform. Instead of using InvoiceNum as the expression for the Count function, you could use any of the other fields displayed in the subform.

You've finished creating the subform's calculated controls.

8. Close the Property Sheet, save your subform changes, and then close the subform. The active object is now the main form in Design view.

   Trouble? The subform in the frmContractsAndInvoices form might appear to be blank after you close the frmInvoiceSubform form. This is a temporary effect; the subform's controls do still exist. Switch to Form view and then back to Design view to display the subform's controls.

9. Switch to Form view. The calculated controls you added in the subform's Form Footer section are *not* displayed in the subform.

10. Switch to Design view.

Next, you'll add two calculated controls in the main form to display the two calculated controls from the subform.

Adding Calculated Controls to a Main Form

The subform's calculated controls now contain a count of the number of invoices and a total of the invoice amounts. However, notice that Daksha's design has the two calculated controls displayed in the main form, *not* in the subform. You need to add two calculated controls in the main form that reference the values in the subform's calculated controls. Because it's easy to make a typing mistake with these references, you'll use Expression Builder to set the Control Source property for the two main form calculated controls.

To add a calculated control to the main form's Detail section:

1. Adjust the length of the Detail section if necessary so that there is approximately 0.5 inch below the frmBillingSubform control. The Detail section should be approximately 5.5 inches.

2. On the Form Design Tools Design tab, in the Controls group, click the **Text Box** tool ab|.

3. Position the pointer's plus symbol below the frmBillingSubform at the 5-inch mark on the vertical ruler and aligned with the 1-inch mark on the horizontal ruler, and then click to insert the text box control and label in the form. Don't be concerned about positioning the control precisely because you'll resize and move the label and text box later.

4. Open the Property Sheet, click the label control for the text box, set its Caption property to **Number of Invoices**, right-click the border of the label control, point to **Size** on the shortcut menu, and then click **To Fit**. Don't worry if the label control now overlaps the text box control.

   You'll use Expression Builder to set Control Source property for the text box control.

5. Click the unbound text box control to select it, click the **Control Source** box in the Property Sheet, and then click the property's **Build** button [...] to open Expression Builder.

6. In the Expression Elements box, click the **expand indicator** [+] next to frmVisitsAndInvoices, and then click **frmBillingSubform** in the Expression Elements box.

7. Scroll down the Expression Categories box, and then double-click **txtInvoiceNumCount** in the Expression Categories box. See Figure 6-41.

Figure 6-41   Text box control's expression in the Expression Builder dialog box

Control Source property setting

selected frmBillingSubform form

selected calculated control

Instead of adding txtInvoiceNumCount to the expression box at the top, the Expression Builder changed it to [frmBillingSubform]. Form![txtInvoiceNumCount]. This expression displays the value of the txtInvoiceNumCount control that is located in the frmBillingSubform form, which is a form object.

You need to add an equal sign to the beginning of the expression.

8. Press the **Home** key, type **=** (an equal sign), and then click the **OK** button. The Expression Builder dialog box closes, and the Control Source property is set.

Next, you'll add a second text box control to the main form, set the Caption property for the label control, and use Expression Builder to set the text box's Control Source property.

Be sure you resize the label to its best fit.

9. Repeat Steps 2 through 4 to add a text box to the main form, positioning the text box at the 3.5-inch mark on the horizontal ruler and approximately the 5-inch mark on the vertical ruler, and setting the label's Caption property to **Invoice Amount Total**.

10. Click the unbound text box control to select it, click the **Control Source** box in the Property Sheet, and then click the property's **Build** button ⋯ to open Expression Builder.

11. In the Expression Builder dialog box, type **=** (an equal sign), in the Expression Elements box, click the **expand indicator** ⊞ next to frmVisitsAndInvoices, click **frmBillingSubform** in the Expression Elements box, scroll down the Expression Categories box, and then double-click **txtInvoiceAmtSum** in the Expression Categories box.

12. Click the **OK** button to accept the expression and close the Expression Builder dialog box, close the Property Sheet, and save the form.

13. Click the **Collapse the Ribbon** button ︿, switch to Form view, and then display the record for VisitID 1048. See Figure 6-42.

Figure 6-42 Form with calculated controls

Now that the calculated controls are in the form, you will modify their appearance. You also will set additional properties for the calculated controls.

Resizing, Moving, and Formatting Calculated Controls

In addition to resizing and repositioning the two calculated controls and their attached labels, you need to change the format of the rightmost calculated control to Currency and to set the following properties for both calculated controls.

- Set the Tab Stop property to a value of No. The **Tab Stop property** specifies whether users can use the Tab key to navigate to a control on a form. If the Tab Stop property is set to No, users can't tab to the control.
- Set the ControlTip Text property to a value of "Calculated total number of invoices for this animal visit" for the calculated control on the left and "Calculated invoice total for this animal visit" for the calculated control on the right. The **ControlTip Text property** specifies the text that appears in a ScreenTip when users position the mouse pointer over a control in a form.

Now you'll resize, move, and format the calculated controls and their attached labels.

To size, move, and format the calculated controls and their attached labels:

▶ **1.** Switch to Layout view, right-click the **Invoice Amount Total** calculated control, and then click **Properties** on the shortcut menu to open the Property Sheet.

2. Click the **All** tab in the Property Sheet (if necessary), set the Format property to **Currency**, and then close the Property Sheet. The value displayed in the calculated control changes from 250 to $250.00.

Now you'll resize and move the controls into their final positions in the form.

3. Individually, reduce the widths of the two calculated controls by dragging the left border to the right to decrease the text box width so that they approximately match those shown in Figure 6-43.

Figure 6-43	Resized calculated controls and labels

4. Switch to Design view, select the **Number of Invoices** label and its related calculated control, and then use the → key to move the label and its related text box to the right, aligning the left edge of the label with the left edge of the Comments label as closely as possible.

5. Press the ↑ key four times to move the selected calculated control and its label until it is two grid dots from the bottom of the subform control.

6. Lengthen the Detail section to approximately the 6-inch marker on the vertical ruler.

7. Click the **Invoice Amount Total** label control, press the **Shift** key, click the corresponding calculated control text box, release the **Shift** key, and then drag the selected calculated control and its label to position them below and left-aligned with the Number of Invoices label control and its calculated control.

TIP

In Design view you must use the move handle to move only a text box or its label, while in Layout view you can use either the move handle or the arrow keys.

> **8.** Switch to Layout view.

> **9.** Click the **Invoice Amount Total** label control, and use the arrow keys to left-align the label control with the Number of Invoices label, select the **Invoice Amount Total** text box, and then use the arrows to left-align the calculated control text box with the Number of Invoices calculated control text box.

> **10.** Deselect all controls, switch to Form view, and then select record 1048. See Figure 6-44.

Figure 6-44	Calculated controls and labels aligned

modified calculated controls and labels

The calculated controls and their labels are properly placed in the form. Next you will set the Tab Stop Property and the ControlTip Text property for both controls, which you can do on the Other tab in the control's Property Sheet.

To set the Tab Stop Property and the ControlTipText property for the calculated controls:

> **1.** Switch to Layout view, right-click the **Invoice Amount Total** calculated control, click **Properties** on the shortcut menu, and then click the **Other** tab in the Property Sheet.

> **2.** Set the Tab Stop property to **No**, and then set the ControlTip Text property to **Calculated invoice total for this animal visit**.

> **3.** Click the **Number of Invoices** calculated control to display this control's properties in the Property Sheet, set the Tab Stop property to **No**, and then set the ControlTip Text property to **Calculated total number of invoices for this animal visit**.

4. Close the Property Sheet, save your form design changes, switch to Form view, and then display visit 1048.

5. Position the pointer on the **Number of Invoices** box to display its ScreenTip, and then position the pointer on the **Invoice Amount Total** box to display its ScreenTip. You may have to pause while you position the pointer over the box, until the ScreenTip appears. See Figure 6-45.

Figure 6-45   **ScreenTip for the calculated control**

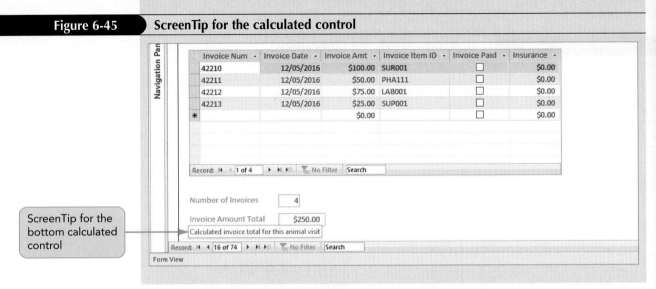

ScreenTip for the bottom calculated control

Daksha asks you to verify that users can't update the calculated controls in the main form and that when users tab through the controls in the form, the controls are selected in the correct order.

Changing the Tab Order in a Form

Pressing the Tab key in Form view moves the focus from one control to another. A control is said to have **focus** when it is active and awaiting user action. The order in which the focus moves from control to control when a user presses the Tab key is called the **tab order**. Setting a logical tab order enables the user to keep his or her hands on the keyboard without reaching for the mouse, thereby speeding up the process of data entry in a form. Daksha wants to verify that the tab order in the main form is top-to-bottom, left-to-right. First, you'll verify that users can't update the calculated controls.

To test the calculated controls and modify the tab order:

1. Select the value in the Number of Invoices box, and then type **8**. The Number of Invoices value remains unchanged, and the message "Control can't be edited; it's bound to the expression '[frmBillingSubform].[Form]![txtInvoiceNumCount]'" is displayed on the status bar. The status bar message warns you that you can't update, or edit, the calculated control because it's bound to an expression. The calculated control in the main form changes in value only when the value of the expression changes in the subform.

2. Click the Invoice Amount Total box, and then type **8**. The value remains unchanged, and a message again displays on the status bar because you cannot edit a calculated control.

Next, you'll determine the tab order of the fields in the main form. Daksha wants the tab order to be down and then across.

3. Select the value in the Visit ID box, press the **Tab** key to advance to the Date of Visit box, and then press the **Tab** key five more times to advance to the Reason/Diagnosis box, Comments text box, OffSite check box, and AnimalID combo box, in order, and then to the subform.

Access sets the tab order in the same order in which you add controls to a form, so you should always check the form's tab order when you create a custom form in Layout or Design view. In this form you can see that the tab order is set such that the user will tab through the field value boxes in the main form before tabbing through the fields in the subform. In the main form, tabbing bypasses the two calculated controls because you set their Tab Stop properties to No, and you bypass the Select Visit combo box because it's an unbound control. Also, you tab through only the field value boxes in a form, not the labels.

The tab order Daksha wants for the field value boxes in the main form (top-to-bottom, left-to-right) should be the following: AnimalID, VisitID, OffSite, VisitDate, Reason, Comments, and then the subform. The default tab order doesn't match the order Daksha wants, so you'll change the tab order. You can change the tab order only in Design view.

4. Double-click the **Home** tab to restore the ribbon, switch to Design view, and then on the Form Design Tools Design tab, in the Tools group, click the **Tab Order** button. The Tab Order dialog box opens. See Figure 6-46.

Figure 6-46   Tab Order dialog box

Because you did not set the Name property for the combo box control and the calculated controls, Access assigned them names that consist of the type of control and number; for example Combo12 for the AnimalID combo box, Text24 for the Number of Invoices calculated control, and Text26 for the Invoice Amount Total calculated control as shown in Figure 6-46. (The numbers assigned to your controls might differ.) The Auto Order button lets you create a left-to-right, top-to-bottom tab order automatically, which is not the order Daksha wants. You need to move the Combo12 entry above the VisitID entry.

5. Click the **row selector** to the left of the Combo12 item (your number might differ), and then drag the row selector up to position it above the VisitID entry.

6. Click the row selector to the left of the OffSite item, and then drag the row selector up to position it above VisitDate. The entries are now correct and in the correct order. See Figure 6-47.

Figure 6-47 **Tab Order dialog box with corrected order**

7. Click the **OK** button to close the Tab Order dialog box, save your form design changes, and then switch to Form view.

8. Tab through the controls in the main form to make sure the tab order is correct, moving from the Animal ID box, to the Visit ID box, then to the Off-Site Visit checkbox, then to Date of Visit box, the Reason/Diagnosis box, to the Comments box, and then finally to the subform.

Trouble? If the tab order is incorrect, switch to Design view, click the Tab Order button in the Tools group, change your tab order in the Tab Order dialog box to match the order shown in Figure 6-47, and then repeat Steps 7 and 8.

Written Communication: Enhancing Information Using Calculated Controls

For a small number of records in a subform, it's easy for users to quickly count the number of records and to calculate numeric total amounts when the form doesn't display calculated controls. For instance, when students have completed few courses or when people have made few tax payments, it's easy for users to count the courses and calculate the student's GPA or to count and total the tax payments. But for subforms with dozens or hundreds of records—for instance, students with many courses, or people with many tax payments—displaying summary calculated controls is mandatory. By adding a few simple calculated controls to forms and reports, you can increase the usefulness of the information presented and improve the ability of users to process the information, spot trends, and be more productive in their jobs.

You've finished adding controls to the form, but the form is plain looking and lacks visual clues organizing the controls in the form. You'll complete the form by making it more attractive and easier for Kimberly and her staff to use.

Improving a Form's Appearance

The frmVisitsAndInvoices form has four distinct areas: the Form Header section containing the title and the Select Visit combo box, the six bound controls in the Detail section, the subform in the Detail section, and the two calculated controls in the Detail section. To visually separate these four areas, you'll increase the height of the Form Header section, add a horizontal line at the bottom of the Form Header section, and draw a rectangle around the calculated controls.

Adding a Line to a Form

You can use lines in a form to improve the form's readability, to group related information, or to underline important values. You use the Line tool in Design view to add a line to a form or report.

Adding a Line to a Form or Report

- Display the form or report in Design view.
- On the Form Design Tools Design tab, in the Controls group, click the More button, and then click the Line tool.
- Position the pointer where you want the line to begin.
- Drag the pointer to the position for the end of the line, and then release the mouse button. If you want to ensure that you draw a straight horizontal or vertical line, press and hold the Shift key as you drag the pointer to draw the line.

You will add a horizontal line to the Form Header section to separate the controls in this section from the controls in the Detail section.

To add a line to the form:

▶ **1.** Switch to Design view, and then drag the bottom border of the Form Header section down to the 1-inch mark on the vertical ruler to make room to draw a horizontal line at the bottom of the Form Header section.

▶ **2.** On the Form Design Tools Design tab, in the Controls group, click the **Line** tool ◻.

▶ **3.** Position the pointer's plus symbol at the left edge of the Form Header section just below the title.

▶ **4.** Press and hold the **Shift** key, drag right to the 6-inch mark on the vertical ruler, release the mouse button, and then release the **Shift** key. See Figure 6-48.

Figure 6-48   **Line added to the form**

Trouble? If the line is not straight or not positioned correctly, click the Undo button on the Quick Access Toolbar, and then repeat Steps 2 through 4. If the line is not the correct length, be sure the line is selected, press and hold the Shift key, and press the left or right arrow key until the line's length is the same as that of the line shown in Figure 6-48.

▶ **5.** Drag the bottom border of the Form Header section up to just below the line.

▶ **6.** Save your form design changes.

Next, you'll add a rectangle around the calculated controls in the Detail section.

Adding a Rectangle to a Form

You can use a rectangle in a form to group related controls and to visually separate the group from other controls. You use the **Rectangle tool** in Design view to add a rectangle to a form or report.

Adding a Rectangle to a Form or Report

- Display the form or report in Design view.
- On the Form Design Tools Design tab, in the Controls group, click the More button, and then click the Rectangle tool.
- Click in the form or report to create a default-sized rectangle, or drag a rectangle in the position and size you want.

You will add a rectangle around the calculated controls and their labels to separate them from the subform and from the other controls in the Detail section.

To add a rectangle to the form:

1. On the Form Design Tools Design tab, in the Controls group, click the **More** button to open the Controls gallery, and then click the **Rectangle** tool ☐.

2. Position the pointer's plus symbol approximately two grid dots above and two grid dots to the left of the Number of Invoices label.

3. Drag the pointer down and to the right to create a rectangle that that has all four sides approximately two grid dots from the two calculated controls and their labels. See Figure 6-49.

Figure 6-49   Rectangle added to the form

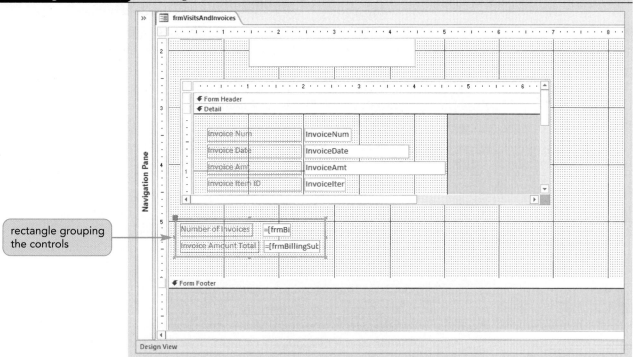

rectangle grouping the controls

Trouble? If the rectangle is not sized or positioned correctly, use the sizing handles on its selection border to adjust its size and the move handle to adjust its position.

Next, you'll set the thickness of the rectangle's lines.

▶ **4.** Click the **Form Design Tools Format** tab.

▶ **5.** In the Control Formatting group, click the **Shape Outline button arrow**, point to **Line Thickness** at the bottom of the gallery, and then click **1 pt** line (second line from the top).

▶ **6.** Click a blank area of the Form window to deselect the control.

Next, you'll add color and visual effects to the form's controls.

Modifying the Visual Effects of the Controls in a Form

Distinguishing one group of controls in a form from other groups is an important visual cue to the users of the form. For example, users should be able to distinguish the bound controls in the form from the calculated controls and from the Select Visit control in the Form Header section. You'll now modify the controls in the form to provide these visual cues. You'll start by setting font properties for the calculated control's labels.

To modify the format of the controls in the form:

▶ **1.** Select the **Number of Invoices** label and the **Invoice Amount Total** label, using the Shift key to select multiple controls.

▶ **2.** On the Form Design Tools Format tab, in the Font group, click the **Font Color button arrow** [A ▾], click the **Blue** color (row 7, column 8 in the Standard Colors palette), and then in the Font group, click the **Bold** button [B]. The labels' captions now appear in bold, blue font.

Next, you'll set properties for the Select Visit label in the Form Header section.

▶ **3.** Select the **Select Visit** label in the Form Header section, change the label's font color to **Red** (row 7, column 2 in the Standard Colors palette), and then apply bold formatting.

Next, you'll set the label's Special Effect property to a shadowed effect. The **Special Effect property** specifies the type of special effect applied to a control in a form or report. The choices for this property are Flat, Raised, Sunken, Etched, Shadowed, and Chiseled.

▶ **4.** Open the Property Sheet for the Select Visit label, click the **All** tab (if necessary), set the Special Effect property to **Shadowed**, and then deselect the label. The label now has a shadowed special effect, and the label's caption now appears in a red, bold font.

Next, you'll set the Special Effect property for the bound control text boxes to a sunken effect.

▶ **5.** Select the **VisitID** text box, the **VisitDate** text box, the **Reason** text box, and the **Comments** text box, set the controls' Special Effect property to **Sunken**, close the Property Sheet, and then deselect the controls.

Finally, you'll set the background color of the Form Header section, the Detail section, the Select Visit combo box, and the two calculated controls. You can use the **Background Color button** in the Font group on the Form Design Tools Format tab to change the background color of a control, section, or object (form or report).

6. Click the **Form Header** section bar.

7. On the Form Design Tools Format tab, in the Font group, click the **Background Color button arrow** , and then click the **Light Blue 2** color (row 3, column 5 in the Standard Colors palette). The Form Header's background color changes to the Light Blue 2 color.

8. Click the **Detail** section bar, and then in the Font Group, click the **Background Color** button to change the Detail section's background color to the **Light Blue 2** color.

9. Select the **Select Visit** combo box, **Number of Invoices** calculated control box, and the **Invoice Amount Total** calculated control box, set the selected controls' background color to the **Light Blue 2** color, and then deselect all controls by clicking to the right of the Detail section's grid.

10. Save your form design changes, switch to Form view, click the **Select Visit** arrow, and then click **1048** in the list to display this visit record in the form. See Figure 6-50.

Figure 6-50 Completed custom form in Form view

background changed to Light Blue 2

red, bold font and shadowed effect

sunken effect

blue, bold font

11. Test the form by tabbing between fields, navigating between records, and using the Select Visit combo box to find records, making sure you don't change any field values and observing that the calculated controls display the correct values.

12. Close the form, make a backup copy of the database, compact and repair the database, and then close the database.

INSIGHT

Applying Styles to Form and Report Controls

You can use the Quick Styles gallery to apply a built-in style reflecting a combination of several formatting options to a control in a form or report. To do this, select the control in either Layout or Design view, and then, on the Form or Report Design Tools Format tab, click the Quick Styles button in the Control Formatting group to display the Quick Styles gallery. Click a style in the gallery to apply it to the selected control.

You can also change the shape of a control in a form or report by clicking the Change Shape button in the Control Formatting group to display the Change Shape gallery, and then clicking a shape to apply it to the selected control.

Kimberly is pleased with the forms you have created. She will show these to her staff, and determine which of the forms will be most effective for using and managing the CareCenter database.

REVIEW

Session 6.3 Quick Check

1. To create a combo box to find records in a form with the Combo Box Wizard, the form's record source must be a(n) _____.
2. You use the _____ tool to add a subform to a form.
3. To calculate subtotals and overall totals in a form or report, you use the _____ function.
4. The Control Source property setting can be either a(n) _____ or a(n) _____.
5. Explain the difference between the Tab Stop property and tab order.
6. What is focus?
7. The _____ property has settings such as Raised and Sunken.

Review Assignments

PRACTICE

Data File needed for the Review Assignments: Supplier.accdb (cont. from Module 5)

Kimberly wants you to create several forms, including a custom form that displays and updates companies and the products they offer. Complete the following steps:

1. Open the **Supplier** database you worked with in the previous module.
2. In the **tblProduct** table, remove the lookup feature from the SupplierID field, and then resize the Supplier ID column in the datasheet to its best fit. Save and close the table.
3. Edit the relationship between the primary tblSupplier and related tblProduct tables to enforce referential integrity and to cascade-update related fields. Create the relationship report, save the report as **rptRelationshipsForProducts**, and then close it.
4. Use the Documenter to document the qryCompanyContacts query. Select all query options; use the Names, Data Types, and Sizes option for fields; and use the Names and Fields option for indexes. Print the report produced by the Documenter, and then close it.
5. Use the Datasheet tool to create a form based on the tblProduct table, save the form as **frmProductDatasheet**, and then close it.
6. Use the Multiple Items tool to create a form based on the qryDuplicateProduct Types query, save the form as **frmProductTypeMultipleItems**, and then close it.
7. Use the Split Form tool to create a split form based on the tblProduct table, and then make the following changes to the form in Layout view:
   a. Remove the two Units controls from the stacked layout, reduce the width of the Units field value box by about half, and then anchor the two Units controls to the bottom left. Depending on the size of your window, the two Units controls may be positioned at the bottom left of the right column.
   b. Remove the four control pairs in the right column from the stacked layout, and then anchor the group to the bottom right. You may see a dotted border outlining the location of the previously removed controls. This may be automatically selected as well.
   c. Remove the ProductName control pair from the stacked layout, move them to the top right, and then anchor them to the top right.
   d. Reduce the widths of the ProductID and SupplierID field value boxes to a reasonable size.
   e. Change the title to **Product**, save the modified form as **frmProductSplitForm**, and then close it.
8. Use Figure 6-51 and the following steps to create a custom form named **frmSuppliersWithProducts** based on the tblSupplier and tblProduct tables.

Figure 6-51 Supplier database custom form design

a. Place the fields from the tblSupplier table at the top of the Detail section. Delete the Contact Last Name label, and change the caption for the Contact First Name label to Contact Name.

b. Move the fields into two columns in the Detail section, as shown in Figure 6-51, resizing and aligning controls, as necessary, and increasing the width of the form.

c. Add the title in the Form Header section.

d. Make sure the form's Record Source property is set to tblSupplier, and then add a combo box in the Form Header section to find Company field values. In the Combo Box Wizard steps, select the Company and SupplierID fields, and hide the key column. Resize and move the control. Ensure the label displays the text "Company Name". Make sure the size of the Company Name field value box can accommodate the largest company name.

e. Add a subform based on the tblProduct table, include only the fields shown in Figure 6-51, link with SupplierID, name the subform **frmPartialProductSubform**, delete the subform label, resize the columns in the subform to their best fit, and resize and position the subform.

f. Add a calculated control that displays the number of products displayed in the subform. Set the calculated control's Tab Stop property to No, and the ControlTip Text property to Calculated number of products.

g. Add a line in the Form Header section, and add a rectangle around the calculated control and its label, setting the line thickness of both controls to 3 pt. Set the rectangle's color the same as the line's color.

h. In the main form, use the Light Gray 1 fill color (row 2, column 1 in the Standard Colors palette) for all form sections, and use the Black font color (row 1, column 2 in the Standard Colors palette) for all the label text, the calculated control, Company Name combo box, and the Title.

i. Make sure the tab order is top-to-bottom, left-to-right for the main form text boxes.

9. Make a backup copy of the database, compact and repair the database, and then close the database.

Case Problem 1

Data File needed for this Case Problem: MoreBeauty.accdb (cont. from Module 5)

APPLY

Beauty To Go   Sue Miller wants you to create several forms, including two custom forms that display and update data in the database. Complete the following steps:

1. Open the **MoreBeauty** database you worked with in the previous module.
2. Use the Documenter to document the qryMemberNames query. Select all query options; use the Names, Data Types, and Sizes option for fields; and use the Names and Fields option for indexes. Print the first page of the report produced by the Documenter.
3. Use the Datasheet tool to create a form based on the tblOption table, and then save the form as **frmOptionDatasheet**.
4. Create a custom form based on the qryUpcomingExpirations query. Display all fields from the query in the form. Create your own design for the form. Add a label to the bottom of the Detail section that contains your first and last names. Change the label's font so that your name appears in bold, red font. Change the OptionEnd text box format so that the field value displays in bold, red font. Save the form as **frmUpcomingExpirations**.
5. Use Figure 6-52 and the following steps to create a custom form named **frmPlansWithMembers** based on the tblOption and tblMember tables.

Figure 6-52   Plans custom form design

a. Place the fields from the tblOption table at the top of the Detail section, and edit the captions in the associated label controls as shown.
b. Selected fields from the tblMember table appear in a subform named **frmPlansWithMembersSubform**.
c. The calculated control displays the total number of records that appear in the subform. Set the calculated control's ControlTip Text property to Total number of members in this plan. Set the calculated control's Tab Stop property to No.

    d. Apply the Organic theme to the frmPlansWithMembers form only.

    e. Save and close the form.

6. Make a backup copy of the database, compact and repair the database, and then close the database.

Case Problem 2

Data File needed for this Case Problem: Tutoring.accdb (cont. from Module 5)

Programming Pros   Brent Hovis wants you to create several forms, including a custom form that displays and updates the tutoring service's contracts with students. Complete the following steps:

1. Open the **Tutoring** database you worked with in the previous module.

2. Remove the lookup feature from the TutorID field in the tblContract table, and then resize the Tutor ID column to its best fit. Save and close the table.

3. Define a one-to-many relationship between the primary tblTutor table and the related tblContract table. Select the referential integrity option and the cascade updates option for this relationship.

4. Use the Documenter to document the tblContract table. Select all table options; use the Names, Data Types, and Sizes option for fields; and use the Names and Fields option for indexes. Print the report produced by the Documenter.

5. Create a query called **qryLessonsByTutor** that uses the tblTutor and tblContract tables and includes the fields FirstName and LastName from the tblTutor table, and the fields StudentID, ContractDate, SessionType, Length, and Cost from the tblContract table.

6. Use the Multiple Items tool to create a form based on the qryLessonsByTutor query, change the title to **Lessons by Tutor**, and then save the form as **frmLessonsByTutorMultipleItems**.

7. Use the Split Form tool to create a split form based on the qryLessonsByTutor query, and then make the following changes to the form in Layout view.

    a. Size the field value boxes in variable lengths to fit a reasonable amount of data.

    b. Remove the SessionType, Length, and Cost controls and their labels from the stacked layout, move these six controls to the right and then to the top of the form, and then anchor them to the top right.

    c. Select the Cost control and its label, and then anchor them to the bottom right.

    d. Remove the Contract Date control and its label from the stacked layout, and then anchor the pair of controls to the bottom left.

    e. Change the title to **Lessons by Tutor**, and then save the modified form as **frmLessonsByTutorSplitForm**.

8. Use Figure 6-53 and the following steps to create a custom form named **frmContract** based on the tblContract table.

Figure 6-53   Tutoring database custom form design

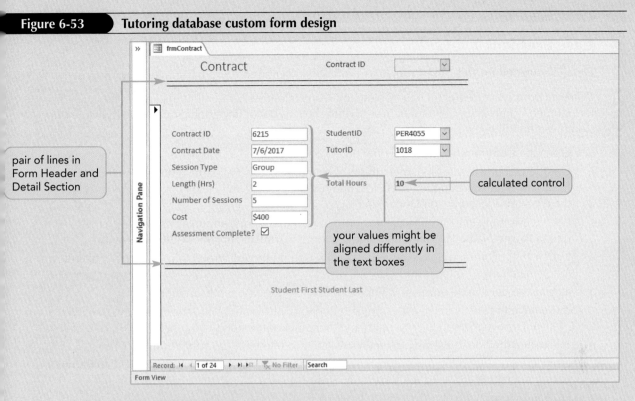

a. For the StudentID combo box, select the LastName, FirstName, and StudentID fields from the tblStudent table, in order, and sort in ascending order by the LastName field and then by the FirstName field.

b. For the TutorID combo box, select the LastName, FirstName, and TutorID fields from the tblTutor table, in order, and sort in ascending order by the LastName field and then by the FirstName field.

c. Make sure the form's Record Source property is set to tblContract, and then add a combo box in the Form Header section to find ContractID field values.

d. Add a calculated control that displays the total number of hours (length multiplied by sessions). *Hint*: Use the * symbol for multiplication. Set the calculated control's Tab Stop property to No, and set the number of decimal places to Auto.

e. Add a line in the Form Header section, add a second line below it, and then add a second pair of lines near the bottom of the Detail section. Set the line thickness of all lines to 1 pt.

f. Use the Label tool to add your name below the pair of lines at the bottom of the Detail section.

g. For the labels in the Detail section, except for the Total Hours label and the label displaying your name, use the Red font color (row 7, column 2 in the Standard Colors palette).

h. For the title and Contract ID label, use the Dark Red font color (row 7, column 1 in the Standard Colors palette).

i. Apply bold to the calculated control and its label.

j. For the background fill color of the sections, the calculated control, and the Contract ID combo box, apply the Medium Gray color (row 1, column 3 in the Standard Colors palette).

k. Make sure the tab order is top-to-bottom, left-to-right for the main form field value boxes.

9. Make a backup copy of the database, compact and repair the database, and then close the database.

Case Problem 3

Data File needed for this Case Problem: Community.accdb (cont. from Module 5)

Diane's Community Center Diane Coleman asks you to create several forms, including a custom form for the Community Center database so that she can better track donations made to the center. Complete the following steps:

1. Open the **Community** database you worked with in the previous module.

2. Use the Documenter to document the tblPatron table. Select all table options; use the Names, Data Types, and Sizes option for fields; and use the Names and Fields option for indexes. Print the report produced by the Documenter.

3. Use the Multiple Items tool to create a form based on the qryPatronNames query, change the title to **Patron Name List**, and then save the form as **frmPatronNamesMultipleItems**.

4. Use the Split Form tool to create a split form based on the tblPatron table, and then make the following changes to the form in Layout view.

   a. Size the field value boxes in variable lengths to fit a reasonable amount of data.

   b. Remove the FirstName, LastName, and Phone controls and their labels from the stacked layout, move them to the top right, and then anchor them to the top right.

   c. Change the title to **Patron**, and then save the modified form as **frmPatronSplitForm**.

5. Use Figure 6-54 and the following steps to create a custom form named **frmPatronDonations** based on the tblPatron and tblDonation tables.

Figure 6-54 **Community database custom form design**

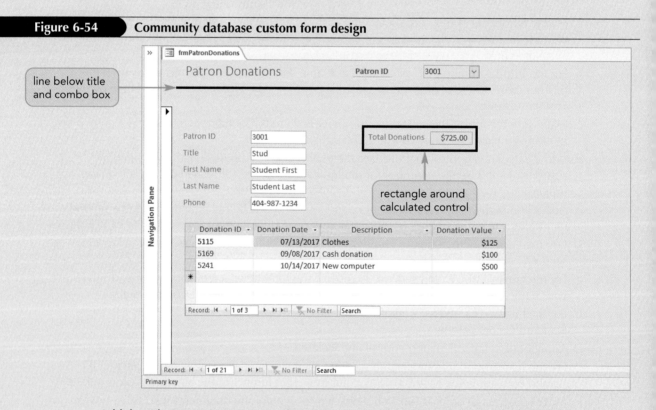

a. Add the title Patron Donations in the Form Header section.

b. Make sure the form's Record Source property is set to tblPatron, and then add a combo box in the Form Header section to find PatronID field values. In the Combo Box Wizard steps, select the PatronID field. Format the label using the Red font (row 7, column 2 in the Standard Colors palette), bold, and the Chiseled special effect.

   c. Add a subform based on the tblDonation table, name the subform **frmPatronDonationsSubform**, delete the subform label, and resize the columns in the subform to their best fit, and resize and position the subform.

   d. Add a calculated control that displays the total of the DonationValue field displayed in the subform with the Currency format. Set the calculated control's Tab Stop property to No and the Border Style property to Transparent.

   e. Add a line in the Form Header section, and add a rectangle around the calculated control and its label, setting the line thickness of both controls to 3 pt. Set the rectangle color to Black (row 1, column 2 in the Standard Colors section) using the Shape Outline button in the Control Formatting group on the Form Design Tools Format tab.

   f. Use the background color Aqua Blue 2 (row 3, column 9 in the Standard Colors palette) for the sections, the calculated control, and the Patron ID combo box.

   g. Make sure the tab order is top-to-bottom for the main form text boxes.

6. Make a backup copy of the database, compact and repair the database, and then close the database.

Case Problem 4

CREATE

Data File needed for this Case Problem: AppTrail.accdb (cont. from Module 5)

Hike Apalachia Molly and Bailey Johnson want you to create several forms, including a custom form that displays and updates guest and reservation data in the AppTrail database. Complete the following steps:

1. Open the **AppTrail** database you worked with in the previous module.

2. Remove the lookup feature from the TourID field in the tblReservation table. Size the TourID field, and save and close the table.

3. Edit the relationship between the primary tblTour and related tblReservation tables to enforce referential integrity and to cascade-update related fields. Create the relationship report, and then save the report as **rptRelationshipsForAppTrail.pdf**, without exporting steps.

4. Use the Documenter to document the qrySelectedStates query. Select all query options; use the Names, Data Types, and Sizes option for fields; and use the Nothing option for indexes. Print the report produced by the Documenter.

5. Use the Datasheet tool to create a form based on the qryHikerLastNameS query, and then save the form as **frmHikerLastNameS**.

6. Create a custom form based on the qryNonHikingTours query. Display all fields in the form. Use your own design for the form, but use the title **Tours with No Hiking** in the Form Header section, and use the Label tool to add your name to the Form Header section. Save the form as **frmNonHikingTours**.

7. Use Figure 6-55 and the following steps to create a custom form named **frmHikersWithReservations** based on the tblHiker and tblReservation tables.

Figure 6-55   **AppTrail database custom form design**

a. Add the title Hikers and Reservations in the Form Header section, and apply bold formatting.

b. Add the fields from the tblHiker table. Size the associated labels so that they're all the same length. Size the field value boxes in variable lengths to fit a reasonable amount of data, as shown in Figure 6-55.

c. Make sure the form's Record Source property is set to tblHiker, and then add a combo box in the Form Header section to find HikerID field values.

d. Add a subform based on the tblReservation table, name the subform **frmHikersWithReservationsSubform**, delete the subform label, resize the columns in the subform to their best fit, and then resize and position the subform.

e. Add a calculated control that displays the total of the People field displayed in the subform. Set the calculated control's Tab Stop property to No, and set the calculated control's Border Style property to Transparent.

f. Add a line in the Form Header section, and add a rectangle around the calculated control and its label, setting the line thickness of both controls to 3 pt. Set the rectangle color to Black (row 1, column 2 in the Standard Colors section) using the Shape Outline button in the Control Formatting group on the Form Design Tools Format tab.

g. Apply the black font color for all controls, including the controls in the subform.

h. Apply the Green 1 fill color (row 2, column 7 in the Standard Colors palette) for the sections and the calculated control.

i. Use the Shadowed special effect for the labels in the Detail section, except for the calculated control label, and the Form Header section, except for the title.

j. Make sure the tab order is top-to-bottom and left-to-right for the main form field value boxes.

8. Make a backup copy of the database, compact and repair the database, and then close the database.

Creating Custom Reports

Creating Custom Reports for Riverview Veterinary Care Center

Case | *Riverview Veterinary Care Center*

At a recent staff meeting, Kimberly Johnson, the office manager, indicated that she would like to make some changes to an existing report in the database. She also requested a new report that she can use to produce a printed list of all invoices for all visits.

In this module, you will modify an existing report and create the new report for Kimberly. In modifying and building these reports, you will use many Access features for customizing reports, including grouping data, calculating totals, and adding lines to separate report sections. These features will enhance the reports and make them easier for Kimberly and her staff to work with.

STARTING DATA FILES

Access2 → Module
CareCenter.accdb (*cont.*)

Review
Supplier.accdb (*cont.*)

Case1
MoreBeauty.accdb (*cont.*)

Case2
Tutoring.accdb (*cont.*)

Case3
Community.accdb (*cont.*)

Case4
AppTrail.accdb (*cont.*)

Session 7.1 Visual Overview:

A report title is placed in either the Report Header section or the Page Header section.

Each column in the report is a field from a table or query.

The report is grouped by AnimalID.

Subtotals sum the values in the grouped columns.

The date appears in the Page Footer section at the bottom of every page in the report.

This report is displayed in Layout view.

The grand total is included when subtotals are added.

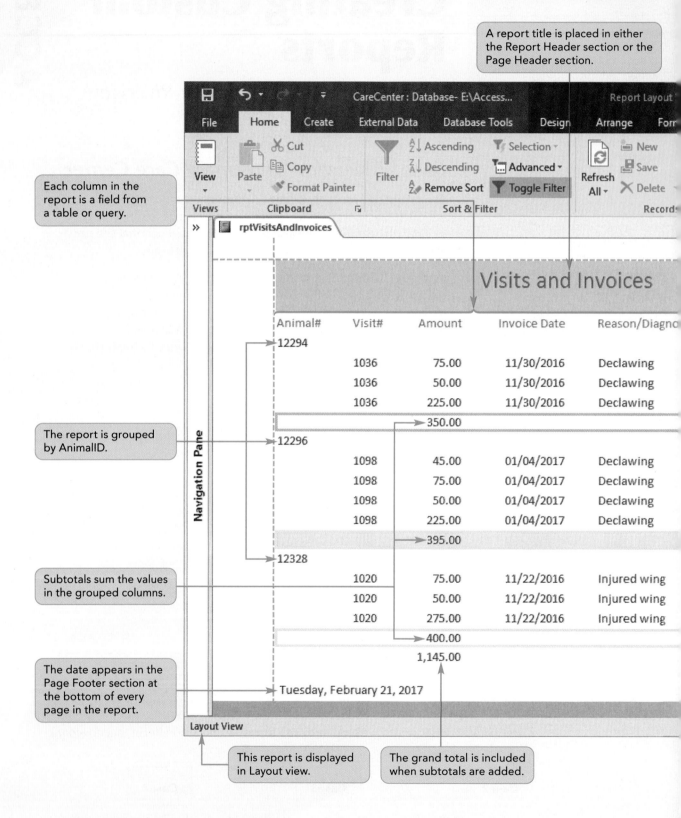

Custom Report in Layout View

The margin guidelines can help you to position the elements inside the page margins.

The column headings are in the Page Header section and will appear at the top of every page in the report.

When you select multiple objects, you can resize or format them together.

The page number appears in the Page Footer section at the bottom of every page in the report.

Customizing Existing Reports

As you know, a report is a formatted output (screen display or printout) of the contents of one or more tables in a database. Although you can format and print data using datasheets, queries, and forms, reports offer greater flexibility and provide a more professional, readable appearance. For example, a billing statement created using a datasheet would not look professional, but the staff at Riverview Veterinary Care Center can easily create professional-looking billing statements from the database using reports.

Before Daksha Yatawara was tasked with enhancing the CareCenter database, Kimberly and her staff created two reports. Kimberly used the Report tool to create the rptVisitsAndInvoices report and the Report Wizard to create the rptAnimalsAndVisits report. One of Kimberly's staff members modified the rptAnimalsAndVisits report in Layout view by changing the title, moving and resizing fields, changing the font color of field names, and inserting a picture. The rptAnimalsAndVisits report is an example of a custom report. When you modify a report created by the Report tool or the Report Wizard in Layout view or in Design view, or when you create a report from scratch in Layout view or in Design view, you produce a **custom report**. You need to produce a custom report whenever the Report tool or the Report Wizard cannot automatically create the specific report you need, or when you need to fine-tune the formatting of an existing report or to add controls and special features.

The rptVisitsAndInvoices report is included in the CareCenter database. Kimberly asks Daksha to review the rptVisitsAndInvoices report and suggest improvements to make it more user friendly. You will make the changes Daksha suggests, but first, you will view and work with the report in Report view.

Viewing a Report in Report View

You can view reports on screen in Print Preview, Layout view, Design view, and Report view. You've already viewed and worked with reports in Print Preview and Layout view. Making modifications to reports in Design view is similar to making changes to forms in Design view. **Report view** provides an interactive view of a report. You can use Report view to view the contents of a report and to apply a filter to its data. You can also copy selected portions of the report to the Clipboard and then use that data in another program.

INSIGHT

Choosing the View to Use for a Report

You can view a report on screen using Report view, Print Preview, Layout view, or Design view. Which view you choose depends on what you intend to do with the report and its data.

- Use Report view when you want to filter the report data before printing a report or when you want to copy a selected portion of a report.
- Use Print Preview when you want to see what a report will look like when it is printed. Print Preview is the only view in which you can navigate the pages of a report, zoom in or out, or view a **multiple-column report**, which is a report that prints the same collection of field values in two or more sets across the page.
- Use Layout view when you want to modify a report while seeing actual report data.
- Use Design view when you want to fine-tune a report's design or when you want to add lines, rectangles, and other controls that are available only in Design view.

You'll open the rptVisitsAndInvoices report in Report view, and then you'll interact with its data in this view.

To view and filter the rptVisitsAndInvoices report in Report view:

1. Start Access, and then open the **CareCenter** database you worked with in the previous two modules.

   Trouble? If the security warning is displayed below the ribbon, click the Enable Content button.

2. Open the Navigation Pane if necessary, double-click **rptVisitsAndInvoices**, and then close the Navigation Pane. The rptVisitsAndInvoices report opens in Report view.

   In Report view, you can view the report prior to printing it, just as you can do in Print Preview. Report view also lets you apply filters to the report before printing it. You'll apply a text filter to the rptVisitsAndInvoices report.

3. Scroll down to Animal ID 12328, which has three report detail lines for Visit ID 1020, right-click **Injured wing** in the Reason column to open the shortcut menu, and then point to **Text Filters**. A submenu of filter options for the Text field opens. See Figure 7-1.

Figure 7-1   **Filter options for a Text field in Report view**

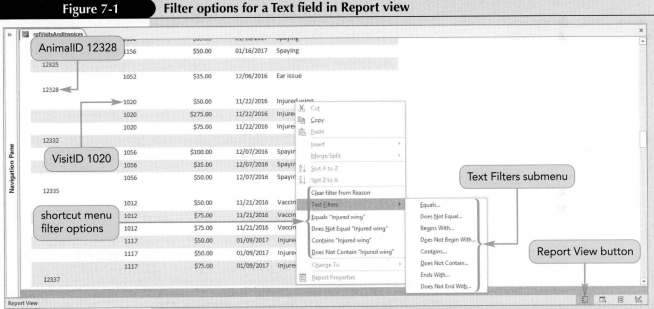

The filter options that appear on the shortcut menu depend on the selected field's data type and the selected value. Because you clicked the Reason field value without selecting a portion of the value, the shortcut menu displays filter options—various conditions using the value "Injured wing"—for the entire Reason field value. You'll close the menus and select a portion of the Reason column value to explore a different way of filtering the report.

4. Click a blank area of the screen to close the menus.

5. For Animal ID 12328: Visit ID 1020, double-click **wing** in the Reason column to select it, and then right-click **wing**. The filter options on the shortcut menu now apply to the selected text, "wing." Notice that the filter options on the shortcut menu include options such as "Ends With" and "Does Not End With" because the text you selected is at the end of the field value in the Reason column.

6. On the shortcut menu, click **Contains "wing"**. The report content changes to display only those visits that contain the word "wing" anywhere in the Reason column. Notice the results also show "Declawing" because the letter string "wing" appear within this word.

7. In the Reason column, double-click the word **Injured** for the Visit ID 1020 report detail line for Animal ID 12328, right-click **Injured** to open the shortcut menu, and then point to **Text Filters**. The filter options now include the "Begins With" and "Does Not Begin With" options because the text you selected is at the beginning of the field value in the Reason column.

   Kimberly wants to view only those visits that contain the phrase "Injured wing" in the Reason column.

8. Click a blank area of the screen to close the menus, and then click in a blank area again to deselect the text.

9. In the report detail line for Visit ID 1020, right-click **Injured wing** in the Reason column, and then click **Equals "Injured wing"** on the shortcut menu. Only the three invoices that contain the selected phrase are displayed in the report. See Figure 7-2.

Figure 7-2	Filter applied to the report in Report View

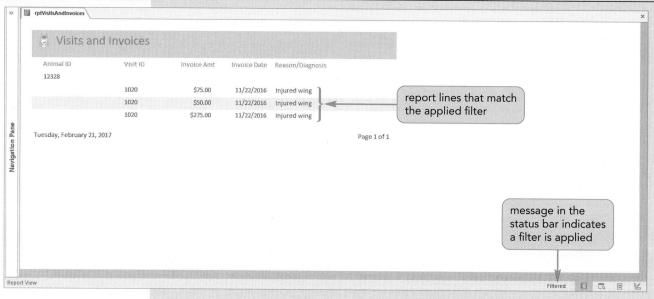

You can print the filtered report, or you can select the entire filtered report or a portion of it and copy it into another file so you can work with it in a different program.

Copying and Pasting a Report into Word

Sometimes it is helpful to copy a filtered report or a portion of a filtered report into another file, such as a Word document or an Excel spreadsheet. This allows you to distribute the report electronically in a format that others can easily access, or you can print the filtered report to distribute on paper. When you copy information contained in an Access object such as a report, it is placed on the Clipboard. The Clipboard is a temporary storage area on your computer on which text or objects are stored when you cut or copy them, and it's contents are available to all Windows programs. You can then paste the text or objects stored on the Clipboard into another file, such as a Word document or an Excel spreadsheet.

Kimberly would like you to create a Word document that contains the records from the Injured wing filter so she can provide this information to the veterinary technician who is monitoring the animal with these injuries. Next, you'll copy the entire filtered report to the Clipboard.

To copy the filtered report and paste it into a Word document:

1. Click to the left of the title graphic at the top of the report to select the report title control, drag down to the end of the last record in the report, and then release the mouse button to select the report title, field titles, and all of the records in the report. See Figure 7-3.

   Trouble? If you selected nothing, you clicked above the title graphic. Make sure the mouse pointer is to the left of the title graphic, but not above it, and then repeat Step 1.

   Trouble? If you selected only a portion of the report, press the Esc key to deselect your selection, and then repeat Step 1.

Figure 7-3   Selected filtered report in Report view

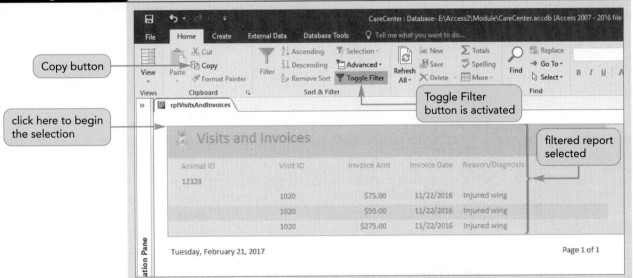

2. On the Home tab, in the Clipboard, click the **Copy** button.

   You'll copy this report data into a Word document.

3. Open Word, and then in Backstage view, click **Blank document**. A blank Word document opens.

4. On the Home tab, in the Clipboard group, click the **Paste** button to paste the report data into the document.

5. Save the Word document with the filename **Injuredwing** in the location where you are saving your files, and then close the Injuredwing document and exit Word. You return to the Access with the rptVisitsAndInvoices filtered report in Report view.

6. To the right of the records, click a blank area of the screen to deselect the report records, and then, in the Sort & Filter group, click the **Toggle Filter** button. The filters are removed from the report.

Viewing and working with a report in Report view often helps you to identify adjustments and modifications you can make to the report to enhance its readability. You can make modifications to a report in Layout view and Design view.

PROSKILLS

Written Communication: Enhancing Reports Created by the Report Tool and the Report Wizard

Creating a report using the Report tool or the Report Wizard can save time, but you should review the report to determine if you need to make any of the following types of common enhancements and corrections:

- Change the report title from the report object name (with an rpt prefix and no spaces) to one that has meaning to the users.
- Reduce the widths of the date and page number controls, and move the controls so that they are not printed on a separate page.
- Review the report in Print Preview, and, if the report displays excess pages, adjust the page margins and the placement of controls.
- Verify that all controls are large enough to fully display their values.
- Use page margins and field widths that display equal margins to the left and right of the data.
- Use a layout for the fields that distributes the data in a balanced way across the report, and use the same spacing between all columns of data.
- The report and page titles can be centered on the page, but do not center the report data. Instead, use spacing between the columns and reasonable column widths to make the best use of the width of the page, extending the data from the left margin to the right margin.

By fine-tuning and correcting the format and layout of your reports, you ensure the report's information is clearly conveyed to users.

Kimberly has identified some changes she would like made to the rptVistsAndInvoices report. Some of the report adjustments you need to make are subtle ones, so you need to carefully review all report controls to ensure the report is completely readable and usable for those using the report.

Modifying a Report in Layout View

You can make the report changes Kimberly wants in Layout view. Modifying a report in Layout view is similar to modifying a form in Layout view. When you open a report in Layout view, the Report Layout Tools Design, Arrange, Format, and Page Setup contextual tabs appear on the ribbon. You use the commands on these tabs to modify and format the elements of the report.

Kimberly wants you to decrease the width of columns and adjust the page margins in the report. She also wants you to rename some of the column headings, format the InvoiceAmt field values using the Standard format, resize the column headings, delete the picture from the Report Header section, remove the alternate row color from the detail and group header lines, and add a grand total of the InvoiceAmt field values. These changes will make the report more useful for Kimberly and her staff.

First, you will view the report in Layout view and observe how the information in the report is grouped and sorted.

To view the report in Layout view:

1. On the status bar, click the **Layout View** button 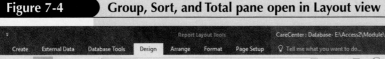, and then scroll to the top of the report (if necessary).

2. On the Report Layout Tools Design tab, in the Grouping & Totals group, click the **Group & Sort** button to open the Group, Sort, and Total pane at the bottom of the window. The Group & Sort button is a toggle button; you click this button to open and close this pane as needed. See Figure 7-4.

Figure 7-4	Group, Sort, and Total pane open in Layout view

The rptVisitsAndInvoices report has a grouping field (the AnimalID field) and a sort field (the VisitID field). At the bottom of the window, the **Group, Sort, and Total pane** provides you with the options to modify the report's grouping fields and sort fields and the report calculations for the groups. A **grouping field** is a report sort field that includes a Group Header section before a group of records having the same sort field value and a Group Footer section after the group of records. These sections are defined with section bars in Design view. A Group Header section usually displays the group name and the sort field value for the group. A Group Footer section usually displays subtotals or counts for the records in that group. The rptVisitsAndInvoices report's grouping field is the AnimalID field, which is displayed in a Group Header section that precedes the set of visits for the Animal; the grouping field does not have a Group Footer section. The VisitID field is a secondary sort key, as shown in the Group, Sort, and Total pane.

Because you don't need to change the grouping or sort fields for the report, you'll close the pane and then make Kimberly's modifications to the report.

3. In the Grouping & Totals group, click the **Group & Sort** button to close the Group, Sort, and Total pane.

Now that you have an understanding of how the information in the report is grouped and sorted, you are ready to make the modifications to the report Kimberly has requested. First, you'll change the column headings for the first three columns to Animal#, Visit#, and Amount. Kimberly prefers to see all the detail data on one line, even when it means abbreviating column headings for columns whose headings are wider than the data. After reducing the column headings, you'll reduce the column widths, freeing up space on the detail lines to widen the Reason column.

To modify the columns in the report in Layout view:

1. Double-click the **Animal ID** column heading to change to editing mode, change it to **Animal#**, and then press the **Enter** key.

2. Repeat Step 1 to change the Visit ID column heading to **Visit#** and the Invoice Amt heading to **Amount**.

Next, you'll change the format of the field values in the Amount column to Standard.

3. Right-click any value in the Amount column to open the shortcut menu, click **Properties** to open the Property Sheet, set the Format property to **Standard**, and then close the Property Sheet. The Standard format adds comma separators and two decimal places.

Now you'll widen the report margins. This will provide room on the printed page for staff to make handwritten notes if necessary.

4. On the ribbon, click the **Report Layout Tools Page Setup** tab.

5. In the Page Size group, click the **Margins** button, and then click **Wide**. This sets page margins to 1" on the top and bottom and 0.75" on the left and right.

Sometimes when margins are decreased, some elements appear outside the margins, and this causes additional pages to be created in the report. This has occurred with the page number, and you'll fix that later. Now you'll adjust the widths of the columns to fit the data better.

6. Click the **Animal#** column heading, press and hold the **Shift** key, click one of the AnimalID values in the column, and then release the **Shift** key. The Animal# column heading and all the values in this column are selected.

7. Position the pointer on the left border of the Animal# column heading selection box, and then when the pointer changes to ↔, drag the left border to the left so it aligns with the left edge of the gray report header box.

8. Drag the right border of the Animal# to the left until the border is just to the right of the # symbol in the column heading text. Now, you'll move the VisitID column to the left, closer to the Animal# column.

9. Click the **Visit#** column heading, press and hold the **Shift** key, click one the VisitID values in the column, and then release the **Shift** key. The Visit# column heading and all the VisitID values in this column are selected.

10. Using the ⬚ pointer, drag the **Visit#** column to the left, until it is positioned such that the left border of the Visit# column heading selection box is aligned with the "t" in the word "Visits" in the report title. The column does not appear to move until you release the mouse button.

Trouble? If the report scrolls to the bottom of the report after you release the mouse button in the drag operation, scroll back to the top of the report.

Now you'll resize and move the Amount heading and InvoiceAmt values to the left, closer to the VisitID column, and then you'll move the Date of Visit and Reason/Diagnosis columns to the left, closer to the Amount column.

11. Select the **Amount** column heading and the **InvoiceAmt** values in the column, and then drag the left border of the Amount column heading selection box to the right until it is positioned just to the left of the "A" in the column heading "Amount." The Amount column is resized to better fit the values in the column.

12. With the Amount column heading and the InvoiceAmt values still selected, drag the column heading to the left until the left border of its selection box aligns with the letter "I" in the word "Invoices" in the report's title.

13. Select the **Invoice Date** column heading and the **InvoiceDate** values, and then resize and reposition the selected column heading and column of values as shown in Figure 7-5.

| Figure 7-5 | Resized columns in Layout view |

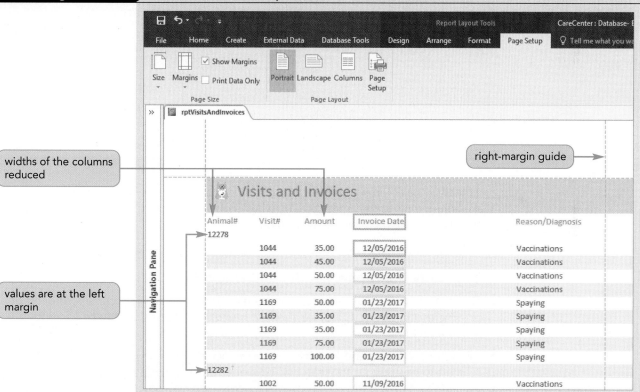

widths of the columns reduced

right-margin guide

values are at the left margin

Now, you'll move the column for the Reason field to the left and resize it to better fit the data, aligning it with the page's right margin.

14. Select the **Reason/Diagnosis** column heading and field values, move them to the left, closer to the Date of Visit column, then resize the column heading and the column of values by dragging the right border of the selected items to the right margin of the report, as shown in Figure 7-6.

Figure 7-6   **Adjusted column width**

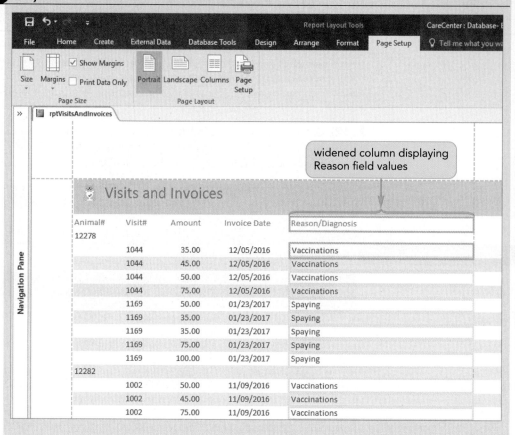

Now that the columns have been resized and repositioned, Kimberly asks you to make adjustments to the report header, which contains a picture and the report's title. You'll also remove the alternate row color.

To modify the report header and row color:

1. If necessary, scroll to the top of the report, right-click the picture to the left of the report title to open the shortcut menu, and then click **Delete** to remove the picture.

2. Click the **Visits and Invoices** title to select it, and then drag the title to the left to position its left selection border at the left-margin guide.

3. Drag the title's right selection border to the right to position it at the right-margin guide to increase the width of the title box to the full width of the page.

4. Click the **Report Layout Tools Format** tab, and then in the Font group, click the **Center** button to center the title in the report header.

   Kimberly finds the alternate row color setting in the group header and detail lines distracting, and asks you to remove this formatting.

5. To the left of the first AnimalID value in the first column, click to the left of the left-margin guide to select the group headers.

6. In the Background group, click the **Alternate Row Color** arrow to display the gallery of available colors, and then at the bottom of the gallery, click **No Color**. The alternate row color is removed from the AnimalID group header rows.

You've removed the alternate row color from the AnimalID values in the report, and next you'll remove the alternate row color from the detail lines. Because the Alternate Row Color button is now set to "No Color," you can just click the button to remove the color.

▶ **7.** Next to the first VisitID in the first AnimalID record detail line, click to the left of the left-margin guide and then in the Background group, click the **Alternate Row Color** button to remove the alternate row color from the detail lines.

Kimberly's last change to the report is to add a grand total for the Amount field values. First, you must select the Amount column or one of the values in the column.

To add a grand total to the report in Layout view:

▶ **1.** In the first detail line for VisitID 1044, click **45.00** in the Amount column. The values in this column are all selected.

▶ **2.** Click the **Report Layout Tools Design** tab, and then in the Grouping & Totals group, click the **Totals** button to display the Totals menu. See Figure 7-7.

Figure 7-7	The Totals menu

Totals menu

selecting one Amount selects the entire column

You can select one of the eight aggregate functions on the Totals menu to summarize values in the selected column. To calculate and display the grand total visit amount, you'll select the Sum aggregate function.

▶ **3.** Click **Sum** in the Totals menu, scroll to the bottom of the report, and then if the last value in the Amount column displays as ######## instead of numbers, click ######## to select it, then drag the left selection border of the selected value to the left until the grand total of 12,015.00 displays.

Notice subtotals for each group of visits are displayed for each AnimalID field value (125.00 for the last animal). See Figure 7-8.

Trouble? If the field value box still contains ###### after you resize it, increase the width again until the grand total value of 12,015.00 is visible.

Figure 7-8   Report showing subtotals and a grand total of the Amount field values

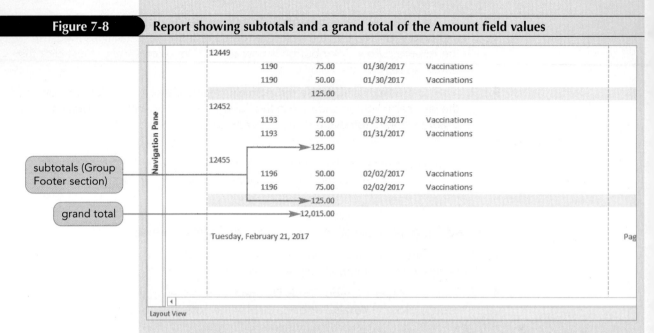

subtotals (Group Footer section)

grand total

Layout View

When you select an aggregate function in Layout view, the results of the function are added to the end of the report, and subtotals for each grouping field are also added. Because each Animal has so few visits, Kimberly asks you to remove the subtotals from the report.

4. Right-click the **125.00** subtotal for the last record to open the shortcut menu, click **Delete** to remove the subtotals, and then scroll to the end of the report. You deleted the subtotals, but the grand total still appears at the end of the report.

Kimberly wants to review the rptVisitsAndInvoices report in Print Preview.

5. Save your report changes, switch to Print Preview, and then use the navigation buttons to page through the report. Viewing the report in Print Preview allows you to identify possible problems that might occur when you print the report. For example, as you navigate through the report, notice that every other page is blank, with just the page number appearing in the footer.

6. Navigate to the second to last page of the report that shows the grand total line, and then click the **Zoom In** button ⊞ on the status bar to increase the zoom percentage to 110%. See Figure 7-9.

Figure 7-9   The rptVisitsAndInvoices report in Print Preview

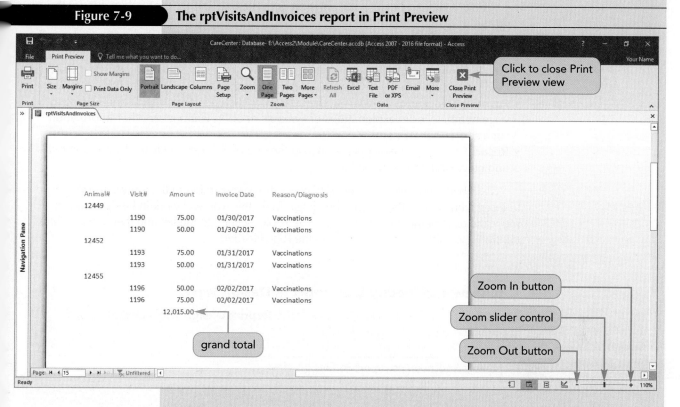

Figure 7-9   The rptVisitsAndInvoices report in Print Preview

Trouble? Depending on the printer you are using, the last page of your report might differ. If so, don't worry. Different printers format reports in different ways, sometimes affecting the total number of pages and the number of records printed per page.

▶ **7.** On the status bar, click the **Zoom Out** button ⊖ to decrease the zoom percentage to 100%, and close the Print Preview view and display the report in Layout view.

As you saw in Print Preview, the page numbers are outside the right margin and are causing extra pages in the report. Therefore, you need to reposition the page number that appears at the bottom of each page. Kimberly suggests you move the page number box to the left so that its right edge is aligned with the right edge of Reason field value box in the Detail section, thereby eliminating the extra pages in the report. She also wants you to add a line below the column heading labels. Although you can make Kimberly's modifications in Layout view, you'll make them in Design view so you can work more precisely.

Modifying a Report in Design View

Design view for reports is similar to Design view for forms, which you used in the previous module to customize forms. When you open a report in Design view, the Report Design Tools contextual tabs—Design, Arrange, Format, and Page Setup—appear on the ribbon, A report in Design view is divided into seven sections:

- **Report Header section**—appears once at the beginning of a report and is used for report titles, company logos, report introductions, dates, visual elements such as lines, and cover pages.
- **Page Header section**—appears at the top of each page of a report and is used for page numbers, column headings, report titles, and report dates.

- **Group Header section**—appears before each group of records that share the same sort field value, and usually displays the group name and the sort field value for the group.
- **Detail section**—contains the bound controls to display the field values for each record in the record source.
- **Group Footer section**—appears after each group of records that share the same sort field value, and usually displays subtotals or counts for the records in that group.
- **Page Footer section**—appears at the bottom of each page of a report and is used for page numbers, brief explanations of symbols or abbreviations, or other information such as a company name.
- **Report Footer section**—appears once at the end of a report and is used for report totals and other summary information.

As Kimberly requested, you need to move the page number in the report, and you need to insert a line below the column headings. To do this, you will work in Design view to move the page number control in the Page Footer section to the left and then create a line control below the column headings in the Page Header.

To view and modify the report in Design view:

1. Switch to Design view, and click the **Report Design Tools Design** tab, if necessary. See Figure 7-10.

Figure 7-10	rptVisitsAndInvoices report in Design view

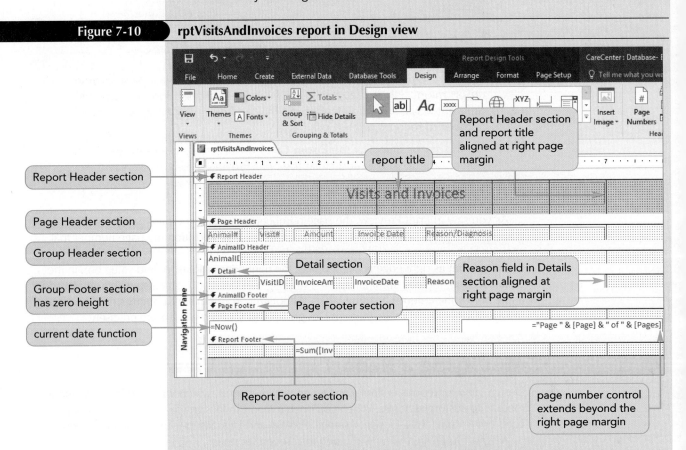

Notice that Design view for a report has most of the same components as Design view for a form. For example, Design view for forms and reports includes horizontal and vertical rulers, grids in each section, and similar buttons in the groups on the Report Design Tools Design tab.

Design view for the rptVisitsAndInvoices report displays seven sections: the Report Header section contains the report title; the Page Header section contains the column heading labels; the Group Header section (AnimalID Header) contains the AnimalID grouping field; the Detail section contains the bound controls to display the field values for each record in the record source (tblVisit); the Group Footer section (AnimalID Footer) isn't displayed in the report; the Page Footer section contains the current date and the page number; and the Report Footer section contains the Sum function, which calculates the grand total of the InvoiceAmt field values.

You will now move the page number control in the Page Footer section so that it is within the report's right page margin. To guide you in this, recall you earlier resized and repositioned the Reason/Diagnosis column in Layout view so it aligned to the right margin of the page. Therefore, you will right-align the page number control to the Reason field value box in the Detail section.

2. Click the **Page Number** control to select it (the control on the right side of the Page Footer section), and then press the ← key to move the control to the left until the right border of its selection box is roughly aligned with the right edge of the Reason field value control box in the Detail section.

   Trouble? If the page number control overlaps the date control in the Report Footer section, don't worry about it. The contents of both will still be displayed.

3. With the Page Number control still selected, press and hold the **Shift** key, click the **Reason** field value control box in the Detail section, and then release the **Shift** key. Both controls are now selected.

4. Right-click one of the selected controls, point to **Align** on the shortcut menu, and then click **Right**. Both controls are now right-aligned.

   Finally, you'll create the line in the Page Header section.

5. Drag the bottom border of the Page Header section down to increase the height approximately half an inch. You'll resize this again after the line is created.

6. On the Report Design Tools Design tab, in the Controls group, click the **More** button, and then click the **Line** tool ◺.

7. In the Page Header section, position the plus symbol of the Line tool pointer approximately two grid dots below the column header boxes, press and hold the **Shift key**, drag to the right page margin, and then release the **Shift** key to create a horizontal line that spans the width of the page. Holding the Shift key while drawing or extending a line snaps the line to either horizontal or vertical—whichever is nearest to the angle at which the line is drawn.

8. If necessary, drag the lower edge of the Page Header section up so it is approximately two grid dots below the line. See Figure 7-11.

Figure 7-11   Modified report in Design view

right-aligned page number and Reason control boxes; page number will now appear within the right page margin

9. Save your report changes, switch to Print Preview, and then scroll and use the navigation buttons to page through the report, paying particular attention to the placement of the line in the Page Header section and the page number in the Page Footer section. The page number is right-aligned in the control box, so the text appears flush with the right margin. The data in the Reason field value text boxes are left-aligned, so this data does not appear flush with the right margin.

Trouble? If you resize a field to position it outside the current margin, the report may widen to accommodate it, triggering a dialog box about the section width being greater than the page width. If this dialog box opens, click OK, manually move form elements as necessary so that no elements extend past 7 inches, and then adjust the report width to 7 inches.

10. Save and close the report.

11. If you are not continuing on to the next session, close the CareCenter database.

Kimberly is happy with the changes you've made to the rptVisitsAndInvoices report. In the next session, you create a new custom report for her based on queries instead of tables.

Session 7.1 Quick Check

1. What is a custom report?

2. Can a report be modified in Layout view?

3. Besides viewing a report, what other actions can you perform in Report view?

4. What is a grouping field?

5. List and describe the seven sections of an Access report.

Session 7.2 Visual Overview:

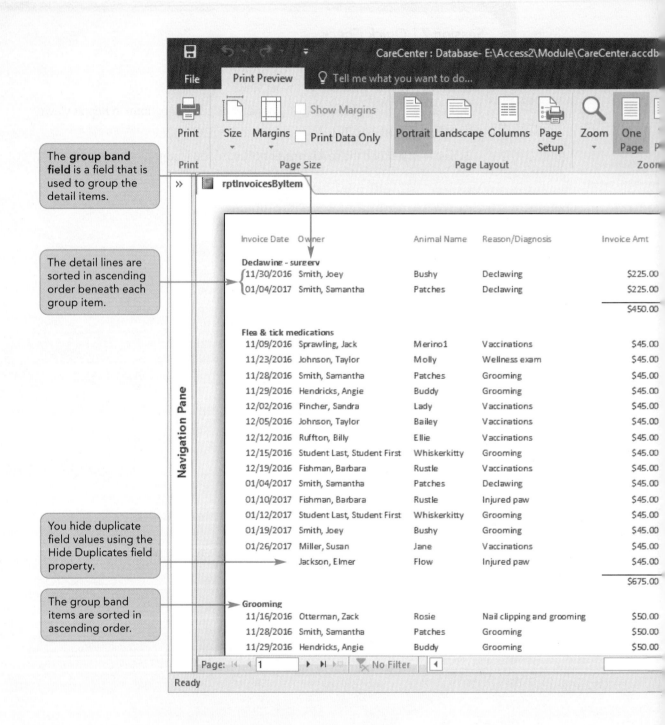

The **group band field** is a field that is used to group the detail items.

The detail lines are sorted in ascending order beneath each group item.

You hide duplicate field values using the Hide Duplicates field property.

The group band items are sorted in ascending order.

CareCenter : Database- E:\Access2\Module\CareCenter.accdb

File   Print Preview   ♀ Tell me what you want to do...

Print   Size   Margins   ☐ Show Margins   Portrait   Landscape   Columns   Page Setup   Zoom   One Page

☐ Print Data Only

Print | Page Size | Page Layout | Zoom

rptInvoicesByItem

Navigation Pane

Invoice Date	Owner	Animal Name	Reason/Diagnosis	Invoice Amt
Declawing - surgery				
11/30/2016	Smith, Joey	Bushy	Declawing	$225.00
01/04/2017	Smith, Samantha	Patches	Declawing	$225.00
				$450.00
Flea & tick medications				
11/09/2016	Sprawling, Jack	Merino1	Vaccinations	$45.00
11/23/2016	Johnson, Taylor	Molly	Wellness exam	$45.00
11/28/2016	Smith, Samantha	Patches	Grooming	$45.00
11/29/2016	Hendricks, Angie	Buddy	Grooming	$45.00
12/02/2016	Pincher, Sandra	Lady	Vaccinations	$45.00
12/05/2016	Johnson, Taylor	Bailey	Vaccinations	$45.00
12/12/2016	Ruffton, Billy	Ellie	Vaccinations	$45.00
12/15/2016	Student Last, Student First	Whiskerkitty	Grooming	$45.00
12/19/2016	Fishman, Barbara	Rustle	Vaccinations	$45.00
01/04/2017	Smith, Samantha	Patches	Declawing	$45.00
01/10/2017	Fishman, Barbara	Rustle	Injured paw	$45.00
01/12/2017	Student Last, Student First	Whiskerkitty	Grooming	$45.00
01/19/2017	Smith, Joey	Bushy	Grooming	$45.00
01/26/2017	Miller, Susan	Jane	Vaccinations	$45.00
	Jackson, Elmer	Flow	Injured paw	$45.00
				$675.00
Grooming				
11/16/2016	Otterman, Zack	Rosie	Nail clipping and grooming	$50.00
11/28/2016	Smith, Samantha	Patches	Grooming	$50.00
11/29/2016	Hendricks, Angie	Buddy	Grooming	$50.00

Page: ◄ 1 ► ►| ▼ No Filter   ◄

Ready

Custom Report in Print Preview

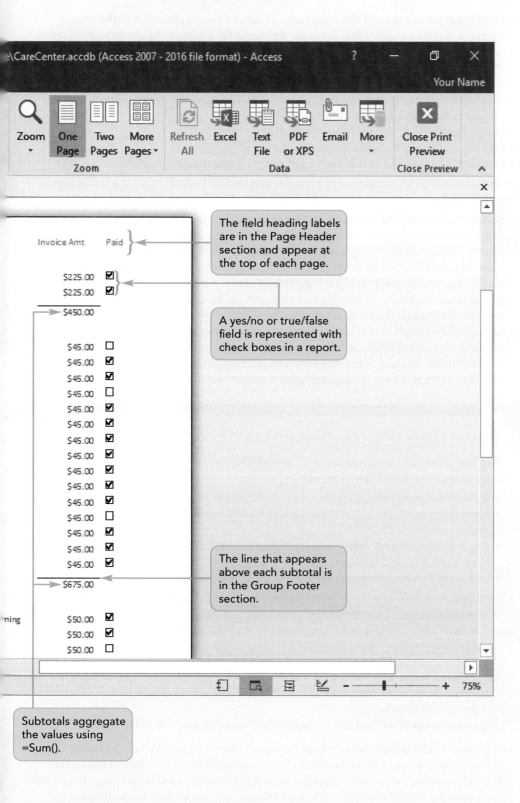

CareCenter.accdb (Access 2007 - 2016 file format) - Access

Your Name

Zoom	One Page	Two Pages	More Pages	Refresh All	Excel	Text File	PDF or XPS	Email	More	Close Print Preview
	Zoom					Data				Close Preview

75%

The field heading labels are in the Page Header section and appear at the top of each page.

A yes/no or true/false field is represented with check boxes in a report.

The line that appears above each subtotal is in the Group Footer section.

Subtotals aggregate the values using =Sum().

Invoice Amt   Paid

$225.00 ☑
$225.00 ☑
$450.00
$45.00 ☐
$45.00 ☑
$45.00 ☑
$45.00 ☐
$45.00 ☑
$45.00 ☑
$45.00 ☑
$45.00 ☑
$45.00 ☑
$45.00 ☑
$45.00 ☑
$45.00 ☐
$45.00 ☑
$45.00 ☑
$45.00 ☑
$675.00

ning
$50.00 ☑
$50.00 ☑
$50.00 ☐

Planning and Designing a Custom Report

Before you create a custom report, you should first plan the report's contents and its layout. When you plan a report, you should follow this general process:

- Determine the purpose of the report and its record source. Recall that the record source is a table or query that provides the fields for a report. If the report displays detailed information (a **detail report**), such as a list of all visits, then the report will display fields from the record source in the Detail section. If the report displays only summary information (a **summary report**), such as total visits by city, then no detailed information appears; only grand totals and possibly subtotals appear based on calculations using fields from the record source.
- Determine the sort order for the information in the report.
- Identify any grouping fields in the report.
- Consider creating a sketch of the report design using pen and paper.

At the same time you are planning a report, you should keep in mind the following layout guidelines:

- Balance the report's attractiveness against its readability and economy. Keep in mind that an attractive, readable, two-page report is more economical than a report of three pages or more. Unlike forms, which usually display one record at a time in the main form, reports display multiple records. Instead of arranging fields vertically as you do in a form, you usually position fields horizontally across the page in a report. Typically, you set the detail lines to be single-spaced in a report. At the same time, make sure to include enough white space between columns so the values do not overlap or run together.
- Group related fields and position them in a meaningful, logical order. For example, position identifying fields, such as names and codes, on the left. Group together all location fields, such as street and city, and position them in their customary order.
- Identify each column of field values with a column heading label that names the field.

PROSKILLS

Written Communication: Formatting a Report

The formatting of a report impacts its readability. Keep in mind the following guidelines when formatting a report:

- Include the report title, page number, and date on every page of the report.
- Identify the end of a report either by displaying grand totals or an end-of-report message.
- Use only a few colors, fonts, and graphics to keep the report uncluttered and to keep the focus on the information.
- Use a consistent style for all reports in a database.

By following these report-formatting guidelines, you'll create reports that make it easier for users to conduct their daily business and to make better decisions.

After working with Kimberly and her staff to determine their requirements for a new report, Daksha prepared a design for a custom report to display invoices grouped by invoice item. Refer to the Session 7.2 Visual Overview, which details Daksha's custom report design in Print Preview.

The custom report will list the records for all invoices and will contain five sections:

- The Page Header section will contain the report title ("Invoices by Item") centered between the current date on the left and the page number on the right. A horizontal line will separate the column heading labels from the rest of the report page. From your work with the Report tool and the Report Wizard, you know that, by default, Access places the report title in the Report Header section and the date and page number in the Page Footer section. Kimberly prefers that the date, report title, and page number appear at the top of each page, so you need to place this information in the custom report's Page Header section.

- The InvoiceItemDesc field value from the tblInvoiceItem table will be displayed in a Group Header section.
- The Detail section will contain the InvoiceDate, InvoiceAmt, and InvoicePaid field values from the tblBilling table; the Reason field value from the tblVisit table; the AnimalName field value from the tblAnimal table; and the Owner calculated field value from the qryOwnersByName query. The detail records will be sorted in ascending order by the InvoiceDate field.
- A subtotal of the InvoiceAmt field values will be displayed below a line in the Group Footer section.
- The grand total of the InvoiceAmt field values will be displayed below a double line in the Report Footer section.

Before you start creating the custom report, you need to create a query that will serve as the record source for the report.

Creating a Query for a Custom Report

As you know, the data for a report can come from a single table, from a single query based on one or more tables, or from multiple tables and/or queries. Kimberly's report will contain data from the tblInvoiceItem, tblBilling, tblVisit, and tblAnimal tables, and from the qryOwnersByName query. You'll use the Simple Query Wizard to create a query to retrieve all the data required for the custom report and to serve as the report's record source. A query filters data from one or more tables using criteria that can be quite complex. Creating a report based on a query allows you to display and distribute the results of the query in a readable, professional format, rather than only in a datasheet view.

To create the query to serve as the custom report's record source:

1. If you took a break after the previous session, make sure that the CareCenter database is open and the Navigation Pane is closed.

2. On the ribbon, click the **Create** tab.

3. In the Queries group, click the **Query Wizard** button to open the New Query dialog box, make sure **Simple Query Wizard** is selected, and then click the **OK** button. The first Simple Query Wizard dialog box opens.

   You need to select fields from the tblInvoiceItem, tblBilling, tblVisit, and tblAnimal tables and from the qryOwnersByName query, in that order.

4. In the Tables/Queries box, select **Table: tblInvoiceItem**, and then move the **InvoiceItemDesc** field from the Available Fields box to the Selected Fields box.

5. In the Tables/Queries box, select **Table: tblBilling**, and then move the **InvoiceItemID**, **InvoiceDate**, **InvoiceAmt**, and **InvoicePaid** fields, in that order, from the Available Fields box to the Selected Fields box.

6. In the Tables/Queries box, select **Table: tblVisit**, and then move the **Reason** field from the Available Fields box to the Selected Fields box.

7. In the Tables/Queries box, select **Table: tblAnimal**, and then move the **AnimalName** field from the Available Fields box to the Selected Fields box.

8. In the Tables/Queries box, select **Query: qryOwnersByName**, move the **Owner** calculated field from the Available Fields box to the Selected Fields box, and then click the **Next** button.

▶ **9.** Make sure the **Detail (shows every field of every record)** option button is selected, and then click the **Next** button to open the final Simple Query Wizard dialog box.

▶ **10.** Change the query name to **qryInvoicesByItem**, click the **Modify the query design** option button, and then click the **Finish** button. The query is displayed in Design view.

Next you need to set the sort fields for the query. The InvoiceItemDesc field will be a grouping field, which means it's the primary sort field, and the InvoiceDate field is the secondary sort field.

To set the sort fields for the query:

▶ **1.** In the design grid, set the value in the InvoiceItemDesc Sort box to **Ascending** and then set the value in the InvoiceDate Sort box to **Ascending**.

▶ **2.** Lengthen the query and table field lists as necessary to view all fields, drag the tables if necessary to position them so the join lines between them are visible, and then save your query changes. The completed query contains eight fields from four tables and one query, and the query includes two sort fields, the InvoiceItemDesc primary sort field and the InvoiceDate secondary sort field. See Figure 7-12.

Figure 7-12	Completed qryInvoicesByItem query in Design View

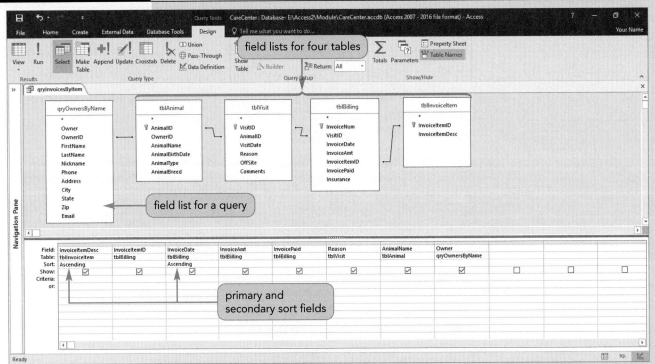

Before closing the query, you'll run it to view the query recordset.

▶ **3.** If necessary, click the **Query Tools Design** tab, run the query, verify that it returns 202 records, and then save and close the query.

You'll use the qryInvoicesByItem query as the record source for the custom report.

Creating a Custom Report

Now that you've created the record source for the custom report, you could use the Report Wizard to create the report and then modify it to match the report design. However, because you need to customize several components of the report, you will create a custom report in Layout view and then switch between Layout and Design view to fine-tune the report.

Making Report Design Modifications

You perform operations in Layout and Design views for reports in the same way that you perform operations in these views for forms. These operations become easier with practice. Remember to use the Undo button when necessary, back up your database frequently, save your report changes frequently, work from a copy of the report for complicated design changes, and compact and repair the database on a regular basis. You can also display the report in Print Preview at any time to view your progress on the report.

You'll create a blank report in Layout view, set the record source, and then add controls to the custom report.

To create a blank report and add bound controls in Layout view:

1. Click the **Create** tab, and then in the Reports group, click the **Blank Report** button. A new report opens in Layout view, with the Field List pane open, and the Report Layout Tools Design tab active on the ribbon. See Figure 7-13.

Figure 7-13	Blank report in Layout view

2. In the Tools group, click the **Property Sheet** button to open the Property Sheet for the report.

3. In the Property Sheet, click the **All** tab (if necessary), click the **Record Source** arrow, click **qryInvoicesByItem**, and then close the Property Sheet.

4. In the Tools group, click the **Add Existing Fields** button to open the Field List pane. The Field List pane displays the eight fields in the qryInvoicesByItem query, which is the record source for the report.

   Referring to Daksha's report design, you'll add six of the eight fields to the report in a tabular layout, which is the default control layout when you add fields to a report in Layout view.

5. In the Field List pane, double-click **InvoiceDate**, and then, in order, double-click **Owner**, **AnimalName**, **Reason**, **InvoiceAmt**, and **InvoicePaid** in the Field List pane. The six bound controls are displayed in a tabular layout in the report. See Figure 7-14.

| Figure 7-14 | Fields added to the report in Layout view |

Trouble? If you add the wrong field to the report, click the field's column heading, press and hold the Shift key, click one of the field values in the column to select the column, release the Shift key, click the Home tab on the ribbon, and then in the Records group, click the Delete button to delete the field. If you add a field in the wrong order, click the column heading in the tabular layout, press and hold the Shift key, click one of the field values in the column, release the Shift key, and then drag the column to its correct position.

Later, you'll add the sixth field, the InvoiceItemDesc field, as a grouping field; for now you are done working with the Field List pane.

6. Close the Field List pane, and then save the report as **rptInvoicesByItem**.

Next, you'll adjust the column widths in Layout view. Also, because the Invoice Amt and Invoice Paid columns are adjacent, you'll change the rightmost column heading to "Paid" to save space.

To resize and rename columns in Layout view:

1. In the right-most column, double-click **Invoice Paid**, delete **Invoice** and the following space, and then press the **Enter** key.

2. Drag the right border of the Paid column heading selection box to the left to decrease the column's width so it just fits the column heading.

3. Click the **Owner** column heading to select the column, and then drag the right edge of the selection box to the right to increase its width, until it accommodates the contents of all data in the column. (You might need to scroll through the report to ensure all Owner field values are visible.)

4. Repeat Step 3 to resize the Animal Name and Reason columns, if necessary, as shown in Figure 7-15. (Note that Whiskerkitty is the longest animal name in the database.) You'll fine-tune the adjustments and the spacing between columns later in Design view.

Figure 7-15 **Resized and renamed columns in Layout view**

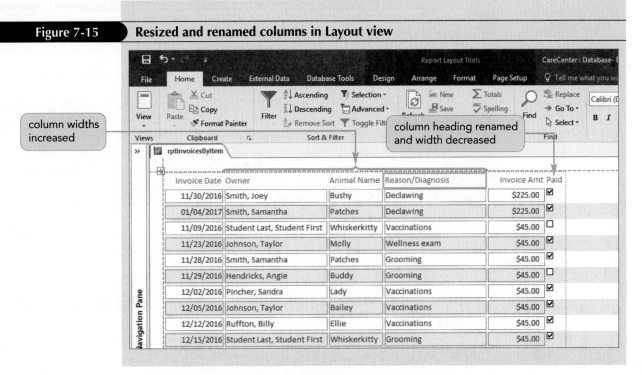

Next you need to add the sorting and grouping data to the report.

Sorting and Grouping Data in a Report

In Access, you can organize records in a report by sorting them using one or more sort fields. Each sort field can also be a grouping field. If you specify a sort field as a grouping field, you can include a Group Header section and a Group Footer section for the group. A Group Header section typically includes the name of the group, and a Group Footer section typically includes a count or subtotal for records in that group. Some reports have a Group Header section but not a Group Footer section, some reports have a Group Footer section but not a Group Header section, and some reports have both sections or have neither section.

You use the Group, Sort, and Total pane to select sort fields and grouping fields for a report. Each report can have up to 10 sort fields, and any of its sort fields can also be grouping fields.

In Daksha's report design, the InvoiceItemDesc field is a grouping field, and the InvoiceDate field is a sort field. The InvoiceItemDesc field value is displayed in a Group Header section, but the InvoiceItemDesc field label is not displayed. The sum of the InvoiceAmt field values is displayed in the Group Footer section for the InvoiceItemDesc grouping field.

Sorting and Grouping Data in a Report

- Display the report in Layout view or Design view.
- If necessary, on the Design tab, click the Group & Sort button in the Grouping & Totals group to display the Group, Sort, and Total pane.
- To select a grouping field, click the Add a group button in the Group, Sort, and Total pane, and then click the grouping field in the list. To set additional properties for the grouping field, click the More button on the group field band.
- To select a sort field that is not a grouping field, click the Add a sort button in the Group, Sort, and Total pane, and then click the sort field in the list. To set additional properties for the sort field, click the More button on the sort field band.

Next, in the report, you'll select the grouping field and the sort field and set their properties.

To select and set the properties for the grouping field and the sort field:

1. On the Report Layout Tools Design tab, in the Grouping & Totals group, click the **Group & Sort** button to open the Group, Sort, and Total pane at the bottom of the Report window.

2. In the Group, Sort, and Total pane, click the **Add a group** button, and then click **InvoiceItemDesc** in the list. A Group Header section is added to the report with InvoiceItem as the grouping field, and group band options appear in the Group, Sort, and Total pane for this section. See Figure 7-16.

Figure 7-16	The InvoiceItemDesc as a grouping field in Layout view

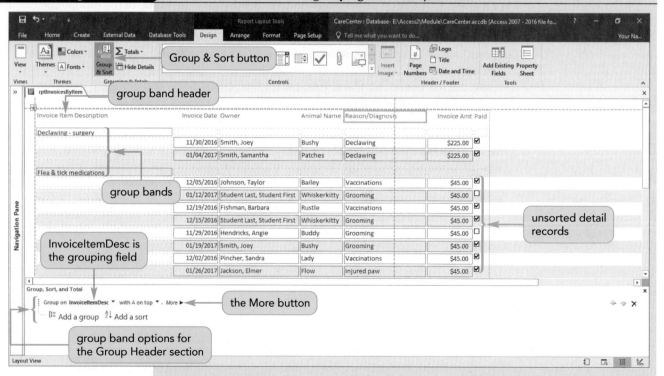

InvoiceItemDesc is now a bound control in the report in a Group Header section that displays a field value box. The group band options in the Group, Sort, and Total pane contain the name of the grouping field (InvoiceItem), the sort order ("with A on top" to indicate ascending), and the More button, which you click to display more options for the grouping field. You can click the "with A on top" arrow to change to descending sort order ("with Z on top").

Notice that the addition of the grouping field has moved the detail records to the right; you'll move them back to the left later in this module. Also, notice that the detail records are unsorted, but Daksha's design specifies an ascending sort on the InvoiceDate field. Next, you'll select this field as a secondary sort field; the InvoiceItem grouping field is the primary sort field.

3. In the Group, Sort, and Total pane, click the **Add a sort** button, and then click **InvoiceDate** in the list. The detail records appear in ascending order by InvoiceDate, and a sort band is added for the InvoiceDate field in the Group, Sort, and Total pane.

Next, you'll display all the options for the InvoiceItemDesc group band field and set group band options as shown in Daksha's report design.

4. In the Group, Sort, and Total pane, click the **Group on InvoiceItemDesc (InvoiceItemDesc)**, and then click the **More** button to display all group band options in an orange bar at the top of the Group, Sort, and Total pane. See Figure 7-17. Next, you need to delete the Invoice Item label.

Figure 7-17	Expanded group band

5. In the "with title Invoice Item Description" option, click the **Invoice Item Description** link to open the Zoom dialog box, press the **Delete** key to delete the expression, and then click the **OK** button. The Invoice Item label is deleted from the report, and the option in the group band options changes to "with title click to add."

Next you'll set the Keep Together property. The **Keep Together property** prints a group header on a page only if there is enough room on the page to print the first detail record for the group; otherwise, the group header prints at the top of the next page.

6. In the group band options, click the **do not keep group together on one page** arrow, and then click **keep header and first record together on one page**.

7. In the group band options, click the **More** button to expand the options (if necessary), click the **without a footer section** arrow, and then click **with a footer section**. A Group Footer section is added to the report for the InvoiceItem grouping band field, but the report will not display this new section until you add controls to it.

8. In the group band options, click the **More** button to expand the options (if necessary), click the **with no totals** arrow to open the Totals menu, click the **Total On** arrow, click **InvoiceAmt**, make sure **Sum** is selected in the Type box, and then click the **Show Grand Total** check box.

9. In the group band options, click the **More** button to expand the options (if necessary), click the **with InvoiceAmt totaled** arrow, click the **Total On** arrow, click **InvoiceAmt**, and then click the **Show subtotal in group footer** check box. This adds subtotals in the Amount column, at the bottom of each group.

10. In the group band options, click the **More** button to expand the options (if necessary). The group band options show the InvoiceAmt subtotals, and a grand total added to the report. See Figure 7-18.

Figure 7-18	Completed properties in the group band

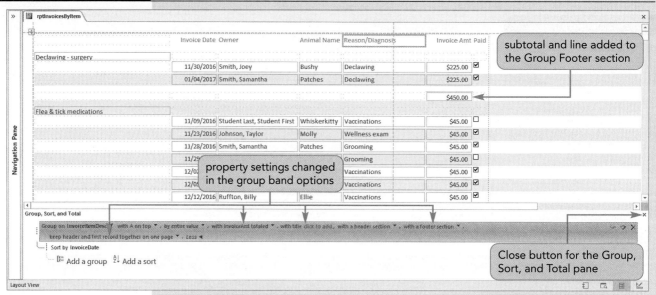

11. Save your report changes, switch to Print Preview, and then use the navigation buttons to review each page until you reach the end of the report—noticing in particular the details of the report format and the effects of the Keep Together property. Also, notice that because the grouping field forces the detail values to the right, the current report design prints the detail values across two pages.

Before you can move the detail values to the left onto one page, you need to remove all controls from the control layout.

To remove controls from a control layout in Layout view:

▶ **1.** Switch to Layout view.

▶ **2.** Click the layout selector ⊞, which is located at the top-left corner of the column heading line, to select the entire control layout. An orange selection border, which identifies the controls that you've selected, appears around the labels and field value boxes in the report, and a yellow outline appears around the other controls in the report.

▶ **3.** Right-click one of the selected controls to open the shortcut menu, point to **Layout**, and then click **Remove Layout**. This removes the selected controls from the layout so they can be moved individually without affecting the other controls.

   Next you'll move all the controls to the left except for the InvoiceItemDesc field value box. You have to be careful when you move the remaining controls to the left. If you try to select all the column headings and the field value boxes, you're likely to miss the subtotal and grand total controls. The safest technique is to select all controls in the report, and then remove the InvoiceItemDesc field value box from the selection. This latter step, removing individual controls from a selection, must be done in Design view.

▶ **4.** Switch to Design view, click the **Report Design Tools Format** tab, and then in the Selection group, click the **Select All** button. All controls in the report are now selected.

▶ **5.** Press and hold the **Shift** key, click the **InvoiceItemDesc** control box in the InvoiceItemDesc Header section to remove this control from the selection, and then release the **Shift** key.

▶ **6.** Press and hold the ← key to move the selected controls rapidly to the left edge of the report, and then release the ← key. See Figure 7-19.

Figure 7-19	All controls repositioned in the report

Select All button

selected form controls moved to the left

InvoiceItemDesc text box is not selected

The grand total of the InvoiceAmt field values is displayed at the end of the report, and subtotals are displayed for each unique InvoiceItemDesc field value in the Group Footer section. It's possible for subtotals to appear in an orphaned footer section. An **orphaned footer section** appears by itself at the top of a page, and the detail lines for the section appear on the previous page. When you set the Keep Together property for the grouping field, you set it to keep the group and the first detail record together on one page to prevent an **orphaned header section**, which is a section that appears by itself at the bottom of a page. To prevent both types of orphaned sections, you'll set the Keep Together property to keep the whole group together on one page.

In addition, you need to fine-tune the sizes of the field value boxes in the Detail section, adjust the spacing between columns, and make other adjustments to the current content of the report design before adding a report title, the date, and page number to the Page Header section. You'll make most of these report design changes in Design view.

Working with Controls in Design View

As you learned when working with forms, Design view gives you greater control over the placement and sizing of controls than you have in Layout view and lets you add and manipulate many more controls; however, this power comes at the expense of not being able to see live data in the controls to guide you as you make changes.

The rptInvoicesByItem report has five sections that contain controls: the Page Header section contains the six column heading labels; the InvoiceItem Header section (a Group Header section) contains the InvoiceItemDesc field value box; the Detail section contains the six bound controls; the InvoiceItem Footer section (a Group Footer section) contains a line and the subtotal control; and the Report Footer section contains a line and the grand total control.

You'll format, move, and resize controls in the report in Design view. The Group, Sort, and Total pane is still open, so first you'll change the Keep Together property setting.

To change the Keep Together property:

▶ **1.** In the Group, Sort, and Total pane, click the **More** button to display all group options.

▶ **2.** Click the **keep header and first record together on one page** arrow, and then click **keep whole group together on one page**.

▶ **3.** Click the **Close** button ☒ in the top-right corner of the Group, Sort, and Total pane to close it.

You'll start improving the report by setting the InvoiceItemDesc label control to bold and then resize the report so it fits on an 8.5-inch-wide page.

To apply bold to a label control and resize the report:

TIP
To copy formatting from one control to another, select the control whose format you wish to copy, click the Format Painter tool on the Form Design Tools Format tab, and then click another control to apply the copied formatting.

▶ **1.** Click the **InvoiceItemDesc** control box in the InvoiceItemDesc Header section, and then on the Report Design Tools Format tab, in the Font group, click the **Bold** button. The placeholder text in the InvoiceItemDesc control box is displayed in bold.

When you bolded the font in the InvoiceItemDesc control box, you increased the size of the characters. You need to increase the height of the control box to fully display all characters.

2. Click the **InvoiceItemDesc** control box, and then increase the height of the control box from the top by one row of grid dots.

The report's width is approximately 16 inches, which is much wider than the width of the contents of the report, so you'll reduce its width to fit a page that is 8.5 inches wide with narrow margins.

3. Click the **Report Design Tools Page Setup** tab, click the **Margins** button, and then click **Narrow**, if necessary.

4. Scroll to the right until you see the right edge of the report (where the dotted grid ends), position the pointer over the right edge of the report until it changes to ↔, drag to the left to the 8-inch mark on the horizontal ruler, and then drag the horizontal scroll box all the way to the left to display the entire report. See Figure 7-20.

| Figure 7-20 | Width of the report reduced |

The field value control boxes in the Detail section are crowded together with little space between them. Your reports shouldn't have too much space between columns, but reports are easier to read when the columns are separated more than they are in the rptInvoicesByItem report. Sometimes the amount of spacing is dictated by the users of the report, but you also need to work with the minimum size of the form controls as well. To design this report to fit on a page with narrow margins, the report width will have to be 8.5 inches minus the left and right margins of 0.25 inches each, which results in a maximum report width of 8 inches (8.5"–0.25"–0.25"). This is the size you already used to reduce the report grid in Design view. Next, you'll add some space between the columns while ensuring they still fit in the 8-inch report width. First, you'll resize the Invoice Date and Owner columns in Layout view, and then you'll arrange the columns in Design view. You'll size the corresponding heading and field value boxes for each column to be the same width.

To move and resize controls in the report:

1. Switch to Layout view, click the **Invoice Date** column heading, press and hold the **Shift** key, and then click one of the **Invoice Date** field values to select all of the Invoice Date field value boxes.

2. Drag the right side of the controls to the left to reduce the size of the field value boxes to fit the data better.

TIP

You can resize labels and controls added with the Label tool using the To Fit command, but you can't resize field value boxes using the To Fit method.

3. Repeat Steps 1 and 2 for the Owner column heading and field values to reduce their widths to fit the data better, if necessary.

Next you'll adjust the spacing between the controls to distribute them evenly across the page.

4. Switch to Design view, click the **Report Design Tools Format** tab, and then in the Selection group, click the **Select All** button to select all controls.

5. Press and hold the **Shift** key, and click the **InvoiceItemDesc** control to deselect it.

6. On the ribbon, click the **Report Design Tools Arrange** tab.

7. In the Sizing & Ordering group, click the **Size/Space** button, and then click **Equal Horizontal**. The form controls are shifted horizontally so the spacing between them is equal. See Figure 7-21.

Figure 7-21	Equal horizontal spacing applied to controls in Design view

The Owner and Reason field value boxes may not be wide enough to display the entire field value in all cases. For the Owner and Reason field value boxes, you'll set their Can Grow property to Yes. The **Can Grow property**, when set to Yes, expands a field value box vertically to fit the field value when the report is printed, previewed, or viewed in Layout and Report views.

TIP

You can select two or more controls, and then set common properties for the selected controls, instead of setting them one control at a time.

8. Click the **Report Design Tools Design** tab, click the **Report Selector** button to deselect all controls, select the **Owner** and **Reason** field value control boxes in the Detail section, right-click one of the selected controls, and then on the shortcut menu click **Properties**.

9. On the Property Sheet, click the **Format** tab, scroll down the Property Sheet to locate the Can Grow property, and then if the Can Grow property is set to Yes, set it to **No**. The default setting for this feature may not work properly, so to ensure the setting is applied correctly, you must make sure it is first set to No.

Trouble? If you don't see the Can Grow property on the Format tab, double-check to ensure you've selected the Owner and Reason controls in the Detail section, not in the Page Header section.

10. Change the Can Grow property value to **Yes**, close the Property Sheet, and then save your report changes.

11. Switch to Print Preview, and then review every page of the report, ending on the last page. See Figure 7-22.

Figure 7-22   The report changes in Print Preview

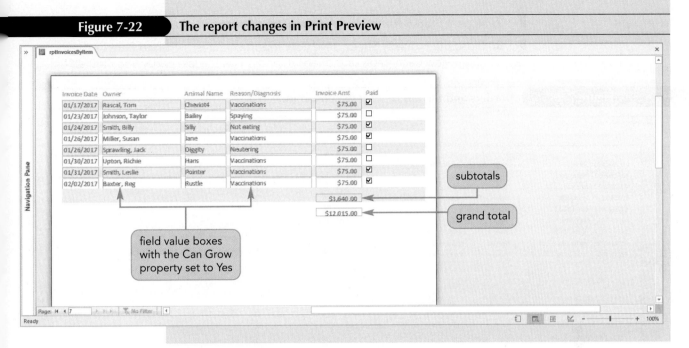

Figure 7-22   The report changes in Print Preview

The groups stay together on one page, except for the groups that have too many detail lines to fit on one page. If necessary, the Can Grow property would expand the height of the Owner and Reason field value boxes.

Also, the lines that were displayed above the subtotals and grand total are no longer displayed, and the commas in the values are not fully visible. You'll add the totals lines back in the report and resize the field value boxes for the totals. First, Daksha thinks the borders around the field value boxes and the alternate row color are too distracting, so you'll remove them from the report.

To remove the borders and alternate row color:

1. Switch to Design view.

2. Click the **Report Design Tools Format tab**, and then in the Selection group, click the **Select All** button.

3. Right-click one of the selected controls, and then click **Properties** on the shortcut menu to open the Property Sheet.

4. Click the **Format** tab (if necessary) in the Property Sheet, click the right side of the Border Style box, and then click **Transparent**. The transparent setting removes the borders from the report by making them transparent.

5. Click the **InvoiceItemDesc Header** section bar, click the right side of the **Alternate Back Color** box in the Property Sheet, and then click **No Color** at the bottom of the gallery. This setting removes the alternate row color from the InvoiceItem Header section. You can also control the Alternate Back Color property using the Alternate Row Color button in the Background group on the Format tab, because the two options set the same property.

6. Click the **Detail** section bar, in the Background group, click the **Alternate Row Color button arrow**, and then click **No Color** at the bottom of the gallery. The Alternate Back Color property setting in the Property Sheet is now set to No Color.

7. Repeat Step 6 for the **InvoiceItemDesc Footer** section.

8. Close the Property Sheet, save your report changes, switch to Print Preview, and review each page of the report, ending on the last page. See Figure 7-23.

Figure 7-23 **Borders and the alternate row color removed**

You still need to resize the subtotal and grand total field value boxes so that the comma separators fully display. In addition, you'll add lines to separate the values from the subtotals and grand total.

To resize the subtotals and grand totals field value boxes and add totals lines to the report:

1. Switch to Design view.

2. In the InvoiceItemDesc Footer section, click the calculated control box to select it, and then drag the upper-right sizing handle up to increase its height by one row of grid dots.

3. Repeat Step 2 to resize the calculated control box in the Report Footer section.

4. On the Report Design Tools Design tab, in the Controls group, click the **More** button to open the Controls gallery.

5. Click the **Line** tool , position the Line tool pointer's plus symbol in the InvoiceItemDesc Footer section in the upper-left corner of the calculated control box, press and hold the **Shift** key, drag from left to right so the line aligns with the top border of the calculated control box and ends at the upper-right corner of the calculated control box, release the mouse button, and then release the **Shift** key.

6. In the Report Footer section, click the calculated control box, press the ↓ key two times to move the control down slightly in the section, and then deselect all controls.

7. In the Controls group, click the **More** button, click the **Line** tool 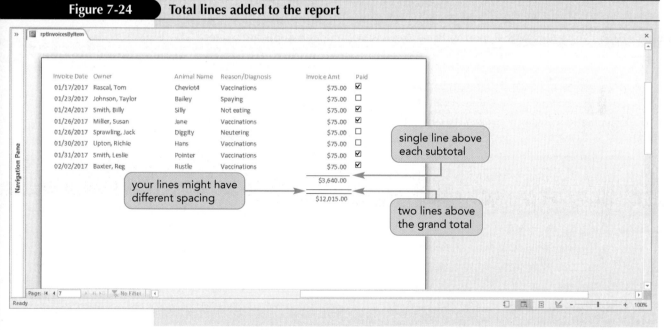, position the pointer's plus symbol in the upper-left corner of the calculated control box, press and hold the **Shift** key, drag left to right so the line aligns with the top border of the calculated control box and ends at the upper-right corner of the calculated control box, release the mouse button, and then release the **Shift** key.

   The grand total line should have two lines separating it from the rest of the report. Next, you'll copy and paste the line you just created in the Report Footer section, and then align the copied line into position.

8. Right-click the selected line in the Report Footer section, and then click **Copy** on the shortcut menu.

9. Right-click the **Report Footer** section bar, and then click **Paste** on the shortcut menu. A copy of the line is pasted in the upper-left corner of the Report Footer section.

10. Press the ↓ key two times to move the copied line down in the section, press and hold the **Shift** key, click the first line in the Report Footer section to select both lines, and then release the **Shift** key.

11. Right-click the selected lines to open the shortcut menu, point to **Align**, and then click **Right**. A double line is now positioned above the grand total box.

12. Save your report changes, switch to Print Preview, and then navigate to the last page of the report. See Figure 7-24.

Figure 7-24   **Total lines added to the report**

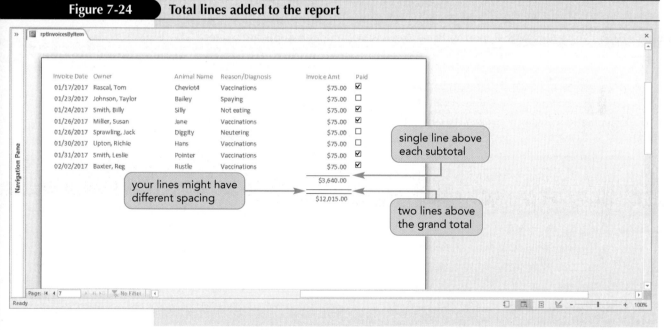

Your next design change to the report is to hide duplicate InvoiceDate field values in the Detail section. This change will make the report easier to read.

Hiding Duplicate Values in a Report

You use the **Hide Duplicates property** to hide a control in a report when the control's value is the same as that of the preceding record in the group. You should use the Hide Duplicates property only on fields that are sorted. Otherwise it may look as if data is missing.

For the rptInvoicesByItem report, the InvoiceDate field is a sort field. Two or more consecutive detail report lines can have the same InvoiceDate field value. In these cases, Daksha wants the InvoiceDate field value to appear for the first detail line but not for subsequent detail lines because he believes it makes the printed information easier to read.

To hide the duplicate InvoiceDate field values:

1. Switch to Design view, and then click a blank area of the screen to deselect all controls.

2. Open the Property Sheet for the InvoiceDate field value box in the Detail section.

3. Click the **Format** tab (if necessary), scroll down the Property Sheet, click the right side of the **Hide Duplicates** box, and then click **Yes**.

4. Close the Property Sheet, save your report changes, switch to Print Preview, navigate to page 1 (the actual page you view might vary, depending on your printer) to the Flea & tick medications group to see the two invoice records for 01/26/2017. The InvoiceDate field value does not display for the second of the two consecutive records with a 01/26/2017 date. See Figure 7-25.

> **TIP**
>
> For properties offering a list of choices, you can double-click the property name repeatedly to cycle through the option in the list.

Figure 7-25	Report in Print Preview with hidden duplicate values

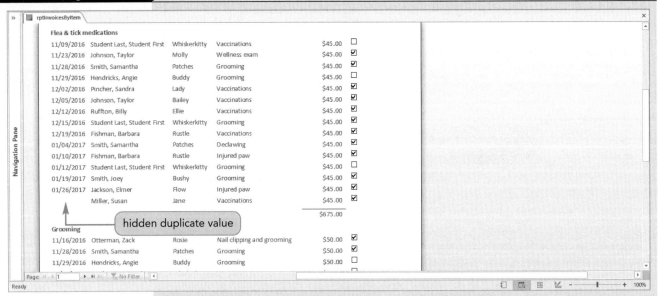

5. If you are not continuing on to the next session, close the CareCenter database.

You have completed the Detail section, the Group Header section, and the Group Footer section of the custom report. In the next session, you will complete the custom report according to Daksha's design by adding controls to the Page Header section.

Session 7.2 Quick Check

1. What is a detail report? A summary report?

2. The _____ property prints a group header on a page only if there is enough room on the page to print the first detail record for the group; otherwise, the group header prints at the top of the next page.

3. A(n) _____ section appears by itself at the top of a page, and the detail lines for the section appear on the previous page.

4. The _____ property, when set to Yes, expands a field value box vertically to fit the field value when a report is printed, previewed, or viewed in Layout and Report views.

5. Why might you want to hide duplicate values in a report?

Session 7.3 Visual Overview:

The content in the Report Header section appears at the top of the first page of the report. This Report Header section has a height of 0 and no content.

The **Date function** displays the current date.

The Group Footer section's content appears at the bottom of each group.

The Report Footer section's content appears at the bottom of the last page of the report.

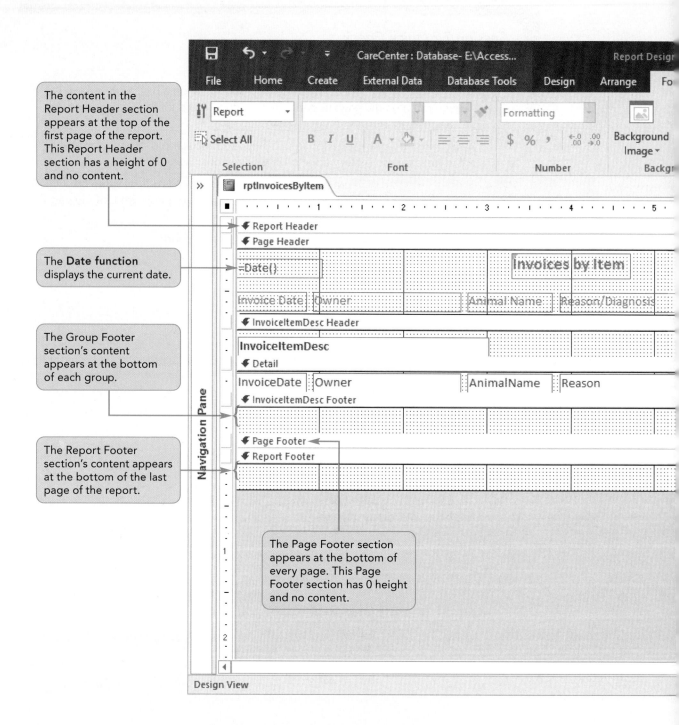

The Page Footer section appears at the bottom of every page. This Page Footer section has 0 height and no content.

Headers and Footers in Reports

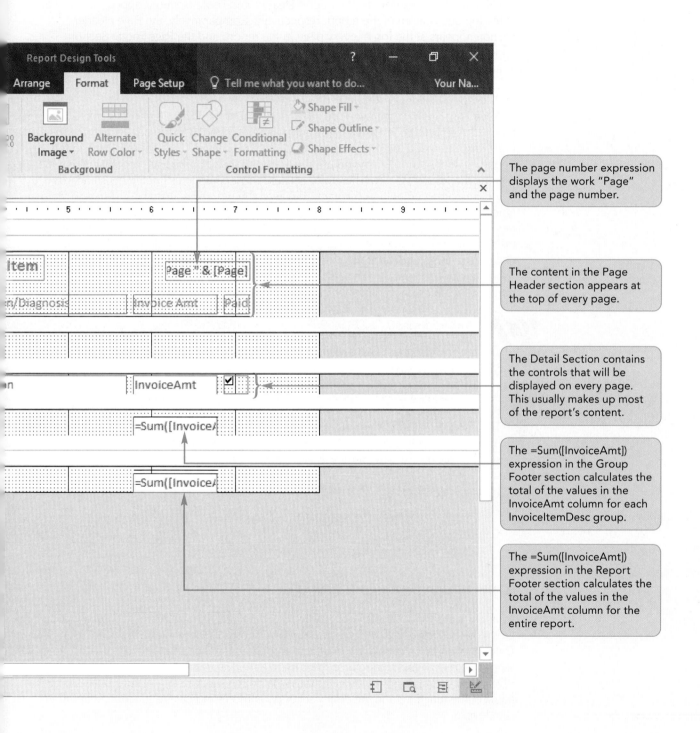

The page number expression displays the work "Page" and the page number.

The content in the Page Header section appears at the top of every page.

The Detail Section contains the controls that will be displayed on every page. This usually makes up most of the report's content.

The =Sum([InvoiceAmt]) expression in the Group Footer section calculates the total of the values in the InvoiceAmt column for each InvoiceItemDesc group.

The =Sum([InvoiceAmt]) expression in the Report Footer section calculates the total of the values in the InvoiceAmt column for the entire report.

Understanding Page Header and Page Footer Sections

Recall that in Access reports, the Report Header and Footer sections appear only once, at the top and bottom of the report, respectively. Comparatively, the Page Header Section appears at the top of every page in the report, and the Page Footer Section appears at the bottom of every page in the report. Therefore, if you want any information to appear consistently on every page in a multipage report, you want to place that information in the Page Header or the Page Footer sections of the report, as opposed to in the Report Header or Report Footer sections.

Keep in mind that when you use the Report tool or the Report Wizard to create a report, the report title is by default displayed in the Report Header section, and the page number is displayed in the Page Footer section. The date and time are displayed in the Report Header section when you use the Report tool and in the Page Footer section when you use the Report Wizard. Therefore, because most companies implement standard report-formatting guidelines that require that all the reports in a database display certain types of controls in consistent positions, you might have to move the date control for reports created by the Report tool or by the Report Wizard so the date is displayed in the same section for all reports. For example, at the Riverview Veterinary Care Center, Daksha's recommendations are that all reports, including the rptInvoicesByItem report, should include the date in the Page Header section, along with the report title, the page number, the column heading labels, and a line below the labels.

Decision Making: Determining Effective Content for the Page Header Section in Reports

Although company standards vary, a common standard for multipage reports places the report title, date, and page number on the same line in the Page Header section. This ensures this critical information appears on every page in the report. For example, placing the report title in the Page Header section, instead of in the Report Header section, allows users to identify the report name on any page without having to turn to the first page. Also, using one line to include this information in the Page Header section saves vertical space in the report compared to placing some of these controls in the Page Header section and others in the Page Footer section.

When you develop reports with a consistent format, the report users become more productive and more confident working with the information in the reports.

Adding the Date to a Report

To add the date to a report, you can click the Date and Time button in the Header/Footer group on the Report Layout Tools or Report Design Tools Design tab. Doing so inserts the Date function in a control (without a corresponding label control) in the Report Header section. The Date function returns the current date. The format of the Date function is =Date(). The equal sign (=) indicates that what follows it is an expression; *Date* is the name of the function; and the empty set of parentheses indicates a function rather than simple text.

Adding the Date and Time to a Report

- Display the report in Layout or Design view.
- In Design view or in Layout view, on the Design tab, in the Header/Footer group, click the Date and Time button to open the Date and Time dialog box.
- To display the date, click the Include Date check box, and then click one of the three date option buttons.
- To display the time, click the Include Time check box, and then click one of the three time option buttons.
- Click the OK button.

In Daksha's design for the report, the date appears on the left side of the Page Header section. You'll add the date to the report and then cut the date from its default location in the Report Header section and paste it into the Page Header section. You can add the current date in Layout view or Design view. However, because you can't cut and paste controls between sections in Layout view, you'll add the date in Design view.

To add the date to the Page Header section:

1. If you took a break after the previous session, make sure that the CareCenter database is open, that the rptInvoicesByItem report is open in Design view, and that the Navigation Pane is closed.

   First, you'll move the column heading labels down in the Page Header section to make room for the controls you'll be adding above them.

2. In Design view, increase the height of the Page Header section by dragging the Page Header's bottom border down until the 1-inch mark on the vertical ruler appears.

3. Select all six label controls in the Page Header section, and then move the controls down until the tops of the label controls are at the 0.5-inch mark on the vertical ruler. You may find it easier to use the arrow keys, rather than the mouse, to position the label controls.

   Daksha's report design calls for a horizontal line below the labels. You'll add this line next.

4. On the Report Design Tools Design tab, in the Controls group, click the **More** button, click the **Line** tool ⬜, and then drag to create a horizontal line positioned one grid dot below the bottom border of the six label controls and spanning from the left edge of the Invoice Date label control and the right edge of the Paid label control.

5. Reduce the height of the Page Header section by dragging the bottom border of the section up until it touches the bottom of the line you just added.

6. In the Header/Footer group, click the **Date and Time** button to open the Date and Time dialog box, make sure the **Include Date** check box is checked and the **Include Time** check box is unchecked, and then click the third date format option button. See Figure 7-26.

Figure 7-26 **Completed Date and Time dialog box**

7. Click the **OK** button. The Date function control is added to the right side of the Report Header section.

8. Click the **Date function** control box, and then click the **layout selector** in the upper-left corner of the Report Header section. The Date function control box is part of a control layout with three additional empty control boxes. See Figure 7-27.

Figure 7-27 **Date function added to the Report Header section**

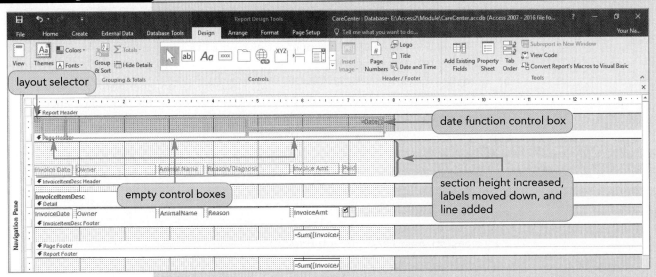

You need to remove these controls from the control layout before you work further with the Date function control box.

9. Right-click one of the selected control boxes, point to **Layout** on the shortcut menu, and then click **Remove Layout**. The three empty cells are deleted, and the Date function control box remains selected.

The default size for the Date function control box accommodates long dates and long times, so the control box is much wider than needed for the date that will appear in the custom report. You'll decrease its width and move it to the Page Header section.

▶ **10.** Drag the left border of the Date function control box to the right until it is 1 inch wide.

▶ **11.** Right-click the selected **Date function** control box to open the shortcut menu, click **Cut** to delete the control, right-click the **Page Header** section bar to select that section and open the shortcut menu, and then click **Paste**. The Date function control box is pasted in the upper-left corner of the Page Header section.

▶ **12.** Save your report changes, and then switch to Print Preview to view the date in the Page Header section. See Figure 7-28.

Figure 7-28 **Date in Page Header Section in Print Preview**

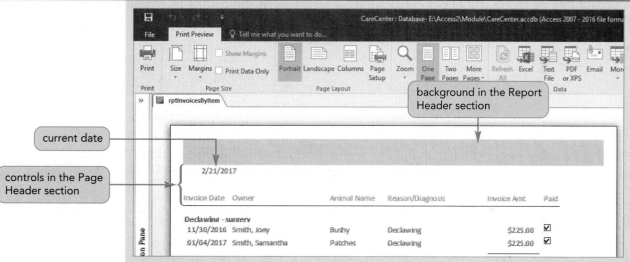

Trouble? Your year might appear with two digits instead of four digits as shown in Figure 7-28. Your date format might also differ, depending on your computer's date settings. These differences do not cause any problems.

Now that the date has been added to the Page Header section, you need to format and position it appropriately.

▶ **13.** Switch to Design view, make sure the **Date function** control box is still selected, click the **Report Design Tools Format** tab, and then in the Font group, click the **Align Left** button ≡.

If a report includes a control with the Date function, the current date will be displayed each time the report is run. If you instead want a specific date to appear each time the report is run, use a label control that contains the date, rather than the Date function.

You are now ready to add page numbers to the Page Header section. You'll also delete the empty Report Header section by decreasing its height to zero.

Adding Page Numbers to a Report

You can display page numbers in a report by including an expression in the Page Header or Page Footer section. In Report Layout Tools or Report Design Tools Design tab, you can click the Page Numbers button in the Header/Footer group to add a page number expression. The inserted page number expression automatically displays the correct page number on each page of a report.

REFERENCE

Adding Page Numbers to a Report

- Display the report in Layout or Design view.
- On the Design tab, click the Page Numbers button in the Header/Footer group to open the Page Numbers dialog box.
- Select the format, position, and alignment options you want.
- Select whether you want to display the page number on the first page.
- Click the OK button to place the page number expression in the report.

Daksha's design shows the page number displayed on the right side of the Page Header section, bottom-aligned with the date.

To add page numbers to the Page Header section:

1. In the Report Header section, drag the bottom border up to the top of the section so the section's height is reduced to zero.

2. Click the **Report Design Tools Design** tab, and then in the Header/Footer group, click the **Page Numbers** button. The Page Numbers dialog box opens.

   You use the Format options to specify the format of the page number. Daksha wants page numbers to appear as Page 1, Page 2, and so on. This is the "Page N" format option. You use the Position options to place the page numbers at the top of the page in the Page Header section or at the bottom of the page in the Page Footer section. Daksha's design shows page numbers at the top of the page.

3. In the Format section, make sure that the **Page N** option button is selected, and then in the Position section, make sure that the **Top of Page [Header]** option button is selected.

   The report design shows page numbers at the right side of the page. You can specify this placement in the Alignment box.

4. Click the **Alignment** arrow, and then click **Right**.

5. Make sure the **Show Number on First Page** check box is checked, so the page number prints on the first page and all other pages as well. See Figure 7-29.

Figure 7-29   Completed Page Numbers dialog box

6. Click the **OK** button. A control box containing the expression =*"Page " & [Page]* appears in the upper-right corner of the Page Header section. The expression =*"Page " & [Page]* in the control box means that the printed report will show the word "Page" followed by a space and the page number. The page number control box is much wider than needed for the page number expression that will appear in the custom report. You'll decrease its width.

7. Click the **Page Number** control box, decrease its width from the left until it is 1 inch wide, and then move it to the left so its right edge aligns with the right edge of the Paid field value box. See Figure 7-30.

Figure 7-30   Page number expression added to the Page Header section

8. Save your report changes, and then switch to Print Preview. See Figure 7-31.

Figure 7-31   Date and page number in the Page Header section

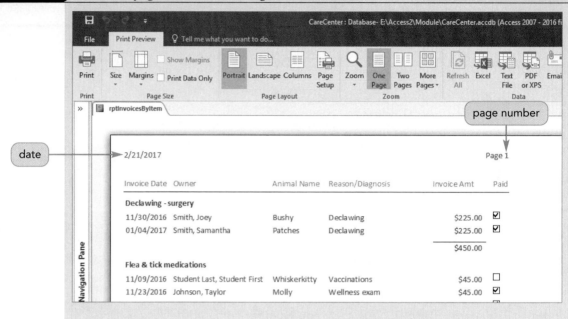

Now you are ready to add the title to the Page Header section.

Adding a Report Title to a Page Header Section

To add a title to a report, you use the Title button in the Header/Footer group on the Report Design Tools Design tab. However, doing so will add the title to the Report Header section, and Daksha's design positions the title in the Page Header section. It will be easier to use the Label tool to add the title directly in the Page Header section.

Daksha's report design includes the title "Invoices by Item" in the Page Header section, centered between the date and the page number.

To add the title to the Page Header section:

1. Switch to Design view.

2. On the Report Design Tools Design tab, in the Controls group, click the **Label** tool *Aa*, position the Label pointer's plus symbol at the top of the Page Header section at the 3-inch mark on the horizontal ruler, and then click the mouse button. The insertion point flashes inside a narrow box, which will expand as you type the report title.

   To match Daksha's design, you need to type the title as "Invoices by Item" and then change its font size to 14 points and its style to bold.

3. Type **Invoices by Item** and then press the **Enter** key.

4. Click the **Report Design Tools Format** tab, in the Font group, click the **Font Size** arrow, click **14**, and then click the **Bold** button *B*.

5. Resize the label control box to display the full title, increase the height of the label control box by two grid dots, and move the label control box to the right so it is centered at the 4-inch mark. See Figure 7-32.

Figure 7-32   **Report title in the Page Header section**

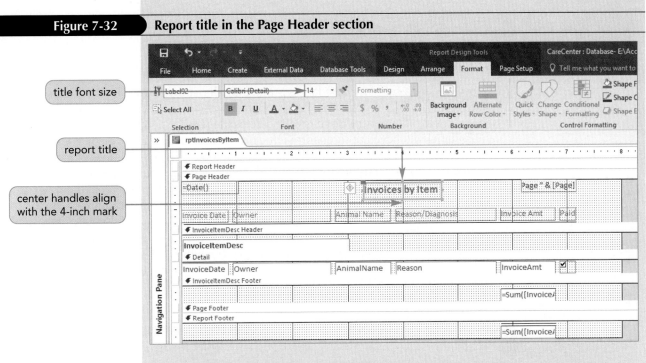

title font size

report title

center handles align
with the 4-inch mark

Finally, you'll bottom-align the date, report title, and page number controls boxes. Yours might appear aligned already, but if not, this step will align the controls.

6. Select the **date**, **report title**, and **page number** control boxes in the Page Header section, right-click one of the selected controls, point to **Align,** and then click **Bottom**.

7. Save your report changes, and then switch to Print Preview to review the completed report. See Figure 7-33.

Figure 7-33   **Completed rptInvoicesByItem report in Print Preview**

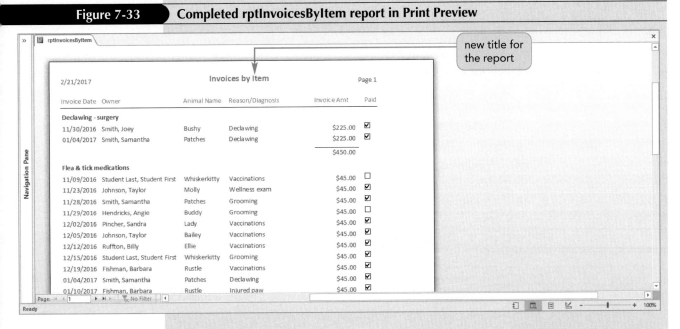

new title for the report

8. Close the report.

Next, Kimberly wants you to create mailing labels that she can use to address materials to the owners of animals seen by the Riverview Veterinary Care Center.

Creating Mailing Labels

Kimberly needs a set of mailing labels printed for all pet owners so she can mail a marketing brochure and other materials to them. The tblOwner table contains the name and address information that will serve as the record source for the labels. Each mailing label will have the same format: first name and last name on the first line; address on the second line; and city, state, and zip code on the third line.

You could create a custom report to produce the mailing labels, but using the Label Wizard is an easier and faster way to produce them. The **Label Wizard** provides templates for hundreds of standard label formats, each of which is uniquely identified by a label manufacturer's name and product number. These templates specify the dimensions and arrangement of labels on each page. Standard label formats can have between one and five labels across a page; the number of labels printed on a single page also varies. Kimberly's mailing labels are manufactured by Avery and their product number is C2163. Each sheet contains 12 labels; each label is 1.5 inches by 3.9 inches, and the labels are arranged in two columns and six rows on the page.

REFERENCE

Creating Mailing Labels and Other Labels

- In the Navigation Pane, click the table or query that will serve as the record source for the labels.
- On the Create tab, click the Labels button in the Reports group to start the Label Wizard and open its first dialog box.
- Select the label manufacturer and product number, and then click the Next button.
- Select the label font, color, and style, and then click the Next button.
- Construct the label content by selecting the fields from the record source and specifying their placement and spacing on the label, and then click the Next button.
- Select one or more optional sort fields, click the Next button, specify the report name, and then click the Finish button.

You'll use the Label Wizard to create a report Kimberly can use to print mailing labels for all animal owners.

To use the Label Wizard to create the mailing label report:

1. Open the Navigation Pane, click **tblOwner** to make it the current object that will serve as the record source for the labels, close the Navigation Pane, and then click the **Create** tab.

2. In the Reports group, click the **Labels** button. The first Label Wizard dialog box opens and asks you to select the standard or custom label you'll use.

3. In the Unit of Measure section make sure that the **English** option button is selected, in the Label Type section make sure that the **Sheet feed** option button is selected, in the Filter by manufacturer box make sure that **Avery** is selected, and then in the Product number box, click **C2163**. See Figure 7-34.

| Figure 7-34 | Label Wizard dialog box |

select this Avery product number

make sure these options are selected

selected manufacturer

TIP

If your label manufacturer or its labels do not appear in the box, you can create your own custom format for them.

The top box shows the Avery product number, dimensions, and number of labels across the page for each of its standard label formats. You can display the dimensions in the list in either inches or millimeters by choosing the appropriate option in the Unit of Measure section. You specify in the Label Type section whether the labels are on individual sheets or are continuous forms.

4. Click the **Next** button to open the second Label Wizard dialog box, in which you choose font specifications for the labels.

   Kimberly wants the labels to use 10-point Arial with a medium font weight and without italics or underlines. The font weight determines how light or dark the characters will print; you can choose from nine values ranging from thin to heavy.

5. If necessary, select **Arial** in the Font name box, **10** in the Font size box, and **Medium** in the Font weight box, make sure the Italic and the Underline check boxes are not checked and that black is the text color, and then click the **Next** button. The third Label Wizard dialog box opens, in which you select the data to appear on the labels.

   Kimberly wants the mailing labels to print the FirstName and LastName fields on the first line, the Address field on the second line, and the City, State, and Zip fields on the third line. A single space will separate the FirstName and LastName fields, the City and State fields, and the State and Zip fields.

6. In the Available fields box, click **FirstName**, click the > button to move the field to the Prototype label box, press the **spacebar**, in the Available fields box click **LastName** (if necessary), and then click the > button. As you select fields from the Available fields box or type text for the label, the Prototype label box shows the format for the label. The braces around the field names in the Prototype label box indicate that the name represents a field rather than text that you entered.

   Trouble? If you select the wrong field or type the wrong text, click the incorrect item in the Prototype label box, press the Delete key to remove the item, and then select the correct field or type the correct text.

7. Press the **Enter** key to move to the next line in the Prototype label box, and then use Figure 7-35 to complete the entries in the Prototype label box. Make sure you type a comma and press the spacebar after selecting the City field, and you press the spacebar after selecting the State field.

Figure 7-35   Completed label prototype

completed label format

insert a comma and a space here

insert a space here

8. Click the **Next** button to open the fourth Label Wizard dialog box, in which you choose the sort fields for the labels.

   Kimberly wants Zip to be the primary sort field and LastName to be the secondary sort field.

9. In the Available fields list, click the **Zip** field, click the ⊳ button to select Zip as the primary sort field, click the **LastName** field, click the ⊳ button to select LastName as the secondary sort field, and then click the **Next** button to open the last Label Wizard dialog box, in which you enter a name for the report.

10. Change the report name to **rptOwnerMailingLabels**, and then click the **Finish** button. The report is saved, and the first page of the report appears in Print Preview. Note that two columns of labels appear across the page. See Figure 7-36.

Figure 7-36   Print Preview of mailing labels

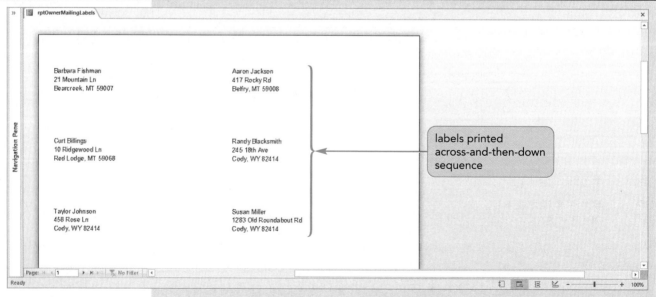

labels printed across-and-then-down sequence

The rptOwnerMailingLabels report is a multiple-column report. The labels will be printed in ascending order by zip code and, within each zip code, in ascending order by last name. The first label will be printed in the upper-left corner on the first page, the second label will be printed to its right, the third label will be printed below the first label, and so on. This style of multiple-column report is the "across, then down" layout. Instead, Kimberly wants the labels to print with the "down, then across" layout because she prefers to pull the labels from the sheet in this manner. In this layout, the first label is printed, the second label is printed below the first, and so on. After the bottom label in the first column is printed, the next label is printed at the top of the second column. The "down, then across" layout is also called **newspaper-style columns** or **snaking columns**.

To change the layout of the mailing label report:

▶ **1.** Switch to Design view. The Detail section, the only section in the report, is sized for a single label.

First, you'll change the layout to snaking columns.

▶ **2.** On the ribbon, click the **Report Design Tools Page Setup** tab.

▶ **3.** In the Page Layout group, click the **Page Setup** button to open the Page Setup dialog box, and then click the **Columns** tab. The Page Setup dialog box displays the column options for the report. See Figure 7-37.

Figure 7-37   Columns tab in the Page Setup dialog box

option to print labels down, then across the page

option to print labels across, then down the page

specifies the number of column

preview of selected column layout

The options in the Page Setup dialog box let you change the properties of a multiple-column report. In the Grid Settings section, you specify the number of columns and the row and column spacing. In the Column Size section, you specify the width and height of each column set. In the Column Layout section, you specify the direction the information flows in the columns.

TIP

When you select a label using a manufacturer's name and product code, the options in the dialog box are set automatically.

▶ **4.** Click the **Down, then Across** option button, and then click the **OK** button.

You've finished the report changes, so you can now save and preview the report.

▶ **5.** Save your report design changes, and then switch to Print Preview. The labels appear in the snaking columns layout.

You've finished all work on Kimberly's reports.

▶ **6.** Close the report, make a backup copy of the database, compact and repair the database, and then close it.

Kimberly is very pleased with the modified report and the two new reports, which will provide her with improved information and expedite her written communications with owners.

REVIEW

Session 7.3 Quick Check

1. What is the function and syntax to print the current date in a report?

2. How do you insert a page number in the Page Header section?

3. Must the page number reside only in the Page Header section?

4. Clicking the Title button in the Header/Footer group on the Report Design Tools Design tab adds a report title to the _____ section.

5. What is a multiple-column report?

Review Assignments

PRACTICE

Data File needed for the Review Assignments: Supplier.accdb (cont. from Module 6)

Kimberly wants you to create a custom report for the Supplier database that prints all companies and the products they offer. She also wants you to customize an existing report. Complete the following steps:

1. Open the **Supplier** database you worked with in the previous two modules.
2. Modify the **rptSupplierDetails** report by completing the following steps:
   a. Change the report title to **Riverview Suppliers**.
   b. Remove the alternate row color from the detail lines in the report.
   c. Change the first column heading to Supplier ID. Change the fifth column heading to First Name and the sixth column heading to Last Name.
   d. In the Report Footer section, add a grand total count of the number of suppliers that appear in the report, make sure the calculated control box has a transparent border, and left-align the count with the left edge of the CompanyName field value box. Left-align the count value in the calculated control box.
   e. Add a label that contains the text **Suppliers:** to the left of the count of the total number of suppliers, aligned to the left margin, and aligned with the bottom of the count calculated control box.
   f. Set the margins to Normal, and adjust the width of the grid to 7.8 inches. Adjust the width of the controls in the Report Header to accommodate the corresponding data, ending up one grid point to the left of the width of the right margin.
   g. Move the page number control to the left until it is one grid dot to the left of the right margin. Right-align the page number value in the control box.
3. After you've completed and saved your modifications to the rptSupplierDetails report, filter the report in Report view, selecting all records that contain the word "supplies" in the Company field. Copy the headings and detail lines of the filtered report, and paste it into a new Word document. Save the document as **Supplies** in the location where you are storing your files. Close Word, save your changes to the Access report, and then close it.
4. Create a query that displays the Company and Category fields from the tblSupplier table and the ProductName, Price, and Units fields from the tblProduct table. Sort in ascending order by the first three fields in the query, and then save the query as **qrySupplierProducts**.
5. Create a custom report based on the qrySupplierProducts query. Figure 7-38 shows a sample of the completed report. Refer to the figure as you create the report. Distribute the fields horizontally to produce a visually balanced report.

Figure 7-38 Supplier database custom report

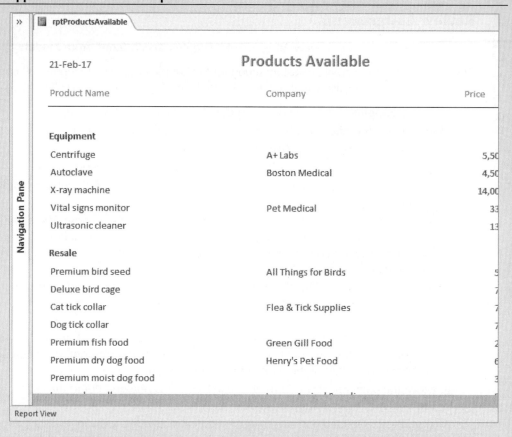

a. Save the report as **rptProductsAvailable**.

b. Use the Category field (from the tblSupplier table) as a grouping field, and use the Company field (from the tblSupplier table) as a sort field.

c. Hide duplicate values for the Company field.

d. Keep the whole group together on one page.

e. Remove the borders from the field value box.

f. Remove the alternate row color from the group header and detail line.

g. Add a Page title **Products Available** using 18-point font, centered horizontally.

h. Apply a text filter for companies that contain "Supplies" in the Company Name.

6. Create a mailing label report according to the following instructions:

a. Use the tblSupplier table as the record source.

b. Use Avery C2160 labels, and use the default font, size, weight, and color.

c. For the prototype label, add the ContactFirst, a space, and ContactLast on the first line; the Company on the second line; the Address on the third line; and the City, a comma and a space, State, a space, and Zip on the fourth line.

d. Sort by Zip and then by Company, and then name the report **rptCompanyMailingLabels**.

e. Format the report with a three-column, across, then down page layout.

7. Make a backup copy of the database, compact and repair, and then close the Supplier database.

Case Problem 1

Data File needed for this Case Problem: MoreBeauty.accdb (cont. from Module 6)

Beauty To Go Sue Miller wants you to create a custom report and mailing labels for the MoreBeauty database. The custom report will be based on the results of a query you will create. Complete the following steps:

1. Open the **MoreBeauty** database you worked with in the previous two modules.
2. Create a query that displays the OptionID, FeeWaived, OptionDescription, and OptionCost fields from the tblOption table, and the FirstName, and LastName fields from the tblMember table. Sort in ascending order by the OptionID, FeeWaived, and LastName fields, and then save the query as **qryOptionMembership**.
3. Create a custom report based on the qryOptionMembership query. Figure 7-39 shows a sample of the first page of the completed report. Refer to the figure as you create the report.

Figure 7-39 **MoreBeauty database custom report**

a. Save the report as **rptOptionMembership**.
b. Use the OptionID field as a grouping field.
c. Select the FeeWaived field as a sort field, and the LastName field as a secondary sort field.
d. Hide duplicate values for the FeeWaived field.
e. Add the OptionDescription field to the Group Header section, and then delete its attached label.
f. Keep the whole group together on one page.
g. Use Narrow margins and spacing to distribute the columns evenly across the page.
h. Remove the alternate row color for all sections.
i. Use black font for all the controls, and set the lines' thickness to 3 pt.
4. Use the following instructions to create the mailing labels:
   a. Use the tblMember table as the record source for the mailing labels.
   b. Use Avery C2160 labels, and use the default font, size, weight, and color.

c. For the prototype label, place FirstName, a space, and LastName on the first line; Street on the second line; and City, a comma and space, State, a space, and Zip on the third line.

d. Sort by Zip and then by LastName, and then name the report **rptMemberLabels**.

e. Format the report with a three-column, across, then down page layout.

5. Make a backup copy of the database, compact and repair it, and then close the MoreBeauty database.

Case Problem 2

Data File needed for this Case Problem: Tutoring.accdb (cont. from Module 6)

Programming Pros   Brent Hovis wants you to modify an existing report and to create a custom report and mailing labels for the Tutoring database. Complete the following steps:

1. Open the **Tutoring** database you worked with in the previous two modules.

2. Modify the **rptTutorList** report. Figure 7-40 shows a sample of the first page of the completed report. Refer to the figure as you modify the report.

Figure 7-40   Tutoring database enhanced report

a. Delete the picture at the top of the report.

b. Set Normal margins and a grid width of 7.8 inches.

c. Center the report title, and ensure the text is "Tutors", formatted in bold and 22-pt font.

d. Move the Hire Date column to the right margin, and center the Hire Date label value. Use horizontal spacing to evenly distribute the columns.

e. Remove the alternate row color from the detail lines in the report.

f. Change the page number format from "Page n of m" to "Page n," and right-align the text.

g. Move the date, time, and page number to the Page Header section.

h. Change the date format to short date, and left-align the date value.

i. Add a grand total control that calculates the total number of tutors, and add a label with the text "Total Tutors".

j. Sort the tutors by Last Name.

3. Create a query that displays, in order, the LastName and FirstName fields from the tblTutor table, the SessionType field from the tblContract table, the FirstName and LastName fields from the tblStudent table, and the NumSessions and Cost fields from the tblContract table. Sort in ascending order by the first three fields in the query, and then save the query as **qryTutorSessions**.

4. Create a custom report based on the qryTutorSessions query. Figure 7-41 shows a sample of the first page of the completed report. Refer to the figure as you create the report.

Figure 7-41   Tutoring database custom report

a. Save the report as **rptTutorSessions**.
b. The LastName field (from the tblTutor table) is a grouping field, and the FirstName field also appears in the Group Header section.
c. The SessionType field is a sort field, and the LastName field (from the tblStudent table) is a sort field.
d. Hide duplicate values for the SessionType field.
e. Use Wide margins, and set the grid width to 6.5 inches. Size fields as shown, and distribute horizontally using spacing to create a balanced look.
f. Set the background color for the grouped header and its controls to Gray-25% - Background 2 in the Theme colors.
g. In addition to the total for each tutor, give a grand total for all tutors with the label "Total for all tutors:"

5. Create a mailing label report according to the following instructions:
a. Use the tblStudent table as the record source.
b. Use Avery C2160 labels, use a 12-point font size, and use the other default font and color options.
c. For the prototype label, place FirstName, a space, and LastName on the first line; Address on the second line; and City, a comma and a space, State, a space, and Zip on the third line.
d. Sort by Zip and then by LastName, and then enter the report name **rptStudentMailingLabels**.
e. Change the page layout of the rptStudentMailingLabels report to three snaking columns.

6. Make a backup copy of the database, compact and repair it, and then close the Tutoring database.

CREATE

Case Problem 3

Data File needed for this Case Problem: Community.accdb (cont. from Module 6)

Diane's Community Center   Diane Coleman asks you to create a custom report for the Community database so that she can better track donations made by donors and to create mailing labels. Complete the following steps:

1. Open the **Community** database you worked with in the previous two modules.
2. Create a query that displays the Description, DonationDate, and DonationValue fields from the tblDonation table, and the FirstName and LastName fields from the tblPatron table. Sort in ascending order by the Description, DonationDate, and LastName fields, and then save the query as **qryPatronDonations**.
3. Create a custom report based on the qryPatronDonations query. Figure 7-42 shows a sample of the first page of the completed report. Refer to the figure as you create the report.

Figure 7-42   **Community database custom report**

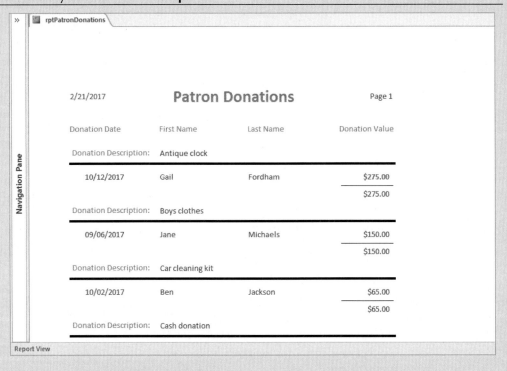

a. Save the report as **rptPatronDonations**.
b. Use the Description field as a grouping field.
c. Select the DonationDate field as a sort field and the LastName field as a secondary sort field.
d. Hide duplicate values for the DonationDate field.
e. Use black font for all the controls.
f. Keep the whole group together on one page.
g. Use Wide margins, and set the grid width to 6 inches. Size fields as shown, and distribute horizontally, using spacing to create a balanced look.
h. Create a conditional formatting rule for the DonationValue field to display the value in blue, bold font when the amount is more than $200.
i. Make any additional changes to the layout and formatting of the report that are necessary for it to match Figure 7-42. Also include a grand total of all donations at the end of the report.

4. After you've created and saved the rptPatronDonations report, filter the report in Report view, selecting all records that contain "Jo" in the LastName field. Copy the entire filtered report, and paste it into a new Word document. Save the document as **PatronJo** in the location where you are storing your files. Close Word, and then save and close the Access report.

5. Diane's Community Center is having a fundraiser dinner, and Diane would like name tags for the patrons. Use the following instructions to create mailing labels that will be used as name tags:

   a. Use the tblPatron table as the record source for the mailing labels.

   b. Use Avery C2160 labels, and use a font size of 16, with Normal weight and black color.

   c. For the prototype label, place FirstName, a space, and LastName on the first line.

   d. Sort by LastName, and then type the report name **rptPatronNameTags**.

   e. Change the page layout of the rptPatronNameTags report to three snaking columns.

6. Make a backup copy of the database, compact and repair it, and then close it.

Case Problem 4

CREATE

Data File needed for this Case Problem: AppTrail.accdb (cont. from Module 6)

Hike Appalachia   Molly and Bailey Johnson want you to create a custom report and mailing labels for the AppTrail database. Complete the following steps:

1. Open the **AppTrail** database you worked with in the previous two modules.

2. Create a query that displays the TourName field from the tblTour table; the HikerFirst, HikerLast, and State field from the tblHiker table; and the TourDate and People fields from the tblReservation table. Sort in ascending order by the TourName, State, and TourDate fields, and then save the query as **qryTourReservations**.

3. Create a custom report based on the qryTourReservations query. Figure 7-43 shows a sample of the first page of the completed report. Refer to the figure as you create the report.

Figure 7-43   **AppTrail database custom report**

a. Save the report as **rptTourReservations**.

b. Use the TourName field as a grouping field.

c. Select the TourDate field as a sort field and the State field as a secondary sort field.

d. Hide duplicate values for the TourDate field.

e. Use black font for all the controls, and display the Tour Name in bold.

f. Keep the whole group together on one page.

g. Add a grand total of all hikers for all dates at the end of the report.

h. Use Wide margins, and set the grid width to 6 inches. Size fields as shown, and distribute horizontally, using spacing to create a balanced look.

i. Remove the color for alternate rows, and then make any other layout and formatting changes necessary to match the report shown in Figure 7-43.

4. Use the following instructions to create the mailing labels:

a. Use the tblHiker table as the record source for the mailing labels.

b. Use Avery C2163 labels, with 12-point font size, Medium weight, and black color settings.

c. For the prototype label, place HikerFirst, a space, and HikerLast on the first line; Address on the second line; City, a comma and a space, State, a space, and Zip on the third line.

d. Sort by Zip, then by HikerLast, and then enter the report name **rptHikerLabels**.

e. Change the page layout for the rptHikerLabels report to snaking columns.

5. Make a copy of the rptTourReservations report using the name **rptTourReservationsSummary**, and then customize it according to the following instructions. Figure 7-44 shows a sample of the first page of the completed report.

Figure 7-44 **AppTrail database custom summary report**

a. Delete the column heading labels and line in the Page Header section, and then reduce the height of the section.

b. Delete the controls from the Detail section, and then reduce the height of that section.

c. Keep the subtotals for the number of reservations per tour and total number of hikers on all tours.

6. Make a backup copy of the database, compact and repair it, and then close the AppTrail database.

MODULE **8**

OBJECTIVES

Session 8.1
- Export an Access query to an HTML document and view the document
- Import a CSV file as an Access table
- Use the Table Analyzer
- Import and export XML files
- Save and run import and export specifications

Session 8.2
- Create a tabbed subform using a tab control
- Create a chart in a tab control using the Chart Wizard
- Create and use an application part
- Export a PDF file
- Understand the difference between importing, embedding, and linking external objects
- Link data from an Excel workbook

Sharing, Integrating, and Analyzing Data

Importing, Exporting, Linking, and Analyzing Data in the CareCenter Database

ACCESS

Case | *Riverview Veterinary Care Center*

Kimberly Johnson is pleased with the design and contents of the CareCenter database. Kimberly feels that other employees would benefit from gaining access to the CareCenter database and from sharing data among the different applications employees use. Kimberly would also like to be able to analyze the data in the database.

In this module, you will import, export, and link data, and you will create application parts. You will also explore the charting features of Access.

STARTING DATA FILES

Module	**Review**	**Case1**	
CareCenter.accdb (*cont.*)	Ads.xlsx	CreditCard.xml	
NewOwnerReferrals.accdb	Partners.accdb	MoreBeauty.accdb (*cont.*)	
PotentialOwners.csv	Payables.csv	Schedule.xlsx	
Referral.xml	Payments.xml		
Volunteer.xlsx	Supplier.accdb (*cont.*)		

Case2	**Case3**	**Case4**
AddSubject.xml	Community.accdb (*cont.*)	AppTrail.accdb (*cont.*)
NewStudentReferrals.accdb	Facility.csv	PotentialTours1.xml
Room.xlsx	Volunteer.accdb	PotentialTours2.xml
Subject.csv		Staff.xlsx
Tutoring.accdb (*cont.*)		

Session 8.1 Visual Overview:

The field names from the table are used as XML tags to identify data.

Each piece of data is encapsulated in paired tags.

Access includes too for exporting data c the External Data ta

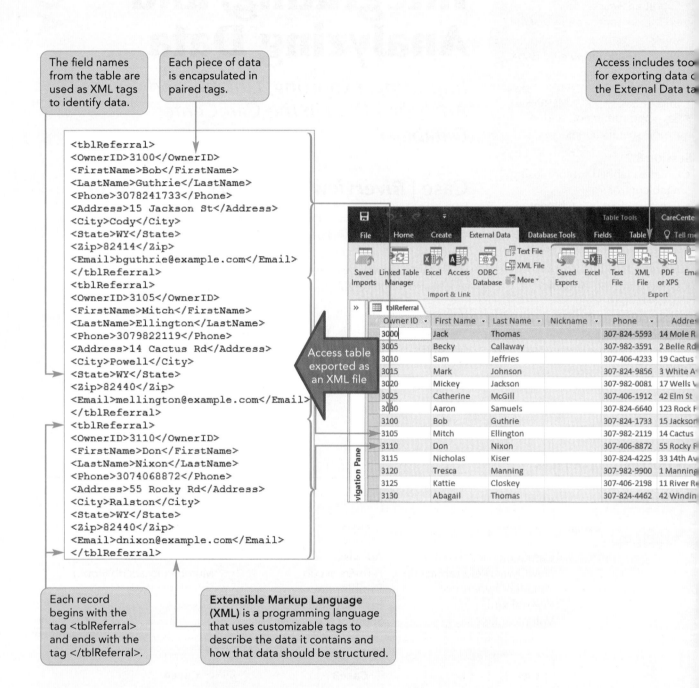

```
<tblReferral>
<OwnerID>3100</OwnerID>
<FirstName>Bob</FirstName>
<LastName>Guthrie</LastName>
<Phone>3078241733</Phone>
<Address>15 Jackson St</Address>
<City>Cody</City>
<State>WY</State>
<Zip>82414</Zip>
<Email>bguthrie@example.com</Email>
</tblReferral>
<tblReferral>
<OwnerID>3105</OwnerID>
<FirstName>Mitch</FirstName>
<LastName>Ellington</LastName>
<Phone>3079822119</Phone>
<Address>14 Cactus Rd</Address>
<City>Powell</City>
<State>WY</State>
<Zip>82440</Zip>
<Email>mellington@example.com</Email>
</tblReferral>
<tblReferral>
<OwnerID>3110</OwnerID>
<FirstName>Don</FirstName>
<LastName>Nixon</LastName>
<Phone>3074068872</Phone>
<Address>55 Rocky Rd</Address>
<City>Ralston</City>
<State>WY</State>
<Zip>82440</Zip>
<Email>dnixon@example.com</Email>
</tblReferral>
```

Access table exported as an XML file

Owner ID	First Name	Last Name	Nickname	Phone	Addres
3000	Jack	Thomas		307-824-5593	14 Mole R
3005	Becky	Callaway		307-982-3591	2 Belle Rd
3010	Sam	Jeffries		307-406-4233	19 Cactus
3015	Mark	Johnson		307-824-9856	3 White A
3020	Mickey	Jackson		307-982-0081	17 Wells V
3025	Catherine	McGill		307-406-1912	42 Elm St
3030	Aaron	Samuels		307-824-6640	123 Rock F
3100	Bob	Guthrie		307-824-1733	15 Jackson
3105	Mitch	Ellington		307-982-2119	14 Cactus
3110	Don	Nixon		307-406-8872	55 Rocky F
3115	Nicholas	Kiser		307-824-4225	33 14th Av
3120	Tresca	Manning		307-982-9900	1 Manning
3125	Kattie	Closkey		307-406-2198	11 River R
3130	Abagail	Thomas		307-824-4462	42 Windin

Each record begins with the tag <tblReferral> and ends with the tag </tblReferral>.

Extensible Markup Language (XML) is a programming language that uses customizable tags to describe the data it contains and how that data should be structured.

Exporting Data to XML and HTML

The table field names are used as column headings in the table on the webpage.

The Export to HTML tool generates an HTML document, embedding the Access content in the document. An **HTML document** contains tags and other instructions that a web browser processes and displays as a webpage.

The name of the table is used as a heading on the webpage.

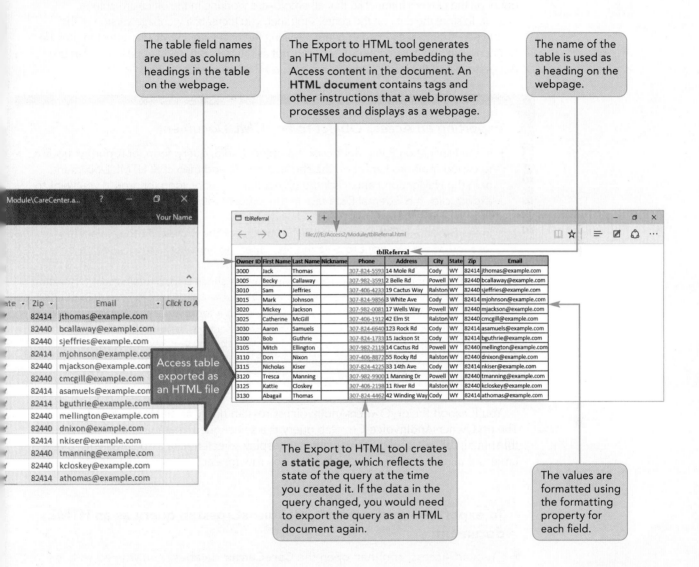

Access table exported as an HTML file

The Export to HTML tool creates a **static page**, which reflects the state of the query at the time you created it. If the data in the query changed, you would need to export the query as an HTML document again.

The values are formatted using the formatting property for each field.

Exporting an Access Query to an HTML Document

An HTML document contains tags and other instructions that a web browser, such as Microsoft Edge, Apple Safari, or Google Chrome, processes and displays as a webpage.

Kimberly wants to display the summary data in the qryOwnersAndInvoicesCrosstab query on the center's intranet so that all employees working in the office are able to view it. To store the data on the center's intranet, you'll create a webpage version of the qryOwnersAndInvoicesCrosstab query. Creating the necessary HTML document to provide Kimberly with the information she wants is not as difficult as it might appear. You can use Access to export the query and convert it to an HTML document automatically.

Exporting an Access Object to an HTML Document

- In the Navigation Pane, right-click the object (table, query, form, or report) you want to export, point to Export on the shortcut menu, and then click HTML Document; or in the Navigation Pane, click the object (table, query, form, or report) you want to export, click the External Data tab, in the Export group, click the More button, and then click HTML Document.
- In the Export – HTML Document dialog box, click the Browse button, select the location where you want to save the file, enter the filename in the File name box, and then click the Save button.
- Click the Export data with formatting and layout check box to retain most formatting and layout information, and then click the OK button.
- In the HTML Output Options dialog box, if using a template, click the Select a HTML Template check box, click the Browse button, select the location for the template, click the template filename, and then click the OK button.
- Click the OK button, and then click the Close button.

You'll export the qryOwnersAndInvoicesCrosstab query as an HTML document. The qryOwnersAndInvoicesCrosstab query is a select query that joins the tblOwner, tblAnimal, tblVisit, and tblBilling tables to display selected data associated with those tables for all invoices. The query displays one row for each unique City field value.

To export the qryOwnersAndInvoicesCrosstab query as an HTML document:

▶ **1.** Start Access, and then open the **CareCenter** database you worked with in the previous three modules.

Trouble? If the security warning is displayed below the ribbon, click the Enable Content button.

▶ **2.** Open the Navigation Pane (if necessary), right-click **qryOwnersAndInvoicesCrosstab** to display the shortcut menu, point to **Export**, and then click **HTML Document**. The Export - HTML Document dialog box opens.

▶ **3.** Click the **Browse** button to open the File Save dialog box, navigate to the location where your Data Files are stored, select the text in the File name box, type **Crosstab**, make sure HTML Documents appears in the Save as type box, and then click the **Save** button. The File Save dialog box closes, and you return to the Export – HTML Document dialog box. See Figure 8-1.

Figure 8-1	Export – HTML Document dialog box

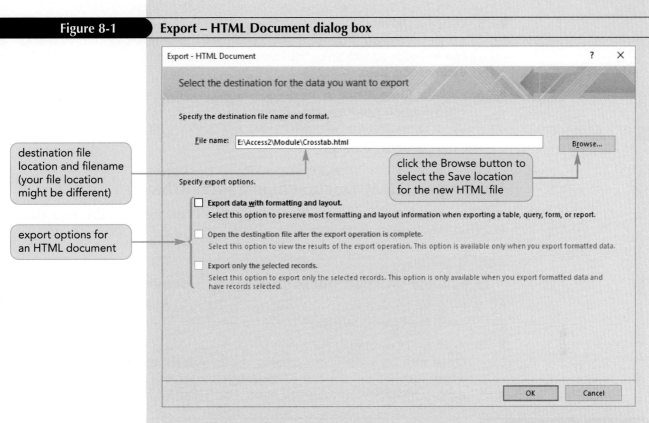

destination file location and filename (your file location might be different)

export options for an HTML document

The dialog box provides options for exporting the data with formatting and layout, opening the exported file after the export operation is complete, and exporting selected records from the source object (available only when you select records in an object instead of selecting an object in the Navigation Pane). You need to select the option for exporting the data with formatting and layout; otherwise the HTML document created will be poorly formatted and difficult to read.

4. Click the **Export data with formatting and layout** check box to select it, and then click the **OK** button. The Export - HTML Document dialog box closes, and the HTML Output Options dialog box opens. See Figure 8-2. In this dialog box you specify the coding to be used to save the HTML file, and you also have the option to save the exported data in a pre-existing HTML document template. The default option, Default encoding, is selected.

Figure 8-2	HTML Output Options dialog box

data encoding options

▶ **5.** Click the **OK** button. The HTML Output Options dialog box closes, the HTML document named Crosstab is saved and the Export - HTML Document dialog box is displayed with an option to save the export steps. You won't save these export steps.

▶ **6.** Click the **Close** button in the dialog box to close it without saving the steps, and then close the Navigation Pane.

Now you can view the webpage.

Viewing an HTML Document in a Web Browser

Kimberly asks to see the webpage you created. You can view the HTML document that you created using any web browser.

To view the Crosstab webpage in a web browser:

▶ **1.** Open Windows File Explorer, and then navigate to the location where you saved the exported Crosstab HTML document.

▶ **2.** Right-click **Crosstab** in the file list to open the shortcut menu, point to **Open with**, and then click the name of your web browser, such as **Microsoft Edge**. Your browser opens the Crosstab webpage that displays the qryOwnersAndInvoicesCrosstab query results. See Figure 8-3.

| Figure 8-3 | qryOwnersAndInvoicesCrosstab query displayed in Edge |

path and filename for selected HTML file (your path might be different)

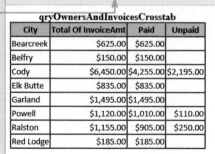

qryOwnersAndInvoicesCrosstab

City	Total Of InvoiceAmt	Paid	Unpaid
Bearcreek	$625.00	$625.00	
Belfry	$150.00	$150.00	
Cody	$6,450.00	$4,255.00	$2,195.00
Elk Butte	$835.00	$835.00	
Garland	$1,495.00	$1,495.00	
Powell	$1,120.00	$1,010.00	$110.00
Ralston	$1,155.00	$905.00	$250.00
Red Lodge	$185.00	$185.00	

Trouble? You may see different column widths than the ones shown in Figure 8-3, depending on the size of your web browser window. This is not a problem.

Any subsequent changes that employees make to the CareCenter database will not appear in the Crosstab webpage that you created because it is a static webpage—that is, it reflects the state of the qryOwnersAndInvoicesCrosstab query in the CareCenter database at the time you created it. If data in the qryOwnersAndInvoicesCrosstab query changes, Kimberly would need to export the query as an HTML document again.

3. Close your browser, and then click the **Close** button X on the Windows File Explorer window title bar to close it and to return to Access.

Trouble? If the Access window is not active on your screen, click the Microsoft Access program button on the taskbar.

Now that you've completed your work creating the webpage, Kimberly has a file containing information for potential new owners that she needs to add to the CareCenter database. Instead of typing the information into new records, she asks you to import the data into the CareCenter database.

Importing a CSV File as an Access Table

Many people use Excel to manage a simple table, such as a table of contact information or product information. Kimberly has been maintaining an Excel workbook containing contact information for people who have called the Riverview Veterinary Care Center clinic to inquire about the services but have not yet booked appointments. Recall from your work in a previous module that she could use the Excel button on the External Data tab to access the Import Spreadsheet Wizard and import the Excel worksheet data. However, in this case, Kimberly has already exported the Excel data to a CSV file. A **CSV (comma-separated values) file** is a text file in which commas separate values, and each line is a record containing the same number of values in the same positions. This is a common format for representing data in a table and is used by spreadsheet applications such as Excel as well as database applications. A CSV file can easily be imported into the CareCenter database as a table. To do so, you use the Import Text Wizard, which you open by clicking the Text File button on the External Data Tab.

REFERENCE

Importing a CSV File into an Access Table

- On the External Data tab, in the Import & Link group, click the Text File button to open the Get External Data - Text File dialog box.
- Click the Browse button in the dialog box, navigate to the location where the file to import is stored, click the filename, and then click the Open button.
- Click the "Import the source data into a new table in the current database" option button, and then click the OK button.
- In the Import Text Wizard dialog box, click the Delimited option button, and then click the Next button.
- Make sure the Comma option button is selected. If appropriate, click the First Row Contains Field Names check box to select it, and then click the Next button.
- For each field, if necessary, select the column, type its field name and select its data type, and then click the Next button.
- Choose the appropriate option button to let Access create a primary key, to choose your own primary key, or to avoid setting a primary key, and then click the Next button.
- Type the table name in the Import to Table box, and then click the Finish button.

Kimberly's CSV file is named PotentialOwners, and you'll import the data as a new table in the CareCenter database.

To view and import the CSV file as an Access table:

▶ **1.** Open Windows File Explorer, navigate to the **Access2 > Module** folder included with your Data Files, right-click **PotentialOwners (CSV)** in the file list to open the shortcut menu, click **Open with**, and then click **Notepad**.

Trouble? If Notepad isn't an option when you click Open with, click Choose another app, click Notepad in the How do you want to open this file dialog box that opens, and then click the OK button.

▶ **2.** Examine the contents of the PotentialOwners file. The file contains rows of data, with commas separating the individual pieces of data.

▶ **3.** Close the Notepad window, and then close the File Explorer window. You return to the Access window.

Trouble? If a dialog box appears prompting you to save the file, click Don't Save. You may have accidentally added or deleted a character, and you don't want to save this change to the file.

▶ **4.** On the ribbon, click the **External Data** tab, and then in the Import & Link group, click the **Text File** button to open the Get External Data - Text File dialog box.

Trouble? If the Export - Text File dialog box opens, you clicked the Text File button in the Export group. Click the Cancel button, and then repeat Step 4, being sure to select the Text File button in the Import & Link group.

▶ **5.** Click the **Browse** button, navigate to the **Access2 > Module** folder included with your Data Files, click **PotentialOwners**, and then click the **Open** button.

▶ **6.** In the Get External Data – Text File dialog box, click the **Import the source data into a new table in the current database** option button (if necessary). The selected path and filename appear in the File name box. See Figure 8-4.

Figure 8-4	**Get External Data – Text File dialog box**

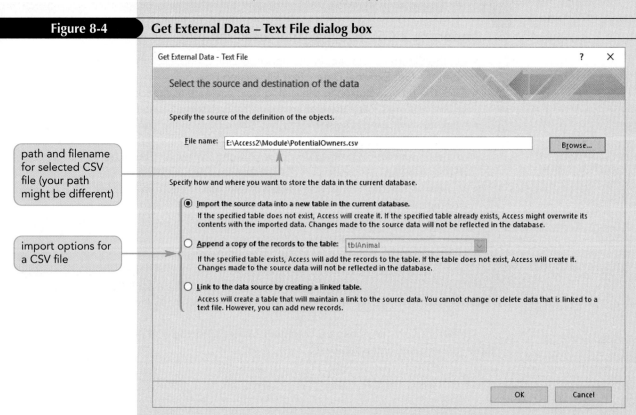

path and filename for selected CSV file (your path might be different)

import options for a CSV file

The dialog box provides options for importing the data into a new table in the database, appending a copy of the data to an existing table in the database, and linking to the source data. In the future, Kimberly wants to maintain the potential new owner data in the CareCenter database, instead of using her Excel workbook, so you'll import the data into a new table.

▶ 7. Click the **OK** button to open the first Import Text Wizard dialog box, in which you designate how to identify the separation between field values in each line in the source data. The choices are the use of commas, tabs, or another character to separate, or delimit, the values, or the use of fixed-width columns with spaces between each column. The wizard has correctly identified that values are delimited by commas.

▶ 8. Click the **Next** button to open the second Import Text Wizard dialog box, in which you verify the delimiter for values in each line. See Figure 8-5.

Figure 8-5	Import Text Wizard dialog box specifying the delimiter for values in the CSV file

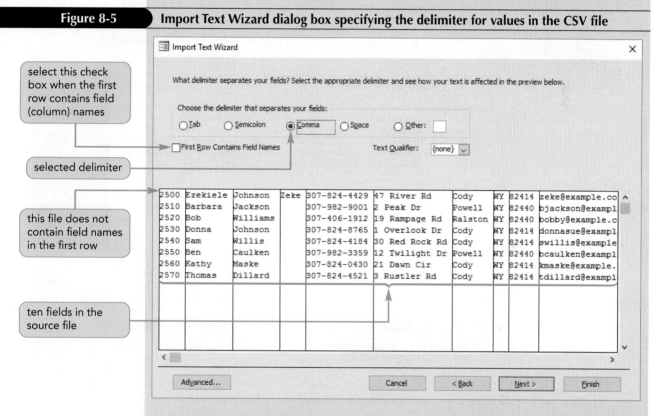

The CSV source file contains eight records with ten fields in each record. A comma serves as the delimiter for values in each line (record), so the Comma option button is selected. The first row in the source file contains the first record, not field names, so the "First Row Contains Field Names" check box is not checked. If the source file used either single or double quotation marks to enclose values, you would click the Text Qualifier arrow to choose the appropriate option.

▶ 9. Click the **Next** button to open the third Import Text Wizard dialog box, in which you enter the field name and set other properties for the imported fields. You will import all fields from the source file and use the default data type and indexed settings for each field, except for the first field's data type.

▶ **10.** In the Field Name box, type **OwnerID**, click the **Data Type** arrow, click **Short Text**, and then click **Field2** in the table list. The heading for the first column changes to OwnerID (partially hidden) in the table list, and the second column is selected.

▶ **11.** Repeat Step 10 for the remaining nine columns, making sure Short Text is the data type for all fields, typing **FirstName**, **LastName**, **Nickname**, **Phone**, **Address**, **City**, **State**, **Zip**, and **Email** in the Field Name box. See Figure 8-6.

Figure 8-6	Field names and options as specified in the Import Text Wizard

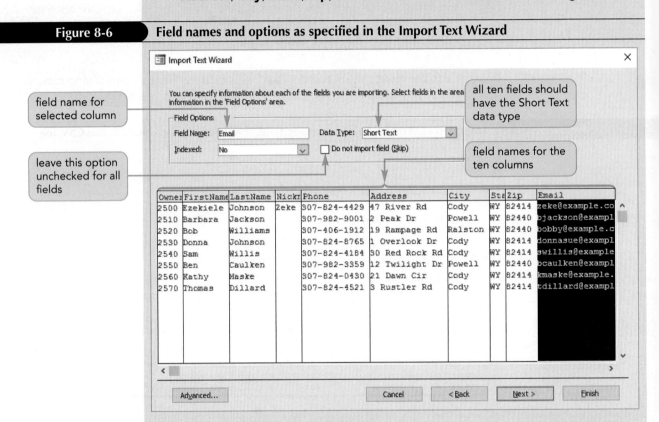

▶ **12.** Click the **Next** button to open the fourth Import Text Wizard dialog box, in which you select the primary key for the imported table. OwnerID, the first column, will be the primary key. When you select this column as the table's primary key, the ID column created by the wizard will be deleted.

▶ **13.** Click the **Choose my own primary key** option button, make sure **OwnerID** appears in the box for the option, click the **Next** button, type **tblPotentialOwners** as the table name in the Import to Table box, click the **I would like a wizard to analyze my table after importing the data** check box to select it, and then click the **Finish** button. An Import Text Wizard dialog box opens, asking if you want to analyze the table.

▶ **14.** Click the **Yes** button to close the dialog box and start the Table Analyzer Wizard. You will continue working with this wizard in the next set of steps.

TIP

You can start the Table Analyzer Wizard directly by clicking the Database Tools tab and then clicking the Analyze Table button in the Analyze group.

After importing data and creating a new table, you can use the Import Text Wizard to analyze the imported table. The Table Analyzer Wizard identifies duplicate data in your table and displays a diagram and explanation in the dialog box describing the potential problem.

Analyzing a Table with the Table Analyzer

Normalizing is the process of identifying and eliminating anomalies, or inconsistencies, from a collection of tables in the database. The **Table Analyzer** analyzes a single table and, if necessary, splits it into two or more tables that are in third normal form. The Table Analyzer looks for redundant data in the table. When the Table Analyzer encounters redundant data, it removes redundant fields from the table and then places them in new tables. The database designer must always review the analyzer results carefully to determine if the suggestions are appropriate.

To use the Table Analyzer Wizard to analyze the imported table:

1. In the first Table Analyzer Wizard dialog box, click the first **Show me an example** button ⟫, read the explanation, close the example box, click the second **Show me an example** button ⟫, read the explanation, close the example box, and then click the **Next** button to open the second Table Analyzer Wizard dialog box. The diagram and explanation in this dialog box describe how the Table Analyzer solves the duplicate data problem.

2. Again, click the first **Show me an example** button ⟫, read the explanation, close the example box, click the second **Show me an example** button ⟫, read the explanation, close the example box, and then click the **Next** button to open the third Table Analyzer Wizard dialog box. In this dialog box, you choose whether to let the wizard decide the appropriate table placement for the fields, if the table is not already normalized. You'll let the wizard decide.

3. Make sure the **Yes, let the wizard decide** option button is selected, and then click the **Next** button. The wizard indicates that the City and State fields should be split into a separate table. Although this data is redundant, it is an industry practice to keep the city, state, and zip information with the address information in a table, so you'll cancel the wizard rather than split the table.

4. Click the **Cancel** button to close the Table Analyzer Wizard. You return to the final Get External Data - Text File dialog box, in which you specify if you want to save the import steps. You don't need to save these steps because you're importing the data only this one time.

5. Click the **Close** button to close the dialog box.

The tblPotentialOwners table is now listed in the Tables section in the Navigation Pane. You'll open the table to verify the import results.

To open the imported tblPotentialOwners table:

1. Open the Navigation Pane, if necessary.

2. Double-click **tblPotentialOwners** to open the table datasheet, and then close the Navigation Pane.

3. Resize all columns to their best fit, and then click **2500** in the first row in the OwnerID column to deselect all values. See Figure 8-7.

| Figure 8-7 | Imported tblPotentialOwners table datasheet |

OwnerID	FirstName	LastName	Nickname	Phone	Address	City	State	Zip	Email	Click to Add
2500	Ezekiele	Johnson	Zeke	307-824-4429	47 River Rd	Cody	WY	82414	zeke@example.com	
2510	Barbara	Jackson		307-982-9001	2 Peak Dr	Powell	WY	82440	bjackson@example.com	
2520	Bob	Williams		307-406-1932	19 Rampage Rd	Ralston	WY	82440	bobby@example.com	
2530	Donna	Johnson		307-824-8765	1 Overlook Dr	Cody	WY	82414	donnasue@example.com	
2540	Sam	Willis		307-824-4184	30 Red Rock Rd	Cody	WY	82414	swillis@example.com	
2550	Ben	Caulken		307-980-3359	12 Twilight Dr	Powell	WY	82440	bcaulken@example.com	
2560	Kathy	Maske		307-824-0430	21 Dawn Cir	Cody	WY	82414	kmaske@example.com	
2570	Thomas	Dillard		307-824-4521	3 Rustler Rd	Cody	WY	82414	tdillard@example.com	

4. Save and close the table.

Next, Kimberly would like you to import data from another file containing new owner referrals from another veterinary care center. However, this data is not in an Access table; instead, it's stored in XML format.

Working with XML Files

Riverview Veterinary Care Center occasionally receives owner referrals from other clinics. Kimberly was provided an XML document that contains owner contact information from another veterinary care center, which she wants to add to the CareCenter database. XML (Extensible Markup Language) is a programming language that is similar in format to HTML but is more customizable and is suited to the exchange of data between different programs. Unlike HTML, which uses a fixed set of tags to describe the appearance of a webpage, developers can customize XML to describe the data it contains and how that data should be structured.

PROSKILLS

Teamwork: Exchanging Data Between Programs

If all companies used Access, you could easily exchange data between any two databases. However, not all companies use Access. One universal and widely used method for transferring data between different database systems is to export data to XML files and import data from XML files. XML files are used to exchange data between companies, and they are also used to exchange data between programs within a company. For example, you can store data either in an Excel workbook or in an Access table or query, depending on which program is best suited to the personnel working with the data and the business requirements of the company. Because the XML file format is a common format for both Excel and Access—as well as many other programs—whenever the data is needed in another program, you can export the data from one program as an XML file and then import the file into the other program. When collaborating with a team of users or sharing database information with other organizations, always consider the characteristics of the programs being used and the best format for exchanging data between programs.

Importing Data from an XML File

In Access, you can import data from an XML file directly into a database table. Kimberly's XML file is named Referral.xml, and you'll import it into a table called tblReferral in the CareCenter database.

REFERENCE

Importing an XML File as an Access Table

- On the External Data tab, in the Import & Link group, click the XML File button to open the Get External Data - XML File dialog box; or right-click the table name in the Navigation Pane, click Import, and then click XML File.
- Click the Browse button, navigate to the location of the XML file, click the XML filename, and then click the Open button.
- Click the OK button in the Get External Data - XML File dialog box, click the table name in the Import XML dialog box, click the appropriate option button in the Import Options section, and then click the OK button.
- Click the Close button; or if you need to save the import steps, click the Save import steps check box, enter a name for the saved steps in the Save as box, and then click the Save Import button.

Now you will import the Referral XML document as an Access table.

To import the contents of the XML document:

1. On the ribbon, click the **External Data** tab if necessary, and then in the Import & Link Group, click the **XML File** button. The Get External Data - XML File dialog box opens.

2. Click the **Browse** button to open the File Open dialog box, navigate to the **Access2 > Module** folder included with your Data Files, click **Referral**, and then click the **Open** button. The selected path and filename now appear in the File name box.

3. Click the **OK** button. The Import XML dialog box opens. See Figure 8-8.

Figure 8-8　**Import XML dialog box**

select to import the structure and data into a new table

From the XML file, you can import only the table structure to a new table, import the table structure and data to a new table, or append the data in the XML file to an existing table. You'll choose to import the data and structure to a new table.

▶ **4.** Make sure the **Structure and Data** option button is selected, click **tblReferral** in the box, and then click the **OK** button. The Import XML dialog box closes, and the last Get External Data - XML File Wizard dialog box displays. You'll continue to work with this dialog box in the next set of steps.

Saving and Running Import Specifications

If you need to repeat the same import procedure many times, you can save the steps for the procedure and expedite future imports by running the saved import steps without using a wizard. Because Kimberly will receive additional lists of owner referrals in the future, you'll save the import steps so she can reuse them whenever she receives a new list.

To save the XML file import steps:

▶ **1.** In the Get External Data – XML File dialog box, click the **Save import steps** check box to select it. The dialog box displays additional options for the save operation. See Figure 8-9.

Figure 8-9   Save Import Steps dialog box in the Get External Data - XML File Wizard

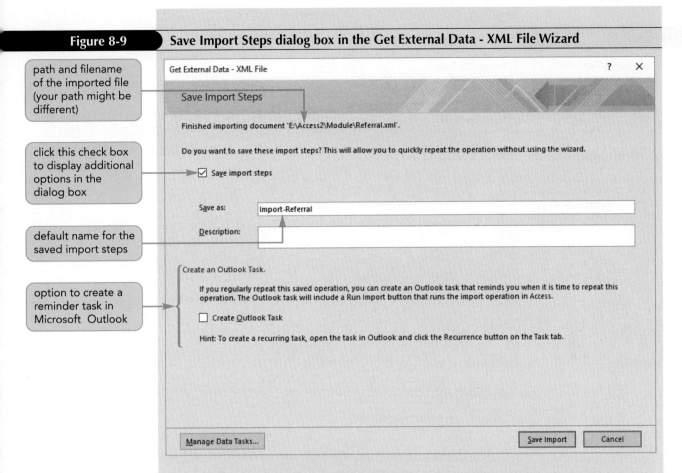

- path and filename of the imported file (your path might be different)
- click this check box to display additional options in the dialog box
- default name for the saved import steps
- option to create a reminder task in Microsoft Outlook

You can accept the default name for the saved import steps or specify a different name, and you can enter an optional description. If the import will occur on a set schedule, you can also create a reminder task in Microsoft Outlook. You'll accept the default name for the saved steps, and you won't enter a description or schedule an Outlook task.

2. Click the **Save Import** button. The import steps are saved as Import-Referral, the Get External Data - XML File dialog box closes, and the data from the Referral.xml file has been imported into the CareCenter database with the name tblReferral. Before reviewing the imported table, you'll add a description to the saved import steps.

3. On the External Data tab, in the Import & Link group, click the **Saved Imports** button to open the Manage Data Tasks dialog box. See Figure 8-10.

   Trouble? If the Saved Exports tab is displayed in the Manage Data Tasks dialog box, then you selected the Saved Exports button instead of the Saved Imports button. Click the Saved Imports tab in the dialog box.

Figure 8-10   **Saved Imports tab in the Manage Data Tasks dialog box**

path and filename
for the saved file
(your path might be
different)

selected saved import

click to add or
modify a description
for the saved import

In this dialog box, you can change the name of a saved import, add or
change its description, create an Outlook task for it, run it, or delete it. You
can also manage any saved export by clicking the Saved Exports tab. You'll
add a description for the saved import procedure.

4. Click the **Click here to edit the description** link to open a box that contains
   an insertion point, type **XML file containing owner referrals from other
   veterinary care centers**, click an unused portion of the highlighted selection
   band to close the box and accept the typed description, and then click
   the **Saved Exports** tab. You have not saved any export steps, so no saved
   exports are displayed.

5. Click the **Close** button to close the Manage Data Tasks dialog box.

6. Open the Navigation Pane, double-click the **tblReferral** table to open the
   table datasheet, close the Navigation Pane, resize all columns to their best
   fit if necessary, and then click **3000** in the first row in the Owner ID column to
   deselect all values. See Figure 8-11.

| Figure 8-11 | Imported XML records in new tblReferral table |

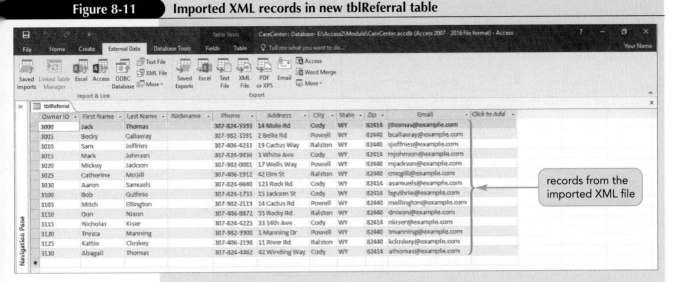

records from the imported XML file

▶ **7.** Save and close the table.

Next, Kimberly asks you to export the tblBilling table as an XML file.

Exporting an Access Table as an XML File

Riverview Veterinary Care Center uses an accounting system that accepts data in XML files. Kimberly wants to export the tblBilling table as an XML file so it can be tested with the accounting system.

Exporting an Access Object as an XML File

- Right-click the object (table, query, form, or report) in the Navigation Pane, point to Export, and then click XML File; or click the object (table, query, form, or report) in the Navigation Pane, and then on the External Data tab, click the XML File button in the Export group.
- Click the Browse button in the Export - XML File dialog box, navigate to the location where you will save the XML file, and then click the Save button.
- Click the OK button in the dialog box, select the options in the Export XML dialog box, or click the More Options button and select the options in the expanded Export XML dialog box, and then click the OK button.
- Click the Close button; or if you need to save the export steps, click the Save export steps check box, enter a name for the saved steps in the Save as box, and then click the Save Export button.

You'll export the tblBilling table as an XML file now.

To export the tblBilling table as an XML file:

1. Open the Navigation Pane (if necessary), right-click **tblBilling**, point to **Export** on the shortcut menu, and then click **XML File**. The Export - XML File dialog box opens.

2. Click the **Browse** button to open the File Save dialog box, navigate to the **Access2 > Module** folder included with your Data Files, change the name in the File name box to **Billing**, make sure **XML** is specified in the Save as type box, and then click the **Save** button. The selected path and filename now appear in the File name box in the Export-XML File dialog box.

3. Click the **OK** button. The Export XML dialog box opens.

   Clicking the More Options button in the Export XML dialog box expands the dialog box and lets you view and select additional options for exporting a database object to an XML file.

4. Click the **More Options** button to display detailed export options in the Export XML dialog box. See Figure 8-12.

Figure 8-12   Data tab in the Export XML dialog box

The Export Data check box, the Export Location box, and the Records To Export option group display the selections you made in the previous steps. You're exporting all records from the tblBilling table, including the data in the records and the structure of the table, to the Billing.xml file in the Access2 > Module folder. The encoding option determines how characters will be represented in the exported XML file. The encoding choices are UTF-8, which uses 8 bits to represent each character, and UTF-16, which uses 16 bits to represent each character. You can also click the Transforms button if you have a special file that contains instructions for changing the exported data.

The accounting software used by the center doesn't have a transform file and requires the default encoding, but Kimberly wants to review the tables that contain lookup data.

5. In the Data to Export box, click the **plus** box to the left of [Lookup Data], and then verify that the tblVisit check box and the tblInvoiceItem check box are not checked. Both the tblVisit table and tblInvoiceItem tables contain lookup data because they are in a one-to-many relationship with the tblBilling table. The accounting program requirements don't include any lookup data from the tblVisit table or tblInvoiceItem table, so you don't want the tblVisit check box or the tblInvoiceItem check box to be checked.

The Data tab settings are correct, so next you'll verify the Schema tab settings.

6. Click the **Schema** tab. See Figure 8-13.

| Figure 8-13 | Schema tab in the Export XML dialog box |

option to export the table structure

option to include the table structure in the XML file

Along with the data from the tblBilling table, you'll be exporting its table structure, including information about the table's primary key, indexes, and table and field properties. An **XSD (XML Structure Definition) file** is a file that defines the structure of the XML file, much like the Design view of a table defines the fields and their data types. You can include this structure information in a separate XSD file, or you can embed the information in the XML file. The accounting software accepts a single XML file, so you'll embed the structure information in the XML file.

7. Click the **Embed schema in exported XML data document** option button. The Create separate schema document option button is now grayed out.

8. Click the **Presentation** tab. See Figure 8-14.

Figure 8-14   **Presentation tab in the Export XML dialog box**

option to export
formatting instructions

Export XML   ×

Data   Schema   Presentation

☐ Export Presentation (HTML 4.0 Sample XSL)

Run from:
  ⦿ Client (HTML)
  ○ Server (ASP)

Include report images:
  ⦿ Put images in:
    [Images   ]   Browse...
  ○ Don't include images

Export Location:
  [Billing.xsl   ]   Browse...

                                    Help   OK   Cancel

The Presentation tab options let you export a separate **XSL (Extensible Stylesheet Language) file** containing the format specifications for the tblBilling table data. The accounting software contains its own formatting instructions for any imported data, so you will not export an XSL file.

9. Make sure that the **Export Presentation (HTML 4.0 Sample XSL)** check box is not checked, and then click the **OK** button. The Export XML dialog box closes, the data in the tblBilling table is exported as an XML file to the Access2 > Module folder, and you return to the final Export - XML File dialog box. You'll see the results of creating this file in the next set of steps.

Kimberly plans to make further tests exporting the tblBilling table as an XML file, so you'll save the export steps.

Saving and Running Export Specifications

Saving the steps to export the tblBilling table as an XML file will save time and eliminate errors when Kimberly repeats the export procedure. You'll save the export steps and then run the saved steps.

To save and run the XML file export steps:

▶ **1.** In the Export – XML File Wizard dialog box, click the **Save export steps** check box. The dialog box displays additional options for the save operation.

The dialog box has the same options you saw earlier when you saved the XML import steps. You'll enter a description, and you won't create an Outlook task because Kimberly will be running the saved export steps only on an as-needed basis.

▶ **2.** In the Description box, type **XML file accounting entries from the tblBilling table**. See Figure 8-15.

Figure 8-15	Saving the export steps

path and filename of the exported file (your path might be different)

click this check box to display additional options in the dialog box

default name of the saved export steps

Export - XML File   ?   ✕

Save Export Steps

Finished exporting 'tblBilling' to file 'E:\Access2\Module\Billing.xml' successfully.

Do you want to save these export steps? This will allow you to quickly repeat the operation without using the wizard.

☑ Save export steps

Save as: Export-Billing

Description: XML file accounting entries from the tblBilling table ◀── description

Create an Outlook Task.

If you regularly repeat this saved operation, you can create an Outlook task that reminds you when it is time to repeat this operation. The Outlook task will include a Run Export button that runs the export operation in Access.

☐ Create Outlook Task

Hint: To create a recurring task, open the task in Outlook and click the Recurrence button on the Task tab.

Manage Data Tasks...   Save Export   Cancel

▶ **3.** Click the **Save Export** button. The export steps are saved as Export-Billing and the Export - XML File dialog box closes.

Now you'll run the saved steps.

▶ **4.** Click the **External Data** tab (if necessary), and then in the Export group, click the **Saved Exports** button. The Manage Data Tasks dialog box opens with the Saved Exports tab selected. See Figure 8-16.

Trouble? If the Saved Imports tab is displayed in the Manage Data Tasks dialog box, then you selected the Saved Imports button instead of the Saved Exports button. Click the Save Exports tab in the dialog box.

Figure 8-16 | **Saved Exports tab in the Manage Data Tasks dialog box**

5. Verify that the Export-Billing export is selected, and then click the **Run** button. The saved procedure runs, and a message box opens, asking if you want to replace the existing XML file you created earlier.

6. Click the **Yes** button to replace the existing XML file. A message box informs you that the export was completed successfully.

7. Click the **OK** button to close the message box, and then click the **Close** button to close the Manage Data Tasks dialog box.

8. Open Windows File Explorer, navigate to the **Access2 > Module** folder included with your Data Files, right-click the **Billing** XML file in the file list to open the shortcut menu, click **Open with**, and then click **Notepad**. See Figure 8-17.

Figure 8-17   Billing XML file in Notepad

Billing XML file

beginning of the
definition of
the data within
the Billing XML file

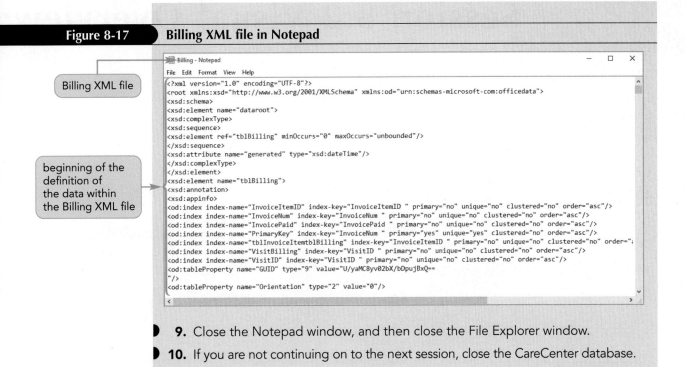

▶ **9.** Close the Notepad window, and then close the File Explorer window.

▶ **10.** If you are not continuing on to the next session, close the CareCenter database.

INSIGHT

Importing and Exporting Data

Access supports importing data from common file formats such as an Excel workbook, a text file, and an XML file. Additional Access options include importing an object from another Access database, importing data from other databases (such as Microsoft SQL Server, mySQL, and others), and importing an HTML document, an Outlook folder, or a SharePoint list.

In addition to exporting an Access object as an XML file or an HTML document, Access includes options for exporting data to another Access database, other databases (Microsoft SQL Server, mySQL), an Excel workbook, a text file, a Word document, a SharePoint list, or a PDF or XPS file. You can also export table or query data directly to Word's mail merge feature or export an object to an email message.

The steps you follow for other import and export options work similarly to the import and export steps you've already used.

You've imported and exported data, analyzed a table's design, and saved and run import and export specifications. In the next session, you will analyze data by working with a chart, creating and using an application part, linking external data, and adding a tab control to a form.

REVIEW

Session 8.1 Quick Check

1. What is HTML?
2. What is an HTML template?
3. What is a static webpage?
4. What is a CSV file?
5. What is the Table Analyzer?
6. _____ is a programming language that describes data and its structure.

Session 8.2 Visual Overview:

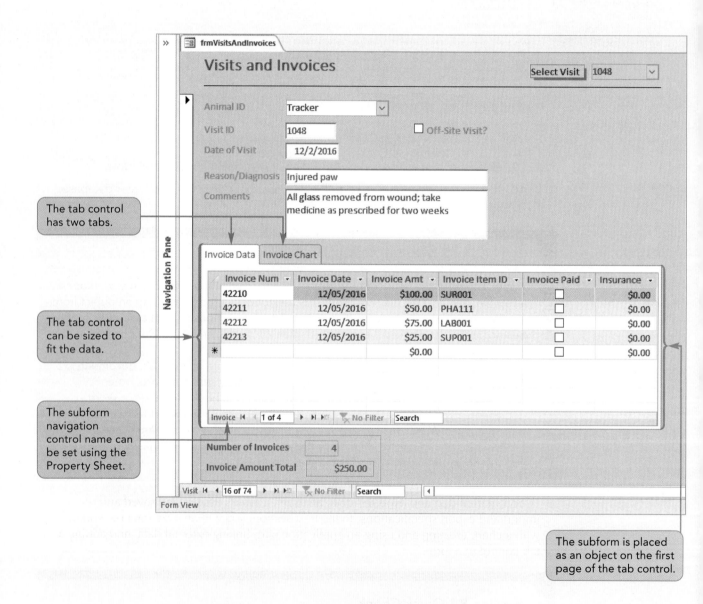

The tab control has two tabs.

The tab control can be sized to fit the data.

The subform navigation control name can be set using the Property Sheet.

The subform is placed as an object on the first page of the tab control.

Tab Control with a Chart

This chart has one data series with four data items.

The Chart Title appears at the top of the chart.

frmVisitsAndInvoices

Visits and Invoices

Select Visit   1048

Animal ID   Tracker

Visit ID   1048

Date of Visit   12/2/2016

Reason/Diagnosis   Injured paw

Comments   All glass removed from wound; take medicine as prescribed for two weeks

☐ Off-Site Visit?

Invoice Data | Invoice Chart

Invoices for this Visit

150
100
50
0
        LAB001   PHA111   SUP001   SUR001

Number of Invoices   4
Invoice Amount Total $250.00

Visit I◄ ◄ 16 of 74 ► ►I ►▸ No Filter   Search

Form View

Navigation Pane

This chart is placed as an object on the second page of the tab control.

Data markers represent the data value of each data item.

The name of each data item is listed under the data marker in a column chart.

The y-axis is the vertical axis containing numbers that represent a range of data values in the data series.

The x-axis is the horizontal axis containing labels that describe each of the data items.

Using a Tab Control in a Form

Kimberly wants you to enhance the frmVisitsAndInvoices form in the CareCenter database to enable users to switch between different content. Recall the frmVistsAndInvoices form currently contains a main form displaying Visit data and the frmBillingSubform subform displaying the information for the billed invoices related to a displayed visit. Specifically, Kimberly wants users to be able to choose between viewing the frmBillingSubform subform or viewing a chart showing the invoices associated with the displayed visit.

You can use the **Tab Control tool** to insert a tab control, which is a control that appears with tabs at the top. Each tab is commonly referred to as a page, or tab page, within the tab control. Users can switch between pages by clicking the tabs. You'll use a tab control to implement Kimberly's requested enhancements. The first page will contain the frmBillingSubform subform that is currently positioned at the bottom of the frmVisitsAndInvoices form. The second page will contain a chart showing the invoice amounts for the invoices associated with the displayed visit.

Working with Large Forms

When you want to work with a form that is too large to display in the Access window, one way to help you navigate the form is to manually add page breaks, where it makes sense to do so. You can use the **Page Break tool** to insert a page break control in the form, which lets users move between the form pages by pressing the Page Up and Page Down keys.

To expedite placing the subform in the first page within the tab control, you'll first cut the subform from the form, placing it on the Clipboard. You'll then add the tab control, and finally you'll paste the subform into the first page on the tab control. You need to perform these steps in Design view.

To add the tab control to the frmVisitsAndInvoices form:

1. If you took a break after the previous session, make sure that the CareCenter database is open with the Navigation Pane displayed.

2. Open the **frmVisitsAndInvoices** form in Form view to review the form and the frmBillingSubform, switch to Design view, and then close the Navigation Pane.

3. Scroll down until the subform is fully visible (if necessary), right-click the top-left corner of the subform control to open the shortcut menu, and then click **Cut** to remove the subform control from the form and place it on the Clipboard.

   Trouble? If you do not see Cut as one of the options on the shortcut menu, you did not click the top edge of the subform control correctly. Right-click the top edge of the subform control until you see this option on the shortcut menu, and then click Cut.

4. Increase the length of the Detail section to **7.0** inches.

5. Select the **Number of Invoices** label and control, the **Invoice Amount Total** label and control, and the rectangle control surrounding them, and then move the selected controls below the 6-inch horizontal line in the grid.

6. On the Form Design Tools Design tab, in the Controls group, click the **Tab Control** tool.

7. Position the + portion of the Tab Control tool pointer in the Detail section at the 2.75-inch mark on the vertical ruler and three grid dots from the left edge of the form, and then click the mouse button. A tab control with two tabs is inserted in the form.

8. Right-click in the middle of the tab control, and then when an orange outline appears inside the tab control, click **Paste** on the shortcut menu. The subform is pasted in the tab control on the left-most tab. See Figure 8-18.

Figure 8-18   Subform in the tab control

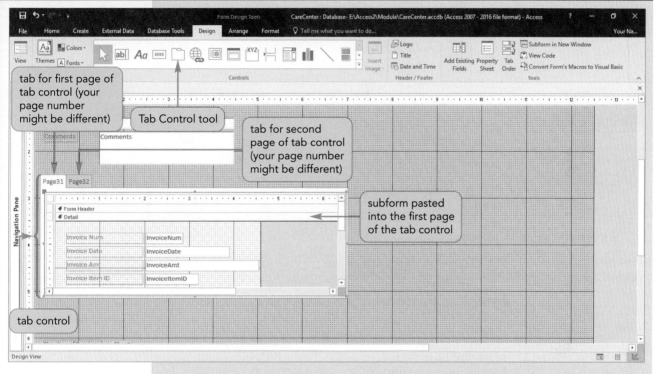

9. Switch to Form view, click the **Select Visit** arrow, click **1048** in the list, and then click **1048** in the Visit ID box to deselect all controls.

10. Scroll down to the bottom of the form. The left tab, which is labeled Page31 (yours might differ), is the active tab. See Figure 8-19.

Figure 8-19   Subform on the tab control in Form view

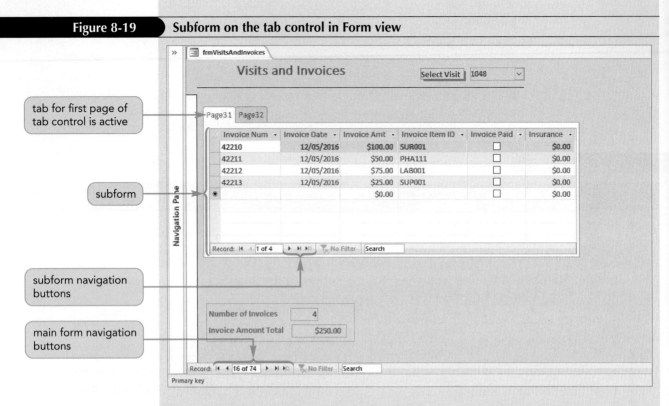

The subform is now displayed on the first page of the tab control.

▶ **11.** Click the **right tab** of the tab control (labeled Page32) to display the second page. The page is empty because you haven't added any controls to it yet.

▶ **12.** Click the **left tab** of the tab control again to display the frmBillingSubform.

After viewing the form and subform in Form view, Kimberly's staff finds the two sets of navigation buttons confusing—they waste time determining which set of navigation buttons applies to the subform and which to the main form. To clarify this, you'll set the Navigation Caption property for the main form and the subform. The **Navigation Caption property** lets you change the navigation label from the word "Record" to another value. Because the main form displays data about visits and the subform displays data about invoices, you'll change the Navigation Caption property for the main form to "Visit" and for the subform to "Invoice."

You'll also set the Caption property for the tabs in the tab control, so they indicate the label on the tabs indicate the contents of each page.

To change the captions for the navigation buttons and the tabs:

▶ **1.** Switch to Design view, and then click the main form's form selector to select the form control in the main form, open the Property Sheet to display the properties for the selected form control, click the **All** tab (if necessary), click the **Navigation Caption** box, and then type **Visit**. See Figure 8-20.

Figure 8-20   Navigation Caption property set for the main form

> **2.** Click the **form selector** for the subform on the left-most tab to select the subform, click the **form selector** for the subform again to select the form control in the subform and to display the Property Sheet for the selected form control, click the **Navigation Caption** box, and then type **Invoice**. Navigation buttons don't appear in Design view, so you won't see the effects of the Navigation Caption property settings until you switch to Form view. Before you do that, you will set the Caption property for the two tabs in the tab control.

> **3.** Click the **left tab** in the tab control, and then click the **left tab** in the tab control again to select it.

> **4.** In the Property Sheet, in the Caption box, type **Invoice Data** and then press the **Tab** key. The Caption property value now appears on the left tab in the tab control. See Figure 8-21.

Figure 8-21   **The Caption property set for the left tab of a tab control**

5. Click the **right tab** in the subform to select it, in the Property Sheet, in the Caption box, type **Invoice Chart**, press the **Tab** key, and then close the Property Sheet.

6. Save your form design changes, and then switch to Form view.

7. Click the **Select Visit** arrow, click **1048** in the list to display the information for this visit, click **1048** in the Visit ID box to deselect all controls, and then scroll to the bottom of the form. The tabs and the navigation buttons now display the new caption values. See Figure 8-22.

Figure 8-22   Modified report with tab control in Form view

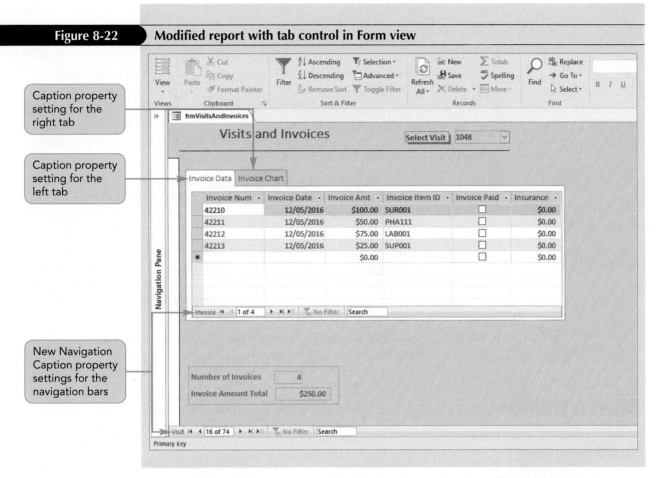

Caption property setting for the right tab

Caption property setting for the left tab

New Navigation Caption property settings for the navigation bars

Next, Kimberly wants you to add a simple chart to the second page of the tab control. You will create the chart using the Chart Wizard.

Creating a Chart Using the Chart Wizard

The Chart Wizard in Access guides you in creating a chart in a form or report based upon data contained in the database. Once the chart is created, you can modify and format the chart using Microsoft Graph, a simple graphing tool included in Microsoft Office 365.

REFERENCE

Embedding a Chart in a Form or Report

- On the Report Design Tools or Form Design Tools Design tab, click the More button in the Controls group, and then click the Chart tool.
- Position the + portion of the pointer in the form or report, and then click the mouse button to start the Chart Wizard.
- Navigate through the Chart Wizard dialog boxes to select the record source, fields, chart type, specify a layout for the chart data, and select the fields that link the records in the database object to the chart's components, if necessary.
- In the Chart Wizard's last dialog box, enter a chart title, select whether to include a legend, and then click the Finish button.

The tblBilling table contains the information Kimberly wants displayed in chart form on the right tab in the tab control.

To create a chart in the tab control using the Chart Wizard:

1. Switch to Design view, click the **Invoice Chart** tab in the tab control, then click the **Invoice Chart** tab again to select it, as indicated by the orange selection border.

2. On the Form Design Tools Design tab, in the Controls group, click the **Chart** tool █, and then position the pointer in the tab control. When the pointer is inside the tab control, the rectangular portion of the tab control you can use to place controls is filled with the color black.

3. Position the + portion of the pointer in the upper-left corner of the black tab control, and then click the mouse button. A chart control appears in the tab control, and the first Chart Wizard dialog box opens, in which you select the source record for the chart.

   Kimberly wants the chart to provide a simple visual display of the relative proportions of the invoice amounts for the invoice items for the currently displayed animal visit. You'll use the tblBilling table as the record source for the chart and select the InvoiceAmt and InvoiceItemID fields as the fields to use in the chart.

4. Click **Table: tblBilling** in the box listing the available tables, and then click the **Next** button to display the second Chart Wizard dialog box, in which you select the fields from the tblBilling table that contain the data to be used to create the chart.

TIP

The order of the items is important. Be sure to add InvoiceItemID first, then InvoiceAmt.

5. From the Available Fields box, add the **InvoiceItemID** and **InvoiceAmt** fields to the Fields for Chart box, in that order, and then click the **Next** button to display the third Chart Wizard dialog box, in which you choose the chart type.

6. Click the **Pie Chart** button (first chart in the fourth row) to select the pie chart as the chart type to use for Kimberly's chart. The box on the right displays a brief description of the selected chart type. See Figure 8-23.

Figure 8-23   **Chart Wizard showing selected chart type**

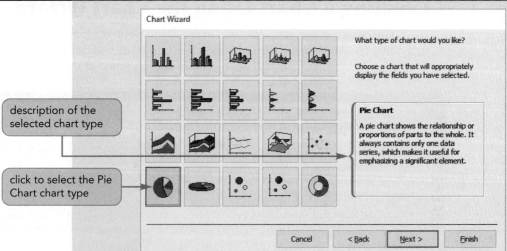

7. Click the **Next** button to display the next Chart Wizard dialog box, which displays a preview of the chart and options to modify the layout of the data in the chart. You'll use the default layout based on the two selected fields.

8. Click the **Next** button to display the next Chart Wizard dialog box, which lets you choose the fields that link records in the main form (which uses the tblVisit table as its record source) to records in the chart (which uses the tblBilling table as its record source). You don't need to make any changes in this dialog box because the wizard has already identified VisitID as the common field linking these two tables. You can use the VisitID field as the linking field even though you didn't select it as a field for the chart.

9. Click the **Next** button to display the final Chart Wizard dialog box, in which you enter the title that will appear at the top of the chart and choose whether to include a legend in the chart.

10. Type **Invoices for this Visit**, make sure the **Yes, display a legend** option button is selected, and then click the **Finish** button. The completed chart appears in the tab control.

You'll view the form in Form view, where it's easier to assess the chart's appearance.

11. Save your form design changes, switch to Form view, display Visit ID **1048** in the main form, click the **Invoice Chart** tab to display the chart, and then scroll down to the bottom of the form (if necessary). See Figure 8-24.

Figure 8-24   **Pie chart in the tab control**

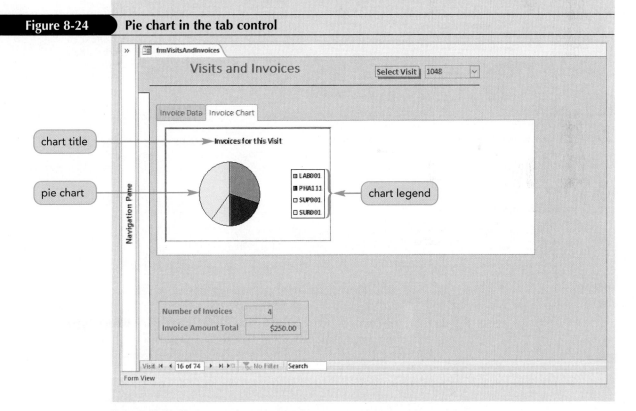

Linking Record Sources

INSIGHT

The record source for a primary main form must have a one-to-many relationship to the record source for a related subform or chart. The subform or chart object has its Link Master Fields property set to the primary key in the record source for the main form and its Link Child Fields property set to the foreign key in the record source for the subform or chart.

After viewing the chart, Kimberly decides it needs some modifications. She wants you to change the chart type from a pie chart to a bar chart, remove the legend, and modify the chart's background color. To make these formatting changes, you'll switch to Design view. To modify the chart, you need to access the Microsoft Graph tools. You can double-click the chart to display the Microsoft Graph menu bar and toolbar on the ribbon and open the datasheet for the chart, or you can right-click the chart and use the shortcut menu to open the chart in a separate Microsoft Graph window.

To edit the chart using Microsoft Graph tools:

▶ 1. Switch to Design view, right-click an edge of the chart object to open the shortcut menu, point to **Chart Object**, and then click **Open**. Microsoft Graph starts and displays the chart and datasheet in a separate window on top of the Access window. See Figure 8-25.

Figure 8-25	Chart in the Microsoft Graph window

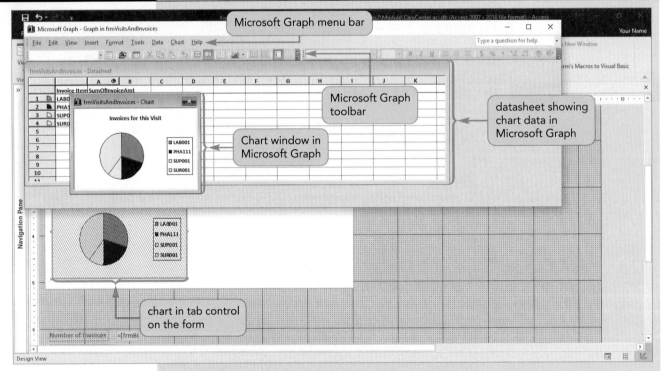

▶ 2. On the Microsoft Graph menu bar, click **Chart**, click **Chart Type** to open the Chart Type dialog box, and then click **Column** in the Chart type box to display the types of column charts. See Figure 8-26.

Figure 8-26 | Microsoft Graph Chart Type dialog box

click to create a custom chart type

selected chart type

subtypes of the selected chart type

description of selected chart subtype

click to view sample of selected chart subtype

The column chart is the selected chart type, and the clustered column chart is the default chart subtype (row 1, column 1). A description of the selected chart subtype appears below the chart subtypes. You can create a custom chart by clicking the Custom Types tab. You can also use the Press and Hold to View Sample button to display a sample of the selected subtype.

3. Click the **Press and Hold to View Sample** button to view a sample of the chart, release the mouse button, and then click the **OK** button to close the dialog box and change the chart to a column chart in the Microsoft Graph window and in the tab control on the form.

4. On the Microsoft Graph menu bar, click **Chart**, click **Chart Options** to open the Chart Options dialog box, click the **Legend** tab to display the chart's legend options, click the **Show legend** check box to uncheck it, and then click the **OK** button. The legend is removed from the chart object in the Microsoft Graph window and in the tab control on the form.

To change the color or other properties of a chart's elements—the chart background (or chart area), axes, labels to the left of the y-axis, labels below the x-axis, or data markers (columnar bars for a column chart)—you need to double-click the chart element.

TIP

A data marker is a bar, dot, segment, or other symbol that represents a single data value.

5. In the Microsoft Graph Chart window, double-click one of the column data markers in the chart to open the Format Data Series dialog box, and then in the Area section, click the **orange** color (row 2, column 2) in the color palette. The sample color in the dialog box changes to orange to match the selected color. See Figure 8-27.

Figure 8-27 **Format Data Series dialog box in Microsoft Graph**

6. Click the **OK** button to close the dialog box. The color of the data markers in the chart in the Microsoft Graph window and in the form's tab control changes to orange.

   Trouble? If only one of the bars changed color, you selected one bar instead of the entire series. Click Edit, click Undo, and then repeat Steps 5 and 6.

7. In the Chart window, double-click the white chart background to the left of the title to open the Format Chart Area dialog box, in the Area section, click the **light orange** color (row 5, column 2) in the color palette, and then click the **OK** button. The chart's background color changes from white to light orange in the chart in the Microsoft Graph window and in the form's tab control.

8. Click **File** on the Microsoft Graph menu bar, and then click **Exit & Return to frmVisitsAndInvoices** to close the Microsoft Graph window and return to the form.

9. Save your form design changes, switch to Form view, display Visit ID **1048** in the main form, and then click the **Invoice Chart** tab to display the chart. Scroll down to the bottom of the form. See Figure 8-28.

Figure 8-28   Completed chart in Form view

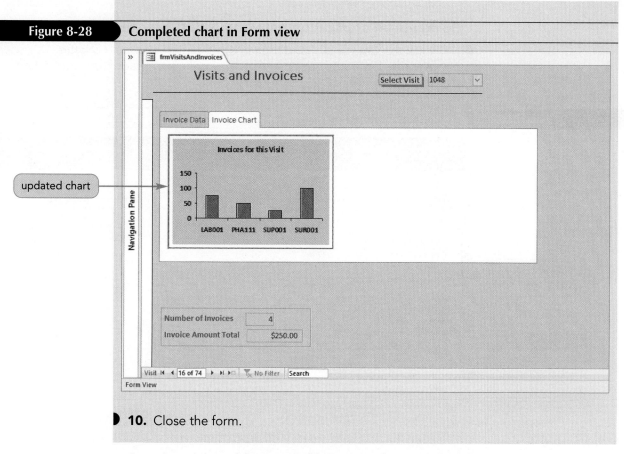

updated chart

▶ **10.** Close the form.

Sometimes it is useful to use a table structure from one database in other databases. One option would be to import the table structure only from the database file into each subsequent database, a method you used in an earlier module. Another option is to create an application part in one database, which can then easily be included in any Access database file on your computer.

Using Templates and Application Parts

A template is a predefined database that can include tables, relationships, queries, forms, reports, and other database objects and is used to create a new database file. On the New tab in Backstage view, a list of predefined templates are displayed. You can also create your own template from an existing database file. In addition to creating a database template, you can also create templates for objects using an **application part**, which is a specialized template for a specific database object that can be imported into an existing database. There are predefined application parts included with Access, and you can also create your own user-defined application part. Once you create a user-defined application part in one database, it is available to all Access databases created and stored on your computer.

You can use an application part to insert a predefined object from another database or template into an existing database. Like a template, an application part can contain tables, relationships, queries, forms, reports, and other database objects.

Kimberly would like to reuse a table structure from another database to create a new table in the CareCenter database. You'll use the NewOwnerReferrals.accdb database file to create an application part for the table structure, and then you'll import the new application part into the CareCenter database to use to create a table of referrals from online veterinary pharmacies.

To create an application part from a database file:

▶ **1.** Click the **Create** tab, and then in the Templates group, click the **Application Parts** button to open the gallery of predefined application parts. See Figure 8-29.

| Figure 8-29 | **Predefined Application Parts** |

templates that create forms

templates that create multiple database objects including tables, forms, and queries

Note that there are Blank Forms and Quick Start Application Parts. If you or another user of your computer has created user-defined application parts, they also will appear in the gallery.

▶ **2.** Close the CareCenter database file.

▶ **3.** Open the **NewOwnerReferrals** database file from the **Access2 > Module** folder included with your Data Files, enabling the content if necessary.

When you save this file as a template, all database objects that are in the file will be included in the template file. This file contains only the tblReferral table.

▶ **4.** Click the **File** tab to open Backstage view, and then in the navigation bar, click **Save As**.

▶ **5.** In Database File Types section of the Save Database As list, click **Template**. See Figure 8-30.

Figure 8-30 Save As options in Backstage View

6. Click the **Save As** button. The Create New Template from This Database dialog box opens.

7. Click in the Name box, type **Referral**, click in the Description box, type **New owner referral**, and then click the **Application Part** check box to select it. See Figure 8-31.

Figure 8-31 Create New Template from This Database dialog box

this text will appear as a ScreenTip for this application part in the Application Parts gallery

check to save this template as an application part

▶ **8.** Click the **OK** button to close the dialog box. An alert box opens, indicating that the application part, as a template, has been saved.

▶ **9.** Click the **OK** button to close the message box, and then close the NewOwnerReferrals database.

Now that you've created the application part, you'll use it in the CareCenter database to create the referral table for owners who have been referred to the care center from online pharmacies.

To use the application part to create the referral table:

▶ **1.** Open the **CareCenter** database, click the **Create** tab, and then in the Templates group, click the **Application Parts** button. The Referral template is displayed in the User Templates section in the Application Parts gallery. See Figure 8-32.

Figure 8-32	Referral template in Application Parts Gallery

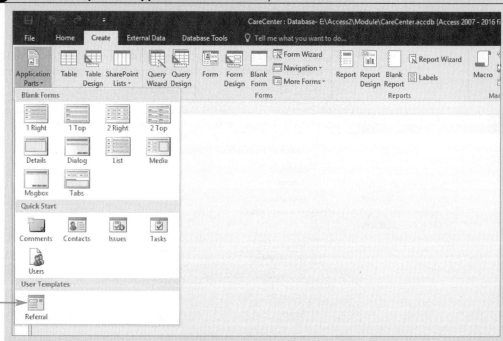

user-defined template added as an application part

▶ **2.** Click **Referral**. The Create Relationship dialog box opens because the application part includes a table.

▶ **3.** Click the **There is no relationship** option button. This indicates that the new table is not related to other tables in the current database. See Figure 8-33.

Figure 8-33 **Create Relationship dialog box**

use these options to create a relationship between the table in the application part and a table in the current database

4. Click the **Create** button to insert the Referral database object into the current database, and then open the Navigation Pane.

Only the tblReferral table will be inserted into the current database because the Referral template contains only one database object, which is the tblReferral table. Because the CareCenter database already contains a table called tblReferral, the newly inserted table is named tblReferral1, to avoid overwriting the table that already exists. The newly inserted tblReferral1 will be used to store the owner information for owners referred by online pharmacists. You'll rename this table as tblReferralPharm.

5. In the Navigation Pane, right-click the **tblReferral1** table, click **Rename**, change the name to **tblReferralPharm**, and then press the **Enter** key.

6. In the Navigation Pane, double-click **tblReferralPharm** to open it in Datasheet view.

Note that the tblReferralPharm table contains the same fields as the tblReferral table but does not contain any records.

7. Close the tblReferralPharm table.

Kimberly would like to be able to send an electronic copy of the rptVisitDetails report that other people can view on their computers, rather than distributing printed reports. You can export tables, queries, reports, and other database objects as files that can be opened in other programs such as Excel and PDF readers. Kimberly would like to distribute rptVisitDetails as a PDF and asks you to export the report in this format.

Exporting a Report to a PDF File

PDF (portable document format) is a file format that preserves the original formatting and pagination of its contents no matter what device is used to view it. Current versions of all major operating systems for computers and handheld devices include software that opens PDF files. Most web browsers allow you to view PDF files as well. You'll create a PDF document from the rptVisitDetails report so Kimberly can send this report to colleagues.

To export the rptVisitDetails report to a PDF file:

1. In the Navigation Pane, right-click **rptVisitDetails**, point to **Export** on the shortcut menu, and then click **PDF or XPS**. The Publish as PDF or XPS dialog box opens.

2. Navigate to the **Access2 > Module** folder included with your Data Files, and then change the name in the File name box to **Visit Details Report**. See Figure 8-34.

Figure 8-34	Publish as PDF or XPS file dialog box

the file structure of your computer drives and folders might differ

file size is reduced to minimize downloading time

Kimberly would like people who are visually impaired to be able to use the PDF document with their screen readers. When a PDF file is saved using the minimum size option, there is no additional functionality for screen readers. You can include document structure tags that allow people using screen readers to navigate the document easily. Screen reader software voices the structure tags, such as a tag that provides a description of an image. Structure tags also reflow text so that screen readers understand the flow of information and can read it in a logical order. For instance, a page with a sidebar shouldn't be read as two columns; the main column needs to be read as a continuation of the previous page.

In order to add this functionality, you'll specify that document structure tags should be included.

▶ **3.** Click the **Options** button. The Options dialog box opens.

▶ **4.** Click the **Document structure tags for accessibility** check box to select it. See Figure 8-35.

Figure 8-35   **Options dialog box for PDF file export**

this option allows you to select individual pages from a multipage report

this option allows you to include the document structure tags

▶ **5.** Click the **OK** button to close the Options dialog box, and then click the **Publish** button to close the Publish as PDF or XPS dialog box and to create the PDF file. The Export - PDF dialog box opens.

Trouble? Depending on the operating system you're using, the PDF file may open. If it does, close the PDF file and return to Access.

▶ **6.** In the Export - PDF dialog box, click the **Close** button to close the dialog box without saving the export steps.

▶ **7.** Open Windows File Explorer, navigate to the **Access2 > Module** folder included with your Data Files, and then double-click the **Visit Details Report.pdf** to open the PDF file and examine the results.

▶ **8.** Close the PDF file, and then close Windows File Explorer.

Kimberly is pleased to know that she can export database objects as PDF files. Now she would like your help with one additional external data issue. Her staff maintains an Excel workbook that contains contact information for people who volunteer at Riverview Veterinary Care Center. Kimberly wants to be able to use this data in the CareCenter database.

Integrating Access with Other Applications

As you know, when you create a form or report in Access, you include more than just the data from the record source table or query. You've added controls such as lines, rectangles, tab controls, and graphics in your forms and reports to improve their appearance and usability. You can also add charts, drawings, and other objects to your forms and reports, but Access doesn't have the capability to create them. Instead, you create these objects using other applications and then place them in a form or report using the appropriate integration method.

When you integrate information between two files created using different software applications, the file containing the original information, or object, is called the **source file**, and the file in which you place the information from the source file is called the **destination file**. In Access there are three ways for you to integrate objects created by other applications—importing, embedding, and linking.

As you know from your work thus far, when you import an object, you include the contents of a file in a new table or append it to an existing table, or you include the contents of the file in a form, report, or field. In this module you imported CSV and XML files as new tables in the CareCenter database, and the CSV and XML files you imported were created by other applications. After importing an object into a destination file, it no longer has a connection to the original object in the source file or the application used to create it. Any subsequent changes you make to the object in the source file using the source application are not reflected in the imported object in the destination file.

When you **embed** an object from the source file into a form, report, or field in the destination file, you preserve its connection to the application used to create it in the source file, enabling you to edit the object, if necessary, using the features of the source application. However, any changes you make to the object are reflected only in the destination file in which it is embedded; the changes do not affect the original object in the source file from which it was embedded. Likewise, if you make any changes to the original object in the source file, these changes are not reflected in the embedded object in the destination file.

When you **link** an object to a form, report, or field in a destination file, you maintain a connection between the object in the destination file to the original object in the source file. You can make changes to a linked object only in the source file. Any changes you make to the original object in the source file using the source application are then reflected in the linked object in the destination file. To view or use the linked object in a form, report, or field in the destination file, you must first open the source file in the source application.

PROSKILLS

Decision Making: Importing, Embedding, and Linking Data

How do you decide which integration method to use when you need to include in an Access database data that is stored in another file created in a different application?

- You should choose to import an object when you want to copy an object from a file created using a different application into a table, form, or report in the Access database, *and* you want to be able to manipulate and work with that object using Access tools, *and* you do not need these changes to the imported object to be reflected in the original object in the source file.

- Conversely, you should choose to embed or link the object when you want to be able to edit the copied object in the table, form, or report using the application with which the source object was created. You should embed the object when you *do not* want your changes to the embedded object in the destination file to affect the original object in the source file. You should choose to link the object when you want the object in the destination file to always match the original object in the source file.

The decision to import, embed, or link to an object containing data depends on how you will use the data in your database and what connection is required to the original data. You should carefully consider the effect of changes to the original data and to the copied data before choosing which method to use.

Linking Data from an Excel Worksheet

Kimberly's staff has extensive experience working with Excel, and one of her staff members prefers to maintain the data for people who volunteer in an Excel file named Volunteer. However, Kimberly needs to reference the volunteer data in the CareCenter database on occasion, and the data she's referencing must always be the current version of the data in the Volunteer Excel file. Importing the Excel workbook data as an Access table would provide Kimberly with data that's quickly out of date unless she repeats the import steps each time the data in the Excel workbook changes. Therefore, you'll link the data in the Excel file to a table in the CareCenter database. When the staff changes data in the Volunteer Excel workbook, the changes will be reflected automatically in the linked version in the database table. In addition, Kimberly won't be able to update the volunteer data from the CareCenter database, which ensures that only the staff members responsible for maintaining the Volunteer Excel workbook can update the data.

To link table data to an Excel file:

▶ **1.** Click the **External Data** tab, and then in the Import & Link group, click the **Excel** button. The Get External Data - Excel Spreadsheet dialog box opens.

   Trouble? If the Export - Excel File dialog box opens, you clicked the Excel button in the Export group. Click the Cancel button and then repeat Step 1, being sure to select the Excel button from the Import & Link group.

▶ **2.** Click the **Browse** button to open the File Open dialog box, navigate to the **Access2 > Module** folder included with your Data Files, click **Volunteer**, click the **Open** button, and then click the **Link to the data source by creating a linked table** option button. This option links to the data instead of importing or appending it. The selected path and filename are displayed in the File name box. See Figure 8-36.

Figure 8-36 **Linking to data in an Excel workbook**

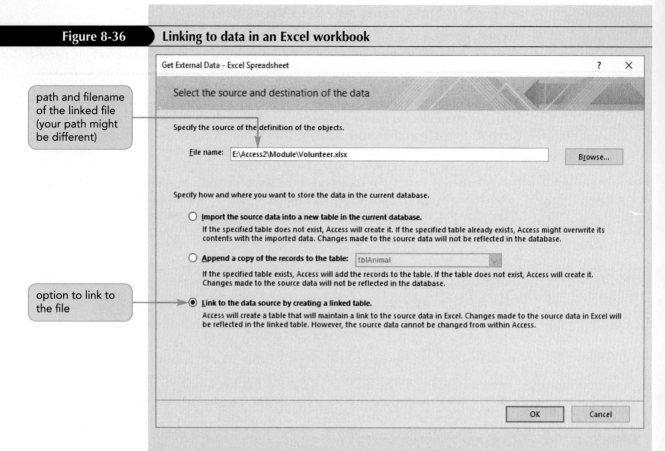

path and filename of the linked file (your path might be different)

option to link to the file

3. Click the **OK** button. The first Link Spreadsheet Wizard dialog box opens.

The first row in the worksheet contains column heading names, and each row in the worksheet represents the data about a single volunteer.

4. Click the **First Row Contains Column Headings** check box to select it. See Figure 8-37.

| Figure 8-37 | Link Spreadsheet Wizard dialog box |

option to use the first row in the worksheet as column heading names

data in the worksheet to be linked

5. Click the **Next** button to open the final Link Spreadsheet Wizard dialog box, in which you choose a name for the linked table.

6. Change the default table name to **tblVolunteer** and then click the **Finish** button. A message box informs you that you've created a table that's linked to the workbook.

7. Click the **OK** button to close the message box. The tblVolunteer table is listed in the Navigation Pane, with an icon to its left indicating it is a linked table.

You can open and view the tblVolunteer table and use fields from the linked table in queries, forms, and reports, but you cannot update the data using the CareCenter database. You can only update the data only from the Excel workbook file. To open and view the tblVolunteer table in the CareCenter database, you must first open and leave open the Excel file to which the table is linked.

Kimberly tells you that the volunteer Hoskins had not been able to volunteer for a while, so her Active status was "no". She's now able to volunteer, and Kimberly would like to change her Active status to "yes". Next, you'll make a change to data in the Excel file and see the update in the linked table.

To update the data in the Excel file and view the data in the linked table:

1. Start Excel and open the **Volunteer** file from the **Access2 > Module** folder included with your Data Files. The Volunteer workbook opens and displays the Volunteer worksheet.

   Trouble? If you attempt to open the table in Access before you open the workbook in Excel, you'll get an error message and won't be able to open the workbook. Make sure you always open the workbook or other source file before you open a linked table.

2. Switch to the CareCenter database, and then open the **tblVolunteer** datasheet. The fields and records in the tblVolunteer table display the same data as the Volunteer worksheet.

3. Switch to the Volunteer Excel workbook, select the value **no** in the Active column for Angela Hoskins (row 4), type **yes** to replace the value, and then press the **Enter** key.

4. Switch to the CareCenter database. The Active status for Angela Hoskins is now **yes**.

   Trouble? If the record is not updated in the tblVolunteer table in the CareCenter database, click the record to show the update.

   You've completed your work for Kimberly and her staff.

5. Close the tblVolunteer table in Access.

6. Switch to the Volunteer workbook, save your changes to the workbook, and then exit Excel.

7. Make a backup copy of the CareCenter database, compact and repair the database, and then close it.

Knowing how to create tab controls and application parts, export data to PDF documents, and link to data maintained by other applications will make it easier for Kimberly and her staff to efficiently manage their data.

REVIEW

Session 8.2 Quick Check

1. The _____ property lets you change the default navigation label from the word "Record" to another value.
2. What is the Microsoft Graph program?
3. What is a PDF file?
4. What is an application part?
5. What is the difference between an application part and a template?
6. How can you edit data in a table that has been linked to an Excel file?

PRACTICE

Review Assignments

Data Files needed for the Review Assignments: Ads.xlsx, Partners.accdb, Payables.csv, Payments. xml, and Supplier.accdb (cont. from previous module)

Kimberly wants you to integrate data in other files created with other applications with the data in the Supplier database, and she wants to be able to analyze the data in the database. Complete the following steps:

1. Open the **Supplier** database you worked with in the previous three modules.

2. Export the qrySupplierProducts query as an HTML document to the Access2 > Review folder provided with your Data Files, saving the file as **qrySupplierProducts**. Save the export steps with the name **Export-qrySupplierProducts**. Once saved, modify the description to be **HTML file containing the qrySupplierProducts query**.

3. Import the CSV file named **Payables**, which is located in the Access2 > Review folder, as a new table in the database. Use the names in the first row as field names, use Currency as the data type for the numeric fields, choose your own primary key, name the table **tblPayables**, run the Table Analyzer, record the Table Analyzer's recommendation, and then cancel out of the Table Analyzer Wizard without making the recommended changes. Do not save the import steps.

4. Import the data and structure from the XML file named **Payments**, which is located in the Access2 > Review folder included with your Data Files, as a new table named **tblPayments** in the database. Do not save the import steps, and then rename the table **tblPayment** (with no "s" on the end of the name).

5. Export the tblSupplier table as an XML file named **Supplier** to the Access2 > Review folder; do not create a separate XSD file. Save the export steps, and use the default name given.

6. The Riverview Veterinary Care Center also pays for advertisements, and information on this activity is contained in an Excel file named Ads. Create a table named **tblAds** in in the CareCenter database that links to the **Ads** Excel file, which is located in the Access2 > Review folder included with your Data Files. Change the cost of the flyer for Ad 5 to **$150**, and save the workbook.

7. Modify the **frmSuppliersWithProducts** form in the following ways:

   a. Add a tab control to the bottom of the Detail section, so the left edge is aligned with the left edge of the Notes label, and then place the existing subform on the first page of the tab control.

   b. Change the caption for the left tab to **Product Data** and for the right tab to **Product Chart.**

   c. Change the caption for the main form's navigation buttons to **Supplier.**

   d. Add a chart to the second page of the tab control. Use the tblProduct table as the record source, select the ProductName and Price, use the 3-D Column Chart type (row 1, column 2), do not include a legend, and use **Products Offered** as the chart title.

   e. Change the chart to a 3-D Clustered Bar chart, and change the purple colored data markers to pink.

8. Export the **tblPayment** table as a PDF file called **Payments**, using document structure tags for accessibility. Do not save the export steps.

9. Open the **Partners** database from the Access2 > Review folder, and then create and implement an application part as follows:

   a. Create an application part called **Vendor** with the description **New Vendor**, and do not include the data.

   b. Close the Partners database.

   c. Open the **Supplier** database and import the Vendor application part, which has no relationship to any of the other tables. Open the tblNewVendor table to verify the structure has been imported, but does not contain any records.

10. Make a backup copy of the database, compact and repair the database, and then close it.

Case Problem 1

Data Files needed for this Case Problem: CreditCard.xml, MoreBeauty.accdb (cont. from previous module), and Schedule.xlsx.

APPLY

Beauty To Go Sue Miller wants you to integrate data from files created with other applications with the data in the MoreBeauty database, and she wants to be able to analyze the data in the database. Complete the following steps:

1. Open the **MoreBeauty** database you worked with in the previous three modules.
2. Export the qryMemberNames query as an HTML document to the Access2 > Case1 folder using a filename of **MemberNames**. Save the export steps.
3. Export the rptOptionMembership report as a PDF document with a filename of **Option** to the Access2 > Case1 folder. Include the document structure tags for accessibility, and do not save the export steps.
4. Import the data and structure from the XML file named **CreditCard**, which is located in the Access2 > Case1 folder provided with your Data Files, as a new table. Save the import steps. Rename the table as **tblCreditCard**.
5. Export the tblOption table as an XML file named **Options** to the Access2 > Case1 folder; do not create a separate XSD file. Save the export steps.
6. Create a new table named **tblSchedule** by linking to the **Schedule** Excel file, which is located in the Access2 > Case1 folder provided with your Data Files. For ScheduleID 105, change the Day value to **Tuesday**.
7. Modify the **frmPlansWithMembers** form in the following ways:
   a. Add a tab control to the bottom of the Detail section, and place the existing subform on the first page tab of the tab control.
   b. Change the caption for the left tab to **Member Data** and for the right tab to **Member Chart**.
   c. Change the caption for the main form's navigation buttons to **Option** and for the subform's navigation buttons to **Member**.
   d. Add a chart to the second page of the tab control. Use the tblOption table as the record source, select the OptionID and OptionCost fields, use the Column Chart chart type, do not include a legend, and use **Option Cost** as the chart title.
   e. Change the color of the data marker to red (row 3, column 1 in the color palette.).
8. Make a backup copy of the database, compact and repair the database, and then close it.

Case Problem 2

Data Files needed for this Case Problem: AddSubject.xml, NewStudentReferrals.accdb, Room.xlsx, Subject.csv, and Tutoring.accdb (cont. from previous module)

CHALLENGE

Programming Pros Brent Hovis wants you to integrate data from other files created with different applications with the data in the Tutoring database, and he wants to be able to analyze the data in the database. Complete the following steps:

1. Open the **Tutoring** database you worked with in the previous three modules.
2. Export the rptTutorSessions report as a PDF document with a filename of **TutorSessions** to the Access2 > Case2 folder provided with your Data Files. Include the document structure tags for accessibility, and do not save the export steps.

3. Import the CSV file named **Subject**, which is located in the Access2 > Case2 folder, as a new table in the database. Use the names in the first row as field names, set the third column's data type to Currency and the other fields' data types to Short Text, choose your own primary key, name the table **tblSubject**, run the Table Analyzer, and record the Table Analyzer's recommendation, but do not accept the recommendation. Do not save the import steps.

4. Export the tblTutor table as an XML file named **Tutor** to the Access2 > Case2 folder; do not create a separate XSD file. Save the export steps.

5. Create a new table named **tblRoom** that is linked to the **Room** Excel file, which is located in the Access2 > Case2 folder provided with your Data Files. Add the following new record to the Room workbook: Room Num **6**, Rental Cost **$25**, and Type **Private**.

⊕ **Explore** 6. Import the XML file named **AddSubject** file, which is located in the Access2 > Case2 folder included with your Data Files, appending the records to the tblSubject table. Do not save any import steps. (*Hint:* Because you cannot import and append the data from the AddSubject XML file directly to the existing tblSubject table, first import the AddSubject XML file into a new table with an appropriate name (such as tblAddSubject), export this new table to an Excel file with an appropriate name (such as AddSubject), and then import and append the Excel data to the tblSubject table. Open the AddSubject table to verify the records with the SubjectID of 124 through 130 were appended. Close the tblAddSubject table. Remove the new table that was temporarily created (tblAddSubject). Finally, close the Tutoring database.)

⊕ **Explore** 7. Open the **NewStudentReferrals** database from the Access2 > Case2 folder provided with your Data Files, and then create and work with an application part as follows:

a. Create an application part called **NewStudentContact** with the description **New student referrals** and include the data.

b. Close the NewStudentReferrals database.

c. Open the **Tutoring** database and import the **NewStudentContact** application part, which has no relationship to any of the other tables. Open the tblContact table to verify the data has been imported.

d. Kimberly would like to import an empty tblContact table in the future. Delete the NewStudentContact application part by clicking the Application Parts button, right-clicking the NewStudentContact template, selecting Delete Template Part from Gallery, and then clicking Yes in the dialog box that opens.

e. Save and close the Tutoring database.

f. Open the **NewStudentReferrals** database, and then create an application part called **Contact** with the description **Contact information**, and do not include the data.

g. Close the NewStudentReferrals database.

h. Open the **Tutoring** database and then add the Contact application part. Note this will create a new table called tblContact1 because the tblContact table already existed. Open the tblContact1 table to verify that it does not contain records.

8. Make a backup copy of the database, compact and repair the database, and then close it.

Case Problem 3

Data Files needed for this Case Problem: Community.accdb (cont. from previous module), Facility. csv, and Volunteer.accdb.

Diane's Community Center   Diane Coleman wants you to integrate data from other files created with different applications with data in the Community database, and she wants to be able to analyze the data in the database. Complete the following steps:

1. Open the **Community** database you worked with in the previous three modules.

2. Export the qryDonationsSeptemberOrLaterCrosstab query as an HTML document named **Crosstab** to the Access2 > Case3 folder. Save the export steps.

3. Export the rptPatronDonations report as a PDF document named **PatronDonations** to the Access2 > Case3 folder. Include the document structure tags for accessibility, and do not save the export steps.

⊕ **Explore** 4. Import the CSV file named **Facility**, which is located in the Access2 > Case3 folder provided with your Data Files, as a new table in the database. Use the Short Text data type for all fields, choose your own primary key, name the table **tblTemporary**, and run the Table Analyzer. Accept the Table Analyzer's recommendations, which will be to create two tables. Rename the tables as **tblStorage** and **tblFacility**. (*Hint*: Use the Rename Table button to the right of "What name do you want for each table?") Make sure each table has the correct primary key. (*Hint*: Use the Set Unique Identifier button to set a primary key if necessary.) Let the Table Analzyer create a query. Do not save the import steps. Review the tblTemporary query, review the tblTemporary table (it might be named tblTemporary_OLD), and then review the tblStorage and tblFacility tables. Close all tables.

5. Export the tblDonation table as an XML file named **Donation** to the Access2 > Case3 folder; do not create a separate XSD file. Save the export steps. Once saved, modify the description as **Exported tblDonation table as an XML file**.

6. Modify the frmPatronDonations form in the following ways:

   a. Add a tab control to the bottom of the Detail section, and place the existing subform on the first page of the tab control.

   b. Change the caption for the left tab to **Donation Data** and for the right tab to **Donation Chart**.

   c. Change the caption for the main form's navigation buttons to **Donor** and for the subform's navigation buttons to **Donation**.

   d. Add a chart to the second page of the tab control. Use the tblDonation table as the record source, select the PatronID, DonationValue, and DonationDate fields, use the 3-D Column Chart type, include a legend, and use **Donations by Patron** as the chart title.

   e. Change the chart to a Clustered Bar chart.

7. Close the Community database.

8. Open the **Volunteer** database, which is located in the Access2 > Case3 folder provided with your Data Files. Create an application part called **Volunteer** with the description **Volunteer information**, and do not include the data. Close the Volunteer database.

9 Open the **Community** database. Create a table called **tblPotentialVolunteer** using the Volunteer application part.

10. Make a backup copy of the database, compact and repair the database, and then close it.

CHALLENGE

Case Problem 4

Data Files needed for this Case Problem: AppTrail.accdb (cont. from previous modules), PotentialTours1.xml, PotentialTours2.xml, and Staff.xlsx

Hike Appalachia Molly and Bailey Johnson want you to integrate data from other files created with different applications with the data in the AppTrail database, and they want to be able to analyze the data in the database. Complete the following steps:

1. Open the **AppTrail** database you worked with in the previous three modules.

2. Export the qryHikersWithoutReservations query as an HTML document named **HikersWithoutReservations** to the Access2 > Case4 folder. Do not save the export steps.

3. Import the data and structure from the XML file named **PotentialTours1**, which is located in the Access2 > Case4 folder provided with your Data Files, as a new table in the database. Do not save the import steps. Rename the new table **PotentialTours**. Open the PotentialTours table to verify the records were imported. Close the PotentialTours table.

✪ **Explore** 4. Import the data from the XML file named **PotentialTours2**, which is located in the Access2 > Case4 folder provided with your Data Files, appending the data to the PotentialTours table. *(Hint:* Because you cannot import and append the data from the PotentialTours2 XML file directly to the existing PotentialTours table, first import the PotentialTours2 XML file into a new table with an appropriate name, export this new table to an Excel file with an appropriate name (such as PotentialTours2), and then import and append the Excel data to the PotentialTours table.) Once the data is appended rename the PotentialTours table as **tblPotentialTours**. Open the tblPotentialTours table to verify the records were appended. Close the tblPotentialTours table. Remove the PotentialTours2 table from the database.

5. Export the qryTourReservations query as an XML file named **TourReservations** to the Access2 > Case4 folder; do not create a separate XSD file. Do not save the export steps.

6. Create a new table named **tblStaff** by linking to the **Staff** Excel file, which is located in the Access2 > Case4 folder provided with your Data Files. In the Staff Excel file, change the Job Title in the last record from Tour Assistant to **Tour Guide**. Open the tblStaff table to ensure the change was reflected. Close the tblStaff table.

7. Modify the frmHikersWithReservations form in the following ways:

   a. Add a tab control to the bottom of the Detail section, and place the existing subform on the first page of the tab control.

   b. Change the caption for the left tab to **Reservation Data** and for the right tab to **Reservation Chart**.

   c. Change the caption for the main form's navigation buttons to **Hiker** and for the subform's navigation buttons to **Reservation**.

   d. Add a chart to the second page of the tab control. Use the tblReservation table as the record source, select the TourDate, TourID, and People fields, use the Column Chart chart type, do not include a legend, and use **Reservations** as the chart title.

8. Export the rptTourReservations report as a PDF document named **TourReservations** to the Access2 > Case4 folder provided with your Data Files. Include the document structure tags for accessibility, and do not save the export steps.

9. Make a backup copy of the database, compact and repair the database, and then close it.

ACCESS

Using Action Queries and Advanced Table Relationships

Enhancing User Interaction with the Veterinary Database

Case | *Riverview Veterinary Care Center*

Riverview Veterinary Care Center in Cody, Wyoming, provides a range of medical services for pets and livestock in the greater Cody area. In addition to caring for household pets, such as dogs and cats, the center specializes in serving the needs of livestock on ranches in the surrounding area. Kimberly Johnson, the office manager for Riverview Veterinary Care Center, oversees a small staff and is responsible for maintaining the medical records for all of the animals the care center serves. The Riverview staff developed the Veterinary database of animal, visit, billing, employee, and treatment data, and use Microsoft Access 2016 (or simply Access) to manage it. Kimberly has been enhancing the Veterinary database containing tables, queries, forms, and reports that she and other staff members use to track animals and their visits. Kimberly has asked you to continue enhancing the database by creating some advanced queries and integrating more tables into the database.

STARTING DATA FILES

Access3 → **Module**	**Review**	**Case1**
Veterinary.accdb	Ordering.accdb	Salon.accdb
Case2	**Case3**	**Case4**
Technology.accdb	Thrift.accdb	BlueRidge.accdb

Session 9.1 Visual Overview:

The selected Make Table button indicates this query is a **make-table query**, which is an action query that creates a new table by copying records from one or more existing tables.

The design grid for a make-table query contains the same elements as the design grid for a select query.

The selected Append button indicates this query is an **append query**, which is an action query that adds records from existing tables or queries to the end of another table.

For an append query, the Append To row replaces the Show row.

Action Queries

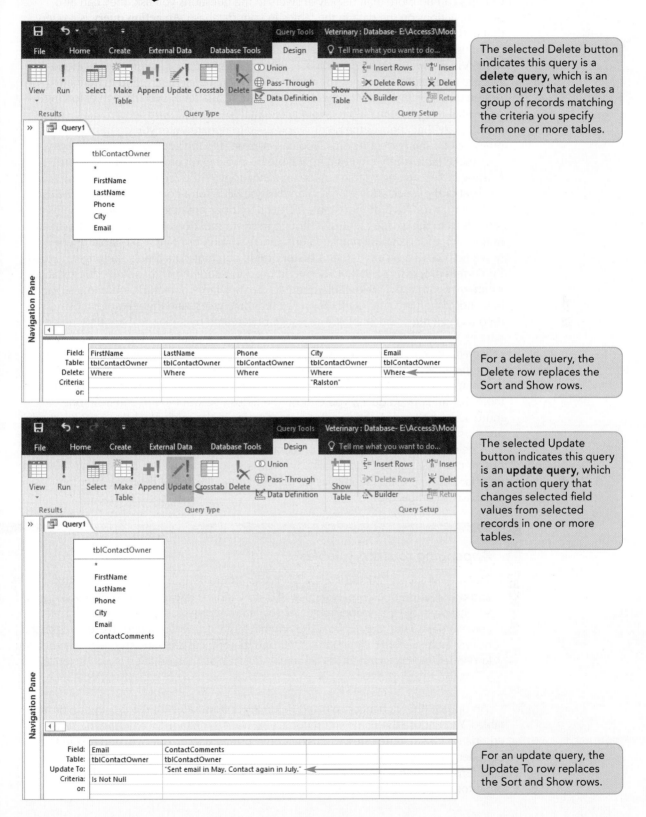

The selected Delete button indicates this query is a **delete query**, which is an action query that deletes a group of records matching the criteria you specify from one or more tables.

For a delete query, the Delete row replaces the Sort and Show rows.

The selected Update button indicates this query is an **update query**, which is an action query that changes selected field values from selected records in one or more tables.

For an update query, the Update To row replaces the Sort and Show rows.

Action Queries

Queries can do more than display answers to the questions you ask; they can also perform actions on the data in the tables in your database. An **action query** is a query that adds, changes, or deletes multiple table records at a time. For example, Kimberly could use an action query to delete all paid invoices from the previous year. As shown in the Visual Overview for Session 9.1, there are four types of action queries available in Access: the make-table query, the append query, the delete query, and the update query. Action queries can modify many records in a table at a time. Even though enforcing referential integrity can help to avoid accidental loss of data, you should first create a select query that chooses the records you need to update. After you confirm that the query selects the correct records, you can convert it to the appropriate action query.

A make-table query creates a new table by copying records from one or more existing tables. The new table can be an exact copy of the records in an existing table, a subset of the fields and records in an existing table, or a combination of the fields and records from two or more tables. The query does not delete the selected fields and records from the existing tables, although in some situations taking this additional step makes sense for database management. One common use of a make-table query is to move records to a history table. A **history table** contains data that is no longer needed for current processing but that you might need to reference in the future. For instance, Kimberly could use a make-table query to create a table of records for animals that have not visited the care center for more than five years, and then remove those records from the source tables. The new table created by a make-table query reflects data at a point in time; future changes made to the original (existing) tables are not reflected in the new table. You need to run the make-table query periodically if you want the newly created table to contain current data.

An append query adds records from existing tables or queries to the end of another table. For an append query, you choose the fields you want to append from one or more tables or queries; the selected data remains in the original tables. Append queries are most often used to append records to existing history tables.

A delete query deletes a group of records matching the criteria you specify from one or more tables. You choose which records you want to delete by entering selection criteria. Deleting records removes them permanently from the database after the database is compacted.

INSIGHT

Appending to History Tables

Tables containing data about cleared checks, former employees, inactive customers, and obsolete products are examples of history tables. Because the records you append to a history table are no longer needed for current processing in the original table, you can delete the records from the original table after you append the records to the history table. Before deleting the data from the original table, be sure to verify that you appended the correct records. When you delete data, the deletion is permanent.

An update query changes selected field values from selected records in one or more tables. You choose the fields and records you want to change by entering the selection criteria and the update rules. Kimberly could use an update query to add text in the comment field of every owner record that contains an email address to note that an email message had been sent to these owners. Update queries are particularly valuable in performing multiple updates to large tables.

Creating a Make-Table Query

Kimberly wants to contact all owners who live in Ralston to remind them about the care center's expanded hours. She would like a table for this purpose, containing the FirstName, LastName, Phone, City, and Email fields from the tblOwner table for all owners whose City field value is Ralston. She believes she needs this table only for this communication, after which she would not need the table anymore. You can create the new temporary table for Kimberly by using a make-table query that uses fields from the tblOwner table in the Veterinary database.

When you run a make-table query, you create a new table. The records in the new table are based on the records in the query's underlying tables. The fields in the new table will have the data type and field size of the fields in the query's underlying tables. The new table will not preserve the primary key designation or field properties such as the format or lookup properties.

You will create a make-table query to create a temporary table Kimberly can modify by adding notes that she will take when she contacts the owners who live in Ralston. By creating a new temporary table using the make-table query, Kimberly won't need to worry about disrupting or changing the data in any existing tables or in any objects on which those existing tables are based. After Kimberly is satisfied that all owners have been contacted and she's gathered their feedback, she can delete the table.

REFERENCE

Creating a Make-Table Query

- Create a select query with the necessary fields and selection criteria.
- On the Query Tools Design tab, click the Run button in the Results group to preview the results.
- Switch to Design view to make any necessary changes to the query, and then, when the query is correct, click the Make Table button located in the Query Type group on the Query Tools Design tab.
- In the Make Table dialog box, type the new table name in the Table Name box, making sure the Current Database option button is selected to include the new table in the current database; or, click the Another Database option button, enter the database name in the File Name box, and then click the OK button.
- Click the Run button, and then click the Yes button to confirm the creation of the new table.

You'll create the new temporary table now using a make-table query. You'll base the make-table query on the tblOwner table.

To create and run the select query based on the tblOwner table:

▶ 1. Start Access, and then open the **Veterinary** database from the **Access3 > Module** folder included with your Data Files.

   Trouble? If you don't have the starting Data Files, you need to get them before you can proceed. Your instructor will either give you the Data Files or ask you to obtain them from a specified location (such as a network drive). If you have any questions about the Data Files, see your instructor or technical support person for assistance.

   Trouble? If the security warning is displayed below the ribbon, click the Enable Content button.

▶ **2.** Make sure the Navigation Pane is closed, click the **Create** tab, and then, in the Queries group, click the **Query Design** button. The Show Table dialog box opens on top of the Query window in Design view.

▶ **3.** Add the **tblOwner** field list to the Query window, and then close the Show Table dialog box.

▶ **4.** Resize the tblOwner field list to display all its fields, and then add the **FirstName**, **LastName**, **Phone**, **City**, and **Email** fields to the design grid in that order.

Next, you'll enter the City field's selection criterion of Ralston.

▶ **5.** In the design grid, click the **City Criteria** box, type **Ralston**, and then press the **Tab** key. The condition changes to "Ralston". See Figure 9-1.

Figure 9-1	Select query on which make-table query will be based

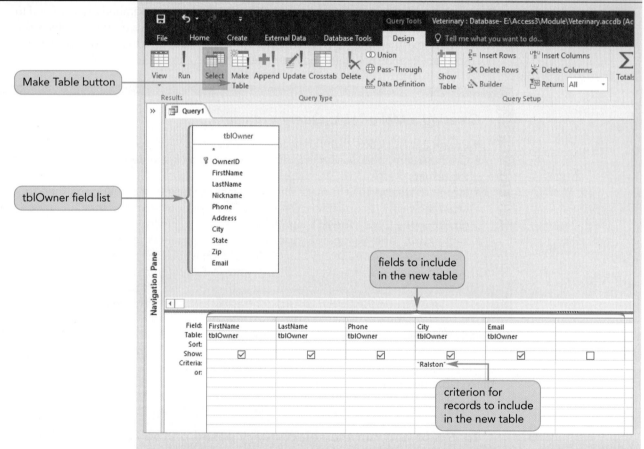

You've completed the select query, so now you can run it to make sure the recordset contains the data Kimberly needs.

▶ **6.** Run the query. The query recordset shows the four records for Ralston owners.

Now that you have verified that the records selected contain the city Ralston, you can be confident these are the same records that will be selected for the make-table query. Next you'll change the query to a make-table query.

To change the query type, and then run and save the make-table query:

▶ **1.** Switch to Design view, and then on the Query Tools Design tab, in the Query Type group, click the **Make Table** button. The Make Table dialog box opens. You use the dialog box to enter a name for the new table and designate the database to be used to store the table. See Figure 9-2.

option to create the
new table in the
Veterinary database

option to create the
new table in
another database

enter the
new table
name here

Be sure to select the
Current Database option
button; otherwise, you will
need to specify the name
of another database file in
which to place the table.

▶ **2.** In the Table Name box, type **tblContactOwner**, make sure the **Current Database** option button is selected, ensuring the new table will be added to the Veterinary database, and then click the **OK** button.

Now that you have created and tested the query, you can run it to create the tblContactOwner table. After you run the query, you can save it, and then you can view the new table. Because the query is not saved, the name on the tab is Query1.

▶ **3.** Run the query. A dialog box opens, indicating that you are about to paste 4 rows into a new table. Because you are running an action query that alters the contents of the database, you have the opportunity to cancel the operation, if necessary, or to confirm it.

▶ **4.** Click the **Yes** button. The dialog box closes, and the make-table query creates the tblContactOwner table. The query is still displayed in Design view.

▶ **5.** Save the query as **qryContactOwnerMakeTable**, close the query, and then open the Navigation Pane. The qryContactOwnerMakeTable query appears in the Queries list with a special icon indicating that it is a make-table query. See Figure 9-3.

Figure 9-3 Query type icons in the Navigation Pane

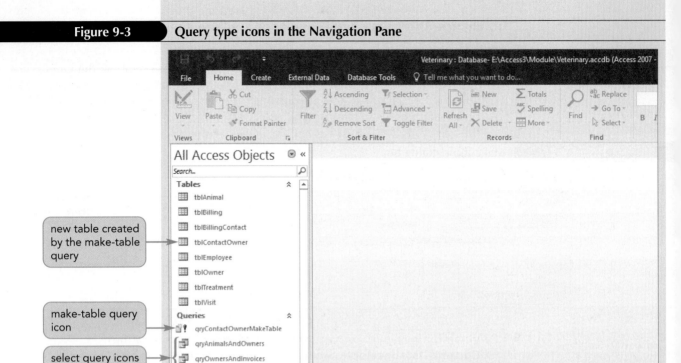

new table created by the make-table query

make-table query icon

select query icons

You can now open the tblContactOwner table to view the results of the make-table query.

6. Open the **tblContactOwner** table in Datasheet view, resize all datasheet columns to their best fit, and then click the first row's **FirstName** field value to deselect all values. See Figure 9-4.

Figure 9-4 tblContactOwner table datasheet

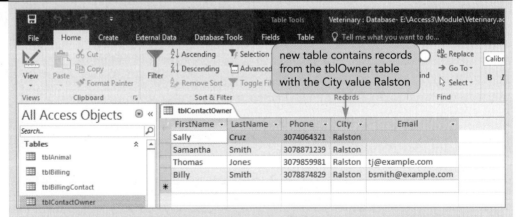

The tblContactOwner table includes the FirstName, LastName, Phone, City, and Email fields for owners who live in Ralston. Make-table queries do not transfer Caption property settings to the created tables, so the FirstName and LastName column headings do not contain spaces. The tblContactOwner table also does not include formatting for the phone number. Other field properties that do not transfer include Decimal Places, Default Value, Format, Input Mask, Validation Rule, and Validation Text.

7. Save your datasheet changes, close the table, and then close the Navigation Pane.

Kimberly can now make any necessary changes to the tblContactOwner table records when she contacts customers without affecting the tblOwner table in the Veterinary database.

PROSKILLS

Decision Making: Determining When to Delete Objects

A database evolves to meet the needs of its users, and eventually some database objects are no longer needed. A table, query, or report created for a special event, for instance, would no longer be useful after that event is over. Likewise, a database might contain a form created to enter data that is no longer relevant. Periodically, you should evaluate the objects in your database and consider if all the objects are still providing useful information. If some are not, you may want to delete such tables, queries, forms, and reports. If the database is a large one and serves a large user base, you will want to gain input from all users before deciding to delete objects.

Creating an Append Query

Kimberly has decided to expand the list of owners that she will contact to include the owners who live in Cody. She asks you to add these new records to the tblContactOwner table. You could make this change by modifying the selection criterion in the qryContactOwnerMakeTable query to select owners with City field values of Cody. If you ran this modified query, however, you would overwrite the existing tblContactOwner table with a new table. If Kimberly had made any changes to the existing tblContactOwner table records, creating a new table would overwrite these changes as well.

Instead, you will create the qryContactOwnerAppend query as a select query to select only owners whose city is Cody, and then you'll change the query to an append query. An append query is a query that adds records from existing tables or queries to the end of another table. When you run this new query, the selected records will be appended to (added to the bottom of) the records in the existing tblContactOwner table.

REFERENCE

Creating an Append Query

- Create a select query with the necessary fields and selection criteria.
- On the Query Tools Design tab, click the Run button in the Results group to preview the results.
- Switch to Design view to make any necessary changes to the query, and then, when the query is correct, click the Append button located in the Query Type group on the Query Tools Design tab.
- In the Append dialog box, select the table name in the Table Name box, making sure the Current Database option button is selected to include the new table in the current database; or click the Another Database option button, enter the database name in the File Name box, and then click the OK button.
- Click the Run button, and then click the Yes button to confirm appending the records to the table.

You can now create the append query you'll use to include the additional customer data Kimberly wants in the tblContactOwner table.

To create the append query:

▶ **1.** Click the **Create** tab, and then, in the Queries group, click the **Query Design** button. The Show Table dialog box opens on top of the Query window in Design view.

▶ **2.** Add the **tblOwner** field list to the Query window, and then close the Show Tables dialog box.

▶ **3.** Resize the tblOwner field list to display all its fields, then add the **FirstName**, **LastName**, **Phone**, **City**, and **Email** fields to the design grid in that order. The selected fields match the fields in the table to which the records will be appended.

Next, you'll enter the selection criterion of Cody for the City field.

▶ **4.** In the design grid, click the **City Criteria** box, type **Cody** and then press the **Tab** key. See Figure 9-5.

| Figure 9-5 | Selection criterion for append query |

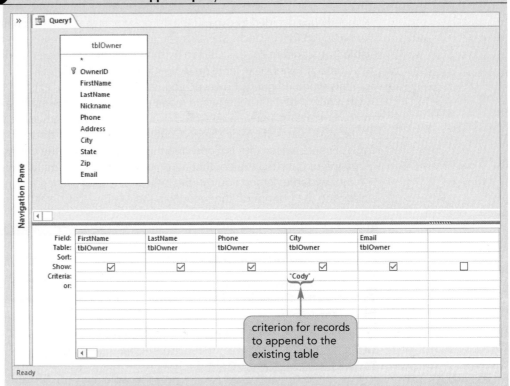

Before you can run the query to append the records to the tblContactOwner table, you have to change the query type to an append query. It is always a good idea to test an action query before you run it, so you will first run this select query to make sure the correct records are selected. Then you will change the query type to an append query and run it to append the new records to the tblContactOwner table.

▶ **5.** On the Query Tools Design tab, in the Query Type group, click the **Select** button to select it (if necessary).

▶ **6.** Run the query. The query recordset shows the 10 records for owners who live in Cody.

These 10 records are the additional records you will append to the tblContactOwner table. Now that you've verified that the results shown in the query are correct, you can change the query type to an append query.

▶ **7.** Switch to Design view, and then on the Query Tools Design tab, in the Query Type group, click the **Append** button. The Append dialog box opens. You use this dialog box to select the name of the table to which you want to append the data and to designate the database to be used to store the table.

▶ **8.** In the Table Name box, click the arrow, click **tblContactOwner**, ensure that the **Current Database** option button is selected, and then click the **OK** button. The Append To row replaces the Show row in the design grid.

The Append To row in the design grid identifies the fields that the query will append to the designated table. The FirstName, LastName, Phone, City, and Email fields are selected and will be appended to the tblContactOwner table, which already contains these same six fields for owners.

You'll run and save the append query now.

To run and save the append query:

▶ **1.** Run the query. A dialog box opens, warning you that you are about to append 10 rows.

▶ **2.** Click the **Yes** button to acknowledge the warning. The dialog box closes, and the append query adds the 10 records to the tblContactOwner table. The Query window is still displayed in Design view.

▶ **3.** Save the query as **qryContactOwnerAppend**, and then close the query.

Next, you'll open the tblContactOwner table to make sure that the 10 records were appended to the table.

▶ **4.** Open the Navigation Pane, open the **tblContactOwner** table datasheet, resize the fields to their best fit, and then click the first row's **FirstName** field value to deselect all values. See Figure 9-6.

Figure 9-6	**tblContactOwner table datasheet after appending records**

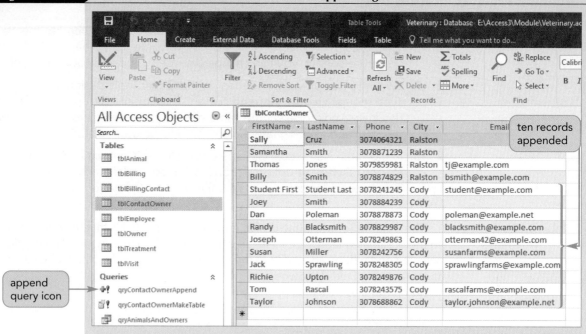

The new records have been added to the tblContactOwner table. Because the tblContactOwner table does not have a primary key, the new records appear at the end of the table.

5. Save your datasheet changes, close the table, and then close the Navigation Pane.

Kimberly has contacted all the owners in the tblContactOwner table who are located in the city of Ralston. She asks you to delete these records from the tblContactOwner table so that the table contains only those records for owners she has not yet contacted.

Creating a Delete Query

You can either delete records in a table individually or create a delete query to remove a group of them all at once. When using a delete query, you specify one or more criteria that identify the records you want to delete. For example, to delete the records Kimberly no longer needs from the tblContactOwner table, you can create a delete query to delete the owner records in the table whose city is Ralston.

REFERENCE

Creating a Delete Query

- Create a select query with the necessary fields and selection criteria.
- On the Query Tools Design tab, click the Run button in the Results group to preview the results.
- Switch to Design view to make any necessary changes to the query, and then, when the query is correct, click the Delete button located in the Query Type group on the Query Tools Design tab.
- Click the Run button, and then click the Yes button to confirm deleting the records.

You will create the delete query next.

To create the delete query:

▶ 1. Click the **Create** tab, and then, in the Queries group, click the **Query Design** button. The Show Table dialog box opens on top of the Query window.

▶ 2. Add the **tblContactOwner** field list to the Query window, and then close the Show Table dialog box.

▶ 3. Resize the tblContactOwner field list if necessary to display all its fields, and then add all the fields in order from the tblContactOwner field list to the design grid.

▶ 4. In the design grid, click the **City Criteria** box, type **Ralston**, and then press the **Tab** key. The criterion changes to "Ralston". Only the records with a City field value of Ralston will be selected when you run the query.

▶ 5. Run the query. The query recordset shows the four records with City field values of Ralston. The select query is correct. See Figure 9-7.

Figure 9-7	Four records to be deleted

Now that you have verified that the correct records are selected, you can change the query to a delete query.

▶ 6. Switch to Design view, and then on the Query Tools Design tab, in the Query Type group, click the **Delete** button. In the design grid, the Delete row replaces the Sort and Show rows.

▶ 7. Run the query. A dialog box opens, warning that you are about to delete four rows from the table.

▶ 8. Click the **Yes** button to acknowledge the warning. The dialog box closes, and the four records are deleted from the tblContactOwner table. The Query window is still displayed in Design view.

▶ 9. Save the query as **qryContactOwnerDelete**, and then close the query.

Next you'll open the tblContactOwner table to verify that the records have been deleted.

▶ 10. Open the Navigation Pane, and then open the **tblContactOwner** table in Datasheet view. The table contains ten records, and the Ralston records were correctly deleted. See Figure 9-8.

Figure 9-8	tblContactOwner table after deleting four records

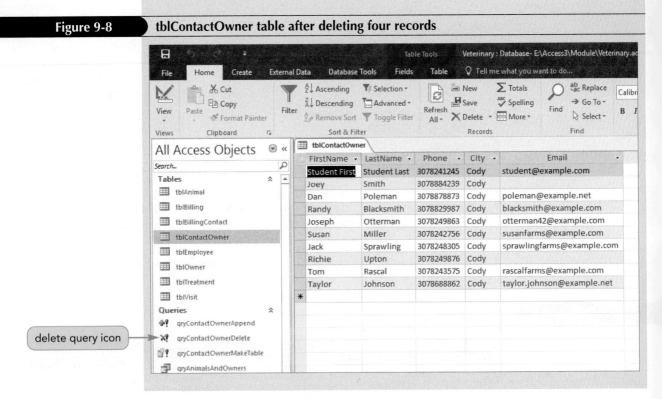

Kimberly wants you to make some structural changes to the tblContactOwner table. First she wants you to add a field named ContactComments to the tblContactOwner table in which she can keep notes about the calls she makes. She also wants you to add appropriate captions to the FirstName and LastName fields. You can add the field and captions to the tblContactOwner table without affecting the other objects in the Veterinary database, including the tblOwner table, because the tblContactOwner table was created as a temporary table to serve a specific, one-time purpose.

To add the new ContactComments field to the tblContactOwner table and add field captions:

1. Switch to Design view.

   You'll set the data type for the new field to Long Text, so that Kimberly is not limited to 255 characters of data in the field, which would be the case with the Short Text data type.

2. Click the **Field Name** box below the Email field, type **ContactComments**, press the **Tab** key, type the letter **l**, and then press the **Tab** key to select the Long Text data type.

3. Press the **F6** key to position the insertion point in the Format box in the Field Properties pane, press the **Tab** key, and then type **Contact Comments** in the Caption box. You've completed adding the ContactComments field to the table. See Figure 9-9.

Figure 9-9   **ContactComments field added to the tblContactOwner table**

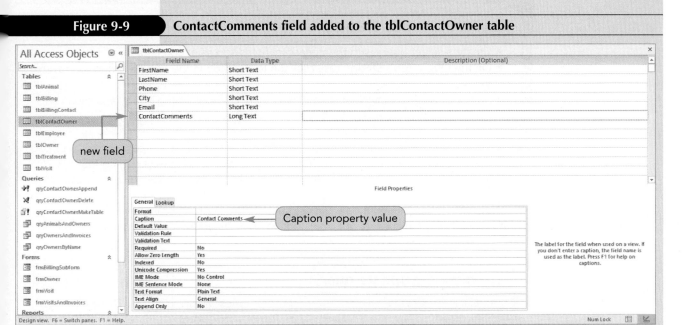

4. Add the caption **First Name** to the FirstName field, and then add the caption **Last Name** to the LastName field.

5. Save your changes to the table structure, switch to Datasheet view, and then resize the columns to their best fit. Notice that the captions and new field are displayed.

6. Save your changes to the table layout, close the table, and then close the Navigation Pane.

Kimberly has sent an email message to each owner who has an email address in the Email field, and she wants to update the ContactComments field in the tblContactOwner table with the same comments for all records with an email address in the Email field. To accomplish this for Kimberly, you'll create an update query.

Creating an Update Query

Recall that an update query changes selected field values and records in one or more tables. An update query is useful when a group of records in a table all require the same change in data for a common field. For example, in the tblContactOwner table, Kimberly wants to enter the same comment in the ContactComment field for those owners who have an email address. She could type the comments in the ContactComments field for one of the records and then copy and paste the comments to the other records. However, performing these steps takes time and could result in incorrectly updating a record or neglecting to update one of the records. Instead, using an update query allows Kimberly to make this change to the table records quickly and accurately.

REFERENCE

Creating an Update Query

- Create a select query with the necessary fields and selection criteria.
- On the Query Tools Design tab, click the Run button in the Results group to preview the results.
- Switch to Design view to make any necessary changes to the query, and then, when the query is correct, click the Update button located in the Query Type group on the Query Tools Design tab.
- Type the updated values in the Update To boxes for the fields you want to update.
- Click the Run button, and then click the Yes button to confirm changing the records.

Now you can create an update query to update the ContactComments field in the tblContactOwner table for records that contain an email address in the EmailAddress field.

To create the update query:

1. Click the **Create** tab, and then in the Queries group, click the **Query Design** button to open the Show Table dialog box on top of the Query window.

2. Add the **tblContactOwner** field list to the Query window, close the Show Table dialog box, and then resize the tblContactOwner field list to display all its fields.

   You will select the Email and ContactComments fields for the query results. The Email field lets you select records for owners who have an email address listed in this field. The ContactComments field is the field Kimberly needs to update.

3. Add the **Email** and **ContactComments** fields, in this order, to the design grid.

4. In the design grid, click the **Email Criteria** box, type **Is Not Null**, and then press the **Tab** key. The query will select a record only if there is a value in the Email field—in other words, if the field is not null.

5. Run the query. The query recordset displays eight records, each of which contains an Email value. The selected query is correct.

   Now that you have verified that the correct records are selected, you can change the query to an update query.

6. Switch to Design view, and then on the Query Tools Design tab, in the Query Type group, click the **Update** button. In the design grid, the Update To row replaces the Sort and Show rows.

   You specify how you want to change a field value for the selected records by entering an expression in the field's Update To box. An expression is a calculation resulting in a single value. You can type a simple expression directly into the Update To box.

7. In the design grid, click the **ContactComments Update To** box, type **"Sent email in May. Contact again in July."** (be sure to type the quotation marks), and then drag the right border of the ContactComments column to the right to display the entire expression value. See Figure 9-10.

Figure 9-10   Update query for the tblContactOwner table

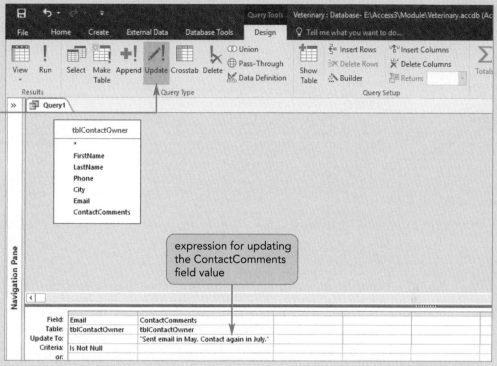

Update button

expression for updating
the ContactComments
field value

8. Run the query. A dialog box opens, warning that you are about to update 8 rows in the tblContactOwner table.

9. Click the **Yes** button. The dialog box closes, and the query updates the ContactComments field values for owners who have an email address in the Email field. The Query window is still displayed in Design view.

You are finished updating the tblContactOwner table, so you'll save and close the query.

10. Save the query as **qryContactOwnerUpdate** and then close the query.

Now you can view the tblContactOwner table to see the results of the update operation.

TIP

For text expressions that contain quotation marks, you need to type the quotation marks twice. For example, to enter the expression A "text" expression, type "A ""text"" expression".

To view the updated tblContactOwner table:

1. Open the Navigation Pane, open the **tblContactOwner** table in Datasheet view, and then resize the Contact Comments column to its best fit. The ContactComments field values for owners who have email addresses have been updated correctly. See Figure 9-11.

Figure 9-11	tblContactOwner table with updated ContactComments field values

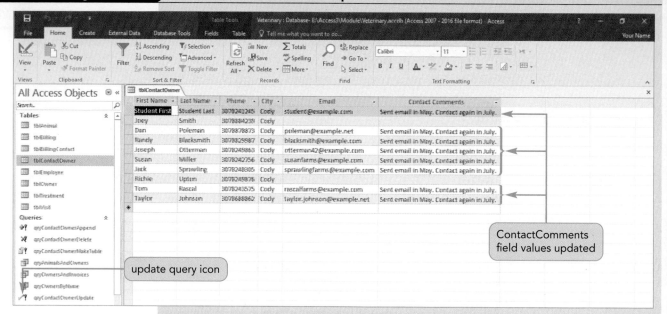

> **2.** Save your table datasheet changes, and close the table.

> **3.** If you are not continuing on to the next session, close the Veterinary database.

INSIGHT

Deleting Action Queries

You usually create an action query and run it for a special purpose, and in most cases you need to run the query only once. If you create and run an action query and then save it, you might accidentally run it again. Doing so would result in the update of tables in unintended ways. Therefore, after you've run an action query, you shouldn't save it in your database; this will prevent users from running it by mistake.

Kimberly can now use action queries in her future work with the Veterinary database. In the next session, you'll learn about the different types of relationships you can create between tables, and you'll view and create indexes to increase a database's efficiency.

REVIEW

Session 9.1 Quick Check

1. What is an action query?

2. What precautions should you take before running an action query?

3. What is the difference between a make-table query and an append query?

4. What does a delete query do?

5. What does an update query do?

6. How does the design grid change when you create an update query?

Session 9.2 Visual Overview:

For a many-to-many relationship, you must create a third table, known as a **relationship table**, and form one-to-many relationships between the two original primary tables and the relationship table. Here, the tblTreatment table exists only because the tblBilling and tblEmployee tables have a many-to-many relationship.

The ∞ symbol indicates there can be many records that contain the same InvoiceNum in the tblTreatment table.

The ∞ symbol indicates there can be many records that contain the same EmployeeID in the tblTreatment table.

A primary table has a one-to-many relationship with a relationship table.

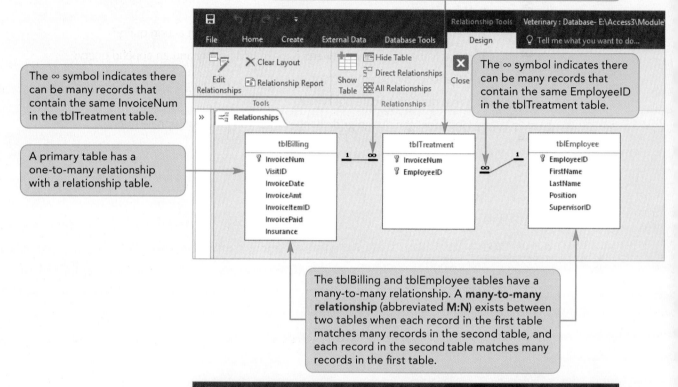

The tblBilling and tblEmployee tables have a many-to-many relationship. A **many-to-many relationship** (abbreviated **M:N**) exists between two tables when each record in the first table matches many records in the second table, and each record in the second table matches many records in the first table.

The tblBilling table contains one record for each invoice and is one of the two primary tables in the many-to-many relationship.

Invoice Num	Visit ID	Invoice Date	Invoice Amt	Invoice Item ID	Invoice Paid
42135	1016	11/21/2016	$75.00	LAB001	☑
42145	1020	11/22/2016	$275.00	SUR002	☑
42146	1020	11/22/2016	$50.00	PHA111	☑
42147	1020	11/22/2016	$75.00	LAB001	☑
42155	1024	11/23/2016	$50.00	LAB001	☑
42156	1024	11/23/2016	$75.00	VAC111	☑
42157	1024	11/23/2016	$45.00	FTM111	☑
42158	1024	11/23/2016	$35.00	HTM111	☑
42159	1024	11/23/2016	$15.00	NTR001	☑
42165	1028	11/29/2016	$50.00	GRM001	☐
42166	1028	11/29/2016	$15.00	NTR001	☐
42167	1028	11/29/2016	$45.00	FTM111	☐
42175	1032	11/28/2016	$50.00	GRM001	☑
42176	1032	11/28/2016	$45.00	FTM111	☑
42182	1036	11/30/2016	$225.00	SUR222	☑
42183	1036	11/30/2016	$50.00	PHA	
42184	1036	11/30/2016	$75.00	LAB	

InvoiceNum 42145 occurs just once in the tblBilling table but twice in the tblTreatment table.

Many-to-Many Relationship

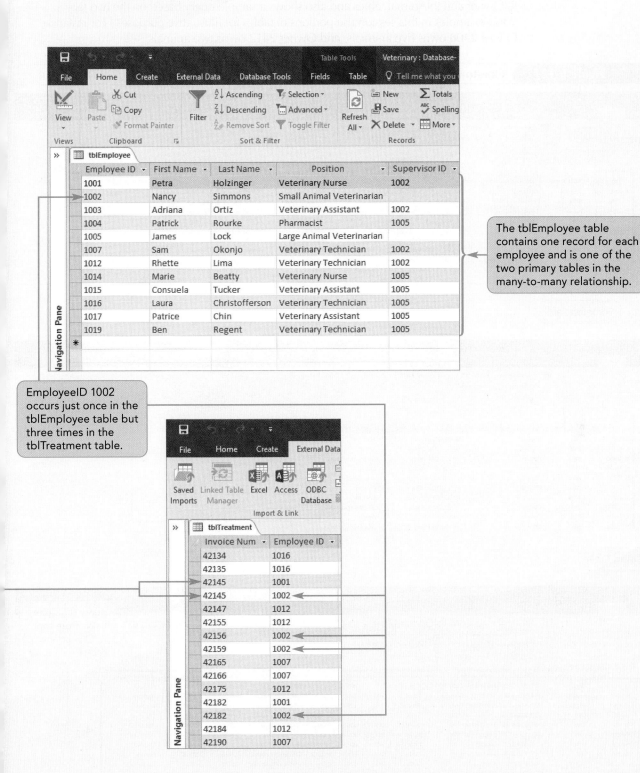

The tblEmployee table contains one record for each employee and is one of the two primary tables in the many-to-many relationship.

EmployeeID 1002 occurs just once in the tblEmployee table but three times in the tblTreatment table.

Understanding Types of Table Relationships

As you know, a one-to-many relationship (abbreviated as 1:M) exists between two tables when each record in the primary table matches zero, one, or more records in the related table, and when each record in the related table matches at most one record in the primary table. For example, Figure 9-12 shows a one-to-many relationship between portions of the tblOwner and tblAnimal tables and also shows a sample query based on the two tables. (Most examples in this session use portions of tables for illustrative purposes.) For instance, Owner 2408 owns five animals, and Owner 2412 owns two animals.

Figure 9-12 One-to-many relationship and sample query

You use the common field—the OwnerID field—to form the one-to-many relationship between the tblOwner and tblAnimal tables. When you join the two tables based on OwnerID field values, you can extract data from them as if they are one larger table. For example, you can join the tblOwner and tblAnimal tables to create the qryAnimalsAndOwners query shown in Figure 9-12. In the qryAnimalsAndOwners query, the Last Name, First Name, Phone, Address, City, State, Zip, and Email columns are from the tblOwner table, and the Animal ID, Owner ID, and Animal Name columns are from the tblAnimal table.

In addition to one-to-many relationships between tables, you can also relate tables through many-to-many and one-to-one relationships.

Many-to-Many Relationships

In the Veterinary database, an invoice can represent treatment performed by many employees, and each employee can provide treatment on many invoiced treatments, so the tblBilling and tblEmployee tables have a many-to-many relationship, as shown in the Session 9.2 Visual Overview.

When you have a many-to-many relationship (abbreviated as M:N) between two tables, you must create a third table, known as a relationship table, and form one-to-many relationships between the two original primary tables and the relationship table. For instance, the tblTreatment table, shown in the Session 9.2 Visual Overview, exists only because the tblBilling and tblEmployee tables have a many-to-many relationship. Each record in the tblTreatment table contains two foreign keys: the EmployeeID field is a foreign key that allows you to join the tblEmployee table to the tblTreatment table; and the InvoiceNum field is a foreign key that allows you to join the tblBilling table to the tblTreatment table. The primary key of the tblTreatment table is a composite key, consisting of the combination of the EmployeeID and InvoiceNum fields. Each pair of values in this primary key is unique.

Unlike a one-to-many or one-to-one relationship, a many-to-many relationship is not represented by a single line between two tables in the Relationships window. Rather, a many-to-many relationship is represented by the two one-to-many relationships between the primary tables and the relationship table. For instance, Visual Overview 9.2 shows a one-to-many relationship line between the tblBilling and tblTreatment tables and another one-to-many relationship line between the tblEmployee and tblTreatment tables. Because the tblTreatment table is a relationship table, these two relationships together represent a many-to-many relationship.

You can see the one-to-many relationship between each primary table and the relationship table by examining the records. For example, the fourth record shown in the tblTreatment table represents major surgery for InvoiceNum 42145 that was performed by Nancy Simmons, who has EmployeeID 1002. EmployeeID 1002 appears in many records in the tblTreatment table that represent treatment Nancy Simmons provided for many other invoices including 42156, 42159, and more. Also, InvoiceNum 42145 appears in two tblTreatment table records, each for a different employee: Petra Holzinger and Nancy Simmons.

PROSKILLS

Decision Making: Identifying Many-to-Many Relationships

Although one-to-many relationships are the most common type of table relationship, many-to-many relationships occur frequently, and most databases have one or more many-to-many relationships. When developing a database, you need to decide when the relationship between two tables should be many-to-many rather than one-to-many. You can recognize when this relationship is appropriate by thinking about how all the pieces of data to be recorded interrelate, as demonstrated by the following examples:

- In a college database, a student takes more than one class, and each class has more than one student enrolled; a course has many prerequisites and can be the prerequisite to many courses.
- In a pharmacy database, a medication is prescribed to many customers, and a customer can take many medications.
- In an airline database, a flight has many passengers, and a passenger can take many flights.
- In a publisher database, an author can write many books, and a book can have multiple authors.
- In a manufacturing database, a manufactured product consists of many parts, and a part can be a component in many manufactured products.
- In a film database, a movie has many actors, and each actor appears in many movies.

Common one-to-many relationships can turn into many-to-many relationships when circumstances change. For example, a department in an organization has many employees, and an employee usually works in a single department. However, an instructor can have a joint appointment to two departments, and some companies hire employees and split their time between two departments. You must carefully analyze each situation and design your table relationships to handle the specific requirements for today and for the future.

When you join tables that have a many-to-many relationship, you can extract data from them as if they were one larger table. For example, you can join the tblBilling and tblEmployee tables to create the qryTreatment query shown in the Session 9.2 Visual Overview. In the tblTreatment table, the EmployeeID field joins the tblEmployee and tblTreatment tables, and the InvoiceNum field joins the tblBilling and tblTreatment tables.

One-to-One Relationships

A **one-to-one relationship** (abbreviated as **1:1**) exists between two tables when each record in the first table matches at most one record in the second table, and each record in the second table matches at most one record in the first table. Most relationships between tables are either one-to-many or many-to-many; the primary use for one-to-one relationships is as entity subtypes. An **entity subtype** is a table whose primary key is a foreign key to a second table and whose fields are additional fields for the second table.

In the Veterinary database, the Address, City, State, and Zip fields in the tblOwner table identify for most owners both the owner's location and billing address, which is where Riverview Veterinary Care Center sends the owner's invoices. In a few cases, however, a friend or relative will be paying the veterinary bills, so the billing name and address is different from the owner's name and address. There are two ways to handle these two sets of names and addresses. One way is to add the BillingFirstName, BillingLastName, BillingAddress, BillingCity, BillingState, and BillingZip fields to the tblOwner table. For each owner with an additional billing name and address, you store the appropriate values in these billing fields. For those owners who do not have additional billing information, you leave these billing fields null.

Another way to handle the two sets of addresses is to create an entity subtype, which in this case could be a table named tblBillingContact. In the tblBillingContact table, the OwnerID field, which is the primary key, is also a foreign key to the tblOwner table. A record appears in the tblBillingContact table only for those owners who have different mailing and billing names and addresses. All billing data appears only in the tblBillingContact table. The tblOwner table and the tblBillingContact table, which is an entity subtype, have a one-to-one relationship, as shown in Figure 9-13.

Figure 9-13   **tblOwner and tblBillingContact tables with a 1:1 relationship**

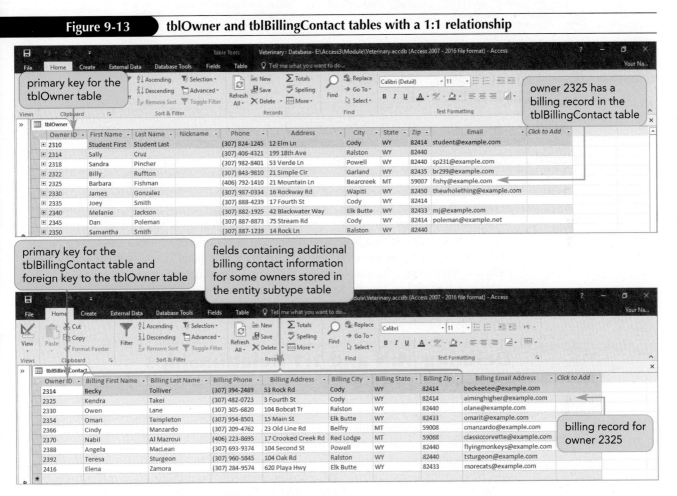

When you define a one-to-one relationship between tables, you can extract data from them as if they were one larger table. For example, you can define a relationship between the tblOwner and tblBillingContact tables to create the qryBillingContactData query shown in Figure 9-14.

Figure 9-14   Query results based upon a 1:1 relationship between tables

fields from the tblOwner table

fields from the tblBilling Contact table

The relationship between the tblOwner and tblBillingContact tables is based upon the common OwnerID field. In the query, the Owner ID, First Name, Last Name, and Phone fields are from the tblOwner table; and the Billing First Name, Billing Last Name, Billing Address, Billing City, Billing State, and Billing Zip fields are from the tblBillingContact table. Only the nine owners who have records in the tblBillingContact table—because they have different billing addresses—appear in the qryBillingContactData query recordset.

Next, you'll define a many-to-many relationship between the tblBilling and tblEmployee tables and a one-to-one relationship between the tblOwner and tblBillingContact tables.

Defining M:N and 1:1 Relationships Between Tables

Similar to the way you define one-to-many relationships, you define many-to-many and one-to-one relationships in the Relationships window. First, you'll open the Relationships window and define the many-to-many relationship between the tblBilling and tblEmployee tables, using the tblTreatment table as the relationship table. You'll start by defining a one-to-many relationship between the tblBilling and tblTreatment tables, with tblBilling as the primary table, tblTreatment as the related table, and InvoiceNum as the common field (the primary key in the tblBilling table and a foreign key in the tblTreatment table). Next, you'll define a one-to-many relationship between the tblEmployee and tblTreatment tables, with tblEmployee as the primary table, tblTreatment as the related table, and EmployeeID as the common field (the primary key in the tblEmployee table and a foreign key in the tblTreatment table).

To define a many-to-many relationship between the tblBilling and tblEmployee tables:

1. If you took a break after the previous session, make sure that the Veterinary database is open.

2. Close the Navigation Pane (if necessary), click the **Database Tools** tab, and then in the Relationships group, click the **Relationships** button to open the Relationships window.

3. On the Relationship Tools Design tab, in the Relationships group, click the **Show Table** button to open the Show Table dialog box.

4. Add the **tblTreatment**, **tblBillingContact**, and **tblEmployee** field lists to the Relationships window, and then close the Show Table dialog box.

5. Resize the tblBillingContact field list so that all field names are visible, and then drag the field list title bars of the field lists for the tblBillingContact, tblBilling, tblEmployee, and tblTreatment tables to arrange them as shown in Figure 9-15.

Figure 9-15	Relationships window with three table field lists added

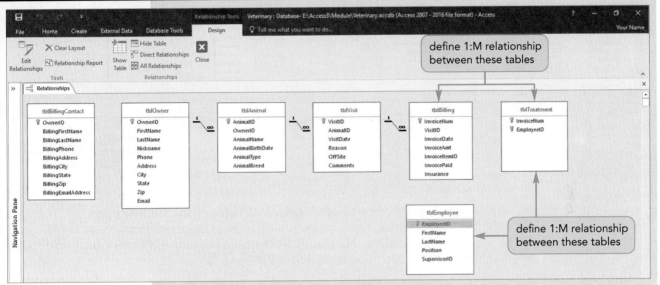

First, you'll define the one-to-many relationship between the tblBilling and tblTreatment tables.

6. In the tblBilling field list, click **InvoiceNum**, and then drag it to **InvoiceNum** in the tblTreatment field list. When you release the mouse button, the Edit Relationships dialog box opens.

The primary table, related table, and common field appear at the top of the dialog box. The Relationship Type box at the bottom of the dialog box lists One-To-Many. You'll enforce referential integrity and cascade updates to related fields, but you won't cascade deletions to related records because you want to preserve the Billing contact information in case it will be used again later.

7. Click the **Enforce Referential Integrity** check box, and then click the **Cascade Update Related Fields** check box. You have now selected all the necessary relationship options.

8. Click the **Create** button to close the dialog box and define the one-to-many relationship between the two tables. The completed relationship appears in the Relationships window.

9. Repeat Steps 6 through 8 to define the one-to-many relationship between the primary tblEmployee table and the related tblTreatment table, using EmployeeID as the common field. See Figure 9-16.

Figure 9-16   **M:N relationship defined between the tblBilling and tblEmployee tables**

Now you'll define a one-to-one relationship between the tblOwner and tblBillingContact tables. Not all owners have billing contact information, so it will be important to create the relationship by dragging from the tblOwner table to the tblBillingContact table to preserve referential integrity.

To define a one-to-one relationship between the tblOwner and tblBillingContact tables:

Be sure to drag from the tblOwner to the tblBillingContact table and not the reverse.

1. In the tblOwner field list, click **OwnerID**, and then drag it to **OwnerID** in the tblBillingContact field list. When you release the mouse button, the Edit Relationships dialog box opens.

   The primary table, related table, and common field appear at the top of the dialog box. The Relationship Type box at the bottom of the dialog box lists One-To-One.

   Trouble? If an error message appears indicating a violation of referential integrity, you mistakenly dragged the OwnerID field from the tblBillingContact table to the tblOwner table. Click the Cancel button and try again, dragging from the tblOwner table to the tblBillingContact table.

2. Click the **Enforce Referential Integrity** check box, click the **Cascade Update Related Fields** check box, and then click the **Create** button to define the one-to-one relationship between the two tables and close the dialog box. The completed relationship appears in the Relationships window. See Figure 9-17.

Figure 9-17   **1:1 relationship defined between the tblOwner and tblBillingContact tables**

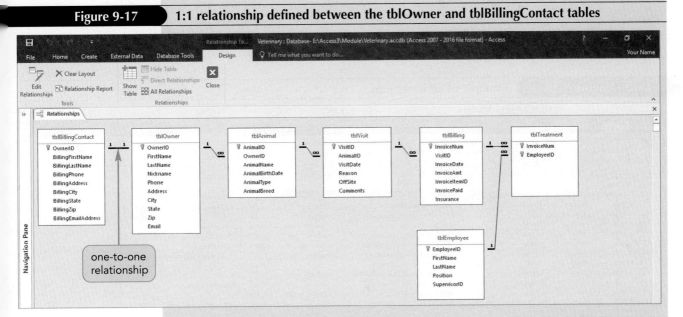

Each side of the relationship has the digit 1 at its end of the join line to indicate a one-to-one relationship between the two tables.

3. Save your relationship changes.

The tblEmployee table contains data about the employees at Riverview Veterinary Care Center who provide veterinary care. Kimberly asks you to create a select query to display the employees in the tblEmployee table and their supervisors. The select query you'll create will require a special join using the tblEmployee table.

Understanding Join Types

The design of the Veterinary database includes a one-to-many relationship between the tblOwner and tblVisit tables using OwnerID as the common field, which allows you to join the two tables to create a query based on data from both tables. While the term *join* is sometimes used to refer to any relationship between tables in a database, **join** is also a technical database term that describes how data from the tables in a relationship is selected and returned. The most common type of join is referred to as an inner join, which is the type of join you have used in your work with the database for the Riverview Veterinary Care Center thus far. Two other types of joins are the outer join and the self-join.

Inner and Outer Joins

An **inner join** is a join in which records are selected from two tables only when the records have the same value in the common field that links the tables. For example, in a database containing a table of student information and a table of class information, an inner join would return all student records that have a matching class record and all class records that have a matching student record. In the Veterinary database, OwnerID is the common field for the tblOwner and tblBillingContact tables. As shown in Figure 9-18, the results of a query based on an inner join of these two tables would return only those records that have a matching OwnerID value. The record in the tblOwner table with an Owner ID column value of 2310 is not included in the query recordset because it fails to match a record with the same Owner ID column value in the tblBillingContact table.

(That owner does not have a different billing address.) Because primary key values can't be null, records with null foreign key values do not appear in a query recordset based on an inner join. You usually use an inner join whenever you perform a query based on more than one table; it is the default join you have used to this point. You can specify or change the join type of a relationship in the Join Properties dialog box.

Figure 9-18	Example of an inner join

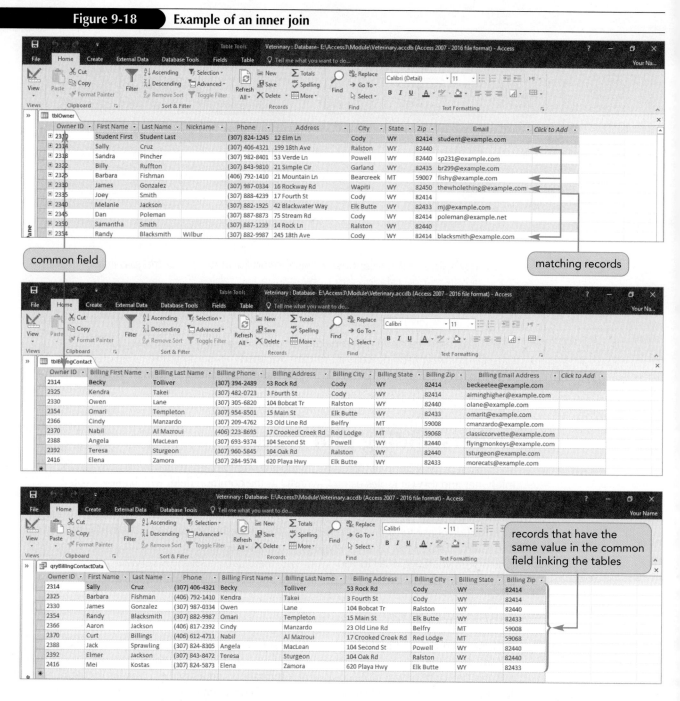

An **outer join** is a join in which *all* records from one table are selected along with only those records from a second table that have matching common field values. For example, in a database containing a student table and a class table, you could create two different outer joins between these two tables. One outer join would return the records for all students whether or not the students are enrolled in classes, and another outer join between these two tables would return all classes whether or not any students are enrolled in them. In the Veterinary database, you would use this kind of join if you wanted to see, for example, all records from the tblOwner table and also any and all matching records from the tblBillingContact table. Figure 9-19 shows an outer join for the tblOwner and tblBillingContact tables. All records from the tblOwner table appear in the query recordset, along with only matching records from the tblBillingContact table. Notice that the record from the tblOwner table for Owner ID 2310 appears in the query recordset even though it does not match a record in the tblBillingContact table.

Figure 9-19   **Example of an outer join**

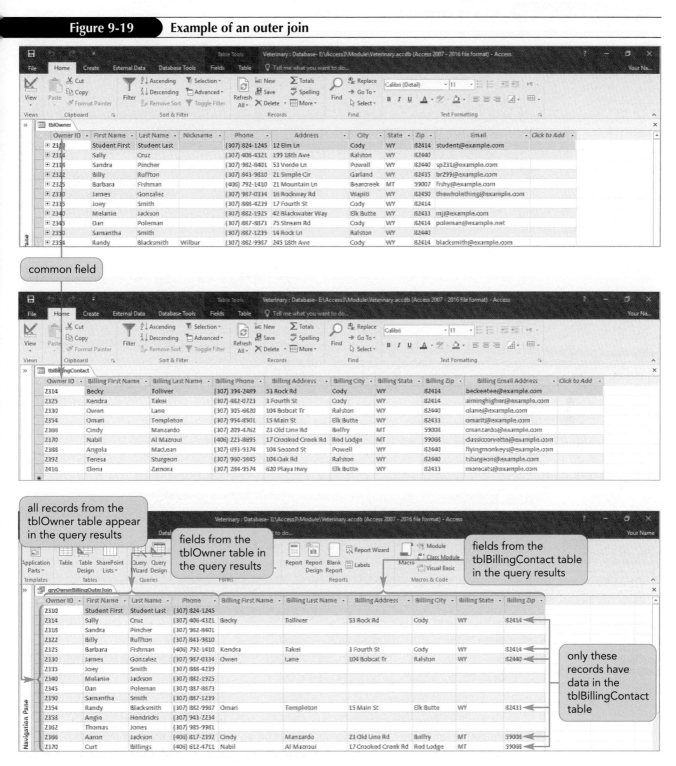

Another example of an outer join using the tblAnimal and tblOwner tables is shown in Figure 9-20. All records from the tblAnimal table appear in the query recordset. If any tblOwner records had an Owner ID that did not match an Owner ID in the tblAnimal table, these records would not be in the query recordset. For example, the Owner ID 2416 record from the tblOwner table does not appear in the query recordset because it does not match a record in the tblAnimal table.

Figure 9-20	Another example of an outer join

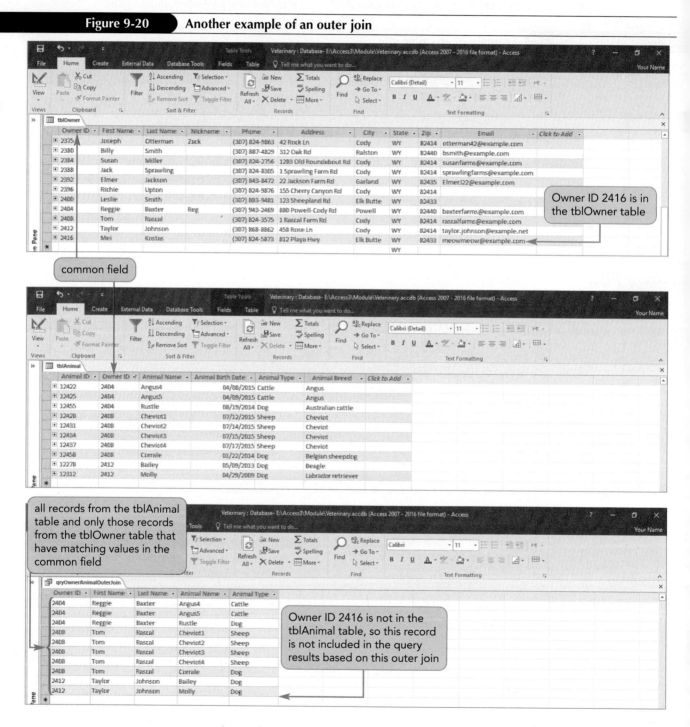

Any relationship you create in Access is by default an inner join, but you can change the join type between two tables to be an outer join in the Join Properties dialog box. You'll view the join type between the tblOwner and tblAnimal tables and examine the options for changing the join type.

To view the join type between the tblOwner and tblAnimal tables:

▶ **1.** Right-click the **join line** between the tblOwner and tblAnimal tables, and then click **Edit Relationship** on the shortcut menu to open the Edit Relationships dialog box.

Trouble? If the Edit Relationship dialog box does not open, click the join line, and then on the Relationship Tools Design tab, in the Tools group, click the Edit Relationships button.

▶ **2.** Click the **Join Type** button in the dialog box to open the Join Properties dialog box. See Figure 9-21.

Figure 9-21	Join Properties dialog box for tblOwner and tblAnimal tables

option button for inner join

option button for outer joins

Join Properties

● 1: Only include rows where the joined fields from both tables are equal.
○ 2: Include ALL records from 'tblOwner' and only those records from 'tblAnimal' where the joined fields are equal.
○ 3: Include ALL records from 'tblAnimal' and only those records from 'tblOwner' where the joined fields are equal.

OK   Cancel

In the Join Properties dialog box, the first option button is selected, indicating that the join type between the tblOwner and tblAnimal tables is an inner join. You would click the second or third option button to establish an outer join between the two tables. You'd select the second option if you wanted to select all records from the tblOwner table and any matching records from the tblAnimal table based on the OwnerID common field. You'd select the third option if you wanted to select all records from the tblAnimal table and any matching records from the tblOwner table based on the OwnerID common field.

When you change the join type for a relationship between two tables in the Relationships window, every new object created based on the two related tables uses the join type you selected in the Join Properties dialog box. Existing queries, reports, or forms based on the two related tables continue to use the join type that was in effect at the time you created these existing items.

Kimberly wants to continue to use an inner join for all queries based on the related tblOwner and tblAnimal tables.

▶ **3.** Click the **Cancel** button to close the Join Properties dialog box without making any changes, and then click the **Cancel** button to close the Edit Relationships dialog box without making any changes.

▶ **4.** Close the Relationships window, and then if you are prompted to save changes, click **No** to ensure that you don't change the relationship type.

Self-Joins

A table can also be joined with itself; this join is called a **self-join**. A self-join can be either an inner or outer join. For example, the tblEmployee table lists all employees, and for each employee who has a supervisor, the SupervisorID is included. The SupervisorID is the EmployeeID of the supervisor. It doesn't make sense to have separate SupervisorID and Employee ID fields. Imagine a situation where there are multiple supervisors, and each of the supervisors also has a supervisor. Separate tables for supervisors would be very confusing. The supervisors are also employees, and thus the EmployeeID for a supervisor is entered in the SupervisorID field. This is a case where a self-join would be used. The tblEmployee table would be joined to itself so the SupervisorID field could be related to the EmployeeID field in order to display the name of the supervisor for each employee. You would use a self-join to relate the SupervisorID field to the EmployeeID field to determine the name of the supervisor if you wanted to see records from the tblEmployee table together with information about each employee's supervisor. Figure 9-22 shows a self-join for the tblEmployee table. In this case, the self-join is an inner join because records appear in the query results only if the SupervisorID field value matches an EmployeeID field value. To create this self-join, you would add two copies of the tblEmployee field list to the Query window in Design view and then join the SupervisorID field of one tblEmployee field list to the EmployeeID field of the other tblEmployee field list.

Figure 9-22   **Example of a self-join**

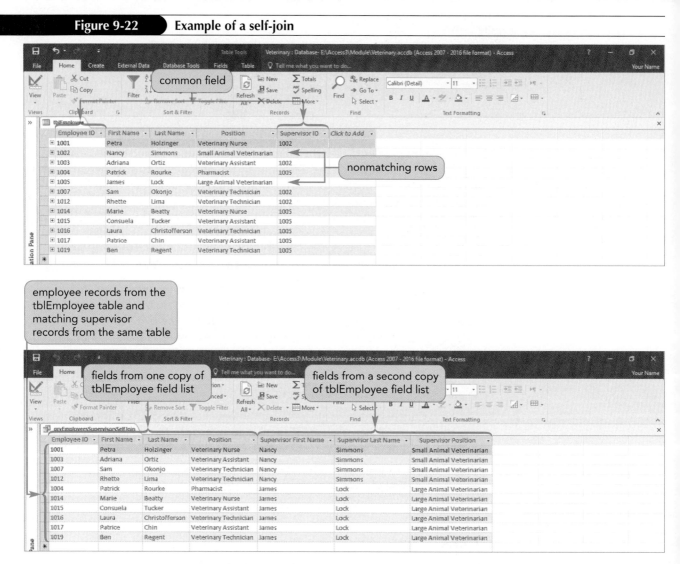

employee records from the tblEmployee table and matching supervisor records from the same table

In Figure 9-22, the query results show the record for each employee in the tblEmployee table with a value in the SupervisorID field, and the detail for each record includes information about the supervisor for that employee. The supervisor information also comes from the tblEmployee table through the SupervisorID field. The join for the query is an inner join, so only employees with nonnull SupervisorID field values appear in the query recordset.

You need to create a query to display the employees and their supervisors in the tblEmployee table. This query requires a self-join. To create the self-join, you need to add two copies of the tblEmployee field list to the Query window in Design view and then add a join line from the EmployeeID field in one field list to the SupervisorID field in the other. The SupervisorID field is a foreign key that matches the primary key field EmployeeID. You can then create a query to display employee information with the related supervisor information.

TIP

You can work with relationships and join properties in the Query window just as you do in the Relationship window, but any relationships you make in the Query window apply only to that query.

REFERENCE

Creating a Query Using a Self-Join

- Click the Create tab on the ribbon.
- In the Queries group, click the Query Design button.
- In the Show Table dialog box, double-click the table for the self-join, double-click the table a second time, and then click the Close button.
- Click and drag the primary key field from one field list to the foreign key field in the other field list.
- Right-click the join line between the two tables, and then click Join Properties to open the Join Properties dialog box.
- Click the first option button to select an inner join, or click the second option button or the third option button to select an outer join, and then click the OK button.
- Select the fields, specify the selection criteria, select the sort options, and set other properties as appropriate for the query.

Now you'll create the query using a self-join to display supervisor information with the relevant employee records.

To create the query using a self-join:

TIP

To remove a table's field list from the Query window, right-click the field list, and then click Remove Table on the shortcut menu.

1. Click the **Create** tab, and then in the Queries group, click the **Query Design** button. The Show Table dialog box opens on top of the Query window in Design view.

2. Double-click **tblEmployee** to add the tblEmployee field list to the Query window.

3. Double-click **tblEmployee** again to add a second copy of the tblEmployee field list to the Query window, and then close the Show Table dialog box. The left field list is identified as tblEmployee, and the right field list is identified as tblEmployee_1 to distinguish the two copies of the table.

   You will now create a join between the two copies of the tblEmployee field list by linking the EmployeeID field in the tblEmployee field list to the SupervisorID field in the tblEmployee_1 field list. The SupervisorID field is a foreign key that matches the primary key field, EmployeeID.

4. In the tblEmployee field list, click the **EmployeeID** field, and then drag it to the **SupervisorID** field in the tblEmployee_1 field list. A join line is created between the two fields. You can verify that this is an inner join query by opening the Join Properties dialog box.

5. Right-click the join line between the two field lists, and then click **Join Properties** on the shortcut menu to open the Join Properties dialog box. See Figure 9-23.

| Figure 9-23 | Join Properties dialog box for tblEmployee table self-join |

titles of the two field lists in the Query window

column names of the fields from both field lists involved in the relationship

The first option button is selected, indicating that this is an inner join. Because the inner join is correct, you can close the dialog box and then add the necessary fields in the design grid.

Your query will use each employee's SupervisorID value to retrieve data associated with the supervisor's corresponding EmployeeID value. To accomplish this, you choose the employee-related records from the tblEmployee_1 field list, which is connected to the other field list using the SupervisorID field.

▶ **6.** Click the **Cancel** button, and then from the tblEmployee_1 field list, add the **EmployeeID**, **FirstName**, **LastName**, and **Position** fields to the design grid.

▶ **7.** From the tblEmployee field list, add the **FirstName** and **LastName** fields to the design grid.

The tblEmployee field list is connected to the other field list using the EmployeeID field, so the FirstName and LastName fields will display the first and last names of the supervisor for each record in the tblEmployee_1 field list.

▶ **8.** Run the query. The query recordset displays six fields and 10 records. See Figure 9-24.

| Figure 9-24 | Initial self-join on the tblEmployee table |

employee data from the tblEmployee_1 table

supervisor data from the tblEmployee table

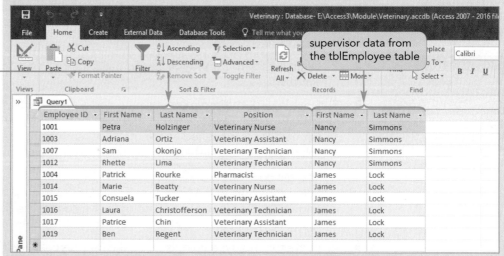

> The query recordset displays all employees and their supervisors with the exception of the records for Nancy Simmons and James Lock because their records contain null SupervisorID field values. (They are supervisors of the other employees and do not have assigned supervisors.) Remember that an inner join doesn't display records from the second table unless it contains a matching value in the common field. In the tblEmployee_1 table, the SupervisorID field values for Nancy Simmons and James Lock are null, so the inner join doesn't select their records in the tblEmployee table.

Two columns in the query recordset are titled "First Name," and two columns are titled "Last Name." Kimberly asks you to rename the two rightmost columns so that the contents of the query recordset will be more clear. After you set the Caption property for the two rightmost fields, the column names in the query recordset will be, from left to right, Employee ID, First Name, Last Name, Position, Supervisor First Name, and Supervisor Last Name. You'll also sort the query in ascending order by EmployeeID.

To set the Caption property for two query fields and sort the query:

1. Switch to Design view.

2. Click the **Field** box for the fifth column.

3. On the Query Tools Design tab, in the Show/Hide group, click the **Property Sheet** button, and then set the Caption property to **Supervisor First Name**.

4. Click the **Field** box for the sixth column, and then set the Caption property to **Supervisor Last Name**.

5. Close the Property Sheet, click the right side of the EmployeeID Sort box to display the sort order options, and then click **Ascending**.

6. Save the query as **qryEmployeesSupervisors**, run the query, resize all columns to their best fit, and then click the first row's Employee ID field value to deselect all values. The query recordset displays the new captions for the fifth and sixth columns. See Figure 9-25.

| Figure 9-25 | Final self-join on the tblEmployee table |

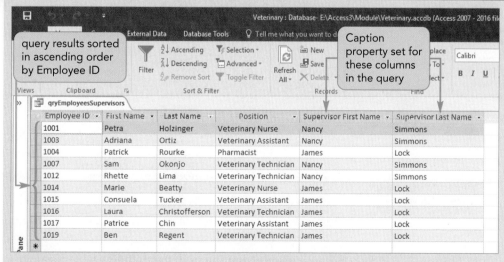

7. Save and close the query.

Kimberly wonders if her staff's work will take longer as the Veterinary database grows in size with the addition of more table records. Specifically, she wants to know if queries will take longer to run. Using indexes will help make her queries run faster.

Using Indexes for Table Fields

Suppose you need to find all the pages in a book that discuss a specific topic. The fastest, most accurate way to perform your search is to look up the topic in the book's index. In a similar fashion, you can create indexes for fields in a table, so that Access can quickly locate all the records in a table that contain specific values for one or more fields. An **index** is a list that relates field values to the records that contain those field values.

In Access, an index is automatically created for a table's primary key. When you view a table in datasheet view, the records are always in primary key order, even though they may not have been entered in that order. This is due to the automatically created index for the primary key. For example, the tblBilling table in the Veterinary database includes an index for the InvoiceNum field, which is the table's primary key. Conceptually, as shown in Figure 9-26, each record in the tblBilling table is identified by its record number, and the InvoiceNum index has two columns. The first column contains a record number in the tblBilling table, and the second column contains the InvoiceNum value for that record number. For instance, InvoiceNum 42100 in the index has a record number value of 3; and record number 3 in the tblBilling table contains the data for InvoiceNum 42100.

| Figure 9-26 | tblBilling table with index for the InvoiceNum field |

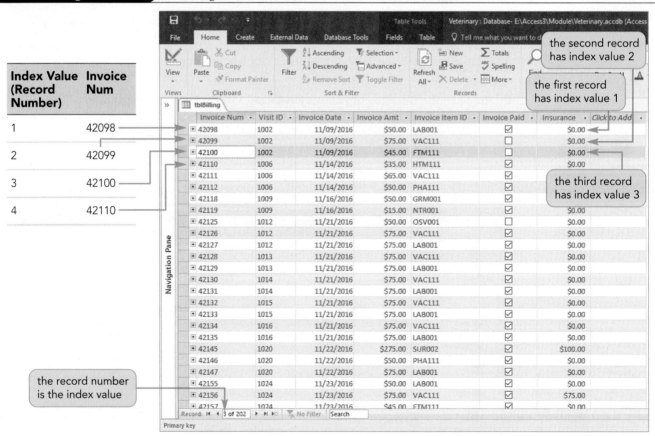

Because InvoiceNum values in the tblBilling table are unique, each row in the InvoiceNum index has a single record number. An index for a non-primary-key field, however, may contain multiple record numbers in a row. Figure 9-27 illustrates a

VisitID index for the tblBilling table. Because VisitID is a foreign key in the tblBilling table (a visit can have many invoices), each VisitID entry in the index can be associated with many record numbers in the tblBilling table. For instance, VisitID 1002 in the index has record number values of 1, 2, and 3, and record numbers 4, 5, and 6 in the tblBilling table contain the invoice data for VisitID 1006.

| Figure 9-27 | tblBilling table with index for the VisitID field |

Index Value (Record Number)	Visit ID
1, 2, 3	1002
4, 5, 6	1006
7, 8	1009
9, 10	1012

Invoice Num	Visit ID	Invoice Date	Invoice Amt	Invoice Item ID	Invoice Paid	Insurance	Click to Add
⊞ 42098	1002	11/09/2016	$50.00	LAB001	☑	$0.00	
⊞ 42099	1002	11/09/2016	$75.00	VAC111	☐	$0.00	
⊞ 42100	1002	11/09/2016	$45.00	FTM111	☐	$0.00	
⊞ 42110	1006	11/14/2016	$35.00	HTM111	☑	$0.00	
⊞ 42111	1006	11/14/2016	$65.00	VAC111	☑	$65.00	
⊞ 42112	1006	11/14/2016	$50.00	PHA111	☑	$0.00	
⊞ 42118	1009	11/16/2016	$50.00	GRM001	☑	$0.00	
⊞ 42119	1009	11/16/2016	$15.00	NTR001	☑	$0.00	
⊞ 42125	1012	11/21/2016	$50.00	OSV001	☐	$0.00	
⊞ 42126	1012	11/21/2016	$75.00	VAC111	☑	$0.00	

If you were to create an index for the VisitID field in the tblBilling table, queries that use VisitID as a sort field or as a selection criterion would run faster.

Benefits and Limitations of Indexes

With small tables, the increased speed associated with indexes is not readily apparent. In practice, tables with hundreds of thousands or millions of records are common. In such cases, the increase in speed is dramatic. In fact, without indexes, many database operations in large tables would not be practical because they would take too long to complete. Why the speed difference in these cases? Sorting or selecting records from a large table without an index requires numerous accesses to storage media to retrieve table records because the entire table can't fit in computer memory. In contrast, indexes are usually small enough to fit completely in computer memory, and records can be sorted and selected based on indexes with minimal need to access storage media. Because accessing storage media is generally slower than performing operations in computer memory, using indexes in large tables is faster.

The speed advantage of using an index must be weighed against two disadvantages: The index adds storage requirements to the database, and it takes time to update the index as you add and delete records. Except for primary key indexes, you can add and delete indexes at any time. Thus, you can add an index if you think searching and querying would be faster as the number of records in the database increases. You can also delete an existing index if you later deem it to be unnecessary.

You can view the existing indexes for a table by opening the table in Design view.

View a Table's Indexes

- Open the table in Design view.
- To view an index for a single field, click the field, and then view the Indexed property in the Field Properties pane.
- To view all the indexes for a table or to view an index consisting of multiple fields, click the Indexes button in the Show/Hide group on the Table Tools Design tab.

You'll view the indexes for the tblTreatment table.

To view the indexes for the tblTreatment table:

1. Open the Navigation Pane, and then open the **tblTreatment** table in Design view.

2. On the Table Tools Design tab, in the Show/Hide group, click the **Indexes** button to open the Indexes: tblTreatment dialog box, and then drag the dialog box to the position shown in Figure 9-28.

Figure 9-28	Indexes for the tblTreatment table

Because the InvoiceNum field was selected when you opened the Indexes: tblTreatment dialog box, the properties in the Field Properties pane pertained to this field. In particular, the Indexed property value of No for the InvoiceNum field specifies there's no index for this field.

In the Indexes: tblTreatment dialog box, the properties in the Index Properties section apply to the selected PrimaryKey index, which consists of the table's composite key of the InvoiceNum and EmployeeID fields. Because EmployeeID in the second row of the dialog box does not have an Index Name property value, both InvoiceNum and EmployeeID make up the PrimaryKey index. The PrimaryKey index was generated automatically when the table was created, and the InvoiceNum and EmployeeID fields were designated as the table's composite key. The properties for the PrimaryKey index indicate that this index is the primary key index (Primary property setting of Yes) and that values in this index must be unique (Unique property setting of Yes)—that is, each InvoiceNum and EmployeeID pair of field values must be unique. The Ignore Nulls property setting of No means that records with null values for the InvoiceNum field or EmployeeID field are included in the index, but this setting is ignored because the Yes setting for the Primary property doesn't allow either field to have a null value.

▶ **3.** Close the Indexes: tblTreatment dialog box, and then close the table.

INSIGHT

Default Automatic Indexes

In addition to the automatically created primary key index, an index is also automatically created for any field name that contains the following letter sequences: "code", "ID", "key", or "num". You can add, change, and delete from this list of letter sequences to manage the automatic indexes created in a database. To do so, click the File tab to open Backstage view, click Options in the navigation bar to open the Access Options dialog box, and then click Object Designers in the left pane. In the Table design view section, the AutoIndex on Import/Create box displays, by default, ID;key;code;num. Modify the entries in the AutoIndex on Import/Create box if you want a different list of letter sequences to be used in automatically created indexes for the fields in your tables.

Over the past few weeks, Kimberly's staff has been monitoring the performance of the Veterinary database by timing how long it takes to run queries. She wants her staff to let her know if the performance changes over the next several days as a result of creating an index for the City field in the tblOwner table. Many queries use the City field as a sort field or selection criterion, and adding an index might speed up those queries.

Creating an Index

You can create an index for a single field in the Indexes dialog box or by setting the Indexed property for the field in Design view. However, for a multiple-field index, you must create the index in the Indexes dialog box.

REFERENCE

Creating an Index

- Open the table in Design view.
- To create an index for a single field, click the field, and then set the Indexed property in the Field Properties pane.
- To create an index consisting of multiple fields, click the Indexes button located on the Table Tools Design tab in the Show/Hide group to open the Indexes dialog box.
- Enter a name for the index in the first Index Name box, and select the first field in the Field Name box.
- In the second Index Name box, leave the name blank, and select the second field in the Field Name box.
- Set additional field names in each row as needed, leaving the Index Name box blank for each row except the first one, set other properties as necessary for the index, and then close the Indexes dialog box.

Next, you'll create an index for the City field in the tblOwner table by setting the field's Indexed property.

To create an index for the City field in the tblOwner table:

1. Open the tblOwner table in Design view, close the Navigation Pane, and then click **City** in the Field Name column.

2. On the Table Tools Design tab, in the Show/Hide group, click the Indexes button to open the Indexes: tblOwner dialog box, and then position the dialog box as shown in Figure 9-29.

Figure 9-29	Indexes list for the tblOwner table

An index was created for the OwnerID field because it is the primary key. The OwnerID index would have been created even if the field wasn't the primary key because the field name has an ID suffix. No other indexes exist for the tblOwner table. You'll create an index for the City field that allows duplicates because the same City field value can appear in many records in the tblOwner table.

3. Click the right side of the **Indexed** box in the Field Properties pane, and then click **Yes (Duplicates OK)**. An index for the City field is created with duplicate values allowed. Setting the Indexed property automatically created the City index in the Indexes: tblOwner dialog box. See Figure 9-30.

| Figure 9-30 | City index added to the tblOwner table |

4. Close the dialog box, save your table design changes, and then switch to Datasheet view.

5. Change the first record in the table so the Last Name and First Name columns contain your last and first names, respectively.

6. Close the table, make a backup copy of the Veterinary database, compact and repair the database, and then close it.

The work you completed with table relationships, table and query joins, and indexes will make it much easier for Kimberly and her staff to enter, retrieve, and view information in the Veterinary database.

Session 9.2 Quick Check

REVIEW

1. What are the three types of relationships you can define between tables?

2. What is an entity subtype?

3. What is the difference between an inner join and an outer join?

4. Describe the results of two different outer joins that you could create between a members table and a classes table in a database for a fitness club.

5. What is a self-join?

6. What is an index?

7. In Access, an index is generated automatically for a table's _____ key.

Review Assignments

PRACTICE

Data File needed for the Review Assignments: Ordering.accdb

The Ordering database contains data about Riverview Veterinary Care Center suppliers and their products, as well as data about the invoices from the suppliers and the payments made by Riverview Veterinary Care Center to the suppliers. The database also contains a form and some reports. Kimberly wants you to define relationships between the tables and to create some new queries for her. Complete the following steps:

1. Open the **Ordering** database located in the Access3 > Review folder provided with your Data Files, and then click the Enable Content button next to the security warning, if necessary.

2. Modify the first record in the tblSupplier table datasheet so the Contact First Name and Contact Last Name columns contain your first and last names, and the Notes field contains your city and state or country. Close the table.

3. Create a make-table query based on the tblProduct table, selecting the ProductID, SupplierID, ProductName, Price, TempControl, and Sterile fields, and selecting only those records for products that require a temperature-controlled environment. Use **tblProductSpecialEnviron** as the new table name, store the table in the current database, and then run the query. Save this query as **qryMakeSpecialEnviron**. Close the query.

4. Open the tblProductSpecialEnviron table, and then adjust the column widths to their best fit. Format the TempControlled and Sterile fields to yes/no. (*Hint*: In Design View, select the fieldname, then select the Format property for yes/no.) Save and close the tblProductSpecialEnviron table.

5. Create an append query based on the tblProduct table, selecting the ProductID, SupplierID, ProductName, Price, TempControl, and Sterile fields, and selecting only those records that are sterile and do not require a temperature-controlled environment. Append the records to the tblProductSpecialEnviron table, run the query, and save it as **qryAppendSterile**. Open the tblProductSpecialEnviron table, and then verify that the records have been added. Close the table and the query.

6. Suppliers are offering a 10 percent discount off the regular price for all products in the tblProductSpecialEnviron table. Create an update query to select all records in the tblProductSpecialEnviron table, decrease the Price field values by 10 percent, run the query, save it as **qrySpecialDiscount**, then close the query. (*Hint*: Use the expression **0.9*[Price].**) Open the tblProductSpecialEnviron table, verify that the Price field values have been reduced by 10 percent, then close the table.

7. Create a delete query that deletes all records in the tblProductSpecialEnviron table in which the Price is less than $20.00. Run the query, save it as **qryDeletePriceLess20**, and the close the query. Open the tblProductSpecialEnviron table, verify that the table now contains 13 records, and then close the table.

8. Define a many-to-many relationship between the tblInvoice and tblPayment tables, using the tblInvoicePayment table as the related table. Define a one-to-one relationship between the primary tblSupplier table and the related tblSupplierCreditLine table. Select the referential integrity option and the cascade updates option for the relationships.

9. Create a query using a self-join that selects all products in the tblProduct table that are included in another product. To do so, add two copies of the tblProduct field list to the query design window, then create a relationship between the ProductID field in the first list and the IncludedIn field in the second list. The query results should display the ProductID and ProductName fields for the included items. (*Hint*: These should come from the second field list.) The query results should also include the ProductID and ProductName fields for the products that are collections, assigning the captions Collection Product ID and Collection Product Name, respectively. Sort the records in ascending order by the Collection Product ID column. Resize all columns in the datasheet to best fit, save the query as **qryProductCollections**, and then close the query.

10. Open the **tblProductSpecialEnviron** table in Design view, specify the primary key, add an index that allows duplicates for the SupplierID field, and then save and close the table.

11. Make a backup copy of the database, compact and repair the database, and then close it.

Case Problem 1

Data File needed for this Case Problem: Salon.accdb

Beauty To Go   Sue Miller, an owner of a nail and hair salon in Orlando, Florida, regularly checks in on her grandmother, who resides in a retirement community. On some of her visits, Sue does her grandmother's hair and nails. Her grandmother told Sue that some of her friends would be glad to pay her and have regularly scheduled services if she could do their hair and nails also. Sue expanded her business to include the services to friends of her grandmother in local retirement communities to meet the needs of these ladies. Sue created an Access database named Salon to store data about members, plans, and contracts. The tblService table contains data about members and the scheduled services, the tblPrepaid table contains data about members' prepaid balances, the tblMember table contains data about members, the tblOption table contains data about options offered to members, and the tblSchedule table contains data about each scheduled service. The database also contains several other objects, including queries, forms, and reports. Sue wants you to define a many-to-many relationship between the tblMember and tblSchedule tables, create a one-to-one relationship between the tblMember and tblPrepaid tables, and create several new queries. To do so, complete the following steps:

1. Open the **Salon** database located in the Access3 > Case1 folder provided with your Data Files, and then click the Enable Content button next to the security warning, if necessary.

2. Modify the first record in the **tblMember** table datasheet so the First Name and Last Name columns contain your first and last names. Close the table.

3. Define a many-to-many relationship between the tblMember and tblSchedule tables, using the tblService table as the related table. Define a one-to-one relationship between the primary tblMember table and the related tblPrepaid table. Select the referential integrity option and the cascade updates option for the relationships.

4. Create a make-table query based on the tblMember table, selecting all fields from the table except the Street, City, State, and Zip fields, and only those records where the MemberStatus field value is **on hold**. Use **tblSpecialMember** as the new table name, store the table in the current database, and then run the query. Save the query as **qryMakeOnHold**, and close the query.

5. Create an append query based on the tblMember table (selecting all fields from the table except the Street, City, State, and Zip fields) that selects only those records where the MemberStatus field value is **inactive**. Append the records to the tblSpecialMember table and run the query. Save the query as **qryAppendInactive** and then close the query.

6. Create an update query to select all records in the tblSpecialMember table in which the MemberStatus field value is **inactive**, changing the MemberComments field value to **Contact member**, and run the query. Save the query as **qryUpdateSpecialOption** and close the query.

7. Create a delete query that deletes all records in the tblSpecialMember table where the OptionID field value equals **128**. Run the query, save it as **qryDelete128**, and close the query. Open the **tblSpecialMember** table, resize all columns to their best fit, and then save and close the table.

8. Create a select query with an outer join between the tblMember and tblPrepaid tables, selecting all records from the tblMember table and any matching records from the tblPrepaid table. Display all fields from the tblMember table and the Balance and ReplenishDate fields from the tblPrepaid table. Save the query as **qryMemberPrepaidOuterJoin**, and then run and close the query.

9. In the tblMember table, add an index that allows duplicates using the OptionBegin field, and then save and close the table.

10. Make a backup copy of the database, compact and repair the database, and then close it.

Case Problem 2

CREATE

Data File needed for this Case Problem: Technology.accdb

Programming Pros   While in college obtaining his bachelor's degree in Raleigh, North Carolina, Brent Hovis majored in computer science. Prior to graduating, Brent began tutoring freshman and sophomore students in programming to make some extra money. When Brent entered graduate school, he started Programming Pros, a company offering expanded tutoring services for high school and college students through group, private, and semiprivate tutoring sessions. The company also offers supplementary sessions for students who are preparing for exams or finishing class projects. Brent created an Access database named Technology, which includes six tables. The tblBillingContact table contains data about billing information for clients whose bills are paid by someone else, the tblContract table contains data about the client contracts, the tblStudent table contains data about the students receiving services, the tblSupplement table contains data about the supplementary sessions students can book, the tblSupplementContract table contains data about the supplementary session agreements, and the tblTutor table contains data about the employees who provide tutoring. Brent asks you to define table relationships and create some new queries for him. To do so, complete the following steps:

1. Open the **Technology** database located in the Access3 > Case2 folder provided with your Data Files, and then click the Enable Content button next to the security warning, if necessary.

2. Change the first record in the **tblStudent** table datasheet so the First Name and Last Name columns contain your first and last names. Close the table.

3. Define a many-to-many relationship between the tblContract and tblSupplement tables, using the tblSupplementContract table as the related table. Define a one-to-one relationship between the primary tblStudent table and the related tblBillingContact table. Select the referential integrity option and the cascade updates option for the relationships.

4. Create a make-table query based on the qryLessonsByTutor query, selecting all fields from the query and only those records where the SessionType field value is **Group**. Use **tblSpecialSession** as the new table name, store the table in the current database, and then run the query. Save the query as **qryMakeSpecialSession**, and close the query. Open the tblSpecialSession table, and verify the SessionType value is Group for all records. Close the tblSpecialSession table.

5. Create an append query based on the qryLessonsByTutor query that selects all fields for only those records where the SessionType field value is **Semi-private**. Append the records to the tblSpecialSession table and run the query. Save the query as **qryAppendSemiPrivate**, and then close the query. Open the tblSpecialSession table and verify that the SessionType column includes values of both Group and Semi-private. Close the tblSpecialSession table.

6. Create an update query to select all records in the tblSpecialSession table where the value in the Length field value is **2**, changing the field value to **3**. Run the query, save it as **qryUpdateLength2to3**, and then close the query. Open the tblSpecialSession table and verify there are no records whose Length field is 2. Close the tblSpecialSession table.

7. Create a delete query that deletes all records in the tblSpecialSession table in which the ContractDate field value is less than **7/31/2017**. Run the query, save it as **qryDeleteBeforeAug2017**, and then close the query. Open the **tblSpecialSession** table, resize all columns to their best fit, and then verify there are no records whose ContractDate is earlier than 7/31/2017. Save your layout changes, and then close the tblSpecialSession table.

8. Create a select query with an outer join between the tblStudent and tblBillingContact tables, selecting all records from the tblStudent table and any matching records from the tblBillingContact table. Display the FirstName and LastName fields from the tblStudent table and the FirstName, LastName, and BillingRelationship fields from the tblBillingContact table. Change the caption for the FirstName and LastName fields from the tblBillingContact table to **Billing First Name** and **Billing Last Name**. Save the query as **qryStudentBillingContactOuterJoin**, run the query, resize all columns to their best fit, and then save and close the query.

9. Create a self-join query based on the tblTutor table that produces the results shown in Figure 9-31.

Figure 9-31   **qryTutorSelfJoin results**

10. Open the **tblSpecialSession** table in Design view, add an index that allows duplicates for the StudentID field, and then save and close the table.

11. Make a backup copy of the database, compact and repair the database, and then close it.

TROUBLESHOOT

Case Problem 3

Data File needed for this Case Problem: Thrift.accdb

Diane's Community Center   Diane Coleman is a successful businesswoman in Dallas, Georgia, but things were not always that way. Diane experienced trying times and fortunately had people in the community come into her life to assist her and her children when times were difficult. To give back to her community and support those in need, Diane has created a community center in Dallas where those in need can come in for goods and services. She has also opened a thrift store to sell and auction donated items to support the center. Diane created an Access database named Thrift to track information for the community center and for the thrift store. In the Thrift database, the tblAuction table contains data about donated items that will be auctioned, the tblDonation table contains data about the donations people make, the tblDonationLocation table contains data about the location of donated items, the tblFacility table contains data about the building locations where donated goods are stored, the tblPatron table contains data about people who donate cash or goods, and the tblStorage table contains data about the storage locations in the facilities for the donated goods. The database also contains other objects, including queries, forms, and reports. Diane wants you to define table relationships and create several new queries. To do so, complete the following steps:

1. Open the **Thrift** database located in the Access3 > Case3 folder provided with your Data Files, and then click the Enable Content button next to the security warning, if necessary.

2. Modify the first record in the **tblPatron** table datasheet so the Title, First Name, and Last Name columns contain your title and name. Close the table.

3. Define a one-to-many relationship between the primary tblFacility table and the related tblStorage table. Define a many-to-many relationship between the tblDonation and tblStorage tables, using the tblDonationLocation table as the related table. Select the referential integrity option and the cascade updates option for the relationships.

⚙ **Troubleshoot** 4. Open the query qryMakeSpecialDonation in Design view. This is a query that Diane created that is not working as she intended. This query should create a new table named **tblSpecialDonation** in the current database, which should contain data from all fields in the tblDonation table. Identify and fix the problems in the query's design, save your changes, and then run the query. Open the tblSpecialDonation table, change the format of the CashDonation and AuctionItem fields to Yes/No, and then verify that the CashDonation value is Yes for all records. Save your changes, and then close the tblSpecialDonation table and the query.

5. Create an append query based on the tblDonation table, selecting all fields from the table and only those records where the Description field value ends with the word **clothes**. (*Hint*: Use the expression *Like "*clothes"*.) Append the records to the **tblSpecialDonation** table, and run the query. Save the query as **qryAppendClothes**, and then close the query. Open the tblSpecialDonation table, and verify the Description field value for all records is either Cash donation or ends with *clothes*. Close the tblSpecialDonation table.

6. Create an update query to select all records in the tblSpecialDonation table in which the Description field value equals **Cash donation**, changing the Description field value to **Money**. Run the query, save it as **qryUpdateMoney**, and then close the query. Open the tblSpecialDonation table, and verify the Description field value for all records is either Money or ends with *clothes*. Close the tblSpecialDonation table.

7. Create a delete query that deletes all records in the **tblSpecialDonation** table in which the DonationValue field value is more than **$100** and the Description value is **Money**. Run the query, save it as **qryDeleteOver100**, and then close the query. Open the **tblSpecialDonation** table, resize all columns to their best fit, save the table, and then verify that all records for money donations have a DonationValue field value of 100 or less. Close the tblSpecialDonation table.

⚙ **Troubleshoot** 8. Open the query **qryDonationAuctionOuterJoin** in Design view. This is a query that Diane created that is not working as she intended. This query should display all records from the tblDonation table and any matching records from the tblAuction table. Identify and fix the problems in the query's design. Save your changes to the query, run it, and then close the query.

9. Add an index that allows duplicate PatronID values in the tblDonation table, and then save and close the table.

10. Make a backup copy of the database, compact and repair the database, and then close it.

Case Problem 4

CHALLENGE

Data File needed for this Case Problem: BlueRidge.accdb

Hike Appalachia   Molly and Bailey Johnson own Hike Appalachia, a business in which they and their staff members guide clients on hikes in the Blue Ridge Mountains of North Carolina. They advertise in local and regional outdoor magazines and field requests from people all around the region. Molly and Bailey created an Access database called BlueRidge to track information for their business. In the BlueRidge database, the tblGuide table contains data about the people who are tour guides, the tblHiker table contains data about clients, the tblReservation table contains data about tours that clients have booked, the tblTour table contains data about the hiking trips the company offers, and the tblTourGuideReservation table contains data about the tour guide assigned to each tour. The database also contains several other objects, including queries, forms, and reports. Molly and Bailey want you to define a many-to-many relationship between the tblReservation and tblGuide tables and to create several new queries. To do so, complete the following steps:

1. Open the **BlueRidge** database located in the Access3 > Case4 folder provided with your Data Files, and then click the Enable Content button next to the security warning, if necessary.

2. Modify the first record in the **tblHiker** table so the Hiker First Name and Hiker Last Name columns contain your first and last names.

3. Define a many-to-many relationship between the tblReservation and tblGuide tables, using the tblTourGuideReservation table as the related table. Select the referential integrity option and the cascade updates option for the relationships.

4. Create a make-table query based on the tblHiker and tblReservation tables, selecting the HikerFirst, HikerLast, and State fields from the tblHiker table and the TourDate and TourID fields from the tblReservation table. Select those records with a State field value of **NC**. Save the table as **tblSelectedReservation** in the current database, and then run the query. Save the query as **qryMakeSelectedReservation**, and close the query. Open the tblSelectedReservation table, and verify that all records have a State field value of NC. Close the tblSelectedReservation table.

5. Create an append query based on the tblHiker and tblReservation tables, selecting the HikerFirst, HikerLast, and State fields from the tblHiker table and the TourDate and TourID fields from the tblReservation table. Select those records with a State field value of **GA** or **MD,** and append the selected records to the tblSelectedReservation table. Run the query, save it as **qryAppendStateReservation**, and then close the query. Open the tblSelectedReservation table, and verify that all records have a State field value of NC, GA, or MD. Close the tblSelectedReservation table.

6. Create a delete query that deletes all records from the tblSelectedReservation table in which the TourDate field value is earlier than **9/8/2017**. Run the query, save it as **qryDeleteBeforeSep8**, and then close the query. Open the **tblSelectedReservation** table, resize all columns to their best fit, verify that all records have TourDate value on or after 9/8/2017, and then close the tblSelectedReservation table.

7. Create a select query with an outer join between the tblHiker and tblReservation tables, selecting all records from the tblHiker table and any matching records from the tblReservation table. Display the HikerFirst, HikerLast, and City fields from the tblHiker table and the TourDate and TourID fields from the tblReservation table. Save the query as **qryHikerReservationOuterJoin**, and then run and close the query.

⊕ **Explore** 8. Create a select query with a self-join based on the tblHiker table that displays records only for those hikers whose City value is the same as the City value for a different hiker in the table. To do this, first create a relationship between the City fields of both field lists. Select the HikerID, HikerFirst, HikerLast, City, and State fields from the primary table (the table *without* _1 at the end of the name). For the HikerFirst field, add the expression **<>[tblHiker_1].[HikerFirst]** as the criteria. For the City field, add the expression **=[tblHiker_1].[City]** as the criteria. Open the Property Sheet for the query. (*Hint*: If the Property Sheet does not say "Query Properties" at the top, click the blank area next to the field lists.) Change the value for Unique Records to **Yes**. Run the query, resize all columns to their best fit, save the query as **qryHikerSameCitySelfJoin**, and then close the query.

⊕ **Explore** 9. Add an index named **Location** to the tblHiker table that consists of the State and City fields and uses the default property settings, delete the Zip index, and then save and close the table. (*Hint*: Create an index named Location using the first field name, and then in the next row, leave the index name blank but specify the second field name.)

10. Make a backup copy of the database, compact and repair the database, and then close the database.

ACCESS

Automating Tasks with Macros

Creating a User Interface for the Veterinary Database

OBJECTIVES

Session 10.1
- View macros in the Macro Designer
- Run and add actions to macros
- Single step a macro
- Create a submacro
- Add a command button to a form
- Attach a submacro to a command button

Session 10.2
- Create an unbound form
- Add a list box control to a form
- Use a SQL statement to fill a list box control with object names
- Create multiple macros for a form
- Create a navigation form

Case | *Riverview Veterinary Care Center*

Kimberly Johnson recently hired new staff at Riverview Veterinary Care Center. The new staff members have limited experience working with databases, so Kimberly consults with Daksha Yatawara, the database developer for the care center, about providing training to the new staff. In addition, Daksha suggests implementing some advanced Access features to automate and control how users interact with the Veterinary database. One of these features makes it possible to create a custom user interface that will make it easier for inexperienced users to access the database and minimize the chance that an unauthorized user could change the design of any database object.

To meet the needs of the less experienced users, he would like the interface to display specific forms and reports and all the queries in the database, so that users can select objects they want to work with from the interface. For more advanced users, Daksha would like a form that has some buttons that users can click to perform common tasks. In this module, you will automate tasks in the Veterinary database by creating and editing macros. You will also modify the user interface for the database by creating buttons that are linked to macros and by creating a navigation form.

STARTING DATA FILES

Access3 → Module
Veterinary.accdb (*cont.*)

Review
Ordering.accdb (*cont.*)

Case1
Salon.accdb (*cont.*)

Case2
Technology.accdb (*cont.*)

Case3
Thrift.accdb (*cont.*)

Case4
BlueRidge.accdb (*cont.*)

Session 10.1 Visual Overview:

Click the Single Step button to **single step**, which executes one macro action at a time, pausing between actions.

The **Action Catalog button** is a toggle to open and close the Action Catalog pane.

Click the Run button to run the macro.

A **macro** is a recorded sequence of commands or keystrokes that can be saved and then executed, or run, by a single action by the user.

The mcr prefix tag identifies the object as a macro.

The instruction that initiates each individual command or keystroke within a macro is called an **action**.

The **OpenForm action** opens a specified form in a specified view.

A piece of data that is required by an action is known as an **argument**.

A **comment** is a text description for the benefit of database developers and has no effect on the macro. A comment starts with /* and ends with */ and contains a description of one or more tasks.

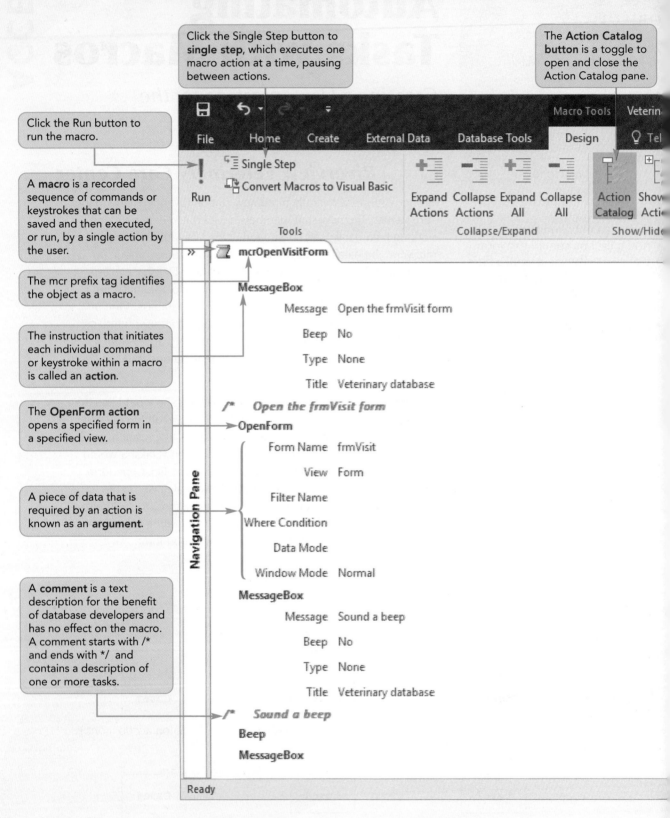

The Macro Designer Window

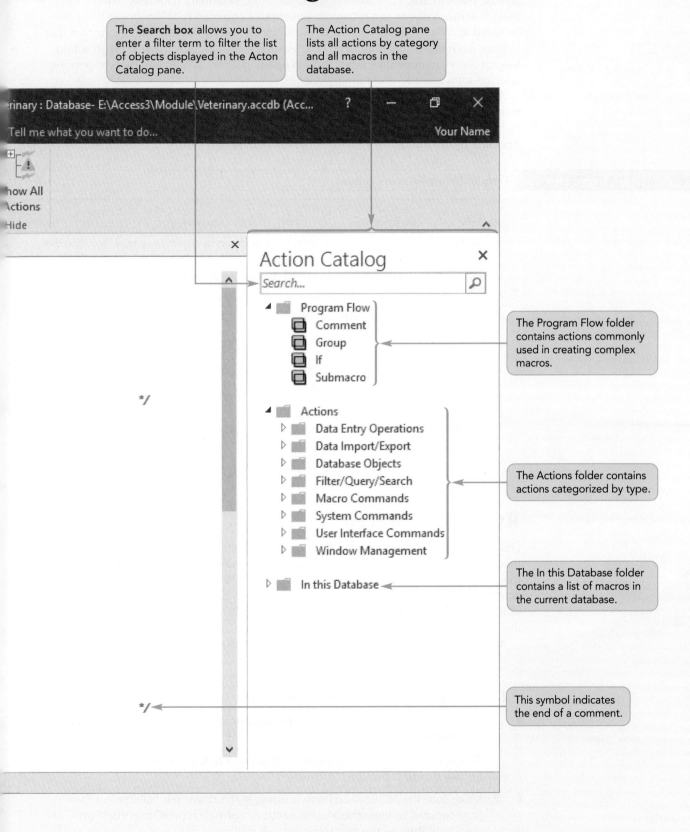

The **Search box** allows you to enter a filter term to filter the list of objects displayed in the Acton Catalog pane.

The Action Catalog pane lists all actions by category and all macros in the database.

The Program Flow folder contains actions commonly used in creating complex macros.

The Actions folder contains actions categorized by type.

The In this Database folder contains a list of macros in the current database.

This symbol indicates the end of a comment.

Introduction to Macros

Daksha plans to automate some of the tasks in the Veterinary database, initially by using macros. A macro is a recorded sequence of commands or keystrokes that can be saved and then executed, or run, by a single action by the user. The instruction that initiates each individual command or keystroke within the macro is called an action. Macros automate repetitive tasks, such as opening forms, tables, and reports; printing selected form records; and running queries.

Access provides more than 80 common actions you can include in your database macros. Each of these actions has a designated name you reference to include its instruction in a macro. Figure 10-1 lists the names and corresponding instructions for Access actions commonly used in macro development.

Figure 10-1   **Frequently used Access actions**

Action	Description
ApplyFilter	Applies a filter to a table, form, or report to restrict or sort the records in the recordset
Beep	Produces a beep tone through the computer's speakers
CloseWindow	Closes the specified window, or the active window if none is specified
FindRecord	Finds the first record (or the next record, if the action is used again) that meets the specified criteria
GoToControl	Moves the focus to a specified field or control on the active datasheet or form
MessageBox	Displays a message box containing a warning or informational message
OpenForm	Opens a form in the specified view
QuitAccess	Exits Microsoft Access
RunMacro	Runs a macro
SelectObject	Selects a specified object so you can run an action that applies to the object
SendKeys	Sends keystrokes to Microsoft Access or another active program

Running a Macro

Daksha created a macro with multiple actions to demonstrate to Kimberly how using macros will make working with the Veterinary database easier for the newer staff members. Daksha's macro is named mcrOpenVisitForm, and it performs multiple actions using the frmVisit form. You can reference and run a macro from within a form or report, or you can run a macro by right-clicking its name in the Macros section of the Navigation Pane.

You will run the mcrOpenVisitForm macro from the Navigation Pane.

To run the mcrOpenVisitForm macro:

▶ 1. Start Access, and then open the **Veterinary** database you worked with in the previous module.

   Trouble? If the security warning is displayed below the ribbon, click the Enable Content button.

▶ 2. Make sure the Navigation Pane is open, scroll down the Navigation Pane (if necessary) to view the Macros section, right-click **mcrOpenVisitForm**, and then click **Run** on the shortcut menu. A message box opens. See Figure 10-2.

| Figure 10-2 | Message box opened by the first action in the mcrOpenVisitForm macro |

Opening the message box is the first action Daksha added to the mcrOpenVisitForm macro. As in other computer applications, a **message box** in Access is a special dialog box that contains a message and a command button, but no options. A **command button** is a button that performs an action when a user clicks it. The message box that Daksha created specifies that the next macro action will open the frmVisit form. When the user clicks the OK button, the message box will close, and the macro will resume with the next action. Daksha added this message box and other message boxes to the macro so that he could demonstrate to Kimberly how macros can execute multiple actions to complete multistep tasks. With macros you create for working databases, you don't include message boxes between steps as Daksha did in his macro.

▶ **3.** Click the **OK** button. The next two actions in the mcrOpenVisitForm macro are performed: the frmVisit form opens, and the second message box opens. See Figure 10-3.

| Figure 10-3 | Second and third actions in the mcrOpenVisitForm macro |

▶ **4.** Click the **OK** button. A beep sounds, and the third message box opens. These are the fourth and fifth actions in the mcrOpenVisitForm macro.

▶ **Trouble?** If your computer doesn't have speakers or if your audio is turned down or muted, you won't hear the beep. If you do hear the beep, it might not sound like a beep at all, depending on your computer and its settings.

▶ **5.** Click the **OK** button, and then drag the message box from its title bar to the right so you can view the values displayed in the form. The frmVisit form now displays record 23 for VisitID 1072. The sixth action in the mcrOpenVisitForm is displaying record 23, and the seventh action is displaying the message box with the message "Close the form."

▶ **6.** Click the **OK** button. The frmVisit form closes, and the mcrOpenVisitForm macro ends.

Now that you have run Daksha's sample macro to view it as a user would, you will view the code, or instructions, for the macro and examine its components.

Viewing a Macro in the Macro Designer

You create, view, and edit a macro using the **Macro Designer**, which is a development environment built into Access. To open the Macro Designer, you'll open the macro in Design view.

To open Macro Designer and view the mcrOpenVisitForm macro:

▶ **1.** Right-click **mcrOpenVisitForm** in the Navigation Pane, click **Design View** on the shortcut menu, and then close the Navigation Pane. The Macro Designer displays the mcrOpenVisitForm macro. See Figure 10-4.

Figure 10-4	Macro Designer showing the mcrOpenVisitForm macro

The Macro Designer lists the actions included in the macro. In addition to actions, a macro can also include arguments and comments, as described in the Session 10.1 Visual Overview. You can change the view of the Macro Designer to display more detail.

> **2.** On the Macro Tools Design tab, in the Collapse/Expand group, click the **Expand All** button to display all the details for the actions, arguments, and comments that make up the mcrOpenVisitForm macro.
>
> If you rest the mouse pointer on the MessageBox action or on any argument line, a ScreenTip displays a brief explanation of the action or argument. You can also use Help to learn about specific actions and their arguments and about macros in general.
>
> **3.** Move the mouse pointer over **MessageBox** action at the top of the Macro Designer. The mouse pointer changes to 🖑, and a ScreenTip appears, describing the action and common ways to use the action.
>
> **4.** Click **MessageBox**. The arguments for the message display in a shaded box.

Once a macro has been created, you can modify it in the Macro Designer. You can add or delete actions, and you can modify the arguments for an action. Daksha asks you to add actions to the mcrOpenVisitForm macro. Before doing so, you need to understand how arguments are used in macros.

Using Arguments in a Macro

Some actions require information. For instance, if an action is going to open a form, the action needs to know the name of the form to open. A piece of data that is required by an action is known as an argument. An action can have more than one argument; multiple arguments are separated by commas.

The mcrOpenVisitForm macro contains a MessageBox action as the first action. The name of the MessageBox action is followed by the four arguments needed by the action—Message, Beep, Type, and Title:

- The Message argument contains the text that appears in the message box when it is displayed.
- The Beep argument is either Yes or No, to specify whether a beep sounds when the message box opens.
- The Type argument determines which icon, if any, appears in the message box to signify the critical level of the message. The icon choices are None (no icon), Critical ⊗, Warning? ❓, Warning! ⚠, and Information ⓘ.
- The Title argument contains the word(s) that will appear in the message box title bar.

Adding Actions to a Macro

Once a macro has been created, you can modify it by adding or deleting actions in the Macro Designer. When you add an action, you use the Add New Action box at the bottom of the Macro Designer window. After entering the appropriate arguments, you use the Move up and Move down buttons for the action to position it within the macro.

You'll add two actions, the MessageBox and FindRecord actions, to the mcrOpenVisitForm macro between the GoToRecord action and the last MessageBox action. You'll start by adding the MessageBox action and then moving it up to the correct position within the macro.

To add the MessageBox action to the mcrOpenVisitForm macro and position it in the macro:

1. On the Macro Tools Design tab, in the Collapse/Expand group, click the **Collapse Actions** button to hide all the detailed argument lines in the macro. Only the lines for the actions and comments are now displayed in the Macro Designer.

   Below the last action in the macro is the Add New Action box, which you use to add actions to the end of the macro.

2. Click the **Add New Action** arrow to display the list of actions, scroll down the list (if necessary), and then click **MessageBox**. The list closes, a new MessageBox action is added to the end of the macro with its four arguments displayed, and two arguments are set with default values. See Figure 10-5.

Figure 10-5	MessageBox action added to mcrOpenVisitForm

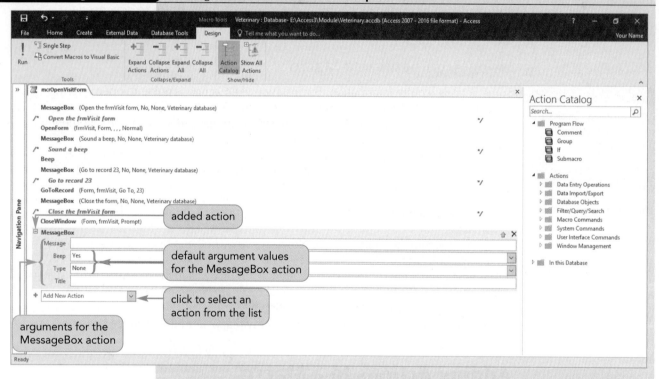

You'll enter values for the Message and Title arguments, change the Beep argument value from Yes to No, and retain the default Type argument value of None.

3. Click in the **Message** box, type **Find visit 1152**, and then press the **Tab** key. The contents of the Beep box are now selected.

4. Click the **Beep** arrow, click **No** in the list, press the **Tab** key twice, and then type **Veterinary database** in the Title box. See Figure 10-6.

Figure 10-6   Argument values added to MessageBox action

This MessageBox action is currently the last action in the mcrOpenVisitForm macro. However, it instead belongs as the seventh action in the macro, so that it takes place after the GoToRecord action that moves to record 23 and before the MessageBox action with the message "Close the form." Therefore you now need to move the new MessageBox action three positions up in the macro.

5. In the upper-right corner of the shaded MessageBox action box, click the **Move up** button three times to move the action to its correct position below the GoToRecord action. See Figure 10-7.

Figure 10-7   New MessageBox action after being moved up

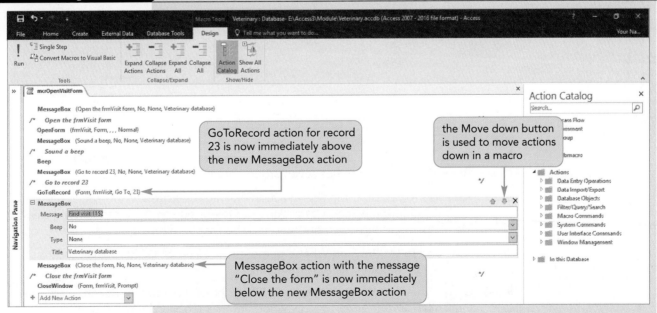

▶ **6.** On the Macro Tools Design tab, in the Collapse/Expand group, click the **Collapse Actions** button to hide all the argument lines in the MessageBox action.

Next you'll add the FindRecord action to the macro to find the record for VisitID 1152. You use the **FindRecord action** to find the first record, or the next record if the action is used again, that meets the criteria specified by the FindRecord arguments.

You could add the FindRecord action to the bottom of the macro and move it up three positions as you did for the MessageBox action. Instead, you'll search for the action in the Action Catalog pane and then drag it to its correct position in the macro.

To add the FindRecord action to the mcrOpenVisitForm macro:

▶ **1.** In the Action Catalog pane, click the **Search** box, and then type **find**. A filtered list of actions containing the search term "find" is displayed.

▶ **2.** Drag the **FindRecord** action from the Action Catalog pane to the Macro Designer window and position it immediately below the newly added MessageBox action until a colored line appears just below the MessageBox action. See Figure 10-8.

Figure 10-8	Dragging the FindRecord action to the macro

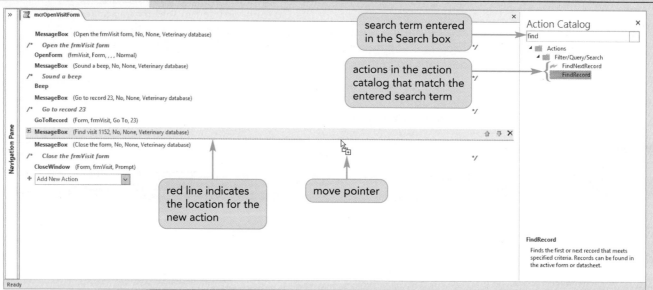

▶ **3.** Release the mouse button to add the FindRecord action to the macro. The FindRecord action has seven arguments.

Trouble? If you drag the wrong action or drag the action to the wrong location, delete the action by clicking its Delete button ☒ to the right of the Move up and Move down buttons, and then repeat Steps 2 and 3.

You need to set the Find What argument to a value of 1152. You'll accept the defaults for the other action arguments.

▶ **4.** Click in the **Find What** box, type **1152**, and then next to FindRecord, click the **Collapse** button ☐ to hide all the argument boxes for the action.

Finally, you'll add a comment above the FindRecord action to document the FindRecord action.

▶ **5.** In the Action Catalog pane, click the **blank square** on the right end of the Search box to clear the contents of the Search box. The Action Catalog pane again displays the categories of available actions.

▶ **6.** In the Program Flow section of the Action Catalog pane, drag **Comment** to the macro, and position it immediately above the FindRecord action. A Comment box is displayed, with move buttons and a Delete button to its right.

▶ **7.** Click in the **Comment** box, type **Find visit 1152**, and then click a blank area of the Macro Designer to close the Comment box. See Figure 10-9.

Figure 10-9	Actions and comment added to the mcrOpenVisitForm macro

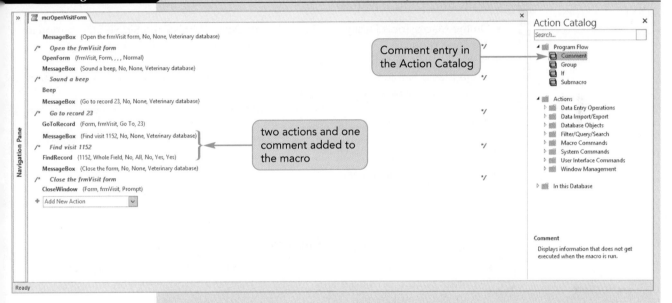

▶ **8.** On the Quick Access Toolbar, click the **Save** button 🖫 to save your macro design changes.

After you create a macro or make changes to an existing macro, you should test it. You can use single step mode to make sure the individual actions in a macro are executed in the proper order and that the arguments for a given action are correctly set.

PROSKILLS

Teamwork: Using Comments to Share Information

When working with a team to develop and maintain a database, you'll be regularly reading and making changes to macros that other team members wrote; in addition, other team members will be changing and extending macros that you created. Therefore, it's important to use comments to document the macros you write. Including a comment before each related set of actions to explain its purpose can help other team members understand the structure of your macro. In addition, including comments makes it easier for everyone on the team to find and fix any errors, because they can compare the explanation of what a section of a macro should do, as given in the comment, with the actions that follow.

Single Stepping a Macro

When you create a complicated macro with many actions, you'll often find it useful to run through the macro one step at a time. In Access, you can do this using single step mode. In **single step mode**, a macro is executed one action at a time, with a pause between actions. Using single step mode is also referred to as single stepping, and allows you to confirm you have placed actions in the right order and with the correct arguments. If you have problems with a macro, you can use single step mode to find the causes of the problems and to determine appropriate corrections. The Single Step button in the Tools group on the Macro Tools Design tab is a toggle you use to turn single step mode on and off. Once you turn on single step mode, it stays on for all macros until you turn it off.

REFERENCE

Single Stepping a Macro

- On the Macro Tools Design tab in the Macro Designer, click the Single Step button in the Tools group.
- In the Tools group, click the Run button.
- In the Macro Single Step dialog box, click the Step button to execute the next action.
- To stop the macro, click the Stop All Macros button.
- To execute all remaining actions in the macro and turn off single step mode, click the Continue button.

Now that you have added actions to the mcrOpenVisitForm macro, you'll single step through it to ensure the actions are in the correct order and the arguments are correctly set.

To single step through the macro:

▶ **1.** On the Macro Tools Design tab, in the Tools group, click the **Single Step** button to turn on single step mode. The button appears selected, indicating that single step mode is on.

▶ **2.** In the Tools group, click the **Run** button. The Macro Single Step dialog box opens. See Figure 10-10.

Figure 10-10   **Macro Single Step dialog box**

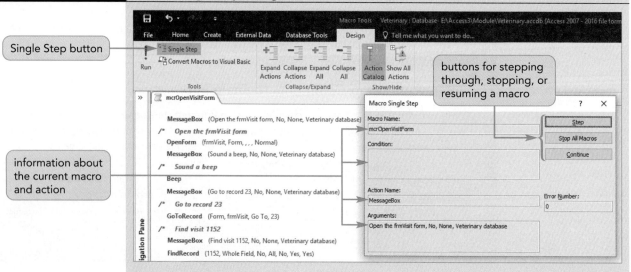

Single Step button

information about the current macro and action

buttons for stepping through, stopping, or resuming a macro

Trouble? If the first message box opens instead of the Macro Single Step dialog box, then you turned off single stepping in Step 1 when you clicked the Single Step button. Click the OK button to run the complete macro, and then repeat Steps 1 and 2.

When you single step through a macro, the Macro Single Step dialog box opens before performing each action. This dialog box shows the macro's name and the action's condition, name, and arguments. The action will be executed or not executed, depending on whether the condition is true or false. From this dialog box, you can step through the macro one action at a time, stop the macro and return to the Macro Designer, or continue by executing all remaining actions without pausing. If you click the Continue button, you also turn off single step mode.

▶ **3.** Click the **Step** button. The first action in the macro (MessageBox) runs. Because the MessageBox action pauses the macro, the Macro Single Step dialog box remains hidden until you click the OK button in the message box.

▶ **4.** Click the **OK** button to close the message box. The Macro Single Step dialog box shows the macro's second action (OpenForm).

▶ **5.** Click the **Step** button. The second action in the macro runs, opening the frmVisit form, and shows the macro's third action (MessageBox) in the Macro Single Step dialog box.

▶ **6.** Continue clicking the **Step** button and the **OK** button until you see the "Find visit 1152" message box, making sure you read the Macro Single Step dialog box carefully and observe the actions that occur. At this point, record 23 is the current record in the frmVisit form.

▶ **7.** Click the **OK** button, and then click the **Step** button. The FindRecord action runs, record 58 for VisitID 1152 is now the current record in the frmVisit form, and the Macro Single Step dialog box shows the macro's last MessageBox action.

▶ **8.** Click the **Step** button, click the **OK** button, and then click the **Step** button. The Macro Single Step dialog box closes automatically after the last macro action is completed; the last macro action closes the frmVisit form.

You've finished checking Daksha's macro and can turn off the single step feature.

▶ **9.** Click the **Macro Tools Design** tab, in the Tools group, click the **Single Step** button to turn off single step feature, and then click the **Close 'mcrOpenVisitForm'** button ☒ to close the macro.

Next, you will review another macro Daksha created for the frmVisit form.

Using a Command Button with an Attached Macro

Daksha created a macro that he associated with a command button on the frmVisit form that you just opened using the mcrOpenVisitForm macro. A command button is a control that runs a macro when you click it. To add a command button to a form, you open the form in Design view and use the Button tool in the Controls group on the Form Design Tools Design tab. After adding the command button to the form and while still in Design view, you attach a macro to the command button. Then, when a user clicks the command button, the macro's actions are executed.

You'll use the Open Animal Table command button on the frmVisit form to see how a command button works.

To use the Open Animal Table command button:

1. Open the Navigation Pane, open the **frmVisit** form in Form view, click **1002** in the Visit ID box to deselect all values, and then close the Navigation Pane. The first visit with VisitID 1002 and AnimalID 12282 is displayed. See Figure 10-11.

Figure 10-11   Open Animal Table command button on the frmVisit form

2. Click the **Open Animal Table** command button. The frmVisit form remains open, and the tblAnimal table opens. The tblAnimal table is the active object. See Figure 10-12.

Figure 10-12   tblAnimal table opened with the Open Animal Table command button

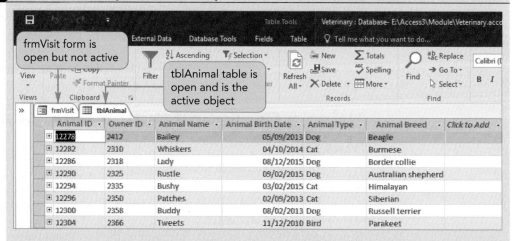

Clicking the Open Animal Table command button triggered an attached macro that opened the tblAnimal table. The tblAnimal table will remain open until it is closed manually or by another macro.

▶ **3.** Close the **tblAnimal** table. The frmVisit form is now the active object.

Understanding Events

Clicking the Open Animal Table command button is an event, and the opening of the tblAnimal table is controlled by setting an event property. An **event** is something that happens to a database object, such as a user clicking a checkbox, or a form being loaded. You can connect an action to a specific event so the action occurs in response to that event. For example, an event occurs when you click a command button on a form, when you use the mouse to position the pointer on a form, or when you press a key to choose an option. In your work with Access, you've initiated hundreds of events on forms, controls, records, and reports without any special effort. For example, events you've triggered in forms include Open, which occurs when you open a form; Activate, which occurs when the form becomes the active window; and Close, which occurs when you close a form and the form is removed from the screen. Each event has an associated event property. An **event property** specifies how an object responds when an event occurs. For example, each form has OnOpen, OnActivate, and OnClose event properties associated with the Open, Activate, and Close events, respectively.

Event properties appear in the Property Sheet when you create forms and reports. Unlike most properties you've used previously in the Property Sheet, event properties do not have an initial value. If an event property contains no value, it means the event property has not been set. In this case, no special action results when the associated event occurs. For example, if the OnOpen event property of a form is not set and you open the form, then the Open event occurs (the form opens), and no special action occurs beyond the opening of the form. You can set an event property value to a macro name, and the named macro will run when the event occurs. For example, you could write a macro that automatically selects a particular field in a form when you open it. You can also create a group of statements using Visual Basic for Applications, or VBA, code and set the event property value to the name of that group of statements. The group of statements, or **procedure**, is then executed when the event occurs. Such a procedure is called an **event procedure**. You will learn more about VBA code and procedures in the next module.

When you clicked the Open Animal Table command button on the frmVisit form, the Click event occurred and triggered an attached macro. This happened because the Open Animal Table command button contains an OnClick event property setting, which you will examine next.

To view the OnClick event property setting for the Open Animal Table command button:

TIP

The Event tab in the Property Sheet lists the names of the event properties with spaces even though you type each event property name without a space.

▶ **1.** Switch to Design view, right-click the **Open Animal Table** command button control, click **Properties** on the shortcut menu to open the Property Sheet (if necessary), and then click the **Event** tab (if necessary).

▶ **2.** Right-click the **On Click** box, click **Zoom** on the shortcut menu to open the Zoom dialog box, and then click to the right of the selected text to deselect it. See Figure 10-13.

Event property values are often longer than the boxes in the Property Sheet can display at once. Working with them in the Zoom dialog box ensures you can always see the entire value.

Figure 10-13   **Macro attached to the OnClick event property**

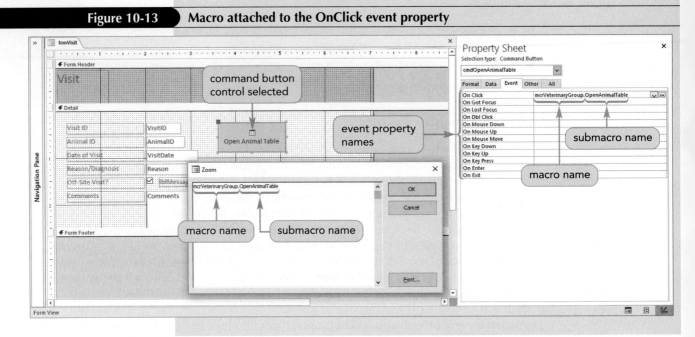

The OnClick event property value shown in the Zoom dialog box is mcrVeterinaryGroup.OpenAnimalTable. This is an example of a reference to a submacro in a macro.

Understanding Submacros

If you need to create several related macros, you can create them as submacros in a single macro instead of creating them as separate macros. A **submacro** is a complete macro with a Submacro header within a macro. Submacros are especially useful in a large database that contains many objects because they allow you to limit the number of objects by consolidating related macros. Because you can specify a submacro to run in response to an event, using submacros gives you more options than simply creating a large macro that performs many actions. For example, if a form's design uses command buttons to open a form with a related record and to print the related record displayed in the form, you can create one macro for the form that contains two submacros—one submacro to open the form, and a second submacro to print the related record. Because you created the macro specifically for the form object, you can store all the submacros you need in a single macro.

When you reference a submacro in an event property value, a period separates the macro name from the submacro name. For the OnClick event property value shown in Figure 10-13, for example, mcrVeterinaryGroup is the macro name, and OpenAnimalTable is the submacro name. When you click the Open Animal Table command button on the frmVisit form, the actions contained in the OpenAnimalTable submacro are processed. This submacro is located in the mcrVeterinaryGroup macro.

You'll now close the Zoom dialog box, and then you'll open the Macro Designer from the Property Sheet.

To open the mcrVeterinaryGroup macro in the Macro Designer:

1. Click the **Cancel** button in the Zoom dialog box to close it. In the Property Sheet for the selected Open Animal Table command button, the On Click box contains an arrow and a Build button. The button is named cmdOpenAnimalTable; *cmd* is a prefix tag to identify a command button control. See Figure 10-14.

Figure 10-14   **Property Sheet Event tab for the Open Animal Table command button**

You click the On Click arrow if you want to change the current macro to a different macro, and you click the Build button if you want to use the Macro Designer to view or change the existing macro. The Build button is also called the **Macro Builder** when you use it to work with macros.

2. Click the **Build** button [...] on the right end of the On Click box. The Macro Designer opens and displays the mcrVeterinaryGroup macro and the OpenAnimalTable submacro. See Figure 10-15.

Figure 10-15   **Macro Designer displaying the mcrVeterinaryGroup macro and its submacro**

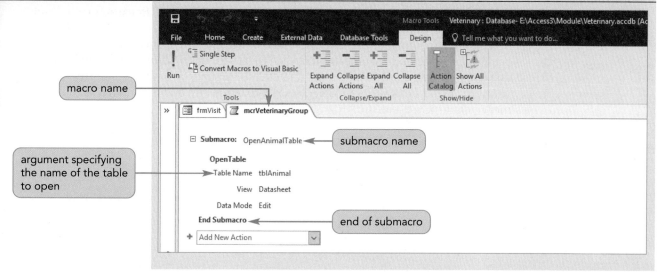

The mcrVeterinaryGroup macro consists of one submacro that starts with the Submacro statement and ends with the End Submacro statement. These statements are not actions; they are control statements to identify the beginning and end of a submacro. If a macro contains several submacros, each submacro starts with a Submacro statement and ends with an End Submacro statement.

The OpenAnimalTable submacro consists of a single action, OpenTable, which opens the tblAnimal table. The OpenTable action arguments are as follows:

- The **Table Name argument** specifies the name of a table that will be opened when the macro is run.
- The **View argument** specifies the view in which the object will open. For tables, you can specify Datasheet, Design, Print Preview, PivotTable, or PivotChart.
- The **Data Mode argument** specifies the table's data entry options. Allowable settings for this argument are Add (users can add new records but can't change or delete existing records), Edit (users can change and delete existing records and can add new records), and Read Only (users can only view records). If you don't select an argument value, Edit is the default setting.

Now that you've seen a macro that's attached to a command button, Daksha asks you to add a command button to the frmVisit form and then attach a new macro to the command button that will enable users to print the current record in the frmVisit form by clicking it. Daksha created the mcrVeterinaryGroup macro to group together all the submacros in the Veterinary database. You'll add a submacro to the mcrVeterinaryGroup macro to print the current record.

Adding a Submacro

To print the contents of a form's current record, normally you have to click the File tab to display Backstage view, click Print in the navigation bar, click Print in the list of options, click Selected Record(s), and then click the OK button—a process that takes five steps and several seconds. Instead of following this process, you can create a command button on the form, create a macro that prints the contents of a form's current record, and then attach the macro to the command button on the form. Instead of following the above steps to print the form's current record, a user could simply click the command button.

First, you'll add a submacro to the mcrVeterinaryGroup macro. You'll use the SelectObject and RunMenuCommand actions for the new submacro. The **SelectObject action** selects a specified object so that you can run an action that applies to the object. The **RunMenuCommand action** selects and runs a command on the ribbon. The specific argument you'll use with the RunMenuCommand action is the **PrintSelection argument**, which prints the selected form record. Because macros and submacros are database objects, you'll follow the naming conventions for database objects when naming macros and submacros. These naming conventions include using descriptive object names so that the object's function is obvious, capitalizing the first letter of each word in the name, and excluding spaces from the name. Therefore, you'll name the submacro PrintSelectedRecord when you add the submacro to the mcrVeterinaryGroup macro.

Adding a Submacro

- Open the macro in the Macro Designer.
- Click the Add New Action arrow, click Submacro, and then type the submacro name in the Submacro box.
- Click the Add New Action arrow above the End Submacro statement, click the action you want to use, and then set the action's arguments.
- If the submacro consists of more than one action, repeat the previous step for each action.
- Add comments as needed to the submacro to document the submacro's function or provide other information.
- Save the macro.

You'll now add the PrintSelectedRecord submacro to the mcrVeterinaryGroup macro.

To add the PrintSelectedRecord submacro to the mcrVeterinaryGroup macro:

1. Click the **Collapse** icon ⊟ to the left of Submacro OpenAnimalTable to collapse the actions and arguments for the submacro.

2. Click the **Add New Action** arrow to display the list of actions and control statements, and then click **Submacro**. A submacro box appears with the default name selected in it, which is Sub followed by one or more numbers. You will replace the default name with a more appropriate name for the submacro.

3. Type **PrintSelectedRecord** in the Submacro box. The Submacro and End Submacro statements are added to the macro, and another Add New Action box is displayed between these two statements. See Figure 10-16.

Figure 10-16   New submacro added

first submacro collapsed

second submacro

submacro name

first action will be added here

You need to select the SelectObject action and set its arguments.

▸ **4.** Between the Submacro and End Submacro statements, click the **Add New Action** arrow, scroll down the list, and then click **SelectObject**. The **SelectObject** action is added to the PrintSelectedRecord submacro. This action has three arguments. The first argument, Object Type, specifies the type of database object to select. The second argument, Object Name, specifies the name of the object to open. The third argument, In Database Window, specifies whether to open the object in the database window (yes) or not (no). You would open a table, form, or report in the database window if it is not already open. If the table, form, or report is already open in the database window, you would select No as the value for the Database Window argument.

You need to open a form named frmVisit, so you'll set these arguments first.

▸ **5.** Click the **Object Type** arrow, click **Form**, click the **Object Name** arrow, and then click **frmVisit**. Because the form will be open when you run the macro, you'll leave the In Database Window argument set to No.

You'll next select the RunMenuCommand action and set its arguments. The RunMenuCommand action lets you add a command available on the ribbon to a submacro. The Command argument in this submacro lets you select the command. In this case, the Command argument is named PrintSelection.

▸ **6.** Below the SelectObject action, click the **Add New Action** arrow, scroll down the list, and then click **RunMenuCommand**. The RunMenuCommand action box appears with the Command box, in which you specify Command argument.

▸ **7.** Click the **Command** arrow, scroll down the list, and then click **PrintSelection**.

You've completed the second action. You'll add another SelectObject action to the submacro to make the frmVisit form the active object after the selected record prints.

▸ **8.** Below the RunMenuCommand action, click the **Add New Action** arrow, scroll down the list, click **SelectObject**, set the Object Type argument to **Form**, and then set the Object Name argument to **frmVisit**. You've finished adding the three actions to the PrintSelectedRecord submacro. See Figure 10-17.

Figure 10-17	Three actions added to the PrintSelectedRecord submacro

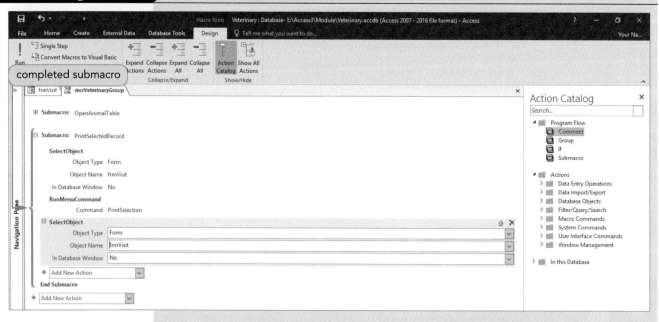

9. Save your macro design changes, and then close the mcrVeterinaryGroup macro. The frmVisit form is the active object.

Next, you'll add a command button to the frmVisit form. After you attach the PrintSelectedRecord macro to the command button control, you'll be able to click the command button to print the current frmVisit form record.

Adding a Command Button to a Form

In Design view for a form, you use the Button tool in the Controls group on the Form Design Tools Design tab to add a command button control to a form. If the Use Control Wizards tool is selected when you click the Button tool, the Command Button Wizard guides you through the process of adding the command button control. You'll explore adding the command button control directly to the frmVisit form without using the wizard, and then you'll set the command button control's properties using its Property Sheet.

To add a command button control to the frmVisit form:

1. Close the Property Sheet, and then click the **Form Design Tools Design** tab.

2. In the Controls group, click the **More** button, and then make sure the **Use Control Wizards** tool is not selected.

Trouble? If the Use Control Wizards tool has an orange background, click it to disable the control wizards, and then continue with Step 3.

3. In the Controls group, click the **Button** tool.

4. Position the pointer's plus symbol (+) to the right of the Open Animal Table button in the Details section, and then click the mouse button. A second command button is added to the form. See Figure 10-18.

Figure 10-18   New command button added to the frmVisit form

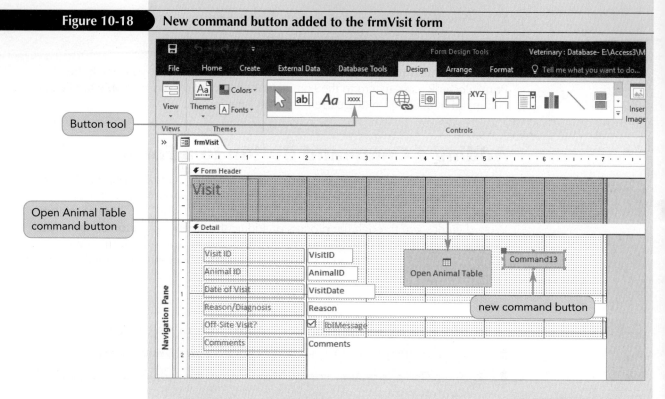

Trouble? If the Command Button Wizard dialog box opens, click the Cancel button to close it, on the Form Design Tools Design tab in the Controls group, click the More button, click the Use Control Wizards tool to deselect it, and then repeat Steps 3 and 4.

Trouble? The command button on your screen might show a different number in its label, depending on how you completed the previous steps. This difference will not affect the command button or macro.

You can now attach the PrintSelectedRecord submacro to the command button.

Attaching a Submacro to a Command Button

So far you've created the PrintSelectedRecord submacro and added the command button to the frmVisit form. Now you'll attach the submacro to the command button control's OnClick property so that the submacro is executed when the command button is clicked.

To attach the PrintSelectedRecord submacro to the command button control:

  1. Make sure the new command button control is selected.

  2. Open the **Property Sheet**, and then, if necessary, click the **Event** tab in the Property Sheet.

3. Click the **On Click** arrow in the Property Sheet to display the macros list, and then click **mcrVeterinaryGroup.PrintSelectedRecord**.

    You can change the text that appears on the command button (also known as the command button's label or caption) by changing its Caption property. You can also replace the text with a picture by setting its Picture property, or you can include both text and a picture. Daksha wants you to place a picture of a printer on the command button and to display text on the command button.

4. In the Property Sheet, click the **Format** tab, click the **Picture** box, and then click the **Build** button ··· that appears on the right side of the Picture box. The Picture Builder dialog box opens. See Figure 10-19.

Figure 10-19   Picture Builder dialog box

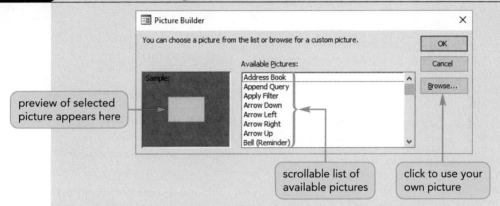

preview of selected picture appears here

scrollable list of available pictures

click to use your own picture

    The Picture Builder dialog box contains an alphabetical list of pictures supplied with Access. You can scroll the list and select one of the pictures, or you can click the Browse button to select your own picture. When you select a picture, a sample of the picture is displayed on the command button in the Sample box on the left.

5. Scroll the Available Pictures box, and then click **Printer**. A picture of a printer is displayed on the command button in the Sample box.

6. Click the **OK** button. The Picture Builder dialog box closes, and the printer picture is displayed on the command button in the form.

7. Change the Caption property to **Print Selected Record**, and then press the **Tab** key.

    The **Picture Caption Arrangement property** specifies how a command button's Caption property value is arranged in relation to the picture placed on the command button. The choices are No Picture Caption, General, Top, Bottom, Left, and Right.

8. Click the **Picture Caption Arrangement** arrow, and then click **Bottom**. The caption will appear below the printer picture. However, the command button is not tall enough or wide enough to display the picture and caption, so you'll resize it.

9. Use the middle-bottom sizing handle and the middle-right sizing handle to increase the width and height of the command button so it is approximately the same size as the Open Animal Table button and looks like the one shown in Figure 10-20.

Figure 10-20 Command button with picture and caption

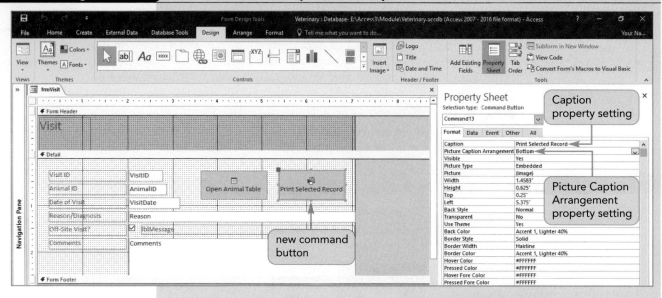

Trouble? If the background color of your button does not match the Open Animal Table button, in the Property Sheet, on the Format tab, click the Use Theme box, click the Use Theme arrow, and then click No.

Next, you'll save the frmVisit form and test the command button.

To save the form and test the command button:

1. Close the Property Sheet, save your form design changes, and then switch to Form view.

2. Navigate to the last visit record, for VisitID 1196.

3. Click the **Print Selected Record** command button on the form to open the Print dialog box. Notice that the submacro correctly set the print range to print the selected record.

TIP

If the Print dialog box contains a Print to File checkbox, you can print to a file instead of printing on paper.

4. Click the **OK** button to print the last visit record. The submacro returns control to the frmVisit form after the record is printed.

5. Close the form.

6. If you are not continuing on to the next session, close the Veterinary database.

In this session, you have learned how to create and use macros in a form to automate tasks. In the next session, you'll create a navigation system that will limit access to the database objects while still allowing users to run queries and view forms and reports. You'll create a form that contains a list box to display specific forms, reports, and queries in the Veterinary database, use a SQL statement to select the values for the list box, and then add command buttons to the form.

Session 10.1 Quick Check

REVIEW

1. What is a macro?
2. What is the Macro Designer?
3. What does the MessageBox action do?
4. What are you trying to accomplish when you single step through a macro?
5. What is an event property?
6. What is the purpose of the Where Condition argument for the OpenForm action?
7. How do you add a picture to a command button?

Session 10.2 Visual Overview:

A **navigation form** is a form with tabs that allows you to display database objects in an organized way to users.

In a navigation form, the active top-level tab is displayed with a different background color than the other top-level tabs.

The frmQueries tab is the active lower-level tab.

Clicking this [Add New] tab label will add a new lower-level tab.

A **list box control** displays a scrollable list of values. When the list of items is too long for the list box control, a scroll bar will appear.

The active button control's properties are displayed in the Property Sheet.

You can drag the name of a form or report from the Navigation Pane to the [Add New] text on a tab to add that object to the tab.

A Navigation Form

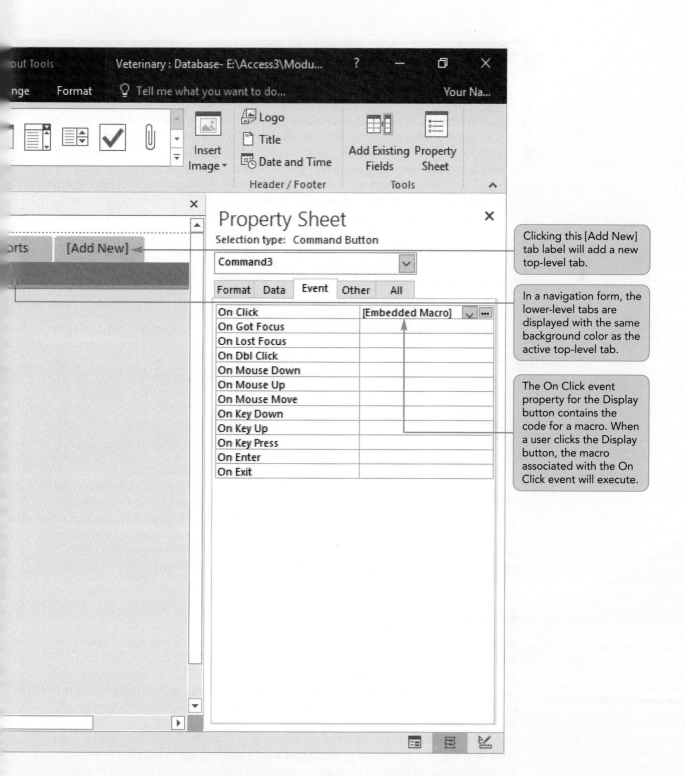

Clicking this [Add New] tab label will add a new top-level tab.

In a navigation form, the lower-level tabs are displayed with the same background color as the active top-level tab.

The On Click event property for the Display button contains the code for a macro. When a user clicks the Display button, the macro associated with the On Click event will execute.

Designing a User Interface

A **user interface** is what you see and use when you communicate with a computer application. Daksha wants to provide a simple user interface for the Veterinary database to assist beginner users as they become familiar with and begin using the database objects.

Problem Solving: Restricting Access to Database Objects and Prohibiting Design Changes

It's important to ensure that data is as accurate as possible. Many database users do not have much experience with database applications and could inadvertently corrupt data. However, database users need to be able to add, change, and delete data. If they make updates using forms and special queries, such as action queries, users can manipulate only the data on forms and queries, without accessing the rest of the data in the tables upon which the forms and queries are built. To minimize the risk of users inadvertently corrupting data, users should be restricted to updating only the data they need. For this reason, a database administrator might create forms and special queries for the purpose of restricting the users' ability to access only authorized data. Users also need to review and print information from a database using reports, forms, and queries. Similarly, users should not be allowed to change the design of any database object or the design of the user interface. You can create a user interface that meets all these needs and restrictions. When users open a database, you can present them with a form that allows them to choose among the available forms, reports, and queries and to navigate from one object to another object as they perform their work. At the same time, you can limit users to this controlled user interface and prevent them from circumventing it, thereby preventing them from changing any aspect of the design of the database. By considering the needs of the users and by using the features and tools provided by the DBMS, you can ensure users can work productively with a database and ensure the integrity of the data stored in the database.

Before he creates the user interface for the Veterinary database, Daksha wants you to create a form to display a list of the queries in the database in a list box, from which users can select and run a query. The list will include only select queries, but not action queries, because you want to prevent inexperienced users from selecting and running action queries. Daksha's technique enables users to choose and run select queries, which select records from tables but do not affect the records in a table.

Creating an Unbound Form

When the form controls in a form do not need data from a table or query, you create an unbound form. The data displayed in an unbound form can be provided by a Structured Query Language (SQL) statement. Recall that SQL is a standard language used in querying, updating, and managing relational databases. To create an unbound form, you create a blank form, add one or more form controls, and then specify SQL statements that provide the form data.

All the objects you've created and used so far are standard objects in which users need to navigate from record to record, or from page to page in the case of reports, and to perform other operations such as copying data and closing the object. For unbound forms, users do not need to perform any of these operations, so when you create an unbound form, you can remove these features from the form.

The Veterinary database contains several queries, and more queries might be added in the future. To allow users to choose from the available queries, Daksha wants you to create a form that will display the queries in a list box. The Session 10.2 Visual Overview shows a preview of the frmQueries form you'll create as part of a navigation form. To create the frmQueries form, you'll begin by creating a blank form. You'll add a list box control and two command buttons to the form, and you'll enter a SQL statement that will provide the contents of the list box.

The Veterinary database contains a few action queries. First, you'll delete any action queries that are in the Veterinary database, then you'll create the frmQueries form.

To delete the action queries in the Veterinary database:

1. If you took a break after the previous session, make sure that the Veterinary database is open and the Navigation Pane is displayed.

2. If you want to keep the action queries you created, make a copy of the Veterinary database.

3. In the Navigation Pane, right-click **qryContactOwnerAppend**, and then click **Delete** on the shortcut menu. A dialog box opens that prompts you to confirm that you want to delete the query.

4. In the dialog box, click the **Yes** button to confirm that you want to delete the query. The qryContactOwnerAppend query is deleted from the database.

5. Repeat Steps 3 and 4 to delete the following queries from the database: **qryContactOwnerDelete**, **qryContactOwnerMakeTable**, and **qryContactOwnerUpdate**.

6. Close the Navigation Pane.

Next, you'll create the frmQueries form.

To create and save the frmQueries form:

1. Click the **Create** tab, and then in the Forms group, click the **Blank Form** button. A blank form opens in the Form window in Layout view, and the Field List pane is displayed.

2. Close the Field List pane, and then switch to Design view.

3. Save the form with the name **frmQueries**.

A number of form properties are available in Access that are especially helpful in designing a user interface; for Daksha's form, you'll use properties that let you disable the display of the Close button, the navigation buttons, the record selector, and the right-click shortcut menu. In addition, to match Daksha's design, you need to set the Caption property to "Queries," which is the value that will appear on the object tab when you open the form. Figure 10-21 shows the form property settings you will use to create the frmQueries form for Daksha.

Figure 10-21   frmQueries form properties

Property	Setting	Function
Caption	Queries	Value that appears on the form's object tab when the form is open
Close Button	No	Disables the display of the Close button on the form's object tab
Navigation Buttons	No	Disables the display of navigation buttons at the bottom of the form
Record Selectors	No	Disables the display of a record selector on the left side of the form
Shortcut Menu	No	Disables the display of the shortcut menu when a user right-clicks the form

Next you'll use the Property Sheet to set the form properties shown in Figure 10-21.

To set the properties for the unbound frmQueries form:

▶ **1.** Right-click the form selector ▣, and then click **Properties** on the shortcut menu to open the form's Property Sheet.

▶ **2.** If necessary, click the **Format** tab in the Property Sheet to display the format properties for the form.

You can now set the Caption property for the form. As you know, the Caption property value will appear on the tab when the form is displayed.

▶ **3.** Click the **Caption** box, and then type **Queries**.

Next, you'll set the Record Selectors property. Because the form does not display any records, there's no need to include a record selector.

▶ **4.** In the Record Selectors box, double-click **Yes** to change the property setting from Yes to No.

Next you'll set the remaining form properties.

▶ **5.** Scrolling as necessary, set the Navigation Buttons property to **No**, and set the Close Button property to **No**.

▶ **6.** Click the **Other** tab in the Property Sheet to display the Other page of the Property Sheet, and then set the Shortcut Menu property to **No**.

▶ **7.** Close the Property Sheet, and then save your form design changes.

Now that you have set the form's properties, you can add a list box control to the form.

Adding a List Box Control to a Form

You can add a list box control to a form using the Control Wizards tool, or you can set the properties for the list box control individually in the control's Property Sheet.

The label associated with the list box control that you will add to the frmQueries form will identify the list box for the user, and the list box control will display the list of queries in the Veterinary database that users can preview or view. A user will be able to click the name of a query to select it and then click one of the command buttons to preview or view the query. Double-clicking a query name in the list box also will open the query datasheet. You will not use the Control Wizards tool to create the list box control because you'll be using a SQL statement to provide the query names for the list box control.

REFERENCE

Adding a List Box Control to a Form

- Switch to Design view, if necessary.
- If necessary, on the Form Design Tools Design tab, in the Controls group, click the More button, and then click the Use Control Wizards tool to select or deselect it, depending on whether you want to use the wizard.
- On the Form Design Tools Design tab, in the Controls group, click the More button, and then click the List Box tool.
- Position the pointer's plus symbol (+) where you want to place the upper-left corner of the list box control, and then click the mouse button.
- If you use the List Box Control Wizard, complete the dialog boxes to choose the source of the list, select the fields to appear in the list box, select a sort order, size the columns, and select the label; or if you do not use the List Box Wizard, set the Row Source property and size the list box control.

Now you'll add the list box control to the form.

To add the list box control to the form and position its label:

1. Click the **Form Design Tools Design** tab, in the Controls group, click the **More** button, and then make sure the **Use Control Wizards** tool is not selected.

2. In the Controls gallery, click the **List Box** tool.

3. Position the pointer's plus symbol (+) approximately ½ inch from the top and ½ inch from the left edge of the Details section, and then click the mouse button. A list box control and attached label control appear in the form. See Figure 10-22.

Figure 10-22   **Form with the list box control and label control**

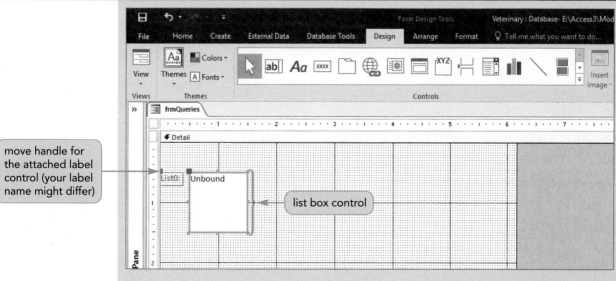

move handle for the attached label control (your label name might differ)

list box control

Trouble? If your list box control is sized or positioned differently, resize it or move it until it matches the list box control shown in Figure 10-22.

Next you'll move the attached label control from its current position to the left of the list box control to above the control.

▶ **4.** Click the **label** control to select it, position the mouse pointer on the move handle in the upper-left corner of the label control, and then drag it to position it two grid dots above the list box control and aligned with the left edge of the list box control.

You can now set the Caption property for the label control.

▶ **5.** Open the Property Sheet, and then click the **Format** tab in the Property Sheet, if necessary.

▶ **6.** Set the label control's Caption property value to **Available Queries**.

▶ **7.** Resize the label control by dragging its right border to the right until it is wide enough to display all of the caption text.

▶ **8.** Close the Property Sheet.

Now you'll save the form and check your progress by switching to Form view.

▶ **9.** Save your form design changes, and then switch to Form view. See Figure 10-23.

Figure 10-23   **frmQueries form displayed in Form view**

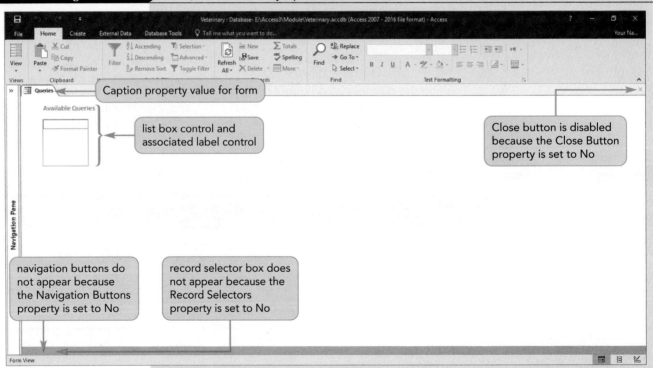

Next you need to enter the SQL statement that will provide the query names for the list box control. Before you do so, you need to become familiar with how SQL statements are structured.

Introduction to SQL

Much of what is accomplished in Access behind the scenes is done with SQL. Whenever you create a query, for example, an equivalent SQL statement is automatically constructed. When you save a query, the SQL statement version of the query is saved.

In viewing the SQL statements, you'll recognize some of the query statement names. This is not a coincidence! There are really only five SQL statement types: select, update, delete, insert, and create. These correspond with the Access queries Select, Update, Delete, Append, and Make Table. For example, the following simple SQL statement selects records in the tblOwner table, selecting the fields OwnerID, LastName, FirstName, and City where the city is Cody:

SELECT tblOwner.OwnerID, tblOwner.LastName, tblOwner.FirstName, tblOwner.City
FROM tblOwner
WHERE ((((tblOwner.City)="Cody"));

INSIGHT

Using SQL

Instead of using an application with a graphical user interface like Access, which allows you to perform database tasks by clicking buttons and completing dialog boxes, a database administrator in a large organization uses a relational DBMS such as mySQL or Oracle and uses SQL statements to query, update, delete, and make tables. Every full-featured relational DBMS has its own version of the current standard SQL. If you learn SQL for one relational DBMS, it's a relatively easy task to begin using SQL for other relational DBMSs. When you work with two or more relational DBMSs, which is the case in most companies, you'll learn that few differences exist among the various SQL versions.

Viewing a SQL Statement for a Query

When you are working in Design view or viewing a query recordset, you can see the SQL statement that is equivalent to your query by switching to SQL view.

You'll start learning about SQL by examining the SQL statements that are equivalent to two existing queries: qryOwnersByName and qryOwnersAndInvoices.

To view the SQL statement for the qryOwnersByName query:

▶ **1.** Open the Navigation Pane, open the **qryOwnersByName** query datasheet, and then close the Navigation Pane. The query displays 26 records from the tblOwner table. The columns displayed are Owner, Owner ID, First Name, Last Name, Nickname, Phone, Address, City, State, Zip, and Email.

▶ **2.** Right-click the **qryOwnersByName** object tab to open the shortcut menu, click **SQL View** to display the query in SQL view, and then click a blank area of the window to deselect the SQL statement. See Figure 10-24.

Figure 10-24   **SQL view for the qryOwnersByName query**

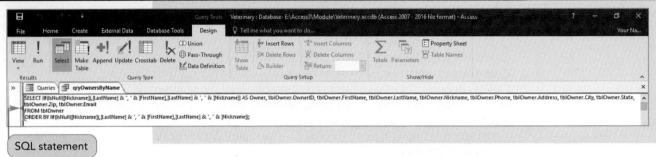

SQL statement

Thus far, you have been able to complete all the Access database tasks using the options on the ribbon, in dialog boxes, and in the Property Sheet. If you learn SQL to the point where you can use it efficiently, you will be able to enter your own SQL statements in SQL view. If you work with more complicated databases, you might find that you need the extra power of the SQL language to implement your database strategies fully.

SQL uses the **SELECT statement** to define what data it retrieves from a database and how it presents the data. A SELECT statement like the one shown in Figure 10-24 must follow these rules:

TIP

The first clause of a SQL statement begins with SELECT, CREATE, UPDATE, DELETE, or INSERT.

- The basic form of a SQL SELECT statement includes four sections, known as clauses. Each clause starts with a different keyword: SELECT, FROM, WHERE, and ORDER BY. After the SELECT keyword, you list the fields you want to display. After FROM, you list the tables used in the query. After WHERE, you list the selection criteria. After ORDER BY, you list the sort fields.
- If a field name includes a space or a special symbol, you enclose the field name in brackets. Because the Veterinary database does not use field names with spaces or special symbols, you don't have to enclose its field names in brackets. However, if your database had a field name such as *Contract Type*, then you would use [Contract Type] in a SQL statement. Some database administrators prefer to enclose every field name in square brackets to make it easier to identify field names in SQL statements.
- You precede a field name with the name of its table by connecting the table name to the field name with a period. For example, you would enter the OwnerID field in the tblVisit table as *tblVisit.OwnerID*.
- You use commas to separate values in a list of field names or a list of table names, and you end the SELECT statement with a semicolon.

The SQL statement shown in Figure 10-24 selects the Owner, OwnerID, FirstName, LastName, Nickname, Phone, Address, City, State, Zip, and Email fields from the tblOwner table; the records are sorted in ascending order by the Owner field. The SQL statement does not contain a WHERE clause, so the recordset includes all records from the tblOwner table when the query is run.

You can enter or change SQL statements directly in SQL view. If you enter a SQL statement and then switch to Design view, you will see its equivalent in the design grid. Next, you'll examine the SQL statement for the qryOwnersAndInvoices query.

To view the SQL statement for the qryOwnersAndInvoices query:

1. Close the qryOwnersByName query, open the Navigation Pane, open the **qryOwnersAndInvoices** query in Design view, and then close the Navigation Pane. The query selects data from the tblOwner and tblBilling tables and does not sort the records. The fields included in the query design are FirstName, LastName, City, InvoiceAmt, and InvoicePaid.

▶ **2.** On the Query Tools Design tab, in the Results group, click the **View** button arrow, click **SQL View** to change to SQL view, and then click a blank area of the window to deselect the SQL statement. See Figure 10-25.

Figure 10-25 **SQL view for the qryOwnersAndInvoices query**

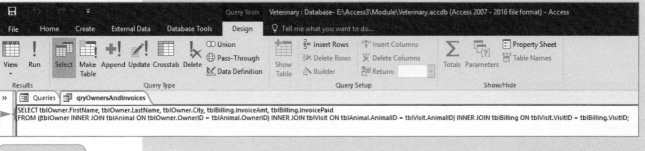

SQL statement

The SELECT statement for this query is similar to the one shown in Figure 10-24, except that it does not include an ORDER BY clause and it includes three INNER JOIN clauses. Together, the INNER JOIN clauses select records from the two tables only when the records have the same value in the common fields that link the tables. The general syntax for a SQL statement with an inner join is the following:

SELECT *field list* FROM *Table1* INNER JOIN *Table2* ON *Table1.Field1* = *Table2.Field2*;

The ON clause is used by Access here instead of the standard SQL WHERE clause.

▶ **3.** Close the query. The frmQueries form in Form view is now the active object.

The SQL SELECT statements mirror the query options you viewed in Design view. In effect, every choice you make in Design view is reflected as part of the SQL SELECT statement. Viewing the SQL statements generated from queries that you design is an effective way to begin learning SQL.

You now can enter the SQL statement that will provide the query names for the list box control.

Using a SQL Statement for a List Box Control

You'll use a SQL SELECT statement to retrieve the list of query names from one of the Access system tables. **System tables** are special tables maintained by Access that store information about the characteristics of a database and about the structure of the objects in the database. Although system tables do not appear in the Navigation Pane, you can retrieve information from system tables using SELECT statements. One of the system tables, the **MSysObjects table**, keeps track of the names, types, and other characteristics of every object in a database. The Name and Type fields are the two MSysObjects table fields you'll use in the SELECT statement. The type field value contains a numeric value that corresponds to an object type. Figure 10-26 shows the numbers that correspond to some commonly used objects. For instance, a table is a type 1 object, and a query is a type 5 object. If the Type value of an MSObject is 5, then we know that the MSObject referred to must be a query. The values may seem cryptic, but think of them as values that Microsoft developers have assigned to these objects so they can use a number instead of a name.

Figure 10-26 **MSysObjects table Type field values**

Object Type	Type Field Value in MSysObjects Table
Table	1
Query	5
Form	-32768
Report	-32764
Macro	-32766
Module	-32761

TIP

SQL is not case sensitive, but typing SQL keywords in uppercase is an industry convention and makes the statements more readable.

Special system queries are created by Access to handle many tasks for you; each of these queries has a name that begins with the tilde (~) character. When a form contains a list box control, combo box control, or subform control, a system query is automatically created by Access to manage the functionality of these controls. For instance, when the frmVisit form was created, a hidden system query called ~sq_ffrmVisit was created by Access. You cannot see these system queries because users should not be able to run them or manipulate them. The purpose of these system queries is to manage the functionality of the form controls. You want to exclude these special system queries from the list box control you've created for the user interface. Because every system query name begins with the ~ character, you'll use the Left function in your SELECT statement to identify the query names that begin with ~ and exclude those from the list of queries to appear in the list box control. The **Left function** provides the first character(s) in a text string. The format of the Left function is *Left*(text string, number of characters). You'll test the first character of the name of each query to determine if it is the ~ character. If the first character is not the ~ character, you'll include the query name in the list box control. You'll use *Left([Name],1)* to retrieve the first character of the Name field, and you'll use the not equal operator (<>). To include only those queries whose names do not begin with the ~ character, you'll use the expression *Left([Name],1)<>"~"*. This expression will be interpreted by Access as "the first character of the Name field does not equal the ~ character." The complete SELECT statement that you will use to select the list of query names is as follows:

SELECT [Name] FROM MSysObjects WHERE [Type]=5 And Left([Name],1)<>"~" ORDER BY [Name];

Recall that the Row Source property for a control specifies the data source, such as a table, a query, or a SQL statement. You'll enter the SELECT statement as the value for the Row Source property for the list box control you created.

To set the Row Source property for the list box control:

1. Switch to Design view, right-click the **list box control** to open the shortcut menu, click **Properties** to open the Property Sheet, and then click the **Data** tab (if necessary).

2. Right-click the **Row Source** box to open the shortcut menu, and then click **Zoom**. The Zoom dialog box opens.

3. In the Zoom dialog box, type **SELECT [Name] FROM MSysObjects WHERE [Type]=5 And Left([Name],1)<>"~" ORDER BY [Name];**

   See Figure 10-27.

Be sure to type the semicolon at the end of the SELECT statement.

Figure 10-27 **SELECT statement for the list box control**

▶ **4.** Click the **OK** button to close the Zoom dialog box.

▶ **5.** Close the Property Sheet, save your form design changes, and then switch to Form view. The queries in the database (excluding system queries) now appear in alphabetical order in the list box control. See Figure 10-28.

Figure 10-28 **List box control displaying query names**

query names retrieved by a SQL statement from the MSysObjects table

Trouble? If a syntax-error message appears, click the OK button, switch to Design view, right-click the list box control, click Properties, right-click the Row Source box, and then click Zoom. Correct the SELECT statement so it's the same as the statement shown in Step 3, click the OK button, and then repeat Step 5.

▶ **6.** Switch to Layout view, and then resize the list box by dragging its right border to the right until the query names are fully displayed.

TIP

If you use the Use Control Wizards tool to add a command button control, you can attach a standard Access action (such as opening a specific query or closing a window) or a macro to the button.

Next you will add the two command button controls to the form that are specified in Daksha's design: Preview and Display. The Preview command button will allow users to view the query in Print Preview, and the Display command button will allow users to view the query as a datasheet. When a user clicks either of the command buttons, the query that will be opened is the query the user has selected in the list box. For the Print Preview button, you'll attach a macro to the command button's On Click property that will display the selected query in Print Preview. Similarly, you'll attach a macro to the Display command button that will display the selected query as a datasheet. You'll add both command button controls and appropriate macros to the form. First, you'll add the Preview command button to the form.

To add the Preview command button control to the form:

▶ **1.** Switch to Design view, click the **Form Design Tools Design** tab, and then increase the width of the form to 4″ and the length of the form to 4″ (if necessary).

▶ **2.** In the Controls group, click the **More** button, make sure the Use Control Wizards tool ◿ is deselected, and then in the Controls group, click the **Button** tool ⊠⊠⊠⊠ .

▶ **3.** Position the pointer's plus symbol (+) below and aligned with the left edge of the list box control in the Details section, and then click the mouse button. A command button control is added to the form.

▶ **4.** If necessary, open the Property Sheet for the command button control.

You can now change the default text that appears on the command button to the word "Preview" and add the Print Preview picture. When you add the picture, the button will be too small to display both the picture and the caption. You'll fix that in subsequent steps.

▶ **5.** In the Property Sheet, click the **Format** tab (if necessary), set the Caption property to **Preview**, click the **Picture** box, and then click the **Build** button ⋯ on the right end of the Picture box. The Picture Builder dialog box opens.

▶ **6.** Scroll the Available Pictures box, and then click **Preview**. A Print Preview picture appears on the command button in the Sample box.

▶ **7.** Click the **OK** button to close the Picture Builder dialog box and to place the Print Preview picture on the command button.

▶ **8.** Click the **Picture Caption Arrangement** box, click its **arrow**, and then click **Bottom**.

Daksha wants you to change the background color of the command button. You'll change the color, then resize the button control to display the caption as well.

▶ **9.** On the Property Sheet, click the **Back Color** box, click its **Build** button ⋯ , in the Theme Colors section click the **Green, Accent 6, Lighter 60%** (third color down in the last column), and then close the Property Sheet.

▶ **10.** Use the bottom-right sizing handle and the middle-right sizing handle to change the size of the command button control to match the size shown in Figure 10-29. The width of the button should be less than half the width of the list box control because you'll be adding another button control of the same size to the right. See Figure 10-29.

Figure 10-29   Preview command button added to the form

resized command
button with new
background color

Instead of repeating the steps to add the command button control for viewing a
query recordset, you'll copy the Preview command button control and paste it in the
Detail section. This will also ensure the button controls are the same dimensions.
After moving the copied button control into position, you can change its properties to
control the text and picture that will appear on it.

To add the Display command button control to the form:

1. Right-click the **Preview** command button control, and then click **Copy** on the
shortcut menu.

2. Right-click a blank area of the grid, and then click **Paste** on the shortcut
menu. A copy of the command button is added in the upper-left corner of
the Detail section.

3. Move the new command button into position to the right of the original
command button, aligning the bottom edges of the two buttons and
aligning the right edge of the new button with the right edge of the list box.
See Figure 10-30.

Figure 10-30 **Command button control duplicated and repositioned**

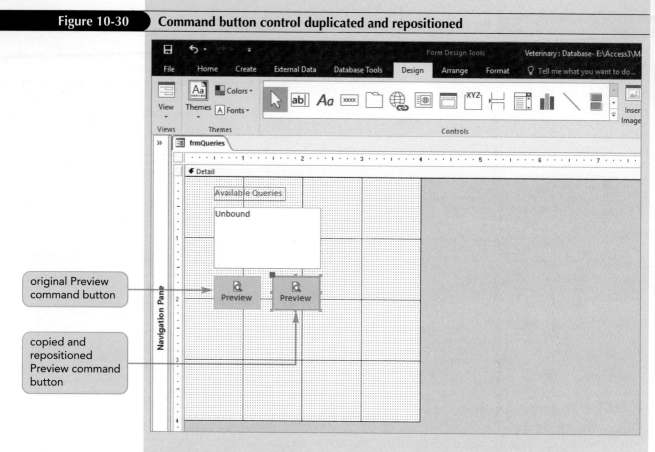

original Preview command button

copied and repositioned Preview command button

▶ **4.** Open the Property Sheet for the new command button, set the Caption property to **Display**, click the **Picture property Build button**, and then in the Picture Builder dialog box, set the Picture property to **MS Access Query**.

▶ **5.** Save your form design changes.

Before creating the macros for the form and for the command button controls to open the query selected by the user, you'll set the Name property for the list box control. The naming convention for a list box control is to use the three-letter prefix LST in lowercase (lst). You'll enter the name lstQueryList for the list box control. You'll also set the background color of the Detail section and the list box control.

To set the Name property for the list box and to set background colors:

▶ **1.** Click the list box control to make it the active control.

Be sure to type the first character as a lowercase L, not as a number 1.

▶ **2.** In the Property Sheet, click the **All** tab, select the value in the **Name** box, and then type **lstQueryList**.

▶ **3.** Click the **Back Color** box, click its **Build** button ⋯ , and then in the Theme Colors section of the color palette, click the **White, Background 1** color (row 1, column 1).

▶ **4.** Click the **Detail** section bar, and then set the section's Back Color property to **White, Background 1, Darker 5%** (row 2, column 1 in the Theme Colors section of the color palette).

▶ **5.** Save your form design changes, and then switch to Form view to display the completed frmQueries form. See Figure 10-31.

| Figure 10-31 | Completed list box control |

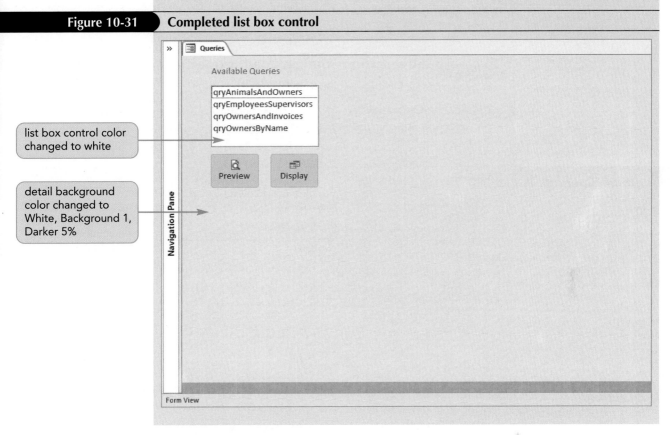

You now can create the macros for the frmQueries form.

Creating Multiple Macros for a Form

Daksha wants the first query name in the list box control to be highlighted when the frmQueries form first opens. You can accomplish this by placing the focus on it. When an item has the focus, it may be selected and appear highlighted, or a flashing insertion point may be visible in the control. In general, it is a good practice to ensure a form element has the focus when the form opens so that if a user presses the Enter key, the default behavior of the element with the focus is executed. If no form controls have the focus when a form opens and a user presses the Enter key, an error message might display, which could confuse or frustrate users. To avoid this situation, you'll place the focus on the first query name in the lstQueryList list box control when the form opens.

When a user double-clicks a query name in the list box or selects a query name and then clicks the Display command button, the selected query should open in Datasheet view. When a user selects a query name in the list box and then clicks the Preview command button, the selected query should open in Print Preview. You'll create and attach four different macros to the objects on your form to enable these behaviors. You'll start by creating and attaching a macro to the On Load property for the form to place the focus on the first query name in the list box control and highlight it when the form opens.

The **Load event** occurs when a form or report opens. When you attach a macro to the Load event through the On Load property for the form, the actions in the macro are processed each time the form is opened. You'll create a macro containing two actions. First, you'll use the GoToControl action to move the focus to the list box control.

This action does not set the focus to any specific query name in the list box control, so you'll use the SendKeys action to send the down arrow keystroke to the list box control. The SendKeys action will result in the first query name in the list box being highlighted. The end result of these two actions will be that when a user opens the frmQueries form, the first query name will have the focus.

To create the macro for the On Load property:

▶ **1.** Switch to Design view, and then, in the Property Sheet, click the **Event** tab.

▶ **2.** Click the **On Load** box, and then click its **Build** button ⋯ . The Choose Builder dialog box opens and includes three options for setting the property value. See Figure 10-32.

Figure 10-32   **Choose Builder dialog box**

You'll attach a macro to the event property.

▶ **3.** Make sure **Macro Builder** is selected, and then click the **OK** button to open the Macro Designer.

▶ **4.** Click the **Add New Action** arrow to display the list of actions, and then click **GoToControl**. The list closes, and a new GoToControl action is added with one argument.

▶ **5.** In the Control Name box, type **lst** and then press the **Tab** key to select the AutoComplete box's value of lstQueryList, which is the Name property setting for the list box control.

Trouble? If you do not see the AutoComplete value, delete the characters you have typed, and retype the first character as a lowercase L, not as a number 1.

The second and final action you need to add is the SendKeys action. The SendKeys action doesn't appear in the Add New Action list. You'll verify this and then use the Show All Actions button to display the SendKeys action.

▶ **6.** Click the **Add New Action** arrow, scroll down the list, notice that the SendKeys action doesn't appear in the list, and then click the **Add New Action** arrow to close the list.

▶ **7.** On the Macro Tools Design tab, in the Show/Hide group, position the mouse pointer over the **Show All Actions** button to display the button's ScreenTip. See Figure 10-33.

Figure 10-33   **Macro for the On Load property of the form**

By default, only trusted actions are displayed in the Add New Action list, but you can display all actions by clicking the Show All Actions button. The actions that are categorized as unsafe actions (not trusted) are not displayed in the list by default; this includes the SendKeys action. This action is considered unsafe because an inexperienced developer could use the SendKeys action to send keystrokes to the database application that could delete data, for instance. Because you need to use the SendKeys action and you understand the risks, you'll display all actions so you can select it from the menu.

▶ **8.** In the Show/Hide group, click the **Show All Actions** button to toggle it on, click the **Add New Action** arrow, scroll the list, and then click **SendKeys**. The list closes, and a SendKeys action is added to the macro with two arguments. You'll use the Keystrokes value of {Down}, which represents the down arrow keystroke, and a Wait value of No, which prevents the macro from pausing when it runs. (If the macro pauses, the down arrow keystroke might not be received right away, and the first query in the list box control may not receive the focus.)

Trouble? If SendKeys isn't in the list, check the Show All Actions button; if it has a white background, it is toggled off. Click it again, click the Add New Action arrow, and then select the SendKeys action.

▶ **9.** In the Keystrokes box, type **{Down}** in the Keystrokes box to complete the macro. See Figure 10-34.

Figure 10-34   **Completed macro for the On Load property of the form**

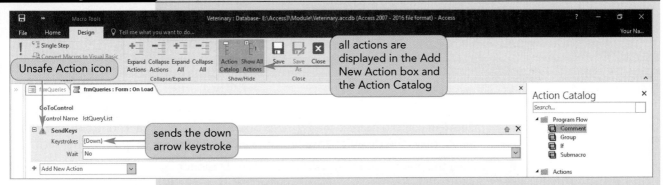

▶ **10.** Position the mouse pointer over the icon to the left of the SendKeys action. The icon's ScreenTip of "Unsafe Action" identifies that the action isn't a trusted action.

▶ **11.** Save the macro, and then close the Macro Designer to return to the frmQueries form in Design view.

Now you'll create the macros for the Preview and Display command button controls.

To create the macros for the command button controls:

▶ **1.** Click the **Preview** command button control.

▶ **2.** In the Properties Sheet, click the **On Click** box (if necessary), click its **Build** button ⎓ to open the Choose Builder dialog box, and then click the **OK** button to open the Macro Designer.

When users click the Preview command button, the query selected in the list box control should open in Print Preview.

▶ **3.** Click the **Add New Action** arrow, scroll the list, and then click **OpenQuery**. The list closes, and a new OpenQuery action is added with three arguments.

You'll enter the expression =[lstQueryList] in the Query Name box to indicate the query to be opened is equal to the name of the query that is selected in the lstQueryList list box control.

▶ **4.** In the Query Name box, type an equal sign (**=**). The Query Name arrow to the right of the Query Name box changes to the Expression Builder button.

▶ **5.** Click the **Expression Builder** button ⎓ to open the Expression Builder dialog box, double-click **lstQueryList** in the Expression Categories list, and then click the **OK** button to close the dialog box. The expression = [lstQueryList] is now displayed in the Query Name box.

▶ **6.** Click the **View** arrow, and then click **Print Preview** to complete the macro. See Figure 10-35.

Figure 10-35   **Completed macro for the Preview command button**

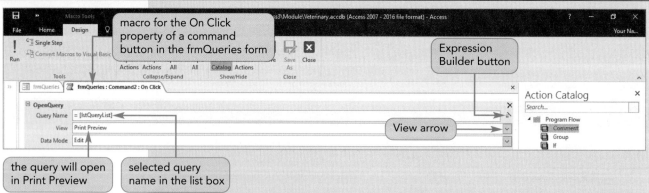

the query will open in Print Preview

selected query name in the list box

Because you did not set the Name property for the command buttons, the tab displays the default name of Command2 (your name might be different).

▶ **7.** Save the macro, and then close the Macro Designer.

Next you'll create the macro for the Display command button.

▶ **8.** Repeat Steps 2 to 5 for the Display command button.

▶ **9.** Set the View property for the OpenQuery action to **Datasheet** (if necessary). See Figure 10-36.

Figure 10-36	Completed macro for the Display command button

▶ **10.** Save the macro, and then close the Macro Designer.

Next you'll add a macro that will open a query in Datasheet view if the user double-clicks a query name in the list box control.

To create the macro for the list box control:

▶ **1.** Click the **list box** control, in the Property Sheet, click the **On Dbl Click** box, click its **Build** button ⋯ to open the Choose Builder dialog box, and then click the **OK** button to open the Macro Designer.

▶ **2.** Click the **Add New Action** arrow, scroll the list, and then click **OpenQuery**. The list closes, and a new OpenQuery action is added with three arguments.

▶ **3.** In the Query Name box, type an equal sign (**=**), click the **Expression Builder** button 🖎 to open the Expression Builder dialog box, double-click **lstQueryList** in the Expression Categories list, and then click the **OK** button to close the dialog box. The expression = *[lstQueryList]* is now displayed in the Query Name box.

▶ **4.** Set the View property for the OpenQuery action to **Datasheet** (if necessary).

▶ **5.** Save the macro, and then close the Macro Designer.

▶ **6.** Close the Property Sheet, save your form changes, and then switch to Form view.

You have finished creating the macros for the form. Next, you will test the list box control and the command button controls.

After creating a custom form, you should test the form in Form view. For the frmQueries form, you need to double-click a query name in the list box to make sure the query datasheet opens. You also need to scroll the list box, click a query name, and then click the Display command button to make sure the query datasheet opens and also click the Preview command button to make sure the query opens in Print Preview.

To test the form's controls:

▶ **1.** Double-click the first query name in the list box to verify that the correct query datasheet opens, and then close the query to make the frmQueries form the active object.

▶ **2.** Repeat Step 1 for each of the other query names in the list box.

▶ **3.** Click a query name in the list box, click the **Preview** command button to verify that the correct query opens in Print Preview, and then close the Print Preview window to make the frmQueries form the active object.

   Note that the Preview command button turns blue when the mouse pointer is positioned on it and when it is clicked. This formatting is applied to the button automatically.

▶ **4.** Repeat Step 3 for the other query names in the list box.

▶ **5.** Click a query name in the list box, click the **Display** command button to verify that the correct query datasheet opens, and then close the query to make the frmQueries form the active object.

▶ **6.** Repeat Step 5 for the other query names in the list box.

   Because the frmQueries form's Close button is disabled, you need to switch to Design view, which still has an enabled Close button, to close the form, or you can close the form by using the shortcut menu for the form object's tab.

▶ **7.** Right-click the **Queries** tab, and then click **Close** on the shortcut menu.

You've completed the custom frmQueries form. The frmQueries form is an example of a form that is designed to allow a user to easily choose a select query and view the records, without having to know how to run a query from the Navigation Pane. Next, Daksha wants you to create the navigation form for the Veterinary database. You'll incorporate the frmQueries form into this overall navigation system.

Creating a Navigation Form

The frmVisit form is a great example of navigation using a single form. You can set properties in Access to display only a single form if that's sufficient to provide the functionality users need and to restrict them from being able to accidentally use other database objects or to corrupt data. If users need access to several queries, forms, reports, or other database objects, though, another option is to build a separate navigation form. A navigation form is a form with tabs that allows you to present database objects in an organized way to users.

A database generally uses either one or more single, independent forms or a navigation form. The choice to use one or the other generally depends on the designer's assessment of the abilities of the users of the database. If the users have little experience with databases, a navigation form approach might be better. If the users have more experience, a few well-designed forms that the users can select themselves might be a better approach.

Daksha wants to restrict the access users have to the Veterinary database to just the queries that will be displayed in the frmQueries form and to selected forms and reports. To control how users interact with the database, he wants you to create a navigation form that provides users access to only those database objects. Six predefined layouts for a navigation form are available in Access, with the layouts differing in the placement of tabs and subtabs. Of the several navigation form styles available, Daksha wants you to use the Horizontal Tabs, 2 Levels layout.

To create the navigation form:

▶ **1.** On the ribbon, click the **Create** tab.

▶ **2.** In the Forms group, click the **Navigation** button. The Navigation gallery opens. See Figure 10-37.

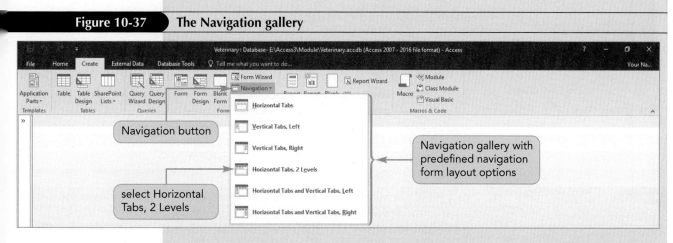

Figure 10-37   **The Navigation gallery**

3. Click **Horizontal Tabs, 2 Levels** in the gallery, and then close the Field List pane. The navigation form with the default title of Navigation Form opens in Layout view. See Figure 10-38.

Figure 10-38   **Initial navigation form**

Because the navigation form won't display data from the database, it will be an unbound form. You'll enter the labels "Forms," "Reports," and "Queries" for the top-level tabs. You'll then drag the forms and reports that Daksha wants to include in the navigation form from the Navigation Pane to the lower-level tabs. The Session 10.2 Visual Overview shows a preview of the completed top-level tabs as well as a lower-level tab. You won't add the frmVisit form to the navigation form because the frmVisit form was created as a manual navigation form for a more advanced user. The macros for previewing and displaying the records would not function in the navigation form because they become submacros of the frmVisit subform of the frmNavigation form. The macros would have to be rewritten to work in a navigation form. If you wanted to have this functionality in a navigation form, you would create a new version of the frmVisit form that is designed to work as a subform of a navigation form. The frmVisit form you created is designed to work as a stand-alone form, not as a subform. However, the simple select queries, simple forms, and reports all work well as subforms in a navigation form.

To add names and objects to the navigation form:

1. Click the top **[Add New]** tab, type **Forms**, and then press the **Enter** key. The name on the first tab changes to Forms, and a second tab appears to its right.

   Trouble? If you type the first letter and it does not appear in the tab, click the tab again to switch to editing mode.

Trouble? If you need to correct or change a tab name, click the name, edit the name, and then press the Enter key.

2. Click the **[Add New]** tab to the right of the Forms tab, type **Queries**, and then press the **Enter** key.

3. Click the **[Add New]** tab to the right of the Queries tab, type **Reports**, and then press the **Enter** key. You have created the top-level tabs and named them Forms, Queries, and Reports. To create the lower-level tabs that will display these respective objects, you will drag some form and report objects from the Navigation Pane to the lower-level tabs. As you drag the objects, their names are added to the tabs.

TIP

You can drag only forms and reports, not queries, to tabs in a navigation form.

4. Open the Navigation Pane, click the **Forms** tab in the navigation form, and then drag the **frmVisitsAndInvoices** form from the Navigation Pane to the lower-level [Add New] tab. The frmVisitsAndInvoices form opens in the first tab below the Forms tab, and the tab displays the form's name.

Trouble? If you drag the wrong object to a tab, right-click the tab, click Delete on the shortcut menu, and then drag the correct object to the tab.

Trouble? You can rearrange the order of objects on the lower-level tabs by dragging the name of an object from its current tab to a new tab.

5. Drag the **frmOwner** form from the Navigation Pane to the next [Add New] tab to the right of the frmVistsAndInvoices tab. You've added the two forms Daksha wants users to work with in the Veterinary database. See Figure 10-39.

Figure 10-39   **Navigation form after adding two forms to lower-level tabs**

Next, you'll drag objects from the Navigation Pane to the lower-level tabs for the Queries and Reports tabs.

6. Click the **Queries** tab at the top of the navigation form, and then drag the **frmQueries** form from the Navigation Pane to the [Add New] tab below the Queries tab. Although you can't drag queries to a navigation form, in this case you're instead dragging the form you created that users can use to view and print queries.

7. Click the **Reports** tab at the top of the navigation form, and then drag from the Navigation Pane to the lower-level tabs, in order, the **rptBillingAndVisits** report and the **rptInvoicesByItem** report. Notice that each report opens as you drag it to the form.

8. Close the Navigation Pane. You've finished adding objects to the navigation form. See Figure 10-40.

Figure 10-40 **Reports added to the navigation form**

Daksha asks you to delete the picture at the top of the navigation form, delete the form title, set the form's Caption property to "Veterinary Database," and then save the form.

To finalize the navigation form:

1. Right-click the **picture** at the top of the form, click **Delete** on the shortcut menu, right-click the **form title**, and then click **Delete** on the shortcut menu.

2. Save the form as **frmNavigation**, and then switch to Design view.

3. Open the Property Sheet for the form, and then set the Caption property to **Veterinary Database**.

4. Switch to Form view. See Figure 10-41.

Figure 10-41   **Completed navigation form**

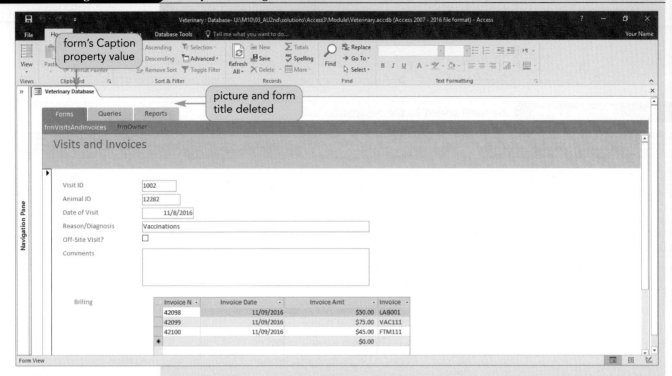

TIP

When you click the Forms tab's lower-level tabs, you need to click a blank area of the form to place the focus in the first field in the record.

5. Navigate through the navigation form by clicking each top-level tab and their respective lower-level tabs.

   When you click the Queries tab you may notice that the first query is not selected. This is because the frmQueries form is a subform of the frmNavigation form, and the Load event occurs on the frmNavigation form but does not occur on its subforms. When you load the frmQueries form itself, the Load event occurs on the frmQueries form. You'll need to click a query in the Available Queries list box before you click one of the command buttons on the form.

6. Save and close the form, make a backup copy of the database, compact and repair the database, and then close it.

   Daksha is happy with the two user interfaces you created for the Veterinary database. He can direct experienced users to the database objects, including the frmVisit form that has some advanced features. He can load the frmNavigation form for users who are less experienced.

Session 10.2 Quick Check

REVIEW

1. What is a list box control?

2. What are system tables?

3. What are the five SQL statement types, and which query types do they correspond to?

4. When does the Load event occur?

5. What is a navigation form?

Review Assignments

Data File needed for the Review Assignments: Ordering.accdb *(cont. from Module 9)*

Daksha wants you to create a user interface for the Ordering database. To help with this request, complete the following steps:

1. Open the **Ordering** database you worked with in the previous module. Delete the action queries qryAppendSterile, qryDeletePriceLess20, qryMakeSpecialEnviron, and qrySpecialDiscount. If you want to keep the action queries, first save a copy of the Ordering database as Ordering_M9, and then delete the action queries.

2. Design and create a form named **frmQueries** that has the following components and characteristics:

   a. Set the form's Caption property to **Ordering Queries**.

   b. Add a list box control with a Name property value of **lstQueryList** that displays all the query names contained in the Ordering database, excluding those that start with a "~" character. To place the query names in the list box control, use a SQL SELECT statement to retrieve the query names from the MSysObjects table, and display the queries in alphabetical order. (*Hint*: Use the same SQL select query that you used in the module.) Widen the list box control to approximately 2.5 inches.

   c. In the attached label control, change the caption to **Queries Available**, formatted with a 12-point, bold font, position the label above the list box control, and increase the width of the label control to fit the text.

   d. Add two command buttons below the list box control. The left command button should display the Preview icon above the word **Preview**, and the right command button should display the MS Access Query icon above the word **Display**.

   e. Create a macro for the form that moves the focus to the first query name in the list box control when the form loads.

   f. Create a macro that causes the query datasheet to display the selected query, then configure the form so the macro runs when a user double-clicks a query name or when a user selects a query name in the list box and clicks the right command button.

   g. Create a macro for the left command button that opens the selected query in Print Preview.

   h. Set the background color of the Detail section to Green 2 in the Standard Colors section and the background color of the list box to Green 1, and then disable the form's shortcut menu, record selectors, Close button, and navigation buttons.

   i. Test the form.

3. Create a navigation form named **frmNavigation**, using the Horizontal Tabs, 2 Levels layout that includes the following tab names and objects:

   a. Use **Forms** as the name for the left-most top-level tab, and place the following forms below it as lower-level tabs, in order: frmSupplier and frmSuppliersWithProducts.

   b. Use **Queries** as the name for the second tab, and place the frmQueries form below it on a lower-level tab.

   c. Use **Reports** as the name for the third tab, and place the following reports below it as lower-level tabs, in order: rptSupplierDetails and rptProductsBySupplier.

   d. Delete the navigation form's picture and title, and set the form's caption to **Ordering Database**.

   e. Test the navigation form, remembering to first select a query in the list on the Queries tab before testing the command buttons.

4. Make a backup copy of the database, compact and repair the database, and then close it.

PRACTICE

Case Problem 1

APPLY

Data File needed for this Case Problem: Salon.accdb *(cont. from Module 9)*

Beauty To Go   To make the Salon database easier to use, Sue Miller wants you to create a user interface for it. To help Sue with her request, complete the following steps:

1. Open the **Salon** database you worked with in the previous module. Delete the action queries qryAppendInactive, qryDelete128, qryMakeOnHold, and qryUpdateSpecialOption. If you want to keep the action queries, first save a copy of the Salon database as Salon_M9, and then delete the action queries.

2. Design and create a form named **frmQueries** that has the following components and characteristics:

   a. Set the form's Caption property to **Salon Queries**.

   b. Add a list box control with a Name property value of **lstQueryList** that displays all the query names contained in the Salon database, excluding those queries that start with a "~" character. To place the query names in the list box control, use a SQL SELECT statement to retrieve the query names from the MSysObjects table, and display the queries in alphabetical order. (*Hint*: Use the same SQL select query that you used in the module.) Widen the list box control to approximately 2.75 inches.

   c. In the attached label control, change the caption to **Select a Query**, formatted with Century Gothic 12-point, bold font, position the label above the list box control, and increase the width of the label to fit the text.

   d. Add two command buttons below the list box control. The left command button should display the Preview icon above the word **Preview**, and the right command button should display the MS Access Query icon above the word **Display**.

   e. Create a macro for the form that moves the focus to the first query name in the list box control when the form loads.

   f. Create a macro that causes the query datasheet to display the selected query, then configure the form so the macro runs when a user double-clicks a query name or when a user selects a query name in the list box and clicks the right command button.

   g. Create a macro for the left command button that opens the selected query in Print Preview.

   h. Set the background color of the Detail section to Light Blue 2 in the Standard Colors section and the background color of the list box to Light Blue 1, and then disable the shortcut menu, navigation buttons, and close button.

   i. Test the form.

3. Create a navigation form named **frmNavigation**, using the Horizontal Tabs, 2 Levels layout that includes the following tab names and objects:

   a. Use **Forms** as the name for the left-most top-level tab, and place the following forms below it on lower-level tabs, in order: frmOptionInfo and frmOptionsWithMembers.

   b. Use **Queries** as the name for the second top-level tab, and place the frmQueries form below it on a lower-level tab.

   c. Use **Reports** as the name for the third top-level tab, and place the following reports below it on lower-level tabs, in order: rptOptionList, rptOptionMembership, and rptMemberLabels.

   d. Delete the navigation form's picture and title, and change the form's caption property to **Salon Database**.

   e. Test the navigation form, remembering to first select a query in the list on the Queries tab before testing the command buttons.

4. Make a backup copy of the database, compact and repair the database, and then close it.

Case Problem 2

TROUBLESHOOT

Data File needed for this Case Problem: Technology.accdb *(cont. from Module 9)*

Programming Pros   Brent Hovis wants the Technology database to include an easy-to-use interface. To help Brent with his request, complete the following steps:

1. Open the **Technology** database you worked with in the previous module.

⚙ **Troubleshoot** 2. Open the **frmQueries** form. Troubleshoot and fix the following problems with this form:

   a. The following action queries appear in the lstQueryList list box control but should not be displayed in the list box and should not be in the database: qryAppendSemiPrivate, qryDeleteBeforeAug2017, qryMakeSpecialSession, and qryUpdateLength2to3.

   b. When you click the Preview button, the query is not displayed in Print Preview.

   c. When you click the Display button, nothing happens. When the user clicks the Display button, the datasheet for the selected query should display.

⚙ **Troubleshoot** 3. Open the navigation form named **frmNavigation.** Troubleshoot and fix the following problems with this form:

   a. The Forms tab should have the following forms below it: frmStudent and frmTutorInfo.

   b. The Queries tab should have the following form below it: frmQueries.

   c. The Reports tab should have the following reports below it: rptTutorList, rptTutorSessions, and rptStudentMailingLabels.

   d. There should be only three tabs; Forms, Queries, Reports.

   e. The text on the tab for the navigation form should be **Technology Database**.

4. Make a backup copy of the database, compact and repair the database, and then close it.

Case Problem 3

APPLY

Data File needed for this Case Problem: Thrift.accdb *(cont. from Module 9)*

Diane's Community Center   Diane Coleman wants the Thrift database to include an easy-to-use user interface. To help her with her request, complete the following steps:

1. Open the **Thrift** database you worked with in the previous module. Delete the action queries qryAppendClothes, qryDeleteOver100, qryMakeSpecialDonation, and qryUpdateMoney. If you want to keep the action queries, first save a copy of the Thrift database as Thrift_M9, and then delete the action queries.

2. Design and create a form named **frmQueries** that has the following components and characteristics:

   a. Set the form's Caption property to **Community Center Queries**.

   b. Add a list box control with a Name property value of **lstQueryList** that displays all the query names contained in the Thrift database, excluding those queries that start with a "~" character. To place the query names in the list box control, use a SQL SELECT statement to retrieve the query names from the MSysObjects table, and display the queries in alphabetical order. (*Hint*: Use the same SQL select query that you used in the module.) Widen the list box to approximately 2.5 inches.

   c. In the attached label control, change the caption to **Choose a query**, formatted with a 14-point, bold font, position the label control above the list box control, and increase the width of the label to fit the text.

   d. Add two command buttons below the list box control. The left command button should display the Preview icon above the word **Preview**, and the right command button should display the MS Access Query icon above the word **Display**.

   e. Create a macro for the form that moves the focus to the first query name in the list box control when the form loads.

   f. Create a macro that causes the query datasheet to display the selected query, then configure the form so the macro runs when a user double-clicks a query name, or when a user selects a query name in the list box and clicks the right command button.

   g. Create a macro for the left command button that opens the selected query in Print Preview.

   h. Set the background color of the Detail section to Brown 2 in the Standard Colors section and the background color of the list box to Brown 1, and then disable the form's shortcut menu, close button, and navigation buttons.

   i. Test the form.

3. Create a navigation form named **frmNavigation**, using the Horizontal Tabs, 2 Levels layout that includes the following tab names and objects:

   a. Use **Forms** as the name for the left-most top-level tab, and place the following forms below it on lower-level tabs, in order: frmPatronDonations and frmPatronInfo.

   b. Use **Queries** as the name for the second top-level tab, and place the frmQueries form below it on a lower-level tab.

   c. Use **Reports** as the name for the third top-level tab, and place the following reports below it on lower-level tabs, in order: rptPatronList and rptPatronDonations.

   d. Delete the navigation form's picture and title, and set the form's Caption property to **Community Center Database**.

   e. Test the navigation form, remembering to first select a query in the list on the Queries tab before testing the command buttons.

4. Make a backup copy of the database, compact and repair the database, and then close it.

Case Problem 4

CREATE

Data File needed for this Case Problem: BlueRidge.accdb (cont. from Module 9)

Hike Appalachia   Molly and Bailey Johnson want you to create a user-friendly interface for the BlueRidge database. To help them with their request, complete the following steps:

1. Open the **BlueRidge** database you worked with in the previous module. Delete the action queries. If you want to keep the action queries, first save a copy of the BlueRidge database as BlueRidge_M9, and then delete the action queries.

2. Design, create, and test a form named **frmQueries** that has the following components and characteristics:

   a. An appropriate Caption property for the form.

   b. A list box control (with an appropriate label control positioned above it) that contains all of the queries except for the system queries. Recall that system query names begin with the ~ character. The list box should be wide enough to display the longest query name. Set an appropriate Caption property for the list box control.

   c. A macro that opens a query in Datasheet view when you double-click the query name in the list box control.

   d. A macro that moves the focus to the first query in the list when the form loads.

   e. Two command buttons below the list box control that have macros that provide appropriate functionality to display the results of the selected query or display the query in Design view.

   f. Appropriate formatting including font, font size, and color for the list box control and appropriate icons and labels for the command buttons.

   g. Disabled shortcut menu, close button, and navigation buttons.

3. Create and test a navigation form named **frmNavigation**, using an appropriate layout that will display the following database objects: frmHikerInfo, frmQueries, rptTourReservations, and rptHikerLabels. Make sure the form's tab displays appropriate text and that the form does not include a picture or a form title.

4. Make a backup copy of the database, compact and repair the database, and then close it.

ACCESS

OBJECTIVES

Session 11.1
- Learn about user-defined functions, Sub procedures, and modules
- Review and modify an existing Sub procedure in an event procedure
- Create a function in a standard module
- Test a procedure in the Immediate window

Session 11.2
- Create event procedures
- Compile and test functions, Sub procedures, and event procedures
- Create a field validation procedure

Using and Writing Visual Basic for Applications Code

Creating VBA Code for the Veterinary Database

Case | *Riverview Veterinary Care Center*

Kimberly Johnson is pleased with your progress in developing the user interface for the Veterinary database. She realizes that many different people will be entering information in the Veterinary database. Whenever there is manual entry of data, there is always the potential for typographical errors. Kimberly wants you to modify the frmVisit, frmOwner, and frmVisitsAndInvoices forms to make data entry easier and to highlight important information on them. To make these modifications, you will write Visual Basic for Applications code.

STARTING DATA FILES

Access3 → Module
Veterinary.accdb (*cont.*)

Review
Ordering.accdb (*cont.*)

Case1
Salon.accdb (*cont.*)

Case2
Technology.accdb (*cont.*)

Case3
Thrift.accdb (*cont.*)

Case4
BlueRidge.accdb (*cont.*)

Session 11.1 Visual Overview:

The **Object box** displays the current object type the procedure acts on.

Each Sub procedure begins with a **Sub statement**, which marks the start of a new Sub procedure.

Each **Case statement** designates the start of an alternative set of actions.

An **assignment statement** assigns the value of an expression to a field, control, or property.

The **End Sub statement** designates the end of a Sub procedure.

The **End Select statement** designates the end of a Case control structure.

A control displays when its Visible property is True and is hidden when its Visible property is False.

You can use the **Immediate window** to test VBA procedures without changing any data in the database.

The function in the Immediate window executes and displays the value returned by the function.

```
Microsoft Visual Basic for Applications - Veterinary - [Form_frmVisit (Code)]
File   Edit   View   Insert   Debug   Run   Tools   Add-Ins   Window   Help

Form

Option Compare Database

Private Sub Form_Current()
    lblMessage.Visible = True
    Select Case [Reason]
    Case "Vaccinations"
        lblMessage.Caption = "Book animal appointment for the
        lblMessage.ForeColor = RGB(0, 0, 255)
    Case "Grooming"
        lblMessage.Caption = "Introduce owner to the home gro
        lblMessage.ForeColor = RGB(0, 150, 0)
    Case Else
        lblMessage.Visible = False
    End Select
End Sub
```

```
Immediate

?LowAll("JDoe@Example.Com")
jdoe@example.com
```

VBA Code Window

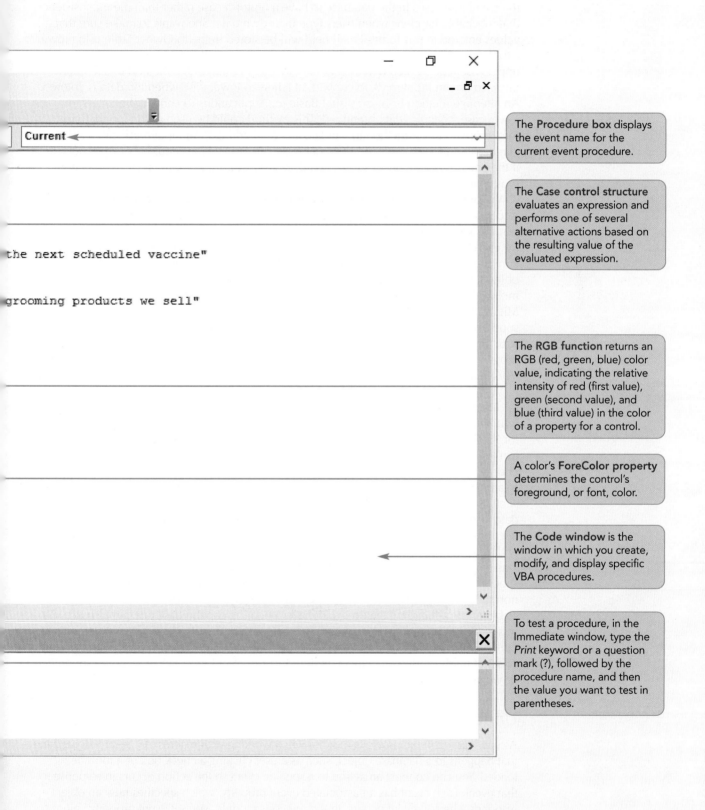

The **Procedure box** displays the event name for the current event procedure.

The **Case control structure** evaluates an expression and performs one of several alternative actions based on the resulting value of the evaluated expression.

The **RGB function** returns an RGB (red, green, blue) color value, indicating the relative intensity of red (first value), green (second value), and blue (third value) in the color of a property for a control.

A color's **ForeColor property** determines the control's foreground, or font, color.

The **Code window** is the window in which you create, modify, and display specific VBA procedures.

To test a procedure, in the Immediate window, type the *Print* keyword or a question mark (?), followed by the procedure name, and then the value you want to test in parentheses.

Current

the next scheduled vaccine"

grooming products we sell"

Introduction to Visual Basic for Applications

Your next task in the development of the Veterinary database is to add a procedure to ensure proper capitalization of data entered using the frmOwner form. Kimberly wants the email addresses in the database to have a uniform case rather than the inconsistency that inevitably happens when users type their own data. She wants to make sure that all values entered in this form's Email field will be stored in the tblOwner table using lower case letters. She asks you to modify the form so that it will automatically convert any upper case letters entered in the Email field to lower case. One method to accomplish this is to use an input mask to convert all letters to lower case when the data is entered. An alternate method is to use Visual Basic for Applications to convert the letters to lower case when the data is entered. This method could be used as the foundation for a more complex method to validate an email address. An input mask can restrict characters during data entry, but Visual Basic for Applications could also check to see if the email address contains the @ symbol and a valid suffix such as .com, which an input mask cannot do.

Visual Basic for Applications (VBA) is the programming language provided with Access and other Office programs. VBA has a common syntax and a set of common features for all Microsoft Office programs, but it also has features that are unique for each Microsoft Office program due to each program's distinct structure and components. For example, because Access has fields, tables, queries, forms, other objects, tab controls, subforms, and other controls that are unique to it, VBA for Access includes features that support these particular components. In contrast, because Microsoft Excel does not have these same Access components, VBA for Excel does not support them, but it does support cells, ranges, and worksheets—three of the basic structures of Excel. The fundamental VBA skills you learn for one of the Microsoft Office programs transfer to any other Microsoft Office program, but to become proficient with VBA in another program, you first need to master its unique aspects.

When you use a programming language, such as VBA, you write a set of instructions to direct the computer to perform specific operations in a specific order, similar to writing a set of instructions for a recipe or an instruction manual. The Visual Overview for Session 11.1 shows the VBA Code window with instructions for Access to use in the frmVisit form. The process of writing instructions in a programming language is called **coding**. You write the VBA instructions, each of which is called a **statement**, to respond to an event that occurs with an object or a form control in a database. A language such as VBA is, therefore, is called an **event-driven language**, because an event in the database triggers a set of instructions. It is also called an **object-oriented language**, because each set of instructions operates on objects in the database. Your experience with macros, which are also event-driven and object-oriented, should facilitate your learning of VBA. Although you must use macros if you need to assign actions to a specific keyboard key or key combination, you can use VBA for everything else you normally accomplish with macros. VBA provides advantages over using macros, such as better error-handling features and easier updating capabilities. You can also use VBA in situations that macros do not handle, such as creating your own set of statements to perform special calculations, verifying a field value based on the value of another field or set of fields, or dynamically changing the color of a form control when a user enters or views a specific field value.

Understanding Procedures

As you learned in the previous module when working with macros, an event is something that happens to a database object, such as a user clicking a check box or a form being loaded. You can connect an action to a specific event so the action occurs in response to that event. Each event has an associated event property, which specifies how an object responds when an event occurs. In the previous module, you set event property values to macro names, and Access executed the macros when those events occurred. You can also create a group of statements, known as a procedure, using VBA code and set an event property value to the name of that procedure. Access then executes the procedure when the event occurs. As you know, such a procedure is called an event procedure. Access has over 60 events and associated event properties. Figure 11-1 describes some frequently used Access events. Each event (such as the AfterUpdate event) has an associated event property (AfterUpdate) and event procedure (ContractNum_AfterUpdate for the AfterUpdate event procedure for the ContractNum control).

Figure 11-1   **Frequently used Access events**

Event	Description
AfterUpdate	Occurs after changed data in a control or a record is updated
BeforeUpdate	Occurs before changed data in a control or a record is updated
Click	Occurs when a user presses and then releases a mouse button over a control in a form
Current	Occurs when the focus moves to a record, making it the current record, or when a form is refreshed or requeried
DblClick	Occurs when a user presses and releases the left mouse button twice over a control in a form within the double-click time limit
Delete	Occurs when a user performs some action, such as pressing the Delete key, to delete a record, but before the record is actually deleted
GotFocus	Occurs when a form or a form control receives the focus
Load	Occurs when a form is opened and its records are displayed
MouseDown	Occurs when a user presses a mouse button
NoData	Occurs after Access formats a report for printing that has no data (the report is bound to an empty recordset), but before the report is printed; you use this event to cancel the printing of a blank report
Open	Occurs when a form is opened, but before the first record is displayed; for reports, the event occurs before a report is previewed or printed

The two types of VBA procedures are Function procedures and Sub procedures. A **user-defined function**, or **function procedure**, performs operations, returns a value, accepts input values, and can be used in expressions (recall that an expression is a calculation resulting in a single value). For example, some of the Veterinary database queries use built-in Access functions, such as Sum, Count, and Avg, to calculate a sum, a record count, or an average. To meet Kimberly's request, you will create a function named LowAll by entering the appropriate VBA statements. The LowAll function will accept the value entered in a field value box—in this case, the Email field—as an input value, convert all characters in the field value to lower case, and then return the changed field value to be stored in the database and displayed in the field value box.

A **Sub procedure** executes instructions and accepts input values but does not return a value and cannot be used in expressions. Most Access procedures are Sub procedures because you need the procedures to perform a series of actions or operations in response to an event. Later in this module, you will create a Sub procedure that displays a message in the frmVisitsAndInvoices form only when the visit date is earlier than a specified date.

Understanding Modules

You store a group of related procedures together in an object called a **module**. Figure 11-2 shows the structure of a typical module.

Figure 11-2	Structure of a VBA module and its procedures

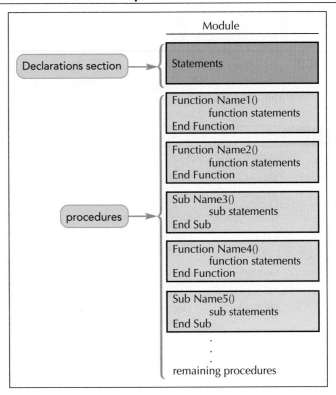

Each module starts with a **Declarations section**, which contains statements that apply to all procedures in the module. One or more procedures, which follow the Declarations section and which can be a mixture of functions and Sub procedures, constitute the rest of the module. The two basic types of modules are standard modules and class modules.

A **standard module** is a database object that is stored in memory with other database objects (queries, forms, and so on) when you open the database. You can use the procedures in a database's standard modules from anywhere in the database—even from procedures in other modules. All standard modules are listed in the Modules section of the Navigation Pane. A procedure that more than one object can use is called a **public procedure**. For example, the LowAll procedure that you will create converts all letters in the value passed to it to lower case. Although you are creating this procedure specifically to work with Email field values, you will place it in a standard module and make it public. You could then use the LowAll procedure for any object in the database.

A **class module** is usually associated with a particular form or report. When you create the first event procedure for a form or report, an associated form or report class module is also created. When you add additional event procedures to the form or report, they are automatically added to the class module for that form or report. Each event procedure in a class module is a **local procedure**, or a **private procedure**, which means that only the form or report for which the class module was created can use the event procedure.

Using an Existing VBA Procedure

Before creating the LowAll procedure for Kimberly, you'll use an existing procedure that Kimberly created in the class module for the frmVisit form. When an owner brings an animal in for care, the Riverview Veterinary Care Center team would like to book an appointment for administering the animal's next required vaccine. For those animals that visit the care center for grooming, the team would like to provide information on available grooming products. To remind the staff to provide information and book the next vaccine visit, Kimberly created a local procedure stored in the class module of the frmVisit form that displays the message about vaccines in blue text in a box to the right of the Off-Site Visit? check box and displays the messages about grooming products in red text. For animals with any other reason for visiting the care center, the class module makes the box invisible.

You'll navigate through the records using the frmVisit form to observe the effects of the procedure.

To navigate a form that uses a VBA procedure:

▶ **1.** Start Access, and then open the **Veterinary** database you worked with in the previous two modules.

▶ **2.** Open the Navigation Pane (if necessary), open the **frmVisit** form in Form view, and then close the Navigation Pane. For the first record for VisitID 1002, the value "Book animal appointment for the next schedule vaccination" is displayed in a blue font to the right of the Off-Site Visit? check box because the Reason field value is "Vaccinations." See Figure 11-3.

Figure 11-3   frmVisit form that uses a VBA procedure

▶ **3.** Click the **Next record** button ▶ twice to move to the third record. The frmVisit form displays record 3 for VisitID 1009. There is no value displayed to the right of the Off-Site Visit? check box because the Reason field is neither "Vaccinations" nor "Grooming."

▶ **4.** Navigate to record 11 for VisitID 1028. Because the Reason value for this visit is "Grooming," the text "Introduce owner to the home grooming products we sell" is displayed in a red font the right of the Off-Site Visit? check box.

Kimberly asks you to change the red color for the display of "Introduce owner to the home grooming products we sell" to green so that it doesn't appear to be an urgent warning.

Examining a VBA Event Procedure

The VBA procedure that controls the display of the message and its color for each record is in the class module for the frmVisit form. The statements in the procedure are processed when you open the frmVisit form and also when the focus leaves one record and moves to another. The event called the **Current event** occurs when the focus shifts to the next record loaded in a form, making it the current record. This also happens when the form loads and when the form is refreshed. The **OnCurrent property** contains a reference to a macro, VBA code, or some other expression that runs when the Current event occurs.

To change the color of the text "Introduce owner to the home grooming products we sell" from red to green, you'll modify the event procedure for the form's OnCurrent property. First, you'll switch to Design view, and then you'll display the event procedure.

To display the event procedure for the form's OnCurrent property:

▶ **1.** Switch to Design view.

▶ **2.** Right-click the **form selector** to display the shortcut menu, and then (if necessary) click **Properties** to open the Property Sheet for the form.

▶ **3.** Click the **Event** tab (if necessary) to display the Event page, click the **On Current** box, and then (if necessary) drag the left border of the Property Sheet to the left until the On Current property value is visible. See Figure 11-4.

Figure 11-4	Event properties for the frmVisit form

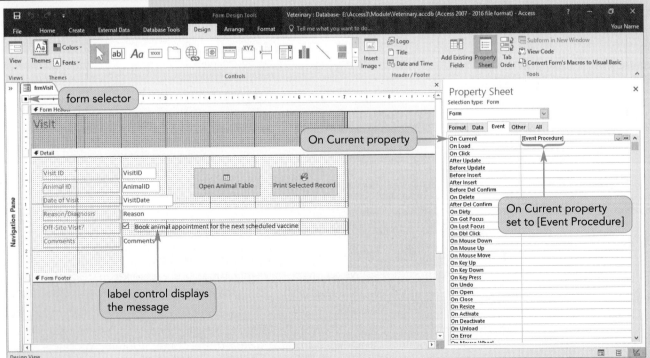

The On Current property is set to [Event Procedure], indicating that a VBA procedure is called when the Current event occurs. You'll click the Build button to display the procedure.

▶ **4.** In the On Current box, click the **Build** button ⋯ . The Code window opens in the Visual Basic window. See Figure 11-5.

Figure 11-5	Code window in the Visual Basic window

current object type in the Object box

form name

event name for the event procedure in the Procedure box

statement in the Declarations sections

Sub procedure for the form's Current event

```
Veterinary - [Form_frmVisit (Code)]
Run  Tools  Add-Ins  Window  Help
                            Ln 4, Col 1
Form                                    Current
Option Compare Database

Private Sub Form_Current()
    lblMessage.Visible = True
    Select Case [Reason]
    Case "Vaccinations"
        lblMessage.Caption = "Book animal appointment for the next scheduled vaccine"
        lblMessage.ForeColor = RGB(0, 0, 255)
    Case "Grooming"
        lblMessage.Caption = "Introduce owner to the home grooming products we sell"
        lblMessage.ForeColor = RGB(255, 0, 0)
    Case Else
        lblMessage.Visible = False
    End Select
End Sub
```

Trouble? If the Project window and/or the Properties windows also appear in your Visual Basic window, click their Close buttons to close them.

Trouble? If the code window isn't maximized within the VBA window, click the maximize button.

The program you use to create and modify VBA code is called the **Visual Basic Editor** (**VBE** or **editor** for short), and the **Visual Basic window** is the program window that opens when you use VBE. As shown in the Session 11.1 Visual Overview, the Code window is the window in which you create, modify, and display specific VBA procedures. You can have as many Code windows open as you have modules in the database. In the Code window, the Object box in the upper-left of the window indicates the current object type (Form), and the Procedure box in the upper-right of the window indicates the event name (Current) for the event procedure you are viewing.

All event procedures are Sub procedures. A horizontal line visually separates each procedure in the Code window. Each Sub procedure begins with a Sub statement and ends with an End Sub statement. The Sub statement includes the scope of the procedure (private or public), the name of the procedure (for example, Form_Current, which means the Current event for the form control), and opening and closing parentheses. The **scope** of a procedure indicates where the procedure is available. If its scope is public, the procedure is available in all objects in the database. If its scope is private, the procedure is available only in the object in which it is created. Event procedures are private by default. For instance, the event procedure in the OnCurrent property in the frmVisit form is private, and other forms do not have access to this procedure code.

Notice the Option Compare statement in the Declarations section above the horizontal line. The Option Compare statement designates the technique used to compare and sort text data. The default method "Database," as shown in Figure 11-5, means letters are compared and sorted in alphabetical order, using the language settings specified for Access on your computer.

The remaining statements in the Form_Current procedure shown in Figure 11-5 use only two controls in the form: The Reason field from the tblVisit table; and lblMessage, which is a label control that displays "Book animal appointment for the next scheduled vaccination" or "Introduce owner to the home grooming products we sell" when it's visible. Based on the Reason field value, the statements in the procedure do the following:

• When the Reason field value is "Vaccinations," set the Caption property for the lblMessage control to "Book animal appointment for the next scheduled vaccination" and set its font color to blue.
• When the Reason field value is "Grooming," set the Caption property for the lblMessage control to "Introduce owner to the home grooming products we sell" and set its font color to red.
• When the Reason field has any other value, hide the lblMessage control.

The statements from the *Select Case [Reason]* statement to the *End Select* statement are an example of a control structure. A **control structure** is a set of VBA statements that work together as a unit. The Case control structure is a conditional control structure. A **conditional control structure** evaluates an expression—the value of the Reason field, in this case—and then performs one of several alternative actions based on the resulting value (or condition) of the evaluated expression. Each Case statement, such as *Case "Vaccinations"* and *Case Else*, designates the start of an alternative set of actions.

Statements such as *lblMessage.Caption = "Book animal appointment for the next scheduled vaccination"* are assignment statements. An assignment statement assigns the value of an expression—"Book animal appointment for the next scheduled vaccination", in this case—to a field, control, or property—the Caption property of the lblMessage control, in this case.

Because a property is associated with a control, you use the general form of *ControlName.PropertyName* to specify a property for a control. An assignment statement such as *lblMessage.ForeColor = RGB(255, 0, 0)*, for example, assigns a value to the ForeColor property of the lblMessage control. A control's ForeColor property determines the control's foreground, or font, color. The expression in this assignment statement uses a built-in VBA function named RGB. The RGB function returns an RGB (red, green, blue) color value, indicating the relative intensity of red (first value), green (second value), and blue (third value) in the color of a property for a control. Figure 11-6 displays a list of some common colors and the red, green, and blue values for the RGB function that produces those colors. Each color component value must be in the range 0 through 255. Instead of using the RGB function for the eight colors shown in Figure 11-6, you can use one of the VBA constants (vbBlack, vbBlue, vbCyan, vbGreen, vbMagenta, vbRed, vbWhite, or vbYellow). A **VBA constant** is a predefined memory location that is initialized to a value that doesn't change. For example, *lblMessage.ForeColor = vbRed* and *lblMessage.ForeColor = RGB(255, 0, 0)* would set the color of the lblMessage control to red. You must use the RGB function when you want colors that differ from the eight colors shown in Figure 11-6.

Figure 11-6   **RGB function values for some common colors**

Color	Red Value	Green Value	Blue Value	VBA Constant
Black	0	0	0	vbBlack
Blue	0	0	255	vbBlue
Cyan	0	255	255	vbCyan
Green	0	255	0	vbGreen
Magenta	255	0	255	vbMagenta
Red	255	0	0	vbRed
White	255	255	255	vbWhite
Yellow	255	255	0	vbYellow

Assigning a Color Value

A color value can be assigned to a control property using a variety of methods. A color value could be one of the following:

- A built-in VB constant such as vbRed, vbWhite, or vbBlack.
- A set of red, green, and blue values, each ranging from 0 to 255, specified in the RGB function. For instance, RGB(0,255,0) represents the color green.
- A hexadecimal value that represents color intensities of red, green, and blue. For instance, 00FF00 represents the color green. The first two characters represent red, the second two characters represent green, and the last two characters represent blue. Similar to the RGB function, these triplets represent the intensity of each color, mixed to form the resulting color.
- A ColorIndex property value, which uses a color code specific to VBA. For instance, the color green has a ColorIndex value of 4.
- A Microsoft Access color code, which is a code specific to Access. For instance, the color green has the Microsoft Access color code 32768.

With all those choices, which one should you use? The most common are the built-in VB constants, RGB function, and hexadecimal values. The RGB function and hexadecimal values are also used in web design and VB.NET programming, so you may find these techniques especially useful if you modify webpage code as well.

The Visible property determines whether or not a control displays. A control displays when its Visible property is True, and the control is hidden when its Visible property is False. The *lblMessage.Visible = True* statement, which is processed before the *Select Case [Reason]* statement, displays the lblMessage control. Because Kimberly doesn't want the lblMessage control to appear for reasons other than Vaccinations and Grooming, the *lblMessage.Visible = False* statement hides the lblMessage control when the Reason field value doesn't equal one of the two reasons.

Modifying an Event Procedure

Kimberly wants you to change the red color for the display of the message "Introduce owner to the home grooming products we sell" to green. This requires changing the red RGB function value of (255, 0, 0) to the green value (0, 150, 0). To make this change, you'll modify the first set of RGB function values in the event procedure. Then you'll close the Visual Basic window and save and test your modifications.

To modify, save, and test the event procedure:

1. In the line lblMessage.Forecolor = RGB(255, 0, 0), double-click **255** to select it, and then type **0** to replace the selected value. The RGB function is now RGB(0, 0, 0).

2. In the same line of code, double-click the next **0**, and then type **150**. The RGB function is now RGB(0, 150, 0), which is a value that will produce a medium shade of green. See Figure 11-7.

Figure 11-7   Modified RGB values

3. On the Code window's toolbar, the **Save** button 🖫 to save your changes.

4. On the Visual Basic window's title bar, the **Close** button ☒ to close it and return to the Form window in Design view.

5. Close the Property Sheet, save your form design changes, and then switch to Form view.

6. Navigate to record 11 for the VisitID 1028. The text "Introduce owner to the home grooming products we sell" displays in green to the right of the Off-Site Visit? check box. Your modification to the event procedure was completed successfully. See Figure 11-8.

Figure 11-8   Forecolor changed in frmVisit form

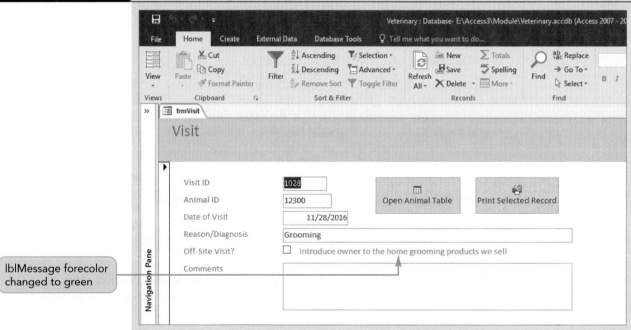

7. Close the frmVisit form.

Now that you have viewed and modified an event procedure, you'll create a function in a standard module.

Creating Functions in a Standard Module

Kimberly wants you to create a VBA procedure for the frmOwner form that will automatically convert the values entered in the Email field to lower case. For example, if a user enters "JDoe@Example.Com" as the email address, the procedure will automatically convert it to "jdoe@example.com". Kimberly feels that this function will make data more uniform in the database. Additionally, she might want to add additional code later that ensures the entry is a valid email address, and this VBA procedure could serve as a foundation for further validation code.

Any user input in the Email Address field is a **string**, which is one or more characters that could include alphabetic characters, numbers, spaces, and punctuation. To accomplish the change Kimberly wants, you will first create a simple function, named LowAll, that accepts a string input value and converts that string to lower case. You will create the function by typing the required statements in the Code window. Then you will create an event procedure that calls the LowAll function whenever a user enters a value in the Email field using the frmOwner form.

Whenever a user enters or changes a field value in a control or in a form and then changes the focus to another control or record, the **AfterUpdate event** is automatically triggered, which, by default, simply accepts the new or changed entry. However, you can set the AfterUpdate event property of a control to a specific event procedure in order to have something else happen when a user enters or changes the field value. In this case, you need to set the Email field's AfterUpdate event property to [Event Procedure] and then code an event procedure to call the LowAll function. Calling the LowAll function will cause the entry in the Email Address field to be converted to lower case letters before storing it in the database.

You could add the LowAll function to the class module for the frmOwner form. However, adding the function to the class module for the frmOwner form would make it a private function, that is, you could not use it in other forms or database objects. Because Kimberly and her staff might use the LowAll function in other forms in the Veterinary database, you'll instead place the LowAll function in a new standard module named basVeterinaryProcedures (*bas* is a standard prefix for modules). Generally, when you enter a procedure in a standard module, it is public, and you can use it in event procedures for any object in the database.

To create a new standard module, you'll begin by opening the Code window.

To create a new standard module:

▶ **1.** On the ribbon, click the **Create** tab.

▶ **2.** In the Macros & Code group, click the **Module** button. A new Code window opens in the Visual Basic window. See Figure 11-9.

Figure 11-9	New standard module in the Code window

default module name

```
Microsoft Visual Basic for Applications - Veterinary - [Module1 (Code)]
File  Edit  View  Insert  Debug  Run  Tools  Add-Ins  Window  Help
                                                          Ln 3, Col 1

(General)                                                 (Declarations)

Option Compare Database
```

default statement in the Declarations sections

Trouble? If other windows appear in your Visual Basic window, click their Close buttons to close them.

In the Code window for the new standard module, the Procedure box indicates the Declarations section as the current procedure in the module. The Option Compare statement is automatically included in the Declarations section of a new module. The LowAll function is a simple function that does not require additional statements in the Declarations section.

Writing Statements in a Function

Each function begins with a **Function statement** and ends with an **End Function statement**. Each procedure in the Code window is separated by a horizontal line. You can view a procedure's statements by selecting the procedure name from the Procedure box.

You'll start the LowAll function with the statement *Function LowAll(FValue)*. LowAll is the function name, and FValue is used as a placeholder for the input value in the function definition. When a user enters a value for the Email field in the frmOwner form, that value will be passed to the LowAll function and substituted for FValue in the function definition. A placeholder like FValue is called a **parameter**. The value passed to the function and used in place of the parameter when the function is executed is called an **argument**. In other words, the value passed to the function is the argument, which is assigned to the parameter named FValue.

INSIGHT

VBA Naming Rules

Each VBA function name, Sub procedure name, argument name, and any other name you create must conform to the following rules:

- It must begin with a letter.
- It cannot exceed 255 characters.
- It can include letters, numbers, and the underscore character (_). You cannot use a space or any punctuation characters.
- It cannot contain keywords—such as Function, Sub, Case, and Option—that VBA uses as part of its language.
- It must be unique, that is, you can't declare the same name twice within the same procedure.

Next you'll enter the LowAll function in the Code window.

To enter the LowAll function in the Code window:

▶ **1.** If necessary, position the insertion point two lines below the Option Compare statement.

▶ **2.** Type **Function LowAll(FValue)** and then press the **Enter** key. The editor displays a horizontal line that visually separates the new function from the Declarations section and adds the End Function statement. See Figure 11-10.

Figure 11-10   **Function entered in the Code window**

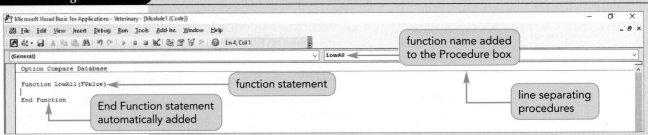

The LowAll function will consist of a single executable assignment statement that you will place between the Function and End Function statements. The assignment statement you'll enter is *LowAll = LCase(FValue)*. The value of the expression, which is LCase(FValue), will be assigned to the function, which is LowAll.

The expression in the assignment statement uses a built-in Access function named LCase. The **LCase function** accepts a single string argument as input, converts the value of the argument to lower case letters, and then returns the converted value. The assignment statement assigns the converted value to the LowAll function. Figure 11-11 illustrates this process.

Figure 11-11 **Evaluation of the assignment statement**

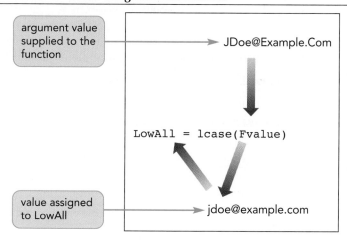

argument value supplied to the function → JDoe@Example.Com

LowAll = lcase(Fvalue)

value assigned to LowAll → jdoe@example.com

TIP

Because VBA ignores the contents of comments, you can include spaces, special characters, and mixed-case strings in your comments.

Before entering the assignment statement, you will add a comment line to explain the procedure's purpose. You can include comments anywhere in a VBA procedure to describe what the procedure does or what a statement does. You begin a comment with the word Rem (for "Remark") or with a single quotation mark ('). VBA ignores anything following the word Rem or the single quotation mark on a single line.

PROSKILLS

Written Communication: Guidelines for Writing VBA Code

It is standard to use proper case in writing VB statements, that is, the first character of each keyword is capitalized, as in the statement End If. In addition, you should use comments in a VBA procedure to explain the purpose of the procedure and to clarify any complicated programming logic used. Comments can be used to identify the name of the original creator of a procedure, the purpose of the procedure, and a history of changes made to the procedure, including who made each change and for what purpose.

Although VBA does not require statements to be indented in procedures, experienced programmers indent statements to make procedures easier to read and maintain. Pressing the Tab key once indents a line four spaces to the right, and pressing the Shift+Tab key combination or the Backspace key once moves the insertion point four spaces to the left. Commenting and indenting your procedures will help you recall the logic of the procedures you created months or years ago and will help others understand your work.

To add a comment and statement to the LowAll function:

▶ **1.** Click in the blank line between the Function and End Function statements (if necessary) to position the insertion point, and then press the **Tab** key.

You will add the comment in this blank line. The single quotation mark is a comment marker, and it indicates that the text that follows is a comment and will not be executed.

▶ **2.** Type '**Convert all letters of a field value to lower case**, and then press the **Enter** key.

Notice that the editor displays the comment in green and moves the insertion point to a new indented line. After entering the comment line, you can enter the assignment statement, which is the executable statement in the function that performs the actual conversion of the argument to lower case.

▶ **3.** Type **LowAll = LCase(**

The editor displays a Quick Info banner with a reminder that LCase accepts a single string argument. See Figure 11-12.

Figure 11-12	The LowAll function entered in the Code window

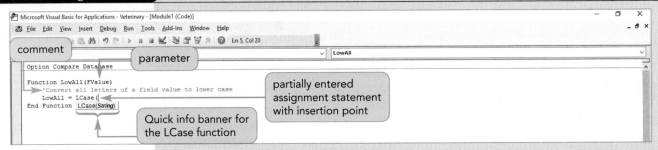

Trouble? If the Quick Info banner does not display, click Tools on the menu bar, click Options, click the Editor tab (if necessary), click the Auto Quick Info check box to select it, and then click the OK button.

You'll now finish typing the assignment statement.

▶ **4.** Type **FValue)** to finish the assignment statement. The editor scans each statement for errors when you press the Enter key or move the insertion point to another line. Because the function is complete and you want the editor to scan the line you just entered for errors, you must move the insertion point to another line.

▶ **5.** Press the ↓ key to move the insertion point to the next line. See Figure 11-13.

Figure 11-13	Complete LowAll statement in the Code window

You have finished entering the function in the module, so you'll save it before continuing with your work. When you click the Save button in the Visual Basic window, the editor saves the module and its procedures. If you are entering a long procedure, it's a good idea to save your work periodically.

> **To save the module:**
> 1. On the Code window toolbar, click the **Save** button 🖫 to open the Save As dialog box.
> 2. In the Module Name box, type **basVeterinaryProcedures**, and then press the **Enter** key. The Save As dialog box closes, the editor saves the module, and the new module name appears in editor the title bar.

After creating a module, you should test its procedures.

Testing a Procedure in the Immediate Window

TIP

VBA functions that you create won't run if the database is not trusted. You must click the Enable Content button that appears below the ribbon when you first open a database that is not stored in a trusted folder

As you just saw, when you finish entering a VBA statement, the editor checks the statement to make sure its syntax is correct. Even though you may have entered all procedure statements with the correct syntax, however, the procedure may still contain logic errors. A **logic error** occurs when a procedure produces incorrect results. For example, the LowAll function would have a logic error if you typed JDoe@Example.Com and the function changed it to JDOE@EXAMPLE.COM or anything other than the correct result of jdoe@example.com. Even the simplest procedure can contain logic errors. Be sure to test each procedure thoroughly to ensure that it does exactly what you expect it to do in all situations.

When working in the Code window, you can use the **Immediate window** to test VBA procedures without changing any data in the database. The Immediate window allows you to run individual lines of VBA code for **debugging**, or testing. In the Immediate window, you can enter different values to test the procedure you just entered. To test a procedure, you type the *Print* keyword or a question mark (?), followed by the procedure name, and then the value you want to test in parentheses. For example, to test the LowAll function in the Immediate window using the test word JDoe@Example.Com, you type *?LowAll("JDoe@Example.Com")* and then press the Enter key. The editor executes the function and displays the value returned by the function (you expect it to return jdoe@example.com). Note that you must enclose a string of characters within quotation marks in the test statement.

REFERENCE

Testing a Procedure in the Immediate Window

- In the Code window, click View on the menu bar, and then click Immediate Window to open the Immediate window.
- Type a question mark (?), the procedure name, and the procedure's arguments in parentheses. If an argument contains a string of characters, enclose the argument in quotation marks.
- Press the Enter key, and verify that the result displayed is the expected output.

Now you'll use the Immediate window to test the LowAll function.

To test the LowAll function in the Immediate window:

▶ **1.** Click **View** on the menu bar, and then click **Immediate Window**. The editor opens the Immediate window below the Code window and places the insertion point inside the window.

▶ **2.** Type **?LowAll("JDoe@Example.Com")** and then press the **Enter** key. The editor executes the function and displays the function result, jdoe@example.com, on the next line. See Figure 11-14.

Figure 11-14 | **LowAll function executed in the Immediate window**

```
?LowAll("JDoe@Example.Com")
jdoe@example.com
```

result of executing the function

Trouble? If a dialog box displays an error message, click the OK button in the dialog box, correct the error in the Immediate window, and then press the Enter key. If the function does not produce the correct output (jdoe@example.com), compare your code to Figure 11-13, correct the LowAll function statements in the Code window as necessary, save your changes, click a blank line in the Immediate window, and then repeat Step 2.

To test the LowAll function further, you could enter several other test values, retyping the entire statement each time. Instead, you'll select the current test value, type another value, and then press the Enter key.

▶ **3.** Delete the email address **JDoe@Example.Com** in the first line of the Immediate window.

▶ **4.** Type **JDOE@EXAMPLE.COM,** move the insertion point to the end of the line, and then press the **Enter** key. The editor executes the function and displays the function result, jdoe@example.com, on a new line.

▶ **5.** On the Immediate window's title bar, click the **Close** button X.

▶ **6.** On the Visual Basic window's title bar, click the **Close** button X to return to the Access window.

▶ **7.** If you are not continuing on to the next session, close the Veterinary database.

INSIGHT

Converting a Macro to Visual Basic

Creating a macro can be a bit more user-friendly than learning VBA code. Some people may find it easier to create a macro and then convert it to VBA. They may find that they have a database with several macros but have learned some VBA and would like to convert the macros to VBA so they can copy them and use them in other databases, or keep as much code as possible in a standard module.

To convert a macro to VBA, you open the macro you'd like to convert, then use the Convert Macros to Visual Basic button in the Tools group on the Macro Tools Design tab.

Your initial test of the LowAll function in the standard module is successful. In the next session, you'll modify the frmOwner form to execute the LowAll function for the Email field in that form.

REVIEW

Session 11.1 Quick Check

1. Why is Visual Basic for Applications called an event-driven, object-oriented language?

2. What is an event procedure?

3. What are the differences between a user-defined function and a Sub procedure?

4. Describe the two different types of modules.

5. The _____ of a procedure is either private or public.

6. What is the Immediate window used for?

Session 11.2 Visual Overview:

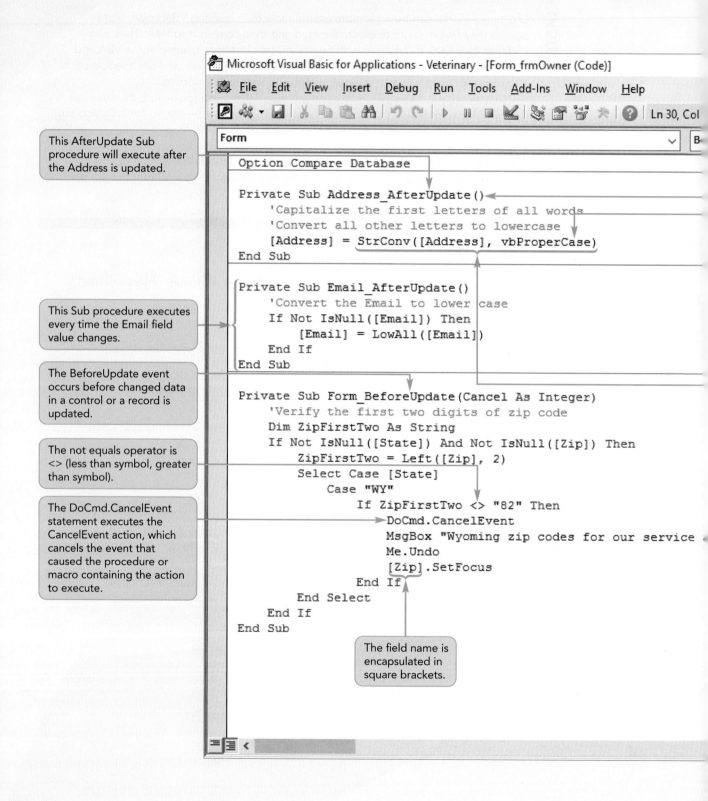

This AfterUpdate Sub procedure will execute after the Address is updated.

This Sub procedure executes every time the Email field value changes.

The BeforeUpdate event occurs before changed data in a control or a record is updated.

The not equals operator is <> (less than symbol, greater than symbol).

The DoCmd.CancelEvent statement executes the CancelEvent action, which cancels the event that caused the procedure or macro containing the action to execute.

The field name is encapsulated in square brackets.

Microsoft Visual Basic for Applications - Veterinary - [Form_frmOwner (Code)]

File   Edit   View   Insert   Debug   Run   Tools   Add-Ins   Window   Help

Ln 30, Col

Form

```
Option Compare Database

Private Sub Address_AfterUpdate()
    'Capitalize the first letters of all words
    'Convert all other letters to lowercase
    [Address] = StrConv([Address], vbProperCase)
End Sub

Private Sub Email_AfterUpdate()
    'Convert the Email to lower case
    If Not IsNull([Email]) Then
        [Email] = LowAll([Email])
    End If
End Sub

Private Sub Form_BeforeUpdate(Cancel As Integer)
    'Verify the first two digits of zip code
    Dim ZipFirstTwo As String
    If Not IsNull([State]) And Not IsNull([Zip]) Then
        ZipFirstTwo = Left([Zip], 2)
        Select Case [State]
            Case "WY"
                If ZipFirstTwo <> "82" Then
                    DoCmd.CancelEvent
                    MsgBox "Wyoming zip codes for our service
                    Me.Undo
                    [Zip].SetFocus
                End If
        End Select
    End If
End Sub
```

Example of an Event Procedure

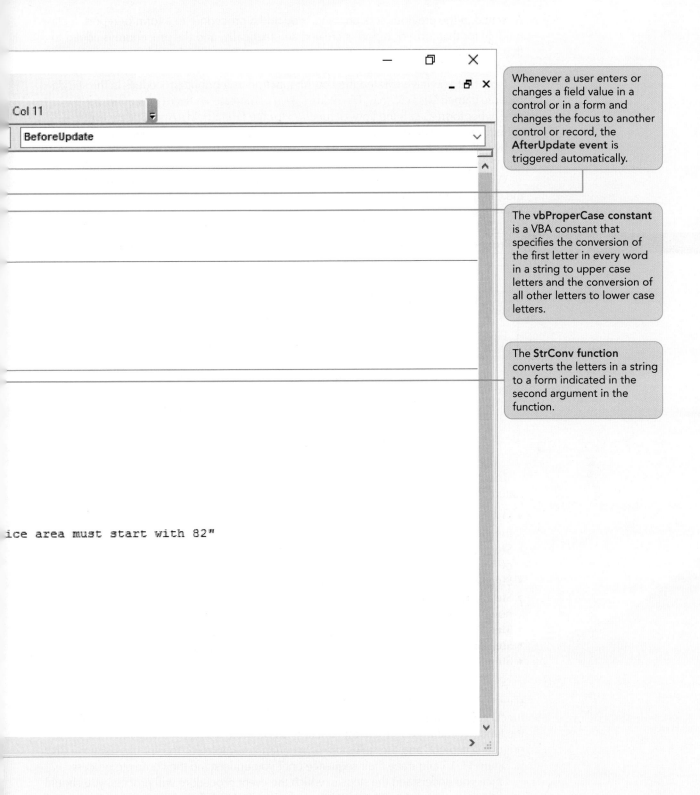

Col 11

BeforeUpdate

ice area must start with 82"

Whenever a user enters or changes a field value in a control or in a form and changes the focus to another control or record, the **AfterUpdate event** is triggered automatically.

The **vbProperCase constant** is a VBA constant that specifies the conversion of the first letter in every word in a string to upper case letters and the conversion of all other letters to lower case letters.

The **StrConv function** converts the letters in a string to a form indicated in the second argument in the function.

Understanding How an Event Procedure Processes

As stated in the previous session, when you add a procedure to a form or report, a class module for that form or report is created automatically, and the procedure is added to that class module. When you create an event procedure, the procedure runs only when a specific event occurs.

Now that you have created the LowAll function as a public procedure in the standard module named basVeterinaryProcedures, you can create an event procedure for the frmOwner form to call the LowAll function for the Email field's AfterUpdate event. Whenever a user enters or changes an Email field value, the AfterUpdate event occurs, so by calling the LowAll function for the Email field's AfterUpdate event, you'll ensure that your event procedure will run whenever this field has a new or changed value.

What exactly happens when a procedure is called? There is an interaction between the calling statement and the function statements. Figure 11-15 shows the process for the LowAll procedure.

| Figure 11-15 | Process of executing the AfterUpdate event procedure for the Email field |

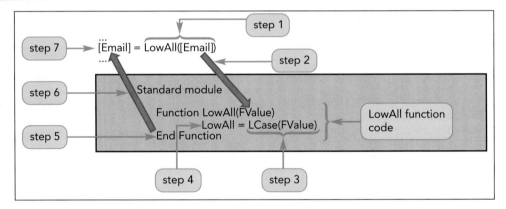

The steps in Figure 11-15 are numbered in the order in which they occur as the statement and the function are processed. These steps are as follows:

- **Step 1:** The call to the function LowAll passes the value of the argument [Email] to the function. This is the value of the Email field that is entered or changed by the user.
- **Step 2:** The function LowAll begins, and the parameter FValue receives the value of [Email].
- **Step 3:** FValue is changed to lower case.
- **Step 4:** The result of function is assigned to the name of the function (LowAll). This is how the result will be returned from the function when the function completes.
- **Step 5:** The function LowAll ends.
- **Step 6:** The value of LowAll is returned to the point of the call to the function.
- **Step 7:** The value of [Email] is set equal to the returned value of LowAll.

Although it might look complicated, the general function process is simple. The statement contains a **function call**, which is a statement that contains the name of the function plus any parameters required by the function. When the statement is executed, the function call is performed, the function is executed, a single value is returned to the original statement, and the statement's execution is completed. You should study the steps in Figure 11-15 and trace their sequence until you understand the complete process.

Once you understand the steps in which the event procedure will process, you should consider how to construct the event procedure in the VB Editor. All event procedures are Sub procedures. The VB editor automatically adds the Sub and End Sub statements to an event procedure. All you need to do is place the statements between the Sub and End Sub statements. Figure 11-16 shows the completed event procedure in the Code window.

Figure 11-16   AfterUpdate event procedure for the Email field

In reviewing the completed event procedure in Figure 11-16, notice the following. Each event procedure is named in a standard way, using the name of the control, an underscore (_), and the event name. No parameters are passed to an event procedure, so nothing is placed in the parentheses following the name of the Sub procedure.

A user might delete an existing Email field value so that it contains no value, or becomes null. In this case, calling the function accomplishes nothing. The procedure is designed to call the LowAll function only when a user changes the Email field to a value that is not null. The If statement screens out the null values. In its simplest form, an **If statement** executes one of two groups of statements based on a condition, similar to common English usage. For example, consider the English statements, "If the door is unlocked, I'll open it and walk through it. Otherwise, I'll knock on the door and wait until someone unlocks it." In these sentences, the two groups of statements come before and after the "otherwise," depending on the condition, "if the door is unlocked." The first group of statements consists of the clause "I'll open it and walk through it." This clause is called the **true-statement group** because it's what happens if the condition ("the door is unlocked") is true. The second group of statements contains "I'll knock on the door and wait until someone unlocks it." This clause is called the **false-statement group** because it is what happens if the condition is false. VBA uses the keyword *If* to precede the condition. The keyword *Then* precedes the true-statement group, and the keyword *Else* precedes the false-statement group. The general syntax of a VBA If statement is:

```
If condition Then
    true-statement group
[Else
    false-statement group]
End If
```

The true-statement group executes when the condition is true, and the false-statement group when the condition is false. In this statement's syntax, the bracketed portions are optional. Therefore, you must omit the *Else* and its related false-statement group when you want a group of statements to execute only when the condition is true.

In Figure 11-16, the If statement uses the VBA **IsNull function**, which returns a value of True when the Email field value is null and False when it is not null. The *Not* in the If statement is the same logical operator you've used previously to negate an expression. So, the statement *[Email] = LowAll([Email])* executes only when the Email field value is not null.

Adding an Event Procedure

To add an event procedure to a control in a form or report, you need to open the form or report in Design view. In this case, you need to add an event procedure to the frmOwner form, specifically to the Email field's AfterUpdate event property.

REFERENCE

Adding an Event Procedure to a Form or Report

- Open the form or report in Design view, select the control whose event property you want to set, open the Property Sheet for the control, and then click the Event tab in the Property Sheet.
- Click the appropriate event property box, click its Build button, click Code Builder in the Choose Builder dialog box, and then click the OK button to open the Code window in the VB editor.
- Enter the Sub procedure statements in the Code window.
- Compile the procedure, fix any statement errors, and then save the event procedure.

Next you'll add the event procedure to the frmOwner form.

To add the event procedure to the frmOwner form:

1. If you took a break after the previous session, make sure that the Veterinary database is open.

2. Open the Navigation Pane (if necessary), open the **frmOwner** form in Design view, and then close the Navigation Pane.

3. Right-click the **Email** field value box to select it and to display the shortcut menu, click **Properties** to open the Property Sheet, and then, if necessary, click the **Event** tab in the Property Sheet. You need to set the AfterUpdate property for the Email field value box.

   Trouble? If you do not see any events on the Event tab, you might have clicked on the Email label control instead of the field value box. Right-click the Email field value box.

4. Click the **After Update** box, click its **Build** button ⋯ to open the Choose Builder dialog box, click **Code Builder**, and then click the **OK** button. The Code window opens in the Visual Basic window. See Figure 11-17.

Figure 11-17   Starting a new event procedure in the Code window

5. Enter the statements shown in Figure 11-18, using the Tab key to indent the lines as shown in the figure (if necessary), pressing the Enter key at the end of each line, and pressing the Backspace key to move one tab stop to the left.

Figure 11-18	Completed event procedure

```
Microsoft Visual Basic for Applications - Veterinary - [Form_frmOwner (Code)]

File   Edit   View   Insert   Debug   Run   Tools   Add-Ins   Window

Email

Option Compare Database

Private Sub Email_AfterUpdate()
    'Convert the Email to lower case
    If Not IsNull([Email]) Then
        [Email] = LowAll([Email])
    End If
End Sub
```

▶ **6.** Compare your screen with Figure 11-18, and make any necessary corrections by selecting the errors and typing the corrections.

Before saving the event procedure, you'll compile the module.

Compiling Modules

The VBA programming language is not the computer's native language. Although you can learn VBA and become fluent in it, computers cannot understand or learn VBA. For a computer to understand the statements in your VBA modules, the statements must be translated into a form that the computer processor can use. The process of translating modules from VBA to a form your computer processor understands is called **compilation**; you say that you **compile** the module when you translate it.

You can compile a procedure at any time as you enter it by clicking the Compile command on the Debug menu in the Visual Basic window. The procedure and all other procedures in all modules in the database are then compiled. Also, when you run a procedure for the first time, the procedure is compiled automatically, and a dialog box will open if any syntax errors exist in the procedure, in which case the computer cannot translate the procedure statements. If no errors are detected, the procedure translates.

You'll now compile the procedures in the Veterinary database and save the class module for the frmOwner form.

> **To compile the procedures in the Veterinary database and save the class module:**
>
> ▶ **1.** Click **Debug** on the menu bar, and then click **Compile Veterinary**. The modules in the database are compiled. Because you have no syntax errors, the VBA statements translate.
>
>   **Trouble?** If any error messages appear, correct the errors in the Code window and repeat Step 1.
>
> ▶ **2.** Save your module changes, close the Visual Basic window, and then close the Property Sheet.

You have created the function and the event procedure and have set the event property. Next, you'll test the event procedure in the frmOwner form to make sure it works correctly.

Testing an Event Procedure

You need to display the frmOwner form in Form view to test the Email field's event procedure by entering a few different test Email field values in the first record of the form. Moving the focus to another control in the form or to another record triggers the AfterUpdate event for the Email field and executes the attached event procedure. Because the LowAll function is attached only to the frmOwner form, the automatic conversion to lower case of Email field values is not in effect when you enter them in the tblOwner table or in any other object in the Veterinary database.

> **To test the event procedure:**
>
> ▶ **1.** Switch to Form view, and navigate to record 2, Owner ID 2314.
>
> ▶ **2.** Click in the empty **Email** box, type **SCRUZ@EXAMPLE.COM** and then press the **Tab** key. The AfterUpdate event procedure for the Email field executes, and the Email box displays "scruz@example.com." See Figure 11-19.

Figure 11-19   frmOwner form after executing the event procedure

Figure 11-19   frmOwner form after executing the event procedure

lower case Email field value

3. Repeat Step 2 again, this time entering **SCruz@Example.com** in the Email box. The correct value of scruz@example.com is displayed in the Email box.

Kimberly is happy with the functionality you've added to the Email box. Next she wants you to create a more complex function for the Zip field in the frmOwner form.

Adding a Second Procedure to a Class Module

Kimberly has found that her staff makes frequent errors when entering Wyoming zip codes, whose first two digits are always 82 in the primary area the Riverview Veterinary Care Center serves. She asks you to create a procedure that will verify that Wyoming zip codes are in the correct range (beginning with 82) when her staff updates the Zip field in the frmOwner form. One option is to use a form validation rule, but Kimberly would like to be able to add complexity later, to validate other zip codes as owners from other areas in Wyoming and other states may visit the care center. Also, Kimberly would like to be able to use this VBA code in other databases. If the validation property is used in the tblOwner table instead of using VBA, then this validation rule would have to be re-created in another database. Instead, by creating an event procedure, Kimberly will be able to copy the VBA code and paste it into another VBA window in another database.

You'll build a simple procedure that can be modified later to add more complexity. For this procedure, you will use an event procedure attached to the BeforeUpdate event for the frmOwner form. The BeforeUpdate event occurs before changed data in a control or a record is updated. You'll use the form's BeforeUpdate event for this new procedure because you want to find data-entry errors for Wyoming zip codes and alert users to the errors before the database is updated.

Designing the Field Validation Procedure

Figure 11-20 shows the procedure that you will create to verify Wyoming zip codes for the area that the Riverview Veterinary Care Center primarily serves. You've already seen several of the statements in this procedure in your work with the LowAll function and with the form's Current event.

Figure 11-20	Zip validation procedure

The Sub and End Sub statements begin and end the Sub procedure. As specified in the Sub statement, the Sub procedure executes when the form's BeforeUpdate event occurs. Within parentheses in the Sub statement, *Cancel As Integer* defines Cancel as a parameter with the Integer data type. VBA has data types that are different from the Access data types you've used to define table fields, but each Access data type is equivalent to one of the VBA data types. For example, the Access Number data type with an Integer field size is the same as the VBA Integer data type, and the Access Short Text data type is the same as the VBA String data type. Figure 11-21 shows the primary VBA data types.

Figure 11-21	Primary VBA data types

Data Type	Stores
Boolean	True/False values
Byte	Integer values from 0 to 255
Currency	Currency values from –922,337,203,685,477.5808 to 922,337,203,685,477.5807
Date	Date and time values from 1 January 100 to 31 December 9999
Decimal	Non-integer values with 0 to 28 decimal places
Double	Non-integer values from $-1.79769313486231*10^{308}$ to $-4.94065645841247*11^{-324}$ for negative values, from $4.94065645841247*11^{-324}$ to $1.79769313486232*10^{308}$ for positive values, and 0
Integer	Integer values from –32,768 to 32,767
Long	Integer values from –2,147,483,648 to 2,147,483,647
Object	Any object reference
Single	Non-integer values from $-3.402823*10^{38}$ to $-1.401298*11^{-45}$ for negative values, from $1.401298*11^{-45}$ to $3.402823*10^{38}$ for positive values, and 0
String	Text values up to 2 billion characters in length
Variant	Any numeric or string data type

When an event occurs, the default behavior for the event is performed. For some events, such as the BeforeUpdate event, the event procedure or macro executes before performing the default behavior. Thus, if something is wrong and the default behavior should not occur, you can cancel the default behavior in the event procedure or macro. For this reason, the Cancel parameter is automatically included for the BeforeUpdate event.

The second procedure statement, which starts with a single quotation mark, is a comment. The third statement, *Dim ZipFirstTwo As String*, declares the String variable named ZipFirstTwo that the Sub procedure uses. A **variable** is a named location in computer memory that can contain a value. If you use a variable in a module, you must explicitly declare it in the Declarations section or in the procedure where the variable is used. You use the **Dim statement** to declare variables and their associated data types in a procedure. The Sub procedure will assign the first two digits of a zip code (the Zip field) to the ZipFirstTwo variable and then use the variable when verifying that a Wyoming zip code the care center primarily serves begins in the correct range. Because the zip code could contain a value that begins with zero (0), the ZipFirstTwo variable uses the String data type instead of a numeric data type. The first two characters of any zip code for Wyoming area primarily served by the care center are represented as the string value "82".

The procedure should not attempt to verify records that contain null field values for the State field and the Zip field. To screen out these conditions, the procedure uses the fourth procedure statement, *If Not IsNull([State]) And Not IsNull([Zip]) Then*, which pairs with the last *End If* statement. The *If* statement determines whether both the State and Zip fields are nonnull. If both conditions are true (both fields contain values), then the next statement in the procedure executes. If either condition is false, then the paired End If statement executes, and the following End Sub statement ends the procedure without the execution of any other statement.

The fifth procedure statement, *ZipFirstTwo = Left([Zip], 2)*, uses a built-in VBA function, the Left function, to assign the first two characters of the Zip field value to the ZipFirstTwo variable. The Left function returns a string containing a specified number of characters from the left side of a specified string. In this case, the Left function returns the leftmost two characters of the Zip field value.

You encountered the Case control structure previously in the frmVisit form's Current event procedure. For the BeforeUpdate event procedure, the *Select Case [State]* statement evaluates the State field value. For a State field value equal to WY (indicating the record should have a Wyoming zip code), the next If statement is executed. For all other State field values, nothing further in the procedure is executed; the default behavior is performed, and control returns back to the form for further processing. The procedure uses the Case control structure because although Kimberly wants the procedure to verify the first two characters of only Wyoming zip codes for now, she might want to expand the procedure in the future to verify the first two digits of zip codes for other areas of Wyoming and other states as Riverview Veterinary Care Center expands its services.

Because valid Wyoming zip codes in the area the care center serves begin with "82", invalid values for the Zip field will not be equal to "82". The not equals operator in VBA is <> (less than symbol followed by the greater than symbol). The next VBA statement, *If ZipFirstTwo <> "82" Then*, is true only for invalid Wyoming zip codes. When the If statement is true, the next four statements are executed. When the If statement is false, nothing further in the procedure is executed, the default behavior performs, and control returns back to the form for further processing.

The first of the four VBA statements that executes for invalid Wyoming zip codes is the DoCmd statement. The DoCmd statement executes an action in a procedure. The *DoCmd.CancelEvent* statement executes the CancelEvent action. The CancelEvent action cancels the event that caused the procedure or macro containing the action to execute. In this case, the BeforeUpdate event cancels and does not update the database with the changes to the current record. In addition, subsequent events are canceled that would have occurred if the BeforeUpdate event had not been canceled. For example, in addition to the form's BeforeUpdate event being triggered when you move to a different record, the following events are also triggered when you move to a different record, in the order listed: BeforeUpdate event for the form, AfterUpdate event for the form, Exit event for the control with the focus, LostFocus event for the control with the focus, RecordExit event for the form, and Current event for the form. When the CancelEvent action is executed, all these events are canceled, and the focus remains with the record being edited.

The second of the four VBA statements that are executed for invalid Wyoming zip codes is the MsgBox statement. The *MsgBox "Wyoming zip codes for our service area must start with 82"* statement displays its message in a message box that remains on the screen until the user clicks the OK button. The message box appears on top of the frmOwner form so the user can view the changed field values in the current record.

For invalid Wyoming zip codes, after the user clicks the OK button in the message box, the *Me.Undo* statement is executed. The Me keyword refers to the current object—in this case, the frmOwner form. Undo is a method that clears all changes made to the current record in the frmOwner form, so that the field values in the record return to the way they were before the user made the current changes. A **method** is an action that operates on specific objects or controls.

Finally, for invalid Wyoming zip codes, the *[Zip].SetFocus* statement is executed. SetFocus is a method that moves the focus to the specified object or control. In this case, the focus is moved to the Zip field in the current record in the frmOwner form.

Adding a Field Value Event Procedure

You can now add an event procedure for the frmOwner form's BeforeUpdate event property that will execute whenever field values in a record are entered or updated.

To add the event procedure for the frmOwner form's BeforeUpdate event property:

▶ 1. Switch to Design view, open the **Property Sheet** for the frmOwner form, and then if necessary, click the **Event** tab in the Property Sheet.

▶ 2. Click the **Before Update** box, click the **Before Update** arrow, click **[Event Procedure]**, and then click the **Build** button ⟦···⟧. The Code window, which contains new Private Sub and End Sub statements, opens in the Visual Basic window. Horizontal lines separate the Option Compare statement from the new procedure and from the AfterUpdate event procedure you entered earlier.

▶ 3. Press the **Tab** key, and then type the Sub procedure statements exactly as shown in Figure 11-22. Press the **Enter** key after you enter each statement, press the **Tab** key to indent lines as necessary, and press the **Backspace** key to move the insertion point one tab stop to the left. When you are finished, your screen should look like Figure 11-22.

Figure 11-22   Event procedure for the fromOwner form's BeforeUpdate event

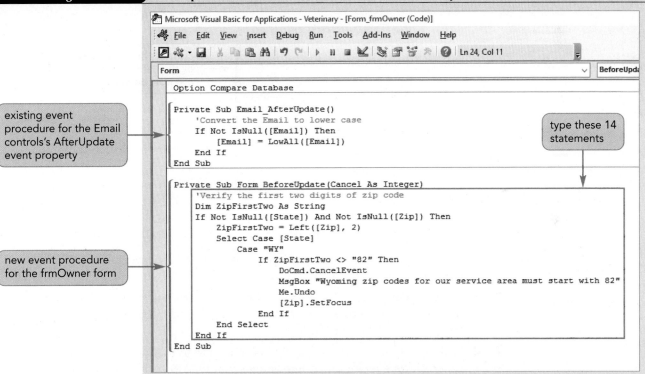

existing event procedure for the Email controls's AfterUpdate event property

type these 14 statements

new event procedure for the frmOwner form

▶ 4. On the menu bar, click **Debug**, and then click **Compile Veterinary** to compile all the modules in the Veterinary database.

   Trouble? If a message box appears identifying an error, click the OK button in the message box, compare your Code window with the one shown in Figure 11-22, make any necessary corrections, and then repeat Step 4 to scan the statements for errors again and to compile the module.

▶ 5. Save your class module changes.

▶ 6. Close the Visual Basic window to return to the Form window, and then close the Property Sheet.

You can now test the BeforeUpdate event procedure. To do so, you'll switch to Form view and enter valid and invalid Zip field values in the frmOwner form.

To test the form's BeforeUpdate event procedure:

1. Switch to Form view with the form displaying record 1. The first two digits of the Zip field value, 82, represent a valid Wyoming zip code.

TIP

You must navigate to another record to trigger a form's BeforeUpdate event procedure.

2. Select **82414** in the Zip box, type **12345**, press the **Tab** key to move to the Email box, and then click the **Next record** button ▶ to move to the next record. The BeforeUpdate event procedure for the frmOwner form executes and determines that the Wyoming zip code's first two digits are incorrect and displays the message box you included in the procedure. See Figure 11-23.

Figure 11-23   **Message box in the frmOwner form indicating an error**

While the message box is displayed, the updated Zip field value of 12345 remains on screen for you to review.

3. Click the **OK** button. The message box closes, the Undo method changes the Zip field value to 82414 (its original value), and the SetFocus method moves the focus to the Zip box.

4. With the Zip field value set to **82414**, navigate to the next record. The form's BeforeUpdate event procedure verifies that the zip code is a valid value for a Wyoming owner in the service area, and the focus moves to the Zip box for the next record.

5. Navigate back to record 1, change the State field value to **TX**, change the Zip field value to **12345**, and then click the **Next record** button ▶ to move to the next record. The form's BeforeUpdate event procedure checks zip codes only when the State field value is "WY" (Wyoming), so even though the zip code 12345 is not valid for Texas (abbreviated TX), the focus moves to the Zip box in the next record anyway.

Next, you'll change the first record's State field value to WY and the Zip field value to 82414, which are the original values for the record.

6. Navigate to the first record, change the State field value to **WY**, and then change the Zip field value to **82414**.

Kimberly is impressed with the zip code validation you've added to the frmOwner form. She has one additional procedure she wants you to create for the form.

Adding an Event Procedure to Change the Case of a Field Value

Kimberly wants to make it quicker for users to enter an address when using the frmOwner form, so she asks you to create a procedure that will automatically convert the case of letters entered in the Address field. This procedure will capitalize the first letter of each word in the field and change all other letters to lower case. For example, if a user enters "12 mAin sT" as the Address field value, the event procedure will correct the field value to "12 Main St".

You'll use an event procedure attached to the AfterUpdate event for the Address field to perform this automatic conversion. You'll use the StrConv function in the event procedure to perform the conversion. The **StrConv function** converts the letters in a string to all upper case letters or to all lower case letters, or converts the first letter of every word in the string to upper case letters and all other letters to lower case letters, which is a pattern known as proper case. The StrConv function ignores numbers. The statement you'll use in the event procedure is *[Address] = StrConv([Address], vbProperCase)*. The StrConv function's second argument, the **vbProperCase constant**, is a VBA constant that specifies the conversion of the first letter in every word in a string to upper case letters and the conversion of all other letters to lower case letters. Recall that the LowAll function you created earlier in this tutorial used the statement *LowAll = LCase(FValue)* to convert every character in a string to lower case. You could also have used the statement *LowAll = StrConv(FValue, vbLower case)* to accomplish the same result. Other VBA constants you can use with the StrConv function are the **vbUpperCase constant**, which specifies the conversion of the string to all upper case letters, and the **vbLower case constant**, which specifies the conversion of the string to all lower case letters.

Next, you'll create the AfterUpdate event procedure for the Address field in the frmOwner form to perform the automatic conversion of entered and updated Address field values.

To add the event procedure for the Address field's AfterUpdate event:

▶ **1.** Switch to Design view.

▶ **2.** Right-click the **Address** field value box to display the shortcut menu, and then click **Properties** to open the Property Sheet for the control.

▶ **3.** If necessary, click the **Event** tab in the Property Sheet.

▶ **4.** Click the **After Update** box, click the **After Update** arrow, click **[Event Procedure]**, and then click the **Build** button [**...**]. The Code window, which contains new Private Sub and End Sub statements, opens in the Visual Basic window. The Code window also contains two other event procedures defined in the form's class module: one event procedure for the form's BeforeUpdate event, and another event procedure for the Email field's AfterUpdate event.

▶ **5.** Press the **Tab** key, and then type the Sub procedure statements exactly as shown in Figure 11-24.

Figure 11-24   **Event procedure for the Address control's AfterUpdate event**

type these three statements

```
Option Compare Database

Private Sub Address_AfterUpdate()
    'Capitalize the first letter of all words
    'Convert all other letters to lower case
    [Address] = StrConv([Address], vbProperCase)
End Sub
```

6. Click **Debug** on the menu bar, click **Compile Veterinary**, save your class module changes, close the Visual Basic window, and then close the Property Sheet.

You can now test the event procedure. To do so, you'll view the frmOwner form in Form view and test the Address field's event procedure by entering different Address field values.

To test the new event procedure for the Address field:

1. Switch to Form view. You'll test the new event procedure by entering Address field values in record 1.

2. Select the current value in Address box, type **12 elm ln** and then press the **Enter** key. The AfterUpdate event procedure for the Address field executes and changes the Address field value to "12 Elm Ln".

3. Repeat Step 2 two more times, entering **12 eLM lN** (correctly changed to "12 Elm Ln"), and then entering **12 ELM LN** (correctly changed to "12 Elm Ln").

4. Close the form.

Hiding a Control and Changing a Control's Color

Kimberly wants you to add a message to the frmVisitsAndInvoices form that will remind her staff when a visit record should be considered for archiving from the tblVisit table. Specifically, when the visit date is prior to the year 2017, Kimberly wants the VisitDate field value displayed in red; all other VisitDate field values should be displayed in black. She also wants to display a message to the right of the VisitDate box in red only when the visit is a candidate for archiving. The red font will help to draw attention to these visit records. Figure 11-25 shows a preview of the formatting she's requesting.

Figure 11-25   **Archive message and red VisitDate field value in frmVisitsAndInvoices form**

In the frmVisitsAndInvoices form, you will add a label to the right of the VisitDate field value box that will display the text "Archive if paid?" in red. Because Kimberly wants the text to appear only when the VisitDate field has a value earlier than 1/1/2017, you will change the label's Visible property during execution. You will also change the foreground color of the value in the VisitDate field value box to red when the VisitDate field value is earlier than 1/1/2017 and to black for all other dates.

Because the change to the Visible property takes place during execution, you will add code to the Current event procedure in the frmVisitsAndInvoices form. To set a property in a VBA statement, you enter the object name followed by a period and the property name. For example, if the label name for the message is lblArchiveMsg, then the statement *lblArchiveMsg.Visible = False* hides the label on the form.

Problem Solving: Using Sample Code from Other Sources

Creating your first few VBA procedures from scratch can be a daunting task. To get started, you should take advantage of the available resources that discuss various ways of designing and programming commonly encountered situations. These resources include the sample databases available from Microsoft, Access VBA books, periodicals, websites that provide sample code, and Access Help. These resources contain sample procedures and code segments, often with commentary about what the procedures and statements accomplish and why. However, when you create a procedure, you are responsible for knowing what it does, how it does it, when to use it, how to enhance it in the future, and how to fix it when problems occur. If you simply copy statements from another source without thoroughly understanding them, you won't be able to enhance or fix the procedure in the future. In addition, you might overlook better ways to accomplish the same thing—better because the procedure would run faster or would be easier to enhance. In some cases, the samples you find might be flawed, so that they won't work properly for you. The time you spend researching and completely understanding sample code will pay dividends in your learning experience to create VBA procedures.

PROSKILLS

First, you'll add a label to the frmVisitsAndInvoices form that will display a message in red for each value that has a VisitDate field value earlier than 1/1/2017. For all other dates, the label will be hidden.

To add the label to the frmVisitsAndInvoices form:

1. Open the Navigation Pane, open the **frmVisitsAndInvoices** form in Design view, and then close the Navigation Pane.

2. On the Form Design Tools Design tab, in the Controls group, click the **Label** tool $\boxed{Aa}$.

3. In the Detail section, position the plus symbol of the Label tool pointer two grid dots to the right of the VisitDate field value box, and then click the mouse button.

4. Type **Archive if paid?** and then press the **Enter** key. The new label control appears in the form and displays the Error Checking Options button. See Figure 11-26.

Figure 11-26	Label control added to the form

Trouble? If you do not see the Error Checking Options button, error checking is disabled in Access. Click the File tab, click Options in the navigation bar, click Object Designers, scroll down the page, click the Enable error checking check box to add a checkmark to it, click the OK button, click a blank area in the form, and then click the "Archive if paid?" label control. Continue with Step 5.

5. Position the pointer on the **Error Checking Options** button ⚠ ▾. The message "This is a new label and is not associated with a control" appears. Because the new label should not be associated with a control, you'll choose to ignore this error.

6. Click the **Error Checking Options arrow** ⚠ ▾, and then click **Ignore Error**. The Error Checking Options button disappears.

7. Press and hold the **Shift key**, click the **VisitDate** field value box to select this control and its label control, release the **Shift** key, right-click one of the selected controls, point to **Align**, and then click **Top** to top-align the selected controls.

Trouble? If the Error Checking Options button appears, click the Error Checking Options button arrow, and then click Dismiss Error.

You'll now set the label control's Name and ForeColor properties, and you'll add the Current event procedure to the frmVisitsAndInvoices form.

To set the label's properties and add the Current event procedure to the form:

1. Deselect all controls, right-click the **Archive if paid?** label control to display the shortcut menu, and then click **Properties** to open the Property Sheet.

2. Click the **All** tab (if necessary), and then set the Name property for the Archive if paid? label control to **lblArchiveMsg**.

You can now set the ForeColor property for the label so that the message is displayed in red.

3. Click the **Fore Color** box, and then click its **Build** button ⋯ to display the color gallery.

4. Click the **Red** color (row 7, column 2 in the Standard Colors palette), and then press the **Enter** key. The ForeColor property value is set to the code for red (#ED1C24), and in the form it now appears in red.

Next you will enter the event procedure for the form's Current event. This event procedure will execute whenever the frmVisitsAndInvoices form is opened or the focus moves from one record to another.

5. Select the form, scroll down the Property Sheet to the On Current box, click the **On Current** box, click the **On Current** arrow, click [**Event Procedure**], and then click the **Build** button ⋯ to open the Code window in the Visual Basic window, displaying the Sub and End Sub statements.

6. Press the **Tab** key, and then type the Sub procedure statements exactly as shown in Figure 11-27.

| Figure 11-27 | Current event procedure for the frmVisitsAndInvoices form |

type these comments

type this statement

```
Microsoft Visual Basic for Applications - Veterinary - [Form_frmVisitsAndInvoices (Code)]
File   Edit   View   Insert   Debug   Run   Tools   Add-Ins   Window   Help
                                                          Ln 12, Col 11

Form                                                                    Current

Option Compare Database

Private Sub Form_Current()
    'For older visits, display a message and the VisitDate field value in red
    'For all other visits, display the VisitDate field value in black without a message
    If VisitDate < #1/1/2017# Then
        lblArchiveMsg.Visible = True
        VisitDate.ForeColor = vbRed
    Else
        lblArchiveMsg.Visible = False
        VisitDate.ForeColor = vbBlack
    End If
End Sub
```

The form's Current procedure uses an If statement to determine whether the current value of the VisitDate field is less than 1/1/2017. If the current value of the VisitDate field is less than 1/1/2017, the procedure sets the lblArchiveMsg control's Visible property to True (which means the "Archive if paid?" message will appear in the frmVisitsAndInvoices form), and it sets the VisitDate control's ForeColor property to vbRed (red). If the current value of the VisitDate field is greater than 1/1/2017, the procedure sets the lblArchiveMsg control's Visible property to False, hiding the message in the form, and sets the VisitDate control's ForeColor property to vbBlack.

▶ **7.** Click **Debug** on the menu bar, and then click **Compile Veterinary** to compile all the modules in the Veterinary database.

▶ **8.** Save your class module changes, close the Visual Basic window, and then close the Property Sheet.

You'll now test the frmVisitsAndInvoices form's Current event procedure.

To test the Current event procedure for the frmVisitsAndInvoices form:

▶ **1.** Switch to Form view. The first record for VisitID 1002 displays in the form with the Date of Visit date prior to 1/1/2017. The "Archive if paid?" message appears in red, as does the VisitDate field value of 11/8/2016.

Trouble? If a dialog box displays indicating a runtime error, the event procedure could not execute. Click the Debug button in the dialog box to open the event procedure in the Code window with the line containing the error highlighted. Check the statements carefully against those shown in Figure 11-27. Make the necessary changes so they match the figure exactly, compile the module, save the module, and then close the Code window. Then repeat Step 1.

▶ **2.** Navigate to the last record to display record 74 for Visit ID 1196, for which the visit date is 2/1/2017. The "Archive if paid?" message is not displayed, and the VisitDate field value is displayed in black.

▶ **3.** Close the form, make a backup copy of the database, compact and repair the database, and then close it.

Kimberly is pleased with the modifications you have made to the forms using Visual Basic code. The forms will be easier for her staff to use and help to minimize errors.

REVIEW

Session 11.2 Quick Check

1. The VBA _____ statement executes one of two groups of statements based on a condition.

2. What happens when you compile a module?

3. What is the purpose of the Dim statement?

4. The _____ function returns a value of true if the field value is empty and false if the field value is not empty.

5. What is the purpose of the DoCmd statement?

6. What is a method?

7. What is a VBA constant?

8. You can use the UCase function or the _____ function to convert a string to all upper case letters.

9. What does the Visible property determine?

10. What does the ForeColor property determine?

PRACTICE

Review Assignments

Data File needed for the Review Assignments: Ordering.accdb (*cont. from Module 10*)

Kimberly asks you to continue your work on the Ordering database by enhancing the usability of the frmSuppliersWithProducts form and the frmSupplier form. To help with this request, complete the following steps:

1. Open the **Ordering** database you worked with in the previous two modules.
2. Create an event procedure on the AfterUpdate event for the frmSuppliersWithProducts form to convert Company field values to proper case—capitalize the first letter of each word, and convert all other letters to lower case. Test the procedure, and then close the form.
3. Create an event procedure on the Current event for the frmSuppliersWithProducts form to do the following:
   a. Display the InitialContact field value in red when the date is March 1, 2017, or later, and in black for earlier dates.
   b. Display the message **Newer Supplier** to the right of the InitialContact box in red text. Display the message only when the InitialContact field value is March 1, 2017, or later. Use **lblSupplierMsg** as the name of the new label control to contain the message.
   c. Test the procedure, and then save and close the form.
4. Create a user-defined function called **CapAll** that will accept one argument called **FValue**, convert it to upper case, and return the upper case value back to the instruction that called it. (*Hint*: Use the UCase function to convert characters to upper case.) Store this user-defined function in a standard module called **basProductProcedures**.
5. In the frmSupplier form, create an event procedure on the AfterUpdate event for the State field that will convert the characters to upper case only if the field value box is not empty. Call the CapAll function to perform the character conversion.
6. Make a backup copy of the database, compact and repair the Product database, and then close the database.

Case Problem 1

APPLY

Data File needed for this Case Problem: Salon.accdb (*cont. from Module 10*)

Beauty To Go Sue Miller asks you to continue your work on the Salon database by enhancing the frmMemberInfo and frmOptionsWithMembers forms. To help Sue with her request, complete the following steps:

1. Open the **Salon** database you worked with in the previous two modules.
2. Create an event procedure in the frmMemberInfo form for the FirstName field's AfterUpdate event to convert the FirstName field values to proper case—capitalize the first letter of each word, and convert all other letters to lower case. Test the procedure.
3. Create an event procedure in the frmMemberInfo form for the form's OnCurrent event to do the following:
   a. If the OptionEnd field value is earlier than May 1, 2017, display the words "Time to renew" in a label control named lblRenewMsg just below the OptionEnd box in bold and red, and display the text in the OptionEnd field value control in red.
   b. No special action is required for other OptionEnd field values.
   c. Test the procedure, and then save your form changes.

4. Create an event procedure in the frmOptionsWithMembers form for the form's Current event to do the following:

   a. If the fee has been waived for the option, display the words "Fee Waived" in red in a label control named lblFeeWaivedMsg to the right of the FeeWaived check box.

   b. No special action is required if the fee for the option is not waived.

   c. Test the procedure, and then save your form changes.

5. Make a backup copy of the database, compact and repair the database, and then close it.

Case Problem 2

Data File needed for this Case Problem: Technology.accdb (*cont. from Module 10*)

Programming Pros   Brent Hovis wants you to continue your work on the Technology database by enhancing the frmTutorInfo, frmStudent, and frmContract forms. To help Brent with his request, complete the following steps:

1. Open the **Technology** database you worked with in the previous two modules.

2. Create an event procedure for the frmTutorInfo form for the AfterUpdate event on the School field to convert School field values to proper case—capitalize the first letter of each word, and convert all other letters to lower case. Test the procedure, and then close the form.

✪ **Explore** 3. In the frmStudent form, create an event procedure for the form's BeforeUpdate event to verify the Zip field values by doing the following:

   a. For a State field value of NC in the area surrounding Raleigh, NC, the first two digits of the Zip field value must equal 27. If the Zip field value is invalid, display an appropriate message, cancel the event, undo the change, and move the focus to the Zip field.

   b. No special action is required for other Zip field values.

   c. Test the procedure, and then save your form changes.

✪ **Explore** 4. In the frmContract form, create an event procedure for the form's Current event for the to do the following:

   a. Display the SessionType field value in a bold, blue text when the value is "Private" and in normal, black text for all other values. (*Hint*: Use the FontBold property set with the value True for bold or False for not bold, and use the color vbBlue for blue.)

   b. Display the message "Small study room" to the right of the SessionType box in a label control called lblSessionTypeMsg, in bold, blue text only when the SessionType field value is "Private".

   c. Test the procedure, and then save your form changes.

5. Make a backup copy of the database, compact and repair the database, and then close it.

Case Problem 3

Data File needed for this Case Problem: Thrift.accdb (*cont. from Module 10*)

Diane's Community Center   Diane Coleman wants you to continue working on the Thrift database by improving the usability of the frmPatronInfo form. To help with her request, complete the following steps:

1. Open the **Thrift** database you worked with in the previous two modules.

2. Create a standard module in the Thrift database called **basThriftProcedures** that contains a function called LowAll that is passed a single string argument as input, converts the value of the argument to lower case letters, and returns the converted value.

3. Using the LowAll function created in the previous step, create an event procedure for the AfterUpdate event for the frmPatronInfo form's Email field to convert the values to lower case. Test the procedure.

CHALLENGE

CHALLENGE

✛ **Explore** 4. In the frmPatronDonations form, create an event procedure for the form's Current event to do the following:

    a. Display the calculated field value (the donation total) in bold, red text when the value is greater than $500 and in regular, black text otherwise. (*Hint*: Use the FontBold property with the value True for bold or False for not bold.)

    b. Display the message "Special donor" below the calculated field box in a label control called lblDonorMsg, in bold, red text only when the calculated field value is greater than $500.

    c. Test the procedure, and then save your form design changes.

  5. Make a backup copy of the database, compact and repair the database, and then close it.

Case Problem 4

TROUBLESHOOT

Data File needed for this Case Problem: BlueRidge.accdb (*cont. from Module 10*)

Hike Appalachia　Molly and Bailey Johnson ask you to continue your work on the BlueRidge database by enhancing the frmGuestInfo form's to increase its usability and improve its appearance. To help them with their request, complete the following steps:

1. Open the **BlueRidge** database you worked with in the previous two modules.

⚙ **Troubleshoot** 2. The event procedure for the frmHikerInfo form to convert the Email field values to all lower case letters is not working correctly. Test the procedure, and fix the event procedure code to convert the Email field values to lower case letters. (*Hint*: Is there a standard module for the BlueRidge database containing the definition of the LowAll function? A proper name for this standard module would be basBlueRidgeProcedures. If not, you need to create one with the LowAll function.) Save your form changes, and then test the procedure.

3. Create an event procedure for the form's OnCurrent event that converts the first name of the hiker to proper case. Save your form changes, and then test the procedure.

4. Create an event procedure for the form's OnCurrent event that converts the last name of the hiker to proper case. Save your form changes, and then test the procedure.

5. Make a backup copy of the database, compact and repair the database, and then close it.

Managing and Securing a Database

Administering the Veterinary Database

OBJECTIVES

Session 12.1
- Filter by form and apply an advanced filter/sort
- Save a filter as a query and apply the saved query as a filter
- Create a subquery
- Create a multivalued field

Session 12.2
- Create an Attachment field
- Use an AutoNumber field
- Save a database as a previous version
- Analyze a database's performance
- Link a database to a table in another database
- Update linked tables
- Split a database
- Encrypt a database with a password
- Set database properties and startup options

Case | *Riverview Veterinary Care Center*

Kimberly Johnson will be offering training sessions for staff members to learn how to use the Veterinary database. Before she begins these training sessions, she asks for your help in finalizing the Veterinary database. Your remaining work will apply advanced Access features for filtering, creating subqueries, and utilizing advanced field types in tables, such as multivalued fields and Attachment fields. In addition, you will learn about database management, database security, and maximizing the database's overall performance. You'll also set database startup options as a final step in the development of the Veterinary database.

STARTING DATA FILES

Access3 → **Module**

James Lock Bachelor Degree.docx
James Lock Expenses.xlsx
James Lock Master Degree.docx
Referral.accdb
Veterinary.accdb (*cont.*)

Review

Ads.accdb
Autoclave.xlsx
Autoclave_Specification_Sheet.pdf
Ordering.accdb (*cont.*)

Case1

NewOptions.accdb
Salon.accdb (*cont.*)

Case2

Bob_Smith_Bachelor_Degree.docx
Bob_Smith_C++_Certificate.pdf
Room.accdb
Technology.accdb (*cont.*)

Case3

Receipt2001.xlsx
Receipt2101.xlsx
StudentVolunteers.accdb
Thrift.accdb (*cont.*)

Case4

BlueRidge.accdb (*cont.*)
Singh_1.txt
Singh_2.txt

Session 12.1 Visual Overview:

The Degree field is defined as a multivalued field. A **multivalued field** is a lookup field that allows you to store more than one value in a field in each record.

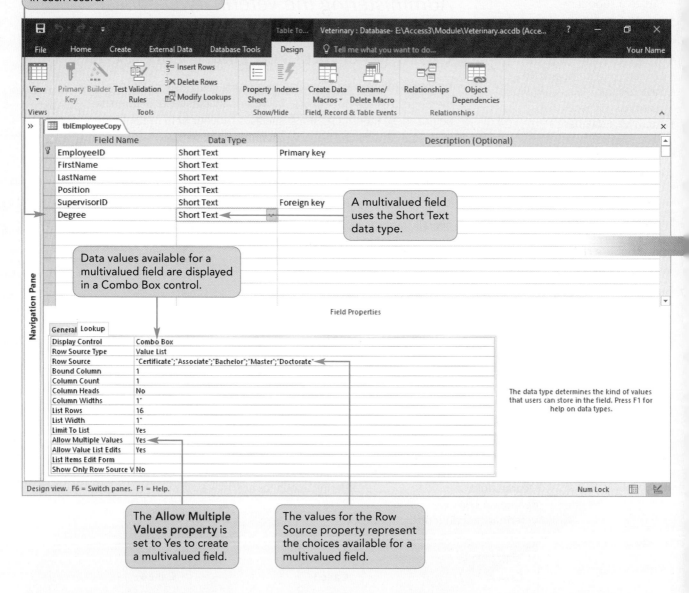

A multivalued field uses the Short Text data type.

Data values available for a multivalued field are displayed in a Combo Box control.

The **Allow Multiple Values property** is set to Yes to create a multivalued field.

The values for the Row Source property represent the choices available for a multivalued field.

Multivalued Fields and Subqueries

The Degree field in this query is the multivalued field.

Field values entered as a multivalued selection appear in a comma-separated list.

The values for the multivalued field contain check boxes to allow you to select more than one value.

When a multivalued field is selected an arrow appears, which when clicked, opens a list of options.

Additional Filtering Options

As you know, you can use a filter to temporarily display specified records from a table or form. In previous modules you used AutoFilter and Filter By Selection. Two additional filtering features in Access are Filter By Form and Advanced Filter/Sort.

Recall Filter By Form filters records that match multiple selection criteria using the same Access logical and comparison operators used in queries. After applying one of these filter tools, you can use the Sort Ascending or Sort Descending buttons in the Sort & Filter group on the Home tab to rearrange the records, if necessary.

Advanced Filter/Sort lets you specify multiple selection criteria and specify a sort order for selected records in the Filter window, in the same way you specify record selection criteria and sort orders for a query in Design view.

Kimberly needs to know which animals visited the Riverview Veterinary Care Center in November 2016, as well as which owners in Cody and Elk Butte have email addresses. She'd like to access this information from the Veterinary database quickly, without creating a query. Although Kimberly has used filters with a query datasheet and a form, she's never used a filter with a table datasheet. You'll use a filter to display all care center visits with November 2016 visit dates in the tblVisit table datasheet.

To filter records in the tblVisit table datasheet:

1. Start Access, and then open the Veterinary database you worked with in the previous three modules.

   Trouble? If the security warning is displayed below the ribbon, click the Enable Content button.

2. Open the Navigation Pane (if necessary), open the **tblVisit** table in Datasheet view, and then close the Navigation Pane.

3. Click the **arrow** on the Date of Visit column heading to open the AutoFilter menu, point to **Date Filters** to open a submenu of context-sensitive options, and then point to **All Dates In Period** to open a submenu. See Figure 12-1.

Figure 12-1   AutoFilter menu and submenus for a date field

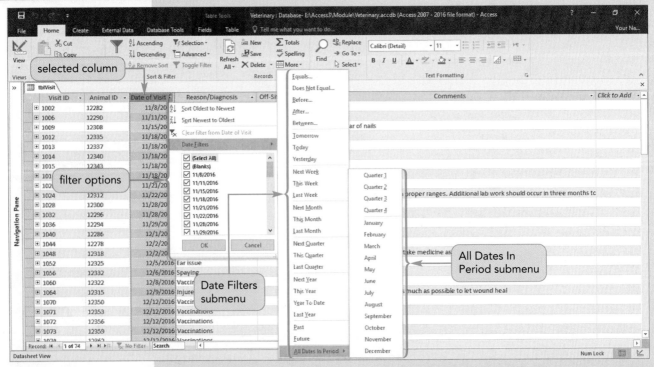

The Date of Visit menu displays all the values that appear in the Date of Visit column; you use the Date of Visit menu when you want to select specific values for the filter. The Date Filters submenu displays filter options that apply to a Date field, and the All Dates In Period submenu displays additional filter options for a Date field.

▶ **4.** In the All Dates In Period submenu, click **November**. Only the 13 records with November visit dates are displayed in the datasheet. If you save a table with an applied filter, the filter is saved, and you can reapply the filter anytime you open the table datasheet.

▶ **5.** Save and close the tblVisit table.

▶ **6.** Open the Navigation Pane, open the **tblVisit** table datasheet to display all 74 records, and then on the Home tab, in the Sort & Filter group, click the **Toggle Filter** button. The VisitDate filter is applied, displaying the 13 records with November visit dates.

▶ **7.** Close the tblVisit table.

Next, you'll use Filter By Form to produce the other results Kimberly wants—the list of owners from Cody or Elk Butte who have email addresses.

Filter By Form

You use the Filter By Form filter option when you need to filter data in a table or form on multiple criteria. When you select the Filter By Form option from the Advanced button menu in the Sort & Filter group, a blank datasheet opens that includes all the fields in the table, and this blank datasheet has two tabs—the Look for datasheet tab and the Or datasheet tab. In the blank datasheet on the Look for tab, you specify multiple selection criteria by entering conditions in the appropriate field value boxes. If you enter criteria in more than one field, you create the equivalent of an And condition—any record that matches all criteria will be selected. To create an Or condition, you enter the criteria for the first part of the condition in the field on the Look for tab's datasheet and then click the Or datasheet tab at the bottom of the datasheet window to display a new blank datasheet. You enter the criteria for the second part of the condition on the Or tab's blank datasheet. Any record that matches all criteria on the Look for datasheet or all criteria on the Or datasheet will be selected.

REFERENCE

Selecting Records Using Filter By Form

- Open the table or query datasheet or the form in Form view.
- On the Home tab, in the Sort & Filter group, click the Advanced button, and then click Filter By Form.
- Enter a simple selection criterion or an And condition in the Look for datasheet tab or form, using the boxes for the appropriate fields.
- If there is an Or condition, click the Or datasheet tab, and then enter the Or condition in the second datasheet or form. Continue to enter Or conditions on separate datasheets or forms by using the Or tab.
- On the Home tab, in the Sort & Filter group, click the Toggle Filter button.

Kimberly wants to display records for only those owners in Cody and Elk Butte with an email address. To accomplish this, the multiple selection criteria you will enter are: Cody *and* Email not blank *or* Elk Butte *and* Email not blank.

To select the records using Filter By Form:

▶ **1.** Open the **tblOwner** table to display the 26 records in the recordset, and then close the Navigation Pane.

▶ **2.** On the Home tab, in the Sort & Filter group, click the **Advanced** button, click **Filter By Form** to display a blank datasheet that has two tabs, the Look for tab and the Or tab. The Look for tab is the active tab. See Figure 12-2.

Figure 12-2   **Blank datasheet for Filter by Form option**

For a criterion, you can select a value from the list of values in a field value box, or you can use a comparison operator (such as <, >=, <>, and Like) and a value, similar to conditions you enter in the query design grid.

▶ **3.** Click the **City** box, click the **City** arrow, and then click **Cody**. The criterion "Cody" appears in the City box.

▶ **4.** Click the **Email** box, and then type **<> ""** in the box. The criterion <> "" is added to the Email box. This represents those email addresses entered that are not blank, with blank represented as "".

Before you add additional options to the filter, you'll verify that the filter is working.

▶ **5.** In the Sort & Filter group, click the **Toggle Filter** button. The records that contain Cody for the city and that also include an email address (meaning the Email field is *not* blank) are displayed. There are eight records. Now you'll return to the Filter by Form window to continue creating the filter.

▶ **6.** On the Home tab, in the Sort & Filter group, click the **Advanced** button, and then click **Filter By Form** to return to the filter.

You've specified the logical operator (And) for the condition "Cody" And "Email not blank". To add the rest of the criteria, you need to display the Or blank datasheet.

TIP

Notice that a third tab, also labeled "Or," is now available in case you need to specify another Or condition.

7. Click the **Or** tab to display a second blank datasheet. The insertion point is in the City box.

8. Click the **City** arrow to display the list, and then click **Elk Butte**.

9. Click the **Email** box, and then type **<> ""**. The filter is now set for second And condition of "Elk Butte" And "Email not blank". See Figure 12-3.

Figure 12-3   Completed filter using Filter by Form option

Combined with the Look for conditions, you now have the Or conditions and the complete Filter By Form conditions. Much like building queries, all data that is on the same line in the criteria must be satisfied in order for the record to satisfy the criteria.

10. In the Sort & Filter group, click the **Toggle Filter** button, and then scroll to the right until both the City and Email columns are visible (if necessary). The filter displays the 10 records that match the selection criteria and displays "Filtered" in the navigation bar. See Figure 12-4.

Figure 12-4   **Records that match the Filter by Form criteria**

Now that you have defined the filter, you can save it as a query, so that Kimberly can easily view the information in the future.

Saving a Filter as a Query

When you save a filter as a query, you can reuse the filter by opening the saved query.

REFERENCE

Saving a Filter as a Query

- Create a filter using Filter By Selection, Filter By Form, or Advanced Filter/Sort.
- If you applied the filter using Filter By Form, click the Advanced button, and then click Filter By Form.
- On the Home tab, in the Sort & Filter group, click the Advanced button, and then click Save As Query.
- Type the name for the query, and then press the Enter key.

Next, you'll save the filter as a query named qryCodyElkButteEmailFilter.

To save the filter as a query:

▶ **1.** On the Home tab, in the Sort & Filter group, click the **Advanced** button, and then click **Filter By Form**. The datasheet displays with the selection criteria.

▶ **2.** In the Sort & Filter group, click the **Advanced** button, and then click **Save As Query**. The Save As Query dialog box opens.

3. Type **qryCodyElkButteEmailFilter** in the Query Name box, and then click the **OK** button. The filter is saved as a query in the Veterinary database.

   Now you can clear the selection criteria, close the Filter by Form window, and return to Datasheet view.

4. In the Sort & Filter group, click the **Advanced** button, and then click **Clear Grid** to remove the selection criteria from the filter datasheet.

5. Close the tblOwner: Filter by Form tab to return to Datasheet view for the tblOwner table. The 10 filtered records are still displayed in the datasheet, and the filter is still applied.

6. In the Sort & Filter group, click the **Toggle Filter** button, click the **Advanced** button, and then click **Clear All Filters**. Because there are no filters applied, the table displays 26 records. Next, you'll leave the tblOwner table open while you open the qryCodyElkButteEmailFilter query in Design view.

7. Open the Navigation Pane, open the **qryCodyElkButteEmailFilter** query, switch to Design view, and then close the Navigation Pane. In the design grid, the first And condition ("Cody" And <> "") appears in the Criteria row, the second And condition ("Elk Butte" And <> "") appears in the or row. You can interpret these criteria as "the records that contain Cody and an email, or contain Elk Butte and an email." See Figure 12-5.

Figure 12-5   **Filter saved as a query in Design view**

8. Run the query to display the 10 records that satisfy the selection criteria, close the query, close the tblOwner table, and then click the **No** button in the dialog box that opens, prompting you to save the table design changes. You don't want to save the filter with the table because you've already saved the filter as a separate query.

The next time Kimberly wants to view the records selected by the filter, she can run the qryCodyElkButteEmailFilter query. She could also open the tblOwner table and apply the qryCodyElkButteEmailFilter query as a filter.

Applying a Query as a Filter

- Open the table to which you want to apply the filter in Datasheet view.
- On the Home tab, in the Sort & Filter group, click the Advanced button, and then click Filter By Form.
- In the Sort & Filter group, click the Advanced button, and then click Load from Query.
- In the Applicable Filter dialog box, click the query you want to apply as a filter, and then click the OK button.
- On the Home tab, in the Sort & Filter group, click the Toggle Filter button to apply the filter.

To apply the qryCodyElkButteEmailFilter query as a filter, you first need to open the tblOwner table.

To apply the query as a filter:

1. Open the Navigation Pane, open the **tblOwner** table, and then close the Navigation Pane.

2. In the Sort & Filter group, click the **Advanced** button, and then click **Filter By Form**. The blank Look for tab in the Filter By Form datasheet displays.

3. In the Sort & Filter group, click the **Advanced** button, and then click **Load from Query**. The Applicable Filter dialog box opens. See Figure 12-6.

Figure 12-6	Applicable Filter dialog box

your list might show the filters in a different order

Applicable Filter ? ✕

Filter:
qryOwnersByName
qryCodyElkButteEmailFilter

click to select the filter saved as a query

OK   Cancel

4. Click **qryCodyElkButteEmailFilter** in the Filter box if necessary to select it, and then click the **OK** button. The query displays in the Filter by Form window.

5. In the Sort & Filter group, click the **Toggle Filter** button. The 10 filtered records are displayed in the datasheet.

6. Click the **Advanced** button, click **Clear All Filters**, and then close the tblOwner table without saving your design changes.

Kimberly finds the qryCodyElkButteEmailFilter useful, but she'd also like a list of the owners who have had animals visit the clinic and their visit information, for owners who live in either Cody or Elk Butte, and who have email addresses. To generate this list, you can use the qryCodyElkButteEmailFilter as a subquery within a query that searches for these animal visit records in the tblVisit table. You'll modify the qryCodyElkButteEmailFilter query to use a subquery.

Creating a Subquery

When you create a query using a SQL SELECT statement, you can place a second SELECT statement inside it; this second query is called a **subquery**. The subquery is run first, and then the results of the subquery are used to run the outer query. A subquery is also known as an **inner query**. It runs inside another query, referred to as a **parent query**, which is simply a query that contains a subquery. A parent query can also be referred to as an **outer query**.

The records that result from the parent query are the only records that will be used as the dataset for the subquery. You can think of this arrangement as a query within a query. For instance, you might have a query that finds all owners from Cody and then use a subquery to find all animals within those records who visited the clinic in November. The subquery would be animals who visited in November, and the parent query would be owners whose city is Cody. This is a simple example, and you could certainly create one query that contains both the tblVisit and tblOwner tables, with criteria that set the city and visit date appropriately. However, in other situations you may be dealing with much more complex parent queries and subqueries. In these cases, rather than dealing with troubleshooting one very complex query, you could build two simpler queries and combine them in this manner. This can be a time-saving technique because you can create a very complex query by combining queries that are easier to understand.

To view the qryCodyElkButteEmailFilter query in SQL view:

▶ **1.** Open the Navigation Pane, open the **qryCodyElkButteEmailFilter** query in Design view, and then close the Navigation Pane. In the design grid, the first And condition ("Cody" And <> "") appears in the Criteria row, the second And condition ("Elk Butte" And <> "") appears in the or row, and the Or condition combines the first And condition with the second And condition.

▶ **2.** On the Query Tools Design tab, in the Results group, click the **View button arrow**, click **SQL View**, and then click a blank area of the window to deselect the SQL SELECT statement. See Figure 12-7.

| Figure 12-7 | SQL statement for the qryCodyElkButteEmail query |

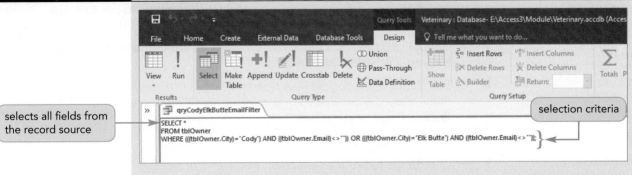

selects all fields from the record source

selection criteria

SELECT * FROM tblOwner selects all fields from the tblOwner table in the order in which they appear in the table. The WHERE clause specifies the selection criteria: records with a City field value of Cody and an Email field value, or records with a City field value of Elk Butte and an Email field value.

In the next set of steps, you'll add the following outer query to modify the query to use it as a subquery:

SELECT * FROM tblAnimal WHERE OwnerID IN (

This will perform a SELECT query to find all fields (*) in the tblAnimal table. The IN function will contain the SQL code for the qryCodyElkButteEmailFilter query, which becomes the subquery. You'll need to add a right parenthesis) before the final semicolon to end the subquery. The finished SQL statement is shown in Figure 12-8.

Figure 12-8	SQL SELECT statement using a subquery

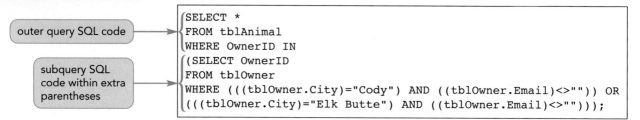

outer query SQL code

subquery SQL code within extra parentheses

```
SELECT *
FROM tblAnimal
WHERE OwnerID IN
(SELECT OwnerID
FROM tblOwner
WHERE (((tblOwner.City)="Cody") AND ((tblOwner.Email)<>"")) OR
(((tblOwner.City)="Elk Butte") AND ((tblOwner.Email)<>"")));
```

To create this query, you'll copy the qryCodyElkButteEmailFilter query and then add to this SQL code to form the query that uses this as a subquery.

To create the query that contains a subquery:

1. Close the qryCodyElkButteEmailFilter query, and then open the Navigation Pane.

2. Right-click **qryCodyElkButteEmailFilter**, and then on the shortcut menu, click **Copy**.

3. On the Home tab, in the Clipboard group, click the **Paste** button to open the Paste As dialog box, and then save as the copy with the name **qryCodyElkButteEmailFilterAnimal**.

4. Open the **qryCodyElkButteEmailFilterAnimal** query in Design view, and then close the Navigation Pane.

5. On the Query Tools Design tab, in the Results group, click the **View button arrow**, click **SQL View**, and then click a blank area of the window to deselect the SQL SELECT statement.

6. Click to the left of the SELECT statement, press the **Enter** key three times, and then click in the top blank line of the SQL window to position the insertion point.

7. Type **SELECT ***, press the ↓ key, type **FROM tblAnimal**, press the ↓ key, and then type **WHERE OwnerID IN**.

8. Edit the next line to add **(** (an open parenthesis) to the left of SELECT, and then delete the asterisk (*) that comes after SELECT, and replace it with **OwnerID** so the statement is:

(SELECT OwnerID

9. Click to the left of the semicolon at the end of the SQL statement and type **)** (close parenthesis). See Figure 12-9.

Figure 12-9	Modified SQL statement

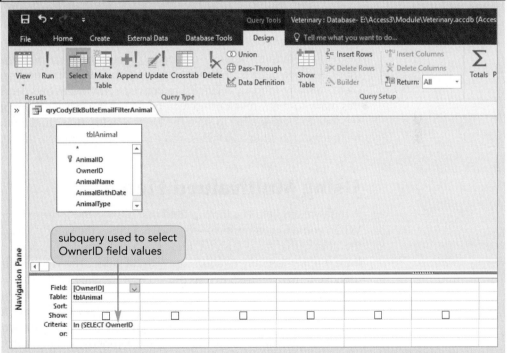

three new lines added

open parentheses added to the left of SELECT

close parentheses added to the left of the semicolon

asterisk replaced with OwnerID

qryCodyElkButteEmailFilterAnimal

```
SELECT *
FROM tblAnimal
WHERE OwnerID IN
(SELECT OwnerID
FROM tblOwner
WHERE (((tblOwner.City)="Cody") AND ((tblOwner.Email) <> "")) OR (((tblOwner.City)="Elk Butte") AND ((tblOwner.Email) <> "")));
```

▶ **10.** Save your query design changes, and then run the query. The query returns 24 records from the tblAnimal table whose OwnerID values are in the qryCodyElkButteEmailFilter.

▶ **11.** Switch to Design view, and then click the first column's **Field** box to deselect all values. The value in the OwnerID Criteria box is a subquery that selects Cody and Elk Butte owners who have email addresses. See Figure 12-10.

Figure 12-10	Query using a subquery in the Design window

subquery used to select OwnerID field values

tblAnimal

*
AnimalID
OwnerID
AnimalName
AnimalBirthDate
AnimalType

Field:	[OwnerID]					
Table:	tblAnimal					
Sort:						
Show:	☐	☐	☐	☐	☐	☐
Criteria:	In (SELECT OwnerID					
or:						

It's unclear from looking at the column in the design grid that all fields are displayed from the tblAnimal table.

▶ **12.** On the Query Tools Design tab, in the Show/Hide group, click the **Property Sheet** button to display the properties for the query. See Figure 12-11.

| Figure 12-11 | Properties for the query |

The Output All Fields property setting of Yes specifies that the query displays all fields from the record source, the tblAnimal table, without these fields being added to the design grid.

▶ **13.** Close the Property Sheet, close the query, and then click the **Yes** button when prompted to save changes to the query design.

Kimberly wants to keep track of the degrees—such as associate's degree, bachelor's degree, and master's degree—earned by employees. Because each employee can earn more than one degree, and each degree can be earned by more than one employee, there's a many-to-many relationship between employees and degrees. To implement this many-to-many relationship, you could use the existing tblEmployee table, create a separate tblDegree table to store the Degree field values, and then create a third table to tie together the other two tables. You could also accomplish this using a multivalued field.

Using Multivalued Fields

A multivalued field is a lookup field that allows you to store more than one value. When you define a multivalued field in a table, the values are not actually stored in the field in that table. Instead, they are stored as hidden values in system tables that have a many-to-many relationship with the table. The values in these system tables are managed, manipulated, and displayed as if the data were stored in the multivalued field in the table.

Using a multivalued field, you can add a Degree field to the tblEmployee table and use the Lookup Wizard to enter the Degree field values and specify that you want to store multiple values in the Degree field. Kimberly and her staff can then select one or more Degree field values from the list of degrees.

Using Multivalued Fields

Users with limited Access and database experience are the intended audience for multivalued fields because understanding the concepts of many-to-many relationships and creating them are difficult for beginning or casual database users. Experienced database users generally avoid multivalued fields and instead implement many-to-many relationships because that method provides total control over the data, rather than limiting options as working with multivalued fields does. One of the limitations of multivalued fields is that except in special circumstances, you can't sort records based on the values stored in a multivalued field in queries, forms, and reports. Also, multivalued fields do not convert properly to a database managed by a DBMS such as SQL Server or Oracle. If you need to convert an Access database using a multivalued field to another DBMS in the future, you'd have to change the multivalued field to many-to-many relationships, which is a change that's much more difficult at that point than if you had avoided using a multivalued field from the beginning. As a precaution, you should save a copy of the database file before you create a multivalued field.

You'll use the multivalued field feature without modifying the existing tables and relationships in the Veterinary database, so Kimberly can decide whether you should keep the multivalued field or use a traditional many-to-many implementation. You'll make a copy of the tblEmployee table, and then you will add the multivalued field to the copied version of the table. This way, you can delete the copy of the tblEmployee table if Kimberly decides not to use a multivalued field. If Kimberly decides to keep it, she has the option to delete the original tblEmployee table and rename this new table as the tblEmployee table.

To create a copy of the tblEmployee table:

1. Open the Navigation Pane, right-click **tblEmployee**, and then on the shortcut menu, click **Copy**.

2. In the Clipboard group, on the Home tab, click the **Paste** button to open the Paste Table As dialog box, and then click the **Table Name** box to deselect the current name. See Figure 12-12.

Figure 12-12   Paste Table As dialog box

When you copy a table to create a new table, you can use the design of the table without copying its data (Structure Only), use the design and copy the data from the table (Structure and Data), or add the data to an existing table (Append Data to Existing Table).

You'll create the new table using the design and data from the tblEmployee table.

▶ **3.** Change the name in the Table Name box to **tblEmployeeCopy**, make sure the **Structure and Data** option button is selected, and then click the **OK** button. A new table named tblEmployeeCopy is created, and it contains the same structure and data as the tblEmployee table.

Now you can add the multivalued field to the tblEmployeeCopy table.

To add the multivalued field to the tblEmployeeCopy table:

▶ **1.** Open the **tblEmployeeCopy** table in Design view, and then close the Navigation Pane.

▶ **2.** In the blank row below the SupervisorID field, click the **Field Name** box, type **Degree**, press the **Tab** key, click the **Data Type** arrow, and then click **Lookup Wizard**. The first Lookup Wizard dialog box opens. You'll type the Degree field values instead of obtaining them from a table or query.

▶ **3.** Click the **I will type in the values that I want** option button, and then click the **Next** button to open the second Lookup Wizard dialog box, in which you'll type the Degree field values.

▶ **4.** Click the **Col1** box in the first row, type **Certificate**, press the **Tab** key, type **Associate**, press the **Tab** key, type **Bachelor**, press the **Tab** key, type **Master**, press the **Tab** key, and then type **Doctorate**. These are the five values that users can choose among for the Degree multivalued field. See Figure 12-13.

Figure 12-13 **Values for the Degree multivalued field**

▶ **5.** Click the **Next** button to open the last Lookup Wizard dialog box, and then click the **Allow Multiple Values** check box to add a checkmark to it, specifying that you want the Degree field to be a multivalued field. See Figure 12-14.

Figure 12-14   Specifying a multivalued field

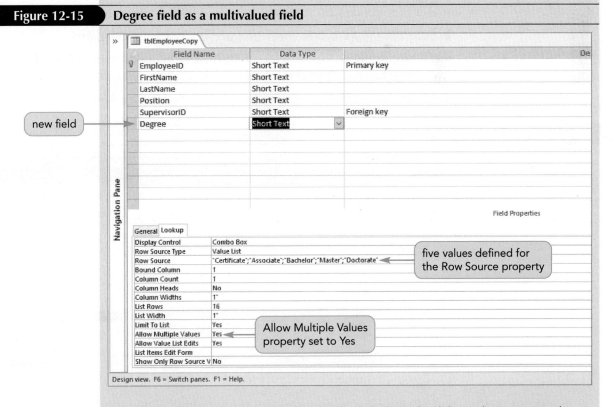

You'll accept the default label name of Degree for the field.

6. Click the **Finish** button to complete the definition of the Degree field as a lookup field that allows multiple values, or a multivalued field.

7. In the Field Properties pane, click the **Lookup** tab. The Degree field has its Row Source property set to the five values you typed in one of the Lookup Wizard dialog boxes, and the Allow Multiple Values property is set to Yes. See Figure 12-15.

Figure 12-15   Degree field as a multivalued field

If you forget to select the Allow Multiple Values check box when you use the Lookup Wizard, you can switch to Design view and set the Allow Multiple

Values property for the field to Yes to change a field to a multivalued field. If you need to add values in the future to the multivalued field, you can add them to the Row Source property.

8. Save your table design changes, and then switch to Datasheet view.

9. Click the right side of the **Degree** box for record 3 (Adriana Ortiz) to open the value list for the field. See Figure 12-16.

Figure 12-16 | **Value list for the Degree multivalued field**

these sort options are unavailable because you cannot sort records based on multivalued fields

10. Click the **Associate** check box, and then click the **OK** button.

11. Repeat Steps 9 and 10 for record 5 (James Lock), selecting **Bachelor**, **Master**, and **Doctorate**, and for record 6 (Sam Okonjo), selecting **Bachelor**.

12. Resize the Degree column to its best fit. See Figure 12-17.

Figure 12-17 | **Values selected for the multivalued field**

records with new values in the Degree field

Next, you'll create queries to display all field values from the tblEmployeeCopy table to display the multivalued field values.

To create queries to display the Degree multivalued field:

1. Save and close the tblEmployeeCopy table, click the **Create** tab, and then in the Queries group, click the **Query Wizard** button to open the New Query dialog box.

2. Make sure the Simple Query Wizard option is selected, click the **OK** button to open the Simple Query Wizard dialog box, from the tblEmployeeCopy table select all fields, click the **Next** button, change the query title to **qryEmployeeCopy**, and then click the **Finish** button.

3. Click the first row's **Employee ID column** value to deselect all values (if necessary), and then resize the Degree.Value column to best fit. The query results include 14 records. See Figure 12-18.

Figure 12-18 ▶ **Query that displays the Degree multivalued field**

Trouble? The rightmost column heading on your screen might be the equivalent tblEmployee-Copy.Degree.Value instead of Degree.Value, indicating the Degree field in the tblEmployeeCopy table. This difference does not affect the contents of the column.

The six fields from the tblEmployeeCopy table are displayed in seven columns in the query recordset because the Degree field is displayed in two columns: the Degree column and the Degree.Value column. The Degree column displays field values exactly as they appear in the tblEmployeeCopy table; all values for the Degree multivalued field, such as those for James Lock, are displayed in one row in the query. The Degree.Value column displays the Degree multivalued field in expanded form so that each value appears in a separate row in the query. "Degree.Value" identifies the Degree field and the Value property for the Degree field.

In queries that contain a multivalued field, you should display the field in a single column, not in two columns, with values appearing as they are in the table or in expanded form. You can eliminate the extra column by deleting it, by clearing its Show check box in Design view, or by selecting just one of the two fields in the Simple Query Wizard when you select the fields for the query.

4. Click the **Home** tab, notice that the Ascending and Descending buttons in the Sort & Filter group are active, click the first row's **Degree** box, notice that the Ascending and Descending buttons are grayed out, and then click the first row's **Degree.Value** box. The Ascending and Descending buttons are active, and you can sort records in the query based on the values in the Degree.Value column.

Next, you'll review the query design.

5. Switch to Design view, and then resize the tblEmployeeCopy field list to display all the values in the list. See Figure 12-19.

Figure 12-19 ▶ **Design of the query containing the Degree multivalued field**

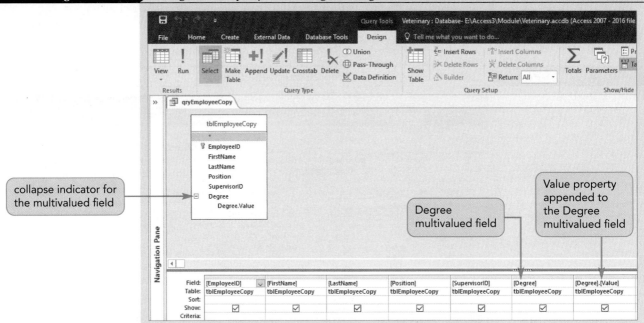

The Degree field in the tblEmployeeCopy field list has a collapse indicator to its left that you can click to hide the Degree.Value entry below it. The rightmost column in the design grid, [Degree].[Value], uses the Value property for the Degree field. Using the **Value property** with a multivalued field displays the multivalued field in expanded form so that each value is displayed in a separate row.

You'll delete the [Degree] column from the query design, retaining the [Degree].[Value] column and setting its Caption property, and then you'll save the query with a new name.

6. Right-click the **column selector bar** for the [Degree] column to select the column and open the shortcut menu, and then click **Cut**.

7. Click the **column selector bar** for the [Degree].[Value] column to select it, open the Property Sheet for the [Degree].[Value] column, set the Caption property to **Degree**, and then close the Property Sheet.

8. Click the **File** tab to open Backstage view, in the navigation bar, click **Save As**, click **Save Object As**, and then click the **Save As** button to open the Save As dialog box.

▶ **9.** Change the query name to **qryEmployeeCopyValue**, click the **OK** button, click the **Home** tab, and then switch to Datasheet view. The datasheet appears, displaying 14 records in the query recordset.

▶ **10.** Close the query, open the Navigation Pane, open the **qryEmployeeCopy** query in Design view, and then close the Navigation Pane.

▶ **11.** Delete the **Degree.Value** column, save the query, and then run the query. The query returns 12 records from the tblEmployeeCopy table and displays the Degree multivalued field values in one row.

▶ **12.** Close the query, and then, if you are not continuing on to the next session, close the Veterinary database.

Kimberly is pleased with your work and will review it as she decides whether to use the multivalued Degree field or a many-to-many relationship. In the next session, you'll add Attachment fields using the tblEmployeeCopy table and evaluate database performance and management options.

Session 12.1 Quick Check

REVIEW

1. Filter By _____ filters records that match multiple selection criteria using the same Access comparison operators used in queries.

2. You can save a filter as a(n) _____ and reuse the filter by opening the saved object.

3. What is a subquery?

4. What is a multivalued field?

5. You use the _____ property to display a multivalued field in expanded form so that each value is displayed in a separate row in a query.

Session 12.2 Visual Overview:

The Current Database option displays options that apply only to the currently open database.

The text you enter for the **Application Title option** appears in the Access window title bar.

The **Use Access Special Keys option** enables or disables the F11 key (show/hide the Navigation Pane), Ctrl+G (show/hide the Immediate window in VB editor), and Alt+F1 (start VB Editor).

The **Display Form option** specifies the form that opens automatically when you open the database.

The **Enable design changes for tables in Datasheet view option** allows you to change a table's design in Datasheet view.

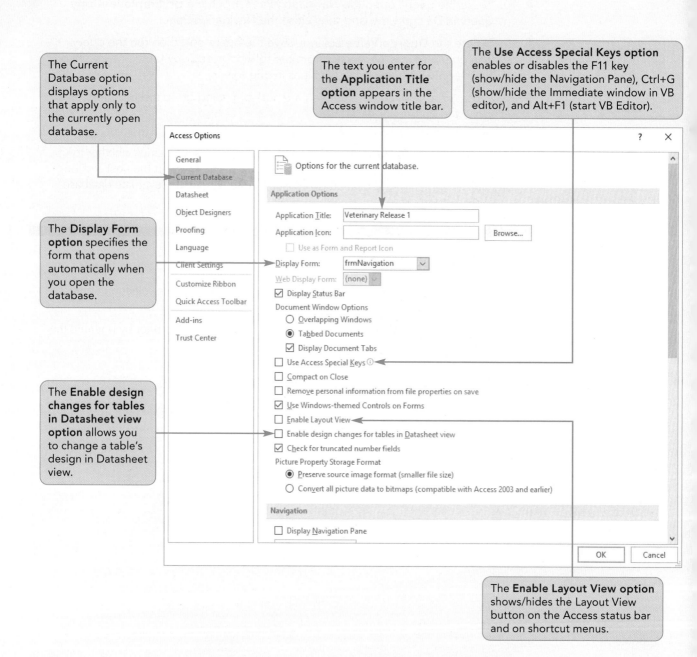

The **Enable Layout View option** shows/hides the Layout View button on the Access status bar and on shortcut menus.

Database Options

The **Display Navigation Pane option** controls whether the Navigation Pane is available in the Access window.

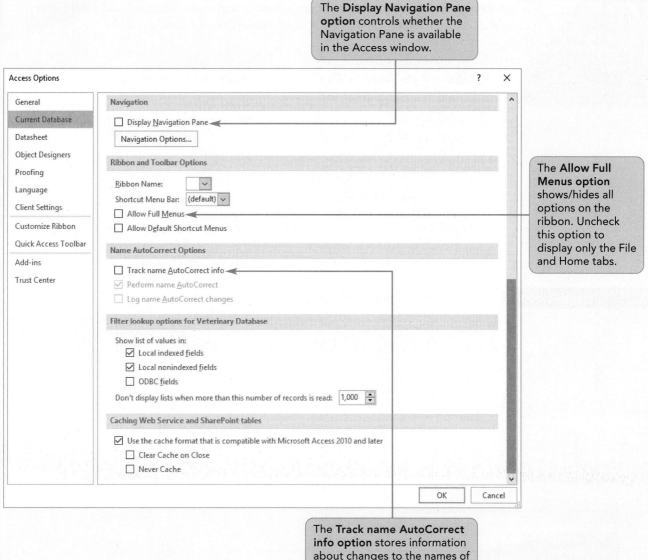

The **Allow Full Menus option** shows/hides all options on the ribbon. Uncheck this option to display only the File and Home tabs.

The **Track name AutoCorrect info option** stores information about changes to the names of fields, controls, and objects.

Creating an Attachment Field

In addition to storing data such as text, numbers, and dates in a database, you can attach external files such as Excel workbooks, Word documents, and images, similar to how you attach external files to email messages. You use the **Attachment data type** to attach one or more files to a table record. The attachments are stored as part of the database. An attachment data field can contain one or more file attachments in a table record.

Kimberly wants to be able to attach documents to the tblEmployeeCopy table that contain information about James Lock's degrees and expenses. You'll add a field with the Attachment data type and use it to attach the documents to the table.

To add a new field with the Attachment data type to the tblEmployeeCopy table:

▶ **1.** If you took a break after the previous session, make sure that the Veterinary database is open.

▶ **2.** Open the Navigation Pane (if necessary), open the **tblEmployeeCopy** table in Design view, and then close the Navigation Pane.

▶ **3.** Click the **Field Name** box for the blank row below the Degree field, type **AddedDocuments**, press the **Tab** key, type **at**, press the **Tab** key to select Attachment as the data type, press the **F6** key to navigate to the Caption box in the Field Properties pane, and then type **Added Documents**. The AddedDocuments field is added to the table. See Figure 12-20.

Figure 12-20   **New AddedDocuments field with the Attachment data type**

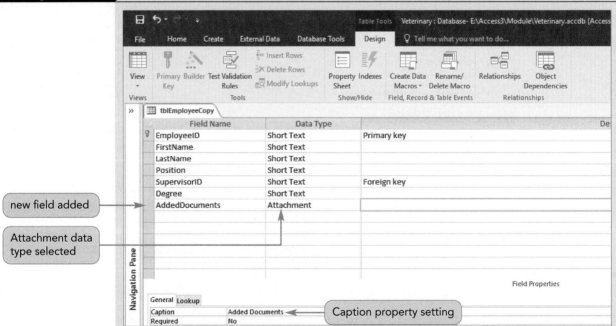

▶ **4.** Save your table design changes, switch to Datasheet view, resize the Added Documents column to its best fit, click the first row's **Employee ID** box to deselect all values, and then save your datasheet format changes. See Figure 12-21.

| Figure 12-21 | Attachment field displayed in the table datasheet |

Each AddedDocuments field value displays an attachment icon in the shape of a paper clip followed by a number in parentheses that indicates the number of files attached in that field for the record. You haven't attached any files, so each record displays zero file attachments. Kimberly has some files from James Lock that she would like you to attach to his record in the Added Documents column.

▶ 5. In the row for James Lock, right-click the **Added Documents** box to open the shortcut menu, and then click **Manage Attachments** to open the Attachments dialog box. You'll add all three of James's files as attachments to the AddedDocuments field for James Lock.

▶ 6. Click the **Add** button to open the Choose File dialog box, navigate to the **Access3 > Module** folder included with your Data Files, click **James Lock Bachelor Degree**, and then click the **Open** button to add the James Lock Bachelor Degree.docx file to the Attachments dialog box.

▶ 7. Click the **Add** button to open the Choose File dialog box, click **James Lock Master Degree**, press and hold the **Ctrl** key, click **James Lock Expenses**, release the **Ctrl** key, and then click the **Open** button. The three files you've added now appear in the Attachments dialog box. See Figure 12-22.

| Figure 12-22 | Attachments dialog box |

▶ 8. Click the **OK** button to close the dialog box. The table datasheet now indicates that three files (as noted by the 3 in parentheses) are attached to the AddedDocuments field in the record for James Lock.

Next, you'll open one of the files attached in the record for James Lock, remove one of the attached files, and save an attached file.

To open, remove, and save files attached in a table field:

▶ **1.** In the row for James Lock, right-click the **Added Documents** box, and then on the shortcut menu click **Manage Attachments** to open the Attachments dialog box.

▶ **2.** Click **James Lock Expenses.xlsx** in the Attachments list, and then click the **Open** button. Excel starts, and the James Lock Expenses workbook opens.

▶ **3.** Exit Excel. You return to the Attachments dialog box open in the Access window.

▶ **4.** Click **James Lock Bachelor Degree.docx** in the Attachments list, and then click the **Remove** button. The James Lock Bachelor Degree document is removed from the Attachments list, and it no longer is attached to the AddedDocuments field for the James Lock record.

▶ **5.** Click **James Lock Master Degree.pdf** in the Attachments list, click the **Save As** button to open the Save Attachment dialog box, if necessary, navigate to the location where you are storing your Data Files, type **James Lock Master Degree Detach** in the File name box, and then click the **Save** button.

▶ **6.** Click the **OK** button to close the Attachments dialog box. Because you removed the James Lock Bachelor Degree.docx file as an attachment, the AddedDocuments field for the James Lock record now shows that there are two attachments.

Kimberly is considering adding an employee number for each employee that could be automatically generated when a new employee record is added. You can do this by adding an AutoNumber field to the tblEmployeeCopy table.

Using an AutoNumber Field

TIP
Read the Natural, Artificial, and Surrogate Keys section in the appendix titled "Relational Databases and Database Design" for more information about AutoNumber fields and primary keys.

As you know, when you create a table in Datasheet view, the AutoNumber data type is assigned to the default ID primary key field because the AutoNumber data type automatically inserts a unique number in this field for every record in the table. Therefore, it can serve as the primary key for any table you create. When defining a field with the AutoNumber data type, you can specify sequential numbering or random numbering, either of which guarantees a unique field value for every record in the table.

You'll add an AutoNumber field to the tblEmployeeCopy table.

To add an AutoNumber field to the tblEmployeeCopy table:

▶ **1.** Switch to Design view, right-click the **row selector** for the EmployeeID field to open the shortcut menu, and then click **Insert Rows**. A blank row is inserted above the EmployeeID row. Next, you'll add the AutoNumber field to this new first row in the table design.

▶ **2.** Click the first row's **Field Name** box, type **EmployeeNum**, press the **Tab** key, type **a**, press the **Tab** key to accept AutoNumber as the data type, press the **F6** key to navigate to the Field Properties pane, press the **Tab** key three times to navigate to the Caption box, and then enter **Employee Num** in the Caption box. You've finished adding the EmployeeNum field to the table. See Figure 12-23.

Figure 12-23   EmployeeNum field added with the AutoNumber data type

3. Save your table design changes, switch to Datasheet view, resize the Employee Num column to its best fit, and then click the first row's **Employee Num** box to deselect all values. The new EmployeeNum field is displayed as the first column in the table, and unique incremental (sequential) numbers appear in the EmployeeNum field for the 12 records in the table. See Figure 12-24.

Figure 12-24   AutoNumber field displayed in the table datasheet

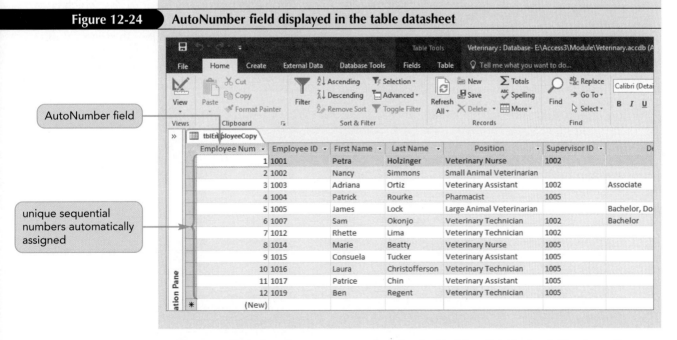

Next, you'll review the property settings for the Position field in the tblEmployeeCopy table to verify they are correct.

To view the property settings for the Position field:

1. Switch to Design view, and then click the Field Name box for the Position field to display its properties. See Figure 12-25.

Figure 12-25 **Property settings for the Position field**

The Position field's Required property is set to No, which means field value entries are optional. The Allow Zero Length property is set to Yes, which is the default setting for Text fields and Memo fields. When a field's **Allow Zero Length property** is set to Yes, the field can store a zero length string value.

2. Save and close the tblEmployeeCopy table.

Setting the Allow Zero Length Property to No

For a Text or Memo field, there is a difference between how you specify a null field value and a zero length value and how the two values are interpreted. Recall that null means that the field does not contain any value at all and describes a text field or a numeric field that is empty. A numeric field that contains the number zero is not empty. Similarly, a text field that contains a zero length value is not empty. You specify a zero length value in a Text or a Memo field by typing two consecutive double quotation marks (""). (You used this method in the previous session.) You specify a null value in a Text or Memo field by entering a No value. When you view a value for a Text or Memo field that has its Allow Zero Length property set to Yes, you can't determine if the field value has been set to null or has a zero length value because both field values look the same—the absence of a visible value.

However, the two values are treated differently. If you run a query to display all records in the table that have a null value in the field using the IsNull function, only the records with null field values appear in the query recordset; the records with zero length values in the field do not appear. And if you change the query to display all records that have a nonnull value, the records with zero length values in the field appear in the query recordset, which often raises questions from users about why those records are displayed. A typical user doesn't understand the distinction between a null value and a zero length value and doesn't need to make this distinction, so you should set the Allow Zero Length property to No for Text and Memo fields.

Kimberly has a previous version of Access on her home computer and wonders if she can open the Veterinary database on that computer.

Saving an Access Database as a Previous Version

The default file format for databases you create in Access 2016 uses the .accdb filename extension and is referred to as the Access 2007 file format because it was introduced with Access 2007. None of the versions of Access prior to Access 2007 can open a database that has the .accdb filename extension. However, you can save an .accdb database to a format that is compatible with previous versions of Access—specifically, to a format that is compatible with Access 2000 or to a format that is compatible with Access 2002-2003; both have the .mdb filename extension. For people who don't have Access 2016, Access 2013, Access 2010, or Access 2007 but do have one of the previous versions of Access, saving the database to a previous version allows them to use the database. Unfortunately, when an Access 2007 file format database uses features such as multivalued and Attachment fields, you cannot save the database in a previous version.

To save an Access 2007 file format database as a previous version, you would complete the following steps (note that you will not actually save the database now):

1. Make sure that the database you want to save is open and all database objects are closed, and that the database does not contain any multivalued fields, Attachment fields, or any other features that are included only in Access 2007 file-formatted databases.
2. Click the File tab to open Backstage view, click Save As in the navigation bar, click Save Database As, and then click Access 2002-2003 Database or click Access 2000 Database, depending on which file format you want to use.
3. Click the Save As button. In the Save As dialog box, navigate to the folder where you want to save the file, enter a name for the database in the File name box, and then click the Save button.

Kimberly is happy to know it's possible for her to open the database on her home computer. Because the Veterinary database currently uses multivalued and Attachment fields, she'll continue to work on the database only at the office, so you don't need to save it as a previous version now.

Next, Kimberly asks you to analyze the performance of the Veterinary database.

Analyzing Database Performance with the Performance Analyzer

Kimberly wants the Veterinary database to respond as quickly as possible to user requests, such as running queries and opening reports. You'll use the Performance Analyzer to check the performance of the Veterinary database. The **Performance Analyzer** is an Access tool that you can use to optimize the performance of an Access database. You select the database objects you want to analyze for performance and then run the Performance Analyzer. You can select tables, queries, forms, reports, and macros either as a group or individually. The Performance Analyzer lists three types of analysis results: Recommendation, Suggestion, and Idea. You can use Access to perform the Recommendation and Suggestion optimizations for you, but you must implement the Idea optimizations. Analysis results include changes such as those related to the storage of fields and the creation of indexes and relationships.

REFERENCE

Using the Performance Analyzer

- Start Access, and open the database you want to analyze.
- On the Database Tools tab, in the Analyze group, click the Analyze Performance button.
- Select the object(s) you want to analyze, and then click the OK button.
- Select the analysis result(s) you want the Performance Analyzer to complete for you, and then click the Optimize button.
- Note the Idea optimizations, and perform those optimizations, as appropriate.
- Click the Close button.

You'll use the Performance Analyzer to optimize the performance of the Veterinary database.

To use the Performance Analyzer to optimize the performance of the Veterinary database:

▶ **1.** Click the **Database Tools** tab, and then in the Analyze group, click the **Analyze Performance** button. The Performance Analyzer dialog box opens. See Figure 12-26.

Figure 12-26   Performance Analyzer dialog box

click this tab to display all the objects in the database

option to select all listed objects

You'll analyze every object in the Veterinary database.

▶ **2.** Click the **All Object Types** tab, and then click the **Select All** button. All objects in the Veterinary database are listed on this tab, and all of them are now selected.

▶ **3.** Click the **OK** button. The Performance Analyzer analyzes all the objects in the Veterinary database and, after a few moments, displays the analysis results. See Figure 12-27.

Figure 12-27   Performance Analyzer analysis results

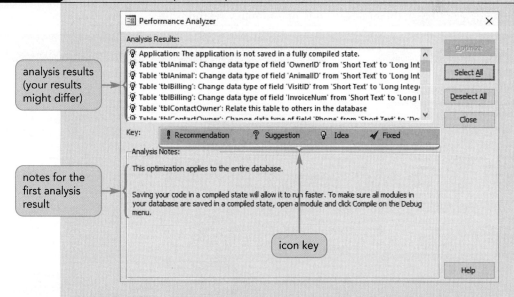

analysis results (your results might differ)

notes for the first analysis result

icon key

Trouble? The contents of the Analysis Results box on your screen might be different from those shown in Figure 12-27, depending on how you've completed the steps in the previous modules.

The icons that appear to the left of each result indicate the type of analysis result. Most of the analysis results are of the Idea type, which means that you have to implement them yourself. You should consider all the Idea type of analysis results, but more important now are the Recommendation and Suggestion types of analysis results, which the Performance Analyzer can complete for you automatically.

▶ **4.** Click several entries in the Analysis Results box, and read each entry and its analysis notes.

You'll let the Performance Analyzer automatically create a relationship between the tblEmployee table and itself because the table has a one-to-many relationship based on the EmployeeID field as the primary key and the SupervisorID field as the foreign key.

▶ **5.** Scroll the Analysis Results box as necessary, click the **Table 'tblEmployee':** **Relate to table 'tblEmployee'** analysis result (its icon is a green question mark, indicating it is a Suggestion type of analysis result) to select it, and then click the **Optimize** button. The Performance Analyzer creates a relationship between the tblEmployee table and itself, and the icon for the selected analysis result changes to a checkmark to indicate a "Fixed" status.

▶ **6.** Click the **Close** button to close the dialog box.

Next, you'll open the Relationships window to view the new relationship created by the Performance Analyzer.

To view the relationship created by the Performance Analyzer:

▶ **1.** Click the **Database Tools** tab, and then in the Relationships group, click the **Relationships** button to open the Relationships window. See Figure 12-28.

Figure 12-28   **tblEmployee table one-to-many relationship**

Trouble? The field lists in the Relationships window might be in different positions from what is shown in Figure 12-28. This difference causes no problems.

The Performance Analyzer added a second copy of the tblEmployee table (named tblEmployee_1) and a join line between the tblEmployee and tblEmployee_1 tables to the Relationships window. The join line connects the primary table (tblEmployee_1) to the related table (tblEmployee) using the EmployeeID field as the primary key and the SupervisorID field as the foreign key. You'll use the Edit Relationships dialog box to view the join properties for the relationship.

▶ **2.** Right-click the join line between the tblEmployee_1 and tblEmployee tables, and then click **Edit Relationship** on the shortcut menu to open the Edit Relationships dialog box. See Figure 12-29.

Figure 12-29   **Edit Relationships dialog box for the new relationship**

The referential integrity options are not selected, so you'll select them now for the new one-to-many relationship to show this as a one-to-many relationship in the Relationship window.

▶ **3.** Click the **Enforce Referential Integrity** check box, click the **Cascade Update Related Fields** check box, and then click the **OK** button to close the dialog box.

▶ **4.** Close the Relationships window, and then click the **Yes** button, if necessary, to save your changes.

Kimberly also has the responsibility at Riverview Veterinary Care Center for maintaining a separate database named Referral in which she stores information about owners who have been referred by other veterinary offices but who have not yet contacted the Riverview Veterinary Care Center. Kimberly wants to be able to retrieve the data in the tblReferral table in the Referral database from within the Veterinary database. To provide Kimberly with access to this table, you'll create a link to the tblReferral table in the Veterinary database.

Linking Tables Between Databases

A **linked table** is a table that is stored in a separate database file than the open database and that can be updated from the open database. You can retrieve and update (add, change, and delete) records in a linked table, but you can't change its structure.

You'll provide Kimberly and other users of the Veterinary database with access to the tblReferral table by using a linked table in the Veterinary database. From the Veterinary database, you'll be able to update the tblReferral table as a linked table, but you won't be able to change its structure. However, from the Referral database, Kimberly will be able to update the tblReferral table *and* change its structure.

Linking to a Table in Another Access Database

- Click the External Data tab.
- In the Import & Link group, click the Access button to open the Get External Data – Access Database dialog box.
- Click the "Link to the data source by creating a linked table" option button.
- Click the Browse button to open the File Open dialog box, select the folder and file containing the linked data, and then click the Open button.
- Click the OK button, select the table(s) in the Link Tables dialog box, and then click the OK button.

You'll link to the tblReferral table in the Referral database from the Veterinary database.

To link to the tblReferral table in the Referral database:

1. Click the **External Data** tab, and then in the Import & Link group, click the **Access** button to open the Get External Data - Access Database dialog box.

2. Click the **Link to the data source by creating a linked table** option button, and then click the **Browse** button to open the File Open dialog box.

3. Navigate to the **Access3 > Module** folder, click **Referral**, and then click the **Open** button to close the File Open dialog box and return to the Get External Data - Access Database dialog box. The path and file you selected now appear in the File name box.

4. Click the **OK** button. The Link Tables dialog box opens. See Figure 12-30.

Figure 12-30	Link Tables dialog box

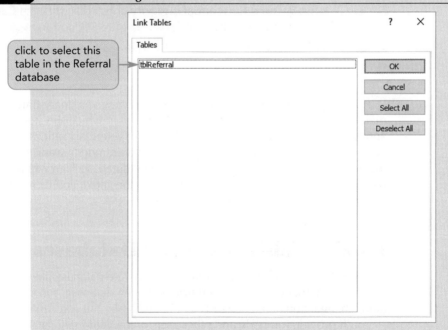

click to select this table in the Referral database

5. Click **tblReferral** in the Tables box, and then click the **OK** button. The Link Tables dialog box closes, and you return to the Access window. A small blue arrow appears to the left of the tblReferral table icon in the Navigation Pane, identifying the tblReferral table as a linked table.

Kimberly will be reorganizing the company network folders soon and might move the Referral database to a different folder. She asks if moving the Referral database would cause a problem for the linked tblReferral table. You'll use the Linked Table Manager to handle this situation. The **Linked Table Manager** is an Access tool you use to change the filename or drive location for linked tables in an Access database. When you use Access to link to data in another file, the file's location (drive, folder, and filename) is stored in the database, and this stored location is used to connect to the linked data. If you change the file's location, you can use the Linked Table Manager to update the stored file location.

REFERENCE

Updating Linked Tables

- In the Navigation Pane, right-click the linked table name, and then click Linked Table Manager on the shortcut menu; or on the External Data tab, in the Import & Link group, click the Linked Table Manager button.
- In the Linked Table Manager dialog box, click the check box(es) for the linked table(s) you want to update, and then click the OK button.
- In the Select New Location dialog box, navigate to the linked table location, click the filename, and then click the Open button.
- Click the OK button, and then close the Linked Table Manager dialog box.

Next, you'll move the Referral database to a different folder, and then you'll use the Linked Table Manager to update the link to the tblReferral table in the Veterinary database.

To move the Referral database and update the link to the tblReferral table:

▶ **1.** Use Windows File Explorer to move the Referral database from the Access3 > Module folder to the Access3 folder, and then switch back to Access.

▶ **2.** In the Navigation Pane, right-click **tblReferral** to open the shortcut menu, and then click **Linked Table Manager**. The Linked Table Manager dialog box opens. See Figure 12-31.

Figure 12-31   Linked Table Manager dialog box

original location of the Referral database (your path may be different)

The tblReferral table is the only linked table, so it's the only table listed. The Access3 > Module folder provided with your Data Files, which is the original location of the Referral database, is listed as the current location for the tblReferral table.

▶ **3.** Click the **Select All** button, and then click the **OK** button. The Select New Location of tblReferral dialog box opens.

▶ **4.** Navigate to the **Access3** folder, click **Referral** in the file list, and then click the **Open** button. A dialog box informs you that all selected linked tables were successfully refreshed, meaning the linked tables were updated.

▶ **5.** Click the **OK** button to close the dialog box. The Linked Table Manager dialog box now displays the Access3 folder as the current location of the linked tblReferral table.

▶ **6.** Close the Linked Table Manager dialog box.

Next, you'll open the tblReferral table to update it as a linked table from the new location.

To update the tblReferral table and view its design in the Veterinary database:

▶ **1.** Open the **tblReferral** table in Datasheet view, and then close the Navigation Pane. The tblReferral table datasheet displays four records. First, you'll add a new record to the tblReferral table.

▶ **2.** Click the **New (blank) record** button ▶▦, type **5005** in the Owner ID column, press the **Tab** key, type **Sarah** in the First Name column, press the **Tab** key, type **Miles** in the Last Name column, press the **Tab** key, type **307-824-1907** in the Phone column, press the **Tab** key, type **134 Jasper Ct** in the Address column, press the **Tab** key, type **Cody** in the City column, press the **Tab** key, type **WY** in the State column, press the **Tab** key, type **82414** in the Zip column, press the **Tab** key, type **smiles@example.org** in the Email Address column, and then press the **Tab** key.

Next, you'll switch to Design view to verify that you can't change the design of the tblReferral table from the Veterinary database.

▶ **3.** Switch to Design view. The OwnerID field is the current field, and the Help message in the Field Properties section indicates that you can't change the Field Name property value for linked tables. See Figure 12-32.

Figure 12-32   Linked table in Design view

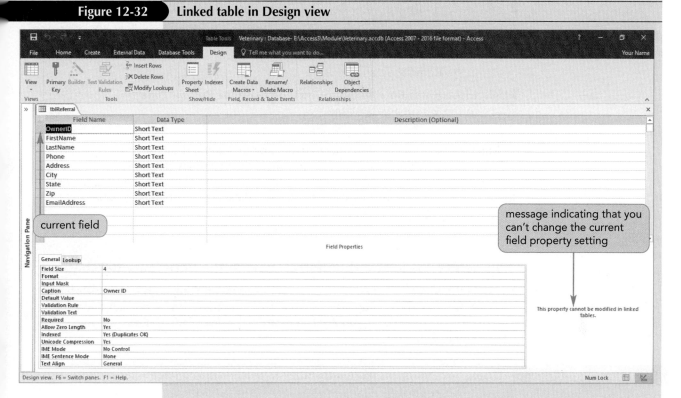

4. Press the **F6** key to select the Field Size property in the Field Properties pane. The Help message indicates that you can't change the Field Size property.

5. Press the **Tab** key to position the insertion point in the Format box. The standard Help message for the Format property appears, which means you can change this field property.

6. Close the table.

Now you'll open the Referral database to see the new record in the tblReferral table that you added from the Veterinary database. Then you'll delete that record and view the table in Design view.

To update the tblReferral table and view its design in the Referral database:

1. Start another instance of Access, keeping the Veterinary database open as well, and then open the Referral database located in the Access3 folder provided with your Data Files.

   Trouble? If the security warning is displayed below the ribbon, click the Enable Content button.

2. Open the Navigation Pane (if necessary), open the **tblReferral** table in Datasheet view, and then click the **row selector** for record 5. The record for Sarah Miles, which you added to the tblReferral linked table in the Veterinary database, appears as record 5 in the tblReferral table in the Referral database.

3. On the Home tab, in the Records group, click the **Delete** button, and then click the **Yes** button in the message box that opens to delete record 5.

▶ **4.** Switch to Design view. Because the tblReferral table is not a linked table in the Referral database (its own database), the Help message in the Field Properties pane does not warn you that you can't change the Field Name property. You can make any design changes you want to the tblReferral table in the Referral database.

▶ **5.** Close the tblReferral table, and then close the Referral database. You return to the Veterinary database.

Kimberly decides that she'd like to maintain the Referral database separately and asks you to delete the linked tblReferral table in the Veterinary database. When you delete the linked tblReferral table in the Veterinary database, you are deleting the *link* to the tblReferral table that exists in the Referral database; the tblReferral table will remain in the Referral database.

To delete the linked tblReferral table in the Veterinary database:

▶ **1.** In the Veterinary database, open the Navigation Pane, right-click **tblReferral** in the Navigation Pane to open the shortcut menu, and then click **Delete**. A dialog box asks if you want to remove the link to the tblReferral table. See Figure 12-33.

Figure 12-33   Dialog box that opens when attempting to delete a linked table

The dialog box confirms that you'll delete only the link to the tblReferral table but not the tblReferral table itself in the Referral database.

▶ **2.** Click the **Yes** button. The link to the tblReferral table is deleted, and the tblReferral table no longer appears in the Navigation Pane for the Veterinary database.

Next, Kimberly wants to create several queries for the Veterinary database, but she doesn't want the user interface for other users to be cluttered with queries they won't need to use. She asks if there's a way for her to have a special user interface to access the data in the Veterinary database. You can accomplish this by splitting the database.

Using the Database Splitter

TIP

Be sure to make a backup before splitting a database.

Users of a particular database might want to customize the user interface to create their own custom versions of the interface, while accessing the same central table data. The **Database Splitter** is an Access tool that splits an Access database into two files: one file contains the tables, and the other file contains the queries, forms, reports, and other database objects. Although a single master copy of the file containing the tables is stored and accessed, users can have their own copies of the other file and add their own queries, reports, and other objects to handle their unique processing needs. Each file created by the Database Splitter is an Access database. The database that contains the tables is called the **back-end database**, and the database that contains the other objects, including the user interface, is called the **front-end database**.

After you split a database, when users open a front-end database, the objects they open use data in the tables in the back-end database. Because the tables in the front-end database are linked tables that are stored in the back-end database, the front-end database contains the physical drive locations of the tables in the back-end database. You can move the front-end database to a different drive location without affecting the physical connections to the back-end database. However, if you move the back-end database to a different drive location, you'll need to use the Linked Table Manager to change the physical drive locations of the back-end database's tables in the front-end database.

People who develop databases and sell them to multiple companies usually split their databases. When a developer delivers a split database, the initial back-end database does not include the company's data, and the initial front-end database is complete as created by the developer. Companies use the front-end database to update their data in the back-end database, but they do not modify the front-end database in any way. Periodically, the database developer improves the front-end database by modifying and adding queries, reports, and other objects without changing the structure of the tables. In other words, the developer changes the front-end database but does not change the back-end database. The developer gives its client companies replacement front-end databases, which continue to work with the back-end database that contains the company's data.

Splitting a database also lets you place the files on different computers. You can place a copy of the front-end database on each user's computer and place the back-end database on a network server that users access through their front-end databases; this arrangement distributes the workload across the network. Finally, as a company grows, it might need a more powerful DBMS such as Oracle, SQL Server, DB2, or MySQL. You could retain the original Access front-end database and replace the Access back-end database with a new non-Access back-end database, which is an easier task than replacing all database objects.

Because splitting an Access database causes minimal disruption to a company's database processing as you periodically enhance the user interface, and because splitting provides greater flexibility for future growth, you should always develop your databases with splitting in mind. The entire process of splitting a database is illustrated in Figure 12-34.

Figure 12-34   Split Access database

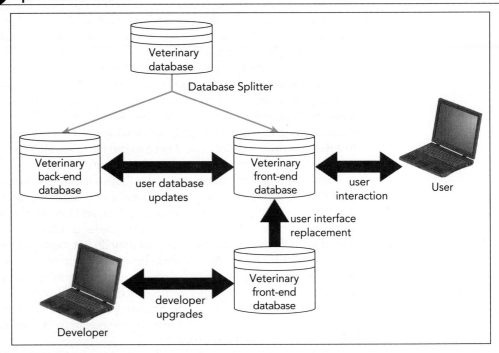

Using the Database Splitter

REFERENCE

- Make a backup copy of the database that you want to split.
- Start Access and open the database you want to split.
- Click the Database Tools tab, and then in the Move Data group, click the Access Database button to start the Database Splitter Wizard.
- Click the Split Database button, select the drive and folder for the back-end database, type a name for the database in the File name box, and then click the Split button.
- Click the OK button.

You'll use the Database Splitter to split the Veterinary database into two files. You will make a backup copy of the database before you split the database.

To use the Database Splitter:

1. Make a backup copy of the Veterinary database.

2. Click the **Database Tools** tab, and then in the Move Data group, click the **Access Database** button. The Database Splitter Wizard opens. See Figure 12-35.

Figure 12-35   Database Splitter Wizard

3. Click the **Split Database** button. The Create Back-end Database dialog box opens. The back-end database will contain the tables from the Veterinary database. You'll use the default filename (Veterinary_be with the .accdb extension) for the back-end database.

4. Navigate to the **Access3 > Module** folder (if necessary), and then click the **Split** button. After a few moments, a dialog box informs you that the database was successfully split.

5. Click the **OK** button to close the dialog boxes, and then scroll up to the top of the Navigation Pane, if necessary. See Figure 12-36.

Figure 12-36   Linked tables in the Veterinary database

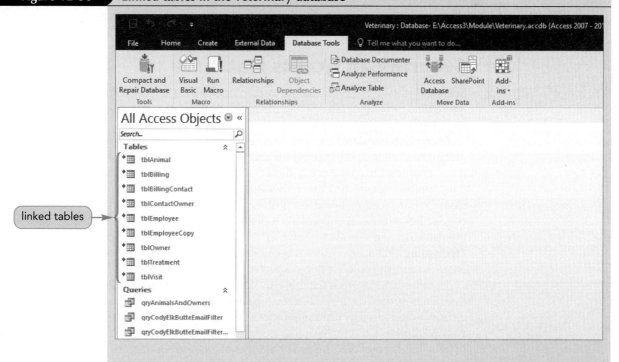

Each table in the Veterinary database has a blue arrow next to its name indicating that there's a link to that table in another file. The tables are no longer stored in the Veterinary database; they are stored in the Veterinary_be database file you just created with the Database Splitter. You can use the linked tables as if they were stored in the Veterinary database, except that you cannot change a table's design from the Veterinary database. You have to close the Veterinary database and open the Veterinary_be database to change a table's design.

▶ **6.** Scroll down the Navigation Pane. The queries, forms, reports, macros, and modules you've created appear in the Navigation Pane and are still stored in the Veterinary database.

You'll close the Veterinary database and then open the Veterinary_be database to verify which objects are stored in the back-end database.

To verify the contents of the back-end database:

▶ **1.** Close the Veterinary database, and then open the **Veterinary_be** database located in the Access3 > Module folder. The tables from the Veterinary database appear in the Navigation Pane with their usual icons, indicating the tables are now stored in the Veterinary_be database. No other objects exist in the Veterinary_be database.

▶ **2.** Open the **tblBilling** table in Design view. You can modify the design of the tables in the Veterinary_be database because they are stored in that database; they are not linked from another database as they are in the Veterinary database.

▶ **3.** Close the tblBilling table, close the Veterinary_be database, and then open the Veterinary database.

Securing an Access Database

Security refers to the protection of a database against unauthorized access, either intentional or accidental. Access provides a unique approach to securing a database by allowing the user to set a password that is used as a key to encrypt the database.

Encryption translates the data in a database to a scrambled format that's indecipherable to another program and stores it in an encrypted format. If unauthorized users attempt to bypass Access and get to the data directly, they will see only the encrypted version of the data. However, users accessing the data using Access and who have the password will have no problem working with the data. When a user stores or modifies data in an encrypted database, Access encrypts the data before updating the database. Once you've encrypted a database, you can use Access to decrypt it. **Decrypting** a database reverses the encryption. Before a user retrieves encrypted data using Access, the data will be decrypted and presented to the user in the normal format.

To prevent access to a database by an unauthorized user through Access, you can assign a password to the database. A **password** is a string of characters assigned to a database that users must enter before they can open the database. As long as the password is known only to authorized users of the database, unauthorized access to the database is prevented. You should use a password that's easily remembered by authorized users but is not obvious or easily guessed by others.

Access provides a single method to encrypt a database and set a password at the same time.

PROSKILLS

Decision Making: Determining When to Encrypt Data Using a Password

You probably are familiar with setting a password and using it to unlock a cell phone or to sign into your email or another device or software application. In these cases, the password acts as an authorization for you to use the device or software. Some software applications use a password for more than simply opening a file. Access uses the password to actually encrypt the data. The password itself isn't stored anywhere. Instead, the password is used as part of a mathematical formula to encrypt the data. When a user tries to open an encrypted file, the user is prompted to provide a password, and attempts to open the file. If the entered password is correct, the password is used to decrypt the data and open the file. If the password is incorrect, the data is not readable, and, therefore, the file will not open.

Because the password itself isn't stored anywhere and the data is actually encrypted, the contents of the database cannot be recovered if a user forgets a password. This is a security feature and also a potential problem if there are concerns about losing the password. Unlike your cell phone, which can be reset and still used if the password is lost, an encrypted Access file cannot be used if the password is lost.

If the data isn't sensitive, it's not as important to encrypt the data with a password. An encrypted Access database provides security for data and should be considered when the data it contains is sensitive, such as credit card information or private health record information. If the database is accessible only from a desktop computer in a secured, locked office, that may be enough security, and it may not be necessary to add encryption.

If you've decided to set a password, therefore encrypting your database, keep in mind that passwords are more secure when they consist of a mixture of numbers, symbols, and both lowercase and uppercase letters.

Access has some built-in security so that users cannot accidentally change data. When you open a database from the Open dialog box in Access, the default setting is for **shared access**; that is, two or more users can open and use the same database at the same time. However, if you want to set a password for encrypting the database, you first need to open the database with exclusive access. You do this by clicking the Open button arrow in the Open dialog box and selecting Open Exclusive on the menu that opens. When you open an Access database with **exclusive access**, you prevent multiple users from opening and using the database at the same time. You must open the database with exclusive access in order to set a password, so that you can guarantee that only one copy of the database is open when you set the password.

If you want someone to be able to view the data without changing it, you can open a database as a read-only file, by selecting the Open Read-Only option from the Open menu in the Open dialog box. **Open Read-Only** includes any database action that does not involve updating the database, such as running queries (but not action queries) and viewing table records. Actions that are prohibited when you open a database as read-only (because they involve updating the database) include changing the database design and updating table records. The other two open options on the Open menu open the selected database with exclusive access for reading and updating (Open Exclusive) or for reading only (Open Exclusive Read-Only).

When multiple users update the database at the same time, row-level locking is enabled so that one user can't change the row content while another user is viewing it. **Locking** denies access by other users to data while one user's updates are processed in the database. **Row-level locking** denies access by other users to the table rows one user is in the process of updating; other users can update the database simultaneously as long as the rows they need to update are not being updated by other users at the same time.

Setting and Removing Password Encryption

In order to set a password, you first open an Access database file with exclusive access to ensure there are no other users who are viewing or manipulating the data when you add or remove the password. After you open the file with exclusive access, you can open Backstage view to access the Encrypt with Password button. If you decide to apply encryption, you are prompted you to type the password twice. This is a security feature to ensure that you did not make a mistake the first time you type the password. Both password entries must be identical in order to set the password encryption. To remove password encryption, you click the Decrypt Database button in Backstage view. Doing so cancels the password protection for the database and also decrypts the database.

Kimberly is pleased with the changes you have made. As a final enhancement to the user interface, she asks you to set Access to open the navigation form you created in a previous module automatically when a user opens the Veterinary database.

Setting the Database Startup Options

In Access you can specify certain actions, called **startup options**, that take place when a database opens. For example, you can specify the name that appears in the Access window title bar, prevent users from using the Navigation Pane, or specify a form that is automatically opened when a user opens a database.

Kimberly wants the navigation form you created in a previous module to display automatically when users open the Veterinary database. This will avoid users having to use the Navigation Pane to access the navigation form.

Setting the Database Startup Options

- Open the database, and then click the File tab to open Backstage view.
- Click Options in the navigation bar to open the Access Options dialog box.
- In the left pane, click Current Database.
- Set the database startup options in the right pane, and then click the OK button to have these options take effect the next time the database is opened.

The Session 12.2 Visual Overview identifies the database startup options Kimberly wants you to set for the Veterinary database. In addition, you'll disable the **Enable error checking option**, which checks for design errors in forms and reports and alerts you to errors by displaying the Error Checking Options button. Disabling the Enable error checking option will suppress the display of the triangle-shaped error indicators that appear in the upper-right or upper-left corner of a control when a potential error occurs. Unlike all the other options, which appear on the Current Database page in the Access Options dialog box, the Enable error checking option appears on the Object Designers page in the Access Options dialog box, and disabling this option will affect all databases you open.

You'll finish developing the Veterinary database by setting the database startup options.

To set the database startup options in the Veterinary database:

▶ **1.** Click the **File** tab to open Backstage view, and then in the navigation bar, click **Options** in the navigation bar to open the Access Options dialog box.

▶ **2.** In the left pane of the dialog box, click **Current Database** to display the list of options for the current database.

▶ **3.** In the Application Title box, type **Veterinary Release 1**, click the **Display Form** arrow, and then click **frmNavigation**. This sets the title in the Access title bar and sets the frmNavigation form as the initial form that loads when the Veterinary database is opened.

▶ **4.** Scrolling as necessary, click the following check boxes to disable (uncheck) the options:

Use Access Special Keys

Enable Layout View

Enable design changes for tables in Datasheet view

Display Navigation Pane

Allow Full Menus

Allow Default Shortcut Menus

Track name AutoCorrect info

▶ **5.** Compare your Access Options dialog box to the Session 12.2 Visual Overview.

▶ **6.** In the left pane of the Access Options dialog box, click **Object Designers** to display the list of options for creating and modifying database objects, and then scroll to the bottom of the dialog box.

▶ **7.** If necessary, click the **Enable error checking** check box to clear it and disable all error checking options. See Figure 12-37.

Trouble? If the Error checking check box does not contain a checkmark, skip Step 7.

Figure 12-37 **Error checking options in the Access Options dialog box**

click to remove the checkmark and disable error checking

> **8.** Click the **OK** button to close the Access Options dialog box. A dialog box informs you that you must close and reopen the Veterinary database for the options you selected to take effect.

> **9.** Click the **OK** button to close the dialog box.

To test the database startup options you have set, you need to close and reopen the Veterinary database.

To test the database startup options:

> **1.** Click the **File** tab to open Backstage view, and then click **Close** in the navigation bar to close the Veterinary database without exiting Access.

> **2.** Click the **File** tab to open Backstage view again, click **Open** in the navigation bar, and then in the Recent list, click **Veterinary** to open the Veterinary database. See Figure 12-38.

Figure 12-38   Veterinary database user interface

The Veterinary database opens and displays the frmNavigation form. Notice the Navigation Pane is not available on the left side of the window, and the ribbon displays only the File and Home tabs. The name "Veterinary Release 1" appears in the Access window title bar.

▶ **3.** Click each of the tabs in the navigation form to verify that all features work properly on the Veterinary database user interface.

Kimberly likes the navigation startup setting but realizes that some of her staff will need access to the ribbon and database objects. One method her staff could use is to press and hold the Shift key when they open the database. You'll open the database using this method to bypass the startup options now.

To bypass the startup options when opening the database:

▶ **1.** Close the Veterinary database. Doing so also closes Access.

▶ **2.** Start Access, and then press and hold the **Shift** key while you click **Veterinary** in the Recent list.

The Veterinary database opens without the startup options you set. For instance, the Navigation Pane is now accessible on the left side of the window, and you can now use the shortcut keys to close a table, which had been disabled previously in the startup options when Allow Default Shortcut Menus was disabled.

▶ **3.** Open the Navigation Pane, open the **tblEmployee** table in Datasheet view, and then right-click the **tblEmployee tab** to display the shortcut menu.

▶ **4.** Click **Close** on the shortcut menu to close the tblEmployee table.

Using the Shift key to open the file bypasses the startup options, but Kimberly thinks this method also defeats the purpose of having startup options. Instead, she would like you to change the database options to fully display the ribbon and enable the database objects again. You'll reset the database startup options.

To reset the database startup options in the Veterinary database:

▶ **1.** Click the **File** tab to open Backstage view, and then in the navigation bar, click **Options** to open the Access Options dialog box.

▶ **2.** In the left pane of the dialog box, click **Current Database** to display the list of options for the current database.

▶ **3.** Click the **Display Form** arrow, and then click **(none)**.

▶ **4.** Scrolling as necessary, click the following check boxes to enable (check) the properties:

Use Access Special Keys

Enable Layout View

Enable design changes for tables in Datasheet view

Display Navigation Pane

Allow Full Menus

Allow Default Shortcut Menus

Track name AutoCorrect info

A dialog box opens that indicates the Track name AutoCorrect info option generates name maps for the database objects and may take several minutes.

▶ **5.** Click **OK** to accept and close the dialog box.

▶ **6.** In the left pane of the Access Options dialog box, click **Object Designers** to display the list of options for creating and modifying database objects, and then scroll to the bottom of the dialog box.

▶ **7.** Click the **Enable error checking** check box to select it and enable all error checking options.

▶ **8.** Click the **OK** button to close the Access Options dialog box. A dialog box may inform you that the Veterinary database must close all objects and update dependency Information.

▶ **9.** Click the **Yes** button to close the dialog box (if necessary). A dialog box informs you that you must close and reopen the Veterinary database for the changes to take effect.

▶ **10.** Click the **OK** button to close the dialog box, and then exit Access.

▶ **11.** Open the **Veterinary** database again to verify the ribbon and database objects are displayed.

▶ **12.** Close the Veterinary database and exit Access.

INSIGHT

Saving a Database as an ACCDE File

If a database contains VBA code, you can save an ACCDE file version of the database to prevent people from viewing or changing the VBA code. Saving an Access database as an **ACCDE file**, which has the .accde extension instead of the .accdb extension, compiles all VBA modules, removes all editable VBA source code, and compacts the resulting database. The database and its VBA code continue to run as normal, but users cannot view or edit the VBA code. Also, users can't view, modify, or create forms, reports, or modules in Design view, nor can they import or export forms, reports, or modules. Because an ACCDE file limits database design changes to tables and queries, saving a database as an ACCDE file is best suited to a front-end database. You should keep a backup copy of the complete front-end database in case you need to modify the database design. To save a database as an ACCDE file, follow these steps:

1. Open the database you want to save as an ACCDE file.
2. Click the File tab to open Backstage view, click Save As in the navigation bar, and then click Make ACCDE.
3. Click the Save As button to open the Save As dialog box.
4. Type the name for the file in the File name box, navigate to the location where you want to store the file, and then click the Save button.

Your work with the Veterinary database is now complete. Kimberly is happy with your work and believes the database will fully satisfy the requirements of the care center.

REVIEW

Session 12.2 Quick Check

1. You can specify sequential numbering or random numbering for a(n) _____ field.
2. What is the Performance Analyzer?
3. When do you use the Linked Table Manager?
4. What is the Database Splitter?
5. _____ refers to the protection of a database against unauthorized access, either intentional or accidental.
6. What is a startup option?

PRACTICE

Review Assignments

Data Files needed for the Review Assignments: *Ads.accdb, Autoclave_Specification_Sheet.pdf, Autoclave.xlsx, and Ordering.accdb (cont. from previous modules)*

Kimberly asks you to complete your work with the user interface for the Ordering database. To meet this request, complete the following steps:

1. Open the **Ordering** database you worked with in the previous three modules.

2. Open the **tblProduct** table datasheet, use an AutoFilter to filter records using the TempControlled field for values of Yes and Sterile field for values of Yes, and then save and close the table.

3. Use Filter By Form with the tblSupplier table to select all records in which the state is NC or SC and the category is Supplies. Apply the filter, save the filter as a query named **qryStateSuppliesFilter**, clear all filters, and then close the table.

4. Create a query named **qryProductSubquery** that selects the SupplierID field from the tblProduct table for all products that weigh 50 pounds or more (*Hint*: Do not show the weight field.) Switch to SQL view, copy the SQL code, and save the qryProductSubquery query.

5. Create a new query in SQL view. Paste the SQL code that you copied in the previous step from qryProductSubquery, and add code that uses the existing code as a subquery and selects all fields from the tblInvoice table where the SupplierID is in the tblInvoice table. Run the query, save the query as **qryProductSubqueryInvoice**, and then close the query.

6. Add a multivalued field to the end of the **tblInvoice** table, defining permitted values of **Courier**, **Email**, **Fax**, and **USPS**, and naming the field **Transmitted**. Save the table, and then add the following values to the field in the table datasheet: for record 4—Email and USPS, for record 8—Courier, and for record 12—Fax and USPS. Close the table.

7. Use the Simple Query Wizard to create a query named **qryInvoiceValue** that displays all fields from the tblInvoice table; for the Transmitted field, display only the version of the field that uses the Value property, and change its Caption property setting to **Transmitted**. Save and close the query.

8. Add an Attachment field named **ProductFiles** to the end of the tblProduct table, using a Caption property setting of **Product Files**. Attach the files **Autoclave_Specification_Sheet.pdf** and **Autoclave.xlsx** to the ProductFiles field for record 2 in the tblProduct table, and then close the table.

9. Add an AutoNumber field named **ProductNum** to the beginning of the tblProductSpecialEnviron table, using a Caption property setting of **Product Num** and a New Values property setting of Random. View the table in Datasheet view to see the random numbers. Save and close the table.

10. Use the Performance Analyzer to analyze the entire Product database, but do not implement any of the analysis results. How many analysis results of the Recommendation type did the Performance Analyzer find? Of the Suggestion type? Of the Idea type? If requested, record the answers in a Word document, and submit it to your instructor. Close the Performance Analyzer dialog box.

11. Use Windows File Explorer to move the Ads database from the Access3 > Review folder to the Access3 folder. Link to the tblAd table, and then move the Ads database to the Access3 > Review folder. Use the Linked Table Manager to update the link to the tblAd table. Open the tblAd table in Datasheet view, and then add a new record to the table: Ad Num **7**, Ad Date **7/12/2017**, Ad Cost **$250.00**, and Placed **Web ad**.

12. Close the Ordering database without exiting Access, create a copy of the Ordering database in the Access3 > Review folder, and then rename the copy as **Sellers**. Open the **Ordering** database in the Access3 > Review folder, and then use the Database Splitter to split the Product database. Use the default name for the back-end database, and store it in the Access3 > Review folder.

13. Set the same database startup options for the Ordering database that you set in Module 12 for the Veterinary database, using a value of **Vendor for Riverview Veterinary Care Center** for the Application Title option.

14. Compact and repair the database, exit Access, open the **Ordering** database, test all the navigation options, and then exit Access.

Case Problem 1

Data Files needed for this Case Problem: NewOptions.accdb and Salon.accdb *(cont. from previous module)*

Beauty To Go   Sue Miller asks you to complete your work with the user interface for the Salon database. To meet her request, complete the following steps:

1. Open the **Salon** database you worked with in the previous three modules.
2. Open the tblMember table datasheet, use an AutoFilter to filter records using the MemberStatus field for values of Inactive and On Hold, and then save and close the table.
3. Use Filter By Form with the **frmMemberInfo** form to select all records in which the Last Name is Sanchez or Smith and the city is Orlando. Apply the filter, save the filter as a query named **qryNameCityFilter**, and then close the form.
4. Create a query named **qryOptionTHSubquery** that selects the ServiceID field from the tblSchedule table for all options that are on ServiceDay TH. (*Hint*: Do not show the ServiceDay field.) Switch to SQL view, copy the SQL code, and then save and close the qryOptionTHSubquery query.
5. Create a new query in SQL view. Paste the SQL code you copied in the previous step from qryOptionTHSubquery, add code that uses the current code as a subquery and selects all fields from the tblService table where the ServiceID is in the tblSchedule table, and then run the query. Save the query as **qryOptionTHSubqueryMemberID**, and then save and close the query.
6. Add an Attachment field named **MemberAttachment** to the end of the tblMember table, using a Caption property setting of **Member Attachment**. Create two Notepad documents named **garcia_1.txt** and **garcia_2.txt**, each containing a thank-you note written by Sandra Garcia, thanking the Beauty To Go team for their wonderful work, and store them in the Access3 > Case1 folder. Attach both documents to the MemberAttachment field for record 3 (Sandra Garcia's record) in the tblMember table, resize the Member Attachment column to its best fit, and then save and close the table.
7. Add an AutoNumber field named **MemberNum** to the beginning of the tblSpecialMember table, using a Caption property setting of **Member Num** and a New Values property setting of Random. Specify the MemberNum field as the primary key. Resize the Member Num column to its best fit in the datasheet, and then save and close the table.
8. Use the Performance Analyzer to analyze the entire Salon database, but do not implement any of the analysis results. How many analysis results of the Recommendation type did the Performance Analyzer find? Of the Suggestion type? Of the Idea type? If requested, record the answers in a Word document, and submit it to your instructor. Close the Performance Analyzer dialog box.
9. Use Windows File Explorer to move the NewOptions database from the Access3 > Case1 folder to the Access3 folder. Link to the table in the **NewOptions** database located in the Access3 folder. Use Windows File Explorer to move the NewOptions database to the Access3 > Case1 folder, and then use the Linked Table Manager to update the link to the tblNewOptions table. Open the tblNewOptions table in Datasheet view, and then add a new record to the table: Option ID **157**, and Option Desc **Massage bi-weekly for 12 months**. Save and close the tblNewOptions table.
10. Close the Salon database without exiting Access, create a copy of the Salon database in the Access3 > Case1 folder, and then rename the copy as **InProgress**. Open the **Salon** database in the Access3 > Case1 folder, and then use the Database Splitter to split the Salon database. Use the default name for the back-end database, and store it in the Access3 > Case1 folder.
11. Set the same database startup options for the Salon database that you set in Module 12 for the Veterinary database, using a value of **Final Exercise** for the Application Title option.
12. Compact and repair the database, exit Access, open the **Salon** database, test all the navigation options, and then exit Access.

Case Problem 2

Data Files needed for this Case Problem: Bob_Smith_Bachelor_Degree.docx, Bob_ Smith_C++_Certificate.pdf, Room.accdb, and Technology.accdb *(cont. from previous module)*

Programming Pros Brent Hovis wants you to complete your work with the user interface for the Technology database. To meet his request, complete the following steps:

1. Open the **Technology** database you worked with in the previous three modules.

2. Open the tblContract table datasheet, use an AutoFilter to filter records using the SessionType field for values of Group or Private, and the Length is one hour. Save and close the table.

3. Use Filter By Form with the **frmStudent** form to select all records in which the city is Apex or Cary and the gender is F. Apply the filter, save the filter as a query named **qryCityGenderFilter**, and then close the form.

🌐 **Explore** 4. Create a query named **qryStudentGenderSubquery** that selects all students from the tblStudent table who are male. Create a query named **qryStudentGenderContracts** that contains all fields from the tblContract table for records whose StudentID is in the subquery qryStudentGenderSubquery. Use SQL view to create the qryStudentGenderContracts query. The results should be sorted in ascending order by StudentID. Save and close the query. (*Hint*: Create the qryStudentGenderSubquery first, copy the SQL code from the subquery to create the new query qryStudentGenderContracts, then open the new qryStudentGenderContracts in Design view to apply the sort order.)

5. Add a multivalued field to the end of the tblTutor table, defining permitted values of **Java, Visual Basic, Visual C++, and Visual C#**, and naming the field **Subject**. Allow the user to choose more than one subject. Save the table, and then add the following values to the field in the table datasheet: for record 1—Java and Visual Basic; for record 2—Visual C#; for record 3—Visual C++; for record 4—Java, Visual C++, and Visual C#; and for record 5—Visual Basic. Resize the Subject column to its best fit, and then save and close the table.

6. Use the Simple Query Wizard to create a query named **qryTutorMultivalued** that displays the TutorID, FirstName, LastName, and Subject from the tblTutor table; for the Subject field, display only the version of the field that displays multiple values in a text box. Resize the Subject column to its best fit, and then save and close the query.

7. Add an Attachment field named **Documents** to the end of the tblTutor table, using a Caption property setting of **Diplomas and References**. Attach two files named **Bob_Smith_C++_Certificate.pdf** and **Bob_Smith_Bachelor_Degree.docx**, to the Documents field for record 3 in the tblTutor table, resize the Documents column to its best fit, and then save and close the table.

8. Add an AutoNumber field named **SpecialNum** to the top of the tblSpecialSession table, using a Caption property setting of **Special Num** and a New Values property setting of Increment. Specify the SpecialNum field as the primary key. Resize the Special Num column to its best fit in the datasheet, and then save and close the table.

🌐 **Explore** 9. Use the Performance Analyzer to analyze the entire Lesson database. How many analysis results of the Recommendation type did the Performance Analyzer find? Of the Suggestion type? Of the Idea type? If requested, record the answers in a Word document, and submit it to your instructor. Use the Performance Analyzer to implement any Suggestion task, and perform any subsequent task(s) required due to implementing the Suggestion(s). Close the Performance Analyzer dialog box.

10. Use Windows File Explorer to move the Room database from the Access3 > Case2 folder to the Access3 folder. Link to the tblRoom table in the Room database located in the Access3 folder. Use Windows File Explorer to move the Room database to the Access3 > Case2 folder, and then use the Linked Table Manager to update the link to the tblRoom table. Open the tblRoom table in Datasheet view, and then add a new record to the table: Room Num **2**, Rental Cost **$75**, and Room Type **Group**. Close the table.

11. Close the Technology database without exiting Access, create a copy of the Technology database in the Access3 > Case2 folder, and then rename the copy as **Sessions**. Open the **Technology** database in the Access3 > Case2 folder, and then use the Database Splitter to split the Lesson database. Use the default name for the back-end database, and store it in the Access3 > Case2 folder.

12. Set the same database startup options for the Technology database that you set in Tutorial 12 for the Veterinary database, using a value of **Programming Pros Final** for the Application Title property.

13. Compact and repair the database, exit Access, open the **Technology** database, test all the navigation options, and then exit Access.

Case Problem 3

APPLY

Data Files needed for this Case Problem: Receipt2100.xlsx, Receipt2101.xlsx, StudentVolunteers.accdb, and Thrift.accdb (*cont. from previous module*)

Diane's Community Center   Diane Coleman wants you to complete your work with the user interface for the Thrift database. To meet her request, complete the following steps:

1. Open the **Thrift** database you worked with in the previous three modules.

2. Open the tblDonation table datasheet, use an AutoFilter to filter records using the Description field for values of New computer and New television, and then save and close the table.

3. Use Filter By Form with the **frmPatronDonations** form to select all records in which the Patron ID is 3022 or 3035 and the Description is Cash donation. Apply the filter, save the filter as a query named **qryPatronDescFilter**, and then close the form.

4. Create a query named **qryPatronOver100Subquery** that selects all PatronIDs from the tblDonation table where the DonationValue Is greater than 100. Use SQL view to create a query named **qryPatronNameOver100** that contains all fields from the tblPatron table for records whose PatronID is in the subquery qryPatronOver100Subquery. Save and close the query.

5. Add a multivalued field to the end of the tblPatron table, defining donation values of **Donor** and **Volunteer**, and naming the field **DonorType** with a Caption property value of **Donor Type**. Save the table, and then add the following values to the field in the table datasheet: for record 2—Donor; for record 3—Volunteer; for record 4—Donor and Volunteer; and for record 5—Volunteer. Resize the Donor Type column to its best fit, and then save and close the table.

6. Create a query named **qryDonorValue** that displays all fields from the tblPatron table; for the DonorType field, display only the version of the field that uses the Value property, and change its Caption property setting to **Donor Type**. Resize the Donor Type column to its best fit in the datasheet, and then save and close the query.

7. Add an Attachment field named **ReceiptFiles** to the end of the tblDonation table, using a Caption property setting of **Receipt Files**. Attach the document named **Receipt2100.xlsx** to record 1 and **Receipt2101.xlsx** to record 2 in the ReceiptFiles field in the tblDonation table, and then close the table.

8. Add an AutoNumber field named **DonationNum** to the top of the tblSpecialDonation table, using a Caption property setting of **Donation Num** and a New Values property setting of Increment. Specify the DonationNum field as the primary key. Resize the Donation Num column to its best fit in the datasheet, and then save and close the table.

9. Use the Performance Analyzer to analyze the entire Thrift database, but do not implement any of the analysis results. How many analysis results of the Recommendation type did the Performance Analyzer find? Of the Suggestion type? Of the Idea type? If requested, record the answers in a Word document, and submit it to your instructor. Close the Performance Analyzer dialog box.

10. Use Windows File Explorer to move the StudentVolunteers database from the Access3 > Case3 folder to the Access3 folder. Link to the tblStudentVolunteers table in the StudentVolunteers database located in the Access3 folder. Use Windows File Explorer to move the StudentVolunteers database to the Access3 > Case3 folder, and then use the Linked Table Manager to refresh the link to the tblStudentVolunteers table.

11. Close the Thrift database without exiting Access, create a copy of the Thrift database in the Access3 > Case3 folder, and then rename the copy as **DianeDonations**. Open the **Thrift** database in the Access3 > Case3 folder, and then use the Database Splitter to split the Thrift database. Use the default name for the back-end database, and store it in the Access3 > Case3 folder.

12. Set the same startup options for the Thrift database that you set in Module 12 for the Veterinary database, using a value of **Diane Donations Final** for the Application Title property.

13. Compact and repair the database, exit Access, open the **Thrift** database, test all the navigation options, and then exit Access.

Case Problem 4

APPLY

Data File needed for this Case Problem: *BlueRidge.accdb (cont. from previous module), Singh_1.txt, and Singh_2.txt*

Hike Appalachia   Molly and Bailey Johnson ask you to complete your work with the user interface for the BlueRidge database. To meet their request, complete the following steps:

1. Open the **BlueRidge** database you worked with in the previous three modules.

2. Open the tblTour table datasheet, use an AutoFilter to filter records using the TourType field for values of Hiking and Climbing, and then save and close the table.

3. Use Filter By Form with the **tblHiker** table to select all records in which the last name is Jackson or Smith and the state is NC or SC. Apply the filter, save the filter as a query named **qryNameStateFilter**, and then save and close the table.

4. Create a query named **qryTour115Subquery** that selects all HikerIDs from the tblReservation table where the TourID is 115. Use SQL view to create a query named **qryTour115Hiker** that contains all fields from the tblHiker table for records whose HikerID is in the subquery qryTour115Subquery. Save and close the query.

5. Add an Attachment field named **Documents** to the end of the tblGuide table, using a Caption property setting of **Medical Documents**. Attach the documents **Singh_1.txt** and **Singh_2.txt** in the Access3 > Case4 folder to the Documents field for record 4 in the tblGuide table, and then close the table.

6. Add an AutoNumber field named **HikerNum** to the beginning of the tblSelectedReservation table, using a Caption property setting of **Hiker Num** and a New Values property setting of Increment. Specify the HikerNum field as the primary key. Save and close the table.

7. Use the Performance Analyzer to analyze the entire BlueRidge database, but do not implement any of the analysis results. How many analysis results of the Recommendation type did the Performance Analyzer find? Of the Suggestion type? Of the Idea type? If requested, record the answers in a Word document, and submit it to your instructor. Use the Performance Analyzer to implement any Suggestion task, and perform any subsequent task(s) required due to implementing the Suggestion(s). Close the Performance Analyzer dialog box.

8. Close the BlueRidge database without exiting Access, create a copy of the BlueRidge database in the Access3 > Case4 folder, and then rename the copy as **Tours**. Open the **BlueRidge** database in the Access3 > Case4 folder, and then use the Database Splitter to split the BlueRidge database. Use the default name for the back-end database, and store it in the Access3 > Case4 folder.

9. Set the same database startup options for the BlueRidge database that you set in Module 12 for the Veterinary database, using a value of **Hike Appalachia Tours** for the Application Title option.

10. Compact and repair the BlueRidge database, close the BlueRidge database without exiting Access, open the **BlueRidge** database, test all the navigation options, and then exit Access.

OBJECTIVES

- Learn the characteristics of a table
- Learn about primary, candidate, alternate, composite, and foreign keys
- Study one-to-one, one-to-many, and many-to-many relationships
- Learn to describe tables and relationships with entity-relationship diagrams and with a shorthand method
- Study database integrity constraints for primary keys, referential integrity, and domains
- Learn about determinants, functional dependencies, anomalies, and normalization
- Understand the differences among natural, artificial, and surrogate keys
- Learn about naming conventions

Relational Databases and Database Design

This appendix introduces you to the basics of database design. Before trying to master this material, be sure you understand the following concepts: data, information, field, field value, record, table, relational database, common field, database management system (DBMS), and relational database management system (RDBMS).

STARTING DATA FILES

There are no starting Data Files needed for this appendix.

Tables

A relational database stores its data in tables. A **table** is a two-dimensional structure made up of rows and columns. The terms table, **record** (row), and **field** (column) are the popular names for the more formal terms **relation** (table), **tuple** (row), and **attribute** (column), as shown in Figure A-1.

Figure A-1	A table (relation) consisting of records and fields

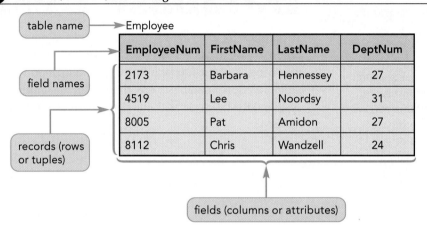

The Employee table shown in Figure A-1 is an example of a relational database table, a two-dimensional structure with the following characteristics:

- Each row is unique. Because no two rows are the same, you can easily locate and update specific data. For example, you can locate the row for EmployeeNum 8005 and change the FirstName value, Pat, the LastName value, Amidon, or the DeptNum value, 27.
- The order of the rows is unimportant. You can add or view rows in any order. For example, you can view the rows in LastName order instead of EmployeeNum order.
- Each table entry contains a single value. At the intersection of each row and column, you cannot have more than one value. For example, each row in Figure A-1 contains one EmployeeNum value, one FirstName value, one LastName value, and one DeptNum value.
- The order of the columns is unimportant. You can add or view columns in any order.
- Each column has a unique name called the **field name**. The field name allows you to access a specific column without needing to know its position within the table.
- Each row in a table describes, or shows the characteristics of, an entity. An **entity** is a person, place, object, event, or idea for which you want to store and process data. For example, EmployeeNum, FirstName, LastName, and DeptNum are characteristics of the employees of a company. The Employee table represents all the employee entities and their characteristics. That is, each row of the Employee table describes a different employee of the company using the characteristics of EmployeeNum, FirstName, LastName, and DeptNum. The Employee table includes only characteristics of employees. Other tables would exist for the company's other entities. For example, a Department table would describe the company's departments and a Position table would describe the company's job positions.

Knowing the characteristics of a table leads directly to a definition of a relational database. A **relational database** is a collection of tables (relations).

Note that this book uses singular table names, such as Employee and Department, but some people use plural table names, such as Employees and Departments. You can use either singular table names or plural table names, as long as you consistently use the style you choose.

Keys

Primary keys ensure that each row in a table is unique. A **primary key** is a column, or a collection of columns, whose values uniquely identify each row in a table. In addition to being *unique*, a primary key must be *minimal* (that is, contain no unnecessary extra columns) and must not change in value. For example, in Figure A-2 the State table contains one record per state and uses the StateAbbrev column as its primary key.

Figure A-2 A table and its keys

alternate keys

State

primary key

StateAbbrev	StateName	EnteredUnionOrder	StateBird	StatePopulation
CT	Connecticut	5	American robin	3,590,347
MI	Michigan	26	robin	9,883,360
SD	South Dakota	40	pheasant	833,354
TN	Tennessee	16	mockingbird	6,456,243
TX	Texas	28	mockingbird	26,059,203

Could any other column, or collection of columns, be the primary key of the State table?

- Could the StateBird column serve as the primary key? No, because the StateBird column does not have unique values (for example, the mockingbird is the state bird of more than one state).
- Could the StatePopulation column serve as the primary key? No, because the StatePopulation column values change periodically and are not guaranteed to be unique.
- Could the StateAbbrev and StateName columns together serve as the primary key? No, because the combination of these two columns is not minimal. Something less, such as the StateAbbrev column by itself, can serve as the primary key.
- Could the StateName column serve as the primary key? Yes, because the StateName column has unique values. In a similar way, you could select the EnteredUnionOrder column as the primary key for the State table. One column, or a collection of columns, that can serve as a primary key is called a **candidate key**. The candidate keys for the State table are the StateAbbrev column, the StateName column, and the EnteredUnionOrder column. You choose one of the candidate keys to be the primary key, and each remaining candidate key is called an **alternate key**. The StateAbbrev column is the State table's primary key in Figure A-2, so the StateName and EnteredUnionOrder columns become alternate keys in the table.

Figure A-3 shows a City table containing the fields StateAbbrev, CityName, and CityPopulation.

Figure A-3   A table with a composite key

composite primary key

City

StateAbbrev	CityName	CityPopulation
CT	Hartford	124,062
CT	Madison	18,803
CT	Portland	9,551
MI	Lansing	119,128
SD	Madison	6,482
SD	Pierre	13,899
TN	Nashville	569,462
TX	Austin	757,688
TX	Portland	16,490

What is the primary key for the City table? The values for the CityPopulation column periodically change and are not guaranteed to be unique, so the CityPopulation column cannot be the primary key. Because the values for each of the other two columns are not unique, the StateAbbrev column alone cannot be the primary key and neither can the CityName column (for example, there are two cities named Madison and two cities named Portland). The primary key is the combination of the StateAbbrev and CityName columns. Both columns together are needed to identify—uniquely and minimally— each row in the City table. A multiple-column key is called a **composite key** or a **concatenated key**. A multiple-column primary key is called a **composite primary key**.

The StateAbbrev column in the City table is also a foreign key. A **foreign key** is a column, or a collection of columns, in one table in which each column value must match the value of the primary key of some table or must be null. A **null** is the absence of a value in a particular table entry. A null value is not blank, nor zero, nor any other value. You give a null value to a column value when you do not know its value or when a value does not apply. As shown in Figure A-4, the values in the City table's StateAbbrev column match the values in the State table's StateAbbrev column. Thus, the StateAbbrev column, the primary key of the State table, is a foreign key in the City table. Although the field name StateAbbrev is the same in both tables, the names could be different. As a rule, experts use the same name for a field stored in two or more tables to broadcast clearly that they store similar values; however, some exceptions exist.

| Figure A-4 | StateAbbrev as a primary key (State table) and a foreign key (City table) |

primary key (State table)

State

StateAbbrev	StateName	EnteredUnionOrder	StateBird	StatePopulation
CT	Connecticut	5	American robin	3,518,288
MI	Michigan	26	robin	9,969,727
SD	South Dakota	40	pheasant	812,383
TN	Tennessee	16	mockingbird	6,296,254
TX	Texas	28	mockingbird	24,782,302

composite primary key (City table)

City

foreign key

StateAbbrev	CityName	CityPopulation
CT	Hartford	124,062
CT	Madison	18,803
CT	Portland	9,551
MI	Lansing	119,128
SD	Madison	6,482
SD	Pierre	13,899
TN	Nashville	596,462
TX	Austin	757,688
TX	Portland	16,490

A **nonkey field** is a field that is not part of the primary key. In the two tables shown in Figure A-4, all fields are nonkey fields except the StateAbbrev field in the State and City tables and the CityName field in the City table. "Key" is an ambiguous word because it can refer to a primary, candidate, alternate, or foreign key. When the word "key" appears alone, however, it means primary key and the definition for a nonkey field consequently makes sense.

Relationships

In a database, a table can be associated with another table in one of three ways: a one-to-many relationship, a many-to-many relationship, or a one-to-one relationship.

One-to-Many Relationship

The Department and Employee tables, shown in Figure A-5, have a one-to-many relationship. A **one-to-many relationship** (abbreviated **1:M** or **1:N**) exists between two tables when each row in the first table (sometimes called the **primary table**) matches many rows in the second table and each row in the second table (sometimes called the **related table**) matches at most one row in the first table. "Many" can mean zero rows, one row, or two or more rows. As Figure A-5 shows, the DeptNum field, which is a foreign key in the Employee table and the primary key in the Department table, is the common field that ties together the rows of the two tables. Each department has many employees; and each employee works in exactly one department or hasn't been assigned to a department, if the DeptNum field value for that employee is null.

| Figure A-5 | A one-to-many relationship |

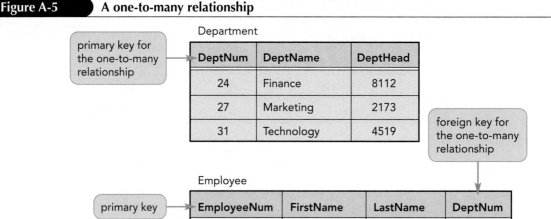

Many-to-Many Relationship

In Figure A-6, the Employee table (with the EmployeeNum field as its primary key) and the Position table (with the PositionID field as its primary key) have a many-to-many relationship. A **many-to-many relationship** (abbreviated as **M:N**) exists between two tables when each row in the first table matches many rows in the second table and each row in the second table matches many rows in the first table. In a relational database, you must use a third table (often called an **intersection table**, **junction table**, or **link table**) to serve as a bridge between the two many-to-many tables; the third table has the primary keys of the two many-to-many tables as its primary key. The original tables now each have a one-to-many relationship with the new table. The EmployeeNum and PositionID fields represent the primary key of the Employment table that is shown in Figure A-6. The EmployeeNum field, which is a foreign key in the Employment table and the primary key in the Employee table, is the common field that ties together the rows of the Employee and Employment tables. Likewise, the PositionID field is the common field for the Position and Employment tables. Each employee may serve in many different positions within the company over time, and each position in the company will be filled by different employees over time.

Figure A-6   A many-to-many relationship

primary key
(Position table)

primary key
(Employee
table)

Employee

EmployeeNum	FirstName	LastName	DeptNum
2173	Barbara	Hennessey	27
4519	Lee	Noordsy	31
8005	Pat	Amidon	27
8112	Chris	Wandzell	24

Position

PositionID	PositionDesc	PayGrade
1	Director	45
2	Manager	40
3	Analyst	30
4	Clerk	20

composite primary
key of the
intersection table

foreign keys related
to the Employee and
Position tables

Employment

EmployeeNum	PositionID	StartDate	EndDate
2173	2	12/14/2011	
4519	1	04/23/2013	
4519	3	11/11/2007	04/22/2013
8005	3	06/05/2012	08/25/2013
8005	4	07/02/2010	06/04/2012
8112	1	12/15/2012	
8112	2	10/04/2011	12/14/2012

One-to-One Relationship

In Figure A-5, recall that there's a one-to-many relationship between the Department table (the primary table) and the Employee table (the related table). Each department has many employees, and each employee works in one department. The DeptNum field in the Employee table serves as a foreign key to connect records in that table to records with matching DeptNum field values in the Department table.

Furthermore, each department has a single employee who serves as the head of the department, and each employee either serves as the head of a department or simply works in a department without being the department head. Therefore, the Department and Employee tables not only have a one-to-many relationship, but these two tables also have a second relationship, a one-to-one relationship. A **one-to-one relationship** (abbreviated **1:1**) exists between two tables when each row in each table has at most one matching row in the other table. As shown in Figure A-7, each DeptHead field value in the Department table represents the employee number in the Employee table of the employee who heads the department. In other words, each DeptHead field value in the Department table matches exactly one EmployeeNum field value in the Employee table. At the same time, each EmployeeNum field value in the Employee table matches at most one DeptHead field value in the Department table—matching one DeptHead field value if the employee is a department head, or matching zero DeptHead field values if the employee is not a department head. For this one-to-one relationship, the EmployeeNum field in the Employee table and the DeptHead field in the Department table are the fields that link the two tables, with the DeptHead field serving as a foreign key in the Department table and the EmployeeNum field serving as a primary key in the Employee table.

Some database designers might use EmployeeNum instead of DeptHead as the field name for the foreign key in the Department table because they both represent the employee number for the employees of the company. However, DeptHead better identifies the purpose of the field and would more commonly be used as the field name.

Figure A-7	A one-to-one relationship

Entity Subtype

Suppose the company awards annual bonuses to a small number of employees who fill director positions in selected departments. As shown in Figure A-8, you could store the Bonus field in the Employee table because a bonus is an attribute associated with employees. The Bonus field would contain either the amount of the employee's bonus (record 4 in the Employee table) or a null value for employees without bonuses (records 1 through 3 in the Employee table).

Figure A-8	Bonus field added to the Employee table

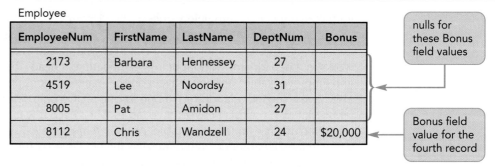

Figure A-9 shows an alternative approach, in which the Bonus field is placed in a separate table, the EmployeeBonus table. The EmployeeBonus table's primary key is the EmployeeNum field, and the table contains one row for each employee earning a bonus. Because some employees do not earn a bonus, the EmployeeBonus table has fewer rows than the Employee table. However, each row in the EmployeeBonus table has a matching row in the Employee table, with the EmployeeNum field serving as the common field; the EmployeeNum field is the primary key in the Employee table and is a foreign key in the EmployeeBonus table.

Figure A-9	Bonus values stored in a separate table, an entity subtype

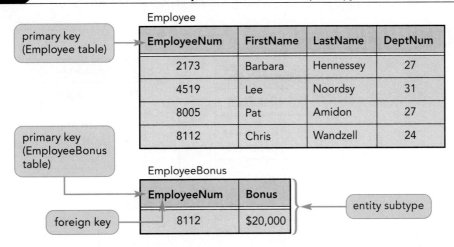

The EmployeeBonus table, in this situation, is called an **entity subtype**, a table whose primary key is a foreign key to a second table and whose fields are additional fields for the second table. Database designers create an entity subtype in two situations. In the first situation, some users might need access to all employee fields, including employee bonuses, while other employees might need access to all employee fields except bonuses. Because most DBMSs allow you to control which tables a user can access, you can specify that some users can access both tables and that other users can access the Employee table but not the EmployeeBonus table, keeping the employee bonus information hidden from the latter group. In the second situation, you can create an entity subtype when a table has fields that could have nulls, as was the case for the Bonus field stored in the Employee table in Figure A-8. You should be aware that database experts debate the validity of the use of nulls in relational databases, and many experts insist that you should never use nulls. This warning against nulls is partly based on the inconsistent way different RDBMSs treat nulls and partly due to the lack of a firm theoretical foundation for how to use nulls. In any case, entity subtypes are an alternative to the use of nulls.

Entity-Relationship Diagrams

A common shorthand method for describing tables is to write the table name followed by its fields in parentheses, underlining the fields that represent the primary key and identifying the foreign keys for a table immediately after the table. Using this method, the tables that appear in Figures A-5 through A-7 and Figure A-9 are described in the following way:

Department (<u>DeptNum</u>, DeptName, DeptHead)
 Foreign key: DeptHead to Employee table
Employee (<u>EmployeeNum</u>, FirstName, LastName, DeptNum)
 Foreign key: DeptNum to Department table
Position (<u>PositionID</u>, PositionDesc, PayGrade)
Employment (<u>EmployeeNum</u>, <u>PositionID</u>, StartDate, EndDate)
 Foreign key: EmployeeNum to Employee table
 Foreign key: PositionID to Position table
EmployeeBonus (<u>EmployeeNum</u>, Bonus)
 Foreign key: EmployeeNum to Employee table

Another popular way to describe tables *and their relationships* is with entity-relationship diagrams. An **entity-relationship diagram (ERD)** shows a database's entities and the relationships among the entities in a symbolic, visual way. In an ERD, an entity and a table are equivalent. Figure A-10 shows an entity-relationship diagram for the tables that appear in Figures A-5 through A-7 and Figure A-9.

Figure A-10 An entity-relationship diagram (ERD)

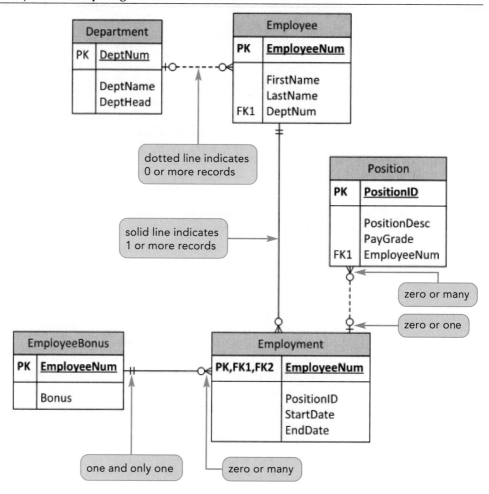

ERDs have the following characteristics:

- A table is represented by a rectangle that contains the table name and lists the field names. Within each rectangle, the primary key is identified with the abbreviation PK, and any foreign keys are designated with FK. Required fields are formatted in bold.
- Relationships are identified by lines joining the tables. A solid relationship line between two tables indicates there could be 1 or more related records. A dotted relationship line between two tables indicates there could be 0 or more related records.

- At the ends of each relationship line, symbols identify the minimum and maximum possible number of related records from each entity in the relationship. A single perpendicular line represents 1 record, a circle represents 0 records, and a group of three branching lines—known as a crow's foot—represents many records. A one-to-many relationship is represented by a 1 at one end of the relationship line and a crow's foot at the opposite end of the relationship line. For example, the Department and Employee tables have a one-to-many relationship. In a similar manner, a many-to-many relationship exists between the Employee and Position entities and one-to-one relationships exist between the Department and Employee entities and between the Employee and EmployeeBonus entities. The relationships in Figure A-10 illustrate all the possible designations for the ends of lines except for "one or many," which is represented by a single perpendicular line with a crow's foot.

Integrity Constraints

A database has **integrity** if its data follows certain rules; each rule is called an **integrity constraint**. The ideal is to have the DBMS enforce all integrity constraints. If a DBMS can enforce some integrity constraints but not others, the other integrity constraints must be enforced by other programs or by the people who use the DBMS. Integrity constraints can be divided into three groups: primary key constraints, foreign key constraints, and domain integrity constraints.

- One primary key constraint is inherent in the definition of a primary key, which says that the primary key must be unique. The **entity integrity constraint** says that the primary key cannot be null. For a composite key, none of the individual fields can be null. The uniqueness and nonnull properties of a primary key ensure that you can reference any data value in a database by supplying its table name, field name, and primary key value.
- Foreign keys provide the mechanism for forming a relationship between two tables, and referential integrity ensures that only valid relationships exist. **Referential integrity** is the constraint specifying that each nonnull foreign key value must match a primary key value in the primary table. Specifically, referential integrity means that you cannot add a row containing an unmatched foreign key value. Referential integrity also means that you cannot change or delete the related primary key value and leave the foreign key orphaned. In some RDBMSs, when you create a relationship, you can specify one of these options: restricted, cascades, or nullifies. If you specify **restricted** and then change or delete a primary key, the DBMS updates or deletes the value only if there are no matching foreign key values. If you choose **cascades** and then change a primary key value, the DBMS changes the matching foreign key values to the new primary key value, or, if you delete a primary key value, the DBMS also deletes the matching foreign key rows. If you choose **nullifies** and then change or delete a primary key value, the DBMS sets all matching foreign key values to null.
- A **domain** is a set of values from which one or more fields draw their actual values. A **domain integrity constraint** is a rule you specify for a field. By choosing a data type for a field, you impose a constraint on the set of values allowed for the field. You can create specific validation rules for a field to limit its domain further. As you make a field's domain definition more precise, you exclude more and more unacceptable values for the field. For example, in the State table, shown in Figures A-2 and A-4, you could define the domain for the EnteredUnionOrder field to be a unique integer between 1 and 50 and the domain for the StateBird field to be any text string containing 25 or fewer characters.

Dependencies and Determinants

Just as tables are related to other tables, fields are also related to other fields. Consider the modified Employee table shown in Figure A-11. Its description is:

Employee (<u>EmployeeNum</u>, <u>PositionID</u>, LastName, PositionDesc, StartDate, HealthPlan, PlanDesc)

Figure A-11   **A table combining fields from three tables**

composite primary key

Employee

EmployeeNum	PositionID	LastName	PositionDesc	StartDate	HealthPlan	PlanDesc
2173	2	Hennessey	Manager	12/14/2011	B	Managed HMO
4519	1	Noordsy	Director	04/23/2013	A	Managed PPO
4519	3	Noordsy	Analyst	11/11/2007	A	Managed PPO
8005	3	Amidon	Analyst	06/05/2012	C	Health Savings
8005	4	Amidon	Clerk	07/02/2010	C	Health Savings
8112	1	Wandzell	Director	12/15/2012	A	Managed PPO
8112	2	Wandzell	Manager	10/04/2011	A	Managed PPO

The modified Employee table combines several fields from the Employee, Position, and Employment tables that appeared in Figure A-6. The EmployeeNum and LastName fields are from the Employee table. The PositionID and PositionDesc fields are from the Position table. The EmployeeNum, PositionID, and StartDate fields are from the Employment table. The HealthPlan and PlanDesc fields are new fields for the Employee table, whose primary key is now the combination of the EmployeeNum and PositionID fields.

In the Employee table, each field is related to other fields. To determine field relationships, you ask "Does a value for a particular field give me a single value for another field?" If the answer is Yes, then the two fields are **functionally** related. For example, a value for the EmployeeNum field determines a single value for the LastName field, and a value for the LastName field depends on the value of the EmployeeNum field. In other words, EmployeeNum functionally determines LastName, and LastName is functionally dependent on EmployeeNum. In this case, EmployeeNum is called a determinant. A **determinant** is a field, or a collection of fields, whose values determine the values of another field. A field is functionally dependent on another field (or a collection of fields) if that other field is a determinant for it.

You can graphically show a table's functional dependencies and determinants in a **bubble diagram**; a bubble diagram is also called a **data model diagram** or a **functional dependency diagram**. Figure A-12 shows the bubble diagram for the Employee table shown in Figure A-11.

| Figure A-12 | A bubble diagram for the modified Employee table |

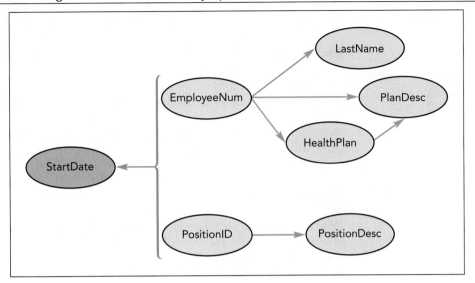

You can read the bubble diagram in Figure A-12 as follows:

- The EmployeeNum field is a determinant for the LastName, HealthPlan, and PlanDesc fields.
- The PositionID field is a determinant for the PositionDesc field.
- The StartDate field is functionally dependent on the EmployeeNum and PositionID fields together.
- The HealthPlan field is a determinant for the PlanDesc field.

Note that EmployeeNum and PositionID together serve as a determinant for the StartDate field and for all fields that depend on the EmployeeNum field alone and the PositionID field alone. Some experts include these additional fields and some don't. The previous list of determinants does not include these additional fields.

An alternative way to show determinants is to list the determinant, a right arrow, and then the dependent fields, separated by commas. Using this alternative, the determinants shown in Figure A-12 are:

EmployeeNum → LastName, HealthPlan, PlanDesc
PositionID → PositionDesc
EmployeeNum, PositionID → StartDate
HealthPlan → PlanDesc

Only the StartDate field is functionally dependent on the table's full primary key, the EmployeeNum and PositionID fields. The LastName, HealthPlan, and PlanDesc fields have partial dependencies because they are functionally dependent on the EmployeeNum field, which is part of the primary key. A **partial dependency** is a functional dependency on part of the primary key, instead of the entire primary key. Does another partial dependency exist in the Employee table? Yes, the PositionDesc field has a partial dependency on the PositionID field.

Because the EmployeeNum field is a determinant of both the HealthPlan and PlanDesc fields, and the HealthPlan field is a determinant of the PlanDesc field, the HealthPlan and PlanDesc fields have a transitive dependency. A **transitive dependency** is a functional dependency between two nonkey fields, which are both dependent on a third field.

How do you know which functional dependencies exist among a collection of fields, and how do you recognize partial and transitive dependencies? The answers lie with the questions you ask as you gather the requirements for a database application. For each field and entity, you must gain an accurate understanding of its meaning and relationships in the context of the application. **Semantic object modeling** is an entire area of study within the database field devoted to the meanings and relationships of data.

Anomalies

When you use a DBMS, you are more likely to get results you can trust if you create your tables carefully. For example, problems might occur with tables that have partial and transitive dependencies, whereas you won't have as much trouble if you ensure that your tables include only fields that are directly related to each other. Also, when you remove data redundancy from a table, you improve that table. **Data redundancy** occurs when you store the same data in more than one place.

The problems caused by data redundancy and by partial and transitive dependencies are called **anomalies** because they are undesirable irregularities of tables. Anomalies are of three types: insertion, deletion, and update.

To examine the effects of these anomalies, consider the modified Employee table that is shown again in Figure A-13.

| Figure A-13 | A table with insertion, deletion, and update anomalies |

composite primary key

Employee

EmployeeNum	PositionID	LastName	PositionDesc	StartDate	HealthPlan	PlanDesc
2173	2	Hennessey	Manager	12/14/2011	B	Managed HMO
4519	1	Noordsy	Director	04/23/2013	A	Managed PPO
4519	3	Noordsy	Analyst	11/11/2007	A	Managed PPO
8005	3	Amidon	Analyst	06/05/2012	C	Health Savings
8005	4	Amidon	Clerk	07/02/2010	C	Health Savings
8112	1	Wandzell	Director	12/15/2012	A	Managed PPO
8112	2	Wandzell	Manager	10/04/2011	A	Managed PPO

- An **insertion anomaly** occurs when you cannot add a record to a table because you do not know the entire primary key value. For example, you cannot add the new employee Cathy Corbett with an EmployeeNum of 3322 to the Employee table if you do not know her position in the company. Entity integrity prevents you from leaving any part of a primary key null. Because the PositionID field is part of the primary key, you cannot leave it null. To add the new employee, your only option is to make up a PositionID field value, until you determine the correct position. This solution misrepresents the facts and is unacceptable, if a better approach is available.

- A **deletion anomaly** occurs when you delete data from a table and unintentionally lose other critical data. For example, if you delete EmployeeNum 2173 because Hennessey is no longer an employee, you also lose the only instance of HealthPlan B in the database. Thus, you no longer know that HealthPlan B is the "Managed HMO" plan.
- An **update anomaly** occurs when a change to one field value requires the DBMS to make more than one change to the database, and a failure by the database to make all the changes results in inconsistent data. For example, if you change a LastName, HealthPlan, or PlanDesc field value for EmployeeNum 8005, the DBMS must change multiple rows of the Employee table. If the DBMS fails to change all the rows, the LastName, HealthPlan, or PlanDesc field now has different values in the database and is inconsistent.

Normalization

Database design is the process of determining the content and structure of data in a database in order to support some activity on behalf of a user or group of users. After you have determined the collection of fields users need to support an activity, you need to determine the precise tables needed for the collection of fields and then place those fields into the correct tables. Understanding the functional dependencies of all fields; recognizing the anomalies caused by data redundancy, partial dependencies, and transitive dependencies when they exist; and knowing how to eliminate the anomalies are all crucial to good database design. Failure to eliminate anomalies leads to data redundancy and can cause data integrity and other problems as your database grows in size.

The process of identifying and eliminating anomalies is called **normalization**. Using normalization, you start with a collection of tables, apply sets of rules to eliminate anomalies, and produce a new collection of problem-free tables. The sets of rules are called **normal forms**. Of special interest for our purposes are the first three normal forms: first normal form, second normal form, and third normal form. First normal form improves the design of your tables, second normal form improves the first normal form design, and third normal form applies even more stringent rules to produce an even better design. Note that normal forms beyond third normal form exist; these higher normal forms can improve a database design in some situations but won't be covered in this section.

First Normal Form

Consider the Employee table shown in Figure A-14. For each employee, the table contains EmployeeNum, which is the primary key; the employee's first name, last name, health plan code and description; and the ID, description, pay grade, and start date of each position held by the employee. For example, Barbara Hennessey has held one position, while the other three employees have held two positions. Because each entry in a table must contain a single value, the structure shown in Figure A-14 does not meet the requirements for a table, or relation; therefore, it is called an **unnormalized relation**. The set of fields that includes the PositionID, PositionDesc, PayGrade, and StartDate fields, which can have more than one value, is called a **repeating group**.

Figure A-14   **Repeating groups of data in an unnormalized Employee table**

repeating group

Employee

EmployeeNum	PositionID	FirstName	LastName	PositionDesc	PayGrade	StartDate	HealthPlan	PlanDesc
2173	2	Barbara	Hennessey	Manager	40	12/14/2011	B	Managed HMO
4519	1 3	Lee	Noordsy	Director Analyst	45 30	04/23/2013 11/11/2007	A	Managed PPO
8005	3 4	Pat	Amidon	Analyst Clerk	30 20	06/05/2012 07/02/2010	C	Health Savings
8112	1 2	Chris	Wandzell	Director Manager	45 40	12/15/2012 10/04/2011	A	Managed PPO

First normal form addresses this repeating-group situation. A table is in **first normal form (1NF)** if it does not contain repeating groups. To remove a repeating group and convert to first normal form, you expand the primary key to include the primary key of the repeating group, forming a composite key. Performing the conversion step produces the 1NF table shown in Figure A-15.

Figure A-15   **After conversion to 1NF**

composite primary key

Employee

EmployeeNum	PositionID	FirstName	LastName	PositionDesc	PayGrade	StartDate	HealthPlan	PlanDesc
2173	2	Barbara	Hennessey	Manager	40	12/14/2011	B	Managed HMO
4519	1	Lee	Noordsy	Director	45	04/23/2013	A	Managed PPO
4519	3	Lee	Noordsy	Analyst	30	11/11/2007	A	Managed PPO
8005	3	Pat	Amidon	Analyst	30	06/05/2012	C	Health Savings
8005	4	Pat	Amidon	Clerk	20	07/02/2010	C	Health Savings
8112	1	Chris	Wandzell	Director	45	12/15/2012	A	Managed PPO
8112	2	Chris	Wandzell	Manager	40	10/04/2011	A	Managed PPO

The alternative way to describe the 1NF table is:

Employee (<u>EmployeeNum</u>, <u>PositionID</u>, FirstName, LastName, PositionDesc, PayGrade, StartDate, HealthPlan, PlanDesc)

The Employee table is now a true table and has a composite key. The table, however, suffers from insertion, deletion, and update anomalies. (As an exercise, find examples of the three anomalies in the table.) The EmployeeNum field is a determinant for the FirstName, LastName, HealthPlan, and PlanDesc fields, so partial dependencies exist in the Employee table. It is these partial dependencies that cause the anomalies in the Employee table, and second normal form addresses the partial-dependency problem.

Second Normal Form

A table in 1NF is in **second normal form (2NF)** if it does not contain any partial dependencies. To remove partial dependencies from a table and convert it to second normal form, you perform two steps. First, identify the functional dependencies for every field in the table. Second, if necessary, create new tables and place each field in a table such that the field is functionally dependent on the entire primary key, not part of the primary key. If you need to create new tables, restrict them to tables with a primary key that is a subset of the original composite key. Note that partial dependencies occur only when you have a composite key; a table in first normal form with a single-field primary key is automatically in second normal form.

First, identifying the functional dependencies leads to the following determinants for the Employee table:

EmployeeNum → FirstName, LastName, HealthPlan, PlanDesc
PositionID → PositionDesc, PayGrade
EmployeeNum, PositionID → StartDate
HealthPlan → PlanDesc

The EmployeeNum field is a determinant for the FirstName, LastName, HealthPlan, and PlanDesc fields. The PositionID field is a determinant for the PositionDesc and PayGrade fields. The composite key EmployeeNum and PositionID is a determinant for the StartDate field. The HealthPlan field is a determinant for the PlanDesc field. Performing the second step in the conversion from first normal form to second form produces the three 2NF tables shown in Figure A-16.

Figure A-16   **After conversion to 2NF**

Employee

primary key →

EmployeeNum	FirstName	LastName	HealthPlan	PlanDesc
2173	Barbara	Hennessey	B	Managed HMO
4519	Lee	Noordsy	A	Managed PPO
8005	Pat	Amidon	C	Health Savings
8112	Chris	Wandzell	A	Managed PPO

Position

primary key →

PositionID	PositionDesc	PayGrade
1	Director	45
2	Manager	40
3	Analyst	30
4	Clerk	20

composite primary key

Employment

EmployeeNum	PositionID	StartDate
2173	2	12/14/2011
4519	1	04/23/2013
4519	3	11/11/2007
8005	3	06/05/2012
8005	4	07/02/2010
8112	1	12/15/2012
8112	2	10/04/2011

The alternative way to describe the 2NF tables is:

Employee (<u>EmployeeNum</u>, FirstName, LastName, HealthPlan, PlanDesc)
Position (<u>PositionID</u>, PositionDesc, PayGrade)
Employment (<u>EmployeeNum</u>, <u>PositionID</u>, StartDate)
    Foreign key: EmployeeNum to Employee table
    Foreign key: PositionID to Position table

All three tables are in second normal form. Do anomalies still exist? The Position and Employment tables show no anomalies, but the Employee table suffers from anomalies caused by the transitive dependency between the HealthPlan and PlanDesc fields. (As an exercise, find examples of the three anomalies caused by the transitive dependency.) That is, the HealthPlan field is a determinant for the PlanDesc field, and the EmployeeNum field is a determinant for the HealthPlan and PlanDesc fields. Third normal form addresses the transitive-dependency problem.

Third Normal Form

A table in 2NF is in **third normal form (3NF)** if every determinant is a candidate key. This definition for 3NF is referred to as **Boyce-Codd normal form (BCNF)** and is an improvement over the original version of 3NF. What are the determinants in the Employee table? The EmployeeNum and HealthPlan fields are the determinants; however, the EmployeeNum field is a candidate key because it's the table's primary key, and the HealthPlan field is not a candidate key. Therefore, the Employee table is in second normal form, but it is not in third normal form.

To convert a table to third normal form, remove the fields that depend on the non-candidate-key determinant and place them into a new table with the determinant as the primary key. For the Employee table, the PlanDesc field depends on the HealthPlan field, which is a non-candidate-key determinant. Thus, you remove the PlanDesc field from the table, create a new HealthBenefits table, place the PlanDesc field in the HealthBenefits table, and then make the HealthPlan field the primary key of the HealthBenefits table. Note that only the PlanDesc field is removed from the Employee table; the HealthPlan field remains as a foreign key in the Employee table. Figure A-17 shows the database design for the four 3NF tables.

| Figure A-17 | After conversion to 3NF |

Employee

	EmployeeNum	FirstName	LastName	HealthPlan
primary key →	2173	Barbara	Hennessey	B
	4519	Lee	Noordsy	A
	8005	Pat	Amidon	C
	8112	Chris	Wandzell	A

HealthBenefits

	HealthPlan	PlanDesc
primary key →	A	Managed PPO
	B	Managed HMO
	C	Health Savings

Position

	PositionID	PositionDesc	PayGrade
primary key →	1	Director	45
	2	Manager	40
	3	Analyst	30
	4	Clerk	20

composite primary key

Employment

EmployeeNum	PositionID	StartDate
2173	2	12/14/2011
4519	1	04/23/2013
4519	3	11/11/2007
8005	3	06/05/2012
8005	4	07/02/2010
8112	1	12/15/2012
8112	2	10/04/2011

The alternative way to describe the 3NF relations is:

Employee (<u>EmployeeNum</u>, FirstName, LastName, HealthPlan)
    Foreign key: HealthPlan to HealthBenefits table
HealthBenefits (<u>HealthPlan</u>, PlanDesc)
Position (<u>PositionID</u>, PositionDesc, PayGrade)
Employment (<u>EmployeeNum</u>, <u>PositionID</u>, StartDate)
    Foreign key: EmployeeNum to Employee table
    Foreign key: PositionID to Position table

The four tables have no anomalies because you have eliminated all the data redundancy, partial dependencies, and transitive dependencies. Normalization provides the framework for eliminating anomalies and delivering an optimal database design, which you should always strive to achieve. You should be aware, however, that experts sometimes denormalize tables to improve database performance—specifically, to decrease the time it takes the database to respond to a user's commands and requests. Typically, when you denormalize tables, you combine separate tables into one table to reduce the need for the DBMS to join the separate tables to process queries and other informational requests. When you denormalize a table, you reintroduce redundancy to the table. At the same time, you reintroduce anomalies. Thus, improving performance exposes a database to potential integrity problems. Only database experts should denormalize tables, but even experts first complete the normalization of their tables.

Natural, Artificial, and Surrogate Keys

When you complete the design of a database, your tables should be in third normal form, free of anomalies and redundancy. Some tables, such as the State table (see Figure A-2), have obvious third normal form designs with obvious primary keys. The State table's description is:

State (StateAbbrev, StateName, EnteredUnionOrder, StateBird, StatePopulation)

Recall that the candidate keys for the State table are StateAbbrev, StateName, and EnteredUnionOrder. Choosing the StateAbbrev field as the State table's primary key makes the StateName and EnteredUnionOrder fields alternate keys. Primary keys such as the StateAbbrev field are sometimes called natural keys. A **natural key** (also called a **logical key** or an **intelligent key**) is a primary key that consists of a field, or a collection of fields, that is an inherent characteristic of the entity described by the table and that is visible to users. Other examples of natural keys are the ISBN (International Standard Book Number) for a book, the SSN (Social Security number) for a U.S. individual, the UPC (Universal Product Code) for a product, and the VIN (vehicle identification number) for a vehicle.

Is the PositionID field, which is the primary key for the Position table (see Figure A-17), a natural key? No, the PositionID field is not an inherent characteristic of a position. Instead, the PositionID field has been added to the Position table only as a way to identify each position uniquely. The PositionID field is an **artificial key**, which is a field that you add to a table to serve solely as the primary key and that is visible to users.

Another reason for using an artificial key arises in tables that allow duplicate records. Although relational database theory and most experts do not allow duplicate records in a table, consider a database that tracks donors and their donations. Figure A-18 shows a Donor table with an artificial key of DonorID and with the DonorFirstName and DonorLastName fields. Some cash donations are anonymous, which accounts for the fourth record in the Donor table. Figure A-18 also shows the Donation table with the DonorID field, a foreign key to the Donor table, and the DonationDate and DonationAmt fields.

Figure A-18   Donor and Donation tables

Donor

DonorID	DonorFirstName	DonorLastName
1	Christina	Chang
2	Franco	Diaz
3	Angie	Diaz
4		Anonymous
5	Tracy	Burns

primary key

Donation

DonorID	DonationDate	DonationAmt
1	10/12/2015	$50.00
1	09/30/2016	$50.00
2	10/03/2016	$75.00
4	10/10/2016	$50.00
4	10/10/2016	$50.00
4	10/11/2016	$25.00
5	10/13/2016	$50.00

duplicate records

What is the primary key of the Donation table? No single field is unique, and neither is any combination of fields. For example, on 10/10/2016, two anonymous donors (DonorID value of 4) donated $50 each. You need to add an artificial key, DonationID for example, to the Donation table. The addition of the artificial key makes every record in the Donation table unique, as shown in Figure A-19.

Figure A-19	Donation table after adding DonationID, an artificial key

Donation

DonationID	DonorID	DonationDate	DonationAmt
1	1	10/12/2015	$50.00
2	1	09/30/2016	$50.00
3	2	10/03/2016	$75.00
4	4	10/10/2016	$50.00
5	4	10/10/2016	$50.00
6	4	10/11/2016	$25.00
7	5	10/13/2016	$50.00

artificial key

The descriptions of the Donor and Donation tables now are:

Donor (DonorID, DonorFirstName, DonorLastName)
Donation (DonationID, DonorID, DonationDate, DonationAmt)
    Foreign key: DonorID to Donor table

For another common situation, consider the 3NF tables you reviewed in the previous section (see Figure A-17) that have the following descriptions:

Employee (EmployeeNum, FirstName, LastName, HealthPlan)
    Foreign key: HealthPlan to HealthBenefits table
HealthBenefits (HealthPlan, PlanDesc)
Position (PositionID, PositionDesc, PayGrade)
Employment (EmployeeNum, PositionID, StartDate)
    Foreign key: EmployeeNum to Employee table
    Foreign key: PositionID to Position table

Recall that a primary key must be unique, must be minimal, and must not change in value. In theory, primary keys don't change in value. However, in practice, you might have to change EmployeeNum field values that you incorrectly entered in the Employment table. Further, if you need to change an EmployeeNum field value in the Employee table, the change must cascade to the EmployeeNum field values in the Employment table. Also, changes to a PositionID field value in the Position table must cascade to the Employment table. For these and other reasons, many experts add surrogate keys to their tables. A **surrogate key** (also called a **synthetic key**) is a system-generated primary key that is hidden from users. Usually you can use an automatic numbering data type, such as the Access AutoNumber data type, for a surrogate key. Figure A-20 shows the four tables with surrogate keys added to each table.

Figure A-20   **Using surrogate keys**

The HealthSK field replaces the HealthPlan field as a foreign key in the Employee table, and the EmployeeSK field replaces the EmployeeNum field in the Employment table. Now when you change an incorrectly entered EmployeeNum field value in the Employee table, you don't need to cascade the change to the Employment table. Likewise, when you change an incorrectly entered HealthPlan field value in the HealthBenefits table, you don't need to cascade the change to the Employee table.

As you design a database, you should *not* consider the use of surrogate keys, and you should use an artificial key only for the rare table that has duplicate records. At the point when you implement a database, you might choose to use artificial and surrogate keys, but be aware that database experts debate their use and effectiveness. You need to consider the following tradeoffs between natural and surrogate keys:

- You use surrogate keys to avoid cascading updates to foreign key values. Surrogate keys can also replace lengthier foreign keys when those foreign keys reference composite fields.
- You don't need a surrogate key for a table whose primary key is not used as a foreign key in another table because cascading updates is not an issue.
- Tables with surrogate keys require more joins than do tables with natural keys. For example, if you need to know all employees with a HealthPlan field value of A, the surrogate key in Figure A-20 requires that you join the Employee and HealthBenefits tables to answer the question. Using natural keys as shown in Figure A-17, the HealthPlan field appears in the Employee table, so no join is necessary.
- Although surrogate keys are meant to be hidden from users, they cannot be hidden from users who create SQL statements and use other ad hoc tools.
- Because you need a unique index for the natural key and a unique index for the surrogate key, your database size is larger and index maintenance takes more time when you use a surrogate key. On the other hand, a foreign key using a surrogate key is usually smaller than a foreign key using a natural key, especially when the natural key is a composite key, so those indexes are smaller and faster to access for lookups and joins.

Microsoft Access Naming Conventions

In the early 1980s, Microsoft's Charles Simonyi introduced an identifier naming convention that became known as Hungarian notation. Microsoft and other companies use this naming convention for variable, control, and other object naming in Basic, Visual Basic, and other programming languages. When Access was introduced in the early 1990s, Stan Leszynski and Greg Reddick adapted Hungarian notation for Microsoft Access databases; their guidelines became known as the Leszynski/Reddick naming conventions. In recent years, the Leszynski naming conventions, the Reddick naming conventions, and other naming conventions have been published. Individuals and companies have created their own Access naming conventions, but many are based on the Leszynski/Reddick naming conventions, as are the naming conventions covered in this section.

An Access database can contain thousands of objects, fields, controls, and other items, and keeping track of their names and what they represent is a difficult task. Consequently, you should use naming conventions that identify the type and purpose of each item in an Access database. You can use naming conventions that identify items generally or very specifically.

For an object, include a prefix tag to identify the type of object, as shown in Figure A-21. In each example in Figure A-21, the final object name consists of a three-character tag prefixed to the base object name. For example, the form name of frmEmployeesAndPositions consists of the frm tag and the EmployeesAndPositions base form name.

Object type	Tag	Example
Form	frm	frmEmployeesAndPositions
Macro	mcr	mcrSwitchboard
Module	bas	basCalculations
Query	qry	qryEmployee
Report	rpt	rptEmployeesAndPositions
Table	tbl	tblEmployee

The tags in Figure A-21 identify each object type in general. If you want to identify object types more specifically, you could expand Figure A-21 to include tags such as fsub for a subform, qxtb for a crosstab query, tlkp for a lookup table, rsub for a subreport, and so on.

For controls in forms and reports, a general naming convention uses lbl as a prefix tag for labels and ctl as a prefix tag for other types of controls. For more specific naming conventions for controls, you'd use a specific prefix tag for each type of control. Figure A-22 shows the prefix tags for some common controls in forms and reports.

Control type	Tag
Check box	chk
Combo box	cbo
Command button	cmd
Image	img
Label	lbl
Line	lin
List box	lst
Option button	opt
Rectangle	shp
Subform/Subreport	sub
Text box	txt

Some database developers use a prefix tag for each field name to identify the field's data type (for example, dtm for Date/Time, num for Number, and chr for Text or Character), others use a prefix tag for each field name to identify in which table the field is located (for example, emp for the Employee table and pos for the Position table), and still others don't use a prefix tag for field names.

You might use suffix tags for controls that might otherwise have identical names. For example, if you have two text boxes in a form for calculated controls that display the average and the sum of the OrderAmt field, both could legitimately be named txtOrderAmt unless you used suffix tags to name them txtOrderAmtAvg and txtOrderAmtSum.

You should ensure that any name you use does not duplicate a property name or any keyword Access reserves for special purposes. In general, you can avoid property and keyword name conflicts by using two-word field, control, and object names. For example, use StudentName instead of Name, and use OrderDate instead of Date to avoid name conflicts.

All database developers avoid spaces in names, mainly because spaces are not allowed in server DBMSs, such as SQL Server, Oracle, and DB2. If you are prototyping a Microsoft Access database that you'll migrate to one of these server DBMSs, or if future requirements might force a migration, you should restrict your Access identifier names so that they conform to the rules common to them all. Figure A-23 shows the identifier naming rules for Access, SQL Server, Oracle, and DB2.

Figure A-23	Identifier naming rules for common database management systems			
Identifier naming rule	Access	SQL Server	Oracle	DB2
Maximum character length	64	30	30	30
Allowable characters	Letters, digits, space, and special characters, except for period (.), exclamation point (!), grave accent ('), and square brackets ([ ])	Letters, digits, dollar sign ($), underscore (_), number symbol (#), and at symbol (@)	Letters, digits, dollar sign ($), underscore (_), and number symbol (#)	Letters, digits, at symbol (@), dollar sign ($), underscore (_), and number symbol (#)
Special rules		No spaces; first character must be a letter or at symbol (@)	No spaces; first character must be a letter; stored in the database in uppercase	No spaces; first character must be a letter, at symbol (@), dollar sign ($), or number symbol (#); stored in the database in uppercase

Review Assignments

1. What are the formal names for a table, for a row, and for a column? What are the popular names for a row and for a column?

2. What is a domain?

3. What is an entity?

4. What is the relationship between a primary key and a candidate key?

5. What is a composite key?

6. What is a foreign key?

7. Look for and describe an example of a one-to-one relationship, an example of a one-to-many relationship, and an example of a many-to-many relationship in a newspaper, magazine, book, or everyday situation you encounter.

8. When do you use an entity subtype?

9. What is the entity integrity constraint?

10. What is referential integrity?

11. What does the cascades option, which is used with referential integrity, accomplish?

12. What are partial and transitive dependencies?

13. What three types of anomalies can be exhibited by a table, and what problems do they cause?

14. Figure A-24 shows the Employee, Position, and Employment tables with primary keys EmployeeNum, PositionID, and both EmployeeNum and PositionID, respectively. Which two integrity constraints do these tables violate and why?

Figure A-24   **Integrity constraint violations**

Employee

EmployeeNum	FirstName	LastName	HealthPlan
2173	Barbara	Hennessey	B
4519	Lee	Noordsy	A
8005	Pat	Amidon	C
8112	Chris	Wandzell	A

Position

PositionID	PositionDesc	PayGrade
1	Director	45
2	Manager	40
3	Analyst	30
4	Clerk	20

Employment

EmployeeNum	PositionID	StartDate
2173	2	12/14/2011
4519	1	04/23/2013
4519		11/11/2007
8005	3	06/05/2012
8005	4	07/02/2010
8112	1	12/15/2012
9876	2	10/04/2011

15. The State and City tables, shown in Figure A-4, are described as follows:
    State (StateAbbrev, StateName, EnteredUnionOrder, StateBird, StatePopulation)
    City (StateAbbrev, CityName, CityPopulation)
    Foreign key: StateAbbrev to State table
    Add the field named CountyName for the county or counties in a state containing the city to this database, justify where you placed it (that is, in an existing table or in a new one), and draw the entity-relationship diagram for all the entities. Counties for some of the cities shown in Figure A-4 are Travis and Williamson counties for Austin TX; Hartford county for Hartford CT; Clinton, Eaton, and Ingham counties for Lansing MI; Davidson county for Nashville TN; Hughes county for Pierre SD; and Nueces and San Patricio counties for Portland TX.

16. Suppose you have a table for a dance studio. The fields are dancer's identification number, dancer's name, dancer's address, dancer's telephone number, class identification number, day that the class meets, time that the class meets, instructor name, and instructor identification number. Assume that each dancer takes one class, each class meets only once a week and has

one instructor, and each instructor can teach more than one class. In what normal form is the table currently, given the following alternative description?

Dancer (<u>DancerID</u>, DancerName, DancerAddr, DancerPhone, ClassID, ClassDay, ClassTime, InstrName, InstrID)

Convert this relation to 3NF and represent the design using the alternative description method.

17. Store the following fields for a library database: AuthorCode, AuthorName, BookTitle, BorrowerAddress, BorrowerName, BorrowerCardNumber, CopiesOfBook, ISBN (International Standard Book Number), LoanDate, PublisherCode, PublisherName, and PublisherAddress. A one-to-many relationship exists between publishers and books. Many-to-many relationships exist between authors and books and between borrowers and books.

   a. Name the entities for the library database.

   b. Create the tables for the library database and describe them using the alternative method. Be sure the tables are in third normal form.

   c. Draw an entity-relationship diagram for the library database.

18. In the database shown in Figure A-25, which consists of the Department and Employee tables, add one record to the end of the Employee table that violates both the entity integrity constraint and the referential integrity constraint.

Figure A-25   **Creating integrity constraint violations**

Department

DeptID	DeptName	Location
M	Marketing	New York
R	Research	Houston
S	Sales	Chicago

Employee

EmployeeID	EmployeeName	DeptID
1111	Sue	R
2222	Pam	M
3333	Bob	S
4444	Chris	S
5555	Pat	R
6666	Meg	R

19. Consider the following table:

Patient (PatientID, PatientName, BalanceOwed, DoctorID, DoctorName, ServiceCode, Service-Desc, ServiceFee, ServiceDate)

This is a table concerning data about patients of doctors at a clinic and the services the doctors perform for their patients. The following dependencies exist in the Patient table:

PatientID → PatientName, BalanceOwed

DoctorID → DoctorName

ServiceCode → ServiceDesc, ServiceFee

PatientID, DoctorID, ServiceCode → PatientName, BalanceOwed, DoctorName, ServiceDesc,
   ServiceFee, ServiceDate

   a. Based on the dependencies, convert the Patient table to first normal form.

   b. Next, convert the Patient table to third normal form.

20. Suppose you need to track data for mountain climbing expeditions. Each member of an
   expedition is called a climber, and one of the climbers is named to lead an expedition. Climbers
   can be members of many expeditions over time. The climbers in each expedition attempt to
   ascend one or more peaks by scaling one of the many faces of the peaks. The data you need to
   track includes the name of the expedition, the leader of the expedition, and comments about
   the expedition; the first name, last name, nationality, birth date, death date, and comments
   about each climber; the name, location, height, and comments about each peak; the name and
   comments about each face of a peak; comments about each climber for each expedition; and
   the highest height reached and the date for each ascent attempt by a climber on a face with
   commentary.

   a. Create the tables for the expedition database and describe them using the alternative method.
   Be sure the tables are in third normal form.

   b. Draw an entity-relationship diagram for the expedition database.

21. What is the difference among natural, artificial, and surrogate keys?

22. Why should you use naming conventions for the identifiers in a database?

INDEX